CANADIAN SIXTH EDITION

COLLEGE ACCOUNTING

A Practical Approach

JEFFREY SLATER
NORTH SHORE COMMUNITY COLLEGE
BEVERLY, MASSACHUSETTS

BRIAN ZWICKER
GRANT MACEWAN COMMUNITY COLLEGE
EDMONTON, ALBERTA

Prentice Hall Canada Inc., Scarborough, Ontario

Canadian Cataloguing in Publication Data

Slater, Jeffrey, 1947–
College Accounting

Canadian 6th ed.
ISBN 0-13-570458-8

1.Accounting. 1. Zwicker, Brian, 1944–
II.Title.

HF5635.S49 1997 657'.044 C96-930672-5

A Division of Simon & Schuster/A Viacom Company

Prentice-Hall, Inc., Upper Saddle River, New Jersey
Prentice-Hall International (UK) Limited, London
Prentice-Hall of Australia, Pty. Limited, Sydney
Prentice-Hall Hispanoamericana, S.A., Mexico City
Prentice-Hall of India Private Limited, New Delhi
Prentice-Hall of Japan, Inc., Tokyo
Simon & Schuster Asia Private Limited, Singapore
Editora Prentice-Hall do Brasil, Ltda., Rio de Janeiro

ISBN 0-13-570458-8

Acquisitions Editor: Patrick Ferrier
Developmental Editor: Lesley Mann
Production Editor: Kelly Dickson
Copy Editor: Rodney Rawlings/Edie Franks
Production Coordinator: Deborah Starks
Cover and Interior Design: Monica Kompter
Cover Image: Jose L. Pelaez/The Stock Market
Page Layout: Joan Morrison/Bill Renaud

Original American edition published by Prentice-Hall, Inc., Upper Saddle River, New Jersey

2 3 4 5 CC 01 00 99 98 97

Printed and bound in the United States

We welcome readers' comments, which can be sent by e-mail to
phcinfo_pubcanada@prenhall.com

To Shelley, with love.
J.S.

To the Memory of Alma Loraine Zwicker.
B.Z.

BRIEF CONTENTS

CONTENTS

CHAPTER 7 PAYROLL CONCEPTS AND PROCEDURES 254

CHAPTER 8 THE EMPLOYER'S TAX RESPONSIBILITIES 288

CHAPTER 9 ACCOUNTING CONCEPTS AND PROCEDURES: SALES AND CASH RECEIPTS 326

Key to use of colour in text

Text	Financial Statements, Ledgers, Worksheets, Registers and Schedules
Text	Journals, Payments and Petty Cash Transactions
Text	Purchase Orders, Sales Invoices and Other Forms and Documents

PREFACE

To the Student

College Accounting: A Practical Approach, Canadian Sixth Edition, was written to introduce you to accounting, a dynamic tool of business. What is accounting and why will you find it useful? Accounting is a planned and orderly way of keeping records for the purpose of seeing how a business is performing. It answers such questions as: Is the business profitable or is it losing money? Which business activities are contributing most to profits and which to losses? Which resources are well employed and which are being wasted? Who owes the business money, and how much? What does the business owe? Accounting is also important for regulatory and tax purposes. You will be surprised at how often your understanding of accounting will work for you on the job.

Learning accounting means familiarizing yourself with many new terms and concepts. Don't be tempted to cut corners and take shortcuts; you will get the most out of your study of accounting if you follow the detailed, step-by-step directions provided in this text. Once you have learned the basic terms and concepts, the rest will quickly fall into place.

We have set up each chapter according to a special format that time has proven makes it easier to learn and remember the material in the chapter. Let's look at each component of a chapter and see why it was set up that way:

- *Broad objectives with page references to introduce the chapter.* These objectives allow you to see where you're headed; they set the stage for the more specific objectives to be found later in the chapter. Page references are given where the material for each objective can be found.
- *Chapter broken down into Learning Units.* Students continually tell us that they learn best when material is broken into small, manageable units. This way, if a question comes up it can be identified and solved immediately without waiting until the whole chapter is read. And, in this way, you can test yourself on smaller amounts of material to be sure that you've mastered each bit before going on to the next.
- *Objectives with page references follow each Unit.* After you have read the Unit, the objectives give you a chance to recap what you've read. Stop to see if you can answer the objective—if not, go back to the page referred to and review the material.
- *Self-review quiz follows each Unit.* This is a chance to test yourself on what you've just learned and try some hands-on applications of the theory just covered. The forms for the quizzes are in your *Study Guide and Working Papers.* The solution to the quiz follows right after the quiz in the text. Don't worry if you get something wrong in the quiz—these quizzes are for you, not for your professor. If you do have trouble with the quiz, go back to the problem area in the unit and review before going on to the next unit.

- *Discussion questions at the end of the chapter.* These questions cover the theory covered in the chapter. It is important to make sure you can answer them before going on to the next chapter.
- *Exercises at the end of the chapter.* Exercises review specific topics covered in the chapter. Notes in the margin identify the topic covered by each exercise—if you know you need more work on a certain topic that you feel uncertain about, seek out those exercises that deal with that topic.
- *Problems at the end of the chapter.* There are A, B, and C problems in the text; forms for the problems are provided in your *Study Guide and Working Papers.* As with the exercises, notes in the margin identify the topic covered by each problem.
- *Practical accounting applications at the end of the chapter.* These give you a way to test your accounting knowledge in a situation that might occur on the job. They're challenging and fun.
- *Ethical case sections.* These allow students to formulate their position on a number of realistic situations which they may someday find themselves in. These are most useful for stimulating classroom discussion.
- *Practice problems follow certain chapters.* These problems give a list of transactions and information needed to perform certain tasks in accounting covered by a set of chapters. At the end of Chapter 5 is a problem that reviews the accounting cycle; in this problem you go through the accounting cycle twice to give you a more complete idea of the procedures involved at the end of each month. At the end of Chapter 8 there is a summary of payroll procedures. After Chapter 13 there is a problem that deals with transactions of a sole proprietorship merchandise company. These problems help put all the theory together in a practical way. Forms for completing the problems are provided in your *Study Guide and Working Papers*.
- *Cumulative review quizzes with page references at the end of the chapter.* Since accounting builds from one chapter to another, it is important to review vocabulary and accounting applications. At the end of each chapter you will find a cumulative review quiz. Each quiz, with page references, will have three parts: vocabulary review, accounting theory, and application problems. The forms for these quizzes, along with the worked-out solutions, will be found in your *Study Guide and Working Papers*.

Perhaps the most valuable change in this edition is the addition of several computer-based simulations at various points in the text. The almost universal reliance upon computer processing in accounting makes it essential for accounting students to have a good exposure to the subject. Since most educational institutions in Canada already own copies of either Simply Accounting or ACCPAC Plus, these two programs from Computer Associates have been selected as the programs of choice. Data diskettes are supplied to adopting institutions who wish to use the computer-based simulations. The purpose of the data diskettes is to relieve students of the task of creating their own sets of data. Not only would that be time-consuming, it could lead to a number of errors. This way, all students begin with the same accurate data and can proceed quickly to learn the essentials. We believe that the two accounting programs chosen, Simply Accounting for Windows (Version 4) and ACCPAC Plus (Version 6.1), are used by the majority of postsecondary educational institutions in Canada. However, there may be a small number who do not. For those institutions it is recommended that the simulations be used, but data diskettes will not be available.

Data sets may be provided in the future for any program or programs which become used by a significant number of institutions. Let Prentice Hall know of your needs.

Some chapters also contain career boxes highlighting individuals who have used their college accounting course work to help them attain a rewarding career. Their advice and experiences are informative, interesting, and inspiring.

If you follow this chapter layout carefully you will find that you learn the basic terms and concepts easily and remember them better, and that the many chances to apply them in a practical way help you to remember them.

TO THE INSTRUCTOR

GENESIS

College Accounting: A Practical Approach, Canadian Sixth Edition, is the result of years of teaching and writing experience in accounting. Our intention in writing this book was to create a vehicle to help maximize student mastery of accounting concepts and procedures.

The needs of students who are not, at this time, considering a career in accounting are unique. It has been our goal in the Canadianization of this text to preserve all of the quality features of the US edition and to insert high-quality Canadian material in order to present the best possible resource for students.

Our approach is based on tried and proven learning techniques, and these techniques have, in turn, been reinforced and shaped by in-class experience with students. We have also listened to a number of concerns from instructors, and this edition incorporates several of your ideas. Among these is the "Type C" problems. This material should greatly benefit the many institutions that have multiple sections and will provide increased choices for all adopters. We have chosen to increase the length and complexity of the Type C problems slightly, but have also tried to be faithful to the text's original purpose— to present accounting for students who are not currently planning a career in the area. A number of other significant features are also incorporated, including integrating GST into Chapters 9, 10, and 11. Most of those reviewers who were approached found this preferable to adding another appendix. We have, however, tried to intelligently compartmentalize the presentation so as not to get in the way of any instructor who may choose to deemphasize the topic of GST.

Of course, the most significant inclusion in this edition is the computer accounting content. Computers are nowadays involved in accounting to a large extent. While it is still true, we believe, that students best learn practical accounting in traditional ways, it is no longer appropriate to leave students with no knowledge of the ways computers can interface with accounting. Accordingly, we have added several excellent computer workshops and an extensive appendix which, taken together, should afford students a unique and valuable learning experience.

There were many options to carefully consider in selecting the software we felt would be most effective in meeting students' needs. Our basic premise was that all, or almost all, institutions which intend to offer computer accounting components already own (or license) accounting software, and most of these depend upon either Simply Accounting or ACCPAC Plus. We have therefore elected to supply data diskettes in these formats. The advantages of these programs include the important option to keep the data sets updated for newer versions of the software, should demand warrant.

The data sets are based upon the latest version of Simply Accounting (Version 4.0) available at the time of writing. The Windows version of ACCPAC—ACCPAC 2000—was not selected, because it is not (yet) a major choice for any significant number of educational institutions.

If our decision does not match your institution's needs, please let your Prentice Hall representative know. The marketplace in this area is very dynamic; we intend to continually revise and enlarge our data sets to better meet your needs.

The end result is, we believe, a clear, accurate, up-to-date, pedagogically effective text, accompanied by a fully articulated package. The text and its ancillaries offer a full range of teaching and learning tools from which the instructor can choose. It's our hope that the Canadian Sixth Edition will continue to be a positive experience for students and instructors alike.

About the Book

College Accounting: A Practical Approach, Canadian Sixth Edition, is set up so that students have small, manageable units of material to learn followed by immediate feedback through the self-review quizzes at the end of each Unit. Each chapter is divided into Learning Units, and is organized in the following way.

Broad Objectives with Page References to Introduce the Chapter These objectives allow students to see where they're headed; they set the stage for the more specific objectives to be found later in the chapter. Page references are given so that the material for each objective can be found easily.

Chapter Broken Down into Learning Units Students continually tell us that they learn best when material is broken into small, manageable units. This way, if a question comes up it can be identified and solved immediately without waiting until the whole chapter is read. And, in this way, students can test themselves on smaller amounts of material, to be sure that they've mastered each bit before going on.

Objectives with Page References Follow Each Unit At the end of each Unit, the objectives are reiterated, giving students a chance to recap what they've read. If they can't answer the objective, they can go back to the page referred to and review the material.

Self-Review Quiz Follows Each Unit This is a chance for students to test themselves on what they've just learned and try some hands-on applications of the theory just covered. The forms for the quiz are in the *Study Guide and Working Papers*. The solution to the quiz follows right after the quiz in the text. If students have trouble with the quiz, they can go back to the problem area in the unit and review before going on to the next unit.

Career Box Profiles Integrated into the text are profiles of people working in the fields of bookkeeping and accounting, showing what their jobs involve and how they used their education to obtain their jobs.

Summary of Key Points and Key Terms at the End of the Chapter The material covered in the chapter is reviewed by Unit at the end of the chapter. The key points of the summary provide one more chance to review and to point up any weak spots in the chapter. Accounting as a discipline is full of new vocabulary. The trick to learning this new vocabulary is to take it slowly and review it often. The terms introduced in the chapter are listed and defined at the end of the chapter by Unit so that students can review them and make sure they know what they mean and how they are used in the chapter.

Blueprint at the End of the Chapter Some people learn better by seeing something in chart or diagram form rather than reading about it. And we all remember things better if we learn them several different ways. The goal of the Blueprint is to review visually the key concepts or procedures in the chapter. It is like a roadmap, showing students in simple steps what they have just been through in the chapter.

Discussion Questions at the End of the Chapter These questions cover the theory covered in the chapter. Students should make sure they can answer them before going on to the next chapter.

Exercises and Mini Exercises at the End of the Chapter Exercises review specific topics covered in the chapter. Notes in the margin identify the topic covered by each exercise—students who know they need more work on a certain topic can seek out those exercises that deal with the topic.

Problems at the End of the Chapter There are A, B, and C problems in the text; forms to be used to answer them are provided in the *Study Guide and Working Papers*. As with the exercises, notes in the margin identify the topic covered by each problem.

Practical Accounting Applications at the End of the Chapter These are a way to test accounting knowledge in a situation that might occur on the job. They're fun and challenging.

Ethical Issues A critical thinking/ethical case is introduced at the end of each chapter. Designed to provoke discussion during class periods, these exercises allow students to grapple with real issues such as those they may face when they enter the workplace.

Practice Problems Follow Certain Chapters These problems, called Mini Practice Sets, give a list of transactions and information needed to perform certain tasks in accounting covered by a set of chapters. At the end of Chapter 5 is a problem that reviews the accounting cycle; in this problem students go through the accounting cycle twice to get a more complete idea of the procedures involved at the end of each month. At the end of Chapter 8 there is a summary of payroll procedures. After Chapter 13 there is a problem that deals with transactions of a sole proprietorship merchandise company. This project covers a three-month period. These problems help put all the theory together in a practical way. Forms for completing the problems are provided in the *Study Guide and Working Papers*. The Mini Practice Sets after Chapters 8 and 13 have been fully revised, and include GST where appropriate.

Computer Workshops At appropriate points in the text special workshops make learning of computer accounting effective, efficient, and as painless as possible. Use of Canada's top two programs ensures that most students gain familiarity with this vital learning component.

Canadian Sixth Edition Highlights

The following are some key features that make the text and its supplements more current and supportive of classroom and homework activities.

Chapter Order Revised In response to feedback we have altered the chapter order so that it better coordinates with your course plans.

Payroll Updated Chapters 7 and 8 have been substantially rewritten to reflect the latest laws in effect in Canada.

GST Accounting This tax is a reality in Canada. The essential details of how to account for GST are covered beginning in Chapter 9. Chapters 9 and 10 have been designed to accommodate instructors who choose either to emphasize or to deemphasize this topic.

Practice Problems Revised The practice problems at the ends of Chapters 8 and 13 have been rewritten and expanded. GST is covered appropriately.

Chapter on Inventory In Chapter 16, students are provided with theory, practice, and applications regarding inventory costing methods and practices.

Accounting Recall: A Cumulative Approach At the end of each chapter students get a chance to cumulatively recall what they've learned in past chapters. The recall is broken into three parts: vocabulary, theory, and practical applications (page references are provided for each question). The *Study Guide and Working Papers* contains the forms as well as solutions for the Accounting Recall materials. It's a great review before beginning the next chapter.

Problem Material Expanded As in previous editions, the A and B sets of problems are designed to reinforce concepts introduced in the chapters. Instructors may also choose from a C set of problems, created to permit a wider choice for institutions which offer multiple sections. These problems are a bit more rigorous than the A and B sets, and will require students to stretch somewhat.

New Study Guide and Working Papers New to this edition are enlarged foldout forms for all worksheets. Forms for all the Exercises and Mini Exercises are also provided. The forms you need for the Accounting Recall, as well as the solutions, have been added. Note that the *Study Guide and Working Papers* is now all-Canadian—customized for Canadian students' needs.

Ethical Issues New as well are the business judgement cases included at the end of each chapter. Students will find these short cases will help them focus on important issues and assist them in forming ethical responses to perplexing challenges we face in the business world.

Comprehensive Computer Coverage While the basic goal of the package has not changed (facilitate the learning of the basics of accounting) it is now time to introduce all students to the realities of the workplace. Hence, we have carefully conceived and integrated appropriate computer accounting workshops into the text. Provision of data sets on diskette allows all students to acquire computer accounting skills in an effective and efficient way. Additionally, when these workshops are used as assignments, instructors can count on all students beginning with identical data—an important consideration when grades are to be assigned.

The Slater/Zwicker Package

The text is just the starting point. Because the needs of Canadian instructors are very high on our priority list, we have taken certain other steps designed to maximize instructor effectiveness and efficiency. These steps include the provision of an *Instructor's Resource Manual,* a Test Item File and PH Custom Test (a computerized test bank). Another significant change is the complete Canadianization of the *Study Guide and Working Papers* and the *Solutions Manual*. We have invested a great many hours into ensuring the highest quality possible and we hope it shows in increased clarity, accuracy, and consistency. Let's look at some of the support systems included in the Slater/Zwicker package.

Learning Aids to Support the Slater/Zwicker System

Instructor's Resource Manual Newly expanded for this edition is the *Instructor's Resource Manual*. It is intended to bring together between two covers all of the materials that act to facilitate and augment each instructor's own special skills, strengths, and experience. The *Instructor's Resource Manual* includes:

- **Class Quizzes** Short exercise or review questions designed to reinforce aspects of the chapter coverage.
- **Class Activities** Something the whole class can take part in. Reviews and reinforces key points.
- **Lesson Outlines** Chapter material is allocated to a variety of classroom situations. There is probably a design that closely fits most educational institutions' scheduling preferences.
- **Typical Student Misconceptions** This identification of common errors gathered from more than 35 years of combined accounting teaching experience may be invaluable—especially to those instructors who are just beginning their careers.

- **Teaching Tips** Valuable suggestions that help students remember and assimilate the material.
- **Business World Notes** What actually happens in accounting in the real world. Takes students beyond the textbook.
- **Lecture Notes** While not intended to replace an appropriate lesson plan, these notes may be very useful as a check that nothing critical is overlooked.

Study Guide and Working Papers This has undergone substantial revision and enhancement. It contains forms for the quizzes at the end of each Learning Unit in the chapter, for all Exercises and Mini Exercises, for the problems (A, B, or C) at the end of each chapter, and for the practice problems that follow Chapters 5, 8, and 13. In addition, all worksheets are now treated as foldouts—a significant enhancement. At the end of each chapter of the *Study Guide and Working Papers*, there is a summary practice test designed to prepare students for in-class exams. It consists of fill-in-the-blank questions, a matching question, and true/false questions. In addition, the forms and solutions to the end-of-chapter Accounting Recalls in the text help students review the concepts covered in each chapter before going on to the next. The answers to the tests are at the end of each chapter of the *Study Guide and Working Papers*. As with the previous edition, the *Study Guide and Working Papers* is a completely Canadian publication. Many changes have been made to help ensure that the student's experience is as effective and efficient as possible.

Solutions Manual This manual provides answers to discussion questions and solutions to exercises, mini exercises, problems, practice problems, practical accounting applications, and ethical cases.

In the front of the Manual is a grid of all problems showing level of difficulty and estimated time needed for completion.

To ensure accurate solutions, each page of the *Solutions Manual* was carefully reviewed by Laurence P. Hanchard, CA. His exacting review will be appreciated by all instructors using this package.

Test Item File Now containing more than 800 questions, the Test Item File has been substantially revised and expanded. Every chapter contains multiple-choice, true/false, and problem/essay questions. Each question is coded by degree of difficulty (easy, moderate, or difficult). We have ensured that topics of special concern to Canadians, such as the GST, CPP contributions, and Canadian tax procedures, are appropriately covered.

PH Custom Test (Windows) Prentice Hall's computerized test file uses a state-of-the-art software program that provides fast, simple, and error-free test generation. Entire tests can be previewed on-screen before printing. PH Custom Test can print multiple variations of the same test, scrambling the order of questions and multiple-choice answers. Tests can be saved to ASCII format and revised in your word-processing system.

Tranparency Masters When producing a text with such a rich support package as *College Accounting,* it is important that we consider the environmental and production costs that result when instructors use only a few transparencies. In response to concerns about these costs, we are offering a special package that contains the *Solutions Manual* and a supply of clear acetates. Thus instructors who adopt the text are provided with the opportunity to produce transparencies for the specific solutiosn that they choose to show in their classroom. We hope you find this a creative response to concerns about waste and the environment.

ACKNOWLEDGEMENTS

The task of publishing a Canadian edition of any textbook is a challenging venture. In this case it helped to be working from an outstanding original and with an outstanding team.

Thanks are certainly due to the many helpful folks at Prentice Hall Canada Inc., including Executive Editor Pat Ferrier, Developmental Editor Lesley Mann, and Production Editor Kelly Dickson.

Thanks are also due to the reviewers for their valuable feedback: Beverly Adamack; Richard F. Barnes, Canadian Institute of Business; Dave Bopara, Toronto School of Business; Richard A. Charron, Cambrian College; and Mel Sparks, Lambton College.

Special recognition is due to Larry Knechtel and Doug Ringrose from Grant MacEwan Community College, who have used portions of the text in their classes. Thanks to Eric Saemisch at Revenue Canada and David Younie from the Canadian Employment Centre for their able assistance in obtaining most of the government forms. Mary Watson of Computer Associates provided her usual sterling assistance in matters relating to her company's computer software.

The *Study Guide and Working Papers* and the *Solutions Manual* were created with able assistance from Pat Leslie.

Closer to home, I would be very remiss if I failed to reflect upon the hours of support and encouragement provided by my wife, Carol, and daughters, Heather and Shannon. Shannon also assisted by creating some of the data sets.

Certain of the other data sets were created by Flora Fitness.

Two freelance editors, Rodney Rawlings and Edie Franks, were actively involved in improving the presentation of the text. Both were unusually thorough and remarkably pleasant in accomplishing their tasks.

My final thanks go to Laurie Hanchard who not only carried out his assigned duties of reviewing both the *Study Guide and Working Papers* and the *Solutions Manual* with remarkable care and attention but also took it as a personal goal to add substantial value to the overall package. The text—indeed, all aspects of this project—is much improved because of Laurie's efforts.

Despite the best efforts of so many talented people, it is inevitable that a few errors will persist in getting into print. I accept responsibility for them and would appreciated your help in identifying them so that they can be totally eliminated in the future.

TESTIMONIAL

As requested, I have read the first pass pages of College Accounting, Canadian Sixth Edition, by Slater and Zwicker, chapters 1-16. I have also read the pages of the Study Guide and the Solutions Manual to *College Accounting*. I checked the arithmetic and logic in all three books with respect to the worked examples and exhibits in the proofed copies. I also ensured that the references to these examples and exhibits within the text were accurate.

Laurence P. Hanchard, C.A.

ACCOUNTING CONCEPTS AND PROCEDURES

1

AN INTRODUCTION

Chapter Objectives

- Defining and listing the functions of accounting. (p. 4)
- Recording transactions in the basic accounting equation. (p. 8)
- Seeing how revenue, expenses, and withdrawals expand the basic accounting equation. (p. 13)
- Preparing an income statement, a statement of owner's equity, and a balance sheet. (p. 18)

Accounting is the language of business; it provides information to managers, owners, investors, governmental agencies, and others inside and outside the organization. Accounting provides answers and insights to questions like these:

- Is Sears' cash balance sufficient?
- Should McDonald's expand its product line?
- Can Canadian Airlines pay its debt obligations?
- What percentage of Apple's marketing budget is for television advertisement? How does this compare with the competition? What is the overall financial condition of Apple?

Smaller businesses also need answers to their financial questions:

- Did business increase enough over the last year to warrant hiring a new assistant?
- Should we spend more money to design, produce, and send out new brochures in an effort to create more business?

Acounting is as important to individuals as it is to businesses; it answers questions like

- Should I take out a loan for a new car or wait until I can afford to pay cash?
- Would my money work better in a savings bank or in a credit union savings plan?

Accounting is the process that analyzes, records, classifies, summarizes, reports, and interprets financial information to decision makers—whether individuals, small business, large corporations, or governmental agencies—in a timely fashion. It is important that students understand the "whys" of the accounting process. Just knowing the mechanics is not enough.

Categories of Business Organization

There are three main categories of business organization: (1) sole proprietorships, (2) partnerships, and (3) corporations. Next, let's define each of them and look at their advantages and disadvantages. This information also appears in Table 1-1.

Sole Proprietorship

A **sole proprietorship** is a business that has one owner. That person is both the owner and the manager of the business. The advantage of a sole proprietorship is that the owner makes all of the decisions for the business. The disadvantage is that if the business cannot pay its obligations, the business owner must pay them. This means that the owner could lose some of his personal assets (e.g., his house or his savings).

TABLE 1-1 TYPES OF BUSINESS ORGANIZATIONS

	Sole Proprietorship	Partnership	Corporation
Ownership	Business owned by one person.	Business owned by more than one person.	Business owned by shareholders.
Formation	Easy to form.	Easy to form.	More difficult to form.
Liability	Owner could lose personal assets to meet obligations of business.	Partners could lose personal assets to meet obligations of partnership.	Limited personal risk. Shareholders' loss is usually limited to their investment in the company.
Closing	Ends with death of owner or closing of business.	Ends with death of partner or exit of a partner.	Can continue indefinitely.

Sole proprietorships are easy to form. They end if the business closes or when the owner dies.

Partnership

A **partnership** is a form of business ownership that has at least two owners (partners). Each partner acts as an owner of the company. This is an advantage because the partners can share the decision making for and the risks of the business. A disadvantage is that as in a sole proprietorship, the partners' personal assets could be lost if the partnership cannot meet its obligations.

Partnerships are easy to form. They end when a partner dies or leaves the partnership.

Disney is an example of a corporation.

Corporation

A **corporation** is a business owned by shareholders. The corporation may have only a few shareholders or it may have many shareholders. The shareholders are not personally liable for the corporation's debts, and they usually do not have input into the business decisions.

Corporations are more difficult to form than sole proprietorships or partnerships. Corporations can exist indefinitely.

CLASSIFYING ORGANIZATIONS BY ACTIVITY

Whether we are looking at a sole proprietorship, a partnership, or a corporation, the business can be classified by what the business does to earn money. Companies are categorized as either service, merchandise, or manufacturing businesses.

TABLE 1-2 EXAMPLES OF SERVICE, MERCHANDISE, AND MANUFACTURING BUSINESSES

Service Businesses	Merchandise Businesses	Manufacturing Businesses
Pete's Taxi Service	Sears	Mattel
Jane's Painting Co.	Eddie Bauer	General Motors
Dr. Wheeler, M.D.	The Bay	Toro

A local cab company is a good example of a **service company** because it provides a service. The first part of this book focusses on service businesses.

Stores like Sears and Eddie Bauer sell products. They are called merchandise companies. **Merchandise companies** can either make their own products or sell products that are made by another supplier. Companies like Mattel and General Motors that make their own products are called **manufacturers.**

Definition of Accounting

Accounting (also called the **accounting process**) is a system that measures the activities of a business in financial terms. It provides various reports and financial statements that show how the various transactions the business undertook

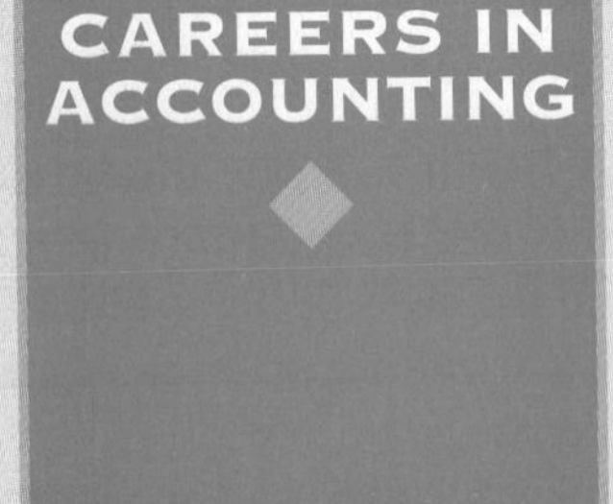

There are many career opportunities in accounting. They vary according to the amount of education and experience required. You should note that while a lot of routine accounting work is now done using computers, this has not lessened the need for all kinds of accounting personnel.

Accounting Clerks Accounting clerks perform most of a business' record-keeping functions. Sometimes, accounting clerks perform specific functions and are given a title that relates to these functions. Payroll clerk and account payable clerk are examples of such titles. Accounting clerks may perform their work manually or by computer.

Accounting clerks generally are required to have completed at least a one-semester accounting course.

Bookkeeping Bookkeepers are sometimes called "general bookkeepers" or "full-charge bookkeepers." That is because they do general accounting work, perform some summarizing and analyzing of accounting information, and supervise the accounting clerks. In some companies, they also may help managers and owners interpret accounting information. The size of the company determines the bookkeeper's responsibility.

Usually, bookkeepers need one or two years of accounting and experience as an accounting clerk. Some computer knowledge may be helpful, too.

Accountants Accountants plan, summarize, analyze, report, and interpret accounting information. Other responsibilities include assisting the owners and managers of the business in making financial decisions and supervising other accounting personnel.

Generally, accountants need a college diploma in accounting. They also may need additional professional credentials.

Accountants fall into three general classifications: public accountants, private accountants, and not-for-profit accountants. The opportunities in these categories are discussed as follows:

(e.g., buying and selling goods) affected the business. It does this by performing the following functions:

- **Analyzing:** Looking at what happened and how the business was affected.
- **Recording:** Putting the information into the accounting system.
- **Classifying:** Grouping all of the same activities (e.g., all purchases) together.
- **Summarizing:** Creating totals by category and/or date which are used in:
- **Reporting:** Issuing the reports that tell the results of the previous functions.
- **Interpreting:** Examining the reports to determine how the various pieces of information they contain relate to each other.

The system communicates the reports and financial statements to people who are interested in the information, such as the business' decision makers, investors, creditors, governmental agencies (e.g., Revenue Canada), and so on.

Public Accountants Public accountants provide services to clients for a fee. They may work alone or work for an accounting firm. Two professional accounting bodies are chiefly concerned with public accounting in Canada: the Certified General Accountants Association and the Canadian Institute of Chartered Accountants. (All professional groups have provincial identities as well.) Membership is restricted to those who have passed a challenging set of qualifying examinations and who have served a period of training in various accounting positions. These professional accountants perform many accounting tasks, but they also provide advice on taxation, perform audits, and consult on many aspects of business operations.

Private Accountants (Managerial Accountants) The main difference between public accountants and private accountants is that most private accountants work for a single business. A business may employ one accountant, or it may have many.

Private accountants who pass an examination prepared by the Society of Management Accountants of Canada can become Certified Management Accountants (CMAs). Those who pass the exam given by the Institute of Internal Auditors can become Certified Internal Auditors (CIAs).

There are many opportunities in private accounting. Private accountants may manage the accounting system, prepare reports and financial statements, prepare budgets, or determine certain costs (e.g., the cost of producing a new product). Some large firms have their own tax accountants and internal auditors.

Nonprofit (Governmental) Accountants Nonprofit accounting is used by governmental agencies and nonprofit agencies such as religious organizations, hospitals, and charitable organizations. These entities use accountants to prepare budgets and to keep records.

It is important to know that some nonprofit agencies do make money. These agencies can keep their nonprofit classifications if they keep the profit in the agency. Also, accounting procedures are similar to—but not quite the same as—procedures for profit-making businesses.

As you can see, a lot of people use these reports. A set of procedures and guidelines exist to make sure that everyone prepares and interprets them the same way. These guidelines are known as **generally accepted accounting principles (GAAP).**

Now let's look at the difference between bookkeeping and accounting. Keep in mind that we will use the terms "accounting" and "the accounting process" interchangeably.

Difference Between Bookkeeping and Accounting

Confusion often arises concerning the difference between bookkeeping and accounting. **Bookkeeping** is the recording (recordkeeping) function of the accounting process; a bookkeeper enters accounting information in the company's books. An accountant takes that information and prepares the financial reports that are used to analyze the company's financial position. **Accounting** involves many complex activities. Often, it includes the preparation of tax and financial reports, budgeting, and analyses of financial information.

Today, computers are used for routine bookkeeping operations that used to take weeks or months to complete. The text takes this into consideration by explaining how the advantages of the computer can be applied to a manual accounting system by using hands-on knowledge of how accounting works. Basic accounting knowledge is needed even though computers can help with routine tasks.

LEARNING UNIT 1-1
The Accounting Equation

ASSETS, LIABILITIES, AND EQUITIES

Let's begin our study of accounting concepts and procedures by looking at a small business: Jill Reed's law practice. Jill decided to open her practice at the end of August. She consulted her accountant before she made her decision. The accountant told her some important things before she made this decision. First, he told her the new business would be considered a separate business entity whose finances had to be kept separate and distinct from Jill's personal finances. The accountant went on to say that all transactions can be analyzed using the basic accounting equation: Assets = Liabilities + Owner's Equity.

Jill had never heard of the basic accounting equation. She listened carefully as the accountant explained the terms used in the equation and how the equation works:

Assets

Cash, land, supplies, office equipment, buildings, and other properties of value *owned* by a firm are called **assets.**

Equities

The rights of financial claim to the assets are called **equities.** Equities belong to those who supply the assets. If you are the only person to supply assets to the firm, you have the sole rights, for financial claims, to them. For example, if you supply the law firm with $3,000 in cash and $2,000 in office equipment, your equity in the firm is $5,000.

Relationship Between Assets and Equities

The relationship between assets and equities is

Assets	=	**Equities**
(Total value of items *owned* by business)		(Total claims against the assets)

The total dollar value of the assets of your law firm will be equal to the total dollar value of the financial claims to those assets, that is, equal to the total dollar value of the equities.

The total dollar value is broken down on the left-hand side of the equation to show the specific items of value owned by the business and on the right-hand side to show the types of claims against the assets owned.

Liabilities

A firm may have to borrow money to buy more assets; when this occurs it means the firm is **buying assets *on account*** (buy now, pay later). Suppose the law firm purchases a desk for $200 on account from Joe's Stationery, and the store is willing to wait 10 days for payment. The law firm has created a **liability:** an obligation to pay that comes due in the future. Joe's Stationery is called the **creditor.** This liability—the amount owed to Joe's Stationery—gives the store the right, or the financial claim, to $200 of the law firm's assets. When Joe's Stationery is paid, the store's rights to the assets of the law firm will end, since the obligation has been paid off.

Basic Accounting Equation

Elements of the basic accounting equation.

To understand better the various claims to a business' assets, accountants divide equities into two parts. The claims of creditors—outside persons or businesses—are labelled **liabilities.** The claims of the business' owner are labelled **owner's equity.** Let's see how the accounting equation looks now. It can be rewritten as follows:

Assets = **Equities**

1. Liabilities: rights of creditors
2. Owner's equity: rights of owner

Assets = Liabilities + Owner's Equity

The purpose of the accounting equation.

The total value of all the assets of a firm equals the combined total value of the financial claims of the creditors (liabilities) and the claims of the owner (owner's equity). This is known as the **basic accounting equation.** The basic accounting equation provides a basis for understanding the conventional accounting system of a business. The equation records business transactions in a logical and orderly way that shows their impact on the company's assets, liabilities, and owner's equity.

Importance of Creditors

Assets
− Liabilities
= Owner's Equity

Another way of presenting the basic accounting equation is:

Assets − Liabilities = Owner's Equity

In accounting, capital does not mean cash. Capital is the owner's current investment, or equity, in the assets of the business.

This form of the equation stresses the importance of creditors. The owner's rights to the business' assets are determined after the rights of the creditors are subtracted. In other words, creditors have first claim on assets. If a firm has no liabilities—and therefore no creditors—the owner has the total rights to assets. Another term for the owner's current investment, or equity, in the business' assets is **capital.**

As Jill Reed's law firm engages in business transactions (paying bills, serving clients, and so on), changes will take place in the assets, liabilities, and owner's equity (capital). Let's analyze some of these transactions.

Transaction A: **Aug. 28: Jill invests $6,000 in cash and $200 of office equipment into the business.**

On August 28, Jill withdraws $6,000 from her personal bank account and deposits the money in the law firm's newly opened bank account. She also invests $200 of office equipment in the business. She plans to be open for business on September 1. With the help of her accountant, Jill begins to prepare the accounting records for the business. We put this information into the basic accounting equation as follows:

Note: Capital is part of owner's equity; it is not an asset.

In our analyses, assume that any number without a sign in front of it is a + amount.

ASSETS		= LIABILITIES + OWNER'S EQUITY
Cash	**+ Office Equipment =**	**Jill Reed, Capital**
$6,000 +	$200 =	$6,200
	$6,200 = $6,200	

Note that the total value of the assets, cash, and office equipment—$6,200—is equal to the combined total value of liabilities (none, so far) and owner's equity ($6,200). Remember, Reed has supplied all the cash and office equipment, so she has the sole financial claim to the assets. Note how the heading "Jill Reed, Capital" is written under the owner's equity heading. The $6,200 is Jill's investment, or equity, in the firm's assets.

Transaction B: **Aug. 29: Law practice buys office equipment for cash, $500.**

From the initial investment of $6,000 cash, the law firm buys $500 worth of office equipment (such as a desk), which lasts a long time, while **supplies** (such as pens) tend to be used up relatively quickly.

	ASSETS		= LIABILITIES + OWNER'S EQUITY
	Cash	**+ Office Equipment =**	**Jill Reed, Capital**
BEGINNING BALANCE	$6,000 +	$200 =	$6,200
TRANSACTION	−500	+500	
ENDING BALANCE	$5,500 +	$700 =	$6,200
		$6,200 = $6,200	

Shift in Assets

As a result of the last transactions, the law office has less cash but has increased its amount of office equipment. This is called a **shift in assets**—the makeup of the assets has changed, but the total of the assets remains the same.

Suppose you go food shopping at the supermarket with $100 and spend $60. Now you have two assets, food and money. The composition of the assets has been *shifted*—you have more food and less money than you did—but the *total* of the assets has not increased or decreased. The total value of the food, $60, plus the cash, $40, is still $100. When you borrow money from the bank, on the other hand, you have an increase in cash (an asset) and an increase in liabilities; overall there is an increase in assets, not just a shift.

An accounting equation can remain in balance even if only one side is affected. The key point to remember is that the left-hand-side total of assets must always equal the right-hand-side total of liabilities and owner's equity.

Transaction C: Aug. 30: Buys additional office equipment on account, $300.

The law firm purchases an additional $300 worth of chairs and desks from Wilmington Company. Instead of demanding cash right away, Wilmington agrees to deliver the equipment and to allow up to 60 days for the law practice to pay the invoice (bill).

This liability, or obligation to pay in the future, has some interesting effects on the basic accounting equation. Wilmington Company has accepted as payment a partial claim against the assets of the law practice. This claim exists until the law firm pays the bill. This unwritten promise to pay the creditor is a liability called **accounts payable.**

	ASSETS		=	LIABILITIES	+	OWNER'S EQUITY
	Cash	**+ Office Equipment**	**=**	**Accounts Payable**	**+**	**Jill Reed, Capital**
BEGINNING BALANCE	$5,500	+ $ 700	=		+	$6,200
TRANSACTION		+300		+300		
ENDING BALANCE	$5,500	+ $1,000	=	$ 300	+	$6,200
		$6,500	=	$6,500		

When this information is analyzed, we can see that the law practice has increased what it owes (accounts payable) as well as increased an asset (office equipment) by $300. The law practice gains $300 in an asset but has an obligation to pay Wilmington Company at a future date.

The owner's equity remains unchanged. This transaction results in an increase of total assets from $6,200 to $6,500.

Finally, note that after each transaction the basic accounting equation remains in balance.

LEARNING UNIT 1-1 REVIEW

AT THIS POINT you should be able to

- List the functions of accounting. (pp.2,4)
- Define and explain the differences between sole proprietorships, partnerships, and corporations. (pp.2,3)
- Compare and contrast bookkeeping and accounting. (p.6)
- Explain the role of the computer as an accounting tool. (p.6)
- State the purpose of the accounting equation. (p.6)
- Explain the difference between liabilities and owner's equity. (p.7)
- Define capital. (p.7)
- Explain the difference between a shift in assets and an increase in assets. (p.8)

To test your understanding of this material, complete Self-Review Quiz 1-1. The blank forms you need are in the *Study Guide and Working Papers* for Chapter 1. The solution to the quiz immediately follows here in the text. If you have difficulty doing the problems, review Learning Unit 1-1 and the solution to the quiz.

Keep in mind that learning accounting is like learning to type—the more you practice, the better you become. You will not be an expert in one day. Be patient. It will all come together.

SELF-REVIEW QUIZ 1-1

(The blank forms you need are on page 1-1 of the *Study Guide and Working Papers.*)

Record the following transactions in the basic accounting equation:

1. Pete O'Brien invests $14,000 to begin a real estate office.
2. The real estate office buys $600 of computer equipment for cash.
3. The real estate company buys $500 of additional computer equipment on account.

Solution to Self-Review Quiz 1-1

	ASSETS		=	LIABILITIES	+	OWNER'S EQUITY
	Cash	+ Computer Equipment	=	Accounts Payable	+	Pete O'Brien, Capital
1.	+$14,000					+$14,000
BALANCE	14,000		=			14,000
2.	−600	+$600				
BALANCE	13,400 +	600	=			14,000
3.		+500		+$500		
ENDING BALANCE	$13,400 +	$ 1,100	=	$ 500	+	$14,000
		$14,500	=	$14,500		

LEARNING UNIT 1-2

The Balance Sheet

The balance sheet shows the company's financial position as of a particular date. (In our example, that date is at the end of August.)

In the first learning unit, the transactions for Jill Reed's law office were recorded in the accounting equation. The transactions we recorded occurred before the law firm opened for business. This report called a **balance sheet** or **statement of financial position** shows the history of the company before it opened. The balance sheet is a formal report that presents the information from the ending balances of both sides of the accounting equation. Think of the balance sheet as a snapshot of the business' financial position as of a particular date.

Let's look at the balance sheet of Jill Reed's law practice for August 31, 19XX, shown in Figure 1-1. The figures in the balance sheet come from the ending balances of the accounting equation for the law practice as shown in Learning Unit 1-1.

Note that in Figure 1-1 the assets owned by the law practice appear on the left-hand side and that liabilities and owner's equity appear on the right-hand side. Both sides equal $6,500. This *balance* between left and right gives the balance sheet its name. In later chapters we will be looking at other ways to set up a balance sheet.

	ASSETS	=	LIABILITIES	+	OWNER'S EQUITY
	Cash + Office Equipment	=	Accounts Payable	+	Jill Reed, Capital
ENDING BALANCES	$5,500 + $1,000	=	$300	+	$6,200

JILL REED, Barrister and Solicitor
BALANCE SHEET
AUGUST 31, 19XX

Assets		Liabilities and Owner's Equity	
Cash	$ 5500 00	Liabilities	
Office Equipment	1000 00	Accounts Payable	$ 300 00
		Owner's Equity	
		Jill Reed, Capital	6200 00
		Total Liabilities and	
Total Assets	$ 6500 00	Owner's Equity	$ 6500 00

Remember: The balance sheet is a formal report.

FIGURE 1-1
The Balance Sheet

Points to Remember in Preparing a Balance Sheet

The Heading

Do you remember the three elements that make up a balance sheet? Assets, liabilities, and owner's equity.

The heading of the balance sheet provides the following information:

- The company name: Jill Reed, Barrister and Solicitor.
- The name of the report: Balance Sheet.
- The date for which the report is prepared: August 31, 19XX.

Use of the Dollar Sign

Note that the dollar sign is not repeated every time a figure appears. As shown in the balance sheet for Jill Reed's law practice, it is usually placed to the left of each column's top figure and to the left of the column's total.

Distinguishing the Total

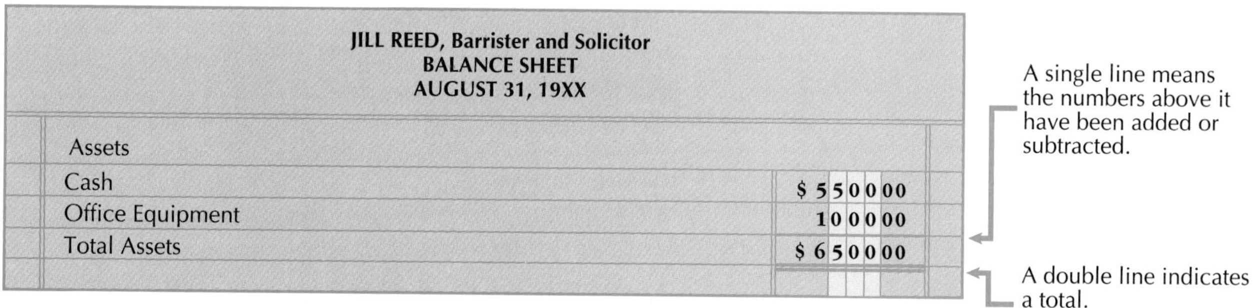

JILL REED, Barrister and Solicitor
BALANCE SHEET
AUGUST 31, 19XX

Assets	
Cash	$ 5500 00
Office Equipment	1000 00
Total Assets	$ 6500 00

A single line means the numbers above it have been added or subtracted.
A double line indicates a total.

When adding numbers down a column, use a single line before the total and a double line beneath it. A single line means that the numbers above it have been added or subtracted. A double line indicates a total. It is important to align the numbers in the column; many errors occur because these figures are not lined up. These rules are the same for all accounting reports.

The balance sheet gives Jill the information she needs to see the law firm's financial position before it opens for business. This information does not tell her, however, whether the firm will make a profit.

LEARNING UNIT 1-2 REVIEW

AT THIS POINT you should be able to

- Define and state the purpose of a balance sheet. (p.10)
- Identify and define the elements making up a balance sheet. (p.10)
- Show the relationship between the accounting equation and the balance sheet. (p.11)
- Prepare a balance sheet in proper form from information provided. (p.11)

SELF-REVIEW QUIZ 1-2

(The blank forms you need are on page 1-2 of the *Study Guide and Working Papers.*)

The date is November 30, 19XX. Use the following information to prepare in proper form a balance sheet for Janning Company:

Accounts Payable	$30,000
Cash	8,000
A. Janning, Capital	9,000
Office Equipment	31,000

Solution to Self-Review Quiz 1-2

JANNING COMPANY
BALANCE SHEET
NOVEMBER 30, 19XX

Assets		Liabilities and Owner's Equity	
Cash	$ 8 000 00	Liabilities	
Office Equipment	31 000 00	Accounts Payable	$ 30 000 00
		Owner's Equity	
		A. Janning, Capital	9 000 00
		Total Liabilities and	
Total Assets	$ 39 000 00	Owner's Equity	$ 39 000 00

Capital does not mean cash. The capital amount is the owner's current investment of assets in the business.

Note: Capital does not mean cash. The capital amount is the owner's current investment of assets in the business. So Janning's $9,000 in capital means the owner may have supplied some cash and some equipment to the business.

LEARNING UNIT 1-3

The Accounting Equation Expanded: Revenue, Expenses, and Withdrawals

As soon as Jill Reed's office opened, she began performing legal services for her clients and earning revenue for the business. At the same time, as a part of doing business, she incurred various expenses, such as rent.

When Jill asked her accountant how these transactions fit into the accounting equation, he began by defining some terms.

KEY TERMS IN THE ACCOUNTING EQUATION

When revenue is earned, it is recorded as an increase in owner's equity and an increase in assets.

Accounts *receivable* is an asset. The law firm expects to be able to *receive* amounts owed from customers at a later date.

Remember: Accounts receivable results from earning revenue even when cash is not yet received.

Record an expense when it is incurred, whether it is paid then or is to be paid later.

Revenue A service company earns **revenue** when it provides services to its clients. Jill's law firm earned revenue when she provided legal services to her clients for legal fees. When revenue is earned, owner's equity is increased. In effect, revenue is a subdivision of owner's equity.

Assets are increased. The increase is in the form of cash if the client pays right away. If the client promises to pay in the future, the increase is called **accounts receivable.** When revenue is earned, the transaction is recorded as an increase in revenue and an increase in assets (either as cash and/or as accounts receivable, depending on whether it was paid right away or will be paid in the future).

Expenses A business' **expenses** are the cost the company incurs in carrying on operations in its effort to create revenue. Expenses are also a subdivision of owner's equity; when expenses are incurred, they *decrease* owner's equity. Expenses can be paid for in cash or they can be charged.

Net Income/Net Loss When revenue totals more than expenses, **net income** is the result; when expenses total more than revenue, **net loss** is the result.

Withdrawals At some point Jill Reed may need to withdraw cash or other assets from the business to pay living or other personal expenses that do not relate to the business. We will record these transactions in an account called **withdrawals.** Sometimes this account is called the *owner's drawing account.* Withdrawals is a subdivision of owner's equity that records personal expenses not related to the business. Withdrawals decrease owner's equity.

It is important to remember the difference between expenses and withdrawals. Expenses relate to business operations; withdrawals are the result of personal needs outside the normal operations of the business.

Now let's analyze the September transactions for Jill Reed's law firm using an **expanded accounting equation** that includes withdrawals, revenues, and expenses.

EXPANDED ACCOUNTING EQUATION

Transaction D: **Sept. 1–30: Provided legal services for cash, $2,000.**

Transactions A, B, and C were discussed earlier, when the law office was being formed in August. See Learning Unit 1-1.

In the law firm's first month of operation a total of $2,000 in cash was received for legal services performed. In the accounting equation the asset Cash is increased by $2,000. Revenue is also increased by $2,000, resulting in an increase in owner's equity.

	ASSETS			= LIABILITIES +	OWNER'S EQUITY			
	Cash	**+ Accts. Rec.**	**+ Office Equip.**	**= Accts. Pay.**	**+ J. Reed, Capital**	**− J. Reed, Withdr.**	**+ Revenue**	**− Expenses**
BAL. FOR.	$5,500		+ $1,000	= $ 300	+ $6,200			
TRANS.	+2,000						+$2,000	
END. BAL.	$7,500		+ $1,000	= $ 300	+ $6,200		+ $2,000	
			$8,500	= $8,500				

A revenue column was added to the basic accounting equation. Amounts are recorded in the revenue column when they are earned. They are also recorded in the assets column, either under Cash and/or under Accounts Receivable. Do not think of revenue as an asset. It is part of owner's equity. It is the revenue that creates an inward flow of cash and accounts receivable.

Transaction E: **Sept. 1–30: Provided legal services on account, $3,000.**

	ASSETS			= LIABILITIES +	OWNER'S EQUITY			
	Cash	**+ Accts. Rec.**	**+ Office Equip.**	**= Accts. Pay.**	**+ J. Reed, Capital**	**− J. Reed, Withdr.**	**+ Revenue**	**− Expenses**
BAL. FOR.	$7,500		+ $ 1,000	= $ 300	+ $6,200		+ $2,000	
TRANS.		+$3,000					+3,000	
END. BAL.	$7,500	+ $3,000	+ $ 1,000	= $ 300	+ $6,200		+ $5,000	
			$11,500	= $11,500				

Jill's law practice performed legal work on account for $3,000. The firm did not receive the cash for these earned legal fees; it accepted an unwritten promise from these clients that payment would be received in the future.

Transaction F: **Sept. 1–30: Received $900 cash as partial payment from previous services performed on account.**

During September some of Jill's clients who had received services and promised to pay in the future decided to reduce what they owed the practice by $900 when their bills came due. This is shown as follows on the expanded accounting equation.

	ASSETS			= LIABILITIES +	OWNER'S EQUITY			
	Cash	**+ Accts. Rec.**	**+ Office Equip.**	**= Accts. Pay.**	**+ J. Reed, Capital**	**− J. Reed, Withdr.**	**+ Revenue**	**− Expenses**
BAL. FOR.	$7,500	+ $3,000	+ $ 1,000	= $ 300	+ $6,200		+ $5,000	
TRANS.	+900	−900						
END. BAL.	$8,400	+ $2,100	+ $ 1,000	= $ 300	+ $6,200		+ $5,000	
			$11,500	= $11,500				

The law firm increased the asset Cash by $900 and reduced another asset, Accounts Receivable, by $900. The *total* of assets does not change. The right-hand side of the expanded accounting equation has not been touched because the total on the left-hand side of the equation has not changed. The revenue was recorded when it was earned, and the *same revenue cannot be recorded twice.* This transaction analyzes the situation *after* the revenue has been previously earned and recorded. Transaction F shows a shift in assets — more cash and less accounts receivable.

Transaction G: **Paid salaries expense, $700.**

	ASSETS			= LIABILITIES +	OWNER'S EQUITY			
	Cash	+ Accts. Rec.	+ Office Equip.	= Accts. Pay.	+ J. Reed, Capital	− J. Reed, Withdr.	+ Revenue	− Expenses
BAL. FOR.	$8,400	+ $2,100	+ $ 1,000	= $ 300	+ $6,200		+ $5,000	
TRANS.	−700							+700
END. BAL.	$7,700	+ $2,100	+ $ 1,000	= $ 300	+ $6,200		+ $5,000	− $700
			$10,800	= $10,800				

As expenses increase, they decrease owner's equity. This incurred expense of $700 reduces the cash by $700. Although the expense was paid, the total of our expenses to date has *increased* by $700. Keep in mind that owner's equity decreases as expenses increase, so the accounting equation remains in balance.

Transaction H: **Paid rent expense, $400.**

	ASSETS			= LIABILITIES +	OWNER'S EQUITY			
	Cash	+ Accts. Rec.	+ Office Equip.	= Accts. Pay.	+ J. Reed, Capital	− J. Reed, Withdr.	+ Revenue	− Expenses
BAL. FOR.	$7,700	+ $2,100	+ $ 1,000	= $ 300	+ $6,200		+ $5,000	− $ 700
TRANS.	−400							+400
END. BAL.	$7,300	+ $2,100	+ $ 1,000	= $ 300	+ $6,200		+ $5,000	− $1,100
			$10,400	= $10,400				

During September the practice incurred rent expenses of $400. This rent was not paid in advance; it was paid when it came due. The payment of rent reduces the asset Cash by $400 as well as increases the expenses of the firm, resulting in a decrease in owner's equity. The firm's expenses are now $1,100.

Transaction I: **Incurred advertising expenses of $200, to be paid next month.**

	ASSETS			= LIABILITIES +	OWNER'S EQUITY			
	Cash	+ Accts. Rec.	+ Office Equip.	= Accts. Pay.	+ J. Reed, Capital	− J. Reed, Withdr.	+ Revenue	− Expenses
BAL. FOR.	$7,300	+ $2,100	+ $ 1,000	= $ 300	+ $6,200		+ $5,000	− $1,100
TRANS.				+200				+200
END. BAL.	$7,300	+ $2,100	+ $ 1,000	= $ 500	+ $6,200		+ $5,000	− $1,300
			$10,400	= $10,400				

Jill ran an ad in the local newspaper and incurred an expense of $200. This increase in expenses caused a corresponding decrease in owner's equity. Since Jill has not paid the newspaper for the advertising yet, she owes $200. Thus her liabilities (Accounts Payable) increase by $200. Eventually, when the bill comes in and is paid, both Cash and Accounts Payable will be decreased.

***Transaction J:* Jill withdrew $100 for personal use.**

	ASSETS			= LIABILITIES +	OWNER'S EQUITY			
	Cash	**+ Accts. Rec.**	**+ Office Equip.**	**= Accts. Pay.**	**+ J. Reed, Capital**	**− J. Reed, Withdr.**	**+ Revenue**	**− Expenses**
BAL. FOR.	$7,300	+ $2,100	+ $ 1,000 =	$ 500	+ $6,200		+ $5,000	− $1,300
TRANS.	−100					+100		
END. BAL.	$7,200	+ $2,100	+ $ 1,000 =	$ 500	+ $6,200	− $100	+ $5,000	− $1,300
			$10,300 =	$10,300				

By taking $100 for personal use, Jill has *increased* her withdrawals from the business by $100 and decreased the asset Cash by $100. Note that as withdrawals increase, the owner's equity will *decrease*. Keep in mind that a withdrawal is *not* a business expense. It is a subdivision of owner's equity that records money or other assets an owner withdraws from the business for *personal* use.

Subdivision of Owner's Equity

Take a moment to review the subdivisions of owner's equity:

- As capital increases, owner's equity increases (see transaction A).
- As withdrawals increase, owner's equity decreases (see transaction J).
- As revenue increases, owner's equity increases (see transaction D).
- As expenses increase, owner's equity decreases (see transaction G).

Jill Reed's Expanded Accounting Equation

The following is a summary of the expanded accounting equation for Jill Reed's law firm.

Jill Reed
Barrister and Solicitor
Expanded Accounting Equation: A Summary

	ASSETS			= LIABILITIES +	OWNER'S EQUITY			
	Cash	**+ Accts. Rec.**	**+ Office Equip.**	**= Accts. Pay.**	**+ J. Reed, Capital**	**− J. Reed, Withdr.**	**+ Revenue**	**− Expenses**
A.	$6,000		+$200 =		+$6,200			
BALANCE	6,000		+ 200 =		6,200			
B.	−500		+500					
BALANCE	5,500		+ 700 =		6,200			
C.			+300	+$300				
BALANCE	5,500		+ 1,000 =	300	+ 6,200			
D.	+2,000						+$2,000	
BALANCE	7,500		+ 1,000 =	300	+ 6,200		+ 2,000	

E.		+$3,000					+3,000	
BALANCE	7,500 +	3,000 +	1,000 =	300	+ 6,200		+ 5,000	
F.	+900	−900						
BALANCE	8,400 +	2,100 +	1,000 =	300	+ 6,200		+ 5,000	
G.	−700							+$700
BALANCE	7,700 +	2,100 +	1,000 =	300	+ 6,200		+ 5,000 −	700
H.	−400							+400
BALANCE	7,300 +	2,100 +	1,000 =	300	+ 6,200		+ 5,000 −	1,100
I.				+200				+200
BALANCE	7,300 +	2,100 +	1,000 =	500	+ 6,200		+ 5,000 −	1,300
J.	−100					+$100		
END. BAL.	$7,200 +	$2,100 +	$1,000 =	$500	+ $6,200 −	$100 +	$5,000 −	$1,300

LEARNING UNIT 1-3 REVIEW

AT THIS POINT you should be able to

- Define and explain the difference between revenue and expenses. (p.13)
- Define and explain the difference between net income and net loss. (p.13)
- Explain the subdivision of owner's equity. (pp.14,16)
- Explain the effects of withdrawals, revenue, and expenses on owner's equity. (p.16)
- Record transactions in an expanded accounting equation and balance the basic accounting equation as a means of checking the accuracy of your calculations. (p. 16)

SELF-REVIEW QUIZ 1-3

(The blank forms you need are on page 1-2 of the *Study Guide and Working Papers.*)

Record the following transactions into the expanded accounting equation for the Bing Company. Note that all titles have a beginning balance.

1. Received cash revenue, $3,000.
2. Billed customers for services rendered, $6,000.
3. Received a bill for telephone expenses (to be paid next month), $125.
4. Bob Bing withdrew cash for personal use, $500.
5. Received $1,000 from customers in partial payment for services performed in transaction 2.

Solution to Self-Review Quiz 1-3

	ASSETS				= LIABILITIES +		OWNER'S EQUITY		
	Cash	+ Accts. Rec.	+ Cleaning Equip.	=	Accts. Pay.	+ B. Bing, Capital	− B. Bing, Withdr.	+ Revenue	− Expenses
BEG. BAL.	$10,000	+ $ 2,500	+ $6,500	=	$1,000	+ $11,800	− $ 800	+ $ 9,000	− $2,000
1.	+3,000		+	=				+3,000	
BALANCE	13,000	+ 2,500	+ 6,500	=	1,000	+ 11,800	− 800	+ 12,000	− 2,000
2.		+6,000						+6,000	
BALANCE	13,000	+ 8,500	+ 6,500	=	1,000	+ 11,800	− 800	+ 18,000	− 2,000
3.					+125				+125
BALANCE	13,000	+ 8,500	+ 6,500	=	1,125	+ 11,800	− 800	+ 18,000	− 2,125
4.	−500						+500		
BALANCE	12,500	+ 8,500	+ 6,500	=	1,125	+ 11,800	− 1,300	+ 18,000	− 2,125
5.	+1,000	−1,000							
END. BAL.	$13,500	+ $ 7,500	+ $6,500	=	$1,125	+ $11,800	− $ 1,300	+ $18,000	− $2,125
		$27,500		=			$27,500		

LEARNING UNIT 1-4

Preparing Financial Reports

Jill Reed would like to be able to find out whether her firm is making a profit, so she asks her accountant whether he can measure the firm's financial performance on a monthly basis. Her accountant replies that there are a number of financial reports that he can prepare, such as the income statement, which shows how well the law firm has performed over a specific period of time. The accountant can use the information in the income statement to prepare other reports.

THE INCOME STATEMENT

The income statement is prepared from data found in the revenue and expense columns of the expanded accounting equation.

An **income statement** is an accounting report that shows business results in terms of revenue and expenses. If revenues are greater than expenses, the report shows net income. If expenses are greater than revenues, the report shows net loss. An income statement can cover one, three, six, or twelve months. It does not usually cover more than one year. The report shows the result of all revenues and expenses throughout the entire period and not just as of a specific date. The income statement for Jill Reed's law firm is shown in Figure 1-2.

FIGURE 1-2
The Income Statement

JILL REED, Barrister and Solicitor
INCOME STATEMENT
FOR MONTH ENDED SEPTEMBER 30, 19XX

Revenue:		
Legal Fees		$ 5000 00
Operating Expenses:		
Salaries Expense	$ 700 00	
Rent Expense	400 00	
Advertising Expense	200 00	
Total Operating Expenses		1300 00
Net Income		$ 3700 00

JILL REED, Barrister and Solicitor STATEMENT OF OWNER'S EQUITY FOR MONTH ENDED SEPTEMBER 30, 19XX		
Jill Reed, Capital, September 1, 19XX		$ 6 2 0 0 00
Net Income for September	$ 3 7 0 0 00	
Less: Withdrawals for September	1 0 0 00	
Increase in Capital		3 6 0 0 00
Jill Reed, Capital, September 30, 19XX		$ 9 8 0 0 00

Comes from income statement.

FIGURE 1-3 Statement of Owner's Equity

Points to Remember in Preparing an Income Statement

Heading The heading of an income statement tells the same three things as all other accounting reports: the company's name, the name of the report, and the period of time the report covers (or the data prepared).

The inside column of numbers ($700, $400, $200) is used to subtotal all expenses ($1,300) before subtracting from revenue.

The Set Up As you can see on the income statement, the inside column of numbers ($700, $400, and $200) is used to subtotal all expenses ($1,300) before subtracting them from revenue ($5,000 − $1,300 = $3,700).

Operating expenses may be listed in alphabetical order, in order of largest amounts to smallest, or in a set order established by the accountant.

THE STATEMENT OF OWNER'S EQUITY

As we said, the income statement is a business report that shows business results in terms of revenue and expenses. But how does net income or net loss affect owner's equity? To find that out we have to look at a second type of report, the **statement of owner's equity.**

If this statement of owner's equity is omitted, the information will be included in the owner's equity section of the balance sheet.

The statement of owner's equity shows for a certain period of time what changes occurred in Jill Reed, Capital. The statement of owner's equity is shown in Figure 1-3.

The capital of Jill Reed can be

Increased by: Owner Investment
Net Income (Revenue − Expenses)

Decreased by: Owner Withdrawals
Net Loss

Remember, a withdrawal is *not* a business expense and thus is not involved in the calculation of net income or net loss on the income statement. It appears on the statement of owner's equity. The statement of owner's equity summarizes the effects of all the subdivisions of owner's equity (revenue, expenses, withdrawals) on beginning capital. The ending capital figure ($9,800) will be the beginning figure in the next statement of owner's equity.

Suppose that Jill's law firm had operated at a loss in the month of September. Suppose instead of net income there was a net loss, and an additional investment of $700 was made on September 15. This is how the statement would look if this had happened.

JILL REED, Barrister and Solicitor
STATEMENT OF OWNER'S EQUITY
FOR MONTH ENDED SEPTEMBER 30, 19XX

Jill Reed, Capital, September 1, 19XX		$6200 00
Additional Investment, September 15, 19XX		700 00
Total Investment for September		$6900 00
Less: Net Loss for September	$400 00	
Withdrawals for September	100 00	
Decrease in Capital		500 00
Jill Reed, Capital, September 30, 19XX		$6400 00

The Balance Sheet

Now let's look at how to prepare a balance sheet from the expanded accounting equation (see Figure 1-4).

Main Elements of the Income Statement, the Statement of Owner's Equity, and the Balance Sheet

In this chapter we have discussed three financial reports: the income statement, the statement of owner's equity, and the balance sheet. (There is a fourth report, called the statement of cash flows, that will not be covered at this time.) Let us review what elements of the expanded accounting equation go into each report, and the usual order in which the reports are prepared. Figure 1-4 presents a diagram of the accounting equation and the balance sheet. Table 1-3 summarizes the following points:

FIGURE 1-4 The Balance Sheet and the Accounting Equation

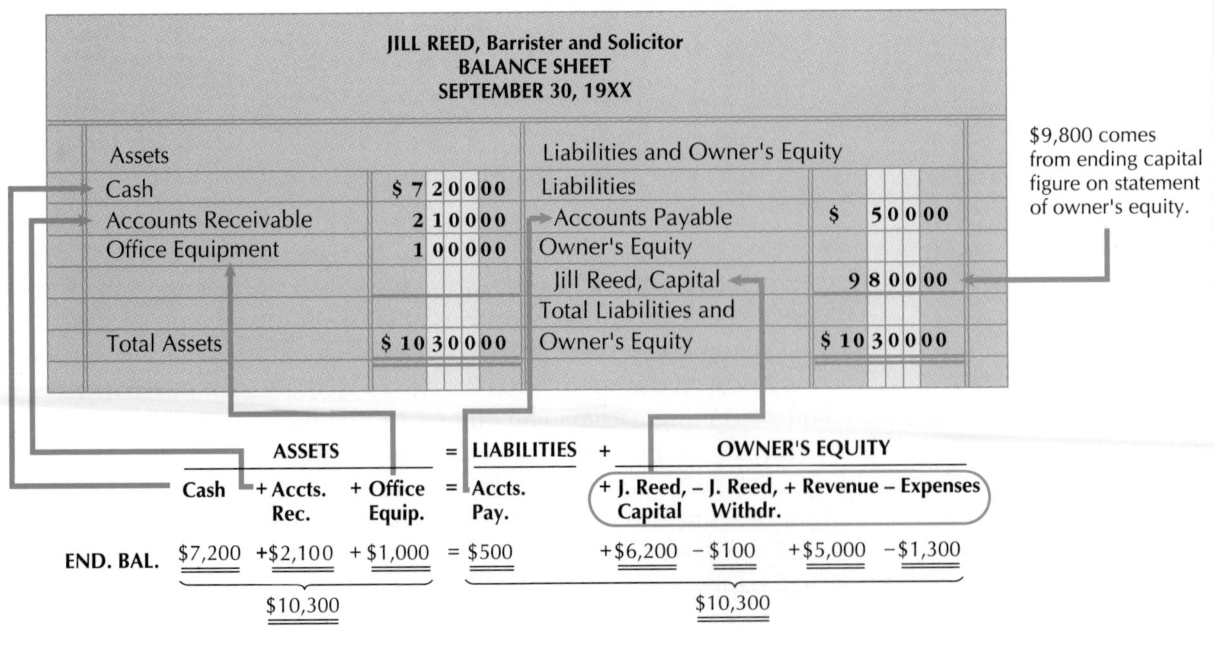

JILL REED, Barrister and Solicitor
BALANCE SHEET
SEPTEMBER 30, 19XX

Assets		Liabilities and Owner's Equity	
Cash	$7200 00	Liabilities	
Accounts Receivable	2100 00	Accounts Payable	$500 00
Office Equipment	1000 00	Owner's Equity	
		Jill Reed, Capital	9800 00
		Total Liabilities and	
Total Assets	$10300 00	Owner's Equity	$10300 00

TABLE 1-3 WHAT GOES ON EACH FINANCIAL REPORT

	Income Statement	Statement of Owner's Equity	Balance Sheet
Assets			X
Liabilities			X
Capital* (beg.)		X	
Capital (end)		X	X
Withdrawals		X	
Revenues	X		
Expenses	X		
Net Income (Loss)	X	X	

* **Note:** Additional investments go on the statement of owner's equity.

- The income statement is prepared first: it includes revenues and expenses and shows net income or net loss. This net income or net loss is used to update the next report, the statement of owner's equity.
- The statement of owner's equity is prepared second; it includes beginning capital and any additional investments, the net income or net loss shown on the income statement, withdrawals, and the total, which is the **ending capital.**
- The balance sheet is prepared last; it includes the final balances of each of the elements listed in the accounting equation under Assets and Liabilities. The balance in Capital comes from the statement of owner's equity.

LEARNING UNIT 1-4 REVIEW

AT THIS POINT you should be able to

- Define and state the purpose of the income statement, the statement of owner's equity, and the balance sheet. (p.18)
- Discuss why the income statement should be prepared first. (p.20)
- Compare and contrast these three financial reports. (p.20)
- Calculate a new figure for capital on the statement of owner's equity and balance sheet. (p. 19)
- Show what happens on a statement of owner's equity if there is a net loss. (p.20)

SELF-REVIEW QUIZ 1-4

(The blank forms you need are on pages 1-3 and 1-4 of the *Study Guide and Working Papers.*)

From the following balances for Rusty Realty prepare:

1. Income statement for month ended November 30, 19XX.
2. Statement of owner's equity for the month ended November 30, 19XX.
3. Balance sheet as of November 30, 19XX.

Cash	$4,000	R. Rusty, Capital, November 1, 19XX	$5,000
Accounts Receivable	1,370	R. Rusty, Withdrawals	100
Store Furniture	1,490	Commissions Earned	1,500
Accounts Payable	900	Rent Expense	200
		Advertising Expense	150
		Salaries Expense	90

Solution to Self-Review Quiz 1-4

RUSTY REALTY
INCOME STATEMENT
FOR MONTH ENDED NOVEMBER 30, 19XX

Revenue:		
Commissions Earned		$ 1 5 0 0 00
Operating Expenses:		
Rent Expense	$ 2 0 0 00	
Advertising Expense	1 5 0 00	
Salaries Expense	9 0 00	
Total Operating Expenses		4 4 0 00
Net Income		$ 1 0 6 0 00

RUSTY REALTY
STATEMENT OF OWNER'S EQUITY
FOR MONTH ENDED NOVEMBER 30, 19XX

R. Rusty, Capital, November 1, 19XX		$ 5 0 0 0 00
Net Income for November	$ 1 0 6 0 00	
Less: Withdrawals for November	1 0 0 00	
Increase in Capital		9 6 0 00
R. Rusty, Capital, November 30, 19XX		$ 5 9 6 0 00

RUSTY REALTY
BALANCE SHEET
NOVEMBER 30, 19XX

Assets		Liabilities and Owner's Equity	
Cash	$ 4 0 0 0 00	Liabilities	
Accounts Receivable	1 3 7 0 00	Accounts Payable	$ 9 0 0 00
Store Furniture	1 4 9 0 00		
		Owner's Equity	
		R. Rusty, Capital	5 9 6 0 00
		Total Liabilities and	
Total Assets	$ 6 8 6 0 00	Owner's Equity	$ 6 8 6 0 00

Chapter Review

COMPREHENSIVE DEMONSTRATION PROBLEM WITH SOLUTION TIPS

(The blank forms you need are on pages 1-5 and 1-6 of the *Study Guide and Working Papers.*)

Michael Brown opened his law office on June 1, 19XX. During the first month of operations Michael conducted the following transactions:

1. Invested $5,000 in cash into the law practice.
2. Paid $600 for office equipment.
3. Purchased additional office equipment on account, $1,000.
4. Performed legal services for clients, receiving cash, $2,000.
5. Paid salaries, $800.
6. Performed legal services for clients on account, $1,000.
7. Paid rent, $1,200.
8. Withdrew $500 from his law practice for personal use.
9. Received $500 from customers in partial payment for legal services performed, transaction 6.

Assignment

a. Record these transactions in the expanded accounting equation.

b. Prepare the financial statements at June 30 for Michael Brown, Barrister and Solicitor.

Solution to Comprehensive Demonstration Problem

	ASSETS			= LIABILITIES +	OWNER'S EQUITY			
A.	**Cash**	**+ Accts. Rec.**	**+ Office Equip. =**	**Accts. Pay.**	**+ M. Brown, Capital**	**− M. Brown, Withdr.**	**+ Revenue**	**− Expenses**
1.	+$5,000				+$5,000			
BAL.	5,000		=		5,000			
2.	−600		+$600					
BAL.	4,400		+ 600 =		5,000			
3.			+1,000	+$1,000				
BAL.	4,400		+ 1,600 =	1,000 +	5,000			
4.	+2,000						+$2,000	
BAL.	6,400		+ 1,600 =	1,000 +	5,000		+ 2,000	
5.	−800							+$800
BAL.	5,600		+ 1,600 =	1,000 +	5,000		+ 2,000 −	800
6.		+$1,000					+1,000	
BAL.	5,600 +	1,000 +	1,600 =	1,000 +	5,000		+ 3,000 −	800
7.	−1,200							+1,200
BAL.	4,400 +	1,000 +	1,600 =	1,000 +	5,000		+ 3,000 −	2,000
8.	−500					+$500		
BAL.	3,900 +	1,000 +	1,600 =	1,000 +	5,000 −	500	+ 3,000 −	2,000
9.	+500	−500						
END. BAL.	$4,400 +	$ 500 +	$1,600 =	$1,000 +	$5,000 −	$500	+ $3,000 −	$2,000
			$6,500 =	$6,500				

Solution Tips to Expanded Accounting Equation

A.

- **Transaction 1:** The business increased its cash by $5,000. Owner's Equity (capital) increased when Michael supplied the cash to the business.
- **Transaction 2:** There was a shift in assets when the equipment was purchased. The business lowered its cash by $600, and a new column—Equipment—was increased for the $600 of equipment that was bought. The amount of capital is not touched because the owner did not supply any new funds.
- **Transaction 3:** When creditors supply $1,000 of additional equipment, the business Accounts Payable shows the debt. The business had increased what it *owes* the creditors.
- **Transaction 4:** Legal Fees, a subdivision of owner's equity, is increased when the law firm provides a service even if no money is received. The service provides an inward flow of $2,000 cash, an asset. Remember, legal fees are *not* an asset. As legal fees increase, owner's equity increases.
- **Transaction 5:** The salary paid by Michael shows an $800 increase in expenses, and a corresponding decrease in cash.
- **Transaction 6:** Michael did the work and earned the $1,000. That $1,000 is recorded as revenue. This time the legal fees create an inward flow of assets called Accounts Receivable for $1,000. Remember legal fees are *not* an asset. They are a subdivision of owner's equity.
- **Transaction 7:** The $1,200 rent expense reduces owner's equity as well as cash.
- **Transaction 8:** Withdrawals are for personal use. Here, business cash decreases by $500 while Michael's cash increases $500. Withdrawals decrease the owner's equity.
- **Transaction 9:** This transaction does not reflect new revenue in the form of legal fees. It is only a shift in assets: more cash and less accounts receivable.

B-1.

Michael Brown, Barrister and Solicitor
Income Statement
For Month Ended June 30, 19XX

Revenue:		
Legal Fees		$3,000
Operating Expenses:		
Salaries Expense	$ 800	
Rent Expense	1,200	
Total Operating Expenses		2,000
Net Income		$1,000

B-2.

Michael Brown, Barrister and Solicitor
Statement of Owner's Equity
For Month Ended June 30, 19XX

Michael Brown, Capital, June 1, 19XX		$5,000
Net Income for June	$1,000	
Less: Withdrawals for June	500	
Increase in Capital		500
Michael Brown, Capital, June 30, 19XX		$5,500

B-3. **Michael Brown, Barrister and Solicitor**
Balance Sheet
June 30, 19XX

Assets		*Liabilities and Owner's Equity*	
Cash	$4,400	Liabilities	
Accounts Receivable	500	Accounts Payable	$1,000
Office equipment	1,600	Owner's Equity	
		M. Brown, Capital	5,500
Total Assets	$6,500	Total Liabilities and Owner's Equity	$6,500

Solution Tips to Financial Reports

B-1. Income statement lists only Revenues and Expenses for a period of time. Inside column for subtotalling. Withdrawals are not listed here.

B-2. The statement of owner's equity takes the net income figure of $1,000 and adds it to Beginning Capital less any withdrawals. This new capital figure of $5,500 will go on the balance sheet. This report shows changes in Capital for a period of time.

B-3. The $4,400, $500, $1,600, and $1,000 came from the totals of the expanded accounting equation. The Capital figure of $5,500 came from the statement of owner's equity. This balance sheet reports Assets, Liabilities, and a new figure for Capital at a specific date.

SUMMARY OF KEY POINTS

Learning Unit 1-1

1. The functions of accounting involve analyzing, recording, classifying, summarizing, and reporting financial information.
2. A sole proprietorship is a business owned by one person. A partnership is a business owned by two or more persons. A corporation is a business owned by shareholders.
3. Bookkeeping is the recording part of accounting.
4. The computer is a tool to use in the accounting process.
5. Assets = Liabilities + Owner's Equity is the basic accounting equation that aids in analyzing business transactions.
6. Liabilities represents amounts owed to creditors while capital represents what is invested by the owner.
7. Capital does not mean cash. Capital is the owner's current investment. The owner could have invested equipment that was purchased before the new business was started.
8. In a shift of assets, the composition of assets changes, but the total of assets does not change. For example, if a bill is paid by a customer, the firm increases cash (an asset) but decreases accounts receivable (an asset), so there is no overall increase in assets; total assets remain the same. When you borrow money from a bank, you have an increase in cash (an asset) and an increase in liabilities: overall there is an increase in assets, not just a shift.

Learning Unit 1-2

1. The balance sheet is a report written as of a particular date. It lists the assets, liabilities, and owner's equity of a business. The heading of the balance sheet answers the questions who, what, and when (as of a specific date).
2. The balance sheet is a formal report of a financial position.

Learning Unit 1-3

1. Revenue generates an inward flow of assets. Expenses generate an outward flow of assets or a potential outward flow. Revenue and expenses are subdivisions of owner's equity. Revenue is not an asset.
2. When revenue totals more than expenses, net income is the result; when expenses total more than revenue, net loss is the result.
3. Owner's equity can be subdivided into four elements: capital, withdrawals, revenue, and expenses.
4. Withdrawals decrease owner's equity; revenue increases owner's equity; expenses decrease owner's equity. A withdrawal is not a business expense; it is for personal use.

Learning Unit 1-4

1. The income statement is a report written for a specific period of time that lists earned revenue and expenses incurred to produce the earned revenue. The net income or net loss will be used in the statement of owner's equity.
2. The statement of owner's equity reveals the causes of a change in capital. This report lists additional investments in the company, net income (or net loss), and withdrawals. The ending figure for capital will be used on the balance sheet.
3. The balance sheet uses the ending balances of assets and liabilities from the accounting equation and the capital from the statement of owner's equity.
4. The income statement should be prepared first because the information on it as to net income or net loss is used to prepare the statement of owner's equity, which in turn provides information about capital for the balance sheet. In this way one builds upon the next, and it begins with the income statement.

KEY TERMS

Accounting A system that measures the business' activities in financial terms, provides written reports and financial statements about those activities, and communicates these reports to decision makers and others.

Accounts payable Amounts owed to creditors that result from the purchase of goods or services on account: a liability.

Accounts receivable An asset that indicates amounts owed by customers.

Assets Properties (resources) of value owned by a business (cash, supplies, equipment, land, etc.).

Balance sheet A report, as of a particular date, that shows the amount of assets owned by a business as well as the amount of claims (liabilities and owner's equity) against these assets.

Basic accounting equation Assets = Liabilities + Owner's Equity.

Bookkeeping The recording function of the accounting process.

Business entity In accounting it is assumed that a business is separate and distinct from the personal assets of the owner. Each unit or entity requires separate accounting functions.

Capital The owner's investment of equity in the company.

Corporation A type of business organization that is owned by shareholders. Usually, shareholders are not personally liable for the corporation's debts.

Creditor Someone who has a claim to assets.

Ending capital Beginning Capital + Additional Investments + Net Income − Withdrawals = Ending Capital. Or: Beginning Capital + Additional Investments − Net Loss − Withdrawals = Ending Capital.

Equities The interest or financial claim of creditors (liabilities) and owners (owner's equity) who supply the assets to a firm.

Expanded accounting equation Assets = Liabilities + Capital − Withdrawals + Revenue − Expenses.

Expense A cost incurred in running a business by consuming goods or services in producing revenue; a subdivision of owner's equity. When expenses increase, there is a decrease in owner's equity.

Generally accepted accounting principles (GAAP) The procedures and guidelines that must be followed during the accounting process.

Income statement An accounting report that details the performance of a firm (revenue minus expenses) for a specific period of time.

Liabilities Obligations that come due in the future. Liabilities result in increasing the financial rights or claims of creditors to assets.

Manufacturing company Business that makes a product and sells it to its customers.

Merchandising company Business that buys a product from a manufacturing company to sell to its customers.

Net income When revenue totals more than expenses, the result is net income.

Net loss When expenses total more than revenue, the result is net loss.

Owner's equity Rights or financial claims to the assets of a business (in the accounting equation, assets minus liabilities).

Partnership A form of business organization that has at least two owners. The partners are usually personally liable for the partnership's debts.

Revenue An amount earned by performing services for customers or selling goods to customers; can be in the form of cash and/or accounts receivable; a subdivision of owner's equity—as revenue increases, owner's equity increases.

Service company Business that provides a service.

Shift in assets A shift that occurs when the composition of the assets has changed, but the total of the assets remains the same.

Sole proprietorship A type of business ownership that has one owner. The owner is personally liable for paying the business' debts.

Statement of financial position Another name for a balance sheet.

Statement of owner's equity A financial report that reveals the change in capital. The ending figure for capital is then placed on the balance sheet.

Supplies One type of asset acquired by a firm; has a much shorter life than equipment and is usually treated as an expense. Sometimes it is treated as an asset–both treatments are possible.

Withdrawals A subdivision of owner's equity that records money or other assets an owner withdraws from a business for personal use.

BLUEPRINT OF FINANCIAL REPORTS

❶ Income Statement

Measuring performance

Revenue:		XXX
Operating	XX	
Expenses	XX	XXX
Net Income		XXX

❷ Statement of Owner's Equity

Calculating new figure for capital

Beginning Capital		XXX
Additional Investments		XXX
Total Investments		XXX
Net Income (or Loss)	XXX	
Less: Withdrawals	XXX	
Change in Capital		XXX
Ending Capital		XXX

❸ Balance Sheet

Showing where we now stand

Assets		Liabilities and Owner's Equity	
	XXX	Liabilities	XXX
	XXX	Owner's Equity	
	XXX	Ending Capital	XXX
Total Assets	XXX	Total Liab. + OE	XXX

QUESTIONS, EXERCISES, AND PROBLEMS

Discussion Questions

1. What are the functions of accounting?
2. Define, compare, and contrast sole proprietorships, partnerships, and corporations.
3. How are businesses classified?

4. What is the relationship of bookkeeping to accounting?
5. List the three elements of the basic accounting equation.
6. Define capital.
7. The total of the left-hand side of the accounting equation must equal the total of the right-hand side. True or false? Please explain.
8. A balance sheet tells a company where it is going and how well it will perform. True or false? Please explain.
9. Revenue is an asset. True or false? Please explain.
10. What categories is owner's equity subdivided into?
11. A withdrawal is a business expense. True or false? Please explain.
12. As expenses increase they cause owner's equity to increase. Defend or reject.
13. What does an income statement show?
14. The statement of owner's equity only calculates ending withdrawals. True or false?

Mini Exercises

(The blank forms you need are on page 1-8 of the *Study Guide and Working Papers.*)

Classifying Accounts

1. Classify each of the following items, as an asset (A), liability (L), or part of owner's equity (OE).
   - **a.** Cash ______
   - **b.** Accounts Payable ______
   - **c.** G. Blue, Capital ______
   - **d.** Supplies ______
   - **e.** Land ______
   - **f.** Office Equipment ______

The Accounting Equation

2. Complete:
   - **a.** Assets − __________ = Owner's Equity.
   - **b.** Capital does not mean __________.
   - **c.** A(n) __________ __________ __________ results when the total of the assets remain the same but the makeup of the assets has changed.

Shift Versus Increase in Assets

3. Identify which transaction results in a shift in assets (S) and which transaction causes an increase in assets (I).
   - **a.** Long Jewelry bought office equipment for cash.
   - **b.** Pete's Appliance bought computer equipment on account.

The Balance Sheet

4. From the following, calculate what would be the total of assets on the balance sheet.

Pete Jean, Capital	$7,000
Desk	500
Accounts payable	1,000
Cash	7,500

The Accounting Equation Expanded

5. From the following, which are subdivisions of owner's equity?

a. Cash ________

b. B. Flynn, Capital ________

c. Accounts Receivable ________

d. B. Flynn, Withdrawals ________

e. Accounts Payable ________

f. Rent Expense ________

g. Office Equipment ________

h. Hair Salon Fees Earned ________

Identifying Assets

6. Identify which of the following are *not* assets.

a. Cash ________

b. Accounts Payable ________

c. Legal Fees Earned ________

d. Accounts Receivable ________

The Accounting Equation Expanded

7. Which of the following statements are false?

a. ____Revenue is an asset.

b. ____Revenue is a subdivision of owner's equity.

c. ____Revenue provides an inward flow of cash and/or accounts receivable.

d. ____Withdrawals are part of total assets.

Preparing Financial Reports

8. Indicate whether the following items would appear on the income statement (IS), statement of owner's equity (OE), or balance sheet (BS).

a. ____R. Spencer, Capital (Beg.)

b. ____Cash

c. ____Accounts Payable

d. ____Computer Equipment

e. ____Commission Fees Earned

f. ____Salaries Expense

g. ____R. Spencer, Withdrawals

h. ____Accounts Receivable

Preparing Financial Reports

9. Indicate next to each statement whether it refers to the Income Statement (IS), statement of owner's equity (OE), or balance sheet (BS).
   - **a.** ____Report listing revenues and expenses
   - **b.** ____Calculate new figure for Capital
   - **c.** ____Prepared as of a particular date
   - **d.** ____Statement that is prepared first

Exercises

(The forms you need are on pages 1-9 and 1-10 of the *Study Guide and Working Papers.*)

The accounting equation.

1-1. Complete the following table:

	ASSETS	= LIABILITIES	+ OWNER'S EQUITY
a.	$6,000 =	?	+ $2,000
b.	? =	$4,000	+ $8,000
c.	$10,000 =	$4,000	+ ?

Recording transactions into the accounting equation.

1-2. Record the following transactions in the basic accounting equation. Treat each one separately.

ASSETS = LIABILITIES + OWNER'S EQUITY

a. Bill invests $40,000 in company.
b. Bought equipment for cash, $600.
c. Bought equipment on account, $900.

Preparing a balance sheet.

1-3. From the following, prepare a balance sheet for Ron's Cleaners at the end of November 19XX: Cash, $21,000; Cleaning Equipment, $6,000; Accounts Payable, $8,000; A. Ron, Capital, ??.

Recording transactions into the expanded accounting equation.

1-4. Record the following transactions into the expanded accounting equation. The running balance may be omitted for simplicity.

ASSETS			= LIABILITIES +	OWNER'S EQUITY			
Cash	+ Accounts Receivable	+ Computer Equipment	= Accounts Payable	+ B. Wong, Capital	– B. Wong, Withdrawals	+ Revenue	– Expenses

a. Bill Wong invested $40,000 in a computer company.
b. Bought computer equipment on account, $7,000.
c. Bill Wong paid personal telephone bill from company chequebook, $200.
d. Received cash for services rendered, $14,000.
e. Billed customers for services rendered for month, $30,000.
f. Paid current rent expense, $4,000.
g. Paid supplies expense, $1,500.

Preparing the income statement, statement of owner's equity, and balance sheet.

1-5. From the following account balances, prepare in proper form (a) an income statement for June, (b) a statement of owner's equity, and (c) a balance sheet for Sullivan Realty.

Cash	$3,310
Accounts Receivable	1,490
Office Equipment	6,700

Accounts Payable	2,000
J. Sullivan, Capital, June 1	8,000
J. Sullivan, Withdrawals	40
Professional Fees	2,900
Salaries Expense	500
Utilities Expense	360
Rent Expense	500

Group A Problems

(The forms you need are on pages 1-11 to 1-17 of the *Study Guide and Working Papers.*)

The accounting equation.

1A-1. Ron Lee decided to open Lee's Realty. Ron completed the following transactions:

a. Invested $18,000 cash from his personal bank account into the business.

b. Bought equipment for cash, $2,000.

c. Bought additional equipment on account, $1,100.

d. Paid $400 cash to partially reduce what was owed from the transaction in **c**.

Based on the above information, record these transactions into the basic accounting equation.

Preparing a balance sheet.

1A-2. Molly Ribbon is the accountant for Blue's Advertising Service. From the following information, her task is to construct a balance sheet as of September 30, 19XX, in proper form. Could you help her?

Building	$20,000
Accounts Payable	30,000
R. Blue, Capital	14,000
Cash	10,000
Equipment	14,000

Recording transactions in the expanded accounting equation.

1A-3. At the end of November, Dan Miller decided to open his own typing service. Analyze the following transactions he completed by recording their effects on the expanded accounting equation.

a. Invested $18,000 in his typing service.

b. Bought new office equipment on account, $4,000.

c. Received cash for typing services rendered, $500.

d. Performed typing services on account, $2,100.

e. Paid secretary's salary, $350.

f. Paid office supplies expense for the month, $210.

g. Rent expenses for office due but unpaid, $900.

h. Dan Miller withdrew cash for personal use, $400.

Preparing the income statement, statement of owner's equity, and balance sheet.

1A-4. Joy Allen, owner of Allen's Stencilling Service, has requested that you prepare from the following balances (a) an income statement for June 19XX, (b) a statement of owner's equity for June, and (c) a balance sheet as of June 30, 19XX.

Cash	$1,300
Accounts Receivable	300

Equipment	685
Accounts Payable	310
J. Allen, Capital, June 1, 19XX	1,200
J. Allen, Withdrawals	300
Stencilling Fees	2,000
Advertising Expense	110
Repair Expense	25
Travel Expense	350
Supplies Expense	190
Rent Expense	250

Comprehensive problem.

1A-5. John, a retired army officer, opened Tobey's Catering Service. As his accountant, analyze the transactions listed below and present in proper form.

1. The analysis of the transactions by utilizing the expanded accounting equation.

2. A balance sheet showing the position of the firm before opening on November 1, 19XX.

3. An income statement for the month of November.

4. A statement of owner's equity for November.

5. A balance sheet as of November 30, 19XX.

19XX		
Oct.	25	John Tobey invested $20,000 in the catering business from his personal savings account.
	27	Bought equipment for cash from Munroe Co., $700.
	28	Bought additional equipment on account from Ryan Co., $1,000.
	29	Paid $600 to Ryan Co. as partial payment of the October 28 transaction.

(You should now prepare your balance sheet as of October 31, 19XX.)

Nov.	1	Catered a graduation and immediately collected cash, $2,400.
	5	Paid salaries of employees, $690.
	8	Prepared desserts for customers on account, $300.
	10	Received $100 cash as partial payment of November 8 transaction.
	15	Paid telephone bill, $60.
	17	John paid his home electric bill from the company's chequebook, $90.
	20	Catered a wedding and received cash, $1,800.
	25	Bought additional equipment on account, $400.
	28	Rent expense due but unpaid, $600.
	30	Paid supplies expense, $400.

Group B Problems

(The forms you need are on pages 1-11 to 1-17of the *Study Guide and Working Papers.*)

The accounting equation.

1B-1. Ron Lee began a new business called Lee's Realty. The following transactions resulted:

a. Ron invested $17,000 cash from his personal bank account into the realty company.

b. Bought equipment on account, $1,800.

c. Paid $800 cash to partially reduce what was owed from transaction B.

d. Purchased additional equipment for cash, $3,000.

Record these transactions into the basic accounting equation.

Preparing a balance sheet.

1B-2. Molly Ribbon has asked you to prepare a balance sheet as of September 30, 19XX, for Blue's Advertising Service. Could you assist Molly?

R. Blue, Capital	$19,000
Accounts Payable	70,000
Equipment	41,000
Building	16,000
Cash	32,000

Recording transactions in the expanded accounting equation.

1B-3. Dan Miller decided to open his own typing service company at the end of November. Analyze the following transactions by recording their effects on the expanded accounting equation.

a. Dan Miller invested $9,000 in the typing service.

b. Purchased new office equipment on account, $3,000.

c. Received cash for typing services rendered, $1,290.

d. Paid secretary's salary, $310.

e. Billed customers for typing services rendered, $2,690.

f. Paid rent expense for the month, $500.

g. Dan withdrew cash for personal use, $350.

h. Advertising expense due but unpaid, $100.

Preparing an income statement, statement of owner's equity, and balance sheet.

1B-4. Joy Allen, owner of Allen's Stencilling Service, has requested that you prepare from the following balances (a) an income statement for June 19XX, (b) a statement of owner's equity for June, and (c) a balance sheet as of June 30, 19XX.

Cash	$2,043
Accounts Receivable	1,140
Equipment	540
Accounts Payable	45
J. Allen, Capital, June 1, 19XX	3,720
J. Allen, Withdrawals	360
Stencilling Fees	1,098
Advertising Expense	135
Repair Expense	45
Travel Expense	90
Supplies Expense	270
Rent Expense	240

Comprehensive problem.

1B-5. John Tobey, a retired army officer, opened Tobey's Catering Service. As his accountant, analyze the transactions and present the following information in proper form:

1. The analysis of the transactions by utilizing the expanded accounting equation.
2. A balance sheet showing the financial position of the firm before opening on November 1, 19XX.
3. An income statement for the month of November.
4. A statement of owner's equity for November.
5. A balance sheet as of November 30, 19XX.

19XX

Oct. 25 John Tobey invested $17,500 in the catering business.
27 Bought equipment on account from Munroe Co., $900.
28 Bought equipment for cash from Ryan Co., $1,500.
29 Paid $300 to Munroe Co. as partial payment of the October 27 transaction.

Nov. 1 Catered a business luncheon and immediately collected cash, $2,000.
5 Paid salaries of employees, $350.
8 Provided catering services to Northwest Community College on account, $4,500.
10 Received from Northwest Community College $1,000 cash as partial payment of November 8 transaction.
15 Paid telephone bill, $95.
17 Tobey paid his home mortgage from the company's chequebook, $650.
20 Provided catering services and received cash, $1,800.
25 Bought additional equipment on account, $300.
28 Rent expense due but unpaid, $750.
30 Paid supplies expense, $600.

Group C Problems

The accounting equation.

1C-1. Fred Potter began a new business called Potter's Realty. The following transactions resulted:

Transaction A: Fred invested $18,000 cash from his personal bank account into the realty company.

Transaction B: Bought equipment on account, $3,000.

Transaction C: Paid $1,400 cash to partially reduce what was owed from transaction B.

Transaction D: Purchased additional equipment for cash, $4,000.

Record these transactions into the basic accounting equation.

Preparing a balance sheet.

1C-2. Gabriella Fortunata has asked you to prepare a balance sheet as of April 30, 19XX, for Fortune Graphics Service. Could you assist her?

Gabriella Fortunata, Capital	$39,000
Accounts Payable	23,000
Equipment	16,000
Building	35,000
Cash	11,000

Recording transactions in the expanded accounting equation.

1C-3. Ray Owens decided to open his own database consulting service company at the end of October. Analyze the following transactions by recording their effects on the expanded accounting equation.

Transaction A: Ray invested $20,000 in the consulting service.

Transaction B: Purchased new office equipment on account, $7,500.

Transaction C: Received cash for services rendered, $2,870.

Transaction D: Paid secretary's salary, $650.

Transaction E: Billed customers for data services rendered, $3,875.

Transaction F: Paid rent expense for the month, $700.

Transaction G: Ray withdrew cash for personal use, $900.

Transaction H: Advertising expense due but unpaid, $350.

Transaction I: Repair to office equipment paid, $268.

Preparing an income statement, statement of owner's equity, and balance sheet.

1C-4. Jennifer Cheung, owner of Jennifer's Fashion Service, has requested that you prepare from the following balances: (a) an income statement for July 19XX; (b) a statement of owner's equity for July; and (c) a balance sheet as of July 31, 19XX.

Cash	$1,746
Accounts Receivable	3,450
Equipment	3,580
Accounts Payable	1,830
Jennifer Cheung, Capital, July 1, 19XX	6,430
Jennifer Cheung, Withdrawals	710
Consulting Fees Earned	4,815
Advertising Expense	635
Repair Expense	165
Travel Expense	1,690
Supplies Expense	484
Rent Expense	440
Office Expenses	175

Comprehensive problem.

1C-5. Jean Vende opened First City Surveying Service. As her accountant, analyze the transactions and present to Ms. Vende the following information, in proper form:

1. The analysis of the transactions by utilizing the expanded accounting equation.
2. A balance sheet showing the financial position of the firm before opening on May 1, 19XX.
3. An income statement for the month of May.
4. A statement of owner's equity for May.
5. A balance sheet as of May 31, 19XX.

April	25	Jean invested $18,000 in the surveying business.
	27	Bought equipment on account from Chapman & Co., $3,700.
	28	Bought equipment for cash from Majestic Co., $3,095.
	29	Paid $1,500 to Chapman & Co. as partial payment of the April 27 transaction.
May	1	Surveyed a new business location and immediately collected cash, $2,100.
	5	Paid salaries of employees, $850.
	8	Provided surveying services to City Community College on account, $5,400.
	10	Received from City Community College $2,000 cash as partial payment of May 8 transaction.
	15	Paid telephone bill, $121.
	17	Jean paid her home mortgage from the company's chequebook, $920.
	20	Provided surveying services and received cash, $1,725.
	25	Bought additional equipment on account from Jensen Bros, $1,400.
	28	Paid rent expense for the month, $750.
	30	Paid supplies expense, $285.
	31	Advertising bill received but not paid, $325.

REAL WORLD APPLICATIONS

1R-1.

You have just been hired to prepare, if possible, an income statement for the year ended December 31, 19XX, for Logan's Window Washing Company. The problem is that Bill Logan kept only the following records (on the back of a piece of cardboard).

Money in:

Window cleaning	*$11,376*
My investment	*1,200*
Loan from brother-in-law	*4,000*

Money out:

Salaries	*$5,080*
Withdrawals	*6,200*
Supplies expense	*1,400*

What I owe or they owe me

A. People that work for me but I still owe salaries to $1,800
B. Owe bank interest of $300
C. Work done but clients still owe me $2,900
D. Advertising bill due but not paid $95

Assume that Logan's Window Washing Company records all revenues when earned and all expenses when incurred.

You feel that it is part of your job to tell Bill how to organize his records better. What would you tell him?

1R-2.

While Jon Lune was on a business trip, he asked Abby Slowe, the bookkeeper for Lune Co., to try to complete a balance sheet for the year ended December 31, 19XX. Abby, who had been on the job only two months, submitted the following.

LUNE CO.
FOR THE YEAR ENDED DECEMBER 31, 19XX

Building	$446 000 00	Accounts Payable	$127 604 00
Land	72 935 00	Accounts Receivable	104 337 00
Notes Payable	75 328 00	Auto	14 268 00
Cash	10 016 00	Desks	6 825 00
J. Lune, Capital	?	Total Equity	$250 034 00

1. Could you help Abby fix as well as complete the balance sheet?
2. What written recommendations would you make about the bookkeeper? Should she be retained?
3. Suppose that (a) Jon Lune invested an additional $20,000 in cash as well as additional desks with a value of $8,000 and (b) Lune Co. bought an auto for $6,000 that was originally marked $8,000, paying $2,000 down and issuing a note for the balance. Could you prepare an updated balance sheet? Assume that these two transactions occurred on January 4.

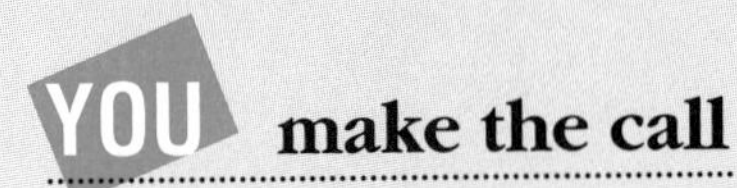

Critical Thinking/Ethical Case

(The forms you need are on page 1-7 of the *Study Guide and Working Papers.*)

1R-3.
Paul Kloss, Accountant for Lowe & Co., travelled to Vancouver on company business. His total expenses came to $350. Paul felt that since the trip extended over the weekend he would "pad" his expense account with an additional $100 of expenses. After all, weekends represent his own time, not the company's. What would you do? Write your specific recommendations to Paul.

ACCOUNTING RECALL

A CUMULATIVE APPROACH

THIS EXAM REVIEWS CHAPTER 1

Your *Study Guide and Working Papers* have forms on page 1-29 to complete this exam, as well as worked-out solutions. The page references next to each question identify what page to turn back to if you answer the question incorrectly.

PART I Vocabulary Review

Match the terms to the appropriate definition or phrase.

Page Ref.	Term		Definition
(8)	1. Capital	A.	Prepared as of a particular date
(13)	2. Accounts receivable	B.	A liability
(2)	3. Sole proprietorship	C.	For personal use
(13)	4. Expense	D.	Provides an inward flow of assets
(19)	5. Balance sheet	E.	Company owned and managed by one person
(13)	6. Revenue	F.	Amount owed by customers
(13)	7. Withdrawals	G.	Owner's investment
(18)	8. Income statement	H.	A cost of running a business
(9)	9. Accounts payable	I.	Broken into four subdivisions
(7)	10. Owner's equity	J.	Prepared for specific period of time

PART II True or False (Accounting Theory)

(13) 11. Revenue is an asset.

(16) 12. The four subdivisions of owner's equity are capital, withdrawals, revenue, and expenses.

(16) 13. As expenses increase, owner's equity increases.

(18) 14 Accounts receivable goes on the income statement.

(19) 15. The statement of owner's equity calculates a new figure for capital.

PART III Applications Problem (p. 1–29)

From the following, prepare the income statement, statement of owner's equity, and balance sheet for Rowe Company.

Cash	$2,000	Jay Rowe, Withdrawals	$100
Accounts Receivable	1,000	Fees Earned	5,000
Office Furniture	1,500	Salaries Expense	700
Accounts Payable	500	Advertising Expense	200
Jay Rowe, Capital, June 1, 19XX	600	Rent Expense	600

DEBITS AND CREDITS

2

ANALYZING AND RECORDING BUSINESS TRANSACTIONS

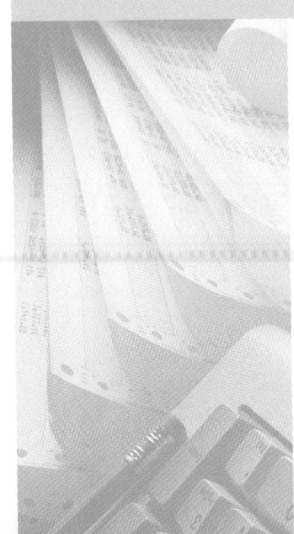

Chapter Objectives

- Setting up and organizing a chart of accounts. (p.44)
- Recording transactions in T accounts according to the rules of debit and credit. (p. 46)
- Preparing a trial balance. (p. 56)
- Preparing financial reports from a trial balance. (p. 57)

In Chapter 1, we used the expanded accounting equation to document the financial transactions performed by Jill Reed's law firm. Remember how long it was: the cash column had a long list of pluses and minuses, and there was no quick system of recording and summarizing the increases and decreases of cash or other items. Can you imagine the problem Canadian Tire or Tim Horton's would have if they used the expanded accounting equation to track the thousands of business transactions they do each day?

LEARNING UNIT 2-1

The T Account

Let's look at the problem a little more closely. Every business transaction is recorded in the accounting equation under a specific **account.** There are different accounts for each of the subdivisions of the accounting equation — there are asset accounts, liabilities accounts, expense accounts, revenue accounts, and so on. What is needed is a way to record the increases and decreases in specific account *categories* and yet keep them together in one place. The answer is the **standard account** form (see Figure 2-1). A standard account is a formal account that includes columns for date, explanation, posting reference, debit, and credit. Each account has a separate form and all transactions affecting that account are recorded on the form. All the business's account forms (which often are referred to as *ledger accounts*) are then placed in a **ledger.** Each page of the ledger contains one account. The ledger may be in the form of a bound or a looseleaf book. If computers are used, the ledger may be part of a computer printout. For simplicity's sake, in this chapter we will use the **T account** form. This form got its name because it looks like the letter T. Generally, T accounts are used for demonstration purposes.

FIGURE 2-1
The Standard Account Form

Account Title							Account No.
Date	Item	PR	Debit	Date	Item	PR	Credit

Debit defined:

1. The *left* side of any T account.
2. A number entered on the left side of any account is said to be *debited* to an account.

Each T account contains three basic parts:

1		
	Title of Account	
2	**Left side**	**Right side** 3

All T accounts have this structure. In accounting, the left side of any T account is called the **debit** side.

Left side	
Dr. (debit)	

Just as the word *left* has many meanings, the word *debit* for now in accounting means a position, the left side of an account. Don't think of it as good (+) or bad (−).

Amounts entered on the left side of any account are said to be *debited* to an account. The abbreviation for debit (Dr.) is from the Latin *debere.*

The right side of any T account is called the **credit** side.

Credit defined:

1. The *right* side of any T account.
2. A number entered on the right side of an account is said to be *credited* to an account.

Dollar signs are not used in standard accounts or T accounts. However, dollar signs are used in formal financial reports.

	Right side
	Cr. (credit)

Amounts entered on the right side of an account are said to be *credited* to an account. The abbreviation for credit (Cr.) is from the Latin *credere.*

At this point, do not associate the definition of debit and credit with the words *increase* or *decrease.* Think of debit or credit as only indicating a *position* (left side or right side) of a T account.

Balancing an Account

No matter which individual account is being balanced, the procedure used to balance it will be the same.

Dr.	Cr.
3,000	**300**
500	**400**
Totals 3,500	700
Bal. 2,800	

In the "real" world, the T account would also include the date of the transaction. The date would appear to the left of the entry:

Dr.		Cr.	
4/2	**3,000**	**4/3**	**300**
4/20	**500**	**4/25**	**400**
Totals	3,500		700
Bal.	2,800		

Footings aid in balancing an account. The ending balance is the difference between the footings.

Note that on the debit (left) side the numbers add up to $3,500. On the credit (right) side the numbers add up $700. The $3,500 and the $700 written in small type are called footings. Footings help in calculating the new (or ending) balance. The **ending balance** ($2,800) is placed on the debit or left side, since the balance of the debit side is greater than that of the credit side.

If the balance was greater on the credit side, that is the side the ending balance would be on.

Remember, the ending balance does not tell us anything about increase or decrease. It only tells us that we have an ending balance of $2,800 on the debit side.

LEARNING UNIT 2-1 REVIEW

AT THIS POINT you should be able to

- Define ledger. (p. 41)
- State the purpose of a T account. (p. 41)
- Identify the three parts of a T account. (p. 42)
- Define debit. (p. 42)
- Define credit. (p. 42)
- Explain footings and calculate the balance of an account. (p. 42)

SELF-REVIEW QUIZ 2-1

(The blank forms you need are on page 2-1 of the *Study Guide and Working Papers.*)

Respond True or False to the following:

1.

Dr.	Cr.
1,000	100
50	50

The balance of the account is $900 Cr.

2. A credit always means increase.

3. A debit is the left side of any account.

4. A ledger can be prepared manually or by computer.

5. Footings replace the need for debits and credits.

Solutions to Self-Review Quiz 2-1

1. False **2.** False **3.** True **4.** True **5.** False

LEARNING UNIT 2-2

Recording Business Transactions: Debits and Credits

Can you get a queen in checkers? In a baseball game does a runner rounding first base skip second base and run over the pitcher's mound to get to third? No—most of us don't do such things because we follow the rules of the game. Usually we learn the rules first and reflect on the reasons for them afterward. The same is true in accounting.

Instead of first trying to understand all the rules of debit and credit and how they were developed in accounting, it will be easier to learn the rules by "playing the game."

T ACCOUNT ENTRIES FOR ACCOUNTING IN THE ACCOUNTING EQUATION

Have patience. Learning the rules of debit and credit is like learning to play any game—the more you play, the easier it becomes. Table 2-1 shows the rules for the side on which you enter an increase or a decrease for each of the separate accounts in the accounting equation. For example, an increase is entered on the debit side in the asset account, but on the credit side for a liability account.

It might be easier to visualize these rules of debit and credit if we look at them in the T account form, using + to show increase and − to show decrease.

ASSETS		= LIABILITIES +		OWNER'S EQUITY							
				+ Capital		− Withdrawals +		Revenue		− Expenses	
Dr.	Cr.	Dr.	Cr.	Dr.	Cr.	Dr.	Cr.	Dr.	Cr.	Dr.	Cr.
+	−	−	+	−	+	+	−	−	+	+	−

Rules for Assets Work in the Opposite Direction to Those for Liabilities When you look at the equation you can see that the rules for assets work in the opposite direction to those for liabilities. That is, for assets the increases appear on the debit side and the decreases are shown on the credit side; the opposite is true for liabilities. As for owner's equity, the rules for withdrawals and expenses, which *decrease* owner's equity, work in the opposite direction to the rules for capital and revenue, which *increase* owner's equity.

Normal Balance

Dr.	Cr.
Assets	Liabilities
Expenses	Capital
Withdrawals	Revenue

A **normal balance of an account** is the side that increases by the rules of debit and credit. For example, the balance of cash is a debit balance, because an asset is increased by a debit. We will discuss normal balances further in Chapter 3.

Balancing the Equation It is important to remember that any amount(s) entered on the debit side of a T account or accounts also must be on the credit side of another T account or accounts. This ensures that the total amount added to the debit side will equal the total amount added to the credit side, thereby keeping the accounting equation in balance.

Chart of Accounts Our job is to analyze Jill Reed's business transactions—the transactions we looked at in Chapter 1—using a system of accounts guided by the rules of debits and credits that will summarize increases and decreases of individual accounts in the ledger. The goal is to prepare an income statement, statement of owner's equity, and balance sheet for Jill Reed. Sound familiar? If this system works, the rules of debits and credits and the use of accounts will give us the same answers as in Chapter 1, but with greater ease.

Jill's accountant developed what is called a **chart of accounts.** The chart of accounts is a numbered list of all of the business's accounts. It allows accounts to

The rules of debit and credit are arbitrary. The rules will aid us in recording information in the ledger.

TABLE 2-1 RULES OF DEBIT AND CREDIT

Account Category	Increase	Decrease	Normal Balance
Assets	Debit	Credit	Debit
Liabilities	Credit	Debit	Credit
Owner's Equity			
Capital	Credit	Debit	Credit
Withdrawals	Debit	Credit	Debit
Revenue	Credit	Debit	Credit
Expenses	Debit	Credit	Debit

TABLE 2-2 CHART OF ACCOUNTS FOR JILL REED, BARRISTER AND SOLICITOR

Balance Sheet Accounts	
Assets	**Liabilities**
111 Cash	211 Accounts Payable
112 Accounts Receivable	
121 Office Equipment	**Owner's Equity**
	311 Jill Reed, Capital
	312 Jill Reed, Withdrawals
Income Statement Accounts	
Revenue	**Expenses**
411 Legal Fees	511 Salaries Expense
	512 Rent Expense
	513 Advertising Expense

The chart of accounts aids in locating and identifying accounts quickly.

Large companies may have up to four digits assigned to each title, and sometimes up to 24 digits (e.g., Exxon).

be located quickly. In Jill's business, for example, 100s are assets, 200s are liabilities, and so on. As you see in Table 2-2, each separate asset and liability has its own number. Note the chart may be expanded as the business grows.

THE ACCOUNTING ANALYSIS: FIVE STEPS

We will analyze the transactions in Jill Reed's law firm using a teaching device called a ***transaction analysis chart*** to record these five steps. (Keep in mind that the transaction analysis chart is not a part of any formal accounting system.) There are five steps to analyzing each business transaction:

Steps to analyze and record transactions. Steps 1 and 2 will come from the chart of accounts.

Remember the rules of debit and credit only tell us on which side to place information. Whether the debit or credit represents increases or decreases depends on the account category—assets, liabilities, capital, and so on. Think of a business transaction as an exchange—you get something and you give or part with something.

Step 1: Determine which accounts are affected. Example: cash, accounts payable, rent expense. A transaction always affects at least two accounts.

Step 2: Determine which categories the accounts belong to—assets, liabilities, capital, withdrawals, revenue, or expenses. Example: Cash is an asset.

Step 3: Determine whether the accounts increase or decrease. Example: If you receive cash, that account is increasing.

Step 4: What do the rules of debits and credits say (Table 2-1)?

Step 5: What does the T account look like? Place amounts into accounts either on the left or right side depending on the rules in Table 2-1.

This is how the five-step analysis looks in chart form:

1 Accounts Affected	2 Category	3 ↓ or ↑ (decrease) (increase)	4 Rules of Dr. and Cr.	5 Appearance of T Accounts

Let us emphasize a major point: *Do not try to debit or credit an account until you have gone through the first three steps of the transaction analysis.*

APPLYING THE TRANSACTION ANALYSIS TO JILL REED'S LAW PRACTICE

Transaction A: Aug. 28: Jill Reed invests $6,000 cash and $200 of office equipment in the business.

1 Accounts Affected	2 Category	3 ↓ ↑	4 Rules of Dr. and Cr.	5 Appearance of T Accounts
Cash	Asset	↑	Dr.	Cash 111 (A) 6,000 |
Office Equipment	Asset	↑	Dr.	Office Equipment 121 (A) 200 |
Jill Reed, Capital	Capital	↑	Cr.	Jill Reed, Capital 311 | 6,200 (A)

Note in column 3 of the chart: It doesn't matter if all arrows go up, as long as the sum of the debits equals the sum of the credits in the T accounts in column 5.

Note again that every transaction affects at least two T accounts, and that the total amount added to the debit side(s) must equal the total amount added to the credit side(s) of the T accounts of each transaction.

Analysis of Transaction A

Step 1: Which accounts are affected? The law firm receives its cash and office equipment, so three accounts are involved: cash, office equipment, and Jill Reed, Capital. These account titles come from the chart of accounts.

Step 2: Which categories do these accounts belong to? Cash and office equipment are assets; Jill Reed, Capital, is capital.

Step 3: Are the accounts increasing or decreasing? The cash and office equipment, both assets, are increasing in the business. The rights or claims of Jill Reed, Capital, are also increasing, since she invested money and office equipment in the business.

Step 4: What do the rules say? According to the rules of debit and credit, an increase in assets (cash and office equipment) is a debit. An increase in capital is a credit. Note that the total dollar amount of debits will equal the total dollar amount of credits when the T accounts are updated in column 5.

Step 5: What does the T account look like? The amount for cash and office equipment is entered on the debit side. The amount for Jill Reed, Capital, goes on the credit side.

A transaction that involves more than one credit or more than one debit is called a **compound entry.** This first transaction of Jill Reed's law firm is a compound entry; it involves a debit of $6,000 to Cash and a debit of $200 to Office Equipment (as well as a credit of $6,200 to Jill Reed, Capital).

As we continue, the explanations will be brief, but do not forget to apply the five steps in analyzing and recording each business transaction.

Transaction B: Aug. 29: Law practice bought office equipment for cash, $500.

1 Accounts Affected	2 Category	3 ↓ ↑	4 Rules of Dr. and Cr.	5 T Account Update
Office Equipment	Asset	↑	Dr.	Office Equipment 121 (A) 200 | (B) 500 |
Cash	Asset	↓	Cr.	Cash 111 (A) 6,000 | 500 (B)

Analysis of Transaction B

Step 1: The law firm paid cash for the office equipment it received.The accounts involved in the transaction are Cash and Office Equipment.

Step 2: The accounts belong to these categories: Office Equipment is an asset; Cash is an asset.

Step 3: The asset Office Equipment is increasing.The asset Cash is decreasing—it is being reduced in order to buy the office equipment.

Step 4: An increase in the asset Office Equipment is a debit; a decrease in the asset Cash is a credit.

Step 5: When the amounts are placed in the T accounts, the amount for office equipment goes on the debit side and the amount for cash on the credit side.

Transaction C: Aug. 30: Bought more office equipment on account, $300.

1 Accounts Affected	2 Category	3 ↓ ↑	4 Rules of Dr. and Cr.	5 T Account Update
Office Equipment	Asset	↑	Dr.	Office Equipment 121 (A) 200 | (B) 500 | (C) 300 |
Accounts Payable	Liability	↑	Cr.	Accounts Payable 211 | 300 (C)

Analysis of Transaction C

Step 1: The law firm receives office equipment by promising to pay in the future. An obligation or liability, Accounts Payable, is created.

Step 2: Office Equipment is an asset. Accounts Payable is a liability.

Step 3: The asset Office Equipment is increasing; the liability Accounts Payable is increasing because the law firm is increasing what it owes.

Step 4: An increase in the asset Office Equipment is a debit. An increase in the liability Accounts Payable is a credit.

Step 5: Enter the amount for office equipment on the debit side of the T account. The amount for the Accounts Payable goes on the credit side.

Transaction D: Sept. 1–30: Provided legal services for cash, $2,000.

1 Accounts Affected	2 Category	3 ↓ ↑	4 Rules of Dr. and Cr.	5 T Account Update
Cash	Asset	↑	Dr.	Cash 111: (A) 6,000 / (D) 2,000 (debit) ; 500 (B) (credit)
Legal Fees	Revenue	↑	Cr.	Legal Fees 411: 2,000 (D) (credit)

Analysis of Transaction D

Step 1: The firm has earned revenue from legal services and receives $2,000 in cash.

Step 2: Cash is an asset. Legal Fees are revenue.

Step 3: Cash, an asset, is increasing. Legal Fees, or revenue, is also increasing.

Step 4: An increase in Cash, an asset, is debited. An increase in Legal Fees, or revenue, is credited.

Step 5: Enter the amount for Cash on the debit side of the T account. Enter the amount for Legal Fees on the credit side.

Transaction E: Sept. 1–30: Provided legal services on account, $3,000.

1 Accounts Affected	2 Category	3 ↓ ↑	4 Rules of Dr. and Cr.	5 T Account Update
Accounts Receivable	Asset	↑	Dr.	Accounts Receivable 112: (E) 3,000 (debit)
Legal Fees	Revenue	↑	Cr.	Legal Fees 411: 2,000 (D) / 3,000 (E) (credit)

Analysis of Transaction E

Step 1: The law practice has earned revenue but has not yet received payment (cash). The amounts owed by these clients are called Accounts Receivable. Revenue is earned at the time the legal services are provided, whether payment is received then or will be received sometime in the future.

Step 2: Accounts Receivable is an asset. Legal Fees are revenue.

Step 3: Accounts Receivable is increasing because the law practice has increased the amount owed to it for legal fees that have been earned but not paid. Legal Fees or revenue are increasing.

Step 4: An increase in the asset Accounts Receivable is a debit. An increase in revenue is a credit.

Step 5: Enter the amount for Accounts Receivable on the debit side of the T account. The amount for Legal Fees goes on the credit side.

Transaction F: Sept. 1–30: Received $900 cash from clients for services rendered previously on account.

1 Accounts Affected	2 Category	3 ↓ ↑	4 Rules of Dr. and Cr.	5 T Account Update
Cash	Asset	↑	Dr.	Cash 111 Dr: (A) 6,000; (D) 2,000; (F) 900 Cr: 500 (B)
Accounts Receivable	Asset	↓	Cr.	Accounts Receivable 112 Dr: (E) 3,000 Cr: 900 (F)

Analysis of Transaction F

Step 1: The law firm collects $900 in cash from previous revenue earned. Since the revenue is recorded at the time it is earned, and not when the payment is made, in this transaction we are concerned only with the payment, which affects the Cash and Accounts Receivable accounts.

Step 2: Cash is an asset. Accounts Receivable is an asset.

Step 3: Since clients are paying what is owed, cash (asset) is increasing and the amount owed (accounts receivable) is decreasing (the total amount owed by clients to Reed is going down). This transaction results in a shift in assets, more cash for less accounts receivable.

Step 4: An increase in Cash, an asset, is a debit. A decrease in Accounts Receivable, an asset, is a credit.

Step 5: Enter the amount for Cash on the debit side of the T account. The amount for Accounts Receivable goes on the credit side.

Transaction G: Sept. 1–30: Paid salaries expense, $700.

1 Accounts Affected	2 Category	3 ↓ ↑	4 Rules of Dr. and Cr.	5 T Account Update
Salaries Expense	Expense	↑	Dr.	Salaries Expense 511 (G) 700 |
Cash	Asset	↓	Cr.	Cash 111 (A) 6,000 | 500 (B) (D) 2,000 | 700 (G) (F) 900 |

Analysis of Transaction G

Step 1: The law firm pays $700 worth of salaries expense by cash.

Step 2: Salaries Expense is an expense. Cash is an asset.

Step 3: The salaries expense of the law firm is increasing, which results in a decrease in cash.

Step 4: An increase in Salaries Expense, an expense, is a debit. A decrease in Cash, an asset, is a credit.

Step 5: Enter the amount for Salaries Expense on the debit side of the T account. The amount for Cash goes on the credit side.

Transaction H: Sept. 1–30: Paid rent expense, $400.

1 Accounts Affected	2 Category	3 ↓ ↑	4 Rules of Dr. and Cr.	5 T Account Update
Rent Expense	Expense	↑	Dr.	Rent Expense 512 (H) 400 |
Cash	Asset	↓	Cr.	Cash 111 (A) 6,000 | 500 (B) (D) 2,000 | 700 (G) (F) 900 | 400 (H)

Analysis of Transaction H

Step 1: The law firm's rent expenses are paid in cash.

Step 2: Rent is an expense. Cash is an asset.

Step 3: The Rent Expense increases the expenses, and the payment for the rent expense decreases the cash.

Step 4: An increase in Rent Expense, an expense, is a debit. A decrease in Cash, an asset, is a credit.

Step 5: Enter the amount for Rent Expense on the debit side of the T account. Place the amount for Cash on the credit side.

Transaction I: Sept. 1–30: Received a bill for Advertising Expense (to be paid next month), $200.

1 Accounts Affected	2 Category	3 ↓ ↑	4 Rules of Dr. and Cr.	5 T Account Update
Advertising Expense	Expense	↑	Dr.	Advertising Expense 513 (I) 200 |
Accounts Payable	Liability	↑	Cr.	Accounts Payable 211 | 300 (C) | 200 (I)

Analysis of Transaction I

Step 1: The advertising bill has come in and payment is due but has not yet been made. Therefore the accounts involved here are Advertising Expense and Accounts Payable; the expense has created a liability.

Step 2: Advertising Expense is an expense. Accounts Payable is a liability.

Step 3: Both the expense and the liability are increasing.

Step 4: An increase in an expense is a debit. An increase in a liability is a credit.

Step 5: Enter the amount for Advertising Expense on the debit side of the T Accounts. Enter amount for Accounts Payable on the credit side.

Transaction J: Reed withdrew cash for personal use, $100.

1 Accounts Affected	2 Category	3 ↓ ↑	4 Rules of Dr. and Cr.	5 T Account Update
Jill Reed, Withdrawals	Withdrawals	↑	Dr.	Jill Reed, Withdrawals 312 (J) 100
Cash	Asset	↓	Cr.	Cash 111 (A) 6,000 | 500 (B) (D) 2,000 | 700 (G) (F) 900 | 400 (H) | 100 (J)

Analysis of Transaction J

Step 1: Jill Reed withdraws cash from business for *personal* use. This withdrawal is not a business expense.

Withdrawals are always increased by debits.

Step 2: This transaction affects Withdrawal and Cash accounts.

Step 3: Jill has increased what she has withdrawn from the business for personal use. The business cash has been decreased.

Step 4: An increase in withdrawals is a debit. A decrease in cash is a credit. (*Remember:* Withdrawals go on the statement of owner's equity; expenses go on the income statement.)

Step 5: Enter the amount for Jill Reed, Withdrawals on the debit side of the T account. The amount for Cash goes on the credit side.

LEARNING UNIT 2-2 REVIEW

AT THIS POINT you should be able to

- State the rules of debit and credit. (p. 44)
- List the five steps of a transaction analysis. (p.45)
- Show how to fill out a transaction analysis chart. (p.45)

SELF-REVIEW QUIZ 2-2

(The blank forms you need are on pages 2-1 and 2-2 of the *Study Guide and Working Papers.*)

O'Malley Company uses the following accounts from its chart of accounts: Cash (111), Accounts Receivable (112), Equipment (121), Accounts Payable (211), Bill O'Malley, Capital (311), Bill O'Malley, Withdrawals (312), Professional Fees (411), Utilities Expense (511), and Salaries Expense (512).

Record the following transactions into transaction analysis charts.

a. Bill O'Malley invested in the business $900 cash and equipment worth $600 from his personal assets.

b. Billed clients for services rendered, $9,000.

c. Utilities bill due but unpaid, $125.

d. Bill O'Malley withdrew cash for personal use, $120.

e. Paid salaries expense, $250.

Solution to Self-Review Quiz 2-2

A.

1 Accounts Affected	2 Category	3 ↓ ↑	4 Rules of Dr. and Cr.	5 T Account Update
Cash	Asset	↑	Dr.	Cash 111 (A) 900 |
Equipment	Asset	↑	Dr.	Equipment 121 (A) 600 |
Bill O'Malley, Capital	Capital	↑	Cr.	Bill O'Malley, Capital 311 | 1,500 (A)

B.

1 Accounts Affected	2 Category	3 ↓ ↑	4 Rules of Dr. and Cr.	5 T Account Update
Accounts Receivable	Asset	↑	Dr.	Accounts Receivable 112 (B) 9,000 |
Professional Fees	Revenue	↑	Cr.	Professional Fees 411 | 9,000 (B)

C.

1 Accounts Affected	2 Category	3 ↓ ↑	4 Rules of Dr. and Cr.	5 T Account Update
Utilities Expense	Expense	↑	Dr.	Utilities Expense 511 (C) 125 |
Accounts Payable	Liability	↑	Cr.	Accounts Payable 211 | 125 (C)

D.

1 Accounts Affected	2 Category	3 ↓ ↑	4 Rules of Dr. and Cr.	5 T Account Update
Bill O'Malley, Withdrawals	Withdrawals	↑	Dr.	Bill O'Malley, Withdrawals 312 (D) 120 |
Cash	Asset	↓	Cr.	Cash 111 (A) 900 | 120 (D)

E.

1 Accounts Affected	2 Category	3 ↓ ↑	4 Rules of Dr. and Cr.	5 T Account Update
Salaries Expense	Expense	↑	Dr.	Salaries Expense 512 (E) 250 |
Cash	Asset	↓	Cr.	Cash 111 (A) 900 | 120 (D) | 250 (E)

LEARNING UNIT 2-3

The Trial Balance and Preparation of Financial Reports

Let us look at all the transactions we have discussed, arranged by T account and recorded using the rules of debit and credit.

Cash 111			
(A)	6,000	500	(B)
(D)	2,000	700	(G)
(F)	900	400	(H)
	8,900	100	(J)
7,200		1,700	

Accounts Receivable 112			
(E)	3,000	900	(F)
2,100			

Office Equipment 121			
(A)	200		
(B)	500		
(C)	300		
	1,000		

Accounts Payable 211			
		300	(C)
		200	(I)
		500	

Jill Reed, Capital 311			
		6,200	(A)

Jill Reed, Withdrawals 312			
(J)	100		

Legal Fees 411			
		2,000	(D)
		3,000	(E)
		5,000	

Salaries Expense 511			
(G)	700		

Rent Expense 512			
(H)	400		

Advertising Expense 513			
(I)	200		

Double-entry bookkeeping system: the *total* of all debits is equal to the *total* of all credits.

This grouping of accounts is much easier to use than the expanded accounting equation because all of the transactions that affect a particular account are in one place. There is a name for this double-entry analysis of transactions, where two or more accounts are affected and the total of debits and credits is equal. It is called **double-entry bookkeeping.** This double-entry system helps in checking the recording of business transactions.

As we saw in Learning Unit 2-2, when all the transactions are recorded in the accounts, the total of all the debits should be equal to the total of all the credits. (If it does not, the accountant must go back and find the error by checking the numbers and adding every column again.)

THE TRIAL BALANCE

Footings are used to obtain the balance of each side of the T account. They are not needed if there is only one entry in the account.

Footings are used to obtain the balance of each side of every T account that has more than one entry. The footings are used to find the ending balance. For example, look at the Cash account above. The footing for the debit side is $8,900 and the footing for the credit side is $1,700. Since the debit side is larger, we sub-

As mentioned earlier, the ending balance of cash, $7,200, is a *normal balance* because it is on the side that increases the asset account.

Only the ending balance of each account is listed.

tract $1,700 from $8,900 to arrive at an *ending balance* of $7,200. Now look at the Rent Expense account. There is no need for a footing because there is only one entry. The amount itself is the ending balance. When the ending balance has been found for every account, we should be able to show that the total of all debits equals the total of all credits.

The ending balances are used to prepare a **trial balance.** The trial balance is not a financial report, although it is used to prepare financial reports. The trial balance lists all of the accounts with their balances in the same order as they appear in the chart of accounts. It proves the accuracy of the ledger.

In the ideal situation, businesses would take a trial balance every day. The large number of transactions most businesses conduct each day makes this impractical. Instead, trial balances are prepared periodically.

Keep in mind that the figure for capital might not be the beginning figure if any additional investment has taken place during the period. You can tell this by looking at the capital account in the ledger.

A more detailed discussion of the trial balance will be provided in the next chapter. For now, notice the heading, how the accounts are listed, the debits in the left column, the credits in the right, and the fact that the total of debits is equal to the total of credits.

LORI LIEVRE

FULL-CHARGE BOOKKEEPER

Lori Lievre started out to be a secretary, but, she says, "I really didn't like the work at all. When I was working for a major supermarket chain, I was put in charge of the books. Even though I didn't know much about bookkeeping, I learned that I loved to work with numbers. But I was very slow because I didn't have the background. So I decided to get a background in the field."

At a local community college, Lori found a 1-year certificate program in accounting that had evening classes. She studied bookkeeping, college accounting, business writing, economics, and other subjects. "The certificate program helped me enormously, " she says. "It gave me the theoretical background I needed. I was working by intuition before. The courses taught me to think things through and follow correct procedures. They also built up my confidence. I know what I'm talking about, and I use the right terminology."

Now working as a full-charge bookkeeper for a paper-converting company, Lori goes through all journals, including cash receipts, disbursements, sales, receivables, payables, and expenses. "I love this job," Lori says. "I got it through an employment agency, and one of the best things about it is that I get to do so many things."

What advice does Lori offer to people starting out in a college accounting course? "If you're working in bookkeeping already, a course like this can be a lifesaver. It fills in the gaps in your knowledge. If you don't have a job in the field yet, the course gives you a combination of practical skills and a strong theoretical foundation. It gives you a sense of what you will be doing in the future. It really does prepare you for the workplace."

Since this is not a formal report, there is no need to use dollar signs; however, the single and double lines under subtotals and final totals are still used for clarity.

JILL REED, Barrister and Solicitor TRIAL BALANCE SEPTEMBER 30, 19XX		
	Dr.	Cr.
Cash	7 200 00	
Accounts Receivable	2 100 00	
Office Equipment	1 000 00	
Accounts Payable		500 00
Jill Reed, Capital		6 200 00
Jill Reed, Withdrawals	100 00	
Legal Fees		5 000 00
Salaries Expense	700 00	
Rent Expense	400 00	
Advertising Expense	200 00	
Totals	11 700 00	11 700 00

FIGURE 2-2
Trial Blance for Jill Reed's Law Firm

A trial balance of Jill Reed's firm's accounts is shown in Figure 2-2.

PREPARING FINANCIAL REPORTS

The trial balance is used to prepare the financial reports. The diagram in Figure 2-3 shows how financial reports can be prepared from a trial balance. Remember, financial reports do not have debit or credit columns. The left column is used only to subtotal numbers.

JILL REED, Barrister and Solicitor
INCOME STATEMENT
FOR MONTH ENDED SEPTEMBER 30, 19XX

Revenue:		
Legal Fees		$5 000 00
Operating Expenses:		
Salaries Expense	$ 700 00	
Rent Expense	400 00	
Advertising Expense	200 00	
Total Operating Expenses		1 300 00
Net Income		$3 700 00

JILL REED, Barrister and Solicitor
TRIAL BALANCE
SEPTEMBER 30, 19XX

	Dr.	Cr.
Cash	7 200 00	
Accounts Receivable	2 100 00	
Office Equipment	1 000 00	
Accounts Payable		500 00
Jill Reed, Capital		6 200 00
Jill Reed, Withdrawals	100 00	
Legal Fees		5 000 00
Salaries Expense	700 00	
Rent Expense	400 00	
Advertising Expense	200 00	
Totals	11 700 00	11 700 00

JILL REED, Barrister and Solicitor
STATEMENT OF OWNER'S EQUITY
FOR MONTH ENDED SEPTEMBER 30, 19XX

Jill Reed, Capital		
September 1, 19XX		$6 200 00
Net Income for September	$3 700 00	
Less: Withdrawals		
for September	100 00	
Increase in Capital		3 600 00
Jill Reed, Capital		
September 30, 19XX		$9 800 00

JILL REED, Barrister and Solicitor
BALANCE SHEET
SEPTEMBER 30, 19XX

Assets		Liabilities and Owner's Equity	
Cash	$7 200 00	Liabilities	
Accounts		Accounts	
Receivable	2 100 00	Payable	$ 500 00
Office		Owner's Equity	
Equipment	1 000 00	Jill Reed,	
		Capital	9 800 00
		Total Liab. and	
Total Assets	$10 300 00	Owner's Equity	$10 300 00

FIGURE 2-3 Steps in Preparing Financial Reports from a Trial Balance

LEARNING UNIT 2-3 REVIEW

AT THIS POINT you should be able to

- Explain double-entry bookkeeping. (p. 54)
- Explain the role of footings. (p. 54)
- Prepare a trial balance from a set of accounts. (p. 55)
- Prepare financial reports from a trial balance. (p. 56)

SELF-REVIEW QUIZ 2-3

(The blank forms you need are on pages 2-2 to 2-4 of the *Study Guide and Working Papers.*)

As the bookkeeper of Pam's Hair Salon you are to prepare from the following accounts on June 30, 19XX, (1) a trial balance as of June 30; (2) an income statement for the month ended June 30; (3) a statement of owner's equity for the month ended June 30; and (4) a balance sheet as of June 30, 19XX.

Cash 111	
4,500	300
2,000	100
1,000	1,200
300	1,300
	2,600

Accounts Payable 211	
300	700

Salon Fees 411	
	3,500
	1,000

Accounts Recievable 121	
1,000	300

Pam Jay, Capital 311	
	4,000 *

Rent Expense 511	
1,200	

Salon Equipment 131	
700	

Pam Jay, Withdrawals 321	
100	

Salon Supplies Expense 521	
1,300	

Salaries Expense 531	
2,600	

* No additional investments.

Solution to Self-Review Quiz 2-3

①

PAM'S HAIR SALON
TRIAL BALANCE
SEPTEMBER 30, 19XX

	Dr.	Cr.
Cash	230000	
Accounts Receivable	70000	
Salon Equipment	70000	
Accounts Payable		40000
Pam Jay, Capital		400000
Pam Jay, Withdrawals	10000	
Salon Fees		450000
Rent Expense	120000	
Salon Supplies Expense	130000	
Salaries Expense	260000	
Totals	890000	890000

②

PAM'S HAIR SALON
INCOME STATEMENT
FOR MONTH ENDED JUNE 30, 19XX

Revenue:		
Salon Fees		$450000
Operating Expenses:		
Rent Expense	$120000	
Salon Supplies Expense	130000	
Salaries Expense	260000	
Total Operating Expenses		510000
Net Loss		$ 60000

③

PAM'S HAIR SALON
STATEMENT OF OWNER'S EQUITY
FOR MONTH ENDED JUNE 30, 19XX

Pam Jay, Capital		
June 1, 19XX		$400000
Less: Net Loss for June	$60000	
Withdrawals for June	10000	
Decrease in Capital		70000
Pam Jay, Capital		
June 30, 19XX		$330000

Note: The net loss results in a decrease in Capital.

④

PAM'S HAIR SALON
BALANCE SHEET
JUNE 30, 19XX

Assets		Liabilities and Owner's Equity	
Cash	$230000	Liabilities	
Accounts Receivable	70000	Accounts Payable	$ 40000
Salon Equipment	70000		
		Owner's Equity	
		Pam Jay, Capital	330000
		Total Liab. and	
Total Assets	$370000	Owner's Equity	$370000

Chapter Review

COMPREHENSIVE DEMONSTRATION PROBLEM WITH SOLUTION TIPS

(The blank forms you need are on pages 2-5 to 2-7 of the *Study Guide and Working Papers.*)

The chart of accounts of Mel's Delivery Service includes the following: Cash, 111; Accounts Receivable, 112; Office Equipment, 121; Delivery Trucks, 122; Accounts Payable, 211; Mel Free, Capital, 311; Mel Free, Withdrawals, 312; Delivery Fees Earned, 411; Advertising Expense, 511; Gas Expense, 512; Salaries Expense, 513; and Telephone Expense, 514. The following transactions resulted for Mel's Delivery Service during the month of July:

Transaction A: Mel invested $10,000 in the business from his personal savings account.

Transaction B: Bought delivery trucks on account, $17,000.

Transaction C: Advertising bill received but unpaid, $700.

Transaction D: Bought office equipment for cash, $1,200.

Transaction E: Received cash for delivery services rendered, $15,000.

Transaction F: Paid salaries expense, $3,000.

Transaction G: Paid gas expense for company trucks, $1,250.

Transaction H: Billed customers for delivery services rendered, $4,000.

Transaction I: Paid telephone bill, $300.

Transaction J: Received $3,000 as partial payment of transaction H.

Transaction K: Mel paid home telephone bill from company chequebook, $150.

As Mel's newly employed accountant, you must do the following:

1. Set up T accounts in a ledger.
2. Record transactions in the T accounts. (Place the letter of the transaction next to the entry.)
3. Foot the T accounts where appropriate.
4. Prepare a trial balance at the end of July.
5. Prepare from the trial balance, in proper form, (a) an income statement for the month of July, (b) a statement of owner's equity, and (c) a balance sheet as of July 31, 19XX.

Solution to Demonstration Problem

1, 2, 3. **GENERAL LEDGER**

Cash 111

Debit	Credit
(A) 10,000	1,200 (D)
(E) 15,000	3,000 (F)
(J) 3,000	1,250 (G)
28,000	300 (I)
22,100	150 (K)
	5,900

Acc. Payable 211

Debit	Credit
	17,000 (B)
	700 (C)
	17,700

Advertising Expense 511

Debit	Credit
(C) 700	

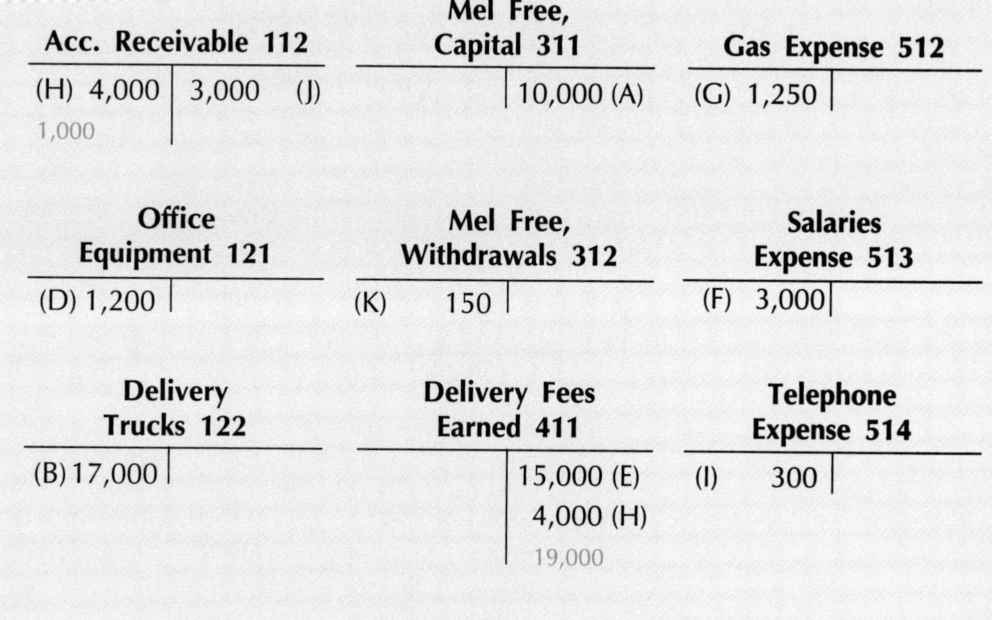

Acc. Receivable 112	
(H) 4,000	3,000 (J)
1,000	

Mel Free, Capital 311	
	10,000 (A)

Gas Expense 512	
(G) 1,250	

Office Equipment 121	
(D) 1,200	

Mel Free, Withdrawals 312	
(K) 150	

Salaries Expense 513	
(F) 3,000	

Delivery Trucks 122	
(B) 17,000	

Delivery Fees Earned 411	
	15,000 (E)
	4,000 (H)
	19,000

Telephone Expense 514	
(I) 300	

Solution Tips to Recording Transactions

	Account	Category	↑↓	Rule
A.	Cash	A	↑	Dr.
	Mel Free, Capital	Cap.	↑	Cr.
B.	Delivery Trucks	A	↑	Dr.
	Accts. Payable	L	↑	Cr.
C.	Advertising Expense	Exp.	↑	Dr.
	Accts. Payable	L	↑	Cr.
D.	Office Equipment	A	↑	Dr.
	Cash	A	↓	Cr.
E.	Cash	A	↑	Dr.
	Del. Fees Earned	Rev.	↑	Cr.
F.	Salaries Expense	Exp.	↑	Dr.
	Cash	A	↓	Cr.
G.	Gas Expense	Exp.	↑	Dr.
	Cash	A	↓	Cr.
H.	Accts. Receivable	A	↑	Dr.
	Del. Fees Earned	Rev.	↑	Cr.
I.	Tel. Expense	Exp.	↑	Dr.
	Cash	A	↓	Cr.
J.	Cash	A	↑	Dr.
	Accts. Receivable	A	↓	Cr.
K.	Mel Free, Withdr.	Withdr.	↑	Dr.
	Cash	A	↓	Cr.

4.

Mel's Delivery Service
Trial Balance
July 31, 19XX

	Dr.	Cr.
Cash	22,100	
Accounts Receivable	1,000	
Office Equipment	1,200	
Delivery Trucks	17,000	
Accounts Payable		17,700
Mel Free, Capital		10,000
Mel Free, Withdrawals	150	
Delivery Fees Earned		19,000
Advertising Expense	700	
Gas Expense	1,250	
Salaries Expense	3,000	
Telephone Expense	300	
TOTALS	46,700	46,700

Solution Tips to Footings and Preparation of a Trial Balance

3. Footings:

Cash	Add left side $28,000.
	Add right side $5,900.
	Take difference $22,100 and stay on side which is larger.
Accounts Payable	Add $17,000 + $700 and stay on same side. Total is $17,700.

4. Trial balance is a list of the ledger's ending balances. The list is in the same order as the chart of accounts. Each title has only one amount listed either as a debit or credit balance.

5. a.

Mel's Delivery Service
Income Statement
for Month Ended July 31, 19XX

Revenue:		
Delivery Fees Earned		$19,000
Operating Expenses:		
Advertising Expense	$ 700	
Gas Expense	1,250	
Salaries Expense	3,000	
Telephone Expense	300	
Total Operating Expenses		5,250
Net Income		$13,750

b.

Mel's Delivery Service
Statement of Owner's Equity
for Month Ended July 31, 19XX

Mel Free, Capital, July 1, 19XX		$10,000
Net Income for July	$13,750	
Less: Withdrawals	150	
Increase in Capital		13,600
Mel Free, Capital, July 31, 19XX		$23,600

c.

Mel's Delivery Service
Balance Sheet
July 31, 19XX

Assets		*Liabilities and Owner's Equity*	
Cash	$22,100	Liabilities	
Accounts Receivable	1,000	Accounts Payable	$17,700
Office Equipment	1,200		
Delivery Trucks	17,000	Owner's Equity	
		Mel Free, Capital	23,600
Total Assets	**$41,300**	**Total Liabilities and Owner's Equity**	**$41,300**

Solution Tips to Prepare Financial Reports from a Trial Balance

		Trial Balance Dr.	Trial Balance Cr.
Balance Sheet	Assets	X	
	Liabilities		X
Statement of Equity	Capital		X
	Withdrawals	X	
Income Statement	Revenues		X
	Expenses	X	
		XX	XX

Net income on the income statement of $13,750 goes on the statement of owner's equity.

Ending capital of $23,600 on the statement of owner's equity goes on the balance sheet as the new figure for capital.

Note: The amounts on Financial Reports are not identified as debits or credits. The inside column is used for subtotalling.

Summary of Key Points

Learning Unit 2-1

1. A T account is a simplified version of a standard account.
2. A ledger is a group of accounts.
3. A debit is the left-hand position (side) of an account and a credit is the right-hand position (side) of an account.

4. A footing is the total of one side of an account: the ending balance is the difference between the footings.

Learning Unit 2-2

1. A chart of accounts lists the account titles and their numbers for a company.
2. The transaction analysis chart is a teaching device, not to be confused with standard accounting procedures.
3. A compound entry is a transaction involving more than one debit or credit.

Learning Unit 2-3

1. In double-entry bookkeeping, the recording of each business transaction affects two or more accounts, and the total of debits equals the total of credits.
2. A trial balance is a list of the ending balances of all accounts, listed in the same order as on the chart of accounts.
3. Any additional investments during the period result in capital on the trial balance not being the beginning figure for capital.
4. There are *no* debit or credit columns on the three financial reports.

KEY TERMS

Account An accounting device used in bookkeeping to record increases and decreases of business transactions relating to individual assets, liabilities, capital, withdrawals, revenue, expenses, and so on.

Chart of accounts A numbering system of accounts that lists the account titles and account numbers to be used by a company.

Compound entry A transaction involving more than one debit or credit.

Credit The right-hand side of any account. A number entered on the right side of any account is said to be credited to that account.

Debit The left-hand side of any account. A number entered on the left side of any account is said to be debited to that account.

Double-entry bookkeeping An accounting system in which the recording of each transaction affects two or more accounts, and the total of the debits is equal to the total of the credits.

Ending balance The difference between footings in a T account.

Footings The totals of each side of a T account.

Ledger A group of accounts that records data from business transactions.

Normal balance of an account The side of an account that increases by the rules of debit and credit.

Standard account A formal account that includes columns for date, explanation, posting reference, debit, and credit.

T account A skeleton version of a standard account, used for demonstration purposes.

Trial balance A list of the ending balances of all the accounts in a ledger. The total of the debits should equal the total of the credits.

Blueprint for Preparing Financial Reports from a Trial Balance

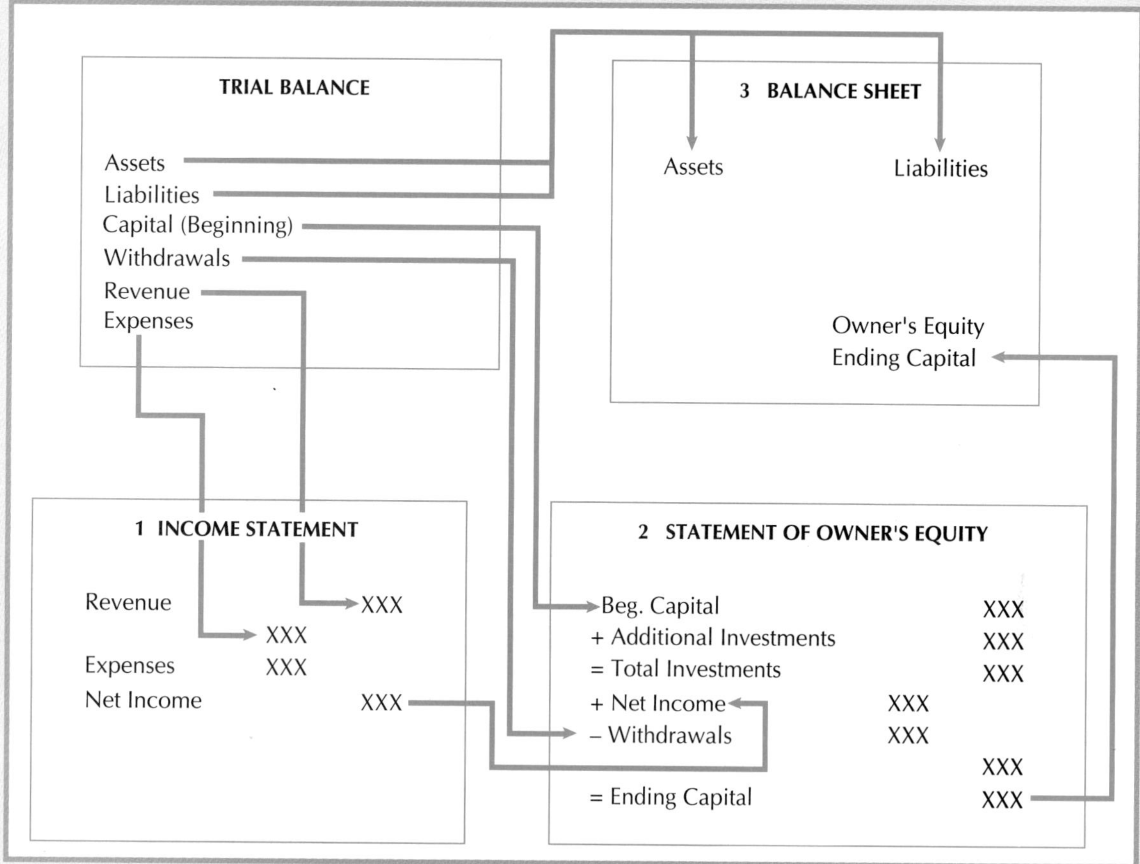

Questions, Exercises, and Problems

Discussion Questions

1. Define a ledger.
2. Why is the left-hand side of an account called a debit?
3. Footings are used in balancing all accounts.True or false? Please explain.
4. What is the end product of the accounting process?
5. What do we mean when we say that a transaction analysis chart is a teaching device?
6. What are the five steps of the transaction analysis chart?
7. Explain the concept of double-entry bookkeeping.
8. A trial balance is a formal report.True or false? Please explain.
9. Why are there no debit or credit columns on financial reports?
10. Compare the financial statements prepared from the expanded accounting equation with those prepared from a trial balance.

Mini Exercises

(The blank forms you need are on pages 2-9 and 2-10 in the *Study Guide and Working Papers.*)

The T Account

1. From the following, foot and balance each account.

Cash 110

4/8	3,000	4/14	2,000
4/12	6,000		

P. Sally, Capital 311

	4,000
	3,000
	6,000

Transaction Analysis

2. Complete the following:

Account	Category	↑	↓	Normal Balance
A. Supplies				
B. Prepaid Rent				
C. Accounts Payable				
D. P. Ring, Capital				
E. P. Ring, Withdrawals				
F. Legal Fees Earned				
G. Rent Expense				

Transaction Analysis

3. Record the following transaction into the transaction analysis chart: Provided legal services for $3,000, receiving $1,000 cash with the remainder to be paid next month.

Accounts Affected	Category	↓ ↑	Rules of Dr. and Cr.	T Accounts

Trial Balance

4. Rearrange the following titles in the order they would appear in on a trial balance:

Rent Expense	Legal Fees Earned
Accounts Receivable	D. Cope, Withdrawals
Accounts Payable	Cleaning Expense
D. Cope, Capital	Advertising Expense
Computer Equipment	Cash

Trial Balance/Financial Reports

5. From the following trial balance identify which report each title will appear on:

- Income Statement (IS)
- Statement of Owner's Equity (OE)
- Balance Sheet (BS)

Blue Co.
Trial Balance
Sept. 30, 19XX

		Dr.	Cr.
A. ______	Cash	390	
B. ______	Supplies	100	
C. ______	Office Equipment	200	
D. ______	Accounts Payable		100
E. ______	A. Ellen, Capital		450
F. ______	A. Ellen, Withdrawals	160	
G. ______	Fees Earned		290
H. ______	Hair Salon Fees		300
I. ______	Salaries Expense	130	
J. ______	Rent Expense	120	
K. ______	Advertising Expense	40	
	TOTALS	1,140	1,140

Exercises

(The blank forms you need are on pages 2-10 and 2-11 in the *Study Guide and Working Papers.)*

Preparing a chart of accounts.

2-1. From the following, prepare a chart of accounts, using the same numbering system as used in this chapter.

Computer Equipment	Professional Fees
Rent Expense	B. Aster, Capital
Accounts Payable	Cash
Accounts Receivable	Salaries Expense
Repair Expense	B. Aster, Withdrawals

Preparing a transaction analysis chart.

2-2. Record the following transaction into the transaction analysis chart: Alice Flynn bought a new piece of office equipment for $9,000, paying $1,000 down and charging the rest.

2-3. Complete the table: for each account listed on the left, fill in what category it belongs to, whether increases and decreases in the account are marked on the debit or credit sides, and which financial report the account appears on. A sample is provided.

Accounts categorizing, rules, and on which reports they appear.

Accounts Affected	Category	↑	↓	Appears on Which Financial Report
Supplies	Asset	Dr.	Cr.	Balance Sheet
Professional Fees Earned				
R. Perez, Withdrawals				
Accounts Payable				
Rent Expense				
Auto				

Rules of debits and credits.

2-4. Given the following accounts, complete the table by inserting appropriate numbers next to the individual transaction to indicate which account is debited and which account is credited.

1. Cash
2. Accounts Receivable
3. Equipment
4. Accounts Payable
5. J. Lowe, Capital
6. J. Lowe, Withdrawals
7. Plumbing Fees Earned
8. Salaries Expense
9. Advertising Expense
10. Supplies Expenses

Transaction	Rules Dr.	Rules Cr.
A. Paid advertising expense.	9	1
B. Jay paid personal utilities bill from company chequebook.		
C. Advertising bill received but unpaid.		
D. Received cash from plumbing fees.		
E. Paid supplies expense.		
F. Jay invested additional equipment into the business.		
G. Billed customers for plumbing services rendered.		
H. Received one-half the balance from transaction G.		
I. Bought equipment on account.		

Preparing financial reports.

2-5. From the following trial balance of Moxie Cleaners, prepare the following:

- Income statement
- Statement of owner's equity
- Balance sheet

MOXIE CLEANERS TRIAL BALANCE JULY 31, 19XX		
	Dr.	Cr.
Cash	450 00	
Equipment	692 00	
Accounts Payable		355 00
J. Moxie, Capital		800 00
J. Moxie, Withdrawals	198 00	
Cleaning Fees		458 00
Salaries Expense	160 00	
Utilities Expense	113 00	
Totals	1613 00	1613 00

Group A Problems

(The forms you need are on pages 2-12 to 2-17 of the *Study Guide and Working Papers.*)

Use of a transaction analysis chart.

2A-1. The following transactions occurred in the opening and operation of Jay's Bookkeeping Service.

a. Jay Miller opened the bookkeeping service by investing $5,000 from his personal savings account.

b. Purchased store equipment on account, $4,000.

c. Rent expense due but unpaid, $400.

d. Received cash for bookkeeping services rendered, $650.

e. Billed a client on account, $700.

f. Jay Miller withdrew cash for personal use, $200.

Complete the transaction analysis chart in the *Study Guide and Working Papers.* The chart of accounts includes Cash; Accounts Receivable; Store Equipment; Accounts Payable; Jay Miller, Capital; Jay Miller, Withdrawals; Bookkeeping Fees Earned; and Rent Expense.

Recording transactions into ledger accounts.

2A-2. Ann Madugo opened a travel agency, and the following transactions resulted:

a. Ann Madugo invested $18,000 in the travel agency.

b. Bought office equipment on account, $3,000.

c. Agency received cash for travel arrangements that it completed for a client, $2,500.

d. Ann Madugo paid a personal bill from the company chequebook, $50.

e. Paid advertising expense for the month, $700.

f. Rent expense for the month due but unpaid, $500.

g. Paid $800 as partial payment of what was owed from the transaction in **b**.

As Ann Madugo's accountant, analyze and record the transactions in T account form. Set up the T accounts and label each entry with the letter of the transaction.

Chart of Accounts

Assets
Cash 111
Office Equipment 121

Liabilities
Accounts Payable 211

Owner's Equity
A. Madugo, Capital 311
A. Madugo, Withdrawals 312

Revenue
Travel Fees Earned 411

Expenses
Advertising Expense 511
Rent Expense 512

Preparing a trial balance from the T accounts.

2A-3. From the following T accounts of Tom's Window Washing Service, (a) record and foot the balances in the *Study Guide and Working Papers* where appropriate, and (b) prepare a trial balance in proper form for May 31, 19XX.

Cash 111

Dr.	Cr.
6,000 (A)	100 (D)
3,500 (G)	200 (E)
	400 (F)
	200 (H)
	900 (I)

Accounts Payable 211

Dr.	Cr.
100 (D)	1,300 (C)

Fees Earned 411

Dr.	Cr.
	7,500 (B)

Accounts Receivable 112

Dr.	Cr.
7,000 (B)	3,000 (G)

Tom Spall, Capital 311

Dr.	Cr.
	5,000 (A)

Rent Expense 511

Dr.	Cr.
400 (F)	

Office Equipment 121

Dr.	Cr.
300 (C)	
200 (H)	

Tom Spall, Withdrawals 312

Dr.	Cr.
900 (I)	

Utilities Expense 512

Dr.	Cr.
200 (E)	

Preparing financial reports from the trial balance.

2A-4. From the trial balance of Walter Lantz, Barrister and Solicitor, prepare (a) an income statement for the month of May, (b) a statement of owner's

WALTER LANTZ, Barrister and Solicitor
TRIAL BALANCE
MAY 31, 19XX

	Dr.	Cr.
Cash	2000 00	
Accounts Receivable	650 00	
Office Equipment	750 00	
Accounts Payable		1300 00
Salaries Payable		675 00
W. Lantz, Capital		1275 00
W. Lantz, Withdrawals	300 00	
Revenue from Legal Fees		1350 00
Utilities Expense	300 00	
Rent Expense	450 00	
Salaries Expense	150 00	
Totals	4600 00	4600 00

equity for the month ended May 31, and (c) a balance sheet as of May 31, 19XX.

Comprehensive problem.

2A-5. The chart of accounts for Angel's Delivery Service is as follows:

Chart of Accounts

Assets	**Revenue**
Cash 111	Delivery Fees Earned 411
Accounts Receivable 112	
Office Equipment 121	**Expenses**
Delivery Trucks 122	Advertising Expense 511
	Gas Expense 512
Liabilities	Salaries Expense 513
Accounts Payable 211	Telephone Expense 514
Owner's Equity	
Alice Angel, Capital 311	
Alice Angel, Withdrawals 312	

Angel's Delivery Service completed the following transactions during the month of March:

Transaction A: Alice Angel invested $16,000 in the delivery service from her personal savings account.
Transaction B: Bought delivery trucks on account, $18,000.
Transaction C: Bought office equipment for cash, $600.
Transaction D: Paid advertising expense, $250.
Transaction E: Collected cash for delivery services rendered, $2,600.
Transaction F: Paid drivers' salaries, $900.
Transaction G: Paid gas expense for trucks, $1,200.
Transaction H: Performed delivery services for a customer on account, $800.
Transaction I: Telephone expense due but unpaid, $700.
Transaction J: Received $300 as partial payment of transaction H.
Transaction K: Alice Angel withdrew cash for personal use, $300.

As Alice's newly employed accountant, you must:

1. Set up T accounts in a ledger.
2. Record transactions in the T accounts. (Place the letter of the transaction next to the entry.)
3. Foot the T accounts where appropriate.
4. Prepare a trial balance at the end of March.
5. Prepare from the trial balance, in proper form, (a) a statement of owner's equity for the month of March, (b) a statement of owner's equity, and (c) a balance sheet as of March 31, 19XX.

Group B Problems

(The forms you need are on pages 2-12 to 2-17 of the *Study Guide and Working Papers.*)

Use of a transaction analysis chart.

2B-1. Jay Miller decided to open a bookkeeping service. Record the following transactions into the transaction analysis charts:

Transaction A: Jay invested $1,500 in the bookkeeping service from his personal savings account.

Transaction B: Purchased store equipment on account, $900.

Transaction C: Rent expense due but unpaid, $250.

Transaction D: Performed bookkeeping services for cash, $1,200.

Transaction E: Billed clients for bookkeeping services rendered, $700.

Transaction F: Jay paid his home heating bill from the company chequebook, $275.

The chart of accounts for the shop includes Cash; Accounts Receivable; Store Equipment; Accounts Payable; Jay Miller, Capital; Jay Miller, Withdrawals; Bookkeeping Fees Earned; and Rent Expense.

Recording transactions into ledger accounts.

2B-2. Ann Madugo established a new travel agency. Record the following transactions for Ann in T account form. Label each entry with the letter of the transaction.

Transaction A: Ann Madugo invested $18,000 in the travel agency from her personal bank account.

Transaction B: Bought office equipment on account, $6,000.

Transaction C: Travel agency rendered service to Jensen Corp. and received cash, $1,200.

Transaction D: Ann Madugo withdrew cash for personal use, $200.

Transaction E: Paid advertising expense, $600.

Transaction F: Rent expense due but unpaid, $500.

Transaction G: Paid $400 in partial payment of transaction B.

The chart of accounts includes Cash, 111; Office Equipment, 121; Accounts Payable, 211; A. Madugo, Capital, 311; A. Madugo, Withdrawals, 312; Travel Fees Earned, 411; Advertising Expense, 511; and Rent Expense, 512.

Preparing a trial balance from the T accounts.

2B-3. From the following T accounts of Tom's Window Washing Service, (a) record and foot the balances in the *Study Guide* where appropriate and (b) prepare a trial balance for May 31, 19XX.

Cash 111	
10,000 (A)	4,000 (C)
4,000 (F)	310 (D)
2,000 (G)	50 (E)
	600 (I)

Accounts Receivable 112	
2,000 (G)	

Office Equipment 121	
2,000 (B)	
4,000 (C)	

Accounts Payable 211	
	2,000 (B)

Tom Spall, Capital 311	
	10,000 (A)

Tom Spall, Withdrawals 312	
600 (I)	

Fees Earned 411	
	4,000 (F)
	4,000 (G)

Rent Expense 511	
310 (D)	

Utilities Expense 512	
50 (E)	

Preparing financial reports from the trial balance.

2B-4. From the trial balance of Walter Lantz, Barrister and Solicitor, prepare (a) an income from the statement for the month of May, (b) a statement of owner's equity for the month ended May 31, and (c) a balance sheet as of May 31, 19XX.

WALTER LANTZ, Barrister and Solicitor
TRIAL BALANCE
MAY 31, 19XX

	Debit	Credit
Cash	6 000 00	
Accounts Receivable	2 400 00	
Office Equipment	2 400 00	
Accounts Payable		200 00
Salaries Payable		600 00
W. Lantz, Capital		4 000 00
W. Lantz, Withdrawals	2 000 00	
Revenue from Legal Fees		8 800 00
Utilities Expense	100 00	
Rent Expense	300 00	
Salaries Expense	400 00	
Totals	13 600 00	13 600 00

Comprehensive problem.

2B-5. The chart of accounts of Angel's Delivery Service includes the following: Cash, 111; Accounts Receivable, 112; Office Equipment, 121; Delivery Trucks, 122; Accounts Payable, 211; Alice Angel, Capital, 311; Alice Angel, Withdrawals, 312; Delivery Fees Earned, 411; Advertising Expense, 511; Gas Expense, 512; Salaries Expense, 513; and Telephone Expense, 514. The following transactions resulted for Angel's Delivery Service during the month of March:

Transaction A: Alice invested $40,000 in the business from her personal savings account.
Transaction B: Bought delivery trucks on account, $25,000.
Transaction C: Advertising bill received but unpaid, $800.
Transaction D: Bought office equipment for cash, $2,500.
Transaction E: Received cash for delivery services rendered, $13,000.
Transaction F: Paid salaries expense, $1,850.
Transaction G: Paid gas expense for company trucks, $750.
Transaction H: Billed customers for delivery services rendered, $5,500.
Transaction I: Paid telephone bill, $400.
Transaction J: Received $1,600 as partial payment of transaction H.
Transaction K: Alice paid home telephone bill from company chequebook, $88.

As Alice's newly employed accountant, you must

1. Set up T accounts in a ledger.
2. Record transactions in the T accounts. (Place the letter of the transaction next to the entry.)
3. Foot the T accounts where appropriate.
4. Prepare a trial balance at the end of March.
5. Prepare from the trial balance, in proper form, (a) a statement of owner's equity for the month of March, (b) a statement of owner's equity, and (c) a balance sheet as of March 31, 19XX.

Group C Problems

Use of a transaction analysis chart.

2C-1. Fran West decided to open a bookkeeping service. Record the following transactions into the transaction analysis charts:

Transaction A: Fran invested $2,500 in the bookkeeping service from her personal savings account.

Transaction B: Purchased office equipment on account, $1,800.

Transaction C: Rent expense due but unpaid, $400.

Transaction D: Performed bookkeeping services for cash, $2,000.

Transaction E: Billed clients for bookkeeping services rendered, $1,300.

Transaction F: Fran paid a home repair bill from the company chequebook, $220.

The chart of accounts for the shop includes Cash; Accounts Receivable; Office Equipment; Accounts Payable; Fran West, Capital; Fran West, Withdrawals; Bookkeeping Fees Earned; and Rent Expense.

Recording transactions into ledger accounts.

2C-2. George Leung established a new travel agency. Record the following transactions for Robert in T account form. Label each entry with the letter of the transaction.

Transaction A: George Leung invested $28,000 in the travel agency from his personal bank account.

Transaction B: Bought office equipment on account, $9,600.

Transaction C: Travel agency rendered service to Portias Corp. and received cash, $2,800.

Transaction D: George Leung withdrew cash for personal use, $800.

Transaction E: Paid advertising expense, $750.

Transaction F: Rent expense due but unpaid, $825.

Transaction G: Paid $2,500 in partial payment of transaction B.

The chart of accounts includes Cash, 111; Office Equipment, 121; Accounts Payable, 211; G. Leung, Capital, 311; G. Leung, Withdrawals, 312; Travel Fees Earned, 411; Advertising Expense, 511; and Rent Expense, 512.

Preparing a trial balance from the T accounts.

2C-3. From the following T accounts of Tod's Small Engine Repair Service, (a) record and foot the balances in the *Study Guide and Working Papers* where appropriate, and (b) prepare a trial balance for October 31, 19XX.

Cash 111	
6,000 (A)	4,000 (C)
4,000 (F)	310 (D)
2,000 (G)	50 (E)
	600 (I)

Accounts Receivable 112	
1,000 (G)	

Office Equipment 121	
2,000 (B)	
4,000 (C)	

Accounts Payable 211	
	2,000 (B)

Tod Tobias, Capital 311	
	6,000 (A)

Tod Tobias, Withdrawals 312	
600 (I)	

Fees Earned 411	
	4,000 (F)
	3,000 (G)

Rent Expense 511	
310 (D)	

Utilities Expense 512	
50 (E)	

Preparing financial reports from the trial balance.

2C-4. From the trial balance of Arnold Gold, Architect, prepare (a) an income statement for the month of June, (b) a statement of owner's equity for the month ended June 30, and (c) a balance sheet as of June 30, 19XX.

ARNOLD GOLD, Architect
TRIAL BALANCE
JUNE 30, 19XX

	Dr.	Cr.
Cash in Bank	140000	
Accounts Receivable	95000	
Supplies	21000	
Equipment	520000	
Accounts Payable		40000
A. Gold, Capital		500000
A. Gold, Withdrawals	80000	
Fees Earned		524000
Rent Expense	110000	
Advertising Expense	42000	
Utilities Expense	56000	
Totals	1064000	1064000

Comprehensive problem.

2C-5. The chart of accounts of Dave's Design Service includes the following: Cash, 111; Accounts Receivable, 112; Office Equipment, 121; Design Equipment, 122; Accounts Payable, 211; Dave Sieg, Capital, 311; Dave Sieg, Withdrawals, 312; Design Fees Earned, 411; Advertising Expense, 511; Repair Expense, 512; Salaries Expense, 513; and Telephone Expense, 514. The following transactions resulted for Dave's Design Service during the month of March:

Transaction A: Dave invested $32,000 in the business from his personal savings account.
Transaction B: Bought design equipment on account, $15,000.
Transaction C: Advertising bill received but unpaid, $600.
Transaction D: Bought office equipment for cash, $3,100.
Transaction E: Received cash for design services rendered, $5,800.
Transaction F: Paid salaries expense, $1,520.
Transaction G:. Paid repair expense for design equipment, $320.
Transaction H: Billed customers for design services rendered, $3,600.
Transaction I: Paid telephone bill, $125.
Transaction J: Received $1,750 as partial payment of transaction H.
Transaction K: Dave paid home telephone bill from company chequebook, $78.
Transaction L: Paid $400 on the bill received in transaction C.

As Dave's newly employed accountant, your task is to

1. Set up T accounts in a ledger.
2. Record transactions in the T accounts. (Place the letter of the transaction next to the entry.)
3. Foot the T accounts where appropriate.
4. Prepare a trial balance at the end of March.
5. Prepare from the trial balance, in proper form, (a) a statement of owner's equity for the month of March, (b) a statement of owner's equity, and (c) a balance sheet as of March 31, 19XX.

REAL WORLD APPLICATIONS

2R-1.

Andy Leaf is a careless bookkeeper. He is having a terrible time getting his trial balance to balance. Andy has asked for your assistance in preparing a correct trial balance. The following is the incorrect trial balance.

RANCH COMPANY TRIAL BALANCE JUNE 30, 19XX		
	Dr.	Cr.
Cash	510 00	
Accounts Receivable		635 00
Office Equipment	360 00	
Accounts Payable	110 00	
Wages Payable	10 00	
H. Clo, Capital	635 00	
H. Clo, Withdrawals	1440 00	
Professional Fees		2240 00
Rent Expense		240 00
Advertising Expense	25 00	
Totals	3090 00	3115 00

Facts you have discovered:

- Debits to the Cash account were $2,640; credits to the Cash account were $2,150.
- Amy Hall paid $15 but was not updated in Accounts Receivable.
- A purchase of office equipment for $5 on account was never recorded in the ledger.
- Revenue was understated in the ledger by $180.

Show how these errors affected the ending balances for the accounts involved, and explain how the trial balance will indeed balance once they are corrected.

Tell Ranch Company how it can avoid this problem in the future. Write out your recommendations.

2R-2.

Alice Groove, owner of Lonton Company, asked her bookkeeper how each of the following situations will affect the totals of the trial balance and individual ledger accounts.

- An $850 payment for a desk was recorded as a debit to Office Equipment, $85, and a credit to Cash, $85.
- A payment of $300 to a creditor was recorded as a debit to Accounts Payable, $300, and a credit to Cash, $100.
- The collection on an Accounts Receivable for $400 was recorded as a debit to Cash, $400, and a credit to J. Ray, Capital, $400.
- The payment of a liability for $400 was recorded as a debit to Accounts Payable, $40, and a credit to Supplies, $40.

- A purchase of equipment of $800 was recorded as a debit to Supplies, $800, and a credit to Cash, $800.
- A payment of $95 to a creditor was recorded as a debit to Accounts Payable, $95, and a credit to Cash, $59.

What did the bookkeeper tell her? Which accounts were overstated and which understated? Which were correct? Explain in writing how mistakes can be avoided in the future.

make the call

Critical Thinking/Ethical Case

2R-3.

Audrey Flet, the bookkeeper of ALN Co., was scheduled to leave on a three-week vacation at 5 o'clock on Friday. She couldn't get the company's trial balance to balance. At 4:30, she decided to put in fictitious figures to make it balance. Audrey told herself she would fix it when she got back from her vacation. Was Audrey right or wrong to do this? Why?

ACCOUNTING RECALL

A CUMULATIVE APPROACH

THIS EXAM REVIEWS CHAPTERS 1 AND 2

Your *Study Guide and Working Papers* (pages 2-27 to 2-29) have forms to complete this exam, as well as worked-out solutions. The page references next to each question identify what page to turn back to if you answer the question incorrectly.

PART I Vocabulary Review

Match the terms to the appropriate definition or phrase.

Page Ref.		Term		Definition
(55)	1.	Trial balance	A.	Total remains the same
(42)	2.	Debit	B.	Entering numbers on right side
(44)	3.	Normal balance	C.	Subdivisions of owner's equity
(13)	4.	Revenue	D.	Group of accounts
(42)	5.	Crediting	E.	Numbering system
(10)	6.	Balance sheet	F.	Left side of an account
(8)	7.	Shift in assets	G.	Prepared as of a particular date
(45)	8.	Chart of accounts	H.	Not an asset
(41)	9.	Ledger	I.	Side of account that increases it
(16)	10.	Capital, withdrawals, revenue, expenses	J.	List of the ledger balances

PART II True or False (Accounting Theory)

(42) 11. A debit always means increase.

(56) 12. There are no debit or credit columns on financial reports.

(55) 13. The trial balance lists only the ending figure for capital that goes on the balance sheet.

(44) 14. An increase in a withdrawal is a credit.

(55) 15. The trial balance is not a formal report.

PART III Applications Problem (p. 2–27)

(1) Record the following transactions into the ledger; (2) prepare a trial balance for July; and (3) prepare the three financial reports for Alice Wong's Bookstore.

Transaction A: On July 1, Alice Wong invested $6,000 in a bookstore.

Transaction B: Completed a sale of books to a school for $3,000. School paid $1,000 down and promised to pay balance in 30 days.

Transaction C: Bought store equipment on account, $500.

Transaction D: Paid utilities bill, $100.

Transaction E: Paid rent, $1,400.

Transaction F: Alice withdrew $500 for personal use.

Transaction G: Paid salaries, $600.

Transaction H: Paid $300 on balance owed in transaction C.

Beginning the Accounting Cycle

3

Journalizing, Posting, and the Trial Balance

Chapter Objectives

- ◆ Journalizing—analyzing and recording business transactions into a journal. (p. 80)
- ◆ Posting—transferring information from a journal to a ledger. (p. 89)
- ◆ Preparing a trial balance. (p. 96)

The normal accounting procedures that are performed over a period of time are called the **accounting cycle.** The accounting cycle takes place in a period of time called an **accounting period.** An accounting period is the period of time covered by the income statement. Although it can be any time period up to one year (e.g., one month or three months), most businesses use a one-year accounting period. The year can be either a **calendar year** (January 1 through December 31) or a **fiscal year.**

A fiscal year is an accounting period that runs for any 12 consecutive months, so it can be the same as a calendar year. A business can choose any fiscal year that is convenient. For example, some retailers may decide to end their fiscal year when inventories and business activity are at a low point, such as after the Christmas season. This is called a **natural business year.** Using a natural business year allows the business to count its year-end inventory when it is easiest to do so.

This chapter covers steps 1 to 4 of the accounting cycle.

Businesses would not be able to operate successfully if they only prepared financial reports at the end of their calendar or fiscal year. That is why most businesses prepare **interim reports** on a monthly, quarterly, or semiannual basis.

In this chapter, as well as in Chapters 4 and 5, we will follow Brenda Clark's new business, Clark's Word Processing Services. We will follow the normal accounting procedures that the business performs over a period of time. Clark has chosen to use a fiscal period of January 1 to December 31, which also is the calendar year.

Table 3-1 lists the steps in the business accounting cycle. This table should be used as a reference table. By the end of Chapter 5, every step will have been explained and illustrated.

LEARNING UNIT 3-1

Analyzing and Recording Business Transactions into a Journal: Steps 1 and 2 of the Accounting Cycle

The General Journal

A business uses a journal to record transactions in chronological order. A ledger accumulates information from a journal. The journal and the ledger are in two different books.

Chapter 2 taught us how to analyze and record business transactions into T accounts, or ledger accounts. However, recording a debit in an account on one page of the ledger and recording the corresponding credit on a different page of the ledger can make it difficult to find errors. It would be much easier if all of the business's transactions were located in the same place. That is the function of the **journal** or **general journal.** Transactions are entered in the journal in chronological order (January 1, 8, 15, etc.), and then this recorded information is used

TABLE 3-1 STEPS OF THE ACCOUNTING CYCLE

Steps	Notes
1. Business transactions occur and generate source documents.	Source documents are cash register tapes, sales tickets, bills, cheques, payroll cards.
↓	↓
2. Analyze and record business transactions into a journal.	Called journalizing.
↓	↓
3. Post or transfer information from journal to ledger.	Copying the debits and credits of the journal entries, placing them into the ledger accounts.
↓	↓
4. Prepare a trial balance.	Summarizing each individual ledger account and listing these accounts and their balances to test for accuracy in recording transactions.
↓	↓
5. Prepare a worksheet.	A multicolumn form that summarizes accounting information to complete the accounting cycle.
↓	↓
6. Prepare financial statements.	Income statement, statement of owner's equity, balance sheet.
↓	↓
7. Journalize and post adjusting entries.	Refers to adjustment columns of worksheet.
↓	↓
8. Journalize and post closing entries.	Refers to income statement and balance sheet columns of worksheet.
↓	↓
9. Prepare a post-closing trial balance.	Proves the equality of debits and credits after adjusting and closing entries are posted.

Use this as a reference table in your study of Chapters 3, 4, and 5.

to update the ledger accounts. In computerized accounting, a journal may be recorded on disk or tape.

We will use a general journal, the simplest form of a journal, to record the transactions of Clark's Word Processing Services. A transaction (debit[s] + credit[s]) that has been analyzed and recorded in a journal is called a **journal entry.** The process of recording the journal entry into the journal is called **journalizing.**

Journal—book of original entry.

The journal is called the **book of original entry,** since it contains the first formal information about the business transactions. The ledger is known as the **book of final entry,** because the information it contains will be transferred from the journal. Like the ledger, the journal may be a bound or looseleaf book. Each of the journal pages looks like the one in Figure 3-1. The pages of the journal are numbered consecutively from page 1. Keep in mind that the journal and

Date		Account Titles and Description	PR	Dr.	Cr.

CLARK'S WORD PROCESSING SERVICES
GENERAL JOURNAL

Page 1

FIGURE 3-1
The General Journal

the ledger are separate books. Also note that both journals and ledgers exist in computerized accounting, although they may look different.

Relationship Between the Journal and the Chart of Accounts

The accountant must refer to the business' chart of accounts for the account name that is to be used in the journal. Every company has its own "unique" chart of accounts.

The chart of accounts for Clark's Word Processing Services appears below. By the end of Chapter 5, we will have discussed each of these accounts.

Note that we will continue to use transaction analysis charts as a teaching aid in the journalizing process.

Clark's Word Processing Services
Chart of Accounts

Assets (100–199)
111 Cash
112 Accounts Receivable
114 Office Supplies
115 Prepaid Rent
121 Word Processing Equipment
122 Accumulated Depreciation, Word Processing Equipment

Liabilities (200–299)
211 Accounts Payable
212 Salaries Payable

Owner's Equity (300–399)
311 Brenda Clark, Capital
312 Brenda Clark, Withdrawals
313 Income Summary

Revenue (400–499)
411 Word Processing Fees

Expenses (500–599)
511 Office Salaries Expense
512 Advertising Expense
513 Telephone Expense
514 Office Supplies Expense
515 Rent Expense
516 Depreciation Expense, Word Processing Equipment

Journalizing the Transactions of Clark's Word Processing Services

Certain formalities must be followed in making journal entries:

- The debit portion of the transaction always is recorded first.
- The credit portion of a transaction is indented 1 cm and placed below the debit portion.
- The explanation of the journal entry follows immediately after the credit and 2 cm from the date column.

◆ A one-line space follows each transaction and explanation. This makes the journal easier to read, and there is less chance of mixing transactions.

◆ Finally, as always, the total amount of debits must equal the total amount of credits. The same format is used for each of the entries in the journal.

May 1, 19XX: Brenda Clark began the business by investing $10,000 in cash.

1 Accounts Affected	2 Category	3 ↑ ↓	4 Rules of Dr. and Cr.
Cash	Asset	↑	Dr.
Brenda Clark, Capital	Owner's Equity	↑	Cr.

For now the PR (posting reference) column is blank; we will discuss it later.

CLARK'S WORD PROCESSING SERVICES
GENERAL JOURNAL

Page 1

Date		Account Titles and Description	PR	Dr.	Cr.
19XX May	1	Cash		10 0 0 0 00	
		Brenda Clark, Capital			10 0 0 0 00
		Initial investment of cash by owner			

Let's now look at the structure of this journal entry. The entry contains the following information:

1. Year of the journal entry	19XX
2. Month of the journal entry	May
3. Day of journal entry	1
4. Name(s) of accounts debited	Cash
5. Name(s) of accounts credited	Brenda Clark, Capital
6. Explanation of transaction	Investment of cash
7. Amount of debit(s)	$10,000
8. Amount of credit(s)	$10,000

May 1: Purchased word processing equipment from Ben Co. for $6,000, paying $1,000 and promising to pay the balance within 30 days.

Note that in this compound entry we have one debit and two credits—but the total amount of debits equals the total amount of credits.

1 Accounts Affected	2 Category	3 ↑ ↓	4 Rules of Dr. and Cr.
Word Processing Equipment	Asset	↑	Dr.
Cash	Asset	↓	Cr.
Accounts Payable	Liability	↑	Cr.

A journal entry that requires three or more accounts is called a compound journal entry.

This transaction affects three accounts. When a journal entry has more than two accounts, it is called a **compound journal entry.**

Date		Account	Dr.	Cr.
	1	Word Processing Equipment	6000 00	
		Cash		1000 00
		Accounts Payable		5000 00
		Purchase of equipment from Ben Co.		

In this entry, only the day is entered in the date column. That is because the year and month were entered at the top of the page from the first transaction. There is no need to repeat this information until a new page is needed or a change of months occurs.

May 1: Rented office space, paying $1,200 in advance for the first three months.

1 Accounts Affected	2 Category	3 ↑ ↓	4 Rules of Dr. and Cr.
Prepaid Rent	Asset	↑	Dr.
Cash	Asset	↓	Cr.

Rent paid in advance is an asset.

In this transaction Clark gains an asset called prepaid rent and gives up an asset, cash. The prepaid rent does not become an expense until it expires.

Date		Account	Dr.	Cr.
	1	Prepaid Rent	1200 00	
		Cash		1200 00
		Rent paid in advance 1 - 3 mo.		

May 3: Purchased office supplies from Norris Co. on account, $600.

1 Accounts Affected	2 Category	3 ↑ ↓	4 Rules of Dr. and Cr.
Office Supplies	Asset	↑	Dr.
Accounts Payable	Liability	↑	Cr.

Supplies become an *expense* when used up.

Remember, supplies are an asset when they are purchased. Once they are used up or consumed in the operation of business, they become an expense.

Date		Account	Dr.	Cr.
	3	Office Supplies	600 00	
		Accounts Payable		600 00
		Purchase of supplies on account		
		from Norris Co.		

Remember, expenses are recorded when they are incurred, no matter when they are paid.

May 7: Completed sales promotion pieces for a client and immediately collected $3,000.

1 Accounts Affected	2 Category	3 ↑ ↓	4 Rules of Dr. and Cr.
Cash	Asset	↑	Dr.
Word Processing Fees	Revenue	↑	Cr.

7	Cash		3 0 0 0 00	
	Word Processing Fees			3 0 0 0 00
	Cash received for services rendered			

May 15: Paid office salaries, $650.

1 Accounts Affected	2 Category	3 ↑ ↓	4 Rules of Dr. and Cr.
Office Salaries Expense	Expense	↑	Dr.
Cash	Asset	↓	Cr.

15	Office Salaries Expense		6 5 0 00	
	Cash			6 5 0 00
	Payment of office salaries			

May 18: Advertising bill from Al's News Co. comes in but is not paid, $250.

1 Accounts Affected	2 Category	3 ↑ ↓	4 Rules of Dr. and Cr.
Advertising Expense	Expense	↑	Dr.
Accounts Payable	Liability	↑	Cr.

18	Advertising Expense		2 5 0 00	
	Accounts Payable			2 5 0 00
	Bill in but not paid from Al's News Co.			

Keep in mind that as withdrawals *increase,* owner's equity *decreases.*

May 20: Brenda Clark wrote a cheque on the bank account of the business to pay her home mortgage payment of $625.

1 Accounts Affected	2 Category	3 ↑ ↓	4 Rules of Dr. and Cr.
Brenda Clark, Withdrawals	Owner's Equity	↑	Dr.
Cash	Asset	↓	Cr.

		Debit	Credit
20	Brenda Clark, Withdrawals	625 00	
	Cash		625 00
	Personal withdrawal of cash		

Reminder: Revenue is recorded when it is earned, no matter when the cash is actually received.

May 22: Billed Morris Company for a sophisticated word processing job, $5,000.

1 Accounts Affected	2 Category	3 ↑ ↓	4 Rules of Dr. and Cr.
Accounts Receivable	Asset	↑	Dr.
Word Processing Fees	Revenue	↑	Cr.

		Debit	Credit
22	Accounts Receivable	5000 00	
	Word Processing Fees		5000 00
	Billed Morris Co. for fees earned		

May 27: Paid office salaries, $650.

1 Accounts Affected	2 Category	3 ↑ ↓	4 Rules of Dr. and Cr.
Office Salaries Expense	Expense	↑	Dr.
Cash	Asset	↓	Cr.

Note: Since we are on page 2 of the journal, the year and month are repeated.

CLARK'S WORD PROCESSING SERVICES
GENERAL JOURNAL

Page 2

Date		Account Titles and Description	PR	Dr.	Cr.
19XX May	27	Office Salaries Expense		65000	
		Cash			65000
		Payment of office salaries			

May 28: Paid half the amount owed for word processing equipment purchased May 1 from Ben Co., $2,500.

1 Accounts Affected	2 Category	3 ↑ ↓	4 Rules of Dr. and Cr.
Accounts Payable	Liability	↓	Dr.
Cash	Asset	↓	Cr.

Date		Account Titles and Description	PR	Dr.	Cr.
	28	Accounts Payable		250000	
		Cash			250000
		Paid half the amount owed Ben Co.			

May 29: Paid telephone bill, $220.

1 Accounts Affected	2 Category	3 ↑ ↓	4 Rules of Dr. and Cr.
Telephone Expense	Expense	↑	Dr.
Cash	Asset	↓	Cr.

Date		Account Titles and Description	PR	Dr.	Cr.
	29	Telephone Expense		22000	
		Cash			22000
		Paid telephone bill			

This concludes the journal transactions of Clark's Word Processing Services. (See page 92 for a summary of all the transactions.)

LEARNING UNIT 3-1 REVIEW

AT THIS POINT you should be able to

- Explain the purpose of the accounting cycle. (p. 80)
- Define and explain the relationship of the accounting period to the income statement. (p.80)
- Compare and contrast a calendar year to a fiscal year. (p. 80)
- Explain the term "natural business year". (p. 80)
- Explain the function of interim reports. (p. 80)
- Define and state the purpose of a journal. (p. 80)
- Compare and contrast a book of original entry to a book of final entry. (p. 81)
- Differentiate between a chart of accounts and a journal. (p.82)
- Explain a compound entry. (p. 84)
- Journalize business transactions. (p.82)

SELF-REVIEW QUIZ 3-1

(The blank forms you need are on pages 3-1 and 3-2 of the *Study Guide and Working Papers.*)

The following are the transactions of Lowe's Repair Service. Journalize the transactions in proper form. The chart of accounts includes Cash; Accounts Receivable; Prepaid Rent; Repair Supplies; Repair Equipment; Accounts Payable; A. Lowe, Capital; A. Lowe, Withdrawals; Repair Fees Earned; Salaries Expense; Advertising Expense; and Supplies Expense.

19XX

June 1 A. Lowe invested $6,000 cash and $4,000 of repair equipment in the business.

1 Paid two months' rent in advance, $1,200.

4 Bought repair supplies from Melvin Co. on account, $600. (These supplies have not yet been consumed or used up.)

15 Performed repair work, received $600 in cash, and had to bill Doe Co. for remaining balance of $300.

18 A. Lowe paid his home telephone bill, $50, with a cheque from the company.

20 Advertising bill for $400 from Jones Co. received but payment not due yet. (Advertising has already appeared in the newspaper.)

24 Paid salaries, $1,400.

Solution to Self-Review Quiz 3-1

LOWE'S REPAIR SERVICE
GENERAL JOURNAL

Page 1

Date		Account Titles and Description	PR*	Dr.	Cr.
19XX June	1	Cash		6 000 00	
		Repair Equipment		4 000 00	
		A. Lowe, Capital			10 000 00
		Owner investment			
	1	Prepaid Rent		1 200 00	
		Cash			1 200 00
		Rent paid in advance			
	4	Repair Supplies		600 00	
		Accounts Payable			600 00
		Purchase of supplies on account			
	15	Cash		600 00	
		Accounts Receivable		300 00	
		Repair Fees Earned			900 00
		Performed repairs			
	18	A. Lowe, Withdrawals		50 00	
		Cash			50 00
		Personal withdrawal			
	20	Advertising Expense		400 00	
		Accounts Payable			400 00
		Advertising bill			
	24	Salaries Expense		1 400 00	
		Cash			1 400 00
		Paid salaries			

*Note that the PR column is left blank in the journalizing process.

LEARNING UNIT 3-2

Posting to the Ledger: Step 3 of the Accounting Cycle

The general journal serves a particular purpose; it puts every transaction the business does in one place.There are things it cannot do, though. For example, if you were asked to find the balance of the cash account from the general journal, you would have to go through the entire journal and look for only the cash entries. Then you would have to add up the debits and credits for the cash account and determine the difference between the two.

What we really need to do to find balances of accounts is to transfer the information from the journal to the ledger.This is called **posting.** In the ledger we will accumulate an ending balance for each account so that we can prepare financial statements.

GENERAL LEDGER

Accounts Payable — Account No. 211

Date 19XX		Explanation	Post. Ref.	Debit	Credit	DR or CR	Balance
May	1		GJ1		6 000 00	CR	6 000 00
	3		GJ1		400 00	CR	6 400 00
	18		GJ1		175 00	CR	6 575 00
	28		GJ2	3 000 00		CR	3 575 00

FIGURE 3-2
Three-Column Account

Footings are not needed in three-column accounts.

In Chapter 2, we used the T account form to make our ledger entries. T accounts are very simple, but they are not used in the real business world. They are only used for demonstration purposes. In practice, accountants often use a **three-column account form** that includes a column for the business's running balance. Figure 3-2 shows a standard three-column account. We will use that format in the text from now on.

FIGURE 3-3
How to Post from Journal to Ledger

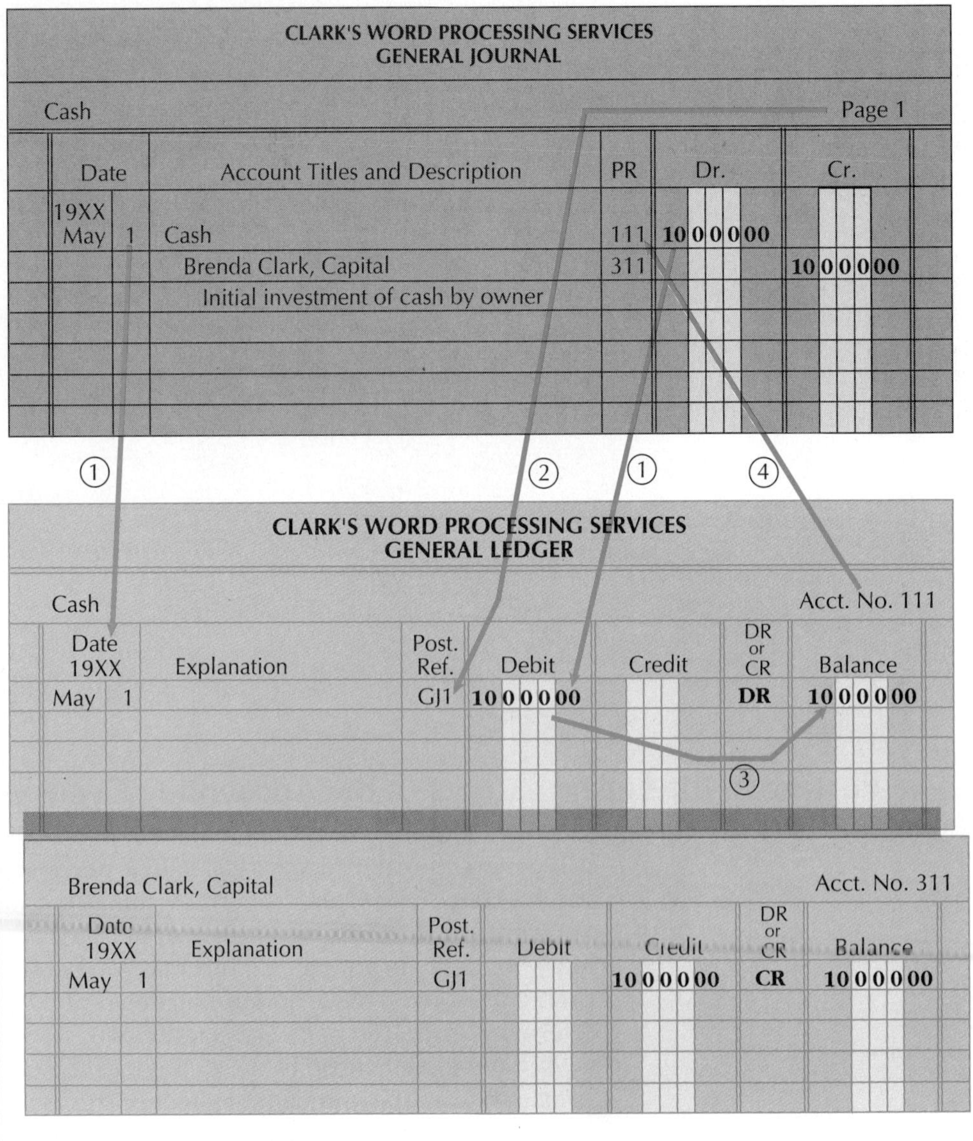

CLARK'S WORD PROCESSING SERVICES
GENERAL JOURNAL

Cash — Page 1

Date		Account Titles and Description	PR	Dr.	Cr.
19XX May	1	Cash	111	10 000 00	
		Brenda Clark, Capital	311		10 000 00
		Initial investment of cash by owner			

CLARK'S WORD PROCESSING SERVICES
GENERAL LEDGER

Cash — Acct. No. 111

Date 19XX		Explanation	Post. Ref.	Debit	Credit	DR or CR	Balance
May	1		GJ1	10 000 00		DR	10 000 00

Brenda Clark, Capital — Acct. No. 311

Date 19XX		Explanation	Post. Ref.	Debit	Credit	DR or CR	Balance
May	1		GJ1		10 000 00	CR	10 000 00

Posting

Now let's look at how to post the transactions of Clark's Word Processing Service from its journal. The diagram in Figure 3-3 shows how to post the cash line from the journal to the ledger. The steps in the posting process are numbered and illustrated in the figure.

Step 1: In the Cash account in the ledger, record the date (May 1, 19XX) and the amount of the entry ($10,000).

Step 2: Record the page number of the journal "GJ1" in the posting reference (PR) column of the Cash account.

Step 3: Calculate the new balance of the account. You keep a running balance in each account as you would in your chequebook. To do this you take the present balance in the account on the previous line and add or subtract the transaction as necessary to arrive at your new balance.

Step 4: Record the account number of Cash (111) in the posting reference (PR) column of the journal. This is called **cross-referencing.**

The same sequence of steps occurs for each line in the journal. In a manual system like Clark's, the debits and credits in the journal may be posted in the order in which they were recorded, or all the debits may be posted first and then all the credits. If Clark used a computer system, the program would post at the press of a menu button.

Using Posting References

The posting references are very helpful. In the journal, the PR column tells us which transactions have or have not been posted and also to which accounts they were posted. In the ledger, the posting reference leads us back to the original transaction in its entirety, so that we can see why the debit or credit was recorded and what other accounts were affected. (It leads us back to the original transaction by identifying the journal and the page in the journal from which the information came.)

Learning Unit 3-2 Review

AT THIS POINT you should be able to

- State the purpose of posting. (p. 89)
- Discuss the advantages of the three-column account. (p. 90)
- Identify the elements to be posted. (p. 91)
- From journalizing transactions, post to the general ledger. (p. 90)

SELF-REVIEW QUIZ 3-2

(The forms you need are on pages 3-3 to 3-6 of the *Study Guide and Working Papers.*)

The following are the journalized transactions of Clark's Word Processing Services. Your task is to post information to the ledger. The ledger in your workbook has all the account titles and numbers that were used from the chart of accounts.

			PR	Dr.	Cr.
	18	Advertising Expense	512	250 00	
		Accounts Payable	211		250 00
		Bill received but not paid from Al's News			
	20	Brenda Clark, Withdrawals	312	625 00	
		Cash	111		625 00
		Personal withdrawal of cash			
	22	Accounts Receivable	112	5000 00	
		Word Processing Fees	411		5000 00
		Billed Morris Co. for fees earned			

CLARK'S WORD PROCESSING SERVICES
GENERAL JOURNAL

Page 2

Date		Account Titles and Description	PR	Dr.	Cr.
19XX May	27	Office Salaries Expense	511	650 00	
		Cash	111		650 00
		Payment of office salaries			
	28	Accounts Payable	211	2500 00	
		Cash	111		2500 00
		Paid half the amount owed Ben Co.			
	29	Telephone Expense	513	220 00	
		Cash	111		220 00
		Paid telephone bill			

CLARK'S WORD PROCESSING SERVICES
PARTIAL GENERAL LEDGER

Cash — Acct. No. 111

Date 19XX		Explanation	Post. Ref.	Debit	Credit	DR or CR	Balance
May	1		GJ1	10000 00		DR	10000 00
	1		GJ1		1000 00	DR	9000 00
	1		GJ1		1200 00	DR	7800 00
	7		GJ1	3000 00		DR	10800 00
	15		GJ1		650 00	DR	10150 00
	20		GJ1		625 00	DR	9525 00
	27		GJ2		650 00	DR	8875 00
	28		GJ2		2500 00	DR	6375 00
	29		GJ2		220 00	DR	6155 00

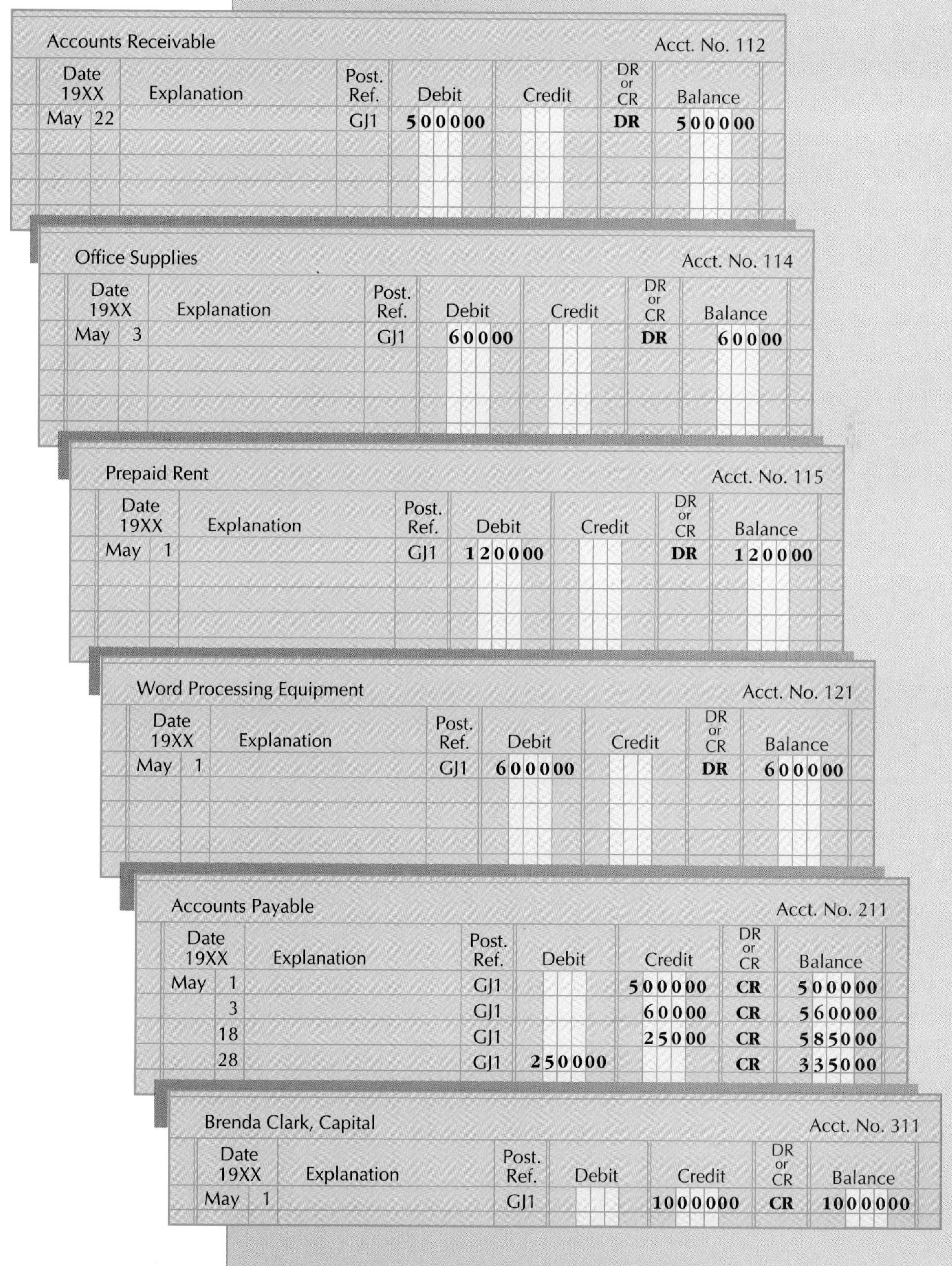

Accounts Receivable — Acct. No. 112

Date 19XX		Explanation	Post. Ref.	Debit	Credit	DR or CR	Balance
May	22		GJ1	5000 00		DR	5000 00

Office Supplies — Acct. No. 114

Date 19XX		Explanation	Post. Ref.	Debit	Credit	DR or CR	Balance
May	3		GJ1	600 00		DR	600 00

Prepaid Rent — Acct. No. 115

Date 19XX		Explanation	Post. Ref.	Debit	Credit	DR or CR	Balance
May	1		GJ1	1200 00		DR	1200 00

Word Processing Equipment — Acct. No. 121

Date 19XX		Explanation	Post. Ref.	Debit	Credit	DR or CR	Balance
May	1		GJ1	6000 00		DR	6000 00

Accounts Payable — Acct. No. 211

Date 19XX		Explanation	Post. Ref.	Debit	Credit	DR or CR	Balance
May	1		GJ1		5000 00	CR	5000 00
	3		GJ1		600 00	CR	5600 00
	18		GJ1		250 00	CR	5850 00
	28		GJ1	2500 00		CR	3350 00

Brenda Clark, Capital — Acct. No. 311

Date 19XX		Explanation	Post. Ref.	Debit	Credit	DR or CR	Balance
May	1		GJ1		10000 00	CR	10000 00

Brenda Clark, Withdrawals — Acct. No. 312

Date 19XX		Explanation	Post. Ref.	Debit	Credit	DR or CR	Balance
May	20		GJ1	625 00		DR	625 00

Word Processing Fees — Acct. No. 411

Date 19XX		Explanation	Post. Ref.	Debit	Credit	DR or CR	Balance
May	7		GJ1		3000 00	CR	3000 00
	22		GJ1		5000 00	CR	8000 00

Office Salaries Expense — Acct. No. 511

Date 19XX		Explanation	Post. Ref.	Debit	Credit	DR or CR	Balance
May	15		GJ1	650 00		DR	650 00
	27		GJ2	650 00		DR	1300 00

Advertising Expense — Acct. No. 512

Date 19XX		Explanation	Post. Ref.	Debit	Credit	DR or CR	Balance
May	18		GJ1	250 00		DR	250 00

Telephone Expense — Acct. No. 513

Date 19XX		Explanation	Post. Ref.	Debit	Credit	DR or CR	Balance
May	29		GJ2	220 00		DR	220 00

LEARNING UNIT 3-3

Preparing the Trial Balance: Step 4 of the Accounting Cycle

Did you note in Self-Review Quiz 3-2 how each account had a running balance figure? Did you know the normal balance of each account in Clark's ledger? As we discussed in Chapter 2, the list of the individual accounts with their balances taken from the ledger is called a **trial balance.**

The trial balance shown in Figure 3-4 was developed from the ledger accounts of Clark's Word Processing Services that were posted and balanced in Self-Review Quiz 3-2. If the information is journalized or posted incorrectly, the trial balance will not be correct.

There are some things the trial balance will not show:

CLARK'S WORD PROCESSING SERVICE
TRIAL BALANCE
MAY 31, 19XX

	Debit	Credit
Cash	6 1 5 5 00	
Accounts Receivable	5 0 0 0 00	
Office Supplies	6 0 0 00	
Prepaid Rent	1 2 0 0 00	
Word Processing Equipment	6 0 0 0 00	
Accounts Payable		3 3 5 0 00
B. Clark, Capital		10 0 0 0 00
B. Clark, Withdrawals	6 2 5 00	
Word Processing Fees		8 0 0 0 00
Office Salaries Expense	1 3 0 0 00	
Advertising Expense	2 5 0 00	
Telephone Expense	2 2 0 00	
Totals	21 3 5 0 00	21 3 5 0 00

The trial balance lists the accounts in the same order as in the ledger. The $6,155 figure of cash came from the ledger.

FIGURE 3-4 The Trial Balance

The totals of a trial balance can balance and yet be incorrect.

- The capital figure on the trial balance may not be the beginning capital figure. For instance, if Brenda Clark had made additional investments during the period, the additional investment would have been journalized and posted to the capital account.The only way to tell if the capital balance on the trial balance is the original balance is to check the ledger capital account to see whether any additional investments were made.This will be important when we make financial reports.
- There is no guarantee that transactions have been properly recorded. For example, the following errors would remain undetected: (1) a transaction that may have been omitted in the journalizing process; (2) a transaction incorrectly analyzed and recorded in the journal; (3) a journal entry journalized or posted twice.

What to Do If a Trial Balance Doesn't Balance

The trial balance of Clark's Word Processing Services shows that the total of debits is equal to the total of credits. But what happens if the trial balance is in balance, but the correct amount is not recorded in each ledger account? Accuracy in the journalizing and posting process will help ensure that no errors are made.

Even if there is an error, the first rule is "Don't panic." Everyone makes mistakes, and there are accepted ways of correcting them. Once an entry had been made in ink, correcting an error must always show that the entry has been changed and who changed it. Sometimes the change has to be explained.

Some Common Mistakes

Correcting the trial balance: What to do if your trial balance doesn't balance.

If the trial balance does not balance, the cause could be something relatively simple. Here are some common errors and how they can be fixed:

- If the difference (the amount you are off) is 10, 100, 1,000, etc., there probably is a mathematical error.

Did you clear your adding machine?

- If the difference is equal to an individual account balance in the ledger, the amount could have been omitted. It is also possible the figure was not posted from the general journal.

- Divide the difference by 2; then check to see if a debit should have been a credit and vice versa in the ledger or trial balance. Example: $150 difference ÷ 2 = $75. This means you may have placed $75 as a debit to an account instead of a credit or vice versa.
- If the difference is evenly divisible by 9, a **slide** or transposition may have occurred. A slide is an error resulting from adding or deleting zeros in writing numbers. For example, $4,175.00 may have been copied as $41.75. A **transposition** is the accidental rearrangement of digits of a number. For example, $4,175 might have been accidentally written as $4,157.
- Compare the balances in the trial balance with the ledger accounts to check for copying errors.
- Recompute balances in each ledger account.
- Trace all postings from journal to ledger.

If you cannot find the error after you have done all of this, take a coffee break. Then start all over again.

Making a Correction Before Posting

Before posting, error correction is straightforward. Simply draw a line through the incorrect entry, write the correct information above the line, and write your initials near the change.

Correcting an Error in an Account Title The following illustration shows an error and its correction in an account title:

	1	Word Processing Equipment		6000 00	
		Cash			1000 00
		Accounts Payable amp ~~Accounts Receivable~~			5000 00
		Purchase of equipment from Ben Co.			

Correcting a Numerical Error Numbers are handled the same way as account titles, as the next change from 520 to 250 shows:

	18	Advertising Expense		250 00	
		Accounts Payable			amp 250 00 ~~520 00~~
		Bill from Al's News			

Correcting an Entry Error If a number has been entered in the wrong column, a straight line is drawn through it, and the number is then written in the correct column:

	1	Word Processing Equipment		6000 00	
		Cash			1000 00
		Accounts Payable		amp ~~5000 00~~	5000 00
		Purchase of equip. from Ben Co.			

MAKING A CORRECTION AFTER POSTING

It is also possible to correct an amount that is properly entered in the journal but posted incorrectly to the proper account in the ledger. The first step is to draw a line through the error and write the correct figure above it. The next step is changing the running balance to reflect the corrected posting. Here, too, a line is drawn through the balance and the corrected balance is written above it. Both changes must be initialed.

Word Processing Fees — Acct. No. 411

Date 19XX		Explanation	Post. Ref.	Debit	Credit	DR or CR	Balance
May	7		GJ1		250000	CR	250000
	22		GJ1		amp 410000 ~~100000~~	CR	660000 ~~260000~~ amp

CORRECTING AN ENTRY POSTED TO THE WRONG ACCOUNT

Drawing a line through an error and writing the correction above it is possible when a mistake has occurred within the proper account, but when an error involves a posting to the wrong account the journal must include a correction accompanied by an explanation. In addition, the correct information must be posted to the appropriate ledgers.

Suppose, for example, that as a result of tracing postings from journal entries to ledgers you find that a $180 telephone bill was incorrectly debited as an advertising expense. The following illustration shows how this is done.

Step 1: The journal entry is corrected and the correction is explained:

GENERAL JOURNAL — Page 1

Date 19XX		Account Titles and Description	PR	Dr.	Cr.
May	29	Telephone Expense	513	18000	
		Advertising Expense	512		18000
		To correct error in which			
		Advertising Exp. was debited			
		for charges to Telephone Exp.			

Step 2: The Advertising Expense ledger account is corrected:

Advertising Expense — Acct. No. 512

Date 19XX		Explanation	Post. Ref.	Debit	Credit	DR or CR	Balance
May	18		GJ1	17500		DR	17500
	23		GJ1	18000		DR	35500
	29	*Correcting entry*	GJ3		18000	DR	17500

Step 3: The Telephone Expense ledger is corrected:

Telephone Expense							Acct. No. 513
Date 19XX		Explanation	Post. Ref.	Debit	Credit	DR or CR	Balance
May	29		GJ3	18000		DR	18000

LEARNING UNIT 3-3 REVIEW

AT THIS POINT you should be able to

- Prepare a trial balance from a ledger, which uses three-column accounts. (p. 96)
- Analyze and correct a trial balance that doesn't balance. (p. 97)
- Correct journal and posting errors. (p. 98)

SELF-REVIEW QUIZ 3-3

(The blank forms you need are on page 3-7 of the *Study Guide and Working Papers.*)

1.

Interoffice Memo

To: Al Vincent

From: Professor Jones

Re: Trial Balance

You have submitted to me an incorrect trial balance. Could you please rework and turn in to me before next Friday?

Note: Individual amounts look OK.

A. RICE
TRIAL BALANCE
OCTOBER 31, 19XX

	Dr.	Cr.
Cash		806000
Operating Expenses		170000
A. Rice, Withdrawals		40000
Service Revenue		540000
Equipment	500000	
Accounts Receivable	354000	
Accounts Payable	200000	
Supplies	30000	
A. Rice, Capital		1160000

2. A $7,000 debit to office equipment was mistakenly posted on June 9, 19XX, to office supplies. Prepare the appropriate journal entry to correct this error.

Solution to Self-Review Quiz 3-3

1.

A. RICE
TRIAL BALANCE
OCTOBER 31, 19XX

	Dr.	Cr.
Cash	8 0 6 0 00	
Accounts Receivable	3 5 4 0 00	
Supplies	3 0 0 00	
Equipment	5 0 0 0 00	
Accounts Payable		2 0 0 0 00
A. Rice, Capital		11 6 0 0 00
A. Rice, Withdrawals	4 0 0 00	
Service Revenue		5 4 0 0 00
Operating Expenses	1 7 0 0 00	
Totals	19 0 0 0 00	19 0 0 0 00

2.

GENERAL JOURNAL Page 4

Date		Account Titles and Description	PR	Dr.	Cr.
19XX June	9	Office Equipment		7 0 0 0 0 0	
		Office Supplies			7 0 0 0 0 0
		To correct error in which office supplies			
		had been debited for purchase of			
		office equipment			

Chapter Review

COMPREHENSIVE DEMONSTRATION PROBLEM WITH SOLUTION TIPS

(The blank forms you need are on pages 3-8 to 3-10 in the *Study Guide and Working Papers.*)

In March, Abby's Employment Agency had the following transactions:

19XX		
Mar.	1	Abby Todd invested $5,000 in the new employment agency.
	4	Bought equipment for cash, $800.
	5	Earned employment fee commission, $200, but payment from Blue Co. will not be received until June.
	6	Paid wages expense, $300.
	7	Abby Todd paid her home utility bill from the company chequebook, $75.
	9	Placed Rick Wool at VCR Corporation, receiving $1,200 cash.
	15	Paid cash for supplies, $600.
	28	Telephone bill received but not paid, $180.
	29	Advertising bill received but not paid, $400.

The chart of accounts includes: Cash, 111; Accounts Receivable, 112; Supplies, 131; Equipment, 141; Accounts Payable, 211; A. Todd, Capital, 311; A. Todd, Withdrawals, 321; Employment Fees Earned, 411; Wage Expense, 511; Telephone Expense, 521; Advertising Expense, 531.

Required

a. Set up a ledger based on the chart of accounts.

b. Journalize (all page 1) and post transactions.

c. Prepare a trial balance for March 31.

ABBY'S EMPLOYMENT AGENCY

Date		Account Titles and Description	PR	Dr.	Cr.
19XX Mar.	1	Cash	111	5 0 0 0 00	
		A. Todd, Capital	311		5 0 0 0 00
		Owner investment			
	4	Equipment	141	8 0 0 00	
		Cash	111		8 0 0 00
		Bought equipment for cash			
	5	Accounts Receivable	112	2 0 0 00	
		Employment Fees Earned	411		2 0 0 00
		Fees on account			
	6	Wage Expense	511	3 0 0 00	
		Cash	111		3 0 0 00
		Paid wages			
	7	A. Todd, Withdrawals	321	7 5 00	
		Cash	111		7 5 00
		Personal withdrawals			
	9	Cash	111	1 2 0 0 00	
		Employment Fees Earned	411		1 2 0 0 00
		Cash fees			
	15	Supplies	131	6 0 0 00	
		Cash	111		6 0 0 00
		Bought supplies for cash			
	28	Telephone Expense	521	1 8 0 00	
		Accounts Payable	211		1 8 0 00
		Telephone bill owed			
	29	Advertising Expense	531	4 0 0 00	
		Accounts Payable	211		4 0 0 00
		Advertising bill received			

GENERAL LEDGER

Cash — Acct. No. 111

Date 19XX		Explanation	Post. Ref.	Debit	Credit	DR or CR	Balance
Mar.	1		GJ1	500000		DR.	500000
	4		GJ1		80000	DR.	420000
	6		GJ1		30000	DR.	390000
	7		G1		7500	DR.	382500
	9		GJ1	120000		DR.	502500
	15		GJ1		60000	DR.	442500

A. Todd, Capital — Acct. No. 311

Date 19XX		Explanation	Post. Ref.	Debit	Credit	DR or CR	Balance
Mar.	1		GJ1		500000	CR.	500000

A. Todd Withdrawals — Acct. No. 321

Date 19XX		Explanation	Post. Ref.	Debit	Credit	DR or CR	Balance
Mar.	7		GJ1	7500		DR.	7500

Accounts Receivable — Acct. No. 112

Date 19XX		Explanation	Post. Ref.	Debit	Credit	DR or CR	Balance
Mar.	5		GJ1	20000		DR.	20000

Employment Fees Earned — Acct. No. 411

Date 19XX		Explanation	Post. Ref.	Debit	Credit	DR or CR	Balance
Mar.	5		GJ1		20000	CR.	20000
Mar.	9		GJ1		120000	CR.	140000

Supplies — Acct. No. 131

Date 19XX		Explanation	Post. Ref.	Debit	Credit	DR or CR	Balance
Mar.	15		GJ1	60000		DR.	60000

Wages Expense — Acct. No. 511

Date 19XX		Explanation	Post. Ref.	Debit	Credit	DR or CR	Balance
Mar.	6		GJ1	30000		DR.	30000

Equipment — Acct. No. 141

Date 19XX		Explanation	Post. Ref.	Debit	Credit	DR or CR	Balance
Mar.	4		GJ1	80000		DR.	80000

Telephone Expense — Acct. No. 521

Date 19XX		Explanation	Post. Ref.	Debit	Credit	DR or CR	Balance
Mar.	28		GJ1	18000		DR.	18000

Accounts Payable — Acct. No. 211

Date 19XX		Explanation	Post. Ref.	Debit	Credit	DR or CR	Balance
Mar.	28		GJ1		18000	CR.	18000
	29		GJ1		40000	CR.	58000

Advertising Expense — Acct. No. 531

Date 19XX		Explanation	Post. Ref.	Debit	Credit	DR or CR	Balance
Mar.	29		GJ1	40000		DR.	40000

Solution Tips to Journalizing

1. When journalizing, the PR column is not filled in.
2. Debits against the date column. Credits indented and listed below the debits. Total of all debits for each transaction should equal total of all credits.
3. Skip a line between each transaction.

The Analysis of the Journal Entries

Date	Account	Category	↑↓	Dr./Cr.	Amount
March 1	Cash	A	↑	Dr.	$5,000
	A. Todd, Capital	O.E.	↑	Cr.	$5,000
4	Equipment	A	↑	Dr.	$ 800
	Cash	A	↓	Cr.	$ 800
5	Accts. Receivable	A	↑	Dr.	$ 200
	Empl. Fees Earned	Rev.	↑	Cr.	$ 200
6	Wage Expense	Exp.	↑	Dr.	$ 300
	Cash	A	↓	Cr.	$ 300
7	A. Todd, Withdrawals	O.E.	↑	Dr.	$ 75
	Cash	A	↓	Cr.	$ 75
9	Cash	A	↑	Dr.	$1,200
	Empl. Fees Earned	Rev.	↑	Cr.	$1,200
15	Supplies	A	↑	Dr.	$ 600
	Cash	A	↓	Cr.	$ 600
28	Telephone Expense	Exp.	↑	Dr.	$ 180
	Accounts Payable	L	↑	Cr.	$ 180
28	Advertising Expense	Exp.	↑	Dr.	$ 400
	Accounts Payable	L	↑	Cr.	$ 400

Solution Tips to Posting

The PR column in the ledger cash account tells you from which page a journal information came (page 1). After the ledger cash account is posted, account number "111" is put in the PR column of the journal. (This is called cross-referencing.)

Note how we keep a running balance in the cash account. A $5,000 Dr. balance and a $200 credit entry result in a new debit balance of $4,800.

Abby's Employment Agency
Trial Balance
March 31, 19XX

	Dr.	Cr.
Cash	4,425	
Accounts Receivable	200	
Supplies	600	
Equipment	800	
Accounts Payable		580
A. Todd, Capital		5,000
A. Todd, Withdrawals	75	
Employment Fees Earned		1,400
Wage Expense	300	
Telephone Expense	180	
Advertising Expense	400	
Totals	**6,980**	**6,980**

Solution Tip to Trial Balance

The trial balance lists the ending balance of each title in the order in which they appear in the ledger. The total of $6,980 on the left equals $6,980 on the right.

SUMMARY OF KEY POINTS

Learning Unit 3-1

1. The accounting cycle is a sequence of accounting procedures that are usually performed during an accounting period.
2. An accounting period is the time period for which the income statement is prepared. The time period can be any period up to one year.
3. A calendar year is from January 1 to December 31. The fiscal year is any 12-month period. A fiscal year could be a calendar year but does not have to be.
4. Interim reports are statements that are usually prepared for a portion of the business's calendar or fiscal year (e.g., a month or a quarter).
5. A general journal is a book that records transactions in chronological order. Here debits and credits are shown together on one page. It is the book of original entry.
6. The ledger is a collection of accounts where information is accumulated from the postings of the journal. The ledger is the book of final entry.
7. Journalizing is the process of recording journal entries.
8. The chart of accounts provides the specific titles of accounts to be entered in the journal.

9. When journalizing, the posting reference (PR) column is left blank.
10. A compound journal entry occurs when more than two accounts are affected in the journalizing process of a business transaction.

Learning Unit 3-2

1. Posting is the process of transferring information from the journal to the ledger.
2. The journal and ledger contain the same information but in a different form.
3. The three-column account aids in keeping a running balance of an account.
4. The normal balance of an account will be located on the side that increases it according to the rules of debits and credits. For example, the normal balances of liabilities occur on the credit side.
5. The mechanical process of posting requires care in transferring appropriate dates, posting references, titles, and amounts.

Learning Unit 3-3

1. A trial balance can balance but be incorrect. For example, an entire journal entry may not have been posted.
2. If a trial balance doesn't balance, check for errors in addition, omission of postings, slides, transpositions, copying errors, and so on.
3. Specific procedures should be followed in making corrections in journals and ledgers.

KEY TERMS

Accounting cycle For each accounting period, the process that begins with the recording of business transactions or procedures into a journal and ends with the completion of a post-closing trial balance.

Accounting period The period of time for which an income statement is prepared.

Book of final entry A ledger that receives information about business transactions from a book of original entry (a journal).

Book of original entry Book that records the first formal information about business transactions. Example: a journal.

Calendar year January 1 to December 31.

Compound journal entry A journal entry that affects more than two accounts.

Cross-referencing Adding to the PR column of the journal the account number of the ledger account that was updated from the journal and inserting the journal page on the ledger account.

Fiscal year The 12-month period a business chooses for its accounting year.

General journal The simplest form of a journal, which records information from transactions in chronological order as they occur. This journal links the debit and credit parts of transactions together.

Interim reports Financial reports that are prepared for a month, quarter, or some other portion of the fiscal year.

Journal A listing of business transactions in chronological order. The journal links on one page the debit and credit parts of transactions.

Journal entry The transaction (debits and credits) that is recorded into a journal once it is analyzed.

Journalizing The process of recording a transaction entry into the journal.

Natural business year A business's fiscal year that ends at the same time as a slow seasonal period begins.

Posting The transferring, copying, or recording of information from a journal to a ledger.

Slide The error that results in adding or deleting zeros in the writing of a number. Example: 79,200→7,920.

Three-column account A running balance account that records debits and credits and has a column for an ending balance (debit or credit). Replaces the standard two-column account we used earlier.

Transposition The accidental rearrangement of digits of a number. Example: 152→125.

Trial balance An informal listing of the ledger accounts and their balances that aids in proving the equality of debits and credits.

BLUEPRINT OF FIRST FOUR STEPS OF ACCOUNTING CYCLE

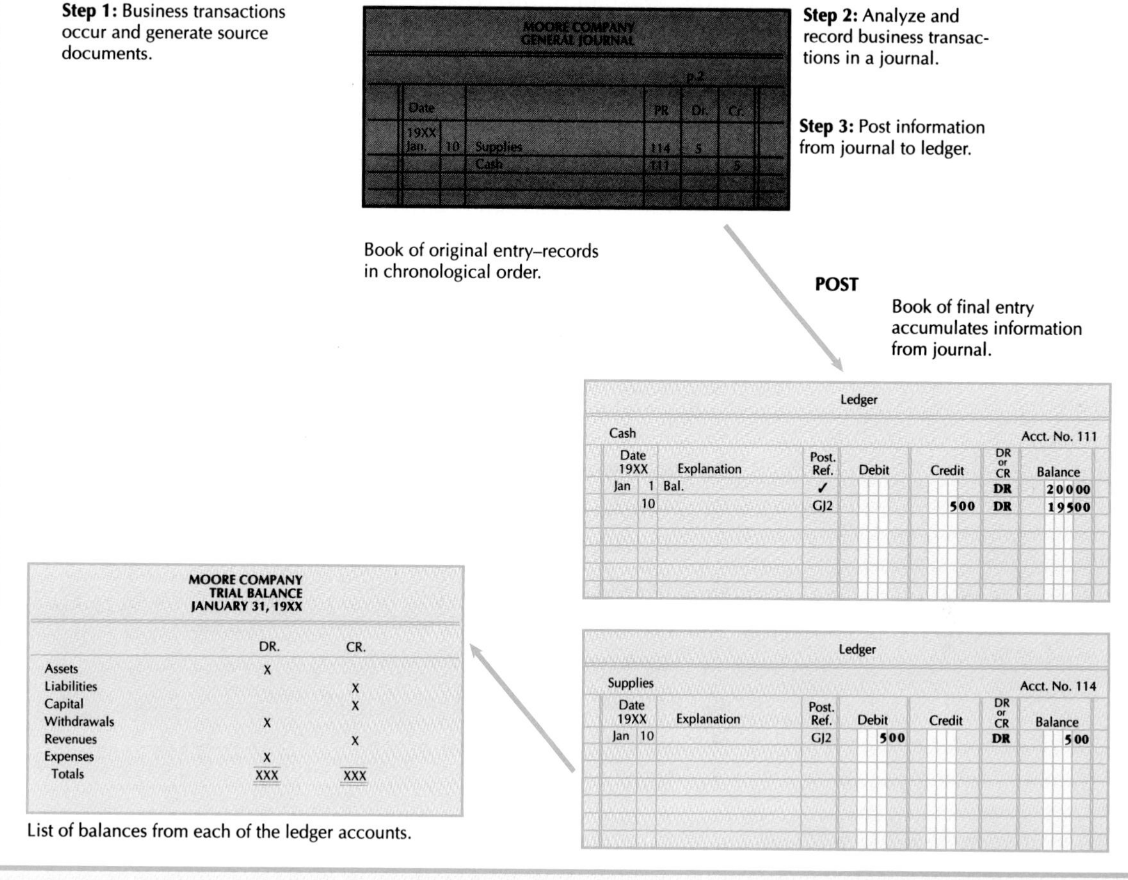

Step 1: Business transactions occur and generate source documents.
MOORE COMPANY
GENERAL JOURNAL
Step 2: Analyze and record business transactions in a journal.
Step 3: Post information from journal to ledger.
Book of original entry–records in chronological order.
POST
Book of final entry accumulates information from journal.
Ledger
Cash
Acct. No. 111
Ledger
Supplies
Acct. No. 114
MOORE COMPANY
TRIAL BALANCE
JANUARY 31, 19XX
List of balances from each of the ledger accounts.

QUESTIONS, EXERCISES, AND PROBLEMS

Discussion Questions

1. Explain the concept of the accounting cycle.
2. An accounting period is based on the balance sheet. Agree or disagree.
3. Compare and contrast a calendar year versus a fiscal year.
4. What are interim reports?
5. Why is the ledger called the book of final entry?
6. How do transactions get "linked" in a general journal?
7. What is the relationship of the chart of accounts to the general journal?
8. What is a compound journal entry?
9. Posting means updating the journal. Agree or disagree. Please comment.
10. The side that decreases an account is the normal balance. True or false?
11. The PR column of a general journal is the last item to be filled in during the posting process. Agree or disagree.
12. Discuss the concept of cross-referencing.
13. What is the difference between a transposition and a slide?

Mini Exercises

(The blank forms you need are on page 3-12 of the *Study Guide and Working Papers.*)

General Journal

1. Complete the following from the general journal of Post Company.

POST COMPANY
GENERAL JOURNAL

Page 1

Date		Account Titles and Descriptions	PR	Dr.	Cr.
19XX April	8	Cash		600000	
		Supplies		10000	
		A. Post, Capital			610000
		Initial investment by owner			

a. Year of journal entry ________
b. Month of journal entry ________
c. Day of journal entry ________
d. Name(s) of accounts debited ________
e. Name(s) of accounts credited ________
f. Explanation of transaction ________
g. Amount of debit(s) ________
h. Amount of credit(s) ________
i. Page of journal ________

General Journal

2. Provide the explanation for each of these general journal entries.

GENERAL JOURNAL

Date		Account Titles and Descriptions	PR	Debit	Credit
19XX June	8	Cash		600000	
		Office Equipment		400000	
		A. Rye, Capital			1000000
		(A)			
	15	Cash		3000	
		Accounts Receivable		6000	
		Hair Fees Earned			9000
		(B)			
	20	Advertising Expense		4000	
		Accounts Payable			4000
		(C)			

Posting and Balancing

3. Balance this three-column account. What function does the PR column serve? When will Account 111 be used in the journalizing and posting process?

Cash						Acct. 111
Date	**Explanation**	**PR**	**Dr.**	**Cr.**	**Dr./Cr.**	**Balance**
19XX						
June 4		GJ 1	10			
5		GJ 1	5			
9		GJ 2		3		
10		GJ 3	2			

The Trial Balance

4. The following trial balance was prepared *incorrectly.*

a. Rearrange the accounts in proper order.

b. Calculate the total of the trial balance. (Small numbers are used intentionally so you can do the calculations in your head.) Assume each account has a normal balance.

Dawn Pisano
Trial Balance
October 31, 19XX

	Dr.	**Cr.**
D. Pisano, Capital	12	
Equipment	8	
Rent Expense		4
Advertising Expense		3
Accounts Payable		7
Taxi Fees	16	
Cash	15	
D. Pisano, Withdrawals	—	5
Totals	**41**	**19**

Correcting Entry

5. On April 1, 1996, a telephone expense for $200 was debited to Repair Expense. On May 8, 1997, this error was found. Prepare the corrected Journal Entry. When would a correcting entry *not* be needed?

Exercises

Preparing journal entries.

(The forms you need are on pages 3-13 to 3-17 of the *Study Guide and Working Papers.*)

3-1. Prepare journal entries for the following transactions that occurred during October:

19XX
Oct. 1 Pete Bard invested $18,000 cash and $1,000 of equipment into his new business.
3 Purchased building for $40,000 on account.
12 Purchased a truck from Smock Co. for $12,000 cash.
18 Bought supplies from Lawn Co. on account, $600.

Preparing journal entries.

3-2. Record the following into the general journal of Jan's Repair Shop.

19XX
Jan. 1 Jan Spice invested $17,000 cash in the repair shop.
5 Paid $8,000 for shop equipment.
8 Bought from Lowell Co. shop equipment for $4,000 on account.
14 Received $700 for repair fees earned.
18 Billed Sullivan Co. $800 for services rendered.
20 Jan withdrew $200 for personal use.

Posting.

3-3. Post the following transactions to the ledger of Long Company. The partial ledger of Long Company is Cash, 111; Equipment, 121; Accounts Payable, 211; and B. Long, Capital, 311. Please use three-column accounts in the posting process.

Page 4

Date 19XX			PR	Dr.	Cr.
Mar.	4	Cash		400000	
		B. Long, Capital			400000
		Cash investment			
	9	Equipment		800000	
		Cash			200000
		Accounts Payable			600000
		Purchase of equipment			

Journalizing, posting, and preparing a trial balance.

3-4. From the following transactions for Lowe Company for the month of July, (a) prepare journal entries (assume that it is page 1 of the journal), (b) post to the ledger (use three-column account), and (c) prepare a trial balance.

19XX
July 1 Joan Lowe invested $6,000 in the business.
4 Bought from Lax Co. equipment on account, $800.
15 Billed Friend Co. for services rendered, $4,000.
18 Received $5,000 cash for services rendered.
24 Paid salaries expense, $1,800.
28 Joan withdrew $400 for personal use.

Chart of accounts includes: Cash, 111; Accounts Receivable, 112; Equipment, 121; Accounts Payable, 211; J. Lowe, Capital, 311; J. Lowe, Withdrawals, 312; Fees Earned, 411; Salaries Expense, 511.

3-5. You have been hired to correct the following trial balance that has been recorded improperly from the ledger to the trial balance.

Correcting the trial balance.

WONG CO.
TRIAL BALANCE
MARCH 31, 19XX

	Dr.	Cr.
Accounts Payable	180000	
F. Wong, Capital		650000
F. Wong, Withdrawals		30000
Services Earned		470000
Concessions Earned	250000	
Rent Expense	40000	
Salaries Expense	250000	
Miscellaneous Expense		130000
Cash	980000	
Accounts Receivable		120000
Totals	1700000	1400000

3-6. On February 6, 19XX, Pete Sanchez made the following journal entry to record the purchase on account of office equipment priced at $1,200. This transaction had not yet been posted when the error was discovered. Make the appropriate correction.

Correcting entry.

GENERAL JOURNAL

Date		Account Titles and Description	PR	Dr.	Cr.
19XX Feb.	6	Office Equipment		80000	
		Accounts Payable			
		Purchase of office equip. on account			80000

Group A Problems

(The forms you need are on pages 3-18 to 3-27 of the *Working Papers and Study Guide.*)

3A-1. Alice Hyer has decided to open Hyer's Dog Grooming Centre. As the bookkeeper, you have been requested to journalize the following transactions:

Journalizing.

19XX

April
- 1 Paid rent for two months in advance, $2,000.
- 3 Purchased grooming equipment on account from Leek's Supply House, $2,800.
- 10 Purchased grooming supplies from Angel's Wholesale for $500 cash.
- 12 Received $1,200 cash from grooming fees earned.
- 20 Alice withdrew $300 for her personal use.
- 21 Advertising bill received from *Daily Sun* but unpaid, $90.
- 25 Paid cleaning expense, $80.
- 28 Paid salaries expense, $400.
- 29 Performed grooming work for $1,500; however, payment will not be received from Rick's Kennel until May.
- 30 Paid Leek's Supply House half the amount owed from April 3 transaction.

Your task is to journalize the above transactions. The chart of accounts for Hyer's Dog Grooming Centre is as follows:

Chart of Accounts

Assets	Owner's Equity
111 Cash	311 Alice Hyer, Capital
112 Accounts Receivable	312 Alice Hyer, Withdrawals
114 Prepaid Rent	
116 Grooming Supplies	**Revenue**
121 Grooming Equipment	411 Grooming Fees Earned
Liabilities	**Expenses**
211 Accounts Payable	511 Advertising Expense
	512 Salaries Expense
	514 Cleaning Expense

Comprehensive problem: Journalizing, posting, and preparing a trial balance.

3A-2. On June 1, 19XX, Dick Reilly opened Reilly's Dance Studio. The following transactions occurred in June:

19XX		
June	1	Dick Reilly invested $7,000 in the dance studio.
	1	Paid three months' rent in advance, $1,000.
	3	Purchased $700 of equipment from Astor Co. on account.
	5	Received $900 cash for fitness training workshop for dancers.
	8	Purchased $300 of supplies for cash.
	9	Billed Lester Co. $2,100 for group dance lesson for its employees.
	10	Paid salaries of assistants, $400.
	15	Dick Reilly withdrew $150 from the business for his personal use.
	28	Paid electrical expense, $125.
	29	Paid telephone bill for June, $190.

Required

a. Set up the ledger based on the charts of accounts below.

b. Journalize (journal is page 1) and post the June transactions.

c. Prepare a trial balance as of June 30, 19XX.

The chart of accounts for Reilly's Dance Studio is as follows:

Chart of Accounts

Assets	Owner's Equity
111 Cash	311 Dick Reilly, Capital
112 Accounts Receivable	312 Dick Reilly, Withdrawals
114 Prepaid Rent	
121 Supplies	**Revenue**
131 Equipment	411 Fees Earned
Liabilities	**Expenses**
211 Accounts Payable	511 Electrical Expense
	512 Salaries Expense
	531 Telephone Expense

Comprehensive problem: Journalizing, posting, and preparing a trial balance.

3A-3. The following transactions occurred in June 19XX for A. French's Placement Agency:

19XX

June
1 A. French invested $9,000 cash in the placement agency.
1 Bought equipment on account from Hook Co., $2,000.
3 Earned placement fees of $1,600, but payment will not be received until July.
5 A. French withdrew $100 for his personal use.
7 Paid wages expense, $300.
9 Placed a client on a local TV show, receiving $600 cash.
15 Bought supplies on account from Lyon Co., $500.
28 Paid telephone bill for June, $160.
29 Advertising bill from Shale Co. received but not paid, $900.

The chart of accounts for A. French Placement agency is as follows:

Chart of Accounts

Assets
111 Cash
112 Accounts Receivable
131 Supplies
141 Equipment

Liabilities
211 Accounts Payable

Owner's Equity
311 A. French, Capital
312 A. French, Withdrawals

Revenue
411 Placement Fees Earned

Expenses
511 Wage Expense
521 Telephone Expense
531 Advertising Expense

Required

a. Set up the ledger based on the chart of accounts.
b. Journalize (page 1) and post the June transactions.
c. Prepare a trial balance as of June 30, 19XX.

Group B Problems

(The forms you need are on pages 3-18 to 3-27 of the *Study Guide and Working Papers.*)

Journalizing.

3B-1. In April Alice Hyer opened a new dog grooming centre. Please assist her by journalizing the following business transactions:

19XX

April
1 Alice Hyer invested $4,000 of grooming equipment as well as $6,000 cash in the new business.
3 Purchased grooming supplies on account from Rex Co., $500.
10 Purchased office equipment on account from Ross Stationery, $400.
12 Alice paid her home telephone bill from the company chequebook, $60.
20 Received $600 cash for grooming services performed.
21 Advertising bill received but not paid, $75.
25 Cleaning bill received but not paid, $90.
28 Performed grooming work for Jay Kennels, $700; however, payment will not be received until May.
29 Paid salaries expense, $400.
30 Paid Ross Stationery half the amount owed from April 10 transaction.

The chart of accounts for Hyer's Dog Grooming Centre includes: Cash, 111; Accounts Receivable, 112; Prepaid Rent, 114; Grooming Supplies, 116; Office Equipment, 120; Grooming Equipment, 121; Accounts Payable, 211; Alice Hyer, Capital, 311; Alice Hyer, Withdrawals, 312; Grooming Fees Earned, 411; Advertising Expense, 511; Salaries Expense, 512; and Cleaning Expense, 514.

Comprehensive problem: Journalizing, posting, and preparing a trial balance.

3B-2. In June the following transactions occurred for Reilly's Dance Studio:

19XX
June
1 Dick Reilly invested $6,000 in the dance studio:
1 Paid four months' rent in advance, $1,200.
3 Purchased supplies on account from A.J.K., $700.
5 Purchased equipment on account from Reese Company, $900.
8 Received $1,300 cash for dance training program provided to Northwest Junior College.
9 Billed Long Co. for dance lessons provided, $600.
10 Dick withdrew $400 from the dance studio to buy a new chainsaw for his home.
15 Paid salaries expense, $400.
28 Paid telephone bill, $118.
29 Electric bill received but unpaid, $120.

Required

a. Set up a ledger.
b. Journalize (all page 1) and post the June transactions.
c. Prepare a trial balance as of June 30, 19XX.

Chart of accounts includes: Cash, 111; Accounts Receivable, 112; Prepaid rent, 114; Supplies, 121; Equipment, 131; Accounts Payable, 211; D. Reilly, Capital, 311; D. Reilly, Withdrawals, 321; Fees Earned, 411; Electrical Expense, 511; Salaries Expense, 521; Telephone Expense, 531.

Comprehensive problem: Journalizing, posting, and preparing a trial balance.

3B-3. In June, A. French's Placement Agency had the following transactions:

19XX
June
1 A. French invested $6,000 in the new placement agency.
2 Bought equipment for cash, $350.
3 Earned placement fee commission, $2,100, but payment from Avon Co. will not be received until July.
5 Paid wages expense, $400.
7 A. French paid his home utility bill from the company chequebook, $69.
9 Placed Jay Diamond on a national TV show, receiving $900 cash.
15 Paid cash for supplies, $350.
28 Telephone bill received but not paid, $185.
29 Advertising bill received but not paid, $200.

The chart of accounts includes: Cash, 111; Accounts Receivable, 112; Supplies, 131; Equipment, 141; Accounts Payable, 211; A. French, Capital, 311; A. French, Withdrawals, 321; Placement Fees Earned, 411; Wage Expense, 511; Telephone Expense, 521; Advertising Expense, 531.

Required

a. Set up a ledger based on the chart of accounts.
b. Journalize (all page1) and post transactions.
c. Prepare a trial balance for June 30, 19XX.

Group C Problems

Journalizing.

3C-1. In August, Bert King opened a personal financial planning centre. Please assist him by journalizing the following business transactions:

19XX		
Aug.	1	Bert King invested $5,000 of computer equipment as well as $8,000 cash in the new business.
	3	Purchased computer supplies on account from Kent Co., $420.
	10	Purchased office equipment on account from Apex Stationery, $1,260.
	12	Bert paid his home telephone bill from the company chequebook, $47.
	20	Received $900 cash for planning services performed.
	21	Advertising bill received but not paid, $220.
	25	Cleaning bill received but not paid, $90.
	28	Performed planning services for Franklin Corp., $2,400; however, payment will not be received until September.
	29	Paid salaries expense, $800.
	30	Paid Apex Stationery half the amount owed from August 10 transaction, $630.
	31	Received bill for repairs on equipment, $275. Not yet paid.

The chart of accounts for the company includes: Cash, 111; Accounts Receivable, 112; Prepaid Rent, 114; Computer Supplies, 116; Office Equipment, 120; Computer Equipment, 121; Accounts Payable, 211; B. King, Capital, 311; B. King, Withdrawals, 312; Planning Fees Earned, 411; Advertising Expense, 511; Salaries Expense, 512; Repairs Expense, 513 and Cleaning Expense, 514.

Comprehensive problem: Journalizing, posting, and preparing a trial balance.

3C-2. In July the following transactions occurred for Joan's Aerobic Studio.

19XX		
June	1	Joan Falk invested $7,200 in the studio.
	1	Paid three months' rent in advance, $1,500.
	3	Purchased supplies on account from Marlin Supplies, $420.
	5	Purchased equipment on account from Brinkley Company, $2,400.
	8	Received $1,800 cash for aerobic training program provided to Anne Webber Dance Group.
	9	Billed Short Co. for aerobic lessons provided, $1,500.
	10	Joan withdrew $1,000 from the dance studio to buy a new sofa for her apartment.
	15	Paid salaries expense, $1,060.
	28	Paid telephone bill for studio, $90.
	28	Electric bill received but unpaid, $172.
	31	Advertising bill received from City Newspaper, $280.

Required

a. Set up a ledger.
b. Journalize (all P. 1) and post the July transactions.
c. Prepare a trial balance as of July 31, 19XX.

Chart of accounts includes: Cash, 111; Accounts Receivable, 112; Prepaid Rent, 114; Supplies, 121; Equipment, 131; Accounts Payable, 211; J. Falk, Capital, 311; J. Falk, Withdrawals, 321; Fees Earned, 411; Advertising Expense, 511; Electrical Expense, 515; Salaries Expense, 521; Telephone Expense, 531.

Comprehensive problem: Journalizing, posting, and preparing a trial balance.

3C-3. In June, Bill Niven Investigative Agency had the following transactions:

19XX

June 1 Bill Niven invested $16,000 in the new agency.
2 Bought equipment for cash, $4,200.
3 Earned investigative fee, $3,100, but payment from client will not be received until later.
5 Paid wages expense, $920.
7 B. Niven paid his home water and gas bill from the company chequebook, $107.
9 Located missing spouse, receiving $950 cash.
15 Paid cash for supplies, $310.
25 Received half of the fee earned on June 3, $1,550.
28 Telephone bill received but not paid, $160.
29 Advertising bill received but not paid, $540.

The chart of accounts includes: Cash, 111; Accounts Receivable, 112; Supplies, 131; Equipment, 141; Accounts Payable, 211; B. Niven, Capital, 311; B. Niven, Withdrawals, 321; Investigative Fees Earned, 411; Wage Expense, 511; Telephone Expense, 521; Advertising Expense, 531.

Required

a. Set up a ledger based on the chart of accounts.
b. Journalize (all page 1) and post transactions.
c. Prepare a trial balance for June 30, 19XX.

Real World Applications

3R-1.

Paul Regan, bookkeeper of Hampton Co., has been up half the night trying to get his trial balance to balance. Here are his results:

HAMPTON CO.
TRIAL BALANCE
JUNE 30, 19XX

	Dr.	Cr.
Office Sales		572000
Cash in Bank	326000	
Accounts Receivable	566000	
Office Equipment	840000	
Accounts Payable		416000
D. Hole, Capital		1156000
D. Hole, Withdrawals		70000
Wage Expense	260000	
Rent Expense	94000	
Utilities Expense	2600	
Office Supplies	12000	
Prepaid Rent	18000	

Ken Small, the accountant, compared Paul's amounts in the trial balance with those in the ledger, recomputed each account balance, and compared postings. Ken found the following errors:

1. A $200 debit to D. Hole, Withdrawals, was posted as a credit.
2. D. Hole, Withdrawals, was listed on the trial balance as a credit.
3. A Note Payable account with a credit balance of $2,400 was not listed on the trial balance.
4. The pencil footings for Accounts Payable were debits of $5,320 and credits of $8,800.
5. A debit of $180 to Prepaid Rent was not posted.
6. Office Supplies bought for $60 was posted as a credit to Supplies.
7. A debit of $120 to Accounts Receivable was not posted.
8. A cash payment of $420 was credited to Cash for $240.
9. The pencil footing of the credits to Cash was overstated by $400.
10. The Utilities Expense of $260 was listed in the trial balance as $26.

Assist Paul Regan by preparing a correct trial balance. What advice could you give Ken about Paul? Can you explain the situation to Paul? Put your answers in writing.

3R-2.

Lauren Oliver, an accountant lab tutor, is having a debate with some of her assistants. They are trying to find out how each of the following five unrelated situations would affect the trial balance:

1. A $5 debit to cash in the ledger was not posted.
2. A $10 debit to Computer Supplies was debited to Computer Equipment.
3. An $8 debit to Wage Expense was debited twice to the account.
4. A $4 debit to Computer Supplies was debited to Computer Sales.
5. A $35 credit to Accounts Payable was posted as a $53 credit.

Could you indicate to Lauren the effect that each situation will have on the trial balance? If a situation will have no effect, indicate that fact. Put in writing how each of these situations could be avoided in the future.

make the call

Critical Thinking/Ethical Case

3R-3.

Jay Simons, the accountant of See Co., would like to buy a new computer software package for his general ledger. He couldn't do it because all funds were frozen for the rest of the fiscal period. Jay called his friend at Joor Industries and asked whether he could copy their software. Why should or shouldn't Jay have done that?

ACCOUNTING RECALL

A CUMULATIVE APPROACH

THIS EXAM REVIEWS CHAPTERS 1 THROUGH 3

Your *Study Guide and Working Papers* has forms (pages 3-40 to 3-44) to complete this exam, as well as worked-out solutions. The page references next to each question identify what page to turn back to if you answer the question incorrectly.

PART I Vocabulary Review

Match the terms to the appropriate definition or phrase.

Page Ref.		
(44)	1. Chart of accounts	A. Process of recording transactions in a journal
(41)	2. Ledger	B. Rearrangement of digits
(98)	3. Slide	C. Book of original entry
(80)	4. Calendar year	D. Running balance
(98)	5. Transposition	E. Transferring information
(90)	6. Three-column account	F. January 1 to December 31
(81)	7. Journalizing	G. Adding or deleting numbers
(84)	8. Compound entry	H. Numbering system
(90)	9. Posting	I. More than two accounts
(80)	10. Journal	J. Book of final entry

PART II True or False (Accounting Theory)

(81) 11. The ledger is located in same book as a journal.

(91) 12. The PR column of a general journal is completed after the posting to the ledger is complete.

(99) 13. Correcting errors in journalizing can only be done before posting.

(80) 14. A calendar year could be a fiscal year.

(97) 15. A trial balance could balance but be incorrect.

PART III Applications Problem

From the following transactions of Jesse Company (a) journalize, (b) post, and (c) prepare a trial balance.

19XX		
May	1	Ray Jesse invests $5,000 in the business.
	4	Bought from Lowe Co., office equipment on account, $700.
	18	Billed Smith for fees earned, $4,000.
	24	Ray Jesse withdrew $600 for personal use.
	28	Paid salaries, $1,400.

Chart of accounts includes: Cash, 111; Accounts Receivable, 112; Office Equipment, 121; Accounts Payable, 211; R. Jesse, Capital, 311; R. Jesse, Withdrawals, 312; Fees Earned, 411; Salaries Expense, 511.

COMPUTER WORKSHOP

Computerized Accounting Application for Chapter 3*

Journalizing, Posting, General Ledger, and Trial Balance

Before starting on this assignment, read and complete the tasks discussed in Parts A, B, and F of Appendix B, "Computerized Accounting" at the back of this book.

How to Open Company Data Files

1. Start Windows; insert your Student Data Files disk into disk drive A or B; then double-click on the CA-Simply Accounting icon.
2. The CA-Simply Accounting copyright screen will appear briefly; then the CA-Simply Accounting Open File dialogue box will appear. Enter one of the following paths into the **Open file name** text box:
   - A:\ATLAS.ASC (if you are storing your student data files on the disk in drive A).
   - B:\ATLAS.ASC (if you are storing your student data files on the disk in drive B).
3. Click on the **Open** button. The program will respond with a request for the **Using date for this session.** The **Using** date is the date associated with the current work session. Once the **Using** date is advanced, it cannot be turned back to an earlier date.
4. Enter "12/31/99" into the **Using date for this session** text box; then click on the **OK** button. Click on the **OK** button in response to the message "The date entered is more than one week past your previous **Using** date of 12/1/99." When you start CA-Simply Accounting for Windows, the file name for the company's data files (in this case ATLAS) will appear in the title bar at the top of the Company Window. Your screen will look like this:

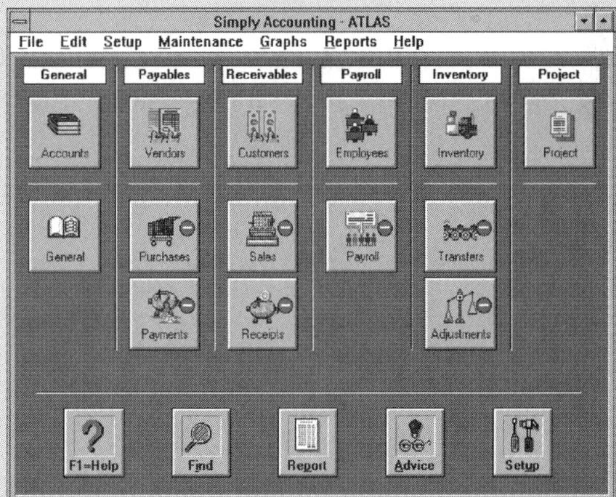

   Note that the icons for Purchases, Payments, Sales, Receipts, Payroll, Transfers, and Adjustments Journals are shown with a lock. The General Journal has no lock. The Atlas Company will only be using the General Journal to record transactions.

How to Add Your Name to the Company Name

5. It is important for you to be able to identify the specific reports that you print for each assignment as your own, particularly if you are using a computer that shares a printer with other computers. The CA-Simply Accounting for Windows program prints the name of the company you are working with at the top of each report. To personalize your reports so that you can identify both the company and your printed reports, the company name needs to be modified to include your name:
   a. Click on the Company Window Setup menu; then click on Company Information. The Company Information dialogue box will appear.

---

*Assuming use of Simply Accounting for Windows. If you are using ACCPAC Plus software, your instructor will supply you with the necessary additonal information.

b. In the Company Information dialogue box use the mouse to position the insertion point immediately after the company name in the **Name** text box; drag through the "Your Name" text to highlight the text; then type your name. Your screen will look similar to the one shown below:

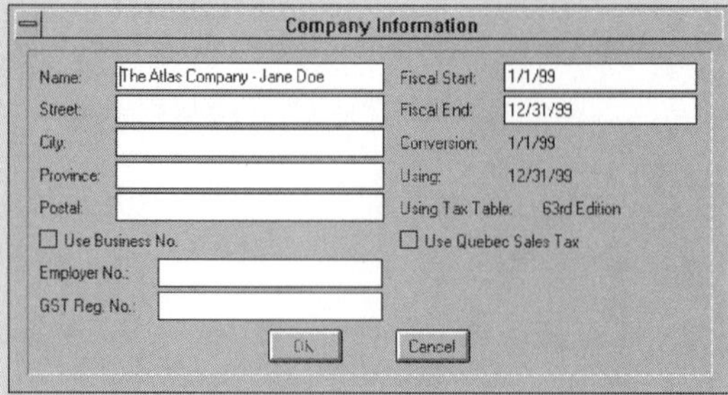

c. Click on the **OK** button to return to the Company window.

How to Record a General Journal Entry

6. The owner of Atlas Company has invested $10,000 in the business. Double-click on the General Journal icon to open the General Journal dialogue box. Enter "Memo" into the **Source** text box; press the TAB key; enter "12/1/99" into the **Date** text box; press the TAB key; enter "Initial investment of cash by owner" into the **Comment** text box; then press the TAB key.

   The **Source** text box can be used for any reference number or notation you wish to associate with a general journal entry and the source document that authorizes the entry. The **Date** text box is used to record the date the transaction occurred. The **Comment** text box can be used for comments related to the journal entry in much the same way that an explanation is used when journal entries are recorded in a manual accounting system. Note that a flashing insertion point is positioned in the **Account** text box.

7. With the flashing insertion point positioned in the **Account** text box, press the ENTER key. The Select Account dialogue box will appear. Double-click on 1110 Cash. The program will enter the account number and name into the **Account** text box, and the flashing insertion point will move to the **Debits** text box.

8. Enter "10000" into the **Debits** text box; then press the TAB key. Dollar amounts can be entered in several ways. For example, to enter $50.00, type 50, 50., or 50.00. To enter an amount containing a decimal point, type the decimal point as part of the amount. For example, enter five dollars and twenty-five cents as 5.25. Do not enter commas. The flashing insertion point will move to **Account** text box ready for the selection of the account to be credited for this entry.

9. With the flashing insertion point positioned in the **Account** text box, press the ENTER key to bring up the Select Account dialogue box. Click on the down arrow button on the scroll bar to the right of the **Select account** listing to advance the display until "3110 Owner's, Capital" appears. Double-click on that. The program will offer the same amount as the **Debits** portion of the entry as a default amount in the **Credits** text box. The **Credits** amount remains highlighted.

10. Press the TAB key to accept the default **Credits** amount. This completes the data you need to enter into the General Journal dialogue box to record the journal entry for the initial investment of cash by the owner. Your screen should look like this:

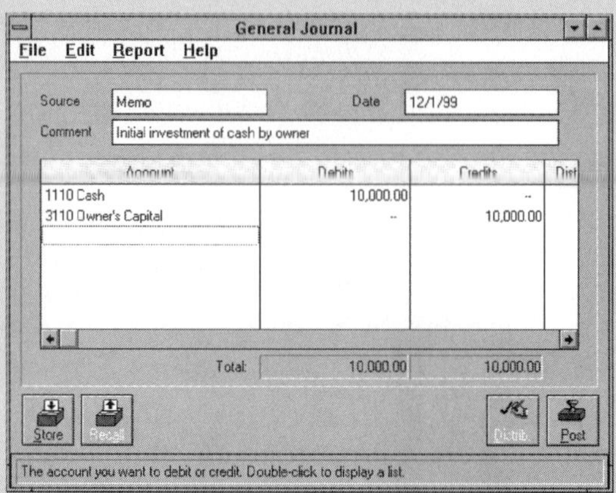

How to Review a Journal Entry

11. Before posting this transaction, you need to verify that the transaction data are correct by reviewing the journal entry. To review the entry, click on the General Journal Report menu; then click on Display General Journal Entry. The journal entry representing the data you have recorded in the General Journal dialogue box is displayed. Review the journal entry for accuracy noting any errors.

How to Edit an Entry Prior to Posting

12. Close the General Journal Entry window by double-clicking on the control menu box. If you have made an error, use the following editing techniques to correct the error.

Editing a General Journal Entry

- Move to the text box that contains the error by either pressing the TAB key to move forward through each text box or the SHIFT and TAB keys together to move to a previous text box. This will highlight the selected text box information so that you can change it. Alternatively, you can use the mouse to point to a text box and drag through the incorrect information to highlight it.
- Type the correct information; then press the TAB key to enter it.
- Note that when editing a dollar amount entered into the **Debits** or **Credits** text box, the program does not automatically change the corresponding **Debits** or **Credits** amount to agree with the new amount you have entered.
- If you have associated a transaction with an incorrect account, double-click on the incorrect account; then select the correct account from the Select Account dialog box. This will replace the incorrect account with the correct account.
- Note that the **Post** button will be dimmed (unavailable) until the journal entry is in balance.
- To discard an entry and start over, double-click on the control menu box. Click on the **Yes** button in response to the question "Are you sure you want to discard this journal entry?"
- Review the journal entry for accuracy after any editing corrections.
- **It is important to note that the only way to edit a journal entry after it is posted is to reverse the entry and enter the correct journal entry.** To correct journal entries posted in error, see Part C "Reversing an Entry Made in the General Journal Dialogue Box" of Appendix B.

How to Post an Entry

13. After verifying that the journal entry is correct, click on the **Post** button to post this transaction. A blank General Journal dialogue box is displayed, ready for additional General Journal transactions to be recorded.

Record Additional Transactions

14. Record the following additional journal entries (enter "Memo" into the **Source** text box for each transaction, then enter the **Date** listed for each transaction):

1992		
Dec.	1	Paid rent for two months in advance, $400.
	3	Purchased office supplies for cash, $100.
	9	Billed a customer for fees earned, $1,500.
	13	Paid telephone bill, $180.
	20	Owner withdrew $500 from the business for personal use.
	27	Received $450 for fees earned.
	31	Paid salaries expense, $700.

15. After you have posted the additional journal entries, double-click on the control menu box to close the General Journal dialogue box. This will restore the Company Window screen, and the General Journal icon will remain highlighted.

How to Display and Print a General Journal

16. With the General Journal icon highlighted, click on the Company Window Report menu; then click on Display General Journal. The General Journal Options dialogue box will appear asking you to define the information you want displayed. Leave the **By posting date** option box checked; leave the **All ledger entries** check box checked; enter 12/1/99 into the **Start** text box; leave the **Finish** text box date set at 12/31/99; then click on the **OK** button. The following General Journal Display will appear on your screen:

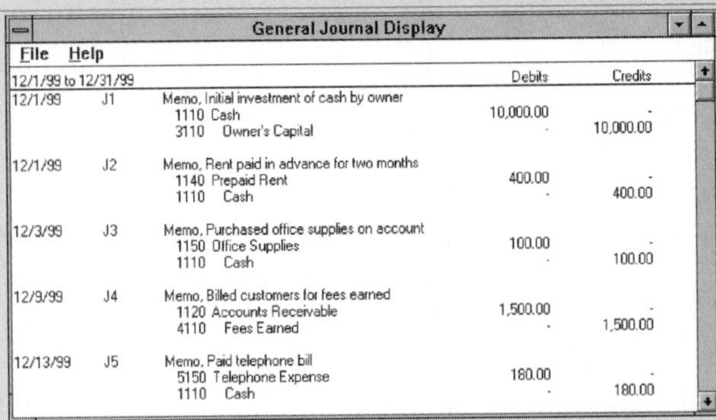

General Journal Display

File Help

12/1/99 to 12/31/99			Debits	Credits
12/1/99	J1	Memo, Initial investment of cash by owner		
		1110 Cash	10,000.00	-
		3110 Owner's Capital	-	10,000.00
12/1/99	J2	Memo, Rent paid in advance for two months		
		1140 Prepaid Rent	400.00	-
		1110 Cash	-	400.00
12/3/99	J3	Memo, Purchased office supplies on account		
		1150 Office Supplies	100.00	-
		1110 Cash	-	100.00
12/9/99	J4	Memo, Billed customers for fees earned		
		1120 Accounts Receivable	1,500.00	-
		4110 Fees Earned	-	1,500.00
12/13/99	J5	Memo, Paid telephone bill		
		5150 Telephone Expense	180.00	-
		1110 Cash	-	180.00

17. The scroll bar can be used to advance the display to view other portions of the report.
18. Click on the General Journal Display File menu; then click on Print to print the General Journal. If you experience any difficulties with your printer (for example, the type size is too small), refer to Part F of Appendix B for information on how to adjust the print and display settings.

What to Do If You Posted an Incorrect Entry

19. Review your printed general journal. If you have made an error in a posted journal entry, see Part C of Appendix B at the back of this book for information on how to correct the error.

How to Display and Print a General Ledger Report

20. Double-click on the control menu box to close the General Journal Display window; click on the Company Window Report menu; then click on General Ledger. The General Ledger Report Options dialogue box will appear. Enter 12/1/99 into the **Start** text box; leave the **Finish** text box date set at 12/31/99; click on the **Select All** button, then click on the **OK** button. Your screen will look like this:

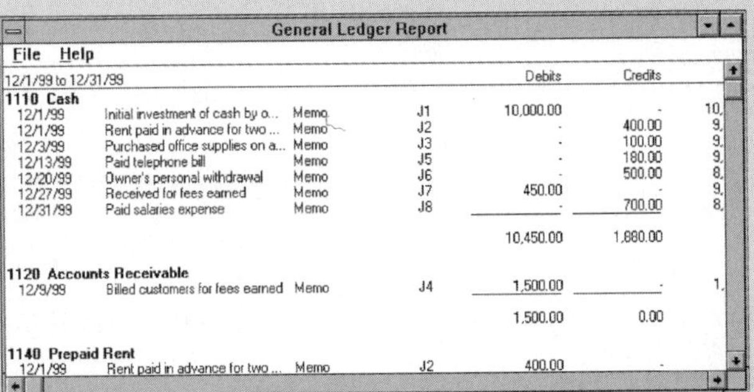

General Ledger Report

File Help

12/1/99 to 12/31/99				Debits	Credits	
1110 Cash						
12/1/99	Initial investment of cash by o...	Memo	J1	10,000.00	-	10,
12/1/99	Rent paid in advance for two ...	Memo	J2	-	400.00	9,
12/3/99	Purchased office supplies on a...	Memo	J3	-	100.00	9,
12/13/99	Paid telephone bill	Memo	J5	-	180.00	9,
12/20/99	Owner's personal withdrawal	Memo	J6	-	500.00	8,
12/27/99	Received for fees earned	Memo	J7	450.00	-	9,
12/31/99	Paid salaries expense	Memo	J8	-	700.00	8,
				10,450.00	1,880.00	
1120 Accounts Receivable						
12/9/99	Billed customers for fees earned	Memo	J4	1,500.00	-	1,
				1,500.00	0.00	
1140 Prepaid Rent						
12/1/99	Rent paid in advance for two ...	Memo	J2	400.00	-	

21. The scroll bars can be used to advance the display to view other portions of the report.
22. Click on the General Ledger Report File menu; then click on Print to print the general ledger report.

How to Display and Print a Trial Balance

23. Double-click on the control menu box to close the General Ledger Report window; click on the Company Window Report menu; then click on Trial Balance. The Trial Balance Options dialogue box will appear. Leave the **As at** date set at 12/31/99; then click on the **OK** button. Your screen will look like this:

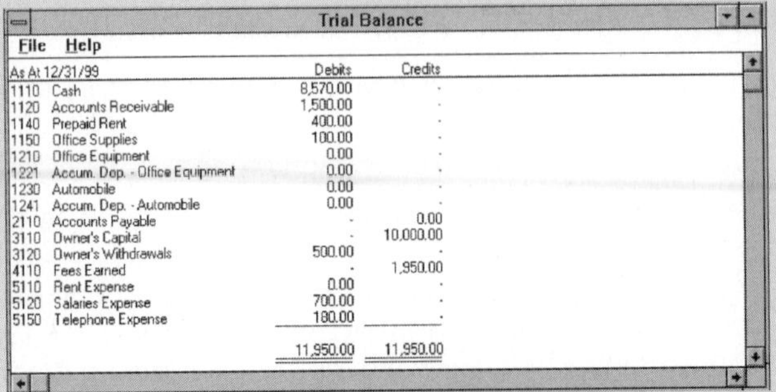

Trial Balance

File Help

As At 12/31/99		Debits	Credits
1110	Cash	8,570.00	-
1120	Accounts Receivable	1,500.00	-
1140	Prepaid Rent	400.00	-
1150	Office Supplies	100.00	-
1210	Office Equipment	0.00	-
1221	Accum. Dep. - Office Equipment	0.00	-
1230	Automobile	0.00	-
1241	Accum. Dep. - Automobile	0.00	-
2110	Accounts Payable	-	0.00
3110	Owner's Capital	-	10,000.00
3120	Owner's Withdrawals	500.00	-
4110	Fees Earned	-	1,950.00
5110	Rent Expense	0.00	-
5120	Salaries Expense	700.00	-
5150	Telephone Expense	180.00	-
		11,950.00	11,950.00

24. The scroll bar can be used to advance the display to view other portions of the report.

25. Click on the Trial Balance File menu; then click on Print to print the Trial Balance.

26. Double-click on the control menu box to close the Trial Balance window and return to the Company Window.

How to Exit from the Program

27. Click on the Company Window File menu; then click on Exit to end the current work session and return to your Windows desktop. Your work will automatically be saved to your Student Data Files disk.

28. You can exit from the CA-Simply Accounting for Windows program at any time during a current work session. Click on the Company Window File menu; then click on Exit. To resume working on an assignment, open the company data files: then leave the **Using date for this session** set at the default date offered.

How to Save your Work During a Current Work Session

29. To save your work during a lengthy current work session, click on the Company Window File menu. Click on Save; then continue with your current work session. It is a good practice to save your work about every 15 minutes when you are involved in a lengthy session.

Complete the Report Transmittal

30. Complete the Atlas Company Report Transmittal located in Appendix A in your *Study Guide and Working Papers.*

The Accounting Cycle Continued

4

Preparing Worksheets and Financial Reports

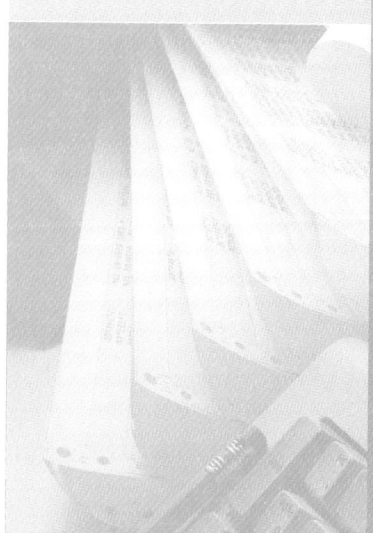

Chapter Objectives

- ◆ Adjustments: prepaid rent, office supplies, depreciation on equipment, and accrued salaries. (p.128)
- ◆ Preparation of adjusted trial balance on the worksheet. (p. 137)
- ◆ The income statement and balance sheet sections of the worksheet. (p. 138)
- ◆ Preparing financial reports from the worksheet. (p. 141)

The accompanying diagram shows the steps of the accounting cycle that were completed for Clark's Word Processing Services in the last chapter. This chapter continues the cycle with the preparation of a worksheet and the three financial reports.

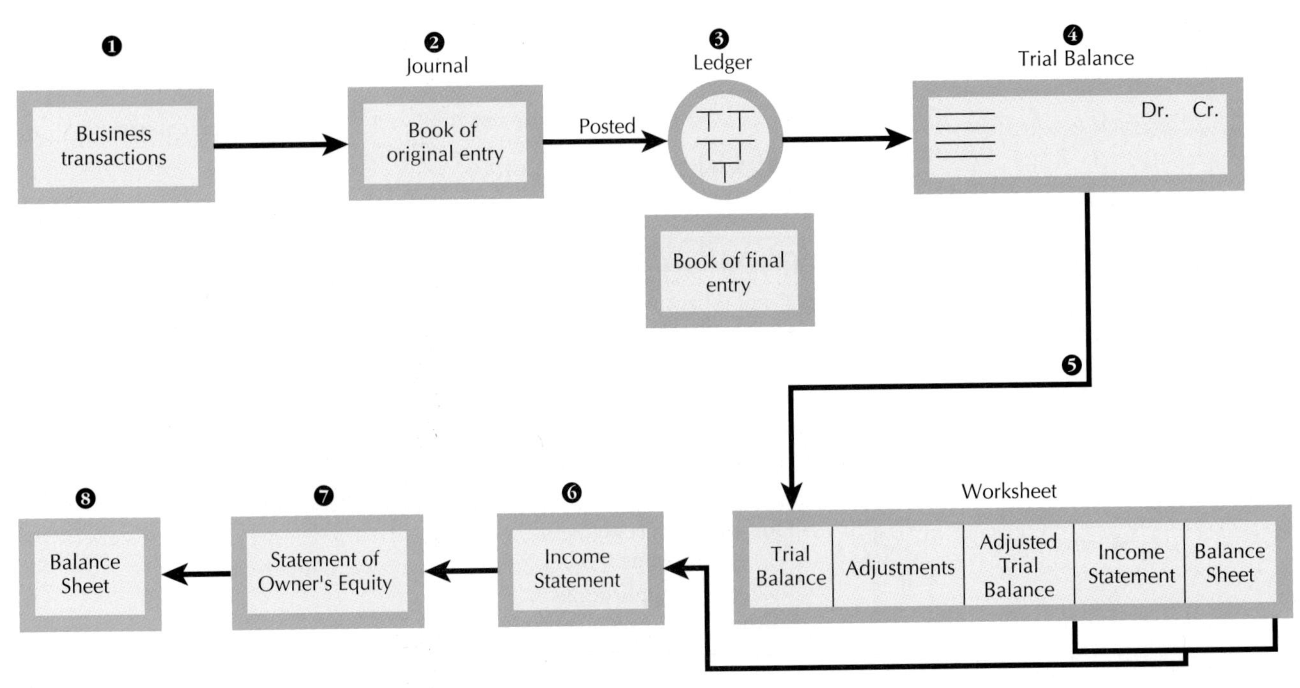

LEARNING UNIT 4-1

Steps of the Accounting Cycle: Preparing Worksheet

The worksheet is not a formal report, so no dollar signs appear on it. Because it is a form, there are no commas, either.

As is true for all accounting reports, the heading includes the name of the company, the name of the report, the date, and the length of the accounting service.

An accountant uses a **worksheet** to organize and check data before preparing financial reports necessary to complete the accounting cycle. The most important function of the worksheet is to allow the accountant to find and correct errors before financial statements are prepared. In a way, a worksheet acts as the accountant's scratch pad. No one sees the worksheet once the formal reports are prepared. A sample worksheet is shown in Figure 4-1.

The accounts listed on the far left of the worksheet are taken from the ledger. The rest of the worksheet has five sections: trial balance, adjustments, adjusted trial balance, income statement, and balance sheet. Each of these sections is divided into debit and credit columns. Refer often to the special overlay in Figure 4-5 as you

CLARK'S WORD PROCESSING SERVICES
WORKSHEET
FOR MONTH ENDING MAY 31, 19XX

Account Titles	Trial Balance Dr.	Trial Balance Cr.	Adjustments Dr.	Adjustments Cr.	Adjusted Trial Balance Dr.	Adjusted Trial Balance Cr.	Income Statement Dr.	Income Statement Cr.
Cash	615500							
Accounts Receivable	500000							
Office Supplies	60000							
Prepaid Rent	120000							
Word Processing Equipment	600000							
Accounts Payable		335000						
B. Clark, Capital		1000000						
B. Clark, Withdrawals	62500							
Word Processing Fees		800000						
Office Salaries Expense	130000							
Advertising Expense	25000							
Telephone Expense	22000							
	2135000	2135000						

FIGURE 4-1
Sample Worksheet

study this learning unit. The transparencies illustrating the completion of a worksheet can be very useful to your understanding of the process.

THE TRIAL BALANCE SECTION

We discussed how to prepare a trial balance in Chapter 2. Some companies prepare a separate trial balance; others, such as Clark's Word Processing Services, prepare the trial balance directly on the worksheet. A trial balance is taken on every account listed in the ledger that has a balance. Additional titles from the ledger are added as they are needed. (We will show this later.)

THE ADJUSTMENTS SECTION

Adjusting is like fine-tuning your TV set.

Chapters 1 to 3 discussed transactions that occurred with outside suppliers and companies. In a real business, though, inside transactions also occur during the accounting cycle. These transactions must be recorded, too. At the end of the worksheet process, the accountant will have all of the business' accounts up to date and ready to be used to prepare the formal financial reports. By analyzing each of Clark's accounts on the worksheet, the accountant will be able to identify specific accounts that must be **adjusted** to bring them up to date. The accountant for Clark's Word Processing Services needs to adjust the following accounts:

- Office Supplies.
- Prepaid Rent.
- Word Processing Equipment.
- Office Salaries Expense.

Let's look at how to analyze and adjust each of these accounts.

Adjusting the Office Supplies Account

On May 31, the accountant found out that the company had only $100 worth of office supplies on hand. When the company originally purchased the $600 of office supplies, they were considered an asset. But as the supplies were used up, they became an expense.

The adjustment for supplies deals with the amount of supplies *used up.*

- Office supplies available, $600.
- Office supplies left or on hand as of May 31, $100.
- Office supplies used up in the operation of the business for the month of May, $500.

Adjustments affect both the income statement and the balance sheet.

Office Supplies Exp. 514

Dr.	Cr.
500	

This is supplies used up.

Office Supplies 114

Dr.	Cr.
600	500
100	

This is supplies on hand.

As a result, the asset Office Supplies is too high on the trial balance (it should be $100, not $600). At the same time, if we don't show the additional expense of supplies used, the company's *net income* will be too high.

If Clark's accountant does not adjust the trial balance to reflect the change, the company's net income would be too high on the income statement and on both sides (assets and owner's equity) of the balance sheet.

Now let's look at the adjustment for office supplies in terms of the transaction analysis chart.

Will go on income statement.

Accounts Affected	Category	↑ ↓	Rules
Office Supplies Expense	Expense	↑	Dr.
Office Supplies	Asset	↓	Cr.

Will go on balance sheet.

The letter A is used to code Office Supplies adjustment because it is the first account to be adjusted.

Note: All accounts listed *below* the trial balance will be *increasing.*

The account Office Supplies is called a **mixed account** because the amount entered on the trial balance is partly a balance sheet amount and partly an income statement amount. On the balance sheet, Office Supplies will be an unexpired cost. On the income statement, Office Supplies Expense will be an expired cost.

The office supplies expense account comes from the Chart of Accounts on page 82. Since it is not listed in the trial balance account titles, it must be listed below the trial balance. Let's see how we enter this adjustment on the worksheet:

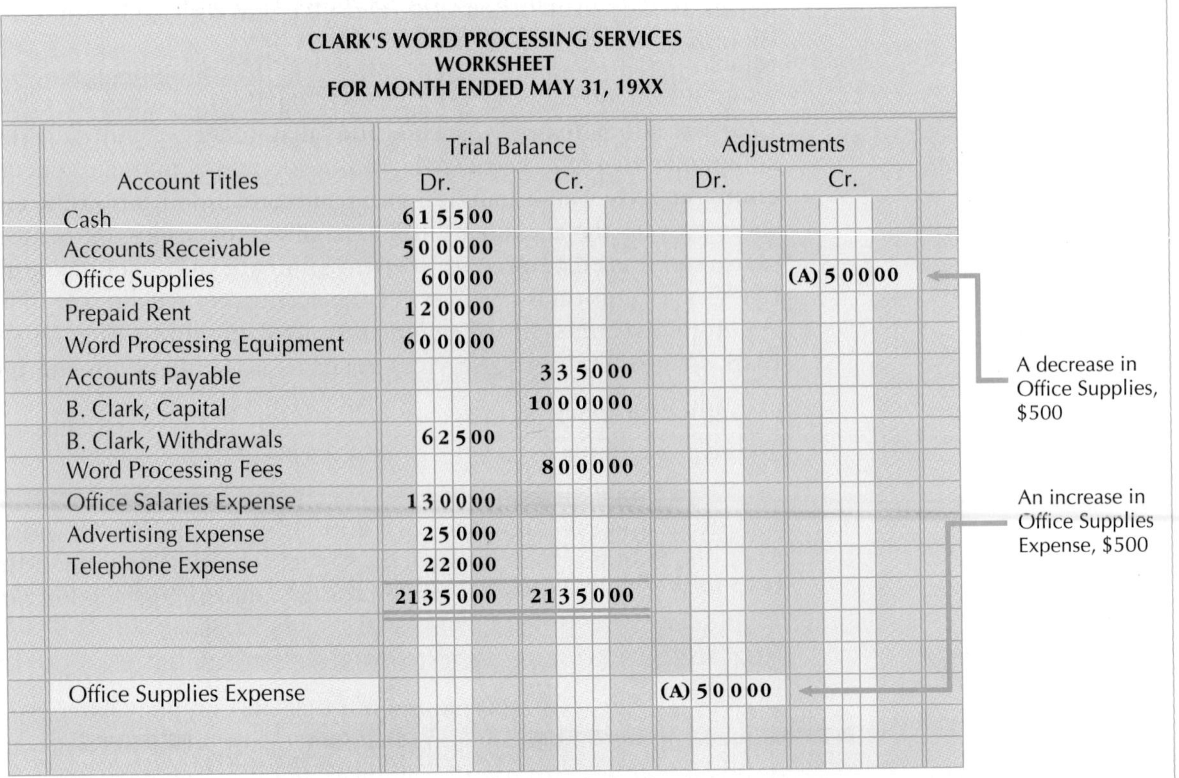

CLARK'S WORD PROCESSING SERVICES
WORKSHEET
FOR MONTH ENDED MAY 31, 19XX

Account Titles	Trial Balance Dr.	Trial Balance Cr.	Adjustments Dr.	Adjustments Cr.
Cash	6155 00			
Accounts Receivable	5000 00			
Office Supplies	600 00			(A) 500 00
Prepaid Rent	1200 00			
Word Processing Equipment	6000 00			
Accounts Payable		3350 00		
B. Clark, Capital		10000 00		
B. Clark, Withdrawals	625 00			
Word Processing Fees		8000 00		
Office Salaries Expense	1300 00			
Advertising Expense	250 00			
Telephone Expense	220 00			
	21350 00	21350 00		
Office Supplies Expense			(A) 500 00	

A decrease in Office Supplies, $500
An increase in Office Supplies Expense, $500

The Office Supplies Expense account indicates the amount of supplies used up. It is listed below other trial balance accounts, since it was not on the original trial balance.
A debit will increase the account Office Supplies Expense; a credit will reduce the account Office Supplies.

Place $500 in the debit column of the adjustments section on the same line as Office Supplies Expense. Place $500 in the credit column of the adjustments section on the same line as Office Supplies. The numbers in the adjustment column show what is used, *not* what is on hand.

Adjusting the Prepaid Rent Account

Adjusting Prepaid Rent: On page 129 the trial balance showed a figure for Prepaid Rent of $1,200. The amount of rent *expired* is the adjustment figure used to update Prepaid Rent and Rent Expense.

Back on May 1, Clark's Word Processing Services paid three months' rent in advance. The accountant realized that the rent expense would be $400 per month ($1,200 ÷ 3 months = $400).

Remember, when rent is paid in advance, it is considered an asset called *prepaid rent.* When the asset, prepaid rent, begins to expire or be used up it becomes an expense. Now it is May 31, and one month's prepaid rent has become an expense.

How is this handled? Should the account be $1,200, or is there really only $800 of prepaid rent left as of May 31? What do we need to do to bring prepaid rent to the "true" balance? The answer is that we must increase Rent Expense by $400 and decrease Prepaid Rent by $400.

Without this adjustment, the expenses for Clark's Word Processing Services for May will be too low, and the asset Prepaid Rent will be too high. If unadjusted amounts were used in the formal reports, the net income shown on the income statement would be too high, and both sides (assets and owner's equity) would be too high on the balance sheet. In terms of our transaction analysis chart, the adjustment would look like this:

Rent Expense 515

Dr.	Cr.
400	

Will go on income statement.

Accounts Affected	Category	↑ ↓	Rules
Rent Expense	Expense	↑	Dr.
Prepaid Rent	Asset	↓	Cr.

Will go on balance sheet.

Prepaid Rent 115

Dr.	Cr.
1,200	400 Adj.
800	

Like the Office Supplies Expense account, the Rent Expense account comes from the chart of accounts on p. 82. It, too, is a mixed account.

Let's look at how we enter this adjustment on the worksheet at the top of page 132.

Adjusting the Word Processing Equipment Account

Take this one slowly.

Original cost of $6,000 for word processing equipment remains *unchanged* after adjustments.

The life of the asset affects how it is adjusted. The two accounts we discussed above, Office Supplies and Prepaid Rent, involved things that are used up relatively quickly. Equipment — like word processing equipment — is expected to last much longer. Also, it is expected to help produce revenue over a longer period. That is why accountants treat it differently. The balance sheet reports the **historical cost,** or original cost, of the equipment. The original cost also is reflected in the ledger. The adjustment shows how the cost of the equipment is allocated (spread) over its expected useful life. This spreading is called **depreciation.** To depreciate the equipment, we have to figure out how much its cost goes down each month. Then we have to keep a running total of how that depreciation mounts up over time. Revenue Canada has a specific set of rules (called Capital Cost Allowance rules) which tell how businesses in Canada must depreciate their assets for tax purposes. For accounting reports however, different methods can be used to calculate depreciation. We will use the simplest method — straight-line depreciation — to calculate the depreciation of Clark Word Processing Service's equipment. Under the straight-line method, equal amounts are taken over successive periods of time.

CLARK'S WORD PROCESSING SERVICES WORKSHEET FOR MONTH ENDED MAY 31, 19XX				
	Trial Balance		Adjustments	
Account Titles	Dr.	Cr.	Dr.	Cr.
Cash	615500			
Accounts Receivable	500000			
Office Supplies	60000			(A) 50000
Prepaid Rent	120000			(B) 40000
Word Processing Equipment	600000			
Accounts Payable		335000		
B. Clark, Capital		1000000		
B. Clark, Withdrawals	62500			
Word Processing Fees		800000		
Office Salaries Expense	130000			
Advertising Expense	25000			
Telephone Expense	22000			
	2135000	2135000		
Office Supplies Expense			(A) 50000	
Rent Expense			(B) 40000	

The Rent Expense is the second account to be adjusted, so the letter B is assigned to it.

Rent expense is listed below other trial balance accounts, since it was not on the original trial balance.

A decrease in Prepaid Rent, $400

An increase in Rent Expense, $400

Again, note that accounts listed below the trial balance are increasing.

The calculation of depreciation for the year for Clark's Word Processing Services is as follows:

$$\frac{\text{Cost of Equipment} - \text{Residual Value}}{\text{Estimated Years of Usefulness}}$$

Assume equipment has a 5-year life.

Word processing equipment has an expected life of approximately five years. At the end of that time, the property's value is called its "residual value." Think of **residual value** as the estimated value of the equipment at end of the fifth year. For Clark, the equipment has an estimated residual value of $1,200.

Clark will record $960 of depreciation each year.

$$\frac{\$6{,}000 - \$1{,}200}{5\text{ Years}} = \frac{\$4{,}800}{5} = \$960 \text{ Depreciation per Year}$$

Our trial balance is for one month, so we must determine the adjustment for that month:

Depreciation is an expense reported on the income statement.

$$\frac{\$960}{12\text{ Months}} = \$80 \text{ Depreciation per Month}$$

This $80 is known as *Depreciation Expense* and will be shown on the income statement.

Next, we have to create a new account that can keep a running total of the depreciation amount apart from the original cost of the equipment. That account is called **Accumulated Depreciation.**

Accumulated Depreciation	
Dr.	Cr.
–	+

is a contra-asset account found on the balance sheet.

The Accumulated Depreciation account shows the relationship between the original cost of the equipment and the amount of depreciation that has been taken or accumulated over a period of time. This is a contra-asset account; it has the opposite balance of an asset such as equipment. Accumulated Depreciation will summarize, accumulate, or build up the amount of depreciation that is taken on the word processing equipment over its estimated useful life.

This is how this would look on a partial balance sheet of Clark's Word Processing Services.

At end of June the accumulated depreciation will be $160, but historical cost will stay at $6,000.

Remember, book value is not the same as market value.

❶ Historical cost of $6,000 of equipment is not changed.

❷ Amount of accumulated depreciation is $80.

❸ This shows the unused amount of the equipment that may be depreciated in future periods of time. This figure, the cost of the asset less its accumulated depreciation, is often termed **book value** or carrying value. In taxation terms, it is referred to as Undepreciated Capital Cost, or UCC.

CLARK'S WORD PROCESSING SERVICES
BALANCE SHEET
MAY 31, 19XX

Assets		
———		XXXX
Word Processing Equip.	$6,000	
Less: Accumulated depreciation	80	
		5,920

Let's summarize the key points before going on to mark the adjustment on the worksheet:

Taking depreciation does not result in any new payment of cash.

1. Depreciation Expense goes on the income statement, which results in
   a. An increase in total expenses.
   b. A decrease in net income.
2. Accumulated depreciation is a contra-asset account found on the balance sheet next to its related equipment account.
3. The original cost of equipment is not reduced; it stays the same until the equipment is sold or removed.
4. Each month the amount in the Accumulated Depreciation account grows larger, while the cost of the equipment remains the same.
5. Businesses may reduce their income tax expense by deducting Capital Cost Allowance (CCA). This CCA is similar to depreciation, and some smaller businesses may use CCA values for their depreciation expense.

Now, let's analyze the adjustment on the transaction analysis chart:

Dep. Expense, W.P. 516
80 |

Accum. Dep., W.P. 122
| 80

Will go on income statement.

Accounts Affected	Category	↑ ↓	Rules
Depreciation Expense, Word Processing Equipment	Expense	↑	Dr.
Accumulated Depreciation, Word Processing Equipment	Contra-Asset	↑	Cr.

Will go on balance sheet.

Note that the original cost of the equipment on the worksheet has *not* been changed ($6,000).

Remember, the original cost of the equipment never changes: (1) the equipment account is not included among the affected accounts because the original cost of equipment remains the same; and (2) the original cost does not change. When the Accumulated Depreciation increases (as a credit), the equipment's *book value* decreases.

This is how we enter the adjustment for depreciation of word processing equipment on the worksheet:

CLARK'S WORD PROCESSING SERVICES
WORKSHEET
FOR MONTH ENDED MAY 31, 19XX

Account Titles	Trial Balance Dr.	Trial Balance Cr.	Adjustments Dr.	Adjustments Cr.
Cash	615500			
Accounts Receivable	500000			
Office Supplies	60000			(A) 50000
Prepaid Rent	120000			(B) 40000
Word Processing Equipment	600000			
Accounts Payable		335000		
B. Clark, Capital		1000000		
B. Clark, Withdrawals	62500			
Word Processing Fees		800000		
Office Salaries Expense	130000			
Advertising Expense	25000			
Telephone Expense	22000			
	2135000	2135000		
Office Supplies Expense			(A) 50000	
Rent Expense			(B) 40000	
Depreciation Exp., W.P. Equip.			(C) 8000	
Accum. Deprec., W.P. Equip.				(C) 8000

An increase in Depreciation Expense, W.P. Equipment

An increase in Accumulated Depreciation, W.P. Equipment

The third account to be adjusted is assigned the letter C.

Because this is a new business, neither account had a previous balance. Therefore, neither is listed in the account titles of the trial balance. The adjustments to these accounts are listed below the Rent Expense. We need to list both accounts below Rent Expense in the account titles section. On the worksheet, put $80 in the debit column of the adjustments section on the same line as Depreciation Expense, W. P. Equipment, and put $80 in the credit column of the adjustments section on the same line as Accumulated Depreciation, W. P. Equipment.

Next month (June in our example), accumulated depreciation will appear listed in the original trial balance.

Next month, on June 30, a further $80 would be entered under Depreciation Expense, and Accumulated Depreciation would show a balance of $160. Remember, in May, Clark was a new company, so no previous depreciation was taken.

Accumulated Depreciation

Dr.	Cr.
	History of amount of depreciation taken to date

Now let's look at the last adjustment for Clark's Word Processing Services.

Adjusting the Salaries Payable Account

Adjusting salaries.

Clark's Word Processing Services paid $1,300 in Office Salaries Expense (see the trial balance of any previous worksheet in this chapter). The last salary cheques for the month were paid on May 27. How can we update this account to show the salary expense as of May 31?

John Murray worked for Clark on May 28, 29, 30, and 31, but his next paycheque is not due until June 3. John earned $350 for these four days. Is the $350 an expense to Clark in May, when it was earned, or in June when it is due and is paid?

May						
S	M	T	W	T	F	S
						1
2	3	4	5	6	7	8
9	10	11	12	13	14	15
16	17	18	19	20	21	22
23	24	25	26	27	28	29
30	31					

An expense can be incurred without being paid as long as it has helped in creating earned revenue for a period of time.

Think back to Chapter 1, when we first discussed revenue and expenses. We noted then that revenue is recorded when it is earned, and expenses are recorded when they are incurred, not when they are actually paid. This principle will be discussed further in a later chapter; for now it is enough to remember that we record revenue and expenses when they occur, because we want to match earned revenue with the expenses that resulted in earning those revenues. In this case, by working those four days, John Murray created some revenue for Clark in May. Therefore, the office salaries expense must be shown in May—the month the revenue was earned.

The results are:

- Office Salaries Expense is increased by $350. This unpaid and unrecorded expense for salaries for which payment is not due is called **accrued salaries.** In effect, we now show the true expense for salaries ($1,650 instead of $1,300):

Office Salaries Expense	
1,300	
350	

- The second result is that salaries payable is increased by $350. Clark's has created a liability called Salaries Payable, meaning that the firm owes money for salaries. When the firm pays John Murray, it will reduce its liability, Salaries Payable, as well as decrease its cash.

In terms of the transaction analysis chart, the following would be done:

Accounts Affected	Category	↑ ↓	Rules
Office Salaries Expense	Expense	↑	Dr.
Salaries Payable	Liability	↑	Cr.

Office Salaries Exp. 511	
1,300	
350	

Salaries Payable 212	
	350

How the adjustment for accrued salaries is entered on the worksheet is shown at the top of page 136.

The account Office Salaries Expense is already listed in the account titles, so $350 is placed in the debit column of the adjustments section on the same line as Office Salaries Expense. However, because the Salaries Payable is not listed in the account titles, it is added to the account title Salaries Payable below the trial balance, below Accumulated Depreciation, W. P. Equipment. Also, $350 is placed in the credit column of the adjustments section on the same line as Salaries Payable.

Now that we have finished all the adjustments that we intended to make, we total the adjustments section, as shown in Figure 4-2.

CLARK'S WORD PROCESSING SERVICES
WORKSHEET
FOR MONTH ENDED MAY 31, 19XX

Account Titles	Trial Balance Dr.	Trial Balance Cr.	Adjustments Dr.	Adjustments Cr.
Cash	615500			
Accounts Receivable	500000			
Office Supplies	60000			(A) 50000
Prepaid Rent	120000			(B) 40000
Word Processing Equipment	600000			
Accounts Payable		335000		
B. Clark, Capital		1000000		
B. Clark, Withdrawals	62500			
Word Processing Fees		800000		
Office Salaries Expense	130000		(D) 35000	
Advertising Expense	25000			
Telephone Expense	22000			
	2135000	2135000		
Office Supplies Expense			(A) 50000	
Rent Expense			(B) 40000	
Depreciation Exp., W.P. Equip.			(C) 8000	
Accum. Deprec., W.P. Equip.				(C) 8000
Salaries Payable				(D) 35000

The Salaries Payable account is coded D because it is the fourth account to be added.

Remember, all accounts added below the trial balance are *increasing*.

An increase in Office Salaries Expense, $350

An increase in Salaries Payable, $350

FIGURE 4-2
The Adjustments Section of The Worksheet

CLARK'S WORD PROCESSING SERVICES
WORKSHEET
FOR MONTH ENDED MAY 31, 19XX

Account Titles	Trial Balance Dr.	Trial Balance Cr.	Adjustments Dr.	Adjustments Cr.
Cash	615500			
Accounts Receivable	500000			
Office Supplies	60000			(A) 50000
Prepaid Rent	120000			(B) 40000
Word Processing Equipment	600000			
Accounts Payable		335000		
B. Clark, Capital		1000000		
B. Clark, Withdrawals	62500			
Word Processing Fees		800000		
Office Salaries Expense	130000		(D) 35000	
Advertising Expense	25000			
Telephone Expense	22000			
	2135000	2135000		
Office Supplies Expense			(A) 50000	
Rent Expense			(B) 40000	
Depreciation Exp., W.P. Equip.			(C) 8000	
Accum. Deprec., W.P. Equip.				(C) 8000
Salaries Payable				(D) 35000
			133000	133000

FIGURE 4-3 The Adjusted Trial Balance Section of the Worksheet

CLARK'S WORD PROCESSING SERVICES
WORKSHEET
FOR MONTH ENDED MAY 31, 19XX

Account Titles	Trial Balance Dr.	Trial Balance Cr.	Adjustments Dr.	Adjustments Cr.	Adjusted Trial Balance Dr.	Adjusted Trial Balance Cr.
Cash	6 1 5 5 00				6 1 5 5 00	
Accounts Receivable	5 0 0 0 00				5 0 0 0 00	
Office Supplies	6 0 0 00			(A) 5 0 0 00	1 0 0 00	
Prepaid Rent	1 2 0 0 00			(B) 4 0 0 00	8 0 0 00	
Word Processing Equipment	6 0 0 0 00				6 0 0 0 00	
Accounts Payable		3 3 5 0 00				3 3 5 0 00
B. Clark, Capital		10 0 0 0 00				10 0 0 0 00
B. Clark, Withdrawals	6 2 5 00				6 2 5 00	
Word Processing Fees		8 0 0 0 00				8 0 0 0 00
Office Salaries Expense	1 3 0 0 00		(D) 3 5 0 00		1 6 5 0 00	
Advertising Expense	2 5 0 00				2 5 0 00	
Telephone Expense	2 2 0 00				2 2 0 00	
	21 3 5 0 00	21 3 5 0 00				
Office Supplies Expense			(A) 5 0 0 00		5 0 0 00	
Rent Expense			(B) 4 0 0 00		4 0 0 00	
Depreciation Exp., W.P. Equip.			(C) 8 0 00		8 0 00	
Accum. Deprec., W.P. Equip.				(C) 8 0 00		8 0 00
Salaries Payable				(D) 3 5 0 00		3 5 0 00
			1 3 3 0 00	1 3 3 0 00	21 7 8 0 00	21 7 8 0 00

If no adjustment is made, just carry over amount from trial balance on same side.

Supplies were $600 but we used up $500, leaving us with a $100 balance in supplies. *Note:* If there are a debit and a credit, take the *difference* between the two and place it on the side that is larger.

Note: Equipment is *not* adjusted here.

Two debits are added together. If two credits, they also would have been added together.

Carry these amounts over to adjusted trial balance in the same positions.

Note: The total of the left (debit) must equal the total of the right (credit) ($21,780).

The Adjusted Trial Balance Section

The adjusted trial balance is the next section on the worksheet. To fill it out, we must summarize the information in the trial balance and adjustments sections, as shown in Figure 4-3.

Note that when the numbers are brought across from the trial balance to the adjusted trial balance, two debits will be added together and two credits will be added together. If the numbers include a debit and a credit, take the difference between the two and place it on the side that is larger.

Now that we have completed the adjustments and adjusted trial balance sections of the worksheet, it is time to move on to the income statement and the balance sheet sections. Before we do that though, look at the chart shown in Table 4-1. This table should be used as a reference to help you in filling out the next two sections of the worksheet.

Keep in mind that the numbers from the adjusted trial balance are carried over to one of the last four columns of the worksheet before the bottom section is completed.

The Income Statement Section

Net income is placed in the debit column of the income statement. Net loss goes on the credit column.

As shown in Figure 4-4 , the income statement section lists only revenue and expenses from the adjusted trial balance. Note that accumulated depreciation and salaries payable do not go on the income statement. Accumulated depreciation is a contra-asset account found on the balance sheet. Salaries payable is a liability found on the balance sheet.

The revenue ($8,000) and all the individual expenses are listed in the income statement section. The revenue is placed in the credit column of the income statement section because it has a credit balance. The expenses have debit balances, so they are placed in the debit column of the income statement section. The following steps must be taken after the debits and credits are placed in the correct columns:

Table 4-1 Normal Balances and Account Categories

Account Titles	Category	Normal Balance on Adjusted Trial Balance	Income Statement		Balance Sheet	
			Dr.	Cr.	Dr.	Cr.
Cash	Asset	Dr.			X	
Accounts Receivable	Asset	Dr.			X	
Office Supplies	Asset	Dr.			X	
Prepaid Rent	Asset	Dr.			X	
Word Proc. Equipment	Asset	Dr.			X	
Accounts Payable	Liability	Cr.				X
B. Clark, Capital	Owner's Equity	Cr.				X
B. Clark, Withdrawals	Owner's Equity	Dr.			X	
Word Proc. Fees	Revenue	Cr.		X		
Office Salaries Expense	Expense	Dr.	X			
Advertising Expense	Expense	Dr.	X			
Telephone Expense	Expense	Dr.	X			
Office Supplies Expense	Expense	Dr.	X			
Rent Expense	Expense	Dr.	X			
Dep. Exp., W. P. Equipment	Expense	Dr.	X			
Acc. Dep., W. P. Equipment	Contra-Asset	Cr.				X
Salaries Payable	Liability	Cr.				X

CLARK'S WORD PROCESSING SERVICES
WORKSHEET
FOR MONTH ENDED MAY 31, 19XX

Account Titles	Adjusted Trial Balance Dr.	Adjusted Trial Balance Cr.	Income Statement Dr.	Income Statement Cr.
Cash	615500			
Accounts Receivable	500000			
Office Supplies	10000			
Prepaid Rent	80000			
Word Processing Equipment	600000			
Accounts Payable		335000		
B. Clark, Capital		1000000		
B. Clark, Withdrawals	62500			
Word Processing Fees		800000		800000
Office Salaries Expense	165000		165000	
Advertising Expense	25000		25000	
Telephone Expense	22000		22000	
Office Supplies Expense	50000		50000	
Rent Expense	40000		40000	
Depreciation Exp., W.P. Equip.	8000		8000	
Accum. Dep., W.P. Equip.		8000		
Salaries Payable		35000		
	2178000	2178000	310000	800000
Net Income			490000	
			800000	800000

FIGURE 4-4 The Income Statement Section of the Worksheet

The difference between $3,100 Dr. and $8,000 Cr. indicates a net income of $4,900. Do not think of the Net Income as a Dr. or Cr. The $4,900 is placed in the debit column to balance both columns to $8,000. Actually, the credit side is larger by $4,900.

Step 1: Total the debits and credits.

Step 2: Calculate the balance between the debit and credit columns and place the difference on the smaller side.

Step 3: Total the columns.

The worksheet in Figure 4-4 shows that the label "Net Income" is added in the account title column on the same line as $4,900. When there is a net income, it will be placed in the debit column of the income statement section of the worksheet. If there is a net loss, it is placed in the credit column. The $8,000 total indicates that the two columns are in balance.

THE BALANCE SHEET SECTION

Remember: The ending figure for capital is not on the worksheet.

To see whether additional investments occurred for the period you must check the capital account in the ledger.

The amounts come from the adjusted trial balance, except the $4,900, which was carried over from the income statement section.

To fill out the balance sheet section of the worksheet, the following are carried over from the adjusted trial balance section: assets, contra assets, liabilities, capital, and withdrawals. Because the beginning figure for capital is used on the worksheet, the net income is brought over to the credit column of the balance sheet so both columns balance.

Let's now look at the completed worksheet in Figure 4-5 to see how the balance sheet section is completed. Note how the net income of $4,900 is brought over to the credit column of the worksheet. The figure for capital is also on the credit column, while the figure for withdrawals is on the debit column. By placing the net income in the credit column both sides total $18,680. If a net loss were to occur it would be placed in the debit column of the balance sheet col-

CLARK'S WORD PROCESSING SERVICES
WORKSHEET
FOR MONTH ENDED MAY 31, 19XX

Account Titles	Trial Balance		Adjustments		Adjusted Trial Balance		Income Statement		Balance Sheet	
	Dr.	Cr.	Dr.	Cr.	Dr.	Cr.	Dr.	Cr.	Dr.	Cr.
Cash	615500									
Accounts Receivable	500000									
Office Supplies	60000									
Prepaid Rent	120000									
Word Processing Equipment	600000									
Accounts Payable		335000								
B. Clark, Capital		1000000								
B. Clark, Withdrawals	62500									
Word Processing Fees		800000								
Office Salaries Expense	130000									
Advertising Expense	25000									
Telephone Expense	22000									
	2135000	2135000								

FIGURE 4-5 Sample Worksheet

Flip to Overlay No. 1 — Adjustments A, B, C, and D

Now that we have completed the worksheet, we can go on to the three financial reports. But first let's summarize our progress.

LEARNING UNIT 4-1 REVIEW

AT THIS POINT you should be able to

- Define and explain the purpose of a worksheet. (p.128)
- Explain the need as well as the process for adjustments. (p.129)
- Define and give an example of a mixed account. (p.130)
- Explain the concept of depreciation. (p. 131)
- Explain the difference between depreciation expense and accumulated depreciation. (p. 132)
- Prepare a worksheet from a trial balance and adjustment data. (p.136–138b)

SELF-REVIEW QUIZ 4-1

From the accompanying trial balance and adjustment data, complete a worksheet for P. Logan Company for the month ended Dec. 31, 19XX. (You can use a blank foldout worksheet located at the end of the *Study Guide and Working Papers.*)

Note: The numbers used on this quiz may seem impossibly small, but we have done that on purpose, so that at this point you don't have to worry about arithmetic, just about preparing the worksheet correctly.

P. LOGAN
TRIAL BALANCE
DECEMBER 31, 19XX

	Dr.	Cr.
Cash	1500	
Accounts Receivable	300	
Prepaid Insurance	300	
Store Supplies	500	
Store Equipment	600	
Accumulated Depreciation, Store Equipment		400
Accounts Payable		200
P. Logan, Capital		1400
P. Logan, Withdrawals	300	
Revenue from Clients		2500
Rent Expense	200	
Salaries Expense	800	
	4500	4500

Adjustment Data

a. Depreciation Expense, Store Equipment, $1.

b. Insurance Expired, $2

c. Supplies on hand, $1.

d. Salaries owed but not paid to employees, $3.

Solution to Self-Review Quiz 4-1

Don't adjust this line! Store Equipment always contains the historical cost.

P. LOGAN COMPANY
WORKSHEET
FOR MONTH ENDED DECEMBER 31, 19XX

Account Titles	Trial Balance		Adjustments		Adjusted Trial Balance		Income Statement		Balance Sheet	
	Dr.	Cr.	Dr.	Cr.	Dr.	Cr.	Dr.	Cr.	Dr.	Cr.
Cash	15 00				15 00				15 00	
Accounts Receivable	3 00				3 00				3 00	
Prepaid Insurance	3 00			(B) 2 00	1 00				1 00	
Store Supplies	5 00			(C) 4 00	1 00				1 00	
Store Equipment	6 00				6 00				6 00	
Accum. Dep., Store Equipment		4 00		(A) 1 00		5 00				5 00
Accounts Payable		2 00				2 00				2 00
P. Logan, Capital		14 00				14 00				14 00
P. Logan, Withdrawals	3 00				3 00				3 00	
Revenue from Clients		25 00				25 00		25 00		
Rent Expense	2 00				2 00		2 00			
Salaries Expense	8 00		(D) 3 00		11 00		11 00			
	45 00	45 00								
Dep. Exp., Store Equipment			(A) 1 00		1 00		1 00			
Insurance Expense			(B) 2 00		2 00		2 00			
Supplies Expense			(C) 4 00		4 00		4 00			
Salaries Payable				(D) 3 00		3 00				3 00
			10 00	10 00	49 00	49 00	20 00	25 00	29 00	24 00
Net Income							5 00			5 00
							25 00	25 00	29 00	29 00

Note that Accumulated Depreciation is listed in trial balance, since this is not a new company. Store Equipment has already been depreciated $4 from an earlier period.

LEARNING UNIT 4-2

Step 6 of the Accounting Cycle: Preparing the Financial Statements from the Worksheet

The formal financial reports can be prepared from the worksheet completed in Learning Unit 4-1. Before beginning, we must check that the entries on the worksheet are correct and in balance. To do this, we have to be sure that (1) all entries are recorded in the appropriate column, (2) the correct amounts are entered in the proper places, (3) the addition is correct across the columns (i.e., from the trial balance to the adjusted trial balance to the financial reports), and (4) the columns are added correctly.

PREPARING THE INCOME STATEMENT

The first report to be prepared for Clark's Word Processing Services is the income statement. When preparing the income statement, it is important to remember that:

1. Every figure on the formal report is on the worksheet. Figure 4-6 shows where each of these figures goes on the income statement.
2. There are no debit or credit columns on the formal report.
3. The inside column on financial reports is used for subtotalling.
4. Withdrawals do not go on the income statement; they go on the statement of owner's equity.

Take a moment to look at the income statement in Figure 4-6. Note which items go where from the income statement section of the worksheet onto the formal report.

PREPARING THE STATEMENT OF OWNER'S EQUITY

Figure 4-7 is the statement of owner's equity for Clark. The figure shows where the information comes from on the worksheet. It is important to remember that if there were additional investments, the figure on the worksheet for capital will not be the beginning figure for capital. Checking the ledger account for capital will tell you whether the amount is correct. Note how net income and withdrawals aid in calculating the new figure for capital.

PREPARING THE BALANCE SHEET

In preparing the balance sheet (page 143), remember that the balance sheet section totals on the worksheet ($18,680) do *not* match the totals on the formal balance sheet ($17,975) because there are no debit or credit columns on the formal report. We must rearrange the information from the worksheet to prepare the balance sheet. For example, at the bottom of the worksheet, Accumulated Depreciation ($80) is in the column opposite Word Processing Equipment ($6,000). However, the $5,920 on the balance sheet is not found on the worksheet. Figure 4-8 shows how to prepare the balance sheet from the worksheet.

Account Titles	Income Statement Dr.	Income Statement Cr.
Cash		
Accounts Receivable		
Office Supplies		
Prepaid Rent		
Word Processing Equipment		
Accounts Payable		
B. Clark, Capital		
B. Clark, Withdrawals		
Word Processing Fees		8000 00
Office Salaries Expense	1650 00	
Advertising Expense	250 00	
Telephone Expense	220 00	
Office Supplies Expense	500 00	
Rent Expense	400 00	
Depreciation Expense, W.P. Equip.	80 00	
Accum. Dep., W.P. Equip.		
Salaries Payable		
	3100 00	8000 00
Net Income	4900 00	
	8000 00	8000 00

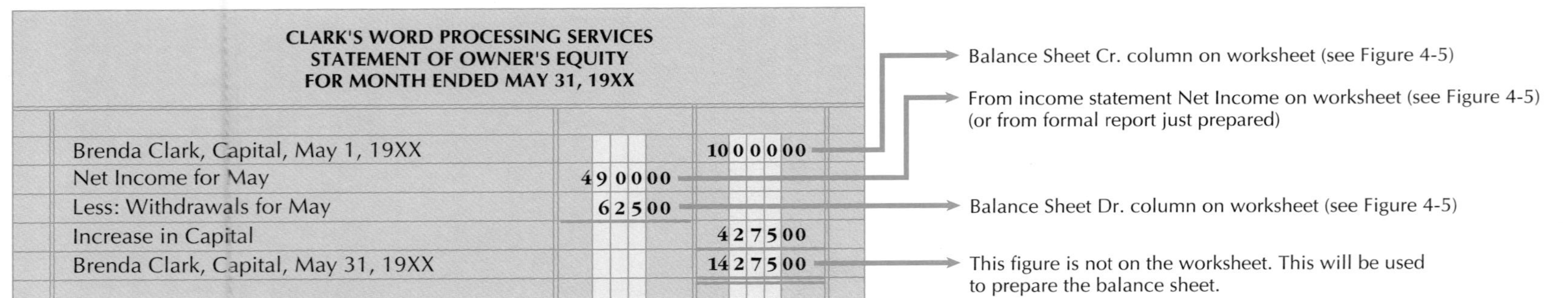

CLARK'S WORD PROCESSING SERVICES
INCOME STATEMENT
FOR MONTH ENDED MAY 31, 19XX

Revenue:		
Word Processing Fees		8000 00
Operating Expenses:		
Office Salaries Expense	1650 00	
Advertising Expense	250 00	
Telephone Expense	220 00	
Office Supplies Expense	500 00	
Rent Expense	400 00	
Depreciation Expense, W.P. Equipment	80 00	
Total Operating Expenses		3100 00
Net Income		4900 00

FIGURE 4-6 From Worksheet to Income Statement

CLARK'S WORD PROCESSING SERVICES
STATEMENT OF OWNER'S EQUITY
FOR MONTH ENDED MAY 31, 19XX

Brenda Clark, Capital, May 1, 19XX		10000 00	Balance Sheet Cr. column on worksheet (see Figure 4-5)
Net Income for May	4900 00		From income statement Net Income on worksheet (see Figure 4-5) (or from formal report just prepared)
Less: Withdrawals for May	625 00		Balance Sheet Dr. column on worksheet (see Figure 4-5)
Increase in Capital		4275 00	
Brenda Clark, Capital, May 31, 19XX		14275 00	This figure is not on the worksheet. This will be used to prepare the balance sheet.

FIGURE 4-7 Completing a Statement of Owner's Equity

Account Titles	Balance Sheet Dr.	Balance Sheet Cr.
Cash	615500	
Accts. Rec.	500000	
Office Supplies	10000	
Prepaid Rent	80000	
Word Proc. Equipment	600000	
Accounts Payable		335000
B. Clark, Capital		1000000
B. Clark, Withdrawals	62500	
Accum. Dep., W.P. Equip.		8000
Salaries Payable		35000
	1868000	1378000
		490000
	1868000	1868000

From Worksheet
From statement of owner's equity or from worksheet:

$10,000	Beg. Capital
+4,900	Net Income
−625	Withdrawals

CLARK'S WORD PROCESSING SERVICES
BALANCE SHEET
MAY 31, 19XX

Assets			Liabilities and Owner's Equity		
Cash		$ 615500	Liabilities		
Accounts Receivable		500000	Accounts Payable	$335000	
Office Supplies		10000	Salaries Payable	35000	
Prepaid Rent		80000	Total Liabilities		$370000
Word Proc. Equip.	$600000				
Less: Accum. Dep.,			Owner's Equity		
W.P.Equip.	8000	592000	Brenda Clark, Capital		1427500
Total Assets		$1797500	Total Liabilities and Owner's Equity		$1797500

FIGURE 4-8 From Worksheet to Balance Sheet

LEARNING UNIT 4-2 REVIEW

AT THIS POINT you should be able to

- Prepare the three financial reports from a worksheet. (p. 141)
- Explain why formal financial reports do not have debit and credit columns. (p. 141)

SELF-REVIEW QUIZ 4-2

(The forms you need are located on pages 4-2- and 4-3 of the *Study Guide and Working Papers.*)

From the worksheet on page 140 for P. Logan, prepare (1) an income statement for December; (2) a statement of owner's equity; and (3) a balance sheet for December 31, 19XX. No additional investments took place during the period.

Solution to Self-Review Quiz 4-2

P. LOGAN
INCOME STATEMENT
FOR THE MONTH ENDED DECEMBER 31, 19XX

Revenue:		
Revenue from clients		$2500
Operating Expenses:		
Rent Expense	$200	
Salaries Expense	1100	
Depreciation Expense, Store Equipment	100	
Insurance Expense	200	
Supplies Expense	400	
Total Operating Expenses		2000
Net Income		$500

P. LOGAN
STATEMENT OF OWNER'S EQUITY
FOR THE MONTH ENDED DECEMBER 31, 19XX

P. Logan, Capital, December 1, 19XX		$1400
Net Income for December	$500	
Less: Withdrawals for December	300	
Increase in Capital		200
P. Logan, Capital, December 31, 19XX		$1600

P. LOGAN
BALANCE SHEET
DECEMBER 31, 19XX

Assets			Liabilities and Owner's Equity		
Cash		$1500	Liabilities		
Accounts Receivable		300	Accounts Payable	$200	
Prepaid Insurance		100	Salaries Payable	300	
Store Supplies		100	Total Liabilities		$500
Store Equipment	$600		Owner's Equity		
Less Accum. Dep.,			P. Logan, Capital		1600
Store Equipment	500	100	Total Liabilities and		
Total Assets		$2100	Owner's Equity		$2100

Chapter Review

Comprehensive Demonstration Problem with Solution Tips

(The blank forms you need are on pages 4-4 and 4-5 of the *Study Guide and Working Papers.*)

From the following trial balance and additional data (1) complete a worksheet and (2) the three financial reports (numbers are intentionally small so you may concentrate on the theory).

Frost Company
Trial Balance
December 31, 19XX

	Dr.	Cr.
Cash	14	
Accounts Receivable	4	
Prepaid Insurance	5	
Plumbing Supplies	3	
Plumbing Equipment	7	
Accumulated Depreciation, Plumbing Equipment		5
Accounts Payable		1
J. Frost, Capital		12
J. Frost, Withdrawals	3	
Plumbing Fees		27
Rent Expense	4	
Salaries Expense	5	
Totals	45	45

Adjustment Data

a. Insurance Expired	$3
b. Plumbing Supplies on Hand	$1
c. Depreciation Expense, Plumbing Equipment	$1
d. Salaries owed but not paid to employees	$2

Solution Tips to Building a Worksheet

1. Adjustments (used up)

a.

Insurance Expense	**Expense**	↑	**Dr.**	**$3**
Prepaid Insurance	**Asset**	↓	**Cr.**	**$3**

Expired means used up.

b.

Plumbing Supplies Expense	**Expense**	↑	**Dr.**	**$2**
Plumbing Supplies	**Asset**	↓	**Cr.**	**$2**

$3 − 1 on hand = $2 *used up!*

FROST COMPANY
WORKSHEET
FOR MONTH ENDED DECEMBER 31, 19XX

Account Titles	Trial Balance		Adjustments		Adjusted Trial Balance		Income Statement		Balance Sheet	
	Dr.	Cr.	Dr.	Cr.	Dr.	Cr.	Dr.	Cr.	Dr.	Cr.
Cash	1400				1400				1400	
Accounts Receivable	400				400				400	
Prepaid Insurance	500			(A) 300	200				200	
Plumbing Supplies	300			(B) 200	100				100	
Plumbing Equipment	700				700				700	
Accum. Dep., Plumb. Equip.		500		(C) 100		600				600
Accounts Payable		100				100				100
J. Frost, Capital		1200				1200				1200
J. Frost, Withdrawals	300				300				300	
Plumbing Fees		2700				2700		2700		
Rent Expense	400				400		400			
Salaries Expense	500		(D) 200		700		700			
	4500	4500								
Insurance Expense			(A) 300		300		300			
Plumbing Supplies Expense			(B) 200		200		200			
Dep. Exp. Plumb. Equip.			(C) 100		100		100			
Salaries Payable				(D) 200		200				200
			800	800	4800	4800	1700	2700	3100	2100
Net Income							1000			1000
							2700	2700	3100	3100

c.

Depreciation Expense, Plumbing Equipment	Expense	↑	Dr.	$1
Accumulated Depreciation, Plumbing Equipment	Contra-Asset	↑	Cr.	$1

The original cost of equipment of $7 is not "touched."

d.

Salaries Expense	Expense	↑	Dr.	$2
Salaries Payable	Liability	↑	Cr.	$2

2. Last four columns of worksheet prepared from adjusted trial balance.
3. Capital of $12 is the old figure. Net income of $10 (revenue − expenses) is brought over to same side as capital on the balance sheet Cr. column to balance columns.

Frost Company
Income Statement
for Month Ended December 31, 19XX

Revenue:		
Plumbing Fees		$27
Operating Expenses:		
Rent Expense	$4	
Salaries Expense	7	
Insurance Expense	3	
Plumbing Supplies Expense	2	
Depreciation Expense, Plumbing Equipment	1	
		17
Net Income		$10

Frost Company
Statement of Owner's Equity
for the Month ended December 31, 19XX

J. Frost, Capital, Dec. 1, 19XX		$12
Net Income for December	$10	
Less: Withdrawals for December	3	
Increase in Capital		7
J. Frost, Capital, Dec. 31, 19XX		$19

Frost Company
Balance Sheet
December 31, 19XX

Assets			Liabilities and Owner's Equity		
Cash		$14	Liabilities:		
Accounts Receivable		4	Accounts Payable	$1	
Prepaid Insurance		2	Salaries Payable	2	
Plumbing Supplies		1	Total Liabilities		$3
Plumbing Equipment	$7				
Less: Accumulated Dep.	6	1	Owner's Equity:		
			J. Frost, Capital		19
Total Assets		$22	Total Liabilities and Owner's Equity		$22

Solution Tips for Preparing Financial Reports from a Worksheet

Inside columns of the three financial reports are used for subtotal. There are no debits or credits on the formal reports.

Report	
Income statement	From income statement columns of worksheet for revenue and expenses.
Statement of owner's equity	From balance sheet Cr. column for old figure for Capital. Net Income from income statement. From balance sheet Dr. column for Withdrawals figure.
Balance sheet	From balance sheet Dr. column for assets. From balance sheet Cr. column for Liabilities and Accumulated Depreciation. New figure for Capital from statement of owner's equity.

Note how Plumbing Equipment $7 and Accumulated Depreciation $6 are rearranged on the formal balance sheet. The total assets of $22 is not on the worksheet. Remember there are no debits or credits on formal reports.

Summary of Key Points

Learning Unit 4-1

1. The worksheet is not a formal report.
2. Adjustments update certain accounts so that they will be up to their latest balance before financial reports are prepared. Adjustments are the result of internal transactions.
3. Adjustments will affect both the income statement and the balance sheet.
4. A mixed account results in balances partly on the balance sheet and partly on the income statement.
5. Accounts listed *below* the account titles on the trial balance of the worksheet are *increasing.*
6. The original cost of a piece of equipment is not adjusted; historical cost is not lost.
7. Depreciation is the process of spreading the original cost of the asset over its expected useful life.
8. Accumulated depreciation is a contra-asset on the balance sheet that summarizes, accumulates, or builds up the amount of depreciation that an asset has accumulated.
9. Book value is the original cost less accumulated depreciation.
10. Accrued salaries are unpaid and unrecorded expenses that are accumulating but for which payment is not yet due.
11. Revenue and expenses go on income statement sections of the worksheet. Assets, contra-assets, liabilities, capital, and withdrawals go on balance sheet sections of the worksheet.

Learning Unit 4-2

1. The formal reports prepared from a worksheet do not have debit or credit columns.
2. Revenue and expenses go on the income statement. Beginning capital plus net income less withdrawals (or: beginning capital minus net loss, less withdrawals) goes on the statement of owner's equity. Be sure to check capital account in ledger to see if any additional investments took place. Assets, liabilities, and the new figure for capital go on the balance sheet.

KEY TERMS

Accrued salaries Salaries that are earned by employees but unpaid and unrecorded during the period (and thus need to be recorded by an adjustment) and will not come due for payment until the next accounting period.

Accumulated depreciation A contra-asset account that summarizes or accumulates the amount of depreciation that has been taken on an asset.

Adjusting The process of calculating the latest up-to-date balance of each account at the end of an accounting period.

Book value Cost of equipment less accumulated depreciation.

Depreciation The allocation (spreading) of the cost of an asset (such as an auto or equipment) over its expected useful life.

Historical cost The actual cost of an asset at time of purchase.

Mixed account An account whose balance is partly an income statement amount and partly a balance sheet amount on the trial balance. Examples: Prepaid Rent, Supplies.

Residual value Estimated value of an asset after all the allowable depreciation has been taken.

Worksheet A columnar device used by accountants to aid them in completing the accounting cycle. It is not a formal report. Often called a spreadsheet.

Blueprint of Steps 5 and 6 of the Accounting Cycle

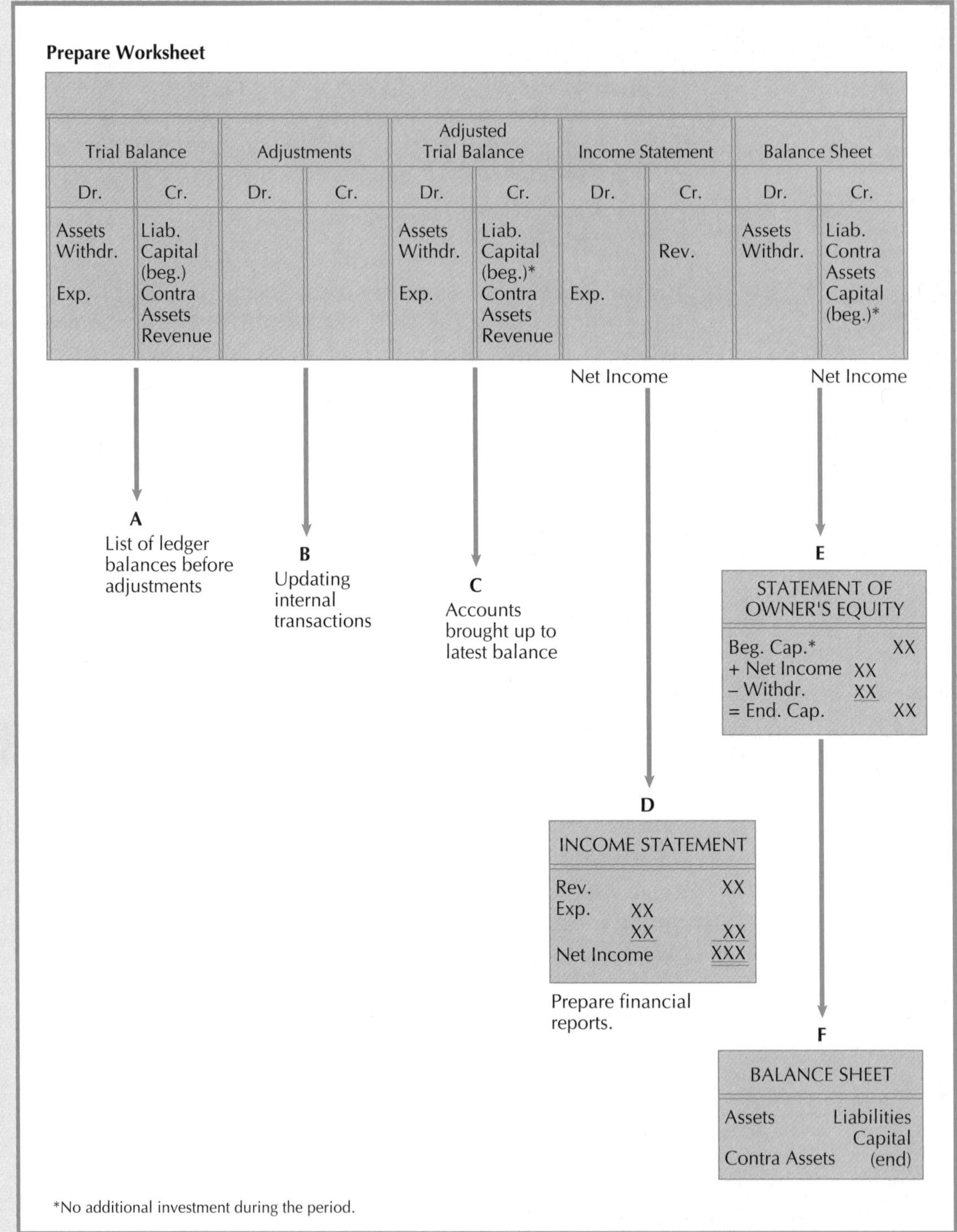

Questions, Exercises, and Problems

Discussion Questions

1. Worksheets are required in every company's accounting cycle. Please agree or disagree and explain why.
2. What is the purpose of adjusting accounts?

3. What is the relationship of internal transactions to the adjusting process?
4. Explain how an adjustment can affect both the income statement and balance sheet. Please give an example.
5. What is a mixed account?
6. Why do we need the accumulated depreciation account?
7. Depreciation expense goes on the balance sheet. True or false? Why?
8. Each month the cost of accumulated depreciation grows while the cost of equipment goes up. Agree or disagree. Defend your position.
9. Define accrued salaries.
10. Why don't the formal financial reports contain debit or credit columns?
11. Explain how the financial reports are prepared from the worksheet.

Mini Exercises

(The blank forms you need are on pages 4-7 and 4-8 of the *Study Guide and Working Papers.*)

Adjustment for Supplies

1. Before Adjustment:

Supplies		Supplies Expense	
500			

Given

At year-end an inventory of supplies showed $100.

Required

a. How much is the adjustment for supplies?
b. Draw a transaction analysis box for this adjustment.
c. What will the balance of supplies be on the adjusted trial balance?

Adjustment for Prepaid Rent

2. Before Adjustment:

Prepaid Rent		Rent Expense	
600			

Given

At year-end rent expired is $400.

Required

a. How much is the adjustment for Prepaid Rent?
b. Draw a transaction analysis box for this adjustment.
c. What will be the balance of Prepaid Rent on the adjusted trial balance?

Adjustment for Depreciation

3. Before Adjustment:

Equip.		Accum. Dep., Equip.		Dep. Exp., Equip.	
5,000			2,000		

Given

At year-end depreciation on Equipment is $1,000.

Required

a. Which of the three T accounts above is not affected?

b. Which title is a contra-asset?

c. Draw a transaction analysis box for this adjustment.

d. What will be the balance of these three accounts on the adjusted trial balance?

Adjustment for Accrued Salaries

4. Before Adjustment:

Salaries Expense		Salaries Payable	
500			

Given

Accrued Salaries, $100.

Required

a. Draw a transaction analysis box for this adjustment.

b. What will be the balance of these two accounts on the adjusted trial balance?

Worksheet

5. From the following adjusted trial balance titles of a worksheet identify in which column each account will be listed on the last four columns of the worksheet.

(ID) Income statement Dr. column

(IC) Income statement Cr. column

(BD) Balance sheet Dr. column

(BC) Balance sheet Cr. column

ATB	ID	IC	BD	BC
a. Cash	_____	_____	_____	_____
b. Acccounts Receivable	_____	_____	_____	_____
c. Supplies	_____	_____	_____	_____
d. Prepaid Rent	_____	_____	_____	_____
e. Equipment	_____	_____	_____	_____
f. Accum. Depreciation	_____	_____	_____	_____
g. B., Capital	_____	_____	_____	_____
h. B., Withdrawals	_____	_____	_____	_____
i. Taxi Fees	_____	_____	_____	_____
j. Advertising Exp.	_____	_____	_____	_____
k. Office Supplies Exp.	_____	_____	_____	_____
l. Rent Expense	_____	_____	_____	_____
m. Depreciation Expense	_____	_____	_____	_____
n. Salaries Payable	_____	_____	_____	_____

6. From the following balance sheet (which was made from the worksheet and other financial reports) explain why the lettered numbers were not found on the worksheet. *Hint*: There are no debits or credits on the formal financial reports.

P. Pool
Balance Sheet
December 31, 19XX

Assets			*Liabilities and Owner's Equity*			
Cash		$5	Liabilities			
Accum. Rec.		3	Accounts Payable	$2		
Supplies		2	Salaries Payable	1		
Equipment	10		Total Liabilities		$3	(B)
Less: Accum. Dep.	4	6	Owner's Equity			
			P. Pool, Capital		13	(C)
			Total Liabilities and			
(A)Total Assets		$16	Owner's Equity		$16	(D)

Exercises

(The blank forms you need are on pages 4-9 and 4-10 of the *Study Guide and Working Papers.*)

4-1. Complete the following table.

Categorizing accounts.

Account	Category	Normal Balance	Which Financial Report(s) Found
Depreciation Expense			
Prepaid Insurance			
Equipment			
Accumulated Depreciation			
P. Mix, Capital			
P. Mix, Withdrawals			
Salaries Payable			
Advertising Expense			

Reviewing adjustments and the transaction analysis charts.

4-2. Use transaction analysis charts to analyze the following adjustments:

a. Depreciation on equipment, $600.

b. Rent expired, $100.

4-3. From the following adjustment data, calculate the adjustment amount and record appropriate debits or credits:

Recording adjusting entries.

a. Supplies purchased, $700.
Supplies on hand, $100.

b. Store equipment, $9,000.
Accumulated depreciation before adjustment, $700.
Depreciation expense, $100.

Preparing a worksheet.

4-4. From the following trial balance and adjustment data, complete a worksheet for A. Lerner as of December 31, 19XX:

a. Depreciation expense, equipment $1.00

b. Insurance expired 3.00

c. Store supplies on hand 2.00

A. LERNER TRIAL BALANCE DECEMBER 31, 19XX		
	Dr.	Cr.
Cash	700	
Accounts Receivable	200	
Prepaid Insurance	500	
Store Supplies	600	
Store Equipment	700	
Accumulated Depreciation, Equipment		200
Accounts Payable		200
A. Lerner, Capital		1700
A. Lerner, Withdrawals	600	
Revenue from Clients		2200
Rent Expense	400	
Wage Expense	600	
	4300	4300

d. Wages owed, but not paid for 3.00 (they are an expense in the old year)

Preparing financial reports from a worksheet.

4-5. From the completed worksheet in Exercise 4-4, prepare

a. An income statement for December.

b. A statement of owner's equity for December.

c. A balance sheet as of December 31, 19XX.

Group A Problems

(The blank forms you need are on pages 4-11 and 4-12 of the *Study Guide and Working Papers.*)

4A-1.

Completing a partial worksheet up to the adjusted trial balance.

GLOW'S FITNESS CENTRE TRIAL BALANCE DECEMBER 31, 19XX		
	Debit	Credit
Cash in Bank	380000	
Accounts Receivable	400000	
Gym Supplies	540000	
Gym Equipment	720000	
Accumulated Depreciation, Gym Equipment		275000
P. Glow, Capital		1040000
P. Glow, Withdrawals	300000	
Gym Fees		1130000
Rent Expense	90000	
Advertising Expense	15000	
	2445000	2445000

Given

The following adjustment data on December 31:

a. Gym supplies on hand, $1,000.

b. Depreciation taken on gym equipment, $700.

Complete a partial worksheet up to the adjusted trial balance.

4A-2. Below is the trial balance for Pat's Plumbing Service for December 31, 19XX.

Completing a worksheet.

PAT'S PLUMBING SERVICE
TRIAL BALANCE
DECEMBER 31, 19XX

	Dr.	Cr.
Cash in Bank	3056 00	
Accounts Receivable	600 00	
Prepaid Rent	800 00	
Plumbing Supplies	742 00	
Plumbing Equipment	1200 00	
Accumulated Depreciation, Plumbing Equipment		960 00
Accounts Payable		242 00
Pat Soll, Capital		2700 00
Plumbing Revenue		4356 00
Heat Expense	400 00	
Advertising Expense	200 00	
Wage Expense	1260 00	
	8258 00	8258 00

Adjustment data to update the trial balance:

a. Rent expired, $300.

b. Plumbing supplies on hand (remaining), $400.

c. Depreciation expense, plumbing equipment, $100.

d. Wages earned by workers but not paid or due until January, $150.

Required

Prepare a worksheet for Pat's Plumbing Service for the month of December.

4A-3. The following is the trial balance for Dan's Moving Co.

Comprehensive problem.

DAN'S MOVING CO.
TRIAL BALANCE
OCTOBER 31, 19XX

	Dr.	Cr.
Cash	4000 00	
Prepaid Insurance	2500 00	
Moving Supplies	1200 00	
Moving Truck	11000 00	
Accumulated Depreciation, Moving Truck		8000 00
Accounts Payable		2768 00
D. Roe., Capital		5442 00
D. Roe., Withdrawals	1400 00	
Revenue from Moving		9000 00
Wages Expense	3712 00	
Rent Expense	1080 00	
Advertising Expense	318 00	
	25210 00	25210 00

Adjustment data to update trial balance:

a. Insurance expired, $600.

b. Moving supplies on hand, $700.

c. Depreciation on moving truck, $300.

d. Wages earned but unpaid, $400.

Required

1. Complete a worksheet for Dan's Moving Co. for the month of October.
2. Prepare an income statement for October, a statement of owner's equity for October, and a balance sheet as of October 31, 19XX.

4A-4.

Comprehensive problem.

DICK'S REPAIR SERVICE
TRIAL BALANCE
NOVEMBER 30, 19XX

	Dr.	Cr.
Cash	3 2 0 0 00	
Prepaid Insurance	4 0 0 0 00	
Repair Supplies	4 6 0 0 00	
Repair Equipment	3 0 0 0 00	
Accumulated Depreciation, Repair Equipment		7 0 0 00
Accounts Payable		5 5 7 0 00
D. Horn, Capital		3 8 0 0 00
Revenue from Repairs		7 0 0 0 00
Wages Expense	1 8 0 0 00	
Rent Expense	3 6 0 00	
Advertising Expense	1 1 0 00	
	17 0 7 0 00	17 0 7 0 00

Adjustment data to update trial balance:

a. Insurance expired, $700.

b. Repair supplies on hand, $3,000.

c. Depreciation on repair equipment, $200.

d. Wages earned but unpaid, $400.

Required

1. Complete a worksheet for Dick's Repair Service for the month of November.
2. Prepare an income statement for November, a statement of owner's equity for November, and a balance sheet as of November 30, 19XX.

Group B Problems

(The blank forms you need are on pages 4-11 and 4-12 of the *Study Guide and Working Papers.*)

Completing a partial worksheet up to adjusted trial balance.

4B-1. Please complete a partial worksheet up to the adjusted trial balance using the following adjustment data:

a. Gym supplies on hand, $2,600.

b. Depreciation taken on gym equipment, $500.

GLOW'S FITNESS CENTRE
TRIAL BALANCE
DECEMBER 31, 19XX

	Dr.	Cr.
Cash	200000	
Accounts Receivable	200000	
Gym Supplies	420000	
Gym Equipment	800000	
Accumulated Depreciation, Gym Equipment		570000
P. Glow, Capital		1100000
P. Glow, Withdrawals	100000	
Gym Fees		140000
Rent Expense	80000	
Advertising Expense	10000	
	1810000	1810000

Completing a worksheet.

4B-2. Given the following trial balance and adjustment data of Pat's Plumbing Service, prepare a worksheet for the month of December.

PAT'S PLUMBING SERVICE
TRIAL BALANCE
DECEMBER 31, 19XX

	Dr.	Cr.
Cash in Bank	39600	
Accounts Receivable	28400	
Prepaid Rent	40000	
Plumbing Supplies	31000	
Plumbing Equipment	100000	
Accumulated Depreciation, Plumbing Equipment		20000
Accounts Payable		34600
Pat Soll, Capital		45600
Plumbing Revenue		468000
Heat Expense	63200	
Advertising Expense	120000	
Wages Expense	146000	
Total	568200	568200

Adjustment Data

a. Plumbing supplies on hand, $60.
b. Rent expired, $150.
c. Depreciation on plumbing equipment, $200.
d. Wages earned but unpaid, $115.

Comprehensive problem.

4B-3. Using the following trial balance and adjustment data of Dan's Moving Co., prepare

1. A worksheet for the month of October.
2. An income statement for October, a statement of owner's equity for October, and a balance sheet as of October 31, 19XX.

Adjustment Data

a. Insurance expired $600
b. Moving supplies on hand $310
c. Depreciation on moving truck $580
d. Wages earned but unpaid $410

DAN'S MOVING CO. TRIAL BALANCE OCTOBER 31, 19XX		
	Dr.	Cr.
Cash	392000	
Prepaid Insurance	328800	
Moving Supplies	140000	
Moving Truck	1065800	
Accumulated Depreciation, Moving Truck		366000
Accounts Payable		131200
D. Roe, Capital		1748200
D. Roe, Withdrawals	424000	
Revenue from Moving		816200
Wages Expense	571200	
Rent Expense	108000	
Advertising Expense	31800	
	3061600	3061600

Comprehensive problem.

4B-4. As the bookkeeper of Dick's Repair Service, use the information that follows to prepare:

1. A worksheet for the month of November.

2. An income statement for November, a statement of owner's equity for November, and a balance sheet as of November 30, 19XX.

DICK'S REPAIR SERVICE TRIAL BALANCE NOVEMBER 30, 19XX		
	Dr.	Cr.
Cash	320400	
Prepaid Insurance	400000	
Repair Supplies	77000	
Repair Equipment	310600	
Accumulated Depreciation, Repair Equipment		65000
Accounts Payable		190400
D. Horn, Capital		625800
Revenue from Repairs		563400
Wages Expense	160000	
Rent Expense	156000	
Advertising Expense	20600	
	1444600	1444600

Adjustment Data

a. Insurance expired $300

b. Repair supplies on hand $170

c. Depreciation on repair equipment $250

d. Wages earned but unpaid $106

Group C Problems

Completing a partial worksheet up to adjusted trial balance.

4C-1. Please complete a partial worksheet up to the adjusted trial balance for Ellen's Art Studio using the following adjustment data:

a. Art supplies on hand, $780.

b. Depreciation taken on equipment, $375.

ELLEN'S ART STUDIO TRIAL BALANCE DECEMBER 31, 19XX		
	Dr.	Cr.
Cash in Bank	1 4 1 0 00	
Accounts Receivable	9 2 0 00	
Art Supplies	1 8 7 0 00	
Equipment	3 9 5 0 00	
Accumulated Depreciation, Equipment		1 8 7 5 00
Ellen Day, Capital		5 6 0 1 00
Ellen Day, Withdrawals	8 5 0 00	
Fees Earned		3 2 5 0 00
Rent Expense	9 0 0 00	
Advertising Expense	3 7 0 00	
Utilities Expense	4 5 6 00	
Totals	10 7 2 6 00	10 7 2 6 00

Completing a worksheet.

4C-2. Given the following trial balance and adjustment data of Carl's Carpentry Service, your task is to prepare a worksheet for the month of November.

CARL'S CARPENTRY SERVICE TRIAL BALANCE NOVEMBER 30, 19XX		
	Dr.	Cr.
Cash in Bank	9 2 4 00	
Accounts Receivable	8 2 0 00	
Prepaid Rent	6 0 0 00	
Carpentry Supplies	7 4 2 00	
Carpentry Equipment	3 8 0 0 00	
Accumulated Depreciation, Carpentry Equipment		2 4 5 0 00
Accounts Payable		3 8 4 00
Carl Weider, Capital		2 7 4 8 00
Carpentry Service Revenue		4 2 5 2 00
Advertising Expense	5 1 0 00	
Utilities Expense	6 7 8 00	
Wages Expense	1 7 6 0 00	
Totals	9 8 3 4 00	9 8 3 4 00

Adjustment Data

a. Carpentry supplies on hand, $320.
b. Rent expired, $300.
c. Depreciation on heating equipment, $700.
d. Wages earned but unpaid, $245.

Comprehensive problem.

4C-3. Using the following trial balance and adjustment data of Fordham's Repair Co., prepare

1. A worksheet for the month of October.
2. An income statement for October, a statement of owner's equity for October, and a balance sheet as of October 31, 19XX.

Adjustment Data

a. Insurance expired, $486
b. Repair supplies on hand, $820.
c. Depreciation on Repair Equipment, $680.

d. Depreciation on Building, $540.

e. Wages earned but unpaid, $926.

FORDHAM'S REPAIR CO.
TRIAL BALANCE
OCTOBER 31, 19XX

	Dr.	Cr.
Cash in Bank	132600	
Prepaid Insurance	94200	
Repair Supplies	114800	
Repair Equipment	846000	
Building	5000000	
Accumulated Depreciation, Repair Equipment		387000
Accumulated Depreciation, Building		1492000
Accounts Payable		72400
Vivian Fordham, Capital		4308500
Vivian Fordham, Withdrawals	840000	
Repair Fees Revenue		1590000
Wages Expense	589000	
Utilities Expense	84100	
Advertising Expense	149200	
Totals	7849900	7849900

Comprehensive problem.

4C-4. As the bookkeeper of Vanessa's Internet Access Service, use the information that follows to prepare

1. A worksheet for the month of August.
2. An income statement for August, a statement of owner's equity for August, and a balance sheet as of August 31, 19XX.

Adjustment Data

a. Insurance expired, $318.

b. Computer supplies on hand, $215.

c. Depreciation on computer equipment, $826.

d. Wages earned but unpaid, $427.

e. Advertising bill received, not paid, $108.

VANESSA'S INTERNET ACCESS
TRIAL BALANCE
AUGUST 31, 19XX

	Dr.	Cr.
Cash in Bank	22800	
Prepaid Insurance	78000	
Computer Supplies	42600	
Computer Equipment	1148000	
Accumulated Depreciation, Computer Equipment		415200
Accounts Payable		84000
Vanessa Roberts, Capital		235700
Vanessa Roberts, Withdrawals	141000	
Revenue from Services Provided		1267000
Wages Expense	326000	
Rent Expense	148500	
Advertising Expense	95000	
Totals	2001900	2001900

REAL WORLD APPLICATIONS

4R-1.

TO:	Hal Hogan, Bookkeeper
FROM:	Pete Tennant, V. P.
RE:	Adjustments for year ended December 31, 19XX

Hal, here is the information you requested. Please supply me with the adjustments needed ASAP. Also, please put in writing why we need to do these adjustments.

Thanks

Attached to memo:

a. Insurance data:

Policy No.	*Date of Policy Purchase*	*Policy Length*	*Cost*
100	November 1 of previous year	4 years	$480
200	May 1 of current year	2 years	600
300	September 1 of current year	1 year	240

b. Rent data: Prepaid rent had a $500 balance at beginning of year. An additional $400 of rent was paid in advance in June. At year-end, $200 of rent had expired.

c. Revenue data: Accrued storage fees of $500 were earned but uncollected and unrecorded at year end.

4R-2.

Hint: Unearned Rent is a liability on the balance sheet.

On Friday, Harry Swag's boss asks him to prepare a special report, due on Monday at 8 a.m. Harry gathers the following material in his briefcase:

		December 31	
		19X1	*19X2*
Prepaid Advertising		$300	$600
Interest Payable		150	350
Unearned Rent		500	300
Cash paid for: Advertising	$1,900		
Interest	1,500		
Cash received for: Rent	2,300		

As his best friend, could you help Harry show the amounts that are to be reported on the 19X2 income statement for (a) Advertising Expense, (b) Interest Expense, and (c) Rent Fees Earned. Please explain in writing why unearned rent is considered a liability.

YOU make the call

Critical Thinking/Ethical Case

4R-3.

Janet Fox, President of Angel Co., went to a tax seminar. One of the speakers at the seminar advised the audience to put off showing expenses until next year because doing so would allow them to take advantage of a new tax law. When Janet returned to the office, she called in her accountant, Frieda O'Riley. She told Frieda to forget about making any adjustments for salaries in the old year so more expenses could be shown in the new year. Frieda told her that putting off these expenses would not follow generally accepted accounting procedures. Janet said she should do it anyway. You make the call. Write your specific recommendations to Frieda.

ACCOUNTING RECALL

A CUMULATIVE APPROACH

THIS EXAM REVIEWS CHAPTERS 1 THROUGH 4

Pages 4-18 and 4-19 of the *Study Guide and Working Papers* have the forms to complete this exam, as well as worked-out solutions. The page references next to each question identify what page to turn back to if you answer the question incorrectly.

PART I Vocabulary Review

Match the terms to the appropriate definition or phrase.

Page Ref.	Term		Definition
(131)	1. Prepaid rent	A.	Estimated value of an asset after all depreciation taken
(134)	2. Accrued salaries	B.	Earned but unpaid
(131)	3. Depreciation expense	C.	Actual cost at time of purchase
(132)	4. Accumulated depreciation	D.	Columnar device
(138)	5. Normal balance	E.	Rent paid in advance
(132)	6. Residual value	F.	Cost — accumulated depreciation
(130)	7. Mixed account	G.	Supplies
(128)	8. Worksheet	H.	Shown on the income statement
(133)	9. Book value	I.	Side that increases it
(131)	10. Historical cost	J.	Contra-asset

PART II True or False (Accounting Theory)

(129) 11. Adjustments are the result of external transactions.

(130) 12. Adjustments affect only the balance sheet.

(132) 13. Accumulated depreciation and equipment will both go on the balance sheet.

(132) 14. The normal balance of accumulated depreciation is a debit.

(142) 15. All financial reports could be prepared from a worksheet.

PART III Applications Problem (4–18)

From the following prepare a worksheet and the three financial reports.

Pete Sove
Trial Balance
December 31, 19XX

Cash	20	
Accounts Receivable	25	
Prepaid Insurance	19	
Store Supplies	18	
Store Equipment	40	
Accumulated Depreciation, Equipment		10
Accounts Payable		30
Pete Sove, Capital		52
Pete Sove, Withdrawals	2	
Fees Earned		49
Rent Expense	10	
Wages Expense	7	
	141	141

Adjustment Data

a. Insurance expired	$4
b. Supplies on hand	4
c. Depreciation expense	5
d. Wages owed, but not paid for	6

COMPUTER WORKSHOP

COMPUTERIZED ACCOUNTING APPLICATION FOR CHAPTER 4

PART A: Compound Journal Entries, Adjusting Entries, and Financial Reports
PART B: Backup Procedures

Before starting on this assignment, read and complete the tasks discussed in Parts A, B, and F of Appendix B, "Computerized Accounting," at the back of this book and complete the "Computerized Accounting Application" assignment in the Computer Workshop at the end of Chapter 3. If you are using ACCPAC Plus software, your instructor will provide necessary details.

Part A: Compound Journal Entries, Adjusting Entries, and Financial Reports

Open the Company Data Files

1. Start Windows; insert your Student Data Files disk into disk drive A or B; then double-click on the CA-Simply Accounting icon. The CA-Simply Accounting-Open File dialogue box will appear.
2. Enter one of the following paths into the **Open file name** text box:
   - A:\ZELL.ASC (if you are storing your student data files on the disk in drive A).
   - B:\ZELL.ASC (if you are storing your student data files on the disk in drive B).
3. Click on the **Open** button; enter "12/31/99" into the **Using date for this session** text box; then click on the **OK** button. Click on the **OK** button in response to the message "The date entered is more than one week past your previous **Using** date of 12/1/99." The Company Window for Zell will appear.

Add Your Name to the Company Name

4. Click on the Company Window Setup menu; then click on Company Information. The Company Information dialogue box will appear. Insert your name in place of the text "Your Name" in the **Name** text box. Click on the **OK** button to return to the Company Window.

How to Record a Compound Journal Entry

5. In the Computerized Accounting Application assignment in Chapter 3 you learned how to record journal entries in the General Journal dialogue box. Compound journal entries can also be recorded in the General Journal dialogue box. The owner of The Zell Company has made an investment in the business consisting of $5,000 in cash and an automobile valued at $12,000. Open the General Journal dialogue box. Enter "Memo" into the **Source** text box; press the TAB key; enter "12/1/99" into the **Date** text box; press the TAB key; enter "Initial investment by owner" into the **Comment** text box; then press the TAB key. The flashing insertion point will be positioned in the **Account** text box.
6. With the flashing insertion point positioned in the **Account** text box, press the ENTER key. The Select Account dialogue box will appear. Double-click on 1110 Cash; enter "5000" into the **Debits** text box; then press the TAB key.
7. Press the ENTER key to bring up the Select Account dialogue box. Double-click on 1230 Automobile. The program will offer 5000.00 as a default amount in the **Credits** text box. The **Credits** amount remains highlighted. You do not want to accept the default. To override the default, enter "-12000" (Be sure to enter the minus sign!); then press the TAB key. The 12000.00 amount will move to the **Debits** text box.
8. Press the ENTER key to bring up the Select Account dialogue box; then double-click on 3110 Owner's Capital. The program will offer the total of the **Debits** portion of the compound journal entry (17000.00) as a default amount in the **Credits** text box. The **Credits** amount remains highlighted. Press the TAB key to accept the default

Credits amount. This completes the data you need to enter into the General Journal dialogue box to record the compound journal entry for the initial investment by the owner. Your screen should look like this:

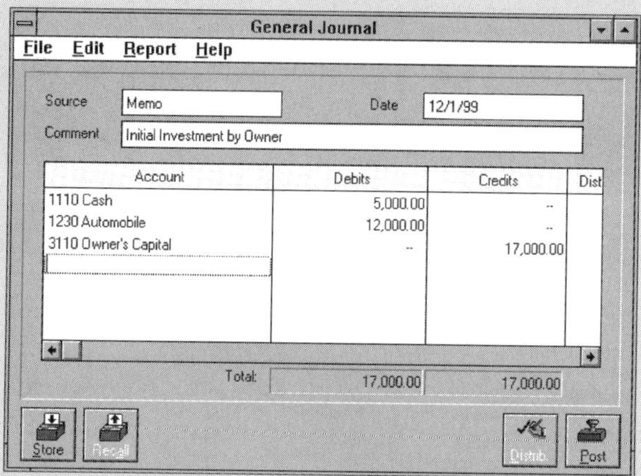

Review the Compound Journal Entry

9. Click on the General Journal Report menu; then click on Display General Journal Entry. Review the compound journal entry for accuracy noting any errors.

10. Close the General Journal Entry window; then make any editing corrections required.

Post the Entry

11. After verifying that the compound journal entry is correct, click on the Post button to post this transaction.

Record Additional Transactions

12. Record the following additional journal entries (enter "Memo" into the **Source** text box for each transaction; then enter the **Date** listed for each transaction):

1999

Dec.	1	Paid rent for two months in advance, $500.
	3	Purchased office supplies ($200) and office equipment ($1,100) both on account.
	9	Billed a customer for fees earned, $2,000.
	13	Paid telephone bill, $150.
	20	Owner withdrew $475 from the business for personal use.
	27	Received $600 for fees earned.
	30	Paid salaries expense, $800.

Display and Print a General Journal and Trial Balance

13. After you have posted the additional journal entries, close the General Journal; then print the following reports:

    a. General Journal (By posting date, All ledger entries, Start: 12/1/99, Finish: 12/31/99).

    b. Trial Balance As at 12/31/99.

14. Review your printed reports. If you have made an error in a posted journal entry, see Part C of Appendix B for information on how to correct the error.

How to Record Adjusting Journal Entries

15. Open the General Journal; then record adjusting journal entries based on the following adjustment data (Source: Memo; Date: 12/31/99; Comment: Adjusting entry):

    a. One month's rent has expired.

    b. An inventory shows $25 of office supplies remaining.

    c. Depreciation on office equipment, $50.

    d. Depreciation on automobile, $150.

Display and Print a General Journal, General Ledger, and Trial Balance

16. After you have posted the adjusting journal entries, close the General Journal; then print the following reports:

    a. General Journal (By posting date, All ledger entries, Start: 12/31/99, Finish: 12/31/99).

    b. General Ledger Report (Start: 12/1/99, Finish: 12/31/99, Select All).

    c. Trial Balance As at 12/31/99.

17. Review your printed reports. If you have made an error in a posted journal entry, see Part C of Appendix B for information on how to correct the error.

How to Display and Print an Income Statement

18. Click on the Company Window Report menu; then click on Income Statement. The Income Statement Options dialogue box will appear asking you to define the information you want displayed. Leave the **Start** text box date set at 12/1/99; leave the **Finish** text box date set at 12/31/99; then click on the **OK** button. Your screen will look like this:

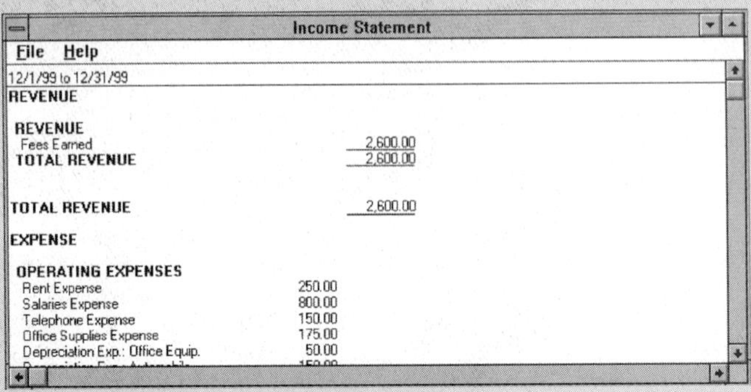

19. The scroll bar can be used to advance the display to view other portions of the report.

20. Click on the Income Statement File menu; then click on Print to print the Income Statement.

How to Display and Print a Balance Sheet

21. Close the Income Statement window; click on the Company Window Report menu; then click on Balance Sheet. The Balance Sheet Options dialogue box will appear asking you to define the information you want displayed. Leave the **As at** date set at 12/31/99; then click on the **OK** button. Your screen will look like this:

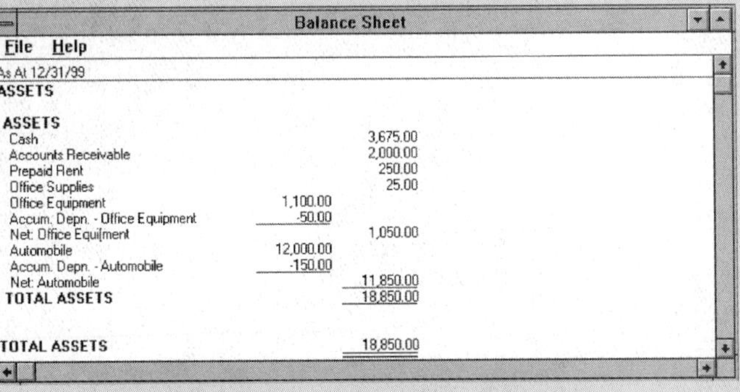

22. Use the scroll bar to advance the display to the Owner's Equity section of the Balance Sheet. Note that the program has included the Statement of Owner's Equity information directly in the Owner's Equity section of the Balance Sheet.

23. Click on the Balance Sheet File menu; click on Print to print the Balance Sheet; then close the Balance Sheet window to return to the Company Window.

Exit from the Program

24. Click on the Company Window File menu; then click on Exit to end the current work session and return to your Windows desktop.

PART B Backup Procedures

Companies that use computerized accounting systems make frequent backup copies of their accounting data for two major reasons:

1. To ensure that they have a copy of the accounting data in case the current data becomes damaged.
2. To permit the printing of historical reports after the **Using** date has been advanced to a new month.

The methods used to make backup copies of company data files vary greatly. Large companies may back up daily using sophisticated high-speed tape backup devices while small companies may back up weekly on floppy disks using the back-up program supplied with their operating system.

Normally all backup copies of a company's data files are stored on a storage medium separate from the original data files in case the original storage medium becomes damaged. However, for the purposes of this introduction to computerized accounting systems, you will be using the working copy of your Student Data Files disk to store backup copies of a company's data files. You will be using a backup method known as the Save As method.

How to Make a Backup Copy of a Company's Data Files

1. Start Windows; insert your Student Data Files disk into disk drive A or B; then double-click on the CA-Simply Accounting icon. The CA-Simply Accounting-Open File dialogue box will appear.
2. Enter one of the following paths into the **Open file name** text box:
   - A:\ZELL.ASC (if you are storing your student data files on the disk in drive A).
   - B:\ZELL.ASC (if you are storing your student data files on the disk in drive B).
3. Click on the **Open** button; leave the **Using date for this session** set at 12/31/99; then click on the **OK** button. The Company Window for Zell will appear on your screen.
4. Click on the Company Window File menu; then click on Save As. The Save As dialogue box will appear. Enter one of the following new file names into the **Save file as** text box:
   - A:\ZELLDEC.ASC (if you are storing your student data files on the disk in drive A).
   - B:\ZELLDEC.ASC (if you are storing your student data files on the disk in drive B).
5. Click on the **Save** button. Note that the company name in the Company Window has changed from Zell to Zelldec. Click on the Company Window File menu again; then click on Save As. Enter one of the following new file names into the **Save file as** text box:
   - A:\ZELL.ASC (if you are storing your student data files on the disk in drive A).
   - B:\ZELL.ASC (if you are storing your student data files on the disk in drive B).
6. Click on the **Save** button. Click on the **Yes** button in response to the question "Replace existing data files with the same name?" Note that the company name in the Company Window has changed back from Zelldec to Zell.
7. You now have two sets of company data files for The Zell Company on your Student Data Files disk. The current data is stored under the file name ZELL.ASC. The backup data for December is stored under the file name ZELLDEC.ASC.

Exit from the Program

8. Click on the Company Window File menu; then click on Exit to end the current work session and return to your Windows desktop.
9. For information on when you might want to use the backup copy of a company's data files, see Part E of Appendix B at the back of this book.

Complete the Report Transmittal

10. Complete the Zell Company Report Transmittal located in Appendix A in your *Study Guide and Working Papers.*

Note: If you are using ACCPAC Plus accounting software, please follow the backup instructions given by your instructor.

THE ACCOUNTING CYCLE COMPLETED

5

ADJUSTING, CLOSING, AND POST-CLOSING TRIAL BALANCE

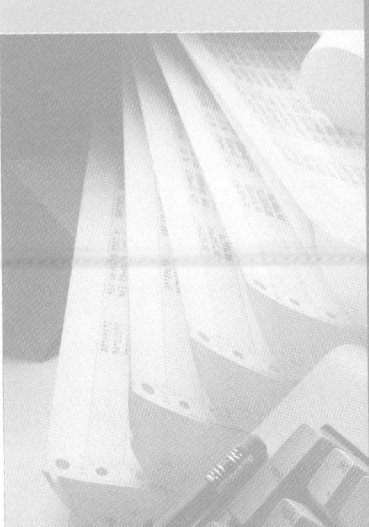

Chapter Objectives

- **Journalizing and posting adjusting entries. (p. 169)**
- **Journalizing and posting closing entries. (p. 173)**
- **Preparing a post-closing trial balance. (p. 183)**

In Chapters 3 and 4 we completed these steps of the accounting cycle for Clark's Word Processing Services:

Remember, for ease of presentation we are using a month as the accounting cycle for Clark. In the "real" world, the cycle can be any time period that does not exceed one year.

Step 1: Business transactions occurred and generated source documents.

Step 2: Business transactions were analyzed and recorded into a journal.

Step 3: Information was posted or transferred from journal to ledger.

Step 4: A trial balance was prepared.

Step 5: A worksheet was completed.

Step 6: Financial statements were prepared.

This chapter covers the following steps. This will complete Clark's accounting cycle for the month of May:

Step 7: Journalizing and posting adjusting entries.

Step 8: Journalizing and posting closing entries.

Step 9: Preparing a post-closing trial balance.

LEARNING UNIT 5-1

Journalizing and Posting Adjusting Entries: Step 7 of the Accounting Cycle

RECORDING JOURNAL ENTRIES FROM THE WORKSHEET

At this point, many ledger accounts are *not up to date.*

Purpose of adjusting entries.

The information in the worksheet is up to date. The financial reports prepared from that information can give the business's management and other interested parties a good idea of where the business stands as of a particular date. The problem is that the worksheet is an informal report. The information concerning the adjustments has not been placed into the journal, or posted to the ledger accounts. This means that the books are not up to date and ready for the next accounting cycle to begin. For example, the ledger shows $1,200 of prepaid rent (p. 95), but the balance sheet we prepared in Chapter 4 shows an $800 balance. Essentially, the worksheet is a tool for preparing financial reports. Now we must use the adjustment columns of the worksheet as a basis for bringing the ledger up to date. We do this by **adjusting journal entries** (see Figure 5-1). Again, the updating must be done before the next accounting period starts. For Clark's Word Processing Services, the next period begins on June 1.

Figure 5-2 shows the adjusting journal entries for Clark taken from the adjustments section of the worksheet. Once the adjusting journal entries are posted to the ledger, the accounts making up the financial statements that were prepared from the worksheet will equal the updated ledger. (Keep in mind that this is the same journal we have been using.) Let's look at some simplified T accounts to show how Clark's ledger looked before and after the adjustments were posted (see adjustments A to D on pp. 170 to 172).

Account Titles	Trial Balance Dr.	Trial Balance Cr.	Adjustments Dr.	Adjustments Cr.
Cash	615500			
Accounts Receivable	500000			
Office Supplies	60000			(A) 50000
Prepaid Rent	120000			(B) 40000
Word Processing Equipment	600000			
Accounts Payable		335000		
B. Clark, Capital		1000000		
B. Clark, Withdrawals	62500			
Word Processing Fees		800000		
Office Salaries Expense	130000		(D) 35000	
Advertising Expense	25000			
Telephone Expense	22000			
	2135000	2135000		
Office Supplies Expense			(A) 50000	
Rent Expense			(B) 40000	
Depreciation Exp., W.P. Equip.			(C) 8000	
Accum. Dep., W.P. Equip.				(C) 8000
Salaries Payable				(D) 35000
			133000	133000

FIGURE 5-1
Journalizing and Posting Adjustments from the Adjustments Section of the Worksheet

Adjustment A

Before posting: Prepaid Rent 114: 600 | — Office Supplies Expense 514: (no entries)

After posting: Office Supplies 114: 600 | 500 — Office Supplies Expense 514: 500 |

CLARK'S WORD PROCESSING SERVICES
GENERAL JOURNAL

Page 2

Date		Account Titles and Description	PR	Dr.	Cr.
		Adjusting Entries			
May	31	Office Supplies Expense	514	50000	
		Office Supplies	114		50000
		Office Supplies used up			
	31	Rent Expense	515	40000	
		Prepaid Rent	115		40000
		Rent expired			
	31	Depreciation Expense, W.P. Equip.	516	8000	
		Accumulated Depreciation, W.P. Equip.	122		8000
		Estimated depreciation of asset			
	31	Office Salaries Expense	511	35000	
		Salaries Payable	212		35000
		Accrued salary to May 31			

FIGURE 5-2
Adjusting Journal Entries

Adjustment B

Before posting:

Prepaid Rent 115		Rent Expense 515	
1,200			

After posting:

Prepaid Rent 115		Rent Expense 515	
1,200	400	400	

Adjustment C

Before posting:

Word Processing Equipment 121		Depreciation Expense, W. P. Equipment 516		Accumulated Depreciation, W. P. Equipment 122	
6,000					

After posting:

Word Processing Equipment 121		Depreciation Expense, W. P. Equipment 516		Accumulated Depreciation, W. P. Equipment 122	
6,000		80			80

TIMOTHY WALKES

WORK-STUDY PROGRAM PARTICIPANT

When he entered university, Timothy Walkes knew he wouldn't be a traditional full-time student as he worked to fulfill his educational goals. "Luckily," he says, "I was able to enter a program in which I studied one semester and worked one semester. I was very fortunate to work at General Motors, where I started as a payroll clerk and worked my way up."

Timothy liked being in the business world while he was in school. "I was able to apply what I learned in school right away. The college accounting course reinforced what I learned on the job, and for the most part the job reinforced what I learned in the course. The best part was being able to go back to the classroom and relate my work experiences to the class. In some cases, I had the opportunity to tell the professor that General Motors handled some things—straight-line depreciation, for instance—differently from the way they were taught in class. I got to explain General Motors' policy, and that was an eye-opener for the professor."

"I felt that I was a role model," he says. "The other students looked to my real-world experience, and I especially enjoyed helping the ones who wanted to work and take classes at the same time. But there's a very practical payoff, too. I've moved and as I look for a new job, I'm finding would-be employers are impressed with my combination of business experience and academic background."

What advice does Timothy have for college accounting students? "Learn all you can about computers. Computer literacy is important in your field, whether you become a bookkeeper or are doing general ledger accounting."

This last adjustment shows the same balances for Depreciation Expense and Accumulated Depreciation. However, in subsequent adjustments the Accumulated Depreciation balance will keep getting larger, but the debit to Depreciation Expense and the credit to Accumulated Depreciation will be the same. We will see why in a moment.

Adjustment D

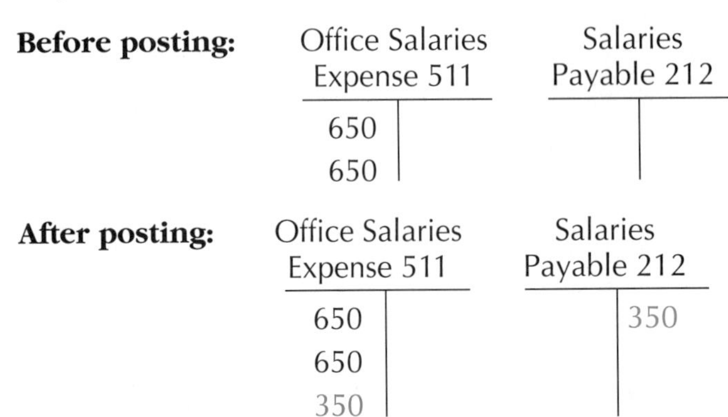

LEARNING UNIT 5-1 REVIEW

AT THIS POINT you should be able to

- Define and state the purpose of adjusting entries. (p. 169)
- Journalize adjusting entries from the worksheet. (p. 170)
- Post journalized adjusting entries to the ledger. (p. 170)
- Compare specific ledger accounts before and after posting of the journalized adjusting entries. (p. 170)

SELF-REVIEW QUIZ 5-1

(The blank forms you need are on pages 5-1 and 5-2 of the *Study Guide and Working Papers.*)

Turn to the worksheet of P. Logan (p. 140) and (1) journalize and post the adjusting entries and (2) compare the adjusted ledger accounts before and after the adjustments are posted. T accounts are provided in your *Study Guide* with beginning balances.

Solution to Self-Review Quiz 5-1

Page 2

Date		Account Titles and Description	PR	Dr.	Cr.
		Adjusting Entries			
May	31	Depreciation Expense, Store Equip.	511	1 00	
		Accumulated Depreciation, Store Equip.	122		1 00
		Estimated depreciation of equipment			
	31	Insurance Expense	516	2 00	
		Prepaid Insurance	116		2 00
		Insurance expired			
	31	Supplies Expense	514	4 00	
		Store Supplies	114		4 00
		Store Supplies used			
	31	Salaries Expense	512	3 00	
		Salaries Payable	212		3 00
		Accrued salaries payable			

Partial Ledger

Before Posting

Depreciation Expense, Store Equipment 511	

Accumulated Depreciation, Store Equipment 122	
	4

Prepaid Insurance 116	
3	

Insurance Expense 516	

Store Supplies 114	
5	

Supplies Expense 514	

Salaries Expense 512	
8	

Salaries Payable 212	

After Posting

Depreciation Expense, Store Equipment 511	
1	

Accumulated Depreciation, Store Equipment 122	
	4
	1

Prepaid Insurance 116	
3	2

Insurance Expense 516	
2	

Store Supplies 114	
5	4

Supplies Expense 514	
4	

Salaries Expense 512	
8	
3	

Salaries Payable 212	
	3

LEARNING UNIT 5-2

Journalizing and Posting Closing Entries: Step 8 of the Accounting Cycle

To make recording of the next fiscal year's transactions easier, a mechanical step, called **closing,** is taken by Clark's accountant. Closing is used to end — or close off — the revenue, expense, and withdrawal accounts at the end of the accounting period. The information needed to complete closing entries will be found in the income statement and balance sheet sections of the worksheet.

To make it easier to understand this process, we will first look at the difference between temporary (nominal) accounts and permanent (real) accounts.

Here is the expanded accounting equation we used in an earlier chapter:

Assets = Liabilities + Capital − Withdrawals + Revenues − Expenses

Permanent accounts are found on the balance sheet.

Three of the items in that equation — assets, liabilities, and capital — are known as **real** or **permanent accounts**, because their balances are carried over from one accounting period to another. The other three items — withdrawals, revenue, and expenses — are called **nominal** or **temporary accounts,** because their balances are not carried over from one accounting period to another. Instead, their balances are set at zero at the beginning of each accounting period. This allows us to accumulate new data about revenue, expenses, and withdrawals, in the new accounting period. The process of closing summarizes the effects of the temporary accounts on capital for that period using **closing journal entries.** When the closing process is complete, the accounting equation will be reduced to:

Assets = Liabilities + Ending Capital

After all closing entries are journalized and posted to the ledger, all temporary accounts have a zero balance in the ledger. Closing is a step-by-step process.

If you look back to page 142 in Chapter 4, you will see that we have calculated the new capital on the balance sheet to be $14,275 for Clark's Word Processing Services. But before the mechanical closing procedures are journalized and posted, the capital account of Clark in the ledger is only $10,000 (Chapter 3, page 95). Let's look now at how to journalize and post closing entries.

How to journalize closing entries

There are four steps to be performed in journalizing closing entries:

An Income Summary is a temporary account located in the chart of accounts under owner's equity. It does not have a normal balance of a debit or a credit.

Step 1: Clear the revenue balance and transfer it to Income Summary. **Income Summary** is a temporary account in the ledger needed for closing. At the end of the closing process there will be no balance in Income Summary.

Revenue → Income Summary

Step 2: Clear the individual expense balances and transfer them to Income Summary.

Expenses → Income Summary

Sometimes, closing the accounts is referred to as "clearing the accounts."

Step 3: Clear the balance in Income Summary and transfer it to Capital.

Income Summary → Capital

Step 4: Clear the balance in Withdrawals and transfer it to Capital.

Withdrawals → Capital

Figure 5-3 is a visual representation of these four steps. Keep in mind that this information must first be journalized and then posted to the appropriate ledger accounts. The worksheet presented in Figure 5-4 contains all the figures we will need for the closing process.

Step 1: Clear Revenue Balance and Transfer to Income Summary

Here is what is in the ledger before closing entries are journalized and posted:

Word Processing Fees 411	
	8,000

Income Summary 313	

Don't forget two goals of closing:

1. Clear all temporary accounts in ledger.
2. Update capital to a new balance that reflects a summary of all the temporary accounts.

All numbers used in the closing process can be found on the worksheet. Note that the *account* Income Summary is *not* on the worksheet.

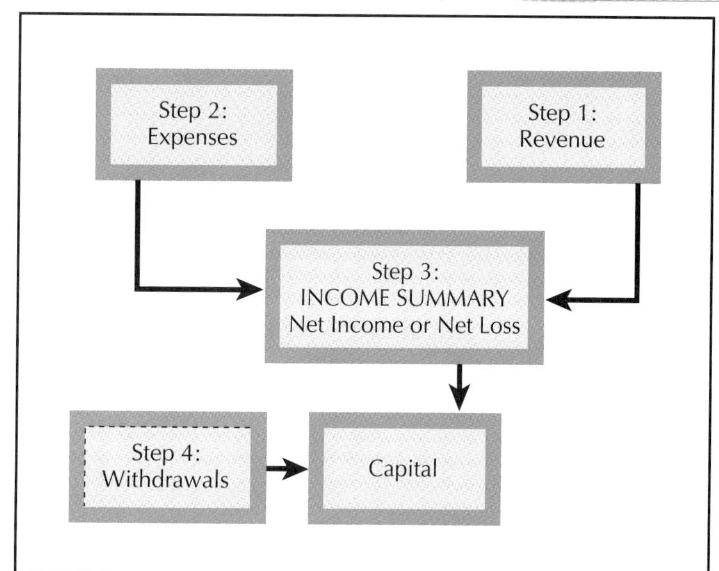

FIGURE 5-3
Four Steps in Journalizing Closing Entries

The income statement section on the worksheet below shows that the Word Processing Fees have a credit balance of $8,000. To close or clear this to zero, a debit of $8,000 is needed. But if we add an amount to the debit side, we must also add a credit — so we add $8,000 on the credit side of the Income Summary.

Account Titles	Income Statement Dr.	Income Statement Cr.	Balance Sheet Dr.	Balance Sheet Cr.
Cash			6155 00	
Accounts Receivable			5000 00	
Office Supplies			100 00	
Prepaid Rent			800 00	
Word Processing Equipment			6000 00	
Accounts Payable				3350 00
B. Clark, Capital		Step 1		10000 00
B. Clark, Withdrawals	Step 2		625 00	
Word Processing Fees		8000 00		
Office Salaries Expense	1650 00		Step 4	
Advertising Expense	250 00			
Telephone Expense	220 00			
Office Supplies Expense	500 00			
Rent Expense	400 00			
Depreciation Exp., W.P. Equip.	80 00			
Accum. Dep., W.P. Equip.		Step 3		80 00
Salaries Payable				350 00
	3100 00	8000 00	18680 00	13780 00
Net Income	4900 00			4900 00
	8000 00	8000 00	18680 00	18680 00

FIGURE 5-4
Closing Figures on the Worksheet

The following is the journalized closing entry for step 1:

May	31	Word Processing Fees	411	800000	
		Income Summary	313		800000
		To close income account			

This is what Word Processing Fees and Income Summary should look like in the ledger after the first step of closing entries is journalized and posted:

Word Processing Fees 411	
8,000 Closing	8,000 Revenue

Income Summary 313	
	8,000 Revenue

Note that the revenue balance is cleared to zero and transferred to Income Summary, a temporary account also located in the ledger.

Step 2: Clear Individual Expense Balances and Transfer the Total to Income Summary

Here is what is in the ledger for each expense before step 2 of closing entries is journalized and posted. Each expense is listed on the worksheet in the debit column of the income statement section on page 175.

Office Salaries Expense 511	
650	
650	
350	

Advertising Expense 512	
250	

Telephone Expense 513	
220	

Office Supplies Expense 514	
500	

Rent Expense 515	
400	

Depreciation Expense, W. P. Equipment 516	
80	

Remember, the worksheet is a tool. The accountant realizes that the information about the total of the expenses will be transferred to Income Summary.

The income statement section of the worksheet lists all the expenses as debits. If we want to reduce each expense to zero, each one must be credited.

The following is the journalized closing entry for step 2:

The $3,100 is the total of the expenses on the worksheet.

	31	Income Summary	313	310000	
		Office Salaries Expense	511		165000
		Advertising Expense	512		25000
		Telephone Expense	513		22000
		Office Supplies Expense	514		50000
		Rent Expense	515		40000
		Depreciation Expense, W.P.Equip.	516		8000
		To close expense accounts			

This is what individual expenses and Income Summary should look like in the ledger after Step 2 of closing entries is journalized and posted:

Office Salaries Expense 511

Dr.	Cr.
650	Closing 1,650
650	
350	

Advertising Expense 512

Dr.	Cr.
250	Closing 250

Telephone Expense 513

Dr.	Cr.
220	Closing 220

Office Supplies Expense 514

Dr.	Cr.
500	Closing 500

Rent Expense 515

Dr.	Cr.
400	Closing 400

Depreciation Expense 516

Dr.	Cr.
80	Closing 80

Income Summary 313

Expenses	Revenue
Step 2 3,100	8,000 Step 1

Step 3: Clear Balance in Income Summary (Net Income) and Transfer It to Capital

This is how the Income Summary and B. Clark, Capital, accounts look before step 3:

Income Summary 313

Dr.	Cr.
3,100	8,000
	4,900

B. Clark, Capital 311

Dr.	Cr.
	10,000

Note that the balance of Income Summary (Revenue minus Expenses or $8,000 − $3,100) is $4,900.That is the amount we must clear from the Income Summary account and transfer to the B. Clark, Capital, account.

In order to transfer the balance of $4,900 from Income Summary (check the bottom of the debit column of the income statement section on the worksheet; see Figure 5-4) to Capital, it will be necessary to debit Income Summary for $4,900 (the difference between the revenue and expenses) and credit or increase Capital of B. Clark for $4,900.

The opposite would take place if the business had a net loss.

This is the journalized closing entry for step 3:

	31	Income Summary	313	490000	
		B. Clark, Capital	311		490000
		Transfer profit for period to Capital account			

This is what the Income Summary and B. Clark, Capital, accounts will look like in the ledger after step 3 of closing entries is journalized and posted:

Income Summary 313

	Dr.	Cr.	
Total of Expenses →	3,100	8,000	← Revenue
Debit to close account →	4,900	4,900	← Net income

B. Clark, Capital 311

Dr.	Cr.	
	10,000	
	4,900	← Net income

At the end of these three steps, Income Summary has a zero balance. If we had a net loss the end result would be to decrease capital. Entry would be debit capital and credit income summary for the loss.

Step 4: Clear the Withdrawals Balance and Transfer It to Capital

Next, we must close the Withdrawals account. The B. Clark, Withdrawals, and B. Clark, Capital, accounts now look like this:

B. Clark, Withdrawals 312	
625	

B. Clark, Capital 311	
	10,000
	4,900

To bring the Withdrawals account to a zero balance, and summarize its effect on Capital, we must credit Withdrawals and debit Capital.

Remember, withdrawals are a nonbusiness expense and thus not transferred to Income Summary. The closing entry is journalized as follows:

31	B. Clark, Capital	311	625 00	
	B. Clark, Withdrawals	312		625 00
	Transfer withdrawals to Capital a/c			

Note that the $10,000 is a beginning balance since no additional investments were made during the period.

At this point the B. Clark, Withdrawals, and B. Clark, Capital, accounts would look like this in the ledger.

B. Clark, Withdrawals 312	
625	Closing 625

B. Clark, Capital 311	
625 (Withdrawals)	10,000 (Beg. balance)
	4,900 (Net income)

Now let's look at the complete ledger for Clark Word Processing Services (see Figure 5-5). Note how the word "adjusting" or "closing" is written in the explanation column of individual ledgers, as for example in the one for Office Supplies. If the goals of closing have been achieved, only permanent accounts will have balances carried to the next accounting period. All temporary accounts should have zero balances.

CLARK'S WORD PROCESSING SERVICE
GENERAL LEDGER

Cash — Account No. 111

Date 19XX		Explanation	Post. Ref.	Debit	Credit	DR or CR	Balance
May	1		GJ1	10000 00		DR	10000 00
	1		GJ1		1000 00	DR	9000 00
	1		GJ1		1200 00	DR	7800 00
	7		GJ1	3000 00		DR	10800 00
	15		GJ1		650 00	DR	10150 00
	20		GJ1		625 00	DR	9525 00
	27		GJ2		650 00	DR	8875 00
	28		GJ2		2500 00	DR	6375 00
	29		GJ2		220 00	DR	6155 00

FIGURE 5-5
Complete Ledger

Accounts Receivable — Acct. No. 112

Date 19XX		Explanation	Post. Ref.	Debit	Credit	DR or CR	Balance
May	22		GJ1	5 0 0 0 00		DR	5 0 0 0 00

Office Supplies — Acct. No. 114

Date 19XX		Explanation	Post. Ref.	Debit	Credit	DR or CR	Balance
May	3		GJ1	6 0 0 00		DR	6 0 0 00
	31	Adjusting	GJ2		5 0 0 00	DR	1 0 0 00

Prepaid Rent — Acct. No. 115

Date 19XX		Explanation	Post. Ref.	Debit	Credit	DR or CR	Balance
May	1		GJ1	1 2 0 0 00		DR	1 2 0 0 00
	31	Adjusting	GJ2		4 0 0 00	DR	8 0 0 00

Word Processing Equipment — Acct. No. 121

Date 19XX		Explanation	Post. Ref.	Debit	Credit	DR or CR	Balance
May	1		GJ1	6 0 0 0 00		DR	6 0 0 0 00

Accumulated Depreciation, Word Processing Equipment — Acct. No. 122

Date 19XX		Explanation	Post. Ref.	Debit	Credit	DR or CR	Balance
May	31	Adjusting	GJ2		80 00	CR	80 00

Accounts Payable — Acct. No. 211

Date 19XX		Explanation	Post. Ref.	Debit	Credit	DR or CR	Balance
May	1		GJ1		5 0 0 0 00	CR	5 0 0 0 00
	3		GJ1		6 0 0 00	CR	5 6 0 0 00
	18		GJ1		2 5 0 00	CR	5 8 5 0 00
	28		GJ2	2 5 0 0 00		CR	3 3 5 0 00

(**FIGURE 5-5** cont.)

Salaries Payable — Acct. No. 212

Date 19XX		Explanation	Post. Ref.	Debit	Credit	DR or CR	Balance
May	31	Adjusting	GJ2		350 00	CR	350 00

Brenda Clark, Capital — Acct. No. 311

Date 19XX		Explanation	Post. Ref.	Debit	Credit	DR or CR	Balance
May	1		GJ1		10000 00	CR	10000 00
	31	Closing (Net Income)	GJ3		4900 00	CR	14900 00
	31	Closing (Withdrawals)	GJ3	625 00		CR	14275 00

Note how this is same ending balance as p. 143.

Brenda Clark, Withdrawals — Acct. No. 312

Date 19XX		Explanation	Post. Ref.	Debit	Credit	DR or CR	Balance
May	20		GJ1	625 00		DR	625 00
	31	Closing	GJ3		625 00		–0–

Income Summary — Acct. No. 313

Date 19XX		Explanation	Post. Ref.	Debit	Credit	DR or CR	Balance
May	31	Closing (Revenue)	GJ2		8000 00	CR	8000 00
	31	Closing (Expense)	GJ2	3100 00		CR	4900 00
	31	Closing (Net Income)	GJ3	4900 00			–0–

Word Processing Fees — Acct. No. 411

Date 19XX		Explanation	Post. Ref.	Debit	Credit	DR or CR	Balance
May	7		GJ1		3000 00	CR	3000 00
	22		GJ1		5000 00	CR	8000 00
	31	Closing	GJ2	8000 00			–0–

Office Salaries Expense — Acct. No. 511

Date 19XX		Explanation	Post. Ref.	Debit	Credit	DR or CR	Balance
May	15		GJ1	650 00		DR	650 00
	27		GJ2	650 00		DR	1300 00
	31	Adjusting	GJ2	350 00		DR	1650 00
	31	Closing	GJ2		1650 00		–0–

Advertising Expense — Acct. No. 512

Date 19XX		Explanation	Post. Ref.	Debit	Credit	DR or CR	Balance
May	18		GJ1	250 00		DR	250 00
	31	Closing	GJ2		250 00		–0–

Telephone Expense — Acct. No. 513

Date 19XX		Explanation	Post. Ref.	Debit	Credit	DR or CR	Balance
May	29		GJ2	220 00		DR	220 00
	31	Closing	GJ2		220 00		–0–

Office Supplies Expense — Acct. No. 514

Date 19XX		Explanation	Post. Ref.	Debit	Credit	DR or CR	Balance
May	31	Adjusting	GJ2	500 00		DR	500 00
	31	Closing	GJ2		500 00		–0–

Rent Expense — Acct. No. 515

Date 19XX		Explanation	Post. Ref.	Debit	Credit	DR or CR	Balance
May	31	Adjusting	GJ2	400 00		DR	400 00
	31	Closing	GJ2		400 00		–0–

Depreciation Expense, Word Processing Equipment — Acct. No. 516

Date 19XX		Explanation	Post. Ref.	Debit	Credit	DR or CR	Balance
May	31	Adjusting	GJ2	80 00		DR	80 00
		Closing	GJ2		80 00		–0–

LEARNING UNIT 5-2 REVIEW

AT THIS POINT you should be able to

- Define closing. (p. 173)
- Differentiate between temporary (nominal) and permanent (real) accounts. (p. 174)
- List the four mechanical steps of closing. (p. 174)
- Explain the role of the Income Summary account. (p. 174)
- Explain the role of the worksheet in the closing process. (p. 174)

SELF-REVIEW QUIZ 5-2

(The blank forms you need are on pages 5-2 and 5-3 of the *Study Guide and Working Papers.*)

Go to the worksheet for P. Logan on page 140. Then (1) journalize and post the closing entries and (2) calculate the new balance for P. Logan, Capital.

Solution to Self-Review Quiz 5-2

		Closing			
Dec.	31	Revenue from Clients	410	25 00	
		Income Summary	312		25 00
		To close income accounts			
	31	Income Summary	312	20 00	
		Rent Expense	518		2 00
		Salaries Expense	512		11 00
		Depreciation Expense, Store Equip.	510		1 00
		Insurance Expense	516		2 00
		Supplies Expense	514		4 00
		To close expense accounts			
	31	Income Summary	312	5 00	
		P. Logan, Capital	310		5 00
		Transfer net income to Capital accounts			
	31	P. Logan, Capital	310	3 00	
		P. Logan, Withdrawals	311		3 00
		Transfer withdrawals to Capital accounts			

Partial Ledger

P. Logan, Capital 310

Dr.	Cr.
3	14
	5
	16

Revenue from Clients 410

Dr.	Cr.
25	25

Supplies Expense 514

Dr.	Cr.
4	4

P. Logan, Withdrawals 311

Dr.	Cr.
3	3

Dep. Exp., Store Equip. 510

Dr.	Cr.
1	1

Insurance Expense 516

Dr.	Cr.
2	2

Income Summary 312	
20	25
5	

Salaries Expense 512	
11	11

Rent Expense 518	
2	2

P. Logan, Capital		$14
Net Income	$5	
Less: Withdrawals	3	
Increase in Capital		2
P. Logan, Capital (ending)		$16

LEARNING UNIT 5-3

The Post-Closing Trial Balance: Step 9 of the Accounting Cycle and the Cycle Reviewed

PREPARING A POST-CLOSING TRIAL BALANCE

The post-closing trial balance helps prove the accuracy of the adjusting and closing process. It contains the true ending figure for capital.

The last step in the accounting cycle is the preparation of a **post-closing trial balance** (sometimes called an opening trial balance) which lists only permanent accounts in the ledger and their balances after adjusting and closing entries have been posted. This post-closing trial balance aids in checking whether the ledger is in balance. This checking is important to do because so many new postings go to the ledger from the adjusting and closing process.

The procedure for taking a post-closing trial balance is the same as for a trial balance, except that, since closing entries have closed all temporary accounts, the post-closing trial balance will contain only permanent accounts (balance sheet). Keep in mind, however, that adjustments have occurred.

THE ACCOUNTING CYCLE REVIEWED

Table 5-1 lists the steps we completed in the accounting cycle for Clark's Word Processing Services for the month of May:

Insight: Most companies journalize and post adjusting and closing entries only at the end of their fiscal year. A company that prepares interim reports may complete only the first six steps of the cycle. Worksheets allow the preparation of interim reports without the formal adjusting and closing of the books. If this happens, footnotes on the interim report will indicate the extent to which adjusting and closing were completed.

Insight: To prepare a financial report for April, the data needed can be obtained by subtracting the worksheet accumulated totals for the end of March from the worksheet prepared at the end of April. In this chapter, we chose a month that would show the completion of an entire cycle for Clark's Word Processing Services.

TABLE 5-1 STEPS OF THE ACCOUNTING CYCLE

Steps	Explanation
1. Business transactions occur and generate source documents.	Source documents are cash register tapes, sales tickets, bills, cheques, payroll cards.
↓	↓
2. Analyze and record business transactions into a journal.	Called journalizing.
↓	↓
3. Post or transfer information from journal to ledger.	Copying the debits and credits of the journal entries into the ledger accounts.
↓	↓
4. Prepare a trial balance.	Summarizing each individual ledger account and listing these accounts and their balances to test for mathematical accuracy in recording transactions.
↓	↓
5. Prepare a worksheet.	A multicolumn form that summarizes accounting information to complete the accounting cycle.
↓	↓
6. Prepare financial statements.	Income statement, statement of ower's equity, and balance sheet.
↓	↓
7. Journalize and post adjusting entries.	Refers to adjustment columns of worksheet.
↓	↓
8. Journalize and post closing entries.	Refers to income statement and balance sheet sections of worksheet.
↓	↓
9. Prepare a post-closing trial balance.	Prove the mathematical accuracy of the adjusting and closing process of the accounting cycle.

LEARNING UNIT 5-3 REVIEW

AT THIS POINT you should be able to

- Prepare a post-closing trial balance. (p. 183)
- Explain the relationship of interim reports to the accounting cycle. (p. 183)

SELF-REVIEW QUIZ 5-3

(The blank forms you need are on page 5-3 of the *Study Guide and Working Papers.*)

From the ledger on pages 178 to 183, prepare a post-closing trial balance.

Note: No revenue, expenses, or withdrawals are found on the post-closing trial balance.

Solution to Self-Review Quiz 5-3

CLARK'S WORD PROCESSING SERVICE
POST-CLOSING TRIAL BALANCE
MAY 31, 19XX

	Dr.	Cr.
Cash	615500	
Accounts Receivable	500000	
Office Supplies	10000	
Prepaid Rent	80000	
Word Processing Equipment	600000	
Accumulated Depreciation, Word Processing Equip.		8000
Accounts Payable		335000
Salaries Payable		35000
Brenda Clark, Capital		1427500
Totals	1805500	1805500

Chapter Review

COMPREHENSIVE DEMONSTRATION PROBLEM WITH SOLUTION TIPS

(The blank forms you need are on pages 5-4 to 5-10 of the *Study Guide and Working Papers.*)

From the following transactions for Rolo Company complete the entire accounting cycle. The chart of accounts includes:

Assets
111 Cash
112 Accounts Receivable
114 Prepaid Rent
115 Office Supplies
121 Office Equipment
122 Accumulated Depreciation, Office Equipment

Liabilities
211 Accounts Payable
212 Salaries Payable

Owner's Equity
311 Rolo Kern, Capital
312 Rolo Kern, Withdrawals
313 Income Summary

Revenue
411 Fees Earned

Expenses
511 Salaries Expense
512 Advertising Expense
513 Rent Expense
514 Office Supplies Expense
515 Depreciation Expense, Office Equipment

We will use unusually small numbers to simplify calculation and emphasize the theory.

19XX

Jan. 2 Rolo Kern invested $1,200 cash and $100 of office equipment to open Rolo Co.
2 Paid rent for three months in advance, $300.
4 Purchased office equipment on account, $50.
6 Bought office supplies for cash, $40.
8 Collected $400 for services rendered.
12 Rolo paid his home electric bill from the company chequebook, $20.
14 Provided $100 worth of services to clients who will not pay until next month.
16 Paid salaries, $60.
18 Advertising bill received for $70 but will not be paid until next month.

Adjustment Data on January 31

a. Supplies on Hand	$6
b. Rent Expired	$100
c. Depreciation, Office Equipment	$20
d. Salaries Accrued	$50

Journalizing Transactions and Posting to Ledger, Rolo Company

General Journal — Page 1

Date		Account Titles and Description	PR	Dr.	Cr.
19XX Jan.	2	Cash	111	1 2 0 0 00	
		Office Equipment	121	1 0 0 00	
		R. Kern, Capital	311		1 3 0 0 00
		Initial investment			
	2	Prepaid Rent	114	3 0 0 00	
		Cash	111		3 0 0 00
		Rent paid in advance			
	4	Office Equipment	121	5 0 00	
		Accounts Payable	211		5 0 00
		Purchased equipment on account			
	6	Office Supplies	115	4 0 00	
		Cash	111		4 0 00
		Supplies purchased for cash			
	8	Cash	111	4 0 0 00	
		Fees Earned	411		4 0 0 00
		Services rendered			
	12	R. Kern, Withdrawals	312	2 0 00	
		Cash	111		2 0 00
		Personal payment of a bill			
	14	Accounts Receivable	112	1 0 0 00	
		Fees Earned	411		1 0 0 00
		Services rendered on account			
	16	Salaries Expense	511	6 0 00	
		Cash	111		6 0 00
		Paid salaries			
	18	Advertising Expense	512	7 0 00	
		Accounts Payable	211		7 0 00
		Advertising bill, but not paid			

Solution Tips to Journalizing and Posting Transactions

Jan. 2

Cash	**Asset**	↑	**Dr.**	**$1,200**
Office Equipment	**Asset**	↑	**Dr.**	**$ 100**
R. Kern, Capital	**Capital**	↑	**Cr.**	**$1,300**

Jan. 2

Prepaid Rent	**Asset**	↑	**Dr.**	**$ 300**
Cash	**Asset**	↓	**Cr.**	**$ 300**

Jan. 4	Office Equipment Accounts Payable	Asset Liability	↑ ↑	Dr. Cr.	$ 50 $ 50
Jan. 6	Office Supplies Cash	Asset Asset	↑ ↓	Dr. Cr.	$ 40 $ 40
Jan. 8	Cash Fees Earned	Asset Revenue	↑ ↑	Dr. Cr.	$ 400 $ 400
Jan. 12	R. Kern, Withdrawals Cash	Owner's Equity Asset	↑ ↓	Dr. Cr.	$ 20 $ 20
Jan. 14	Accounts Receivable Fees Earned	Asset Revenue	↑ ↑	Dr. Cr.	$ 100 $ 100
Jan. 16	Salaries Expense Cash	Expense Asset	↑ ↓	Dr. Cr.	$ 60 $ 60
Jan. 18	Advertising Expense Accounts Payable	Expense Liability	↑ ↑	Dr. Cr.	$ 70 $ 70

Note: All account titles come from the Chart of Accounts. When journalizing, the PR column of the general journal is blank. It is in the posting process that we update the ledger. The PR column in the ledger accounts tell us from what journal page the information came. After posting to the account in the ledger, we fill in the PR column of the journal telling us to what account number the information was transferred.

COMPLETING THE WORKSHEET

See worksheet on page 189.

Solution Tips to the Trial Balance and Completion of the Worksheet

After the posting process is complete from the journal to the ledger, we take the ending balance in each account and prepare a trial balance on the worksheet. If a title has no balance, it is not listed on the trial balance. New titles on the worksheet will be added below as needed.

ROLO CO.
WORKSHEET
FOR MONTH ENDED JANUARY 31, 19XX

Account Titles	Trial Balance Dr.	Trial Balance Cr.	Adjustments Dr.	Adjustments Cr.	Adjusted Trial Balance Dr.	Adjusted Trial Balance Cr.	Income Statement Dr.	Income Statement Cr.	Balance Sheet Dr.	Balance Sheet Cr.
Cash	118000				118000				118000	
Accounts Receivable	10000				10000				10000	
Prepaid Rent	30000			(B) 10000	20000				20000	
Office Supplies	4000			(A) 3400	600				600	
Office Equipment	15000				15000				15000	
Accounts Payable		12000				12000				12000
R. Kern, Capital		130000				130000				130000
R. Kern, Withdrawals	2000				2000				2000	
Fees Earned		50000				50000		50000		
Salaries Expense	6000		(D) 5000		11000		11000			
Advertising Expense	7000				7000		7000			
	192000	192000								
Office Supplies Expense			(A) 3400		3400		3400			
Rent Expense			(B) 10000		10000		10000			
Dep. Exp., Office Equip.			(C) 2000		2000		2000			
Accum. Dep., Office Equip.				(C) 2000		2000				2000
Salaries Payable				(D) 5000		5000				5000
			20400	20400	199000	199000	33400	50000	165600	149000
Net Income							16600			16600
							50000	50000	165600	165600

ADJUSTMENTS

On hand of $6 is *not* the adjustment. Need to calculate amount used up.

Office Supplies Expense	**Expense**	↑	**Dr.**	**$ 34**	**($40 − $6)**
Office Supplies	**Asset**	↓	**Cr.**	**$ 34**	

Expired.

Rent Expense	**Expense**	↑	**Dr.**	**$100**	
Prepaid Rent	**Asset**	↓	**Cr.**	**$100**	

Do not touch original cost of equipment.

Depr. Exp., Office Equip.	**Expense**	↑	**Dr.**	**$ 20**	
Accum. Dep., Office Equip.	**Asset (Contra)**	↑	**Cr.**	**$ 20**	

Owed but not paid.

Salaries Expense	**Expense**	↑	**Dr.**	**$ 50**	
Salaries Payable	**Liability**	↑	**Cr.**	**$ 50**	

Note: This information is on the worksheet but has *not* been updated in the ledger. (This will happen when we journalize and post adjustments at end of cycle.)

Note that the last four columns of the worksheet come from numbers on the adjusted trial balance.

We move Net Income of $166 to the balance sheet credit column, since the capital figure is the old one on the worksheet.

PREPARING THE FORMAL FINANCIAL REPORTS

ROLO CO.
INCOME STATEMENT
FOR MONTH ENDED JANUARY 31, 19XX

Revenue:		
Fees Earned		$500 00
Operating Expenses:		
Salaries Expense	$110 00	
Advertising Expense	70 00	
Office Supplies Expense	34 00	
Rent Expense	100 00	
Depr. Expense, Office Equip.	20 00	
Total Operating Expenses		334 00
Net Income		$166 00

ROLO CO.
STATEMENT OF OWNER'S EQUITY
FOR MONTH ENDED JANUARY 31, 19XX

R. Kern, Capital, Jan. 1, 19XX		$1300 00
Net Income for January	$166 00	
Less: Withdrawals for January	20 00	
Increase in Capital		146 00
R. Kern, Capital, Jan. 31, 19XX		$1446 00

ROLO CO. BALANCE SHEET JANUARY 31, 19XX					
Assets			Liabilities and Owner's Equity		
Cash		$1180 00	Liabilities:		
Accounts Receivable		100 00	Accounts Payable	$120 00	
Prepaid Rent		200 00	Salaries Payable	50 00	
Office Supplies		6 00	Total Liabilities		$ 170 00
Office Equipment	$150 00		Owner's Equity:		
Less: Acc. Dep.	20 00	130 00	R. Kern, Capital		1446 00
			Total Liabilities and		
Total Assets		$1616 00	Owner's Equity		$1616 00

Solution Tips to Preparing the Financial Reports

The reports are prepared from the worksheet. (Many of the ledger accounts are not up to date.) The income statement lists revenue and expenses. The net income figure of $166 is used to update the statement of owner's equity. The statement of owner's equity calculates a new figure for Capital, $1,446 (Beginning Capital + Net Income − Withdrawals). This new figure is then listed on the balance sheet (Assets, Liabilities, and a new figure for Capital).

JOURNALIZING AND POSTING ADJUSTING AND CLOSING ENTRIES

See journal at top of page 192.

Solution Tips to Journalizing and Posting Adjusting and Closing Entries

ADJUSTMENTS

The adjustments from the worksheet are journalized (same journal) and posted to the ledger. Now ledger accounts will be brought up to date. Remember, we have already prepared the financial reports from the worksheet. Our goal now is to get the ledger up to date.

CLOSING

Note Income Summary is a temporary account located in the ledger.

Goals

Where do I get my information for closing?

1. Wipe out all temporary accounts in the ledger to zero balances.
2. Get a new figure for capital in the ledger.

General Journal					Page 2
Date		Account Titles and Description	PR	Dr.	Cr.
		Adjusting Entries			
Jan.	31	Office Supplies Expense	514	3400	
		Office Supplies	115		3400
		Supplies used			
	31	Rent Expense	513	10000	
		Prepaid Rent	114		10000
		Rent expired			
	31	Dep. Expense, Office Equipment	515	2000	
		Accum. Dep., Office Equip.	122		2000
		Estimated Depreciation			
	31	Salaries Expense	511	5000	
		Salaries Payable	212		5000
		Accrued salaries			
		Closing Entries			
	31	Fees Earned	411	50000	
		Income Summary	313		50000
		To close income accounts			
	31	Income Summary	313	33400	
		Salaries Expense	511		11000
		Advertising Expense	512		7000
		Office Supplies Expense	514		3400
		Rent Expense	513		10000
		Dep. Expense, Office Equip.	515		2000
		To close expense accounts			
	31	Income Summary	313	16600	
		R. Kern, Capital	311		16600
		Transfer profit to Capital			
	31	R. Kern, Capital	311	2000	
		R. Kern, Withdrawals	312		2000
		Transfer withdrawals to Capital			

Steps in the Closing Process

Step 1: Close revenue to Income Summary.

Step 2: Close individual expenses to Income Summary.

Step 3: Close balance of Income Summary to Capital. (This really is the net income figure on the worksheet.)

Step 4: Close balance of Withdrawals to Capital.

All the journal closing entries (no new calculations are needed, since all figures are on the worksheet) are posted. The result in the ledger is that all temporary accounts have a zero balance.

GENERAL LEDGER

Cash — Acct. No. 111

Date 19XX		Explanation	Post. Ref.	Debit	Credit	DR or CR	Balance
Jan.	1		GJ1	1200 00		DR.	1200 00
	1		GJ1		300 00	DR.	900 00
	6		GJ1		40 00	DR.	860 00
	8		G1	400 00		DR.	1260 00
	12		GJ1		20 00	DR.	1240 00
	16		GJ1		60 00	DR.	1180 00

Accounts Receivable — Acct. No. 112

Date 19XX		Explanation	Post. Ref.	Debit	Credit	DR or CR	Balance
Jan.	14		GJ1	100 00		DR.	100 00

Prepaid Rent — Acct. No. 114

Date 19XX		Explanation	Post. Ref.	Debit	Credit	DR or CR	Balance
Jan.	14		GJ1	300 00		DR.	300 00
	31	Adjustment	GJ1		100 00	DR.	200 00

Office Supplies — Acct. No. 115

Date 19XX		Explanation	Post. Ref.	Debit	Credit	DR or CR	Balance
Jan.	6		GJ1	40 00		DR.	40 00
	31	Adjustment	GJ2		34 00	DR.	6 00

Office Equipment — Acct. No. 121

Date 19XX		Explanation	Post. Ref.	Debit	Credit	DR. CR.	Balance
Jan.	1		GJ1	100 00		DR.	100 00
	4		GJ1	50 00		DR.	150 00

Fees Earned — Acct. No. 411

Date 19XX		Explanation	Post. Ref.	Debit	Credit	DR. CR.	Balance
Jan.	8		GJ1		400 00	CR.	400 00
	24		GJ1		100 00	CR.	500 00
	31	Closing	GJ2	500 00			–0–

Salaries Expense — Acct. No. 511

Date 19XX		Explanation	Post. Ref.	Debit	Credit	DR. CR.	Balance
Jan.	14	Closing	GJ1	60 00		DR.	60 00
	31	Adjusting	GJ2	50 00		DR.	110 00
	31	Closing	GJ2		110 00		–0–

Advertising Expense — Acct. No. 512

Date 19XX		Explanation	Post. Ref.	Debit	Credit	DR. CR.	Balance
Jan.	18		GJ1	70 00		DR.	70 00
	31	Closing	GJ2		70 00		–0–

Accumulated Depreciation, Equipment — Acct. No. 122

Date 19XX		Explanation	Post. Ref.	Debit	Credit	DR or CR	Balance
Jan.	31	Adjustment	GJ2		20 00	CR.	20 00

Accounts Payable — Acct. No. 211

Date 19XX		Explanation	Post. Ref.	Debit	Credit	DR or CR	Balance
Jan.	4		GJ1		50 00	CR.	50 00
	18		GJ1		70 00	CR.	120 00

Salaries Payable — Acct. No. 212

Date 19XX		Explanation	Post. Ref.	Debit	Credit	DR or CR	Balance
Jan.	31	Adjustment	GJ2		50 00	CR.	50 00

Rolo Kern, Capital — Acct. No. 311

Date 19XX		Explanation	Post. Ref.	Debit	Credit	DR or CR	Balance
Jan.	1		GJ1		1300 00	CR.	1300 00
	31	Closing	GJ2		166 00	CR.	1466 00
	31	Closing	GJ2	20 00		CR.	1446 00

Rolo Kern, Withdrawals — Acct. No. 312

Date 19XX		Explanation	Post. Ref.	Debit	Credit	DR or CR	Balance
Jan.	12		GJ1	20 00		DR.	20 00
	31	Closing	GJ2		20 00		–0–

Income Summary — Acct. No. 313

Date 19XX		Explanation	Post. Ref.	Debit	Credit	DR or CR	Balance
Jan.	31	Closing	GJ2		500 00	CR.	500 00
	31	Closing	GJ2	334 00		CR.	166 00
	31	Closing	GJ2	166 00			–0–

Rent Expense — Acct. No. 513

Date 19XX		Explanation	Post. Ref.	Debit	Credit	DR. CR.	Balance
Jan.	31	Adjusting	GJ2	100 00		DR.	100 00
	31	Closing	GJ2		100 00		–0–

Office Supplies Expense — Acct. No. 514

Date 19XX		Explanation	Post. Ref.	Debit	Credit	DR. CR.	Balance
Jan.	31	Adjusting	GJ2	34 00		DR.	34 00
	31	Closing	GJ2		34 00		–0–

Depreciation Expense, Office Equipment — Acct. No. 515

Date 19XX		Explanation	Post. Ref.	Debit	Credit	DR. CR.	Balance
Jan.	31	Adjusting	GJ2	20 00		DR.	20 00
	31	Closing	GJ2		20 00		–0–

These are all permanent accounts.

ROLO CO. POST-CLOSING TRIAL BALANCE JANUARY 31, 19XX		
	Dr.	Cr.
Cash	1 1 8 0 00	
Accounts Receivable	1 0 0 00	
Prepaid Rent	2 0 0 00	
Office Supplies	6 00	
Office Equipment	1 5 0 00	
Accumulated Depreciation, Office Equipment		2 0 00
Accounts Payable		1 2 0 00
Salaries Payable		5 0 00
R. Kern, Capital		1 4 4 6 00
Total	1 6 3 6 00	1 6 3 6 00

Solution Tips for the Post-Closing Trial Balance

The post-closing trial balance is a list of the ledger *after* adjusting and closing entries have been completed. Note the figure for capital $1,446 is the new figure.

Beg. Capital	$1,300
+ Net Income	166
− Withdrawals	20
= Ending Capital	$1,446

Next accounting period we will enter new amounts in the Revenues, Expenses, and Withdrawal accounts. For now, the post-closing trial balance is only made up of permanent accounts.

SUMMARY OF KEY POINTS

Learning Unit 5-1

1. After formal financial reports have been prepared, the ledger has still not been brought up to date.
2. Information for journalizing adjusting entries comes from the adjustments section of the worksheet.

Learning Unit 5-2

1. Closing is a mechanical process that is completed before the accountant can record transactions for the next fiscal year.
2. Assets, Liabilities, and Capital are permanent (real) accounts; their balances are carried over from one accounting period to another. Withdrawals, Revenue, and Expenses are nominal (temporary) accounts; their balances are *not* carried over from one accounting period to another.
3. Income Summary is a temporary account in the general ledger and does not have a normal balance. It will summarize revenue and expenses and transfer the balance to capital. Withdrawals do not go into Income Summary, because they are *not* business expenses.

4. All information for closing can be obtained from the worksheet.
5. When closing is complete, all temporary accounts in the ledger will have a zero balance, and all this information will be updated in the Capital account.
6. Closing entries are usually done only at year-end. Interim reports can be prepared from worksheets that are prepared monthly, quarterly, etc.

Learning Unit 5-3

1. The post-closing trial balance is prepared from the ledger accounts after the adjusting and closing entries have been posted.
2. The accounts on the post-closing trial balance are all permanent titles.

Key terms

Adjusting journal entries Journal entries that are needed in order to update specific ledger accounts to reflect correct balances at the end of an accounting period.

Closing journal entries Journal entries that are prepared to (a) reduce or clear all temporary accounts to a zero balance or (b) update capital to a new closing balance.

Income Summary A temporary account in the ledger that summarizes revenue and expenses and transfers its balance (net income or net loss) to capital. Does not have a normal balance.

Permanent accounts (real) Accounts whose balances are carried over to the next accounting period. Examples: assets, liabilities, capital.

Post-closing trial balance The final step in the accounting cycle that lists only permanent accounts in the ledger and their balances after adjusting and closing entries have been posted.

Temporary accounts (nominal) Accounts whose balances at end of an accounting period are not carried over to the next accounting period. These accounts — revenue, expenses, withdrawals — help to provide a new or ending figure for capital to begin the next accounting period. Keep in mind that Income Summary is also a temporary account.

Blueprint of Closing Process from the Worksheet

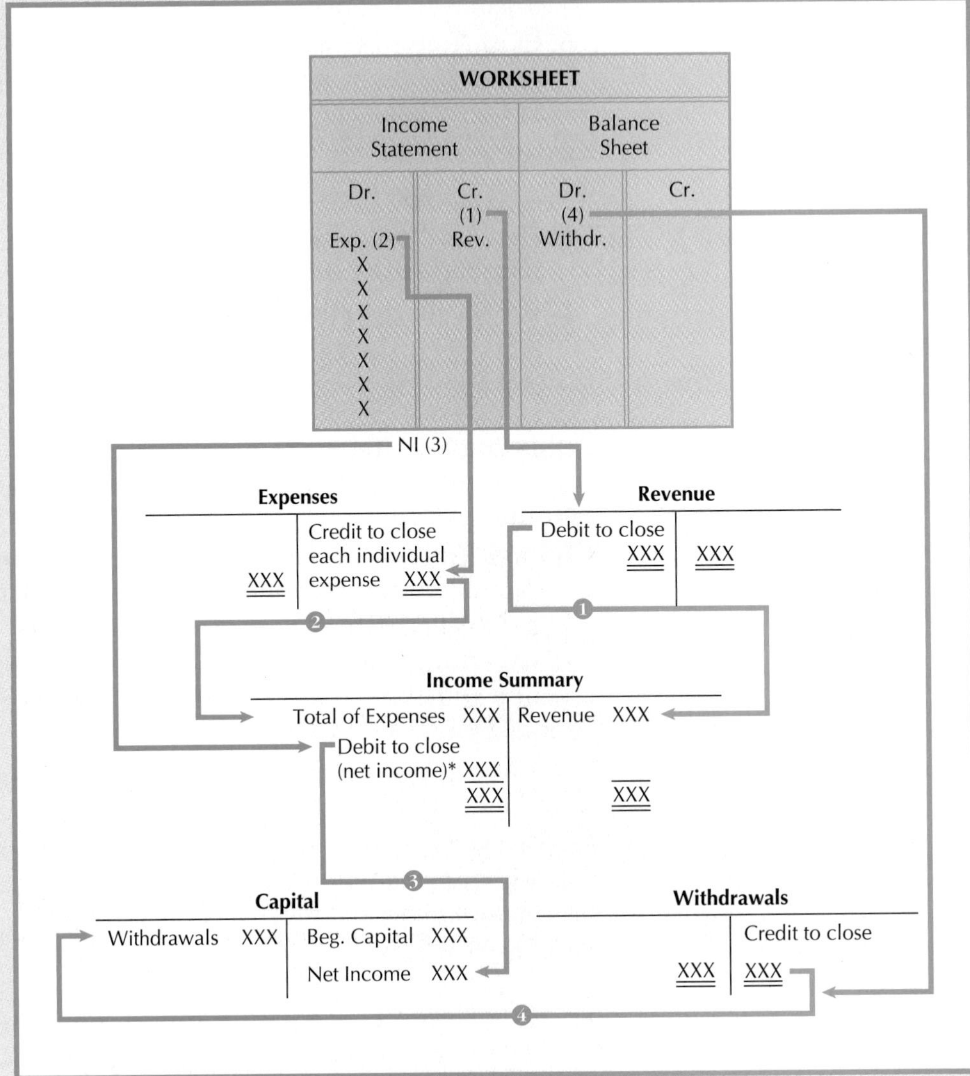

*If a net loss, it would be a credit to close.

The Closing Steps

1. Close revenue balance to Income Summary.
2. Close each *individual* expense and transfer *total* of all expenses to Income Summary.
3. Transfer balance in Income Summary (Net Income or Net Loss) to Capital.
4. Close Withdrawals to Capital.

Questions, Exercises, and Problems

Discussion Questions

1. When a worksheet is completed, what balances are found in the general ledger?
2. Why must adjusting entries be journalized even though the formal reports have already been prepared?
3. "Closing slows down the recording of next year's transactions." Defend or reject this statement with supporting evidence.
4. What is the difference between temporary and permanent accounts?

5. What are the two major goals of the closing process?
6. List the four steps of closing.
7. What is the purpose of Income Summary and where is it located?
8. How can a worksheet aid the closing process?
9. What accounts are usually listed on a post-closing trial balance?
10. Closing entries are always prepared once a month. Agree or disagree. Why?

Mini Exercises

(The blank forms you need are on pages 5-12 and 5-13 of the *Study Guide and Working Papers.*)

Journalizing and Posting Adjusting Entries

1. Post the following adjusting entries (be sure to cross-reference back to journal) that came from the Adjustment columns of the worksheet.

General Journal — Page 3

Date		Account Titles and Description	PR	Dr.	Cr.
Dec.	31	Insurance Expense		3 00	
		Prepaid Insurance			3 00
		Insurance expired			
	31	Supplies Expense		4 00	
		Store Supplies			4 00
		Supplies used			
	31	Dep. Exp., Store Equipment		6 00	
		Accum. Dep., Store Equipment			6 00
		Estimated depreciation			
	31	Salaries Expense		2 00	
		Salaries Payable			2 00
		Accrued salaries			

Steps of Closing and Journalizing Closing Entries

2.

Worksheet

IS		BS	
Dr.	Cr.	Dr.	Cr.
(2)	Rev. (1)	Withdr.	(4)
E X P E N S E S			
NI (3)			

Goals of Closing

1. Temporary accounts in the ledger should have a zero balance.
2. New figure for capital in closing.

Note: All closing can be done from the worksheet. Income Summary is a temporary account in the ledger.

From the above worksheet explain the four steps of closing. Keep in mind that each *individual* expense normally would be listed in the closing process.

Journalizing Closing Entries

3. From the following accounts, journalize the closing entries (assume December 31).

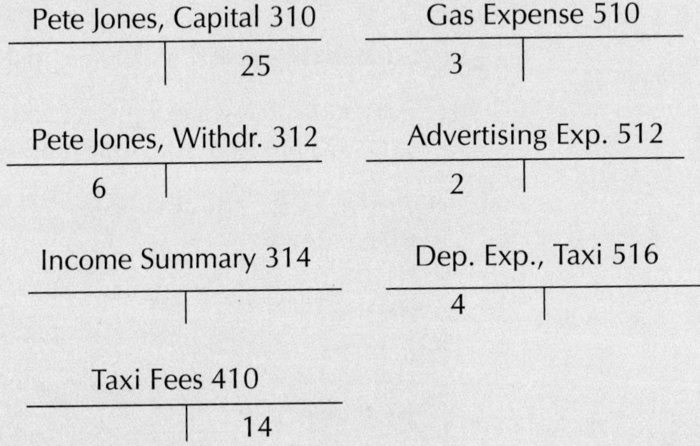

Posting to Income Summary

4. Draw a T account of Income Summary and post to it all entries from question 3 that affect it. Is Income Summary a temporary or permanent account?

Posting to Capital

5. Draw a T account for Pete Jones, Capital, and post to it all entries from question 3 that affect it. What is the final balance of the capital account?

Exercises

(The blank forms you need are on pages 5-14 and 5-15 of the *Study Guide and Working Papers.*)

5-1. From the adjustments section of a worksheet presented here, prepare adjusting journal entries for end of December.

Journalize adjusting entries.

	Adjustments Dr.	Adjustments Cr.
Prepaid Rent		(A) 70000
Office Supplies		(B) 10000
Accumulated Depreciation, Equipment		(C) 40000
Salaries Payable		(D) 10000
Rent Expense	(A) 70000	
Office Supplies Expense	(B) 10000	
Depreciation Expense, Equipment	(C) 40000	
Salaries Expense	(D) 10000	
	130000	130000

Temporary vs. permanent accounts.

5-2. Complete the following table by placing an X in the correct column.

	Temporary	*Permanent*	*Will Be Closed*
Example: **Accounts Receivable**		**X**	
1. Income Summary			
2. A. Flynn, Capital			
3. Salary Expense			
4. A. Flynn, Withdrawals			
5. Fees Earned			
6. Accounts Payable			
7. Cash			

Closing entries.

5-3. From the following T accounts, journalize the four closing entries on December 31, 19XX.

Ed Foley, Capital	
	12,000

Rent Expense	
4,100	

Ed Foley, Withdrawals	
5,200	

Wages Expense	
3,000	

Income Summary	

Insurance Expense	
1,400	

Fees Earned	
	40,500

Dep. Expense, Office Equipment	
800	

Reconstructing closing entries.

5-4. From the following posted T accounts, reconstruct the closing journal entries for December 31, 19XX.

Linn Adams, Capital	
Withdrawals 90	2,000 (Dec. 1)
	700 Net Income

Insurance Expense	
50	Closing 50

Linn Adams, Withdrawals	
90	Closing 90

Wages Expense	
100	Closing 100

Income Summary	
Expenses 600	Revenue 1,300
700	

Rent Expense	
200	Closing 200

Salon Fees	
Closing 1,300	1,300

Depreciation Expense, Equipment	
250	Closing 250

Post-closing trial balance.

5-5. From the following accounts (not in order), prepare a post-closing trial balance for Joy Co. on December 31, 19XX. ***Note:*** These balances are ***before*** closing.

Legal Fees Earned	$12,000
Accounts Payable	45,000
Cash	22,000
Accounts Receivable	18,875
Legal Library	14,250
Office Equipment	59,700
Repair Expense	2,850
Salaries Expense	1,275
J. Joy, Capital	63,450
J. Joy, Withdrawals	1,500

Group A Problems

(The blank forms you need are on pages 5-16 to 5-31 of the *Study Guide and Working Papers.*)

Review in preparing a worksheet and journalizing adjusting and closing entries.

5A-1. Given the following data for Lou's Consulting Service:

LOU'S CONSULTING SERVICE
TRIAL BALANCE
JUNE 30, 19XX

	Dr.	Cr.
Cash	1500000	
Accounts Receivable	600000	
Prepaid Insurance	40000	
Supplies	150000	
Equipment	300000	
Accumulated Depreciation, Equipment		90000
Accounts Payable		700000
L. Long, Capital		1230000
L. Long, Withdrawals	30000	
Consulting Fees Earned		900000
Salaries Expense	140000	
Telephone Expense	100000	
Advertising Expense	60000	
	2920000	2920000

Adjustment Data

a. Insurance expired, $250.
b. Supplies on hand, $600.
c. Depreciation on equipment, $200.
d. Salaries earned by employees but not to be paid till July, $160.

Required

1. Prepare a worksheet.
2. Journalize adjusting and closing entries.

Journalizing and posting adjusting and closing entries. Preparing a post-closing trial balance.

5A-2. Enter beginning balance in each account in your working papers from the trial balance columns of the worksheet on page 202. Then (1) journalize and post adjusting and closing entries and (2) prepare from the ledger a post-closing trial balance for the month of March.

Comprehensive review of the entire accounting cycle, Chapters 1–5.

5A-3. As the bookkeeper of Pete's Plowing, you have been asked to complete the entire accounting cycle for Pete from the following information:

19XX		
Jan.	1	Pete invested $7,000 cash and $6,000 worth of snow equipment into the plowing company.
	1	Paid rent in advance for garage space, $2,000.
	4	Purchased office equipment on account from Ling Corp., $7,200.
	6	Purchased snow supplies for $700 cash.
	8	Collected $15,000 from plowing local shopping centres.
	12	Pete Mack withdrew $1,000 from the business for personal use.
	20	Plowed North East Co. parking lots, payment not to be received until March, $5,000.
	26	Paid salaries to employees, $1,800.

SPEEDY CLEANING SERVICE
WORKSHEET
FOR MONTH ENDED MARCH 31, 19XX

Account Titles	Trial Balance		Adjustments		Adjusted Trial Balance		Income Statement		Balance Sheet	
	Dr.	Cr.	Dr.	Cr.	Dr.	Cr.	Dr.	Cr.	Dr.	Cr.
Cash	40000				40000				40000	
Prepaid Insurance	52000			(A) 18000	34000				34000	
Cleaning Supplies	14400			(B) 10000	4400				4400	
Auto	272000				272000				272000	
Accum. Dep. Auto		86000		(C) 15000		101000				101000
Accts. Payable		22400				22400				22400
J. Speedy, Cap.		54000				54000				54000
J. Speedy, Withdr.	46000				46000				46000	
Cleaning Fees		468000				468000		468000		
Salaries Exp.	144000		(D) 16000		160000		160000			
Telephone Exp.	26400				26400		26400			
Advertising Exp.	19600				19600		19600			
Gas Exp.	16000				16000		16000			
	630400	630400								
Insurance Exp.			(A) 18000		18000		18000			
Cleaning Supplies Exp.			(B) 10000		10000		10000			
Dep. Exp. Auto			(C) 15000		15000		15000			
Salaries Payable				(D) 16000		16000				16000
			59000	59000	661400	661400	265000	468000	396400	193400
Net Income							203000			203000
							468000	468000	396400	396400

28 Paid Ling Corp. one-half amount owed for office equipment.
29 Advertising bill received from Bush Co. but will not be paid until March, $900.
30 Paid telephone bill, $210.

Adjustment Data

a. Snow supplies on hand, $400.
b. Rent expired, $600.
c. Depreciation on office equipment, $120. ($7,200 ÷ 5 yr. ➜ $1,440/12 mo. = $120)
d. Depreciation on snow equipment, $100. ($6,000 ÷ 5 yr. ➜ $1,200/12 mo. = $100)
e. Accrued salaries, $190.

Chart of Accounts

Assets
111 Cash
112 Accounts Receivable
114 Prepaid Rent
115 Snow Supplies
121 Office Equipment
122 Accumulated Depreciation, Office Equipment
123 Snow Equipment
124 Accumulated Depreciation, Snow Equipment

Liabilities
211 Accounts Payable
212 Salaries Payable

Owner's Equity
311 Pete Mack, Capital
312 Pete Mack, Withdrawals
313 Income Summary

Revenue
411 Plowing Fees

Expenses
511 Salaries Expense
512 Advertising Expense
513 Telephone Expense
514 Rent Expense
515 Snow Supplies Expense
516 Depreciation Expense, Office Equipment
517 Depreciation Expense, Snow Equipment

Group B Problems

(The blank forms you need are on pages 5-16 to 5-31 of the *Study Guide and Working Papers.*)

5B-1.

Review in preparing a worksheet and journalizing and closing entries.

To: Ron Ear
From: Sue French
Re: Accounting Needs

Please prepare ASAP from the following information (attached) (1) a worksheet along with (2) journalized adjusting and closing entries.

LOU'S CONSULTING SERVICE
TRIAL BALANCE
JUNE 30, 19XX

	Dr.	Cr.
Cash	10 1 5 0 00	
Accounts Receivable	5 0 0 0 00	
Prepaid Insurance	7 0 0 00	
Supplies	3 0 0 00	
Equipment	12 9 5 0 00	
Accumulated Depreciation, Equipment		4 0 0 0 00
Accounts Payable		5 7 5 0 00
Lou Long, Capital		15 1 5 0 00
Lou Long, Withdrawals	4 0 0 00	
Consulting Fees Earned		5 2 0 0 00
Salaries Expense	4 5 0 00	
Telephone Expense	7 0 00	
Advertising Expense	8 0 00	
	30 1 0 0 00	30 1 0 0 00

Adjustment Data

a. Insurance expired, $100.
b. Supplies on hand, $20.
c. Depreciation on equipment, $200.
d. Salaries earned by employees but not due to be paid till July, $490.

Journalizing and posting adjusting and closing entries. Preparing a post-closing trial balance.

5B-2. Enter the beginning balance in each account in your working papers from the trial balance columns of the worksheet.on page 205.Then (1) journalize and post adjusting entries and (2) prepare from the ledger a post-closing trial balance at end of March.

Comprehensive review of entire accounting cycle. Review of Chapters 1–5.

5B-3. From the following transactions as well as additional data, complete the entire accounting cycle for Pete's Plowing (use the chart of accounts on page 203).

19XX

Jan.	1	To open the business, Pete invested $8,000 cash and $9,600 worth of snow equipment.
	1	Paid rent for five months in advance, $3,000.
	4	Purchased office equipment on account from Russell Co., $6,000.
	6	Bought snow supplies, $350.
	8	Collected $7,000 for plowing during winter storm emergency.
	12	Pete paid his home telephone bill from the company chequebook, $70.
	20	Billed Eastern Freight Co. for plowing fees earned but not to be received until March, $6,500.
	24	Advertising bill received from Jones Co. but will not be paid until next month, $350.
	26	Paid salaries to employees, $1,800.
	28	Paid Russell Co. one-half of amount owed for office equipment.
	29	Paid telephone bill of company, $165.

Adjustment Data

a. Snow supplies on hand, $200.
b. Rent expired, $600.

SPEEDY CLEANING SERVICE
WORKSHEET
FOR MONTH ENDED MARCH 31, 19XX

Account Titles	Trial Balance Dr.	Trial Balance Cr.	Adjustments Dr.	Adjustments Cr.	Adjusted Trial Balance Dr.	Adjusted Trial Balance Cr.	Income Statement Dr.	Income Statement Cr.	Balance Sheet Dr.	Balance Sheet Cr.
Cash	172400				172400				172400	
Prepaid Insurance	35000			(A) 20000	15000				15000	
Cleaning Supplies	80000			(B) 60000	20000				20000	
Auto	122000				122000				122000	
Accumulated Depreciation, Auto		66000		(C) 15000		81000				81000
Accounts Payable		67400				67400				67400
J. Speedy, Capital		248000				248000				248000
J. Speedy, Withdrawals	60000				60000				60000	
Cleaning Fees		370000				370000		370000		
Salaries Expense	200000		(D) 17500		217500		217500			
Telephone Expense	28400				28400		28400			
Advertising Expense	27600				27600		27600			
Gas Expense	26000				26000		26000			
	751400	751400								
Insurance Expense			(A) 20000		20000		20000			
Cleaning Supplies Expense			(B) 60000		60000		60000			
Depreciation Expense, Auto			(C) 15000		15000		15000			
Salaries Payable				(D) 17500		17500				17500
			112500	112500	783900	783900	394500	370000	389400	413900
Net Loss								24500	24500	
							394500	394500	413900	413900

c. Depreciation on office equipment ($6,000 ÷ 4 yr. ➔ $1,500 ÷ 12 = $125), $125.

d. Depreciation on snow equipment ($9,600 ÷ 2 yr. ➔ $4,800 ÷ 12 = $400), $400.

e. Salaries accrued, $300.

Group C Problems

Review in preparing a worksheet and journalizing adjusting and closing entries.

5C-1.

To: Brian Botsford

From: Victoria Stamwell

Re: Accounting Procedures

Please prepare from the following information (attached) (1) a worksheet along with (2) journalized adjusting and closing entries for the period ending May 31, 19XX.

Adjustment Data

a. Insurance expired, $286.

b. Supplies on hand, $820.

c. Depreciation on storage equipment, $520.

d. Depreciation on building, $940.

e. Wages earned by employees but not due to be paid till June, $1,250.

VICTORIA STORAGE COMPANY
TRIAL BALANCE
MAY 31, 19XX

	Debit	Credit
Cash in Bank	1 8 6 0 00	
Prepaid Insurance	6 8 1 00	
Storage Supplies	1 7 4 2 00	
Storage Equipment	9 7 4 0 00	
Building	58 0 0 0 00	
Accumulated Depreciation, Storage Equipment		4 2 1 8 00
Accumulated Depreciation, Building		21 4 7 0 00
Accounts Payable		2 8 6 0 00
Victoria Stamwell, Capital		41 3 3 5 00
Victoria Stamwell, Withdrawals	5 7 4 2 00	
Storage Fees Revenue		17 9 2 0 00
Wages Expense	8 2 4 0 00	
Utilities Expense	9 2 6 00	
Advertising Expense	8 7 2 00	
Totals	87 8 0 3 00	87 8 0 3 00

Journalizing and posting adjusting and closing entries. Preparing a post-closing trial balance.

5C-2. Refer to the worksheet for Wilson Computer Repair Service on page 207. The balances (from the trial balance column) in each account are already entered in your working papers. (1) Journalize and post adjusting and closing entries to each account in the ledger, and (2) prepare from the ledger a post-closing trial balance at the end of November.

WILSON COMPUTER REPAIR SERVICE
WORKSHEET
NOVEMBER 30, 19XX

Account Titles	Trial Balance Dr.	Trial Balance Cr.	Adjustments Dr.	Adjustments Cr.	Adjusted Trial Balance Dr.	Adjusted Trial Balance Cr.	Income Statement Dr.	Income Statement Cr.	Balance Sheet Dr.	Balance Sheet Cr.
Cash	136648			(A) 4827	131821				131821	
Prepaid Insurance	71456			(C) 23455	48001				48001	
Accounts Receivable	527742				527742				527742	
Repair Parts and Supplies	159747			(D) 84240	75507				75507	
Van	2167500				2167500				2167500	
Accumulated Depreciation, Van		810365		(B) 61875		872240				872240
Accounts Payable		377260		(F) 24300		401560				401560
Tom Wilson, Capital		1266358				1266358				1266358
Tom Wilson, Withdrawals	260000				260000				260000	
Repair Revenue		1645870				1645870		1645870		
Advertising Expense	71438		(F) 24300		95738		95738			
Automotive Expense	234551				234551		234551			
Cleaning Expense	37500				37500		37500			
Miscellaneous Expense	17814				17814		17814			
Postage and Office Expense	28417				28417		28417			
Salaries Expense	387040		(E) 42000		429040		429040			
	4099853	4099853								
Insurance Expense			(C) 23455		23455		23455			
Bank Charges Expense			(A) 4827		4827		4827			
Depreciation Expense, Van			(B) 61875		61875		61875			
Salaries Payable				(E) 42000		42000				42000
Supplies Expense			(D) 84240		84240		84240			
			240697	240697	4228028	4228028	1017457	1645870		
Net Income							628413			628413
							1645870	1645870	3210571	3210571

Comprehensive review of the entire accounting cycle, Chapters 1–5.

5C-3. From the following transactions as well as additional data, please complete the entire accounting cycle for Clyde's Plumbing (use a chart of accounts similar to the one on page 203).

May	1	To open the business, Clyde Nott invested $12,000 cash and $5,400 worth of plumbing equipment.
	1	Paid rent for 4 months in advance, $2,400.
	4	Purchased office equipment on account from MacKenzie Co., $4,100.
	6	Bought plumbing supplies, $870.
	8	Collected $3,600 for plumbing services provided.
	9	Clyde paid his home utility bill from the company chequebook, $122.
	10	Billed Western Construction Co. for plumbing fees earned but not to be received until later, $9,600.
	14	Advertising bill received from ABCD Radio Co. but not to be paid until next month, $420.
	21	Peceived cheque from Western Construction Co. in partial payment on transaction dated May 10, $4,800.
	26	Paid salaries to employees, $2,650.
	28	Paid MacKenzie Co. one-half of amount owed for office equipment, $2,050.
	29	Paid telephone bill of company, $176.
	31	Peceived bill from George's Cleaning to be paid in June, $215.

Adjusting Data

a. Plumbing supplies on hand, $310.

b. Rent expired, $600.

c. Depreciation on office equipment, $68.33.
($4,100 ÷ 5 yr. ➜ $820 ÷ 12 = $68.33)

d. Depreciation on plumbing equipment, $150.
($5,400 ÷ 3 yr. ➜ $1,800 ÷ 12 = $150)

e. Salaries accrued, $520.00.

REAL WORLD APPLICATIONS

5R-1.

Ann Humphrey needs a loan from the Charles Bank to help finance her business. She has submitted to the Charles Bank the following unadjusted trial balance. As the loan officer, you will be meeting with Ann tomorrow. Could you make some specific written suggestions to Ann regarding her loan report?

Cash in Bank	770	
Accounts Receivable	1,480	
Office Supplies	3,310	
Equipment	7,606	
Accounts Payable		684
A. Humphrey, Capital		8,000
Service Fees		17,350
Salaries	11,240	
Utilities Expense	842	
Rent Expense	360	
Insurance Expense	280	
Advertising Expense	146	
Totals	26,034	26,034

5R-2.

Janet Smothey is the new bookkeeper who replaced Dick Burns, owing to his sudden illness. Janet finds on her desk a note requesting that she close the books and supply the ending capital figure. Janet is upset, since she can only find the following:

a. Revenue and expense accounts were all zero balance.

b. **Income Summary**

14,360	19,300

c. Owner withdrew $8,000.

d. Owner's beginning capital was $34,400.

Could you help Janet accomplish her assignment? What written suggestions should Janet make to her supervisor so that this situation will not happen again?

make the call

Critical Thinking/Ethical Case

5R-3.

Todd Silver is the purchasing agent for Moore Company. One of his suppliers, Gem Company, offers Todd a free vacation to France if he buys at least 75 percent of Moore's supplies from Gem Company. Todd, who is angry because Moore Company has not given him a raise in over a year, is considering the offer. Write out your recommendation to Todd.

ACCOUNTING RECALL

A CUMULATIVE APPROACH

THIS EXAM REVIEWS CHAPTERS 1 THROUGH 5

Page 5-52 of the *Study Guide and Working Papers* has forms to complete this exam, as well as worked-out solutions. The page references next to each question identify what page to turn back to if you answer the question incorrectly.

PART I Vocabulary Review

Match the terms to the appropriate definition or phrase.

Page Ref.

(173) 1. Closing Entries
(132) 2. Book value
(177) 3. Income summary
(131) 4. Contra-asset
(129) 5. Supplies
(80) 6. Journal
(183) 7. Post-closing trial balance
(169) 8. Adjusting journal entries

A. Updates specific ledger accounts
B. A temporary account with debit balance
C. A permanent account
D. Lists only permanent account
E. Clears all temporary accounts
F. Book of original entry
G. A temporary account in the ledger

(81) 9. Ledger

(13) 10. Withdrawals

H. Cost-accumulated depreciation

I. Book of final entry

J. Accumulated depreciation

PART II True or False (Accounting Theory)

(174) 11. Income summary has a normal balance of a debit.

(174) 12. After closing, all temporary accounts will be cleared to zero balance.

(168) 13. Closing entries cannot be made from a worksheet.

(141) 14. The worksheet shows the beginning figure for capital.

(184) 15. Financial reports are prepared after journalizing and posting adjusting and closing entries.

PART III Applications Problem (5–52)

From the following worksheet journalize the adjusting and closing entries for December 31.

WORKSHEET

Account Titles	Trial Balance		Adjustments		Adjusted Trial Balance		Income Statement		Balance Sheet	
	Dr.	Cr.	Dr.	Cr.	Dr.	Cr.	Dr.	Cr.	Dr.	Cr.
Cash	2000				2000				2000	
Accounts Receivable	2500				2500				2500	
Prepaid Insurance	1900			(A) 400	1500				1500	
Store Supplies	1800			(B) 1400	400				400	
Store Equipment	4000				4000				4000	
Accum. Dep., Equipment		1000		(C) 500		1500				1500
Accounts Payable		3000				3000				3000
P. Sove, Capital		5200				5200				5200
P. Sove, Withdrawals	200				200				200	
Fees Earned		4900				4900		4900		
Rent Expense	1000				1000		1000			
Wage Expense	700		(D) 600		1300		1300			
	14100	14100								
Insurance Expense			(A) 400		400		400			
Supplies Expense			(B) 1400		1400		1400			
Depreciation Expense			(C) 500		500		500			
Wages Payable				(D) 600		600				600
			2900	2900	15200	15200	4600	4900	10600	10300
Net Income							300			300
							4900	4900	10600	10600

MINI PRACTICE SET

Valdez Realty

Reviewing the Accounting Cycle Twice

This comprehensive review problem requires you to complete the accounting cycle for Valdez Realty twice. This will allow you to review Chapters 1 to 5 while reinforcing the relationships between all parts of the accounting cycle. By completing two cycles, you will see how the ending June balances in the ledger are used to accumulate data in July. (The blank forms you need are on pages 5-54 to 5-70 of the *Study Guide and Working Papers.*)

The following chart shows the steps of the accounting cycle and the pages in the text where each step is covered. You can use it to review the accounting cycle before you start and as a reference while you are working.

Steps in the Accounting Cycle	Page in Text Where Covered
1. Business transactions occur and generate source documents.	**1.** p. 81
↓	
2. Analyze and record business transactions into a journal.	**2.** p. 83
↓	
3. Post or transfer information from journal to ledger.	**3.** p. 89
↓	
4. Prepare a trial balance.	**4.** p. 97
↓	
5. Prepare a worksheet.	**5.** p. 127
↓	
6. Prepare financial statements.	**6.** p. 141
↓	
7. Journalize and post adjusting entries.	**7.** p. 169
↓	
8. Journalize and post closing entries.	**8.** p. 173
↓	
9. Prepare a post-closing trial balance.	**9.** p. 183

First, let's look at the chart of accounts for Valdez Realty (top of page 212).

On June 1 Juan Valdez opened a real estate office called Valdez Realty. The following transactions were completed for the month of June:

19XX

June 1 Juan Valdez invested $6,000 cash in the real estate agency along with $3,000 of office equipment.

1 Rented office space and paid three months rent in advance, $2,100.

Valdez Realty
Chart of Accounts

Assets
111 Cash
112 Accounts Receivable
114 Prepaid Rent
115 Office Supplies
121 Office Equipment
122 Accumulated Depreciation, Office Equipment
123 Automobile
124 Accumulated Depreciation, Automobile

Liabilities
211 Accounts Payable
212 Salaries Payable

Owner's Equity
311 Juan Valdez, Capital
312 Juan Valdez, Withdrawals
313 Income Summary

Revenue
411 Commissions Earned

Expenses
511 Rent Expense
512 Salaries Expense
513 Gas Expense
514 Repairs Expense
515 Telephone Expense
516 Advertising Expense
517 Office Supplies Expense
518 Depreciation Expense, Office Equipment
519 Depreciation Expense, Automobile
524 Miscellaneous Expense

19XX		
June	1	Bought an automobile on account, $12,000.
	4	Purchased office supplies for cash, $300.
	5	Purchased additional office supplies on account, $150.
	6	Sold a house and collected a $6,000 commission.
	8	Paid gas bill, $22.
	15	Paid the salary of the office secretary, $350.
	17	Sold a building lot and earned a commission, $6,500. Payment is to be received on July 8.
	20	Juan Valdez withdrew $1,000 from the business to pay personal expenses.
	21	Sold a house and collected a $3,500 commission.
	22	Paid gas bill, $25.
	24	Paid $600 to repair automobile.
	30	Paid the salary of the office secretary, $350.
	30	Paid the June telephone bill, $510.
	30	Received advertising bill for June, $1,200. The bill is to be paid on July 2.

Required Work for June

1. Journalize transactions and post to ledger accounts.
2. Prepare a trial balance in the first two columns of the worksheet and complete the worksheet using the following adjustment data:
   - **a.** One month's rent had expired.
   - **b.** An inventory shows $50 of office supplies remaining.
   - **c.** Depreciation on office equipment, $100.
   - **d.** Depreciation on automobile, $200.
3. Prepare a June income statement, statement of owner's equity, and balance sheet.

4. From the worksheet, journalize and post adjusting and closing entries (page 3 of journal).
5. Prepare a post-closing trial balance.

During July, Valdez Realty completed these transactions:

19XX		
July	1	Paid for June office supplies purchased on account, $150.
	1	Purchased additional office supplies on account, $700.
	2	Paid advertising bill for June.
	3	Sold a house and collected a commission, $6,600.
	6	Paid for gas expense, $29.
	8	Collected commission from sale of building lot on June 17.
	9	Paid $2,000 of the balance owing on automobile purchased June 1.
	12	Paid $300 to send employees to realtor's workshop.
	15	Paid the salary of the office secretary, $350.
	17	Sold a house and earned a commission of $2,400. Commission to be received on August 10.
	18	Sold a building lot and collected a commission of $7,000.
	22	Sent a cheque for $40 to help sponsor a local road race to aid the poor. (This is not to be considered an advertising expense, but it is a business expense.)
	24	Paid for repairs to automobile, $590.
	28	Juan Valdez withdrew $1,800 from the business to pay personal expenses.
	30	Paid the salary of the office secretary, $350.
	30	Paid the July telephone bill, $590.
	30	Advertising bill for July, $1,400. The bill is to be paid on August 2.

Required Work for July

1. Journalize transactions in a general journal (pages 4 and 5) and post to ledger accounts.
2. Prepare a trial balance in the first two columns of the worksheet and complete the worksheet using the following adjustment data:
   - **a.** One month's rent had expired.
   - **b.** An inventory shows $90 of office supplies remaining.
   - **c.** Depreciation on office equipment, $100.
   - **d.** Depreciation on automobile, $200.
3. Prepare a July income statement, statement of owner's equity, and balance sheet.
4. From the worksheet, journalize and post adjusting and closing entries (page 6 of journal).
5. Prepare a post-closing trial balance.

COMPUTER WORKSHOP

Computerized Accounting Application for Valdez Realty Mini Practice Set (Chapter 5)

Closing Process and Post-Closing Trial Balance

Before starting on this assignment, read and complete the tasks discussed in Parts A, B, and F of Appendix B, "Computerized Accounting" at the back of this book and complete the Computerized Accounting Application assignments at the ends of Chapters 3 and 4.

This comprehensive review problem requires you to complete the accounting cycle for Valdez Realty twice. This will allow you to review Chapters 1 to 5 while reinforcing the relationships between all parts of the accounting cycle. By completing two cycles, you will see how the ending June balances in the ledger are used to accumulate data in July. If you are using ACCPAC Plus software, please proceed as your instructor directs.

PART A The June Accounting Cycle

On June 1, Juan Valdez opened a real estate office called Valdez Realty.

Open the Company Data Files

1. Start Windows; insert your Student Data Files disk into disk drive A or B; then double-click on the CA-Simply Accounting icon. The CA-Simply Accounting-Open File dialogue box will appear.
2. Enter one of the following paths into the **Open file name** text box:
   - A:\VALDEZ.ASC (if you are storing your student data files on the disk in drive A).
   - B:\VALDEZ.ASC (if you are storing your student data files on the disk in drive B).
3. Click on the **Open** button, enter "6/30/99" into the **Using date for this session** text box; then click on the **OK** button. Click on the **OK** button in response to the message "The date entered is more than one week past your previous **Using** date of 6/1/99." The Company Window for Valdez will appear.

Add Your Name to the Company Name

4. Click on the Company Window Setup menu; then click on Company Information. The Company Information dialogue box will appear. Insert your name in place of the text "Your Name" in the **Name** text box. Click on the **OK** button to return to the Company Window. Your instructor may suggest you do a **File; Save As** procedure here (using a different file name) to make it easier to start over if a mistake is made later on.

Record June Transactions

5. Open the General Journal dialogue box; then record the following journal entries (enter "Memo" into the **Source** text box for each transaction; then enter the **Date** listed for each transaction):

1999		
June	1	Juan Valdez invested $6,000 cash in the real estate agency along with $3,000 in office equipment.
	1	Rented office space and paid three months rent in advance, $2,100.
	1	Bought an automobile on account, $12,000.
	4	Purchased office supplies for cash, $300.
	5	Purchased additional office supplies on account, $150.
	6	Sold a house and collected a $6,000 commission.
	8	Paid gas bill, $22.
	15	Paid the salary of the office secretary, $350.
	17	Sold a building lot and earned a commission, $6,500. Expected receipt 7/8/99.
	20	Juan Valdez withdrew $1,000 from the business to pay personal expenses.

21 Sold a house and collected a $3,500 commission.
22 Paid gas bill, $25.
24 Paid $600 to repair automobile.
30 Paid the salary of the office secretary, $350.
30 Paid the June telephone bill, $510.
30 Peceived advertising bill for June, $1,200. The bill is to be paid on 7/2/99.

Print Reports

6. After you have posted the journal entries, close the General Journal; then print the following reports:
   a. General Journal (By posting date, All ledger entries, Start: 6/1/99, Finish: 6/30/99).
   b. Trial Balance As at 6/30/99.

   Review your printed reports. If you have made an error in a posted journal entry, see Part C of Appendix B for information on how to correct the error.

Record June Adjusting Entries

7. Open the General Journal; then record adjusting journal entries based on the following adjustment data (Source: Memo; Date: 6/30/99; Comment: Adjusting entry):
   a. One month's rent has expired.
   b. An inventory shows $50 of office supplies remaining.
   c. Depreciation on office equipment, $100.
   d. Depreciation on automobile, $200.

Print Reports

8. After you have posted the adjusting journal entries, close the General Journal; then print the following reports:
   a. General Journal (By posting date, All ledger entries, Start: 6/1/99, Finish: 6/30/99).
   b. Trial Balance As at 6/30/99.
   c. General Ledger Report (Start: 6/1/99, Finish: 6/30/99, Select All).
   d. Income Statement (Start: 6/1/99, Finish: 6/30/99).
   e. Balance Sheet As at 6/30/99.

   Review your printed reports. If you have made an error in a posted journal entry, see Part C Appendix B for information on how to correct the error.

How to Close the Accounting Records

9. The CA-Simply Accounting for Windows program has the capability of performing the first three steps of the closing process automatically.

   Done automatically by the program.

   Step 1: Clear Revenue Balance and Transfer to Income Summary.

   Step 2: Clear Individual Expense Balances and Transfer the Total to Income Summary.

   Step 3: Clear Balance in Income Summary and Transfer it to Capital

   It does not have the capability of performing the fourth step of the closing process automatically, so you will need to record this closing journal entry.

   You need to record this closing entry.

   Step 4: Clear the Withdrawals Balance and Transfer it to Capital.

Record Entry to Close Withdrawals Account

10. Open the General Journal; then record the closing journal entry for Juan Valdez's Withdrawals account.
11. After you have posted the closing entry for Juan Valdez's Withdrawals account, close the General Journal to return to the Company Window.

Make a Backup Copy of June Accounting Records

12. Click on the Company Window File menu; click on Save As; then enter one of the following new file names into the **Save file as** text box:
    - A:\VALDJUNE.ASC (if you are storing your student data files on the disk in drive A).
    - B:\VALDJUNE.ASC (if you are storing your student data files on the disk in drive B).
13. Click on the **Save** button. Note that the company name in the Company Window has changed from Valdez to Valdjune. Click on the Company Window File menu

again; then click on Save As. Enter one of the following new file names into the **Save file as** text box:

- A:\VALDEZ.ASC (if you are storing your student data files on the disk in drive A).
- B:\VALDEZ.ASC (if you are storing your student data files on the disk in drive B).

14. Click on the **Save** button. Click on the **Yes** button in response to the question "Replace existing datafiles with the same name?" Note that the company name in the Company Window has changed back from Valdjune to Valdez.

15. You now have two sets of company data files for Valdez Realty on your Student Data Files disk. The current data is stored under the file name VALDEZ.ASC. The backup data for June is stored under the file name VALDJUNE.ASC.

Important Information About the Closing Process

16. The next instruction will ask you to advance the **Using** date to a new month. It is this procedure that instructs the program to complete the first three steps in the closing process. It is important that you make a backup copy of a company's data files prior to advancing the **Using** date to a new month. When you advance the **Using** date to a new month the program will permanently remove all journal entries from all journals and all individual postings of journal entries to the general ledger accounts. You will not be able to display or print a General Journal or General Ledger report based on dates in the prior month, nor will you be able to record journal entries for dates in the prior month. If for some reason you need to print a General Journal or General Ledger, or record a transaction that occurred in the prior month, you can do so by using the backup copy of the company's data files that you created prior to advancing the **Using** date. See Part E of Appendix B at the end of this book for information on how and when to use a backup copy of a company's data files.

How to Advance the Using Date

17. Click on the Company Window Maintenance menu; then click on Advance Using Date. Enter 7/1/99 into the **New using date** text box; then click on the **OK** button. Click on the **OK** button in response to the message "You have entered both a new calendar quarter and a new fiscal year. If you proceed, the program will zero all existing quarter-to-date payroll information for all employees, close all Revenue and Expense account balances into the Retained Earnings integration account, and reset the Fiscal Start and Fiscal End dates for the new fiscal year. Print all employee reports and make a backup before proceeding."

18. The warning message stated that the revenue and expense accounts would be closed to an account titled Retained Earnings. This is the account that corporations use to accumulate earnings. Valdez Realty is a sole proprietorship, and the program will correctly close the revenue and expense accounts to Income Summary and close Income Summary to the Juan Valdez, Capital account even though the message used a different account name. The backup you created using the Save As method will serve as the backup suggested in the warning message.

Print a Post-Closing Trial Balance

19. Print a post-closing Trial Balance As at 7/1/99.

Exit from the Program

20. Click on the Company Window File menu; then click on Exit to end the current work session and return to your Windows desktop.

Complete the Report Transmittal

21. Complete the Valdez Realty Report Transmittal for June located in Appendix A of your *Study Guide and Working Papers.*

PART B The July Accounting Cycle

Open the Company Data Files

1. Start Windows; insert your Student Data Files disk into disk drive A or B; then double-click on the CA-Simply Accounting icon.
2. Enter one of the following paths into the **Open file name** text box:
   - A:\VALDEZ.ASC (if you are storing your student data files on the disk in drive A).
   - B:\VALDEZ.ASC (if you are storing your student data files on the disk in drive B).
3. Click on the **Open** button; enter "7/31/99" into the **Using date for this session** text box; then click on the **OK** button. Click on the **OK** button in response to the message "The date entered is more than one week past your previous **Using** date of 7/1/99." The Company Window for Valdez Realty will appear.

Modify the Fiscal End Date

4. Click on the Company Window Setup menu; then click on Company Information. The Company Information dialogue box will appear. Enter "7/31/99" as the new **Fiscal end** date; then click on the **OK** button.

Record July Transactions

5. Open the General Journal dialogue box; then record the following journal entries (enter "Memo" into the **Source** text box for each transaction; then enter the **Date** listed for each transaction):

1999		
July	1	Paid for June office supplies purchased on account, $150.
	1	Purchased additional office supplies on account, $700.
	2	Paid advertising bill for June.
	3	Sold a house and collected a commission, $6,600.
	6	Paid for gas expense, $29.
	8	Collected commission from sale of building lot on 6/17/99.
	9	Paid $2,000 of balance owing on automobile purchased June 1.
	12	Paid $300 to send employees to realtor's workshop.
	15	Paid the salary of the office secretary, $350.
	17	Sold a house and earned a commission of $2,400. Expected receipt 8/10/99.
	18	Sold a building lot and collected a commission of $7,000.
	22	Sent a cheque for $40 to help sponsor a local road race to aid the poor. (This is not to be considered an advertising expense, but it is a business expense.)
	24	Paid for repairs to automobile, $590.
	28	Juan Valdez withdrew $1,800 from the business to pay personal expenses.
	30	Paid the salary of the office secretary, $350.
	30	Paid the July telephone bill, $590.
	30	Advertising bill for July, $1,400. The bill is to be paid on 8/2/99.

Print Reports

6. After you have posted the journal entries, close the General Journal; then print the following reports:
   - **a.** General Journal (By posting date, All ledger entries, Start: 7/1/99, Finish: 7/31/99).
   - **b.** Grial Balance As at 7/31/99.

   Review your reports. If you have made an error in a posted journal entry, see Part C of Appendix B for information on how to correct the error.

Record July Adjusting Entries

7. Open the General Journal; then record adjusting journal entries based on the following adjustment data (Source: Memo; Date: 7/31/99; Comment: Adjusting entry):
   - **a.** One month's rent has expired.
   - **b.** An inventory shows $90 of office supplies remaining.
   - **c.** Depreciation on office equipment, $100.
   - **d.** Depreciation on automobile, $200.

Print Reports

8. After you have posted the adjusting journal entries, close the General Journal; then print the following reports:
   - **a.** Deneral Journal (By posting date, All ledger entries, Start: 7/1/99, Finish: 7/31/99).
   - **b.** Trial Balance As at 7/31/99.
   - **c.** General Ledger Report (Start: 7/1/99, Finish: 7/31/99, Select All).
   - **d.** Income Statement (Start: 7/1/99, Finish: 7/31/99).
   - **e.** Balance Sheet As at 7/31/99.

   Review your reports. If you have made an error in a posted journal entry, see Part C of Appendix B for information on how to correct the error.

Record Entry to Close Withdrawals Account

9. Record the closing journal entry for Juan Valdez's Withdrawals account.
10. After you have posted the closing entry for Juan Valdez's Withdrawals account, close the General Journal to return to the Company Window.

Make a Backup Copy of July Accounting Records

11. Click on the Company Window File menu; click on Save As; then enter one of the following new file names into the **Save file as** text box:

- A:\VALDJULY.ASC (if you are storing your student data files on the disk in drive A).
- B:\VALDJULY.ASC (if you are storing your student data files on the disk in drive B).

12. Click on the **Save** button. Note that the company name in the Company Window has changed from Valdez to Valdjuly. Click on the Company Window File menu again; then click on Save As. Enter one of the following new file names into the **Save file as** text box:

- A:\VALDEZ.ASC (if you are storing your student data files on the disk in drive A).
- B:\VALDEZ.ASC (if you are storing your student data files on the disk in drive B).

13. Click on the **Save** button. Click on the **yes** button in response to the question "Replace existing data files with the same name?" Note that the company name in the Company Window has changed back from Valdjuly to Valdez.

14. You now have three sets of company data files for Valdez Realty on your Student Data Files disk. The current data is stored under the file name VALDEZ.ASC. The backup data for June is stored under the file name VALDJUNE.ASC and the backup data for July is stored under the file name VALDJULY.ASC.

Advance the Using Date

15. Click on the Company Window Setup menu; then click on Advance Using Date. Enter 8/1/99 into the **New using date** text box; then click on the **OK** button. Click on the **OK** button in response to the warning message. The backup you created using the Save As method will serve as the backup suggested in the warning message.

Print a Post-Closing Trial Balance

16. Print a post-closing Trial Balance As at 8/1/99.

Exit from the Program

17. Click on the Company Window File menu; then click on Exit to end the current work session and return to your Windows desktop.

Complete the Report Transmittal

18. Complete the Valdez Realty Report Transmittal for July located in Appendix A of your *Study Guide and Working Papers.*

BANKING PROCEDURES AND CONTROL OF CASH

6

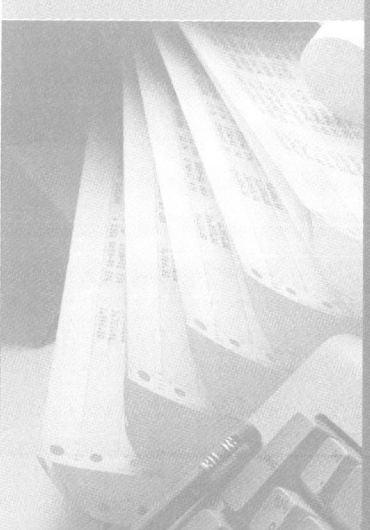

Chapter Objectives

- Depositing, writing, and endorsing cheques for a chequing account. (pp. 220 to 223)
- Reconciling a bank statement. (p. 223)
- Establishing and replenishing a petty cash fund; setting up an auxiliary petty cash record. (pp. 231 to 234)
- Establishing and replenishing a change fund. (p. 235)
- Handling transactions involving cash short and over. (pp. 235 and 236)

The internal control policies of a company will depend on things such as number of employees, company size, sources of cash, and so on.

In this chapter we introduce Art's Wholesale Clothing Company. As Art Newner finds his business increasing, he is becoming quite concerned about developing a system of procedures and records for close control over the cash receipts and cash payments of the business. This is called **internal control** and includes control over the store's assets as well as a way of monitoring the company's operations. (Certain details of the journalizing process used in Art's company are covered in detail in Chapters 9 and 10. Some instructors may take a few minutes from coverage of Chapter 6 material to briefly cover the essentials of special journals, while others may take up this chapter following Chapter 10.)

Art, his accountant, and a consultant studied the situation and developed the following company policies:

1. Responsibilities and duties of employees will be divided. For example, the person receiving the cash, whether at the register or by opening the mail, will not record this information into the accounting records. The accountant, on the other hand, will not be handling the cash receipts.
2. All cash receipts of Art's Wholesale will be deposited into the bank the same day they arrive.
3. All payments will be made by cheque (except petty cash, which will be discussed later in this chapter).
4. Employees will be rotated between jobs. This allows workers to become acquainted with the work of others as well as to prepare for a possible changeover of jobs.
5. Art Newner will sign all cheques after receiving authorization to pay from the departments concerned.
6. At time of payment, all supporting invoices or documents will be stamped paid. That will show when the invoice or document is paid as well as the number of the cheque used.
7. All cheques will be prenumbered. This will control the use of cheques and make it difficult to use a cheque fraudulently without its being revealed at some point.

Let's now look at the chequing account of Art's Wholesale along with specific bank procedures.

LEARNING UNIT 6-1

Bank Procedures, Chequing Accounts, and Bank Reconciliations

Before Art's Wholesale opened on April 1, Art had a meeting at Royal Bank to discuss the steps in opening and using a chequing account for the company.

Opening a chequing account

Purpose of a signature card.

The manager of the bank gave Art a signature card to fill out. The signature card includes space for signature(s), business and home addresses, references, type of account, and so on. The manager explained that this was for Art to sign (since he would be signing cheques for the company) so that the bank could check and validate his signature when cheques were presented for payment. The signature card would be kept in the bank's files so that possible forgeries could be spotted.

Art also received preprinted **deposit slips** and a set of cheques. The deposit slips are to be used when Art's Wholesale receives cash or cheques from any source and deposits them into the chequing account. One copy of the deposit slip stays with the bank and a duplicate copy remains with the company. Thus it can be verified that items in the cash receipts journal that make up the deposit have actually been deposited correctly.

When a bank credits your account, it is increasing the balance.

Notice on the deposit slip in Figure 6-1 that much of the information is preprinted. This saves time as well as labour in processing the deposit. If the bank is closed Art will place a locked bag (provided by the bank) in a night depository so that the deposit bag is in a safe place overnight. The bank will credit (increase) his account balance when the deposit is processed on the next banking day.

Types of cheque endorsement

Endorsements can be made by using a rubber stamp instead of a handwritten signature.

Before any cheque can be deposited or cashed, the bank requires that it be *endorsed*. Endorsement is the signing of one's name on the *back* of the cheque. This process transfers ownership to the bank, which can collect the money from the person or company that issued the cheque. Figure 6-2 shows several common types of **endorsement** that Art's Wholesale could use.

Now let's look at Art's chequebook to see how payments will be recorded.

The chequebook

Drawer—one who writes the cheque.

Drawee—one who pays money to payee.

Payee—one to whom cheque is payable.

Figure 6-3 is an example of the type of cheque used by Art's Wholesale. This **cheque** is a written order signed by Art Newner (the **drawer** or one who writes the cheque) instructing Royal Bank (**the drawee**) to pay a specific sum of money to Joe Francis Company, the **payee**, the one to whom the cheque is payable. Note some of the following key points:

1. The number of the cheque is preprinted, along with the company's address.
2. The cheque stub is filled out first. The stub will be used in recording transactions as well as for future reference. Note here that the beginning balance is $7,100; a deposit of $784 brought the balance to $7,884 before the cheque for $4,000 was written, leaving an ending balance of $3,884.
3. The long line inserted before XX/100 is meant to fill space up in the cheque so that changes cannot easily be made in the amount.
4. When the cheque is handwritten, the amount written in words should start on the far left and should use only one "and" to signify the decimal position, as in "one hundred seventeen dollars *and* 42/100".

If the written amount on the cheque doesn't match the amount expressed in figures, Royal Bank will pay the amount written in words, or will return the cheque unpaid, or will check with the drawer to see which amount is correct.

Many companies use chequewriting machines, which impress the amount of the cheque in figures and words on the cheque itself. This prevents anyone from making fraudulent changes by hand on the cheque.

Now let's turn our attention to look at the transactions of Art's Wholesale that affect the chequing account.

FIGURE 6-1 A Deposit Slip

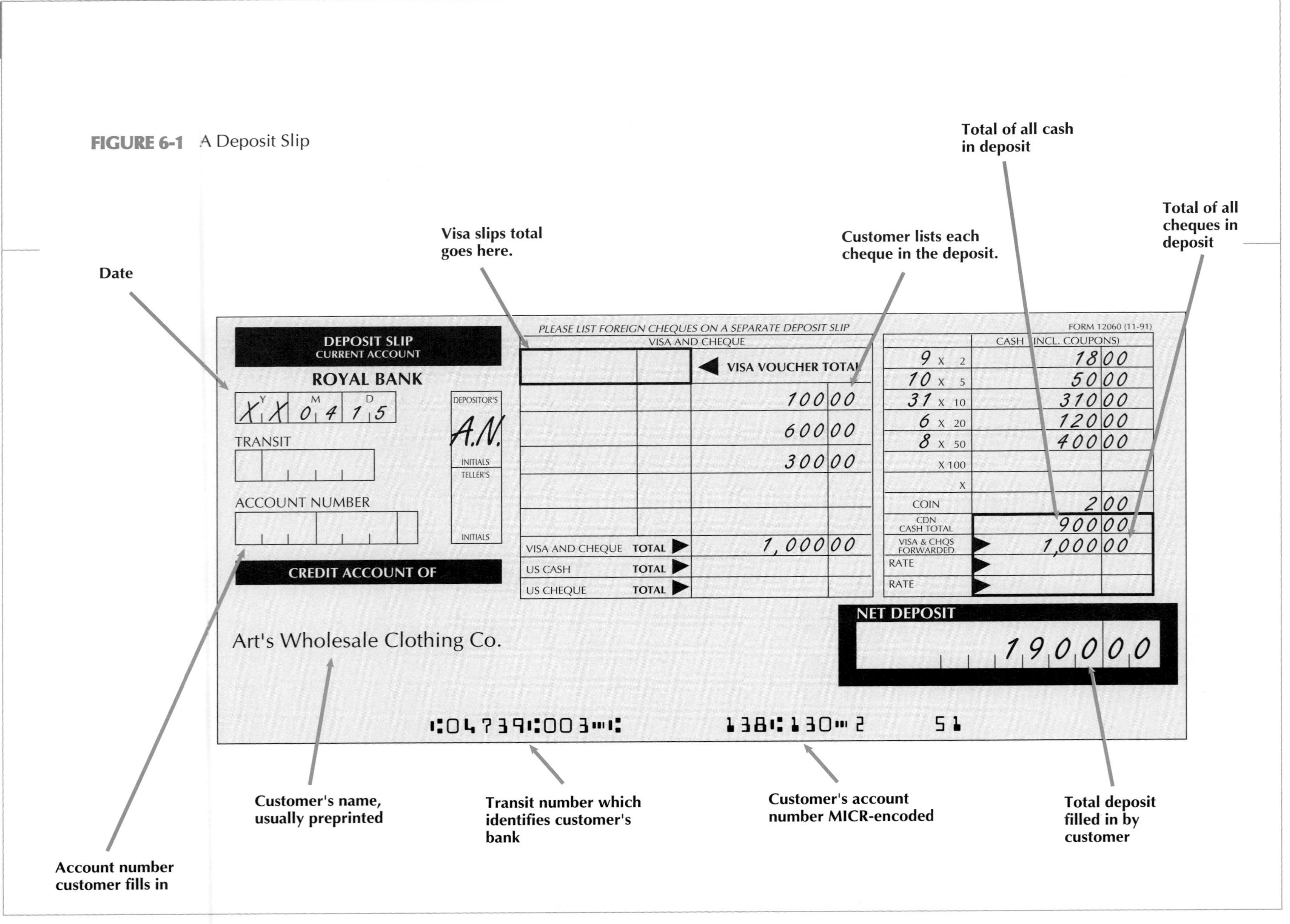

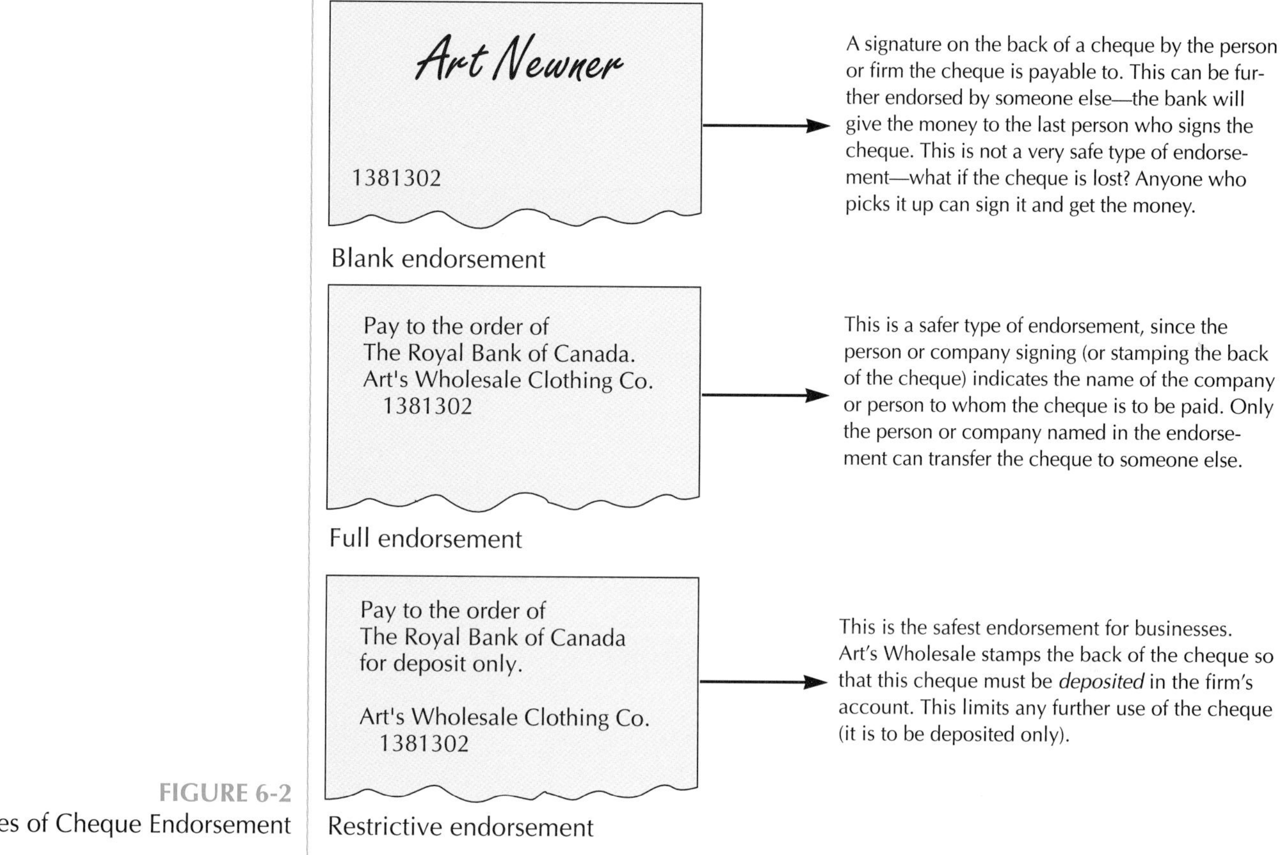

Art Newner
1381302
A signature on the back of a cheque by the person or firm the cheque is payable to. This can be further endorsed by someone else—the bank will give the money to the last person who signs the cheque. This is not a very safe type of endorsement—what if the cheque is lost? Anyone who picks it up can sign it and get the money.
Blank endorsement
Pay to the order of
The Royal Bank of Canada.
Art's Wholesale Clothing Co.
1381302
This is a safer type of endorsement, since the person or company signing (or stamping the back of the cheque) indicates the name of the company or person to whom the cheque is to be paid. Only the person or company named in the endorsement can transfer the cheque to someone else.
Full endorsement
Pay to the order of
The Royal Bank of Canada
for deposit only.
Art's Wholesale Clothing Co.
1381302
This is the safest endorsement for businesses. Art's Wholesale stamps the back of the cheque so that this cheque must be deposited in the firm's account. This limits any further use of the cheque (it is to be deposited only).
Restrictive endorsement

FIGURE 6-2
Types of Cheque Endorsement

TRANSACTIONS AFFECTING THE CHEQUEBOOK

The figures used for deposits in this chapter differ from the figures to be used in Chapter 9 mainly because of the GST — to be covered on Chapters 9 and 10.

The transactions of Art's Wholesale for the month of April that affect the chequing account (p. 218) are the same transactions that will be shown in Chapters 9 and 10 in the cash receipts and cash payments journal. Remember, all payments of money are by written cheque (except petty cash), and all money (cheques) received is deposited in the bank account.

Today some chequing accounts earn interest. The type of chequing account used by Art's Wholesale has a monthly service charge, but we assume that there is no individual charge for each cheque written, and the account does not pay interest.

Differences may result because of timing considerations.

Note in Figure 6-4 that the bank deposits ($15,324) minus the cheques written ($6,994) give an ending chequebook balance of $8,330.

At the end of April the bank sends Art a statement that the balance of the cash account is $7,919. How can this be? The following section discusses how this occurs and how it should be handled. Let's now look at the process to reconcile the difference between the bank and chequebook balances.

THE BANK RECONCILIATION PROCESS

The bank statement or report shows the beginning balance of the cash at the start of the month, along with the cheques the bank has paid and any deposits received (see Figure 6-5). Any other charges or additions to the bank balance are indicated by codes found on the statement. All cheques that have been paid by the bank are sent back to Art's Wholesale. These are called **cancelled cheques** because they have been processed by the bank and are no longer negotiable.

The problem is that this ending bank balance of $7,919 does not agree with the amount in Art's chequebook, $8,330, or the balance in the cash account in the ledger, $8,330.

FIGURE 6-3 A Typical Cheque and Cheque Stub

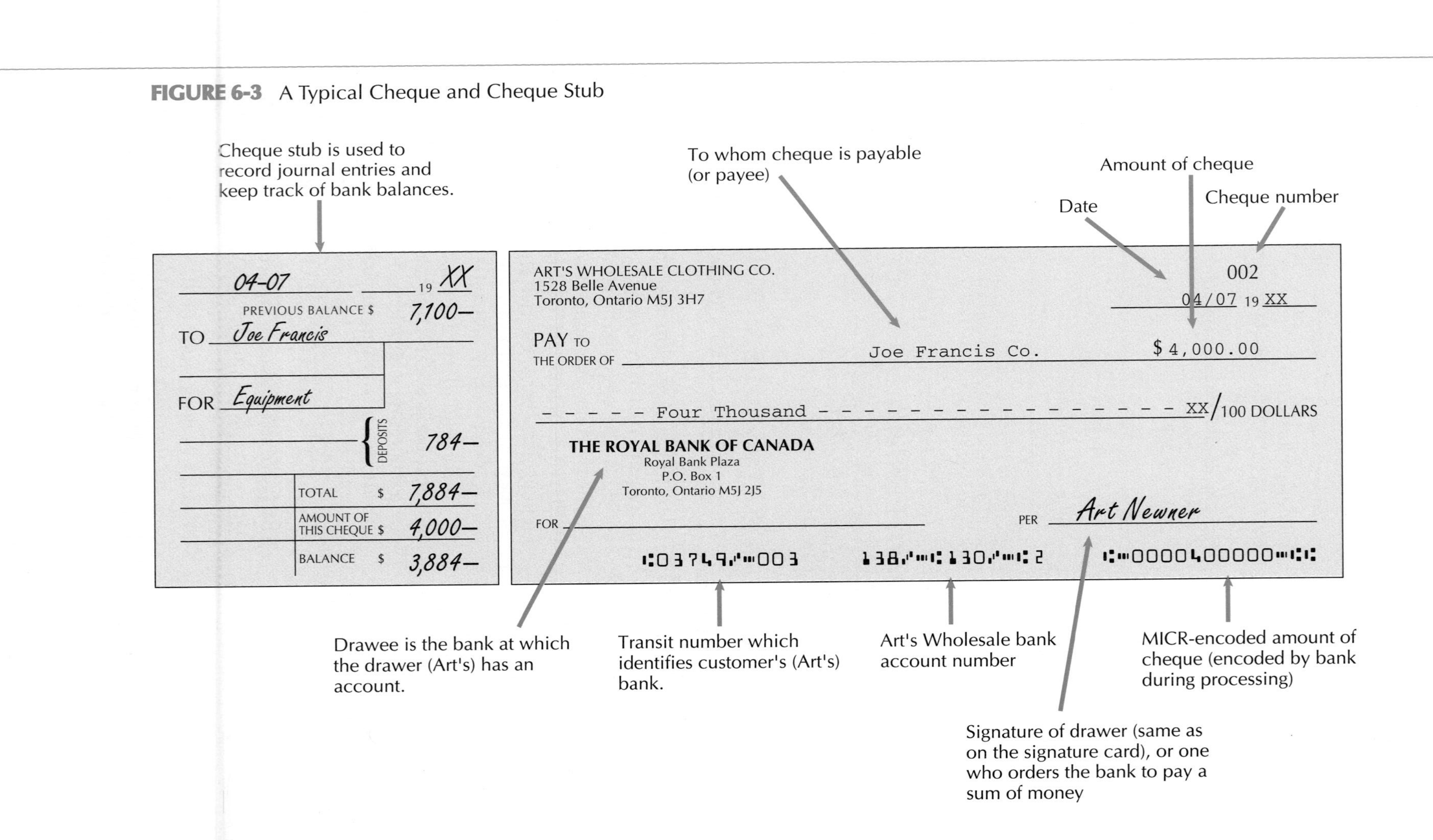

Cheque stub is used to record journal entries and keep track of bank balances.
04-07
19 XX
PREVIOUS BALANCE $ 7,100—
TO Joe Francis
FOR Equipment
DEPOSITS 784—
TOTAL $ 7,884—
AMOUNT OF THIS CHEQUE $ 4,000—
BALANCE $ 3,884—
ART'S WHOLESALE CLOTHING CO.
1528 Belle Avenue
Toronto, Ontario M5J 3H7
002
04/07 19 XX
PAY TO THE ORDER OF Joe Francis Co.
$ 4,000.00
- - - - - Four Thousand - - - - - - - - - - - - - - - - - XX/100 DOLLARS
THE ROYAL BANK OF CANADA
Royal Bank Plaza
P.O. Box 1
Toronto, Ontario M5J 2J5
FOR
PER Art Newner
To whom cheque is payable (or payee)
Date
Amount of cheque
Cheque number
Drawee is the bank at which the drawer (Art's) has an account.
Transit number which identifies customer's (Art's) bank.
Art's Wholesale bank account number
MICR-encoded amount of cheque (encoded by bank during processing)
Signature of drawer (same as on the signature card), or one who orders the bank to pay a sum of money

YVONNE JAMES

OFFICE MANAGER, BOOKKEEPER

Yvonne James was working as a secretary at a bank when her supervisor suggested that she try bookkeeping. "I learned everything on the job," she says, "and within two months I was a section head. I used to take the manuals home to try to figure out the theory behind what I was doing."

Because she had little experience, Yvonne decided to take some accounting courses at her local community college. "The College Accounting course was helpful because it gave me the fundamental background I needed," she says. "I found that the things I was feeling intuitively were correct. I learned the theory to back up my real-life experience."

Yvonne feels that in each of her jobs she has built up her knowledge, and she has reinforced her experience with the courses she needed. For example, a job as a bookkeeper at Nardi Pontiac led her to a course in automotive bookkeeping given by General Motors. "The courses provided a framework, but I also put in a good deal of hard labour. I taught myself," she says. "I was not afraid to make mistakes. I was not afraid to take work home and figure out how to do a task. I also asked a lot of questions."

Yvonne is now Office Manager, Bookkeeper at R. J. Performance Company. As an additional tip for people who want to work in bookkeeping and accounting, she advises, "Learn how to use a computer. It is vital in this field especially if you work for a small company. Knowledge of computers is essential to employers and will make you invaluable."

FIGURE 6-4
Transactions Affecting Chequebook Balance

Bank Deposits Made for April

Date of Deposit	*Amount*	*Received From:*
April 1	$8,000	Art Newner, Capital
4	784	Cheque–Hal's Clothing
15	1,900	Cash sales
16	980	Cheque–Bevans Company
22	1,960	Cheque–Roe Company
27	500	Sale of equipment
30	1,200	Cash sales
Total deposits for month:	$15,324	

Cheques Written for Month of April

Date	*Cheque No.*	*Payment To:*	*Amount*	*Description*
April 2	1	Peter Blum	$ 900	Insurance paid in advance
7	2	Joe Francis Co.	4,000	Paid equipment
9	3	Rick Flo Co.	800	Cash purchases
12	4	Thorpe Co.	594	Paid purchases
28	5	Payroll	700	Salaries
		Total amount of cheques written:	$ 6,994	

Cash/cheque	$15,324
Cheques paid	– 6,994
Balance in company chequebook	$ 8,330

ROYAL BANK PLAZA BRANCH
P.O. BOX 1
TORONTO, ONTARIO
M5J 3H7

03749

ART'S WHOLESALE CLOTHING CO.
1528 BELLE AVENUE
TORONTO, ONTARIO
M5J 3H7

Account Statement

Account No.	
138 130 2	
Period	
From	To
Apr 01/XX	Apr 25/XX
Enclosures	Page
3	1

Date	Transaction Description		Cheques & Debits	Deposits & Credits	Balance
Apr 01	Balance Forward				.00
Apr 01	Deposit			8,000.00	8,000.00
Apr 02	Cheque -	001	900.00		7,100.00
Apr 04	Deposit			784.00	7,884.00
Apr 07	Cheque -	002	4,000.00		3,884.00
Apr 09	Cheque -	003	800.00		3,084.00
Apr 15	Deposit			1,900.00	4,984.00
Apr 16	Deposit			980.00	5,964.00
Apr 22	Deposit			1,960.00	7,924.00
Apr 25	SERVICE CHARGE		5.00		7,919.00

No. of Debits	Total Amount	No. of Credits	Total Amount
4	5,705.00	5	13,624.00

FIGURE 6-5 Bank Statement

Art's accountant has to find out why there is a difference between the balances and how the records can be brought into balance. This process of reconciling the bank balance on the bank statement vs. the company's chequebook balance is called a bank reconciliation, which must be done monthly. To prepare the bank reconciliation Art's accountant takes a number of steps.

Deposits in Transit

Relationship of cash receipts journal to bank reconciliation.

Deposits in transit: These unrecorded deposits could result if a deposit were placed in a night depository on the last day of the month.

In comparing the list of deposits received by the bank with the cash receipts journal* (Figure 6-6), the accountant notices that the two deposits made on April 27 and 30 for $500 and $1,200 are not on the bank's statement. The accountant realizes that in order to prepare this statement, the bank only included information about Art's Wholesale up to April 25. These two deposits made by Art were not shown on the monthly bank statement, since they arrived at the bank after the statement was printed. This timing becomes a consideration in the reconciliation process. The deposits not yet added on to the bank balance are called **deposits in transit**. These two deposits need to be added to the bank balance shown on the bank statement.

Art's Wholesale's chequebook is not affected, since the two deposits have already been added to its balance. The bank has no way of knowing that the deposits are coming until they are received.

* To be covered in detail in Chapter 9.

ART'S WHOLESALE CLOTHING COMPANY
CASH RECEIPTS JOURNAL

Page 1

Date 19XX		Cash Dr.	Sales Discounts Dr.	Accounts Receivable Cr.	Sales Cr.	Sundry Account Name	Post. Ref.	Amount Cr.
April	1	✓800000				Art Newner, Capital	311	800000
	4	✓ 78400	1600	80000		Hal's Clothing	✓	
	15	✓190000			190000	Cash Sales	✗	
	16	✓ 98000	2000	100000		Bevans Company	✓	
	22	✓196000	4000	200000		Roe Company	✓	
	27	50000				Store Equipment	121	50000
	30	120000			120000	Cash Sales	✗	
	30	1532400	7600	380000	310000			850000
		(111)	(413)	(113)	(411)			(X)

FIGURE 6-6
Cash Receipts Journal

Outstanding Cheques

Relationship of cash payments journal to bank reconciliation.

The accountant places the cheques returned by the bank in numerical order (1, 2, 3, etc.). He opens the cash payments journal* (Figure 6-7) and places a checkmark (√) next to each payment cheque that was returned by the bank. This indicates that the amount shown in the cash payments journal has been paid and the bank has returned the cheques processed (or cancelled after payment). The accountant notices in the cash payments journal that two payments were not made by the bank and that these cheques, nos. 4 and 5, were not returned by the bank. On Art's Wholesale's books these two cheques have been deducted from the chequebook balance; therefore, these **outstanding cheques**, or cheques that have not been presented to the bank for payment, need to be deducted from the bank balance. At some point these cheques will reach the bank. Keep in mind that the chequebook balance has already subtracted the amount of these two cheques; it is the *bank* that has no idea that these cheques have been written. When they are presented for payment, then the bank will reduce the amount of the balance.

Cheque nos. 4 and 5 are outstanding.

Cheques outstanding: Drawn by depositor but have not reached bank for payment.

Note in Figure 6-6 how the $500 and $1,200 are not checked off, since they did not appear on the bank statement.

The accountant also notices a bank service charge of $5. This means that Art's wholesale's chequebook balance should be lowered by $5.

The accountant is continually on the lookout for **NSF (nonsufficient funds)** cheques. This means that when the company deposits a cheque, occasionally it

ART'S WHOLESALE CLOTHING COMPANY
CASH PAYMENTS JOURNAL

Page 1

Date 19XX		Chq. No.	Account Debited	Post. Ref.	Sundry Payable Dr.	Accounts Payable Dr.	Purchases Discount Cr.	Cash Cr.	
April	2	1	Prepaid Insurance	116	90000			90000	✓
	7	2	Joe Francis Company	✓		400000		400000	✓
	9	3	Purchases, Thor. Co.	511	80000			80000	✓
	12	4	Thorpe Company	✓		60000	600	59400	
	28	5	Salaries Expense, ABH	611	70000			70000	
	30				240000	460000	600	699400	
					(X)	(211)	(512)	(111)	

FIGURE 6-7
Cash Payments Journal

* To be covered in detail in Chapter 10.

Debit memorandum: Deducted from balance.

will be returned due to the customer's lack of sufficient funds. If this happens, it will result in Art's Wholesale having less money than was thought and thus having to (1) lower the chequebook balance and (2) try to collect the amount from the customer. The bank would notify Art's Wholesale of an NSF (or other deductions) cheque by a **debit memorandum**. Think of a debit memorandum as a deduction from the depositor's balance. Since to a bank, a customer's account represents a liability (the bank must pay out funds if the customer so directs), any reduction in the fund balance requires a debit — hence the term "debit memorandum". Of course, a debit memorandum is recorded by a credit (to cash) on the books of the customer.

Credit memorandum: Addition to balance.

If the bank acts as a collecting agent for Art's Wholesale, say in collecting notes, it will charge Art a small fee, and the net amount collected will be added to the bank balance. The bank will send to Art a **credit memorandum** verifying the increase in the depositor's balance. This would be recorded by a debit in the company's books as the bank account (an asset) is increasing.

A bank reconciliation can be done on the back of the bank statement (see Figure 6-8. Note that the chequebook balance of $8,330 less the $5 service charge will in fact equal the adjusted balance.

A journal entry is also needed to bring the ledger accounts of cash and service charge expense up to date. Any adjustment to the chequebook balance results in a journal entry. The following entry was made to accomplish this:

Adjustments to the chequebook balance must be journalized and posted. This keeps the depositor's ledger accounts (especially cash) up to date.

April	30	Service Charge Expense*	5 00	
		Cash		5 00

* Could be recorded as miscellaneous expense, or bank charges expense.

Example of a More Comprehensive Bank Reconciliation

Keep in mind that both the bank and the depositor can make mistakes that will not be discovered until the reconciliation process.

The bank reconciliation of Art's Wholesale, which we have just prepared, was not as complicated as it might have been for many other companies. Let's take a

HOW TO BALANCE THIS STATEMENT WITH YOUR RECORD OF DEPOSITS AND WITHDRAWALS

1. Mark off on your account record all deposits and withdrawals appearing on the front of this account statement.
2. Enter any deposits and withdrawals not recorded in your account record (i.e., bank interest or fees).
3. Complete the worksheet below. If we can be of assistance to you, please contact us.

ACCOUNT RECONCILIATION WORKSHEET

ENTER the closing balance shown on the front of this account statement:			7,919.00
ADD all deposits/credits which do not appear on this account statement:		500.00	
		1,200.00	
TOTAL additions:		> +	1,700.00
SUB TOTAL:			9,619.00
SUBTRACT all withdrawals/debits which do not appear on this account statement:	4	594.00	
	5	700.00	
TOTAL subtractions:		> −	1,294.00
This balance should agree with your record of deposits and withdrawals:			8,325.00

FIGURE 6-8
Bank Reconciliation Using Back of Bank Statement

moment to look at the bank reconciliation for Monroe Company, which is based on the following:

1. Chequebook balance: $3,978.
2. Balance reported by bank: $5,230.
3. Recorded in journal cheque no. 108 for $54 *more* than should have been when store equipment was purchased.
4. Bank collected a note ($2,000) for Monroe, charging a collection fee of $10.
5. A bounced cheque for $252 (NSF) has to be covered by Monroe. The bank has lowered Monroe's balance by $252 (see Figure 6-9).
6. Bank service charge of $10.
7. Deposits in transit, $1,084.
8. Cheques not yet processed by the bank:

Cheque	*Amount*
191	$204
198	250
201	100

DM: Remember, a debit memorandum is sent by the bank indicating a reduction in depositor's balance. Examples: NSF, cheque printing.

FIGURE 6-9
Bank Reconciliation of Monroe Company

MONROE COMPANY
BANK RECONCILIATION AS OF JUNE 30, 19XX

Chequebook Balance			Balance per Bank		
Ending Chequebook Balance		$3,978	Bank Statement Balance		$5,230
Add:			Add:		
Error in recording Cheque no. 108	$54		Deposits in Transit		1,084
					$6,314
Proceeds of a note* less collection charge by bank	1,990	2,044	Deduct:		
		$6,022	Cheque no.	191..$204	
				198.. 250	
Deduct:				201.. 100	554
NSF Cheque	$252				
Bank Service Charge	10	262			
Reconciled Balance		$5,760	Reconciled Balance		$5,760

* We will discuss Notes Receivable in a later chapter—for now, think of it as a kind of written Accounts Receivable.

Note the following journal entries needed to update Monroe Company's books. *Every time an adjustment is made in the reconciliation process to the chequebook balance, a journal entry will be needed.*

CM: A credit memorandum is sent by a bank indicating an increase in depositor's balance. Example: collecting a note.

Remember: If Monroe Company's chequing account was the type that earned interest, it would have increased the chequebook balance.

19XX				Dr.	Cr.
June	30	Cash		1 9 9 0 00	
		Collection Expense		1 0 00	
		Notes Receivable*			2 0 0 0 00
	30	Cash		5 4 00	
		Store Equipment			5 4 00
	30	Acct. Rec., Alvin Sooth		2 5 2 00	
		Cash			2 5 2 00
	30	Miscellaneous Expense		1 0 00	
		Cash			1 0 00

* We will discuss Notes Receivable in a later chapter—for now, think of it as a kind of written Accounts Receivable.

Before summing up this unit, let's look at two interesting trends in the banking field.

New trends in banking

Electronic Funds Transfer

Many financial institutions have developed or are developing a way to transfer funds among parties electronically, without the use of paper cheques. The system that does this is called **electronic funds transfer (EFT)**. Let's look at an example.

Grant MacEwan Community College, with appropriate authorization from its employees, deposits payroll cheques directly into each employee's bank account, rather than issuing paper cheques. The bank, on receiving computer-coded payroll data, adds each employee's payroll amount to his or her account. This saves time and the possible loss or theft of payroll cheques.

Another good example is the **automatic teller machine (ATM)**. Expect to see these machines used for more transactions than simple banking chores. Sale of stamps, bus passes, and similar items is a real possibility. We now also see bank cards used in fast food chains and other retail establishments (the term **debit card** is used in connection with these transactions as a substitute for cash).

We may also see increased use of "smart cards" where the amount of cash is electronically embedded in the card itself and is read by an electronic device at a check-out to pay for purchases.

Cheque Truncation (Safekeeping)

Some banks do not return cancelled cheques to the depositor but use a procedure called **cheque truncation** or **safekeeping**. What this means is that the bank holds a cancelled cheque for a specific period of time (usually 90 days) and then keeps a microfilm copy handy. What happens if a copy of a cheque is needed? For a small fee the bank provides the depositor with the cheque or a photocopy. (Photocopies will be accepted as evidence by the Revenue Canada for tax returns and audits.)

Truncation cuts down on the amount of "paper" that is returned to customers and thus provides substantial cost savings. It is estimated that over five million cheques are written each day in Canada.

LEARNING UNIT 6-1 REVIEW

AT THIS POINT you should be able to

- Define and explain the need for deposit slips. (p. 221)
- Explain where the bank's transit number is located on the cheque and what its purpose is. (p. 222)
- List and compare and contrast the three common types of cheque endorsement. (p. 223)
- Explain the structure of a cheque. (p. 224)
- Define and state the purpose of a bank statement. (p. 223)
- Explain the relationship of special journals to the bank reconciliation process. (p. 227)
- Explain deposits in transit, cheques outstanding, service charge, and NSF. (pp. 226–227)

- Explain the difference between a debit memorandum and a credit memorandum. (p. 228)
- Explain how to do a bank reconciliation. (p. 229)
- Explain electronic funds transfer and cheque truncation. (p. 230)

SELF-REVIEW QUIZ 6-1

Indicate, by placing an X under it, the heading that describes the appropriate action for each of the following situations:

Situation	Add to Bank Balance	Deduct from Bank Balance	Add to Chequebook Balance	Deduct from Chequebook Balance
1. Bank service charge				
2. Deposits in transit				
3. NSF cheque				
4. A $50 cheque written and recorded by the company as $60				
5. Proceeds of a note collected by the bank				
6. Cheque outstanding				

Solution to Self-Review Quiz 6-1

Situation	Add to Bank Balance	Deduct from Bank Balance	Add to Chequebook Balance	Deduct from Chequebook Balance
1				X
2	X			
3				X
4			X	
5			X	
6		X		

LEARNING UNIT 6-2

The Establishment of a Petty Cash Fund

Petty Cash is an asset on the balance sheet.

Art realized how time-consuming and expensive it would be to write cheques for small amounts to pay for postage, small supplies, delivery charges, and so on. What was needed was a **petty cash fund**. It was estimated that for any given month, Art's Wholesale would need a fund of $60 to cover small expenditures. A cheque payable to the order of the custodian was drawn and cashed to establish the fund. The cash was placed in a small metal box with a simple lock which gave control of the fund to the custodian. Payments out of the fund were only made when a receipt or other supporting documentation was presented by the person requesting the money.

Petty Cash is an asset which is established by writing a new cheque. The Petty Cash account is debited only once unless a greater or lesser amount of petty cash is needed on a regular basis.

Setting up the Fund

Shown here is the transaction analysis chart for the establishment of a $60 petty cash fund, which would be entered in the cash payments journal on May 1, 19XX.

1 Accounts Affected	2 Category	3 ↑↓	4 Rules
Petty Cash	Asset	↑	Dr.
Cash (cheques)	Asset	↓	Cr.

CASH PAYMENTS JOURNAL

Page 2

Date		Chq. No.	Account Debited	PR	Sundry Dr.	Accounts Payable Dr.	Purchases Discount Cr.	Cash Cr.
May	1	6	Petty Cash	112	60 00			60 00

Note the new asset called *Petty Cash*; this new asset was created by writing cheque no. 6, thereby reducing the asset Cash. In reality, the total assets stay the same; what has occurred is a shift from the asset Cash (cheque no. 6) to a new asset account called Petty Cash.

The cheque for $60 is drawn to the order of the custodian, cashed, and the proceeds turned over to John Sullivan, the custodian.

The Petty Cash account is not debited or credited again if the size of the fund is not changed. If the $60 fund is used up very quickly, the fund should be increased. If the fund is too large, the Petty Cash account should be reduced.

But who is responsible for controlling the petty cash fund? Art gives his office manager, John Sullivan, the responsibility and the authority to make payments from the petty cash fund. In other companies the cashier or secretary may be in charge of petty cash.

Making Payments from the Petty Cash Fund

John Sullivan has the responsibility for filling out a **petty cash voucher** for each cash payment made from the petty cash fund.

Note that the voucher (shown in Figure 6-10) when completed will include

1. The voucher number (which will be in sequence): 1.
2. The date: May 2.
3. The person or organization to whom the payment was made: Al's Cleaners.
4. The amount of payment: $3.00.
5. The reason for payment: cleaning.
6. The signature of the person who approved the payment: John Sullivan.
7. The signature of the person who received the payment from petty cash: Art Newner.
8. The account to which the expense will be charged.

Vouchers in box
+ Cash in box
= Original amount placed in petty cash

The completed vouchers are placed in the petty cash box. No matter how many vouchers John Sullivan fills out, *the total of (1) the vouchers in the box and (2) the cash on hand should equal the original amount of petty cash with which the fund was established ($60).*

Petty Cash Voucher No. 1

Date: May 2, 19XX   Amount: $3.00

Paid To: Al's Cleaners

For: Cleaning Package

Approved By: John Sullivan

Payment Received By: Art Newner

Debit Account No.: 619

FIGURE 6-10
Petty Cash Voucher

Assume that at the end of May the following items are documented by petty cash vouchers in the petty cash box as having been paid by John Sullivan:

19XX

May 2 Cleaning package, $3.00.
5 Postage stamps, $9.00.
8 First aid supplies, $15.00.
9 Delivery expense, $6.00.
14 Delivery expense, $15.00.
27 Postage stamps, $6.00.

Think of the auxiliary petty cash record as a worksheet that gathers information for the journal entry.

John records this information in the auxiliary petty cash record shown in Figure 6-11. It is not a special journal, but an aid to John—an auxiliary record that is not essential but is quite helpful as part of the petty cash system. You may want to think of the auxiliary petty cash as an optional worksheet. Let's look at how to replenish the petty cash fund.

How to replenish the petty cash fund

No postings will be done from the auxiliary book; it is not a journal. At some point the summarized information found in the auxiliary petty cash record will be used as a basis for a journal entry in the cash payments journal and eventually posted to appropriate ledger accounts to reflect up-to-date balances.

This $54 of expenses (see Figure 6-11) is recorded in the cash payments journal (Figure 6-12) and a new cheque, no. 17, for $54 is cashed and returned to John Sullivan. The petty cash box now once again reflects $60 cash. The old vouchers that were used are stamped to indicate that they have been processed and the fund replenished.

FIGURE 6-11 Auxiliary Petty Cash Record

Date 19XX		Voucher No.	Description	Receipts	Payments	Category of Payments			
						Postage Expense	Delivery Expense	Sundry	
								Account	Amount
May	1		Establishment	60 00					
	2	1	Cleaning		3 00			Cleaning	3 00
	5	2	Postage		9 00	9 00			
	8	3	First Aid		15 00			Misc.	15 00
	9	4	Delivery		6 00		6 00		
	14	5	Delivery		15 00		15 00		
	27	6	Postage		6 00	6 00			
			Total	60 00	54 00	15 00	21 00		18 00

CASH PAYMENTS JOURNAL

Establishment | Page 2

Date 19XX		Chq. No.	Accounts Debited	PR	Sundry Cr.	Accounts Payable Dr.	Purchase Discount Cr.	Cash Cr.
								60 00
May	1	6	Petty Cash	112	60 00			
Replenishment								
	31		Postage Expense	616	15 00			
			Delivery Expense	620	21 00			
			Cleaning Expense	619	3 00			
		17	Misc. Expense	617	15 00			54 00

FIGURE 6-12
Establishment and Replenishment of Petty Cash Fund

In replenishment, old expenses are updated in journal and ledger to show where money has gone.

Note that in the replenishment process the debits in the cash payments journal (Figure 6-12) are a summary of the totals (except sundry) of expenses or other items from the auxiliary petty cash record. Posting of these specific expenses will assure that the expenses will not be understated on the income statement. *The end result is that our petty cash box is filled, and we have justified which accounts the petty cash money was spent for. Think of replenishment as a single, summarizing entry.*

A new cheque is written in the replenishment process, which is payable to the custodian, cashed by Sullivan, and the cash placed in the petty cash box.

Remember, if at some point the petty cash fund is to be greater than $60, a cheque can be written that will increase Petty Cash and decrease Cash. If the Petty Cash account balance is to be reduced, we can credit or reduce Petty Cash. But for our present purpose Petty Cash will remain at $60.

The auxiliary petty cash record after replenishment would look as follows (keep in mind no postings are made from the auxiliary):

AUXILIARY PETTY CASH RECORD

Date 19XX		Voucher No.	Description	Receipts	Payments	Category of Payments: Postage Expense	Delivery Expense	Sundry: Account	Amount
May	1		Establishment	60 00					
	2	1	Cleaning		3 00			Cleaning	3 00
	5	2	Postage		9 00	9 00			
	8	3	First Aid		15 00			Misc.	15 00
	9	4	Delivery		6 00		6 00		
	14	5	Delivery		15 00		15 00		
	27	6	Postage		6 00	6 00			
			Totals	60 00	54 00	15 00	21 00		18 00
			Ending Balance		6 00				
				60 00	60 00				
			Ending Balance	6 00					
	31		Replenishment	54 00					
	31		Balance (New)	60 00					

The diagram in Figure 6-13 may help you put the sequence together.

Before concluding this unit, let's look at how Art will handle a change fund and problems with cash shortages and overages.

FIGURE 6-13
Steps Involving Petty Cash

Date 19XX		Description	New Cheque Written	Recorded in Cash Payments Journal	Petty Cash Voucher Prepared	Recorded in Auxiliary Petty Cash Record
May	1	Establishment of petty cash for $60	X	X		X
	2	Paid salaries, $2,000	X	X		
	13	Paid $10 from petty cash for bandages			X	X
	19	Paid $8 from petty cash for postage			X	X
	24	Paid light bill, $200	X	X		
	29	Replenishment of petty cash to $60	X	X		X

Has nothing to do with petty cash. (→ May 2 and May 24)

In this step the old expenses are listed in cash payments journal and a new cheque is written to replenish. (→ May 29)

THE CHANGE FUND AND CASH SHORT AND OVER

Change Fund is an asset on the balance sheet.

If a company like Art's Wholesale expects to have many cash transactions occurring, it may be a good idea to establish a **change fund** or float. This is a fund that is placed in the cash register drawer and used to make change for customers who pay cash. Art decides to put $120 in the change fund, made up of various denominations of bills and coins. Let's look at a transaction analysis chart for this sort of procedure.

1 Accounts Affected	2 Category	3 ↑↓	4 Dr./Cr.
Change Fund	Asset	↑	Dr.
Cash	Asset	↓	Cr.

At the close of the business day Art will deposit in the bank the cash taken in for the day but will place the amount of the change fund back in the safe in the office. He will set up the change fund (the same $120) in the appropriate denominations for the next business day.

Now let's look at how to record errors that are made in making change, called *cash short and over*.

Cash short and over

Beg. change fund
+ Cash register total
= Cash should have on hand
– Counted cash
= Shortage or overage of cash

Errors often occur in making change, and so the amount of cash will often be higher or lower than it should be. An account called **Cash Short and Over** will accumulate these shortages or overages. Shortages are debited to the account; overages are credited. At the end of the accounting period, if there are more shortages than overages (debit balance), the net shortage is shown on the income statement as a miscellaneous expense. If the ending balance is an overage (credit balance), it is reported on the income statement as miscellaneous income.

Cash Short and Over

Shortages	Overages
↑	↑
Misc. Expense	Misc. Income

Example 1: Cash register tapes don't agree with cash receipts.

SITUATION 1: OVERAGE

Dec.	5	Cash	550	
		Cash Short and Over		1
		Sales		549

SITUATION 2: SHORTAGE

Dec.	15	Cash	600	
		Cash Short and Over	5	
		Sales		605

Using Cash Short and Over with Petty Cash.

Example 2: Petty Cash has a shortage of $8. The facts are:

$200	Petty Cash account
160	in receipts for expenses
32	in coin and currency

A general journal entry would look as follows:

Individual Expenses	160	
Cash Short and Over	8	
Cash		168

Keep in mind that in actuality we would use a cash payments journal as well as debit *each* individual expense.

If an auxiliary petty cash record is used to record the cash short and over, it would be recorded as a payment of $8 under the category of payments in the sundry column.

LEARNING UNIT 6-2 REVIEW

AT THIS POINT you should be able to

- State the purpose of a petty cash fund. (p. 231)
- Prepare a journal entry to establish a petty cash fund. (p. 232)
- Prepare a petty cash voucher. (p. 233)
- Explain the relationship of the auxiliary petty cash record to the petty cash process. (p. 234)
- Prepare a journal entry to replenish Petty Cash to its original amount. (p. 234)
- Explain why individual expenses are debited in the replenishment process. (p. 235)
- Explain how a change fund is established. (p. 235)
- Explain how Cash Short and Over could be a miscellaneous expense. (p. 235)

SELF-REVIEW QUIZ 6-2

As the custodian of the petty cash fund it is your task to prepare entries to establish the fund on October 1, as well as to replenish the fund on October 31. Please keep an auxiliary petty cash record.

19XX

Oct. 1 Establish petty cash fund for $90, cheque no. 8.

5 Voucher 1, delivery expense, $21.

9 Voucher 2, delivery expense, $15.

10 Voucher 3, office repair expense, $24.

17 Voucher 4, general expense, $12.

25 Voucher 5, general expense, $6.

30 Replenishment of petty cash fund, $78, cheque no. 108. (Cheque would be payable to the custodian.)

Cheques to establish and replenish Petty Cash would be made out to the custodian.

Solution to Self-Review Quiz 6-2

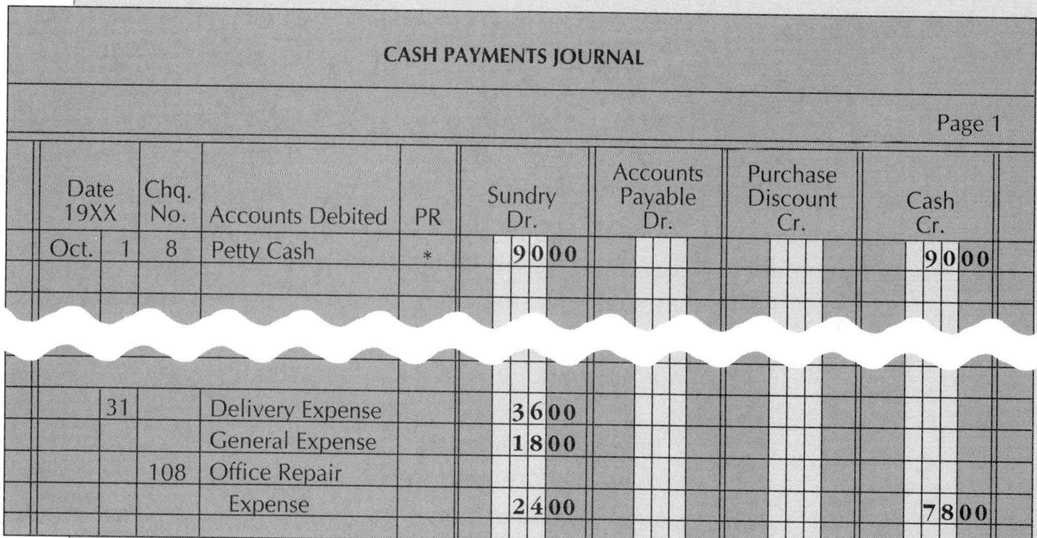

CASH PAYMENTS JOURNAL

Page 1

Date 19XX		Chq. No.	Accounts Debited	PR	Sundry Dr.	Accounts Payable Dr.	Purchase Discount Cr.	Cash Cr.
Oct.	1	8	Petty Cash	*	90 00			90 00
	31		Delivery Expense		36 00			
			General Expense		18 00			
		108	Office Repair Expense		24 00			78 00

* The PR would show posting. Deleted for simplicity at this point.

AUXILIARY PETTY CASH RECORD

Date 19XX		Voucher No.	Description	Receipts	Payments	Delivery Expense	General Expense	Sundry Account	Sundry Amount
Oct.	1		Establishment	90 00					
	5	1	Delivery		21 00	21 00			
	9	2	Delivery		15 00	15 00			
	10	3	Repairs		24 00			Office Repairs	24 00
	17	4	General		12 00		12 00		
	25	5	General		6 00		6 00		
			Totals	90 00	78 00	36 00	18 00		24 00
			Ending Balance		12 00				
				90 00	90 00				
	30		Ending Balance	12 00					
	31		Replenishment	78 00					
Nov.	1		Balance (New)	90 00					

Chapter Review

Summary of key points

Learning Unit 6-1

1. Restrictive endorsement limits any further negotiation of a cheque.
2. Cheque stubs are filled out first before a cheque is written.
3. The payee is the person to whom the cheque is payable.The drawer is the one who orders the bank to pay a sum of money.The drawee is the bank where the drawer has an account.
4. The process of reconciling the bank balance with the company's balance is called bank reconciliation.The timing of deposits, when the bank statement was issued, etc., often result in differences between the bank balance and the chequebook balance.
5. Deposits in transit are added to the bank balance.
6. Cheques outstanding are subtracted from the bank balance.
7. NSF means that an account has insufficient funds to pay a cheque; therefore the amount is not included in the recipient's bank balance and the chequing account balance is lowered.
8. When a bank debits your account they are deducting an amount from your balance.A credit to the account is an increase to your balance.
9. All adjustments to the chequebook balance require journal entries.

Learning Unit 6-2

1. Petty Cash is an asset found on the balance sheet.
2. The auxiliary petty cash record is an auxiliary book; thus no postings are done from this book.Think of it as an optional worksheet.
3. When a petty cash fund is established, the amount is entered as a debit to Petty Cash and a credit to Cash in the cash payments journal.
4. At time of replenishment of the petty cash fund, all expenses are debited (by category) and a credit to Cash (a new cheque) results.This replenishment, when journalized and posted, updates the ledger from the journal.
5. The only time the Petty Cash account is used is to establish the fund to begin with or bring the fund to a higher or lower level. If the petty cash level is deemed sufficient, all replenishments will debit specific expenses and new cheques written.The asset Petty Cash will remain the same.
6. A change fund is an asset that is used to make change for customers.
7. Cash Short and Over is an account that is either a miscellaneous expense or miscellaneous income, depending on whether the ending balance is shortage or overage.

Key terms

ATM Automatic teller machine.

Auxiliary petty cash record A supplementary record for summarizing petty cash information.

Bank reconciliation This is the process of reconciling the chequebook balance with the bank balance given on the bank statement.

Bank statement A report sent by a bank to a customer indicating the previous balance, individual cheques processed, individual deposits received, service charges, and ending bank balance.

Cancelled cheque A cheque that has been processed by a bank and is no longer negotiable.

Cash Short and Over The account that records cash shortages and overages. If ending balance is a debit, it is recorded on the income statement as a miscellaneous expense; if it is a credit, it is recorded as miscellaneous income.

Change fund Fund made up of various denominations of bills and coins that is used to make change to customers.

Cheque A form used to indicate a specific amount of money that is to be paid by the bank to a named person or company.

Cheque truncation (safekeeping) Procedure whereby cheques are not returned to drawer with the bank statement but are instead kept at the bank for a certain amount of time before being first transferred to microfilm and then destroyed.

Credit memorandum Increase in depositor's balance.

Debit memorandum Decrease in depositor's balance.

Deposits in transit Deposits that were made by customers of a bank but did not reach, or were not processed by, the bank before the preparation of the bank statement.

Deposit slip A form provided by a bank for use in depositing money or cheques into a chequing account.

Drawee Bank that drawer has an account with.

Drawer Person who writes a cheque.

Endorsement *Blank*—could be further endorsed. *Full*—restricts further endorsement to only the person or company named. *Restrictive*—restricts any further endorsement.

EFT (electronic funds transfer) An electronic system that transfers funds without use of paper cheques.

Internal control A system of procedures and methods to control a firm's assets as well as monitor its operations.

NSF (Nonsufficient Funds) Notation indicating that a cheque has been written on an account that lacks sufficient funds to back it up.

Outstanding cheques Cheques written by a company or person that were not received or not processed by the bank before the preparation of the bank statement.

Payee The person or company the cheque is payable to.

Petty cash fund A fund (source) that allows payment of small amounts without the writing of cheques.

Petty cash voucher A petty cash form to be completed when money is taken out of petty cash.

Blueprint of a Bank Reconciliation

			Balance per Bank		
Ending Balance per Books		$XXX	Ending Bank Statement Balance (last figure on bank statement)		$XXX
Add:			Add:		
Recording of errors that understate balance	XXX		Deposits in transit (amount not yet credited by bank)	XXX	
Proceeds of notes collected by bank or other items credited (added) by bank but not yet updated in chequebook	XXX	XXX	Bank errors	XXX	XXX
Deduct:			Deduct:		
Recording of errors that overstate balance	XXX		List of outstanding cheques (amount not yet debited by bank)	XXX	
Service charges	XXX		Bank errors	XXX	XXX
Printing charges	XXX				
NSF cheque, etc., or other items debited (charged) by bank but not yet updated in chequebook	XXX	XXX			
Reconciled Balance (Adjusted Balance)		$XXX	Reconciled Balance (Adjusted Balance)		$XXX

Questions, Exercises, and Problems

Discussion Questions

1. What is the purpose of internal control?
2. What is the advantage of having preprinted deposit slips?
3. Explain the difference between a blank endorsement and a restrictive endorsement.
4. Explain the difference between payee, drawer, and drawee.
5. Why should cheque stubs be filled out first, before the cheque itself is written?
6. "A bank statement is sent twice a month." True or false? Please explain.
7. Explain the end product of a bank reconciliation.
8. Why are cheques outstanding subtracted from the bank balance?
9. "An NSF results in a bank issuing the depositor a credit memorandum." Agree or disagree. Please support your response.
10. Why do adjustments to the chequebook balance in the reconciliation process need to be journalized?
11. What is EFT?
12. What is meant by cheque truncation or safekeeping?
13. "Petty cash is a liability." Accept or reject.
14. Explain the relationship of the auxiliary petty cash record to the cash payments journal.

15. At time of replenishment, why are the totals of individual expenses debited?
16. Explain the purpose of a change fund.
17. Explain how Cash Short and Over can be a miscellaneous expense.

Mini Exercises

(The blank forms you need are on page 6-4 in the *Study Guide and Working Papers.*)

Bank Reconciliation

1. Indicate what effect each situation will have on the bank reconciliation process:

   1. Add to bank balance
   2. Deduct from bank balance
   3. Add to chequebook balance
   4. Deduct from chequekbook balance

   ____ **a.** $5 bank service charge
   ____ **b.** $100 deposit in transit
   ____ **c.** $30 NSF cheque
   ____ **d.** A $15 cheque was written and recorded as $25
   ____ **e.** Bank collected a $1,000 note less $50 collection fee
   ____ **f.** Cheque no. 111 was outstanding for $55

Journal Entries in Reconciliation Process

2. Which of the transactions in question 1 above would require a journal entry?

Bank Reconciliation

3. From the following construct a bank reconciliation for Woody Co. as of May 31, 19XX.

Chequebook balance	$10
Bank statement balance	15
Deposits in transit	5
Outstanding cheques	15
Bank service charge	5

Petty Cash

4. Indicate what effect each situation will have:

   1. New cheque written
   2. Recorded in general journal
   3. Petty cash voucher prepared
   4. Recorded in auxiliary petty cash record.

   ____ **a.** Established petty cash
   ____ **b.** Paid $1,000 bill
   ____ **c.** Paid $2 for band-aids from petty cash

____ **d.** Paid $3,000 for stamps from petty cash

____ **e.** Paid electric bill, $250

____ **f.** Replenished petty cash

Replenishment of Petty Cash

5. Petty cash was originally established for $20. During the month $5 was paid out for band-aids and $6 for stamps. During replenishment custodian discovered balance in petty cash was $8. Record using a general journal entry the replenishment of petty cash back to $20.

Increasing Petty Cash

6. In question 5 above, if the custodian decided to raise the level of petty cash to $30, what would be the journal entry to replenish (use a general journal entry)?

Exercises

Bank reconciliation.

6-1. From the following information, construct a bank reconciliation for Norry Co. as of July 31, 19XX. Then prepare journal entries if needed.

Ending chequebook balance	$465
Ending bank statement balance	393
Deposits (in transit)	180
Outstanding cheques	125
Bank service charge (debit memo)	17

Establishing and replenishing petty cash.

6-2. In general journal form, prepare journal entries to establish a petty cash fund on July 1 and replenish it on July 31.

19XX

July 1 A $50 petty cash fund is established.

31 At end of month $16 cash plus the following paid vouchers exist: donations expense, $10; postage expense, $11; office supplies expense, $9; miscellaneous expense, $4.

Cash overage in replenishment.

6-3. If in Exercise 6-2 cash on hand was $14, prepare the entry to replenish the petty cash on July 31.

Cash shortage in replenishment.

6-4. If in Exercise 6-2 cash on hand was $18, prepare the entry to replenish the petty cash on July 31.

Calculate cash shortage with Change Fund.

6-5. At the end of the day the clerk for Pete's Variety Shop noticed an error in the amount of cash he should have had. Total cash sales from the sales tape were $1,100 while the total cash in the till was $1,058. Pete also keeps a $30 change fund in his shop. Prepare an appropriate general journal entry to record the cash sale as well as reveal the cash shortage.

Group A Problems

Preparing a bank reconciliation including collection of a note.

6A-1. Rose Company received a bank statement from TD Bank indicating a bank balance of $7,013. Based on Rose's cheque stubs, the ending chequebook balance was $5,840. Your task is to prepare a bank reconciliation for Rose Company as of July 31, 19XX, from the following information (please journalize entries as needed):

a. Cheques outstanding: no. 124, $620; no. 126, $870.
b. Deposits in transit, $975.
c. Bank service charge, $14.
d. TD Bank collected a note for Rose, $680, less an $8 collection fee.

Preparing a bank reconciliation with NSF using the back of a bank statement.

6A-2. From the bank statement on the next page, please (1) complete the bank reconciliation for Rick's Deli found on the reverse of the bank statement and (2) journalize the appropriate entries as needed.

a. A deposit of $2,000 is in transit.
b. Rick's Deli has an ending chequebook balance of $4,845.
c. Cheques outstanding: no. 111, $725; no. 119, $1,100; no. 121, $360.
d. Jim Rice's cheque for $400 bounced due to lack of sufficient funds.

Establishing and replenishing of petty cash. Relationship to special journals (see Chapter 10 for details) and auxiliary petty cash record.

6A-3. The following transactions occurred in April and were related to the cash payments journal and petty cash fund of Merry Co.:

19XX

April	1	Issued cheque no. 14 for $75 to establish a petty cash fund.
	5	Paid $5 from petty cash for postage, voucher no. 1.
	8	Paid $10 from petty cash for office supplies, voucher no. 2.
	17	Paid $8 from petty cash for office supplies, voucher no. 3.
	24	Paid $6 from petty cash for postage, voucher no. 4.
	26	Paid $9 from petty cash for local church donation, voucher no. 5 (this is a miscellaneous payment).
	28	Issued cheque no. 15 to Roy Kloon to pay for office equipment, $700.

From the chart of accounts: Petty Cash, 120; Office Equipment, 130; Postage Expense, 610; Office Supplies Expense, 620; Miscellaneous Expense, 630. The headings of the cash payments and auxiliary petty cash records are as follows:

CASH PAYMENTS JOURNAL Page 2

Date 19XX	Cheque No.	Accounts Debited	PR	Sundry Dr.	Accounts Payable Dr.	Purchases Discounts Cr.	Cash Cr.

AUXILIARY PETTY CASH RECORD

Date 19XX	Voucher No.	Description	Receipts	Payments	Category of Payments			
					Postage Expense	Office Supplies Expense	Sundry	
							Account	Amount

Required

1. Record the appropriate entries in the cash payments journal as well as the auxiliary petty cash record as needed.
2. Be sure to replenish the petty cash fund on April 30 (cheque no. 16).

BANK OF SASKATCHEWAN
10050 - 101 Street
Regina, Saskatchewan
S4J 6E2

Account Statement

Account No.	
241 673 6	
Period	
From	To
Feb 01/XX	Feb 28/XX
Enclosures	Page
2	1

03749

RICK'S DELI
8811 - 102 Street
Regina, SA
S3A 3G6

Date	Transaction Description		Cheques & Debits	Deposits & Credits	Balance
Feb 01	Balance Forward				5,200.00
Feb 02	Cheque -	108	90.00		
Feb 03	Cheque -	114	210.00		4,900.00
Feb 10	Deposit			300.00	
Feb 10	Cheque -	116	150.00		5,050.00
Feb 14	Deposit			600.00	5,650.00
Feb 15	Cheque -	113	600.00		5,050.00
Feb 20	Deposit			400.00	
Feb 20	NSF Returned Item		400.00		5,050.00
Feb 22	Deposit			1,200.00	6,250.00
Feb 24	Cheque -	117	1,200.00		5,050.00
Feb 26	Deposit			180.00	5,230.00
Feb 28	Cheque -	120	600.00		
Feb 28	Service Charge		30.00		4,600.00

No. of Debits	Total Amount	No. of Credits	Total Amount
8	3,280.00	5	2,680.00

Establishing and replenishing petty cash including a cash shortage.

6A-4. From the following, record the transactions into Logan's auxiliary petty cash record and cash payments journal (pp. 6-11 and 6-12) as appropriate (see Chapter 10 for details of the cash payments journal):

19XX

Oct.	1	A cheque was drawn (no. 444) payable to Roberta Floss, petty cashier, to establish a $150 petty cash fund.
	5	Paid $24 for postage stamps, voucher no. 1.
	9	Paid $15 for delivery charges on goods for resale, voucher no. 2.
	12	Paid $10 for donation to a mission (Miscellaneous Expense), voucher no. 3.
	14	Paid $12 for postage stamps, voucher no. 4.
	17	Paid $10 for delivery charges on goods for resale, voucher no. 5.
	27	Purchased computer supplies from petty cash for $11, voucher no. 6.
	28	Paid $6 for postage, voucher no. 7.
	29	Drew cheque no. 610 to replenish petty cash and a $2 shortage.

Group B Problems

Preparing a bank reconciliation including collection of a note.

6B-1. As the bookkeeper of Rose Company you received the bank statement from TD Bank indicating a balance of $5,344. The ending chequebook balance was $4,835. Prepare the bank reconciliation for Rose Company as of July 31, 19XX, and prepare journal entries as needed based on the following:

a. Deposits in transit, $2,850.

b. Bank service charges, $24.

c. Cheques outstanding: no. 111, $478; no. 115, $1,147.

d. TD Bank collected a note for Rose, $1,770, less a $12 collection fee.

Preparing a bank reconciliation with NSF using back side of a bank statement.

6B-2. Based on the following, please (1) complete the bank reconciliation for Rick's Deli found on the reverse of the bank statement below, and (2) journalize the appropriate entries as needed.

a. Cheques outstanding: no. 110, $92; no. 116, $140; no. 118, $76.

b. A deposit of $420 is in transit.

c. The chequebook balance of Rick's Deli shows an ending balance of $976.

d. Jim Rice's cheque for $50 bounced due to lack of sufficient funds.

Establishment and replenishment of petty cash. Relationship to special journals (see Chapter 10 for details) and auxiliary petty cash record.

6B-3. From the following transactions, (1) record the entries as needed in the cash payments journal of Merry Co. as well as the auxiliary petty cash record and (2) replenish the petty cash fund on April 30 (cheque no. 6).

BANK OF SASKATCHEWAN
10050 - 101 Street
Regina, Saskatchewan
S4J 6E2

03749

Account Statement

Account No.	
241 673 6	
Period From	To
Apr 01/XX	Apr 30/XX
Enclosures	Page
2	1

RICK'S DELI
8811 - 102 Street
Regina, SA
S3A 3G6

Date	Transaction Description		Cheques & Debits	Deposits & Credits	Balance
Apr 01	Balance Forward				898.00
Apr 02	Cheque -	108	12.00		
Apr 03	Cheque -	114	36.00		850.00
Apr 10	Deposit			40.00	
Apr 10	Cheque -	115	20.00		870.00
Apr 14	Deposit			80.00	950.00
Apr 15	Cheque -	113	80.00		870.00
Apr 20	Deposit			50.00	
Apr 20	NSF Returned Item		50.00		870.00
Apr 22	Deposit			160.00	1030.00
Apr 24	Cheque -	117	160.00		870.00
Apr 26	Deposit			24.00	894.00
Apr 28	Cheque -	109	80.00		
Apr 28	Service Charge		4.00		810.00

No. of Debits	Total Amount	No. of Credits	Total Amount
8	442.00	5	354.00

19XX

April 1	Issued cheque no. 4 for $80 to establish a petty cash fund.
5	Paid $9 from petty cash for postage, voucher no. 1.
8	Paid $12 from petty cash for office supplies, voucher no. 2.
17	Paid $9 from petty cash for office supplies, voucher no. 3.
24	Paid $6 from petty cash for postage, voucher no. 4.
26	Paid $12 from petty cash for local church donation, voucher no. 5 (this is a miscellaneous payment).
28	Issued cheque no. 5 to Roy Kloon to pay office equipment, $800.

Chart of accounts includes: Petty Cash, 120; Office Equipment, 130; Postage Expense, 610; Office Supplies Expense, 620; Miscellaneous Expense, 630. Use the same headings as in Problem 6A-3.

Establishing and replenishing petty cash including a cash shortage.

6B-4. From the following, record the transactions into Logan's auxiliary petty cash record and cash payments journal (pp. 6-11 and 6-12) as appropriate (see Chapter 10 for details of the cash payments journal):

19XX

Oct. 1	Roberta Floss, the petty cashier, cashed a cheque, no. 444, to establish a $100 petty cash fund.
5	Paid $18 for postage stamps, voucher no. 1.
9	Paid $12 for delivery charges on goods for resale, voucher no. 2.
12	Paid $10 for donation to a church (Miscellaneous Expense), voucher no. 3.
14	Paid $14 for postage stamps, voucher no. 4.
17	Paid $5 for delivery charges on goods for resale, voucher no. 5.
27	Purchased computer supplies from petty cash for $7, voucher no. 6.
28	Paid $4 for postage, voucher no. 7.
29	Drew cheque no. 618 to replenish petty cash and a $3 shortage.

Group C Problems

Preparing a bank reconciliation including collection of a note.

6C-1. Regina Company received a bank statement from Royal Bank indicating a bank balance of $4,791. Based on Regina's cheque stubs, the ending chequebook balance was $4,100. Your task is to prepare a bank reconciliation for Regina Company as of May 31, 19XX, from the following information (please journalize entries as needed):

a. Cheques outstanding: no. 354, $287; no. 356, $496; no. 347, $748

b. Deposits in transit, $1,418.

c. Bank service charge, $43.

d. Royal Bank collected a note for Regina, $768, less a $12 collection fee.

e. Notice received that a cheque from Fred Brown, a customer, was returned NSF, $135.

Preparing a bank reconciliation with NSF using the back of a bank statement.

6C-2. From the following June 29, 19XX, bank statement, please (1) complete a bank reconciliation for Freda's Flower Shop and (2) journalize the appropriate entries as needed.

a. A deposit of $2,180 is in transit.

b. Freda's Flower Shop has an ending chequebook balance of $4,891.

c. Cheques outstanding: no. 231, $312; no. 245, $750; no. 246, $82; no 24 $254.

d. Joan Brice's cheque for $225 bounced due to nonsufficient funds.

e. Cheque no. 241 for utilities expense was entered in the cash payments journal as $358.

BANK OF INDUSTRY AND COMMERCE
48 JAMES STREET
HALIFAX, NOVA SCOTIA
B4T 2L0

08179

FREDA'S FLOWER SHOP
121 SPRING GARDEN ROAD
HALIFAX, NS
B5H 3E6

Account Statement

Account No.	
914 817 2	
Period From	To
Jun 29/XX	Jul 28/XX
Enclosures	Page
2	1

Date	Transaction Description		Cheques & Debits	Deposits & Credits	Balance
Jul 01	Balance Forward				2,824.00
Jul 02	Cheque -	241	385.00		2,439.00
Jul 03	Cheque -	240	410.00		2,029.00
Jul 10	Deposit			1,712.00	
Jul 10	Cheque -	243	250.00		3,491.00
Jul 14	Deposit			950.00	4,441.00
Jul 15	Cheque -	242	1,214.00		3,227.00
Jul 16	Deposit			225.00	3,452.00
Jul 20	NSF Returned Item		225.00		3,227.00
Jul 22	Deposit			1,260.00	4,487.00
Jul 24	Cheque -	248	1,410.00		3,077.00
Jul 26	Deposit			780.00	3,857.00
Jul 28	Cheque -	1126	672.00		
Jul 28	Service Charge		21.00		3,164.00

No. of Debits	Total Amount	No. of Credits	Total Amount
8	4,587.00	5	4,927.00

f. The cheque for $672 shown by the bank as paid on July 28 was actually a cheque of the Acme Machine Shop. This error will be corrected by the bank next month. The bank apologized for the error.

Establishment and replenishment of petty cash. Relationship to special journals (see Chapter 10 for details) and auxiliary petty cash record.

6C-3. The following transactions occurred in March and were related to the cash payments journal and petty cash fund of Jenkins & Co.:

19XX

March 1 Issued cheque no. 314 for $200 to establish a petty cash fund.

5 Paid $45 from petty cash for postage, voucher no. 1.

8 Paid $32 from petty cash for office supplies, voucher no. 2.

17 Paid $34 from petty cash for office supplies, voucher no. 3.

24 Paid $44 from petty cash for postage, voucher no. 4.

26 Paid $20 from petty cash for local church donation, voucher no. 5 (this is a miscellaneous payment).

28 Issued cheque no. 315 to Klondike Office Equipment to pay for office equipment, $1,800.

From the chart of accounts: Petty Cash, 105; Office Equipment, 170; Postage Expense, 645; Office Supplies Expense, 640; Miscellaneous Expense, 630. The headings of the cash payments and auxiliary petty cash records are the same as for 6A-3.

Required

1. Record the appropriate entries in the cash payments journal and the auxiliary petty cash record as needed.
2. Be sure to replenish the petty cash fund on March 31 (cheque no. 316).

Establishing and replenishing petty cash including a cash shortage.

6C-4. From the following, record the transactions into Brennan Co.'s auxiliary petty cash record and cash payments journal (pp. 6-11 and 6-12) as appropriate (see Chapter 10 for details of the cash payments journal).

19XX

Oct. 1 A cheque was drawn (no. 772) payable to Rob Kiriak, petty cashier, to establish a $250 petty cash fund.

5 Paid $42 for postage stamps, voucher no. 1.

9 Paid $18 for delivery charges on goods for resale, voucher no. 2.

12 Paid $20 for donation to a church (Miscellaneous Expense), voucher no. 3.

14 Paid $54 for postage stamps, voucher no. 4.

17 Paid $11 for delivery charges on goods for resale, voucher no. 5.

27 Purchased computer supplies from petty cash for $16, voucher no. 6.

28 Paid $28 for postage, voucher no. 7.

29 Drew cheque no. 813 to replenish petty cash (a $5 shortage was apparent when the cash was balanced).

Real world applications

6 R-1.

Karen Johnson, the bookkeeper of Hoop Co., has appointed Jim Pool as the petty cash custodian. The following transactions occurred in November:

19XX

Nov. 25 Cheque no. 441 was written and cashed to establish a $50 petty cash fund.

27 Paid $8.50 delivery charge for goods purchased for resale.

29 Purchased office supplies for $12 from petty cash.

30 Purchased postage stamps for $15 from petty cash.

On December 3 Jim received the following internal memo:

> To: Jim Pool
>
> From: Karen Johnson
>
> Re: Petty Cash
>
> Jim, I'll need $5 for postage stamps. By the way, I noticed that our petty cash account seems to be too low. Let's increase its size to $100.

Could you help Jim replenish petty cash on December 3 by providing him with a general journal entry? Support your answer and indicate whether Karen was correct.

6R-2.

Ginger Company has a policy of depositing all receipts and making all payments by cheque. On receiving the bank statement, Bill Free, a new bookkeeper, is quite upset that the balance in cash in the ledger is $4,209.50 while the ending bank balance is $4,440.50. Bill is convinced the bank has made an error. Based on the following facts, is Bill's concern warranted? What other suggestions could you offer Bill in the bank reconciliation process?

a. The Nov. 30 cash receipts, $611, had been placed in the bank's night depository after banking hours and consequently did not appear on the bank statement as a deposit.

b. Two debit memorandums and a credit memorandum were included with the returned cheque. None of the memorandums had been recorded at the time of the reconciliation. The first debit memorandum had a $130 NSF cheque written by Abby Ellen. The second was a $6.50 debit memorandum for service charges. The credit memorandum was for $494 and represented the proceeds less a $6 collection fee from a $500 noninterest-bearing note collected for Ginger Company by the bank.

c. It was also found that cheques no. 942 for $71.50 and no. 947 for $206.50, both written and recorded on November 28, were not among the cancelled cheques returned.

d. Bill found that cheque no. 899 was correctly drawn for $1,094, in payment for a new cash register. However, this cheque had been recorded as though it were for $1,148.

e. The October bank reconciliation showed two cheques outstanding on September 30, no. 621 for $152.50 and no. 630 for $179.30. Cheque no. 630 was returned with the November bank statement, but cheque no. 621 was not.

6R-3.

On March 2, 19XX, the accountant for Mansfield Carpet Co. was injured in a skiing accident and was advised not to return to work for six weeks. The owners of the company are anxious to ensure that the company's bank account statement is reconciled and have asked you to perform this task. You are presented with the following information:

a. Bank reconciliation prepared by the regular accountant at January 31, 19XX:

Mansfield Carpet Co.
Bank Reconciliation
January 31, 19XX

Balance per Bank Statement:			$ 8,364.02
Add: Deposit in Transit:			2,576.03
			10,940.05
Less: Outstanding Cheques:			
	No. 417	$ 28.30	
	419	1,043.25	
	423	1,722.30	2,793.85
Balance per General Ledger:			$ 8,146.20

b. General ledger listing of Bank Account (#110) for the month of February (see p. 250).

c. Bank statement from the Royal Bank for the month ending February 26, 19XX (see p.251).

Required

Prepare the necessary reconciliation and any journal entries necessary at February 28, 19XX.

make the call

Critical Thinking/Ethical Case

Jerry Ary, the bookkeeper of Logan Co., received a bank statement from Ajax Bank. Jerry noticed a $200 mistake made by the bank in the company's favour. Jerry called his supervisor, who said that as long as it benefits the company, he should not tell the bank about the error. You make the call. Write your specific recommendations to Jerry.

Date: 11 Mar. XX 11:06 am
G/L Listing

MANSFIELD CARPET CO.

General Ledger Listing as of 28 Feb XX

Page: 1

G/L listing for account [110] to [110]
for department [ ] to [222] ,
for fiscal period [2] 0 [2] ,
sorted by [Account] .

Last posting sequence number: 4

Acct. Dept.

Pd	Srce	Date	Description	Reference	Posting Entry	Batch Entry	Debits	Credits	Net Change/ Balance
	110	Bank							8,146.20
2	GL-GJ	01 Feb XX	KING PROPERTY	CHQ 404	2 - 1	2 - 1		974.15	
2	GL-GJ	01 Feb XX	SANDRA SMYTHE - Deposit	1007	2 - 2	2 - 2	8,145.38		
2	GL-GJ	02 Feb XX	INGRID LUNDREN - Deposit	1008	2 - 3	2 - 3	909.50		
2	GL-GJ	02 Feb XX	CAMPUS COPY SHOPPE	CHQ 424	2 - 4	2 - 4		133.75	
2	GL-GJ	02 Feb XX	BENJAMIN YEE	02 - 05	2 - 5	2 - 5	4,381.65		
2	GL-GJ	05 Feb XX	LITEMORE NEON SIGNS	CHQ 425	2 - 6	2 - 6		80.25	
2	GL-GJ	05 Feb XX	NORM & JANET TAYLOR - Deposit	1009	2 - 7	2 - 7	969.01		
2	GL-GJ	06 Feb XX	NAME - IT!	CHQ 426	2 - 9	2 - 9		240.75	
2	GL-GJ	07 Feb XX	JERRY SIMON - Deposit	1011	2 - 10	2 - 10	2,782.00		
2	GL-GJ	07 Feb XX	SAXONY WOOL MILLS	CHQ 427	2 - 11	2 - 11		4,559.11	
2	GL-GJ	07 Feb XX	QUALITY CARPET COMPANY	CHQ 428	2 - 12	2 - 12		6,829.28	
2	GL-GJ	07 Feb XX	JODY ARCHER	CHQ 429	2 - 13	2 - 13		25.00	
2	GL-GJ	08 Feb XX	CITY PHONE COMPANY	CHQ 430	2 - 14	2 - 14		121.75	
2	GL-GJ	08 Feb XX	CITY UTILITY COMPANY	CHQ 431	2 - 15	2 - 15		111.14	
2	GL-GJ	08 Feb XX	JOE'S GAS BAR	CHQ 432	2 - 16	2 - 16		94.66	
2	GL-GJ	08 Feb XX	WOOD'S STATIONERY	CHQ 433	2 - 17	2 - 17		1,091.40	
2	GL-GJ	02 Feb XX	CASH	CHQ 434	2 - 18	2 - 18		100.00	
2	GL-GJ	09 Feb XX	IVY LEUNG - Deposit	1012	2 - 19	2 - 19	2,169.96		
2	GL-GJ	09 Feb XX	EMILY MANSFIELD - Salary	CHQ 435	2 - 20	2 - 20		697.35	
2	GL-GJ	09 Feb XX	JAMES MANSFIELD - Salary	CHQ 436	2 - 21	2 - 21		697.35	
2	GL-GJ	09 Feb XX	RBC/TERMPLAN LOAN PAYMENT	02 - 22	2 - 22	2 - 22		601.87	
2	GL-GJ	09 Feb XX	RBC/DEMAND LOAN INTEREST	02 - 23	2 - 23	2 - 23		695.20	
2	GL-GJ	13 Feb XX	PAT HARPER - Deposit	1013	2 - 27	2 - 27	404.46		
2	GL-GJ	15 Feb XX	CITY LIGHTING	CHQ 437	2 - 29	2 - 29		112.50	
2	GL-GJ	15 Feb XX	FREDDY DUNCAN	CHQ 438	2 - 30	2 - 30		2,010.40	
2	GL-GJ	15 Feb XX	RECEIVER GENERAL FOR CANADA	CHQ 439	2 - 31	2 - 31		993.04	
2	GL-GJ	15 Feb XX	VOID	CHQ 440	2 - 32	2 - 32	0.00		
2	GL-GJ	16 Feb XX	WILSON INSURANCE AGENCY	CHQ 441	2 - 33	2 - 33		802.50	
2	GL-GJ	16 Feb XX	COMMUNITY CALENDAR	CHQ 442	2 - 34	2 - 34		246.10	
2	GL-GJ	16 Feb XX	STANDARD NEWS	CHQ 443	2 - 35	2 - 35		909.50	
2	GL-GJ	16 Feb XX	T C CHURCHILL - Deposit	1015	2 - 36	2 - 36	3,610.18		
2	GL-GJ	16 Feb XX	RBC/LOAN PROCESSING CHARGE	02 - 37	2 - 37	2 - 37		40.00	
2	GL-GJ	19 Feb XX	BEATRICE DAY - Deposit	1016	2 - 38	2 - 38	4,068.68		
2	GL-GJ	22 Feb XX	JOAN ANDERSON - Deposit	02 - 44	2 - 44	2 - 44	2,569.07		
2	GL-GJ	23 Feb XX	EMILY MANSFIELD - Salary	CHQ 444	2 - 46	2 - 46		697.35	
2	GL-GJ	23 Feb XX	JAMES MANSFIELD - Salary	CHQ 445	2 - 47	2 - 47		697.35	
2	GL-GJ	24 Feb XX	BOB JONES	CHQ 446	2 - 49	2 - 49		240.00	
2	GL-GJ	26 Feb XX	MICHEL ROBICHAUD - Deposit	02 - 53	2 - 53	2 - 53	3,456.10		
2	GL-GJ	26 Feb XX	JUDY CARMICHAEL - Deposit	1022	2 - 54	2 - 54	1,218.20		
2	GL-GJ	28 Feb XX	DMJ CONSTRUCTION - Deposit	02 - 55	2 - 55	2 - 55	1,786.90		
2	GL-GJ	28 Feb XX	FREDDY DUNCAN	CHQ 447	2 - 56	2 - 56		1,950.90	
2	GL-GJ	28 Feb XX	GEORGE BETTS	CHQ 448	2 - 57	2 - 57		1,213.20	
2	GL-GJ	28 Feb XX	GREENBRIAR RESTAURANT	CHQ 449	2 - 58	2 - 58		76.15	9,429.09
			Acct 110 - Balance, Feb 28, 19XX						17,575.29

ROYAL BANK
MAIN BRANCH
10107 JASPER AVENUE
EDMONTON ALTA
T5J 1W9 03749

Account Statement

Account No.	
124-629-7	
Period	
From	To
Jan 27/XX	Feb 26/XX
Enclosures	Page
	1

MANSFIELD CARPET CO
BAY 215
10620 - 104 AVENUE
EDMONTON AB
T5J 3G2

Date	Transaction Description		Cheques & Debits	Deposits & Credits	Balance
	Balance Forward				8,364.02
Jan 27	Deposit			2,576.03	10,940.05
Jan 28	Cheque -	404	974.15		
	Cheque -	419	1,043.25		8,922.65
Jan 29	Cheque -	423	1,722.30		7,200.35
Jan 30	Cheque -	424	133.75		7,066.60
Feb 01	Deposit			8,145.38	15,211.98
Feb 02	Deposit			5,291.15	
	Cheque -	434	100.00		20,403.13
Feb 03	Deposit			969.01	21,372.14
Feb 06	Deposit			2,782.00	
	Cheque -	425	80.25		
	Loan Payment - Principal		601.87		
	Loan Interest		695.20		22,776.82
Feb 07	Cheque -	430	121.75		
	Cheque -	436	697.35		
	Cheque -	435	697.35		21,260.37
Feb 08	Deposit			2,169.96	
	Cheque -	431	111.14		23,319.19
Feb 10	Cheque -	433	1,091.40		
	Cheque -	432	94.66		
	Cheque -	428	6,829.28		
	Cheque -	426	240.75		15,063.10
Feb 13	Deposit			404.46	
	Loan Management Fee		40.00		
	Cheque -	438	2,010.40		
	Cheque -	427	4,559.11		
	Cheque -	437	112.50		8,745.55
Feb 14	Deposit			3,610.18	12,355.73
Feb 15	Deposit			4,068.68	
	Cheque -	429	25.00		16,399.41
Feb 17	Cheque -	441	802.50		15,596.91
Feb 20	Cheque -	422	246.10		
	NSF Returned		404.46		14,946.35
Feb 21	NSF Charge		15.00		14,931.35
Feb 24	Cheque -	444	697.35		
	Cheque -	445	697.35		13,536.65
Feb 25	Deposit			2,569.07	
	Cheque -	439	993.04		15,112.68
Feb 26	Deposit			4,674.30	
	Cheque -	446	240.00		
	Service Charge		18.45		19,528.53

No. of Debits	Total Amount	No. of Credits	Total Amount
30	26,095.71	11	37,260.22

ACCOUNTING RECALL

A CUMULATIVE APPROACH

THIS EXAM REVIEWS CHAPTERS 1 THROUGH 6

Your *Study Guide and Working Papers* has forms to complete this exam, as well as worked-out solutions. The page references next to each question identify what page to turn back to if you answer the question incorrectly.

PART I Vocabulary Review

Match the terms to the appropriate definition or phrase.

Page Ref.			
(235)	1. Cash short and over	A.	A supplementary record
(223)	2. Blank endorsement	B.	Person who writes a cheque
(221)	3. Payee	C.	A process of reconciling
(221)	4. Drawer	D.	Recorded on the income statement
(227)	5. Outstanding cheques	E.	Person or company to whom the cheque is payable
(226)	6. Bank reconciliation	F.	Lacks sufficient funds
(234)	7. Auxiliary petty cash record	G.	Cheque truncation
(230)	8. Safekeeping	H.	Add to bank balance
(226)	9. Deposits in transit	I.	Cheques written but not processed by bank
(227)	10. NSF	J.	Could be further endorsed

PART II True or False (Accounting Theory)

(232) 11. Petty cash is a liability.

(233) 12. The auxiliary petty cash record is a special journal.

(223) 13. Restrictive endorsements limit any further negotiation of a cheque.

(227) 14. NSF result in lowering the bank balance in the reconciliation process.

(234) 15. In replenishment, the old expenses are shown and a new cheque is written.

PART III Applications Problem (p. 6–21)

From the following calculate the reconciled balance:

Chequebook balance	$755.09
Bank balance	602.05
Interest earned	12.42
Deposits in transit	401.95
Service charge	13.05
Cheques outstanding	249.54

PAYROLL CONCEPTS AND PROCEDURES

7

EMPLOYEE TAXES

Chapter Objectives

- How to calculate gross pay, routine deductions, and net pay for an employee. (p. 256)
- How to prepare a company's payroll summary. (p. 262)
- How to record a typical payroll from a summary. (p. 264)
- How to maintain an individual's earnings record. (p. 266)

Becoming an expert in the subject of payroll and related issues can take a long time. This is because:

1. There are many federal and provincial laws which affect payroll, and they change periodically.
2. Sometimes employers and employees view each other with suspicion in matters concerning payroll. This requires special care to get the figures correct.
3. The actual computation and payment of a payroll is quite detailed, leaving room for a number of mistakes to occur.

In Canada today a company has two common alternatives to processing a payroll manually:

- Use a microcomputer with appropriate software.
- Contract with a payroll service (either an independent service or one connected with a chartered bank).

Either alternative is attractive to medium- or large-sized companies. Many smaller companies continue to process their payroll manually, thus avoiding the costs of the more sophisticated alternatives. Programs like Simply Accounting also can help in processing a payroll for smaller companies with simple payroll needs.

In this chapter we will examine the details of a payroll for ABC Company Ltd. for the first week in March. We will stress those things which affect individual employees. The next chapter examines the same subject from the employer's point of view.

In this chapter and the next, many deductions, maximum amounts, and minimum amounts are obtained from recently published figures from Revenue Canada. Students should be aware that these will change at least annually. Your instructor may supply you with the most up-to-date figures, but remember that you should concentrate on learning the principles involved, not on matching the exact figures illustrated in this chapter and the next.

LEARNING UNIT 7-1

Important Laws and How They Affect Payroll

A number of laws and regulations at the federal and provincial level govern payroll. We will look at several of them here.

MINIMUM WAGE LAWS

Every province has a law which sets the lowest hourly wage that can legally be paid to an employee. The actual **minimum wage** varies somewhat from province to province and has a very small effect on the subject of payroll.

However, such laws also set out the maximum number of hours an employee can be asked to work per day and per week before an *overtime* premium must be paid. A typical requirement (and the one we shall adopt) is that employees who work more than 8 hours per day or 40 hours per week must be paid at time-and-a-half for the overtime hours.

Suppose Janet Johnson worked the following hours during our example week:

Monday	7 hours	
Tuesday	8 hours	
Wednesday	11 hours	
Thursday	8 hours	
Friday	7 hours	
Saturday	4 hours	
Total	45 hours	for the week

If Janet's hourly rate were $10 per hour, her gross wages for the week would be computed as follows:

Regular time	40 h @ $10.00/h	$400
Overtime	5 h @ $15.00/h	75
Total earnings		$475

Sometimes employers arrive at the same total by a slightly different calculation:

Regular rate	45 h @ $10.00/h	$450
Overtime rate (or premium)	5 h @ $5.00/h	25
Total earnings		$475

This second approach stresses the cost of overtime. A manager can more easily recognize the added cost of asking employees to work longer hours. We will use the first approach in this chapter, since it reflects the point of view of the employee.

FEDERAL AND PROVINCIAL INCOME TAX

The federal and provincial governments each require employees to pay a tax based on the income they earn. The details of our **income tax** system are not covered here, but we need to know a few essentials:

1. Taxes are *calculated* once a year: employees must file a tax return by April 30 for the year ended on the previous December 31. However, the tax is *collected* from employees by payroll deductions each pay period.
2. The federal and provincial governments (except Quebec) cooperate by having a single tax deduction which is then divided up according to a legal formula. The amount of income tax an employee must pay is determined by a large number of factors such as number of dependents, level of earnings, other sources of income, permitted deductions, and so on. The amount of income tax deducted from an employee's pay for a week is found by consulting the tables in a booklet called *Payroll Deductions Tables (T4032)*, which is provided by Revenue Canada Taxation. These tables vary somewhat from province to province but the example shown (based on the province of

Payroll periods can be:
Weekly: 52 pay periods/year.
Biweekly: 26 pay periods/year.
Semimonthly: 24 pay periods/year.
Monthly: 12 pay periods/year.

The employer is not responsible for verifying the claims made by employees on their TD1 forms.

Ontario) is typical (see Appendix 7-1 at the end of this chapter). The ranges of earnings per week are shown on the left and the figures in the 11 columns of deductions shown across the page get smaller as they go from left to right. These figures correspond to increasing levels of exemptions claimed by an employee on a form called a **TD1** (Figure 7-1). In our example, Janet Johnson is claiming the normal deduction for a single person, **net claim code 1**. Actually, she may be divorced, separated, or married to a husband who is also earning income, thus making him ineligible as a dependent.

Notice that the procedure for deducting income tax is not very precise. The actual tax that Janet will have to pay for the year will depend on dozens of factors, some of them quite personal (such as whether she has paid any deductible tuition fees during the taxation year, or whether she has charitable donations to claim). The purpose of the deduction tables is to ensure that wage earners pay about as much tax as they would owe on their earnings for the week. Sometimes employees have to pay extra tax when they file their annual tax returns, but usually they get a refund. This is because the tables tend to ignore many allowable tax deductions.

In our example, Janet Johnson will have $89.60 in tax deducted from her pay this week. Refer to Appendix 7-1 and be sure you see where this figure is obtained.

Canada or Quebec Pension Plan

About 25 years ago the **Canada and Quebec Pension Plans** were introduced. Their purpose was to provide a pension benefit (as well as certain other benefits) for Canadians at retirement. The law requires a deduction of 2.8 percent from the earnings of each taxpayer in Canada who is at least 18 years of age but not 70 years or older and who is not in receipt of a disability or retirement pension from CPP. (Earnings of less than $67.31 per week are not subject to this deduction. Likewise, earnings in excess of $35,400 per year are not subject to the 2.8 percent levy.) The rate is in the process of being gradually increased, to top out at just over 4 percent around the turn of the century. This increase is necessary to ensure that funds are available to meet the requirements of Canadians who will be claiming benefits early in the next century.

Recently, the government has been sending a summary of CPP contributions made to each worker in Canada.

In an effort to conserve resources, the government has begun to publish the various tables of deductions in computer-readable format. Your instructor may arrange to supply you with a copy, or make a copy available for the duration of the course.

It is possible to compute the necessary deduction for the Canada Pension Plan (CPP) for each employee, but the federal government has provided detailed tables in the booklet *Payroll Deductions Tables (T4032)* to make this unnecessary (see Appendix 7-2 and Learning Unit 7-2). As you can see, Janet Johnson will have a CPP deduction of $11.42—($475 - 67.31) × 0.028—made from her wages this pay period. The federal government maintains a precise record of the CPP payments made by each Canadian because the benefits we will receive are related to the contributions we make plus the amounts contributed by our employers on our behalf—by law, the same amount as is deducted. There are more details on this in the next chapter.

Unemployment Insurance Plan

It is a requirement for virtually all employees, regardless of age, to participate in Canada's **unemployment insurance (UI) plan**. (Employees working less than 15 hours in a week and earning less than 20 percent of the maximum weekly insurable earnings are not required to pay UI premiums. There are a number of other exceptions as well.) This plan entitles workers to a certain level of income if they become unemployed. The details are very complex and a full discussion of the plan is beyond the scope of this text.

Changes to UI Laws
Very recent changes to Canada's UI laws will see significant alteration to this aspect of payroll. Even the name will be changed–it will now be known as Employment Insurance or EI. Details are not available at this

TD1(E)
Rev. 96

Revenue Canada Revenu Canada

PERSONAL TAX CREDITS RETURN

Instructions

Complete this return if you have a new employer or payer, and you will receive one or more of the following types of income:

- salary, wages, commissions, pensions, or any other remuneration; or
- Unemployment Insurance benefits, including training allowances.

You **do not** have to file a new return every year unless your marital status changes or you expect a change in your personal credits for that year. Complete a new return no later than seven days after the change. It is an offence to file a false return.

If you make regular alimony or maintenance payments, or if you regularly contribute to a registered retirement savings plan (RRSP) during the year, you can reduce the amount of tax to be withheld from your income.To make this request, you have to write to your tax services office for a letter of authority. A letter of authority is not needed if:

- your employer deducts RRSP contributions from your salary; or
- a court order states that alimony or maintenance payments have to be deducted at source from your salary.

If you receive non-employment income, such as a pension or Old Age Security, and you want to have extra tax deducted at source, you can complete Form TD3, *Request for Income Tax Deduction on Non-Employment Income.*

If you need help, ask your employer or payer, or call your tax services office or tax centre. You can find the phone numbers listed for "Revenue Canada" in the Government of Canada section of your telephone book.

Confidential calculation on back - Employee's copy

- -

Employer's or payer's copy

TD1(E)
Rev. 96

Revenue Canada Revenu Canada

PERSONAL TAX CREDITS RETURN

After you complete this return, give it to your employer or payer.

Last name (capital letters)		Usual first name and initials	Employee number
JOHNSON		JANET	N/A
Address		For non-residents only - country of permanent residence	Social insurance number
123 Main Street			1 2 3 4 5 6 7 8 9
	Postal code		Date of birth (Year / Month / Day)
Any City, Province	X1X 1X1		1966 / 03 / 12

1. Basic personal amount

Everyone can claim **$6,456** as the basic personal amount.

- If you choose to claim this amount, **enter $6,456.**
- If you choose not to claim this amount (e.g., when you have more than one employer or payer and you have already claimed the basic personal amount), **enter 0** in box **A** on the other side of this return. Do not complete sections 2 to 8. You may want to complete sections 9 to 11.
- If you are a non-resident, and you are including 90% or more of your annual world income when determining your taxable income in Canada, you can claim certain personal amounts. If you are including less than 90% of your annual world income, **enter 0** in box **A** on the other side of this return. If you are not sure about your non-resident status, or need more information, call your tax services office or tax centre.

Credit claimed $6,456

2. Spousal amount or equivalent-to-spouse amount

You can claim an amount for supporting your spouse if you are **married or have a common-law spouse.**

Generally, a common-law spouse is a person of the opposite sex with whom you live in a common-law relationship for any continuous period of at least 12 months, including any period of separation (due to a breakdown in the relationship) of less than 90 days, or with whom you live in a common-law relationship and who is the natural or adoptive parent of your child. If you are not sure about your status, or need more information, call your tax services office or tax centre.

You can claim an equivalent-to-spouse amount if you are **single, divorced, separated, or widowed,** and you support a relative who is:

- under 18, unless the relative is your parent or grandparent, or has a mental or physical infirmity;
- related to you by blood, marriage, or adoption;
- living with you in a home you maintain; and
- residing in Canada (if the relative is your child, the child does not have to reside in Canada).

Calculating the amount

If you marry during the year, your spouse's net income includes the income earned before and during the marriage.

If the net income for the year of your spouse or relative will be:

- over $5,918, **enter 0;**
- $538 or less, **enter $5,380;** or
- more than $538, complete calculation 2 on the back of this return and **enter** the result as credit claimed.

Any person you claim here cannot be claimed again in section 3. **Credit claimed** $

3. Amount for disabled dependent relatives

You can claim an amount for each disabled dependant who is your or your spouse's:

- child or grandchild,18 years old or older, and has a physical or mental infirmity; or
- parent, grandparent, brother, sister, aunt, uncle, niece, or nephew, who is 18 years old or older, resides in Canada, and has a physical or mental infirmity.

Calculating the amount for a disabled dependent relative:

If your dependant's net income for the year will be:

- $2,690 or less, **enter $1,583,** or
- more than $2,690, complete calculation 3 on the back of this return and **enter** the result as credit claimed.

You can claim an amount for each disabled dependent relative you have. **Credit claimed** $

4. Amount for eligible pension income

Eligible pension income includes pension payments received from a pension plan or fund as a life annuity, and foreign pension payments. It does not include payments from the Canada Pension Plan or Quebec Pension Plan, Old Age Security, guaranteed supplements, or lump-sum withdrawals from a pension fund.

If you receive an eligible pension income, you can claim your eligible pension income or $1,000, whichever amount is less. **Credit claimed** $

5. Age amount

If you will be 65 or older at the end of the year and your estimated net income from all sources for the year will be:

- $25,921 or less, **enter $3,482;**
- over $25,921, but less than $49,134.33, complete calculation 5 on the back of this return and **enter** the result as credit claimed; or
- over $49,134.33, **enter $0.**

Credit claimed $

Ce formulaire existe aussi en français.

FIGURE 7-1
TD1 Form

Calculation 2: more than $538, calculate:	$ 5,918	
Minus: net income of spouse or relative		
Total		
Report total in section 2 as credit claimed		
Calculation 3: more than $2,690, calculate:	$ 4,273	
Minus: dependant's net income		
Total		
Report total in section 3 as credit claimed		
Calculation 5: over $25,921, but less than $49,134.33, calculate basic age amount	$ 3,482	A
Reduced by:		
1. Annual estimated net income $		
2. Less base amount $ – 25,921		
3. Line 1 minus line 2 $		
4. Multiply line 3 ______ by 15%		B
Total : A minus B. If negative, **enter 0**	$	
Report total in section 5 as credit claimed		

Claim Codes

Total claim amount	Claim codes
No claim amount	0
Minimum $ 6,456	1
$ 6,456.01 - 8,037	2
8,037.01 - 9,619	3
9,619.01 - 11,202	4
11,202.01 - 12,783	5
12,783.01 - 14,364	6
14,364.01 - 15,946	7
15,946.01 - 17,527	8
17,527.01 - 19,109	9
19,109.01 - 20,693	10
$ 20,693.01 - and over Manual calculation required by employer	X
No tax withholding required	E

6. Tuition fees and education amount

Enter your tuition fees, for courses you will take in the year, to attend a university, college, or an institution that the Minister of Human Resources Development has certified ______

Add $80 for each month in the year that you will be enrolled full-time in a qualifying educational program at a university, college, or a school offering job retraining courses or correspondence courses ______

Subtotal ______

Subtract any scholarships, fellowships, or bursaries you will receive in the year (do not report the first $500) ______

Enter the total amount claimed. If the amount is negative, **enter 0**. **Credit claimed** $ ______

7. Disability amount

You can claim $4,233 for a person who is severely impaired, mentally or physically, and for whom you will claim the disability amount by using Form T2201, *Disability Tax Credit Certificate.*

Such an impairment has to markedly restrict the person in his or her daily living activities. The impairment has to last, or be expected to last, for a continuous period of at least 12 months.

Enter the total amount claimed: **Credit claimed** $ ______

8. Amounts transferred from your spouse, relatives, or dependants

You can transfer any of the following amounts that your spouse, relative, or dependants do not need to reduce their federal income tax to zero.

Age amount - If your spouse will be 65 or older this year, you can claim any unused balance of the age amount to a maximum of **$3,482** ______

Pension income amount - If your spouse receives eligible pension income, you can claim any unused balance of the eligible pension amount to a maximum of **$1,000** ______

Disability amount - If your spouse, relatives, or dependants are disabled, you can claim their unused balance of the disability amount to a maximum of **$4,233** for each person ______

Tuition fees and education amount - If you are supporting a spouse, relative, or dependants who are attending a university, college, or a certified educational institution, you can claim their unused balance of tuition fees and education amount to a maximum of **$4,000** for each person ______

Enter the total amount calculated **Credit claimed** $ ______

Total all your personal tax credit amounts from sections 1 to 8 **Total of credits** $ *6,456*

See the claim codes at the top of this return to determine the claim code that applies to you. Enter this code in box A. If the total of your tax credits is greater than your total employment income from all sources for the year, your claim code is "E." *1* A

Additional information

9. Additional tax to be deducted

If you receive other income you may want to have more tax deducted from each pay. By doing this, you may not have to pay extra tax when you file your income tax return. To choose this option, state the amount of additional tax you want to have deducted from each pay. To change this deduction later, you have to complete a new TD1 return. $ ______

10. Deduction for living in a designated area (e.g., Yukon Territory, or Northwest Territories)

If you live in the Yukon Territory, Northwest Territories, or another designated area for more than six months in a row, beginning or ending this year, you can claim:

- $7.50 for each day that you live in the designated area; or
- $15 for each day that you live in the designated area, if during that time you live in a dwelling that you maintain, and you are the only person living in that dwelling who is claiming this deduction.

For more information, including a list and categories of designated areas, see the income tax guide called *Northern Residents Deductions*, available at any tax services office or tax centre. $ ______

11. If you reside in **Ontario, Manitoba, Saskatchewan,** or **British Columbia**, enter the number of your dependants under 18 years old at the end of the year. ☐

For **Ontario, Manitoba,** and **Saskatchewan** residents, only the spouse with the higher net income can enter an amount. **If you reside in Ontario, Manitoba,** or **British Columbia**, the number of children indicated should not include a child claimed for the equivalent-to-spouse amount.

I certify that the information given in this return is, to the best of my knowledge, correct and complete.

Signature *Janet Johnson* Date *Jan. 7, 19XX*

FIG. 7-1, (cont.)

time but preliminary information suggests that the changes will make the new EI deduction similar to the CPP deduction. When final details become available, they will be included in the Instructor's Resource Guide so that all students can have access to the latest information.

In each pay period an amount of 2.95 percent is deducted from employees' wages. This deduction applies only to the first $39,000 per year (or $750 per week) according to the tables we are using. Fortunately, the deductions are rather straightforward for most employees and can be found in the same booklet as the CPP deductions (see Appendix 7-3 at the end of this chapter). In Janet Johnson's case, she will have a UI deduction of $14.01 ($\$475 \times 0.0295$) made from her wages for this week.

CPP and UI: Some additional information

Students should be aware that unique CPP deduction tables are supplied for weekly, biweekly, semimonthly, and monthly pay periods. In calculating the CPP deduction per pay period there is no maximum contribution per period—just an annual upper limit ($893.20 for 1996).

The UI deduction, however, is different. A single table is used for all pay periods. As can be seen from the bottom of any UI table, there are maximum deductions which vary according to pay period. This takes some getting used to, but is probably not as complex as it seems, since if the company has only a single pay period (ABC Company Ltd.'s is weekly, for instance), there will be only one single maximum to remember ($22.13 for ABC Company Ltd., since it has a weekly pay period).

Workers' compensation plans

In all provinces, workers' incomes are protected in the event of an injury which occurs on the job. Since the cost of this protection is typically paid by the employer, no deductions are made from employees' wages. We will not pursue this matter further in this textbook.

Various union agreements

Most unions operate under laws which are enacted provincially or federally. In many businesses, workers have been organized into bargaining units, or unions. Normally, the union and the employer agree that **union dues** be deducted from the employees' wages and forwarded to the union treasurer, usually monthly. In our example, the ABC Company Ltd. does not have unionized employees and therefore no deductions are shown.

Other deductions

Other deductions are sometimes made from an employee's earnings. Details will vary from one employer to another but the following deductions are normal in Canada:

1. Medical and dental insurance premiums.
2. Company pension plan—current service.
3. Company pension plan—past service.
4. Charitable donations.
5. Canada Savings Bonds installments.
6. Parking charges.
7. Social fund charges.
8. Repayment of loans or advances.
9. Long-term income replacement premiums.
10. Life insurance premiums.

LEARNING UNIT 7-1 REVIEW

AT THIS POINT you should be able to

- Calculate regular and overtime earnings. (p. 256)
- Explain the purpose of a TD1 form. (p. 257)
- Determine income tax deductions given a completed TD1 form and total earnings. (pp. 256–257)
- Determine a deduction for CPP from tables supplied. (p. 257)
- Determine a deduction for UI from tables supplied. (p. 257)
- Explain the operation of maximum deductions for both CPP and UI. (p. 260)
- Describe in general terms the nature of certain other routine deductions. (p. 260)

SELF-REVIEW QUIZ 7-1

Using the tables in Appendices 7-1, 7-2, and 7-3, determine the gross pay and deductions for income tax, CPP, and UI for Peter Black, a single taxpayer who worked 42 hours last week at a wage rate of $10 per hour.

Solution to Self-Review Quiz 7-1

Gross pay:		
40 h @ $10/h		$400.00
2 h @ $15/h		30.00
Gross pay		$430.00
Deductions:		
Income tax (from Appendix 7-1)	$77.70	
CPP (from Appendix 7-2)	10.16	
UI (from Appendix 7-3)	12.69	
Total deductions		100.55
Net pay ($430 - $100.55)		$329.45

LEARNING UNIT 7-2

A Typical Payroll

The ABC Company Ltd. has six employees to be paid for the first week of March. They are listed below, together with the number of hours each worked and their rates of pay:

To keep things simple, we assume no carryforward balances into the month of March. In reality there would usually be such balances (tax, CPP, and UI payable, for example).

Name	Hours	Rate
Janet Johnson	45	$10/h
Peter Black	42	10/h
John Chernochan	44	8/h
Tony Chui	40	11/h
Beth Madora	35	8/h
Elaine Dumont, Manager	40	800/wk.

				ABC Company Ltd. Employee Earnings Record For the Calendar Year 19XX		
Employee Name	Net Claim Code	Rate of Pay	Hours Worked	Earnings		
				Regular	Overtime	Gross Pay
Janet Johnson	1	10/h	45	400 00	75 00	475 00
Peter Black	1	10/h	42	400 00	30 00	430 00
John Chernochan	4	8/h	44	320 00	48 00	368 00
Tony Chui	1	11/h	40	440 00		440 00
Beth Madora	1	8/h	35	280 00		280 00
Elaine Dumont	3	800/wk	40	800 00		800 00
				2 640 00	153 00	2 793 00
	(A)	(B)	(C)	(D)	(E)	(F)

FIGURE 7-2
Payroll Summary

Employees are paid weekly at the ABC Company Ltd. The following payroll summary (Figure 7-2) has been prepared based upon tables and calculations covered earlier in this chapter. Don't worry if the summary appears a bit complicated—we will deal with each column in turn.

THE PAYROLL SUMMARY IN DETAIL

Many medium- to large-sized companies use a computer to help prepare their payroll. The data output from a computerized payroll is often remarkably similar to the illustrations in this chapter.

A. Net Claim Code Employers require employees to complete and sign a TD1 exemption form at the beginning of employment and in early January each year thereafter. As can be seen from Figure 7-1, this form allows employees to specify their exemption status so that an appropriate amount of income tax can be deducted. The net claim code for each employee is shown in this column. You can see that four of the employees are claiming a net claim code of 1, resulting in the maximum income tax deduction at their earnings level. The other two employees (John and Elaine) presumably have dependents which allow them to specify a higher net claim code, with a lower income tax deduction at their earnings level. A new TD1 can be filed at any time and, if no new form is filed in January of a given year, then the old claim code continues. If a form is not filed, the employee is treated as if he or she has a claim code of 1.

B. Rate of Pay The rates of pay are as set out above. Notice that all employees except Elaine are paid on an hourly basis. Elaine, as manager, receives a weekly salary.

C. Hours Worked Each employee may work a different number of hours in each week. Remember that *overtime rates* will apply to hours in excess of 40 per week or 8 per day. Notice also that Elaine's hours are shown even though she is not paid according to the number of hours she worked. It is typical to record daily the hours worked by each employee. A weekly total is then transferred to this column in the payroll summary.

D. Regular Earnings Regular earnings are computed based upon regular hours per week—or, as in Elaine's case, a salary.

E. Overtime Earnings The segregation of overtime earnings helps the owners of ABC Company Ltd. to control this expensive use of employees' time. A common practice is to hire an additional employee when this figure becomes too high.

F. Gross Pay Each employee earns a total amount per week. It is this figure which governs the legally required deductions.

FIG. 7-2, (cont.)

Deductions						
FIT	CPP	UI	Medical	Charitable	Net Pay	Chq. No.
89 60	11 42	14 01		2 00	357 97	1407
77 70	10 16	12 69	9 00	2 00	318 45	1408
40 40	8 42	10 86	17 00	2 00	289 32	1409
79 80	10 44	12 98		2 00	334 78	1410
38 50	5 96	8 26	9 00	2 00	216 28	1411
193 95	20 49	22 13	17 00	2 00	544 43	1412
519 95	66 89	80 93	52 00	12 00	2061 23	
(G)	(H)	(I)	(J)	(K)	(L)	(M)

G. Income Tax Deduction From Appendix 7-1 we have already seen that Janet's income tax deduction is $89.60. Make sure that you can find the amounts deducted from the other employees in Appendix 7-1.

H. CPP Deduction Appendix 7-2 is the source for these CPP deductions.

I. UI Deduction See Appendix 7-3 to trace each employee's UI deductions. Remember that UI deductions are not required on earnings over $750 per week. This is why Elaine's deduction for UI is $22.13—the maximum for any one week.

J. Medical Deduction The law regarding medical deductions varies from one province to another. Some provinces do not require a deduction for provincial health care plans. In our example, a deduction is required from each household. This explains why no deductions are made from Janet's and Tony's wages. We may assume that they are covered by their spouses' deductions.

K. Charitable Deduction Each employee has agreed to a weekly deduction to support a charitable cause—perhaps world hunger relief.

L. Net Pay This is each employee's gross pay less all deductions, often known as **take-home pay**.

M. Cheque Number A cheque is issued to each employee for the exact amount due. When the cheques are issued, their numbers are written here.

LEARNING UNIT 7-2 REVIEW

AT THIS POINT you should be able to

- Calculate earnings, deductions, and net pay for an employee. (pp. 256–263)
- Describe the preparation of a payroll summary. (pp. 261–262)
- Explain the purpose of each column in a payroll summary. (pp. 262–263)

SELF-REVIEW QUIZ 7-2

If a new employee, Robert Meade, begins employment next week, calculate his gross and net pay assuming a TD1 net claim code of 3, 40 hours worked, a wage of $8/h, and no medical or charitable deduction.

Solution to Self-Review Quiz 7-2

Did you calculate a net pay of $267.13? Details are:

Gross pay: 40 h @ $8/h		$320.00
Deductions:		
Income tax (from Appendix 7-1)	$36.35	
CPP (from Appendix 7-2)	7.08	
UI (from Appendix 7-3)	9.44	
Medical	0.00	
Charitable	0.00	
Total deductions		52.87
Net pay ($320.00 - $52.87)		$267.13

LEARNING UNIT 7-3

Recording and Payment

The details in Figure 7-2 are used to make the journal entry shown below which records the payroll for the first week in March for the ABC Company Ltd.:

Account	Debit	Credit
Salaries and Wages Expense	279300	
Income Taxes Payable		51995
CPP Payable		6689
UI Payable		8093
Medical Plan Payable		5200
Charitable Contributions Payable		1200
Salaries and Wages Payable		206123
To record payroll for first week in March		

Some companies keep track of different salary or wage expenses separately. For instance, it is useful to separate Elaine's salary from the wages of the other workers. The owners can then separate the cost of management from the cost of labour. It is also useful to further break down the labour cost into more detail. Consider the additional information available to the owners if we assume that Tony and Beth are sales personnel. The debit to **Sales Wage Expense** would be $720 ($440 + $280). Instead of the single debit of $2,793 to an account called **Salaries and Wages Expense**, we would now have three debits:

Account	Debit	Credit
Management Salaries Expense	80000	
Sales Wage Expense	72000	
Wages Expense	127300	

(The credit side of the entry would not change.)

If we assume that the ABC Company Ltd. uses this more detailed method, then the entry would be posted to the ledger accounts as summarized below (opening balances are ignored):

Mgmt. Salaries Expense		Sales Wages Expense		Wages Expense	
800.00		720.00		1,273.00	
Expense on the Income Statement		Expense on the Income Statement		Expense on the Income Statement	

Income Taxes Payable		CPP Payable		UI Payable	
	519.95		66.89		80.93
Liability on the Balance Sheet		Liability on the Balance Sheet		Liability on the Balance Sheet	

Medical Plan Payable		Charitable Donations Payable		Salaries and Wages Payable	
	52.00		12.00		2,061.23
Liability on the Balance Sheet		Liability on the Balance Sheet		Liability on the Balance Sheet	

Figure 7-3 summarizes the main elements of the payroll process.

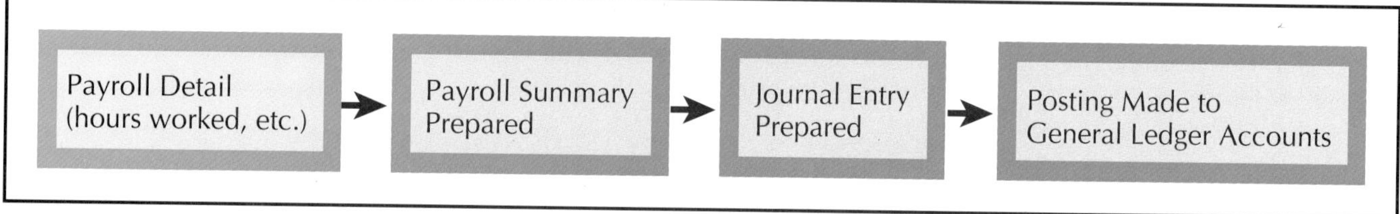

FIGURE 7-3 The Payroll Recording and Posting Process

LAST STEP DIRECTLY AFFECTING EMPLOYEES

From the employees' point of view the best part of the payroll process is receiving their net pay each week. The ABC Company Ltd. writes a cheque to each employee in payment of his or her weekly **take-home pay** (see columns L and M, Figure 7-2). As each cheque is written, it is recorded in the **cash disbursements journal,** as shown in Figure 7-4, below.

CASH DISBURSEMENTS JOURNAL

Date 19XX		Chq. No.	Accounts Payment To:	PR	Sundry Dr.	Accounts Payable Dr.	Salaries and Wages Payable Dr.	Purchases Discount Cr.	Cash Cr.
Mar.	9	1407	Janet Johnson				357 97		357 97
	9	1408	Peter Black				318 45		318 45
	9	1409	John Chernochan				289 32		289 32
	9	1410	Tony Chui				334 78		334 78
	9	1411	Beth Madora				216 28		216 28
	9	1412	Elaine Dumont				544 43		544 43

FIGURE 7-4 Cash Disbursements Journal

The total of Salaries and Wages Payable is posted at the end of the month as a debit.

When the **cash disbursements journal** is posted, the balance in the **Salaries and Wages Payable** account will be reduced to zero. This is as it should be, since the amount recorded as payable, $2,061.23, has been paid by cheques 1407-1412 and the amount remaining to be paid is nil. Please remember that the **cash disbursements journal** is posted at the end of the month. It is only after the cheques have been issued, recorded, and posted that the balance in the **Salaries and Wages Payable** account will be zero.

Most companies pay their employees by cheque, although in a very few cases, companies pay out actual cash. Many large companies transfer wages directly to their employees' bank accounts. Some companies have a separate bank account on which they issue their payroll cheques. The main reason for this practice is to simplify the payment process and reconciliation of bank accounts, especially when the number of employees is large.

EMPLOYEE EARNINGS RECORD

In order to meet legal requirements, the ABC Company Ltd. must keep a separate record of each employee's earnings. This **employee earnings record** is essential for the following reasons:

1. Every year (by February 28), ABC Company Ltd. must prepare and deliver to each employee a summary of the previous calendar year's earnings and related deductions. This form is known as a **T4** (or **T4A** slip or **T4 Supplementary**). Refer to Figure 7-5 for a sample of this form. Notice that in order to complete this form accurately, a detailed record of each employee's earnings and deductions must be kept.

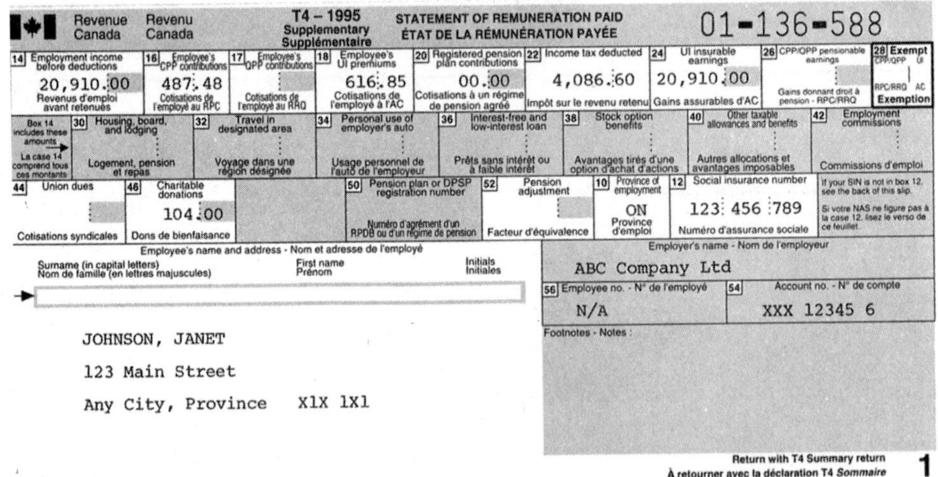

Revenue Canada / Revenu Canada
T4 – 1995 Supplementary / Supplémentaire
STATEMENT OF REMUNERATION PAID / ÉTAT DE LA RÉMUNÉRATION PAYÉE
01-136-588

Box	Item	Amount
14	Employment income before deductions / Revenus d'emploi avant retenues	20,910.00
16	Employee's CPP contributions / Cotisations de l'employé au RPC	487.48
17	Employee's QPP contributions / Cotisations de l'employé au RRQ	
18	Employee's UI premiums / Cotisations de l'employé à l'AC	616.85
20	Registered pension plan contributions / Cotisations à un régime de pension agréé	00.00
22	Income tax deducted / Impôt sur le revenu retenu	4,086.60
24	UI insurable earnings / Gains assurables d'AC	20,910.00
26	CPP/QPP pensionable earnings / Gains donnant droit à pension - RPC/RRQ	
28	Exempt CPP/QPP UI / Exemption RPC/RRQ AC	
30	Housing, board, and lodging / Logement, pension et repas	
32	Travel in designated area / Voyage dans une région désignée	
34	Personal use of employer's auto / Usage personnel de l'auto de l'employeur	
36	Interest-free and low-interest loan / Prêts sans intérêt ou à faible intérêt	
38	Stock option benefits / Avantages tirés d'une option d'achat d'actions	
40	Other taxable allowances and benefits / Autres allocations et avantages imposables	
42	Employment commissions / Commissions d'emploi	
44	Union dues / Cotisations syndicales	
46	Charitable donations / Dons de bienfaisance	104.00
50	Pension plan or DPSP registration number / Numéro d'agrément d'un RPDB ou d'un régime de pension	
52	Pension adjustment / Facteur d'équivalence	
10	Province of employment / Province d'emploi	ON
12	Social insurance number / Numéro d'assurance sociale	123 456 789

Box 14 includes these amounts / La case 14 comprend tous ces montants

If your SIN is not in box 12, see the back of this slip. / Si votre NAS ne figure pas à la case 12, lisez le verso de ce feuillet.

Employee's name and address - Nom et adresse de l'employé
Surname (in capital letters) / Nom de famille (en lettres majuscules) — First name / Prénom — Initials / Initiales

JOHNSON, JANET
123 Main Street
Any City, Province X1X 1X1

Employer's name - Nom de l'employeur: ABC Company Ltd
56 Employee no. - N° de l'employé: N/A
54 Account no. - N° de compte: XXX 12345 6
Footnotes - Notes :

Return with T4 Summary return
À retourner avec la déclaration T4 *Sommaire* 1

FIGURE 7-5
T4 Slip

2. When an employee leaves his or her employment for any reason, a special form is required to comply with the unemployment insurance laws. This form, called a **Record of Employment**, is shown in Figure 7-6.
3. In deducting CPP, it is necessary to keep deducting only as long as an employee's earnings are below a certain level. CPP is payable up to a maximum of $893.20 in 1996. Therefore it is necessary to stop making deductions when this amount is reached.

   For UI there is a maximum per pay period, hence the total per year depends on the number of pay periods occurring in that year.

Figure 7-7 shows a partial employee earnings record for Janet Johnson for the latest year.

Employment and Immigration Canada / Emploi et Immigration Canada

RECORD OF EMPLOYMENT (ROE) / *RELEVÉ D'EMPLOI (RE)*

EMPLOYER: THE GUIDE – HOW TO COMPLETE THE RECORD OF EMPLOYMENT, PROVIDES DETAILED INSTRUCTIONS
EMPLOYEUR: LE GUIDE – COMMENT REMPLIR LE RELEVÉ D'EMPLOI, FOURNIT DES INSTRUCTIONS PRÉCISES

IF COMPLETING THIS FORM BY HAND, USE A PEN AND PRESS FIRMLY / *SI VOUS REMPLISSEZ LE FORMULAIRE À LA MAIN UTILISEZ UN STYLO À BILLE ET APPUYEZ*

1 SERIAL NO. / *N° DE SÉRIE* — *T00008616

2 SERIAL NO. OF RECORD AMENDED OR REPLACED / *N° DE SÉRIE DU RELEVÉ MODIFIÉ OU REMPLACÉ*

3 EMPLOYER'S PAYROLL REFERENCE NO. / *N° DE RÉFÉRENCE DU RÉGISTRE DE PAYE DE L'EMPLOYEUR*

4 EMPLOYER'S NAME AND ADDRESS / *NOM ET ADRESSE DE L'EMPLOYEUR*

SAMPLE
ÉCHANTILLON

5 REVENUE CANADA, TAXATION ACCT. NO. / *N° DE COMPTE À REVENU CANADA, IMPÔT*

6 COMMUNICATION PREFERRED IN / *COMMUNICATIONS DE PRÉFÉRENCE EN*
☐ ENGLISH / *ANGLAIS* ☐ FRENCH / *FRANÇAIS*

7 POSTAL CODE / *CODE POSTAL*

8 PAY PERIOD TYPE / *GENRE DE PÉRIODE DE PAYE*

9 EMPLOYEE'S NAME AND ADDRESS / *NOM ET ADRESSE DE L'EMPLOYÉ(E)*

9 A – OCCUPATION / *PROFESSION*

10 SOCIAL INSURANCE NO. / *N° D'ASSURANCE SOCIALE*

11 FIRST DAY WORKED / *PREMIER JOUR DE TRAVAIL* — D/J M Y/A

12 LAST DAY WORKED / *DERNIER JOUR DE TRAVAIL* — D/J M Y/A

13 U.I. PREMIUMS PAYABLE UP TO / *COTISATIONS D'ASSURANCE-CHÔMAGE PAYABLES JUSQU'AU* — D/J M Y/A

14 FINAL PAY PERIOD ENDING DATE / *DATE DE LA FIN DE LA DERNIÈRE PÉRIODE DE PAYE* — D/J M Y/A

15 STARTING WITH THE FINAL PAY PERIOD (P.P.), ENTER THE INSURABLE EARNINGS UP TO A MAXIMUM OF 20 WEEKS. FOR MONTHLY AND SEMI-MONTHLY PAYROLLS, RECORD THE FULL P.P., IN WHICH THE 20th WEEK FALLS. IF THE INSURABLE EARNINGS TO BE REPORTED ARE AT THE MAXIMUM FOR EACH P.P., CHECK HERE ☐ AND ENTER ONLY THE TOTAL IN BLOCK 15A.

EN COMMENÇANT PAR LA DERNIÈRE PÉRIODE DE PAYE (P.P.), INSCRIRE LE MONTANT DE LA RÉMUNÉRATION ASSURABLE JUSQU'À UN MAXIMUM DE 20 SEMAINES. POUR LES REGISTRES DE PAYE MENSUELS ET BIMENSUELS, CONSIGNER TOUTE LA P.P. PENDANT LAQUELLE TOMBE LA 20e SEMAINE. SI LA RÉMUNÉRATION ASSURABLE À DÉCLARER CORRESPOND AU MAXIMUM AU COURS DE CHAQUE P.P., COCHER ICI ☐ ET INSCRIRE SEULEMENT LE TOTAL À LA CASE 15A.

P.P.	INSURABLE EARNINGS / *RÉMUNÉRATION ASSURABLE*	PAY PERIOD EXCEPTION / *EXCEPTION DE PÉRIODE DE PAYE*	P.P.	INSURABLE EARNINGS / *RÉMUNÉRATION ASSURABLE*	PAY PERIOD EXCEPTION / *EXCEPTION DE PÉRIODE DE PAYE*	P.P.	INSURABLE EARNINGS / *RÉMUNÉRATION ASSURABLE*	PAY PERIOD EXCEPTION / *EXCEPTION DE PÉRIODE DE PAYE*	P.P.	INSURABLE EARNINGS / *RÉMUNÉRATION ASSURABLE*	PAY PERIOD EXCEPTION / *EXCEPTION DE PÉRIODE DE PAYE*
1			2			3			4		
5			6			7			8		
9			10			11			12		
13			14			15			16		
17			18			19			20		

15 A TOTAL (ROUND TO THE NEAREST DOLLAR) / *TOTAL (ARRONDIR AU DOLLAR PRÈS)* $. 0 0

16 INSURABLE WEEKS IN THE LAST 52 WEEKS OR SINCE THE LAST ROE WAS ISSUED, WHICHEVER IS LESS / *SEMAINES ASSURABLES AU COURS DES 52 DERNIÈRES SEMAINES OU DEPUIS LE DERNIER RE, LE NOMBRE LE MOINS ÉLEVÉ ÉTANT RETENU*

17 PAYMENTS OR BENEFITS (OTHER THAN REGULAR PAY) PAID IN THE FINAL PAY PERIOD OR PAYABLE AT A LATER DATE
PAIEMENTS OU AVANTAGES (AUTRES QUE LE SALAIRE HABITUEL) PAYÉS AU COURS DE LA DERNIÈRE PÉRIODE DE PAYE OU PAYABLES À UNE DATE ULTÉRIEURE

A – VACATION PAY / *INDEMNITÉ DE VACANCES* $ ....

B – STATUTORY HOLIDAY PAY FOR / *JOUR(S) FÉRIÉ(S) PAYÉ(S) POUR LE(S)* — D/J M Y/A $ .... D/J M Y/A $ .... D/J M Y/A $ ....

C – OTHER MONIES (SPECIFY) / *AUTRES SOMMES (PRÉCISER)* $ .... $ .... $ ....

IMPORTANT
IF THE ABOVE PAYMENTS ARE INSURABLE, HAVE THEY BEEN ALLOCATED TO THE FINAL PAY PERIOD:
SI LES PAIEMENTS SUSMENTIONNÉS SONT ASSURABLES, ONT-ILS ÉTÉ RÉPARTIS SUR LA DERNIÈRE PÉRIODE DE PAYE: ☐ YES / *OUI* ☐ NO / *NON* IF NO, EXPLAIN IN COMMENTS SECTION / *SI NON, PRÉCISER À LA CASE "OBSERVATIONS"*

18 PAID SICK / MATERNITY / PATERNITY LEAVE OR GROUP WAGE LOSS INDEMNITY PAYMENTS (AFTER THE LAST DAY WORKED)
CONGÉ DE MALADIE / MATERNITÉ / PATERNITÉ PAYÉ OU INDEMNITÉS PAYABLES EN VERTU D'UN RÉGIME COLLECTIF D'ASSURANCE-SALAIRE (APRÈS LE DERNIER JOUR DE TRAVAIL)

PAYMENT START DATE / *DATE DE DÉBUT DU PAIEMENT* — D/J M Y/A — FOR / *POUR* .... WEEKS / DAYS / *SEM. / JOURS* — AMOUNT / *MONTANT* $ ....

19 REASON FOR ISSUING THIS ROE / *RAISON DU PRÉSENT RELEVÉ* — ENTER CODE / *INSCRIRE LE CODE*

FOR FURTHER INFORMATION, CONTACT / *POUR PLUS DE RENSEIGNEMENTS, APPELER* — TELEPHONE / *TÉLÉPHONE*

20 EXPECTED DATE OF RECALL / *DATE PRÉVUE DE RAPPEL* — D/J M Y/A ☐ NOT RETURNING / *RETOUR NON PRÉVU* ☐ UNKNOWN / *DATE NON CONNUE*

21 I AM AWARE THAT IT IS AN OFFENCE TO MAKE FALSE ENTRIES AND HEREBY CERTIFY THAT ALL STATEMENTS ON THIS FORM ARE TRUE.
JE RECONNAIS QUE TOUTE FAUSSE DÉCLARATION CONSTITUE UNE INFRACTION ET J'ATTESTE, PAR LES PRÉSENTES, QUE TOUTES LES DÉCLARATIONS FAITES SUR CE FORMULAIRE SONT VÉRIDIQUES.

SIGNATURE OF ISSUER / *SIGNATURE*

NAME OF ISSUER (please print) / *NOM DU SIGNATAIRE (en lettres moulées)*

22 COMMENTS / *OBSERVATIONS*

23 TELEPHONE NUMBER / *NUMÉRO DE TÉLÉPHONE*

24 DATE / *DATE* — D/J M Y/A

INS 2498 (9-91) B

Canada

NOTE TO EMPLOYEE
THIS IS A VALUABLE DOCUMENT. KEEP IT IN A SAFE PLACE. IF YOU INTEND TO FILE A CLAIM FOR UI BENEFITS YOU SHOULD DO SO IMMEDIATELY. THE REVERSE OF PART 2 CONTAINS IMPORTANT INFORMATION.

À L'EMPLOYÉ(E)
IL S'AGIT D'UN DOCUMENT PRÉCIEUX – CONSERVEZ-LE EN LIEU SÛR. SI VOUS COMPTEZ PRÉSENTER UNE DEMANDE DE PRESTATIONS VEUILLEZ LE FAIRE IMMÉDIATEMENT. D'IMPORTANTS RENSEIGNEMENTS VOUS SONT FOURNIS AU VERSO DE LA PARTIE 2.

EMPLOYEE'S COPY / *COPIE DE L'EMPLOYÉ(E)* PART / *PARTIE* 1

FIGURE 7-6 Record of Employment

Name of Employee	Janet Johnson
Social Insurance Number	123 456 789
Date of Birth	03/12/66

ABC Company Ltd.
Employee Earnings Record
For the Calendar Year 19XX

Employee Address:
123 Main Street
Any City, Province
A1B 1C1

Week	Net Claim Code	Rate of Pay	Hours Worked	Earnings: Regular	Earnings: Overtime	Earnings: Gross Pay	Deductions: FIT	Deductions: CPP	Deductions: UI	Deductions: Medical	Deductions: Charitable	Net Pay	Chq. No.
1	1	10/h	40	400 00		400 00	69 45	9 32	11 80	0 00	2 00	307 43	1061
2			40	400 00		400 00	69 45	9 32	11 80	0 00	2 00	307 43	1102
3			42	400 00	30 00	430 00	77 70	10 16	12 69	0 00	2 00	327 45	1150
4			40	400 00		400 00	69 45	9 32	11 80	0 00	2 00	307 43	1194
5			40	400 00		400 00	69 45	9 32	11 80	0 00	2 00	307 43	1237
6			36	360 00		360 00	59 15	8 20	10 62	0 00	2 00	280 03	1291
7			40	400 00		400 00	69 45	9 32	11 80	0 00	2 00	307 43	1322
8			41	400 00	15 00	415 00	73 60	9 74	12 24	0 00	2 00	317 42	1368
9			45	400 00	75 00	475 00	89 60	11 42	14 01	0 00	2 00	357 97	1407
10			40	400 00		400 00	69 45	9 32	11 80	0 00	2 00	307 43	1451
11			40	400 00		400 00	69 45	9 32	11 80	0 00	2 00	307 43	1490
49		11/h	46	440 00	99 00	539 00	106 10	13 21	15 90	0 00	2 00	401 79	3021
50			40	440 00		440 00	79 80	10 44	12 98	0 00	2 00	334 78	3101
51			38	418 00		418 00	74 60	9 82	12 33	0 00	2 00	319 25	3154
52			40	440 00		440 00	79 80	10 44	12 98	0 00	2 00	334 78	3214
	Totals for the Year			20280 00	630 00	20910 00	4086 60	487 48	616 85	0 00	104 00	15615 07	

FIGURE 7-7 Employee Earnings Record

LEARNING UNIT 7-3 REVIEW

AT THIS POINT you should be able to

- Record a payroll from a payroll summary. (p. 264)
- Break down gross wages into more detail. (p. 264)
- Post the entry recording the payroll into appropriate ledger accounts. (p. 265)
- Demonstrate the payment of net pay to employees by cheque. (p. 255)
- Record the cheques to employees in the cash disbursements journal. (p. 255)
- Illustrate the employee's earnings record. (pp. 266–268)
- Describe the Record of Employment form. (pp. 266–267)
- State the upper limit of UI and CPP deductions. (p. 266)

SELF-REVIEW QUIZ 7-3

Indicate whether the following statements are true or false:

1. All payroll registers are special journals. This means no payroll entry is ever needed.
2. Income Tax Payable is a liability on the balance sheet.
3. Salaries and Wages Expense has a normal balance of a credit.
4. Employee earnings records are optional for an employer.
5. The Record of Employment form must be completed annually for each employee.
6. All wages must be paid by cheque.
7. Cheques paying wages must be recorded in the cash disbursements journal.

Solution to Self-Review Quiz 7-3

1. False
2. True
3. False
4. False
5. False. The Record of Employment is required only when an employee leaves.
6. False. Cash or automatic bank transfers are also normal.
7. True, in general, although other possibilities exist, such as special payroll journals.

Chapter Review

SUMMARY OF KEY POINTS

Learning Unit 7-1

1. The minimum wage law sets the lowest hourly wage that can be paid to an employee and establishes the maximum number of hours per day and per week that an employee may work before an overtime premium must be paid.
2. Employers may calculate overtime pay separately from regular pay in order to highlight the cost of having employees work overtime.
3. Each pay period, employees are required to pay income tax and to contribute to the Canada Pension and unemployment insurance plans according to their level of earnings. The amount to be deducted for each is found in tables published by the federal government.
4. A TD1 form specifies the net claim code for each employee. This in turn governs the income tax deducted each pay period.
5. CPP and UI have a maximum contribution of $893.20 per year and $1,150.76 per year respectively. (These maximums will change annually.)
6. Other deductions (for example, union dues or company-related matters) may also be made from an employee's earnings.

Learning Unit 7-2

1. Each pay period a payroll summary is prepared. It includes the following information for each employee: net claim code; rate of pay; hours worked; regular earnings; overtime earnings; gross pay; income tax deduction; CPP deduction; UI deduction; other deductions such as medical and charitable; net pay; and cheque number.
2. Gross pay determines the level of deductions.
3. Gross pay less deductions equals net, or "take-home," pay.

Learning Unit 7-3

1. The payroll register is completed each pay period and provides basic data for recording the payroll.
2. The Salaries and Wages Expense entry is made and posted to ledger accounts. In addition to summarizing the deductions payable, the ledger accounts are used to classify wage expenses by type.
3. Each payroll cheque written is recorded in the cash disbursements journal. Journal totals are posted to the general ledger monthly.
4. Employers must maintain an Employee Earnings Record for each employee. The source of the information summarized here is the payroll register.
5. Each year employers must prepare and deliver to each employee a T4 or T4A form which summarizes the employee's earnings and deductions for the calendar year.
6. When an employee leaves, is laid off, or is terminated, the employer must complete a Record of Employment form.

Key Terms

Canada (or Quebec) Pension Plan Designed to provide a retirement benefit for all Canadians who contribute to the plan during their employment years. Requires a payroll deduction from each employee until a yearly maximum is reached. (The maximum we are using is $893.20, but a new maximum is used each year.)

Employee earnings record A page, or sheet, or computer file which records and totals the details concerning an employee's earnings, deductions, net pay, and identification details for a calendar year. Used in preparing T4 slips.

Income tax deductions Amounts withheld from employees' wages each period and sent (on behalf of the employees) to the federal government. The amount of the deduction is determined by tables published by the federal government, customized for each province.

Minimum wage laws Laws which govern the lowest wage legally payable in a province. Also states the province's rules about overtime premiums and maximum weekly working hours.

Other deductions Most employees have a variety of items for which a deduction is required. The exact type and amount of these deductions will vary a great deal from one employer to another. Common examples are union dues and provincial health care premiums.

Payroll summary Sometimes known as the payroll journal or payroll register. This document lists in considerable detail the income, deductions, net pay, and other information for each employee for a given pay period. A total for all employees per category is always shown. Forms the basis for posting to appropriate ledger accounts.

Record of Employment Special form to be completed for each employee at the end of their employment. Used in helping to prevent abuses to the Unemployment Insurance Act.

TD1 form A form completed by an employee upon commencement of employment (and annually thereafter) which sets out the deductions claimed by each employee. A net claim code determined by this form affects the amount of income tax deducted.

T4 slip or T4 Supplementary A special form issued annually to each employee summarizing their annual earnings and deductions. Used by employees as a basic document in filing their annual income tax return.

Unemployment insurance plan A plan which all employees must contribute towards and which provides a certain level of income for those workers who are unemployed. Contributions are made up to a maximum per pay period. (The maximum we are using is $22.13 per week or $95.88 per month.)

Blueprint for recording, posting, and paying the payroll

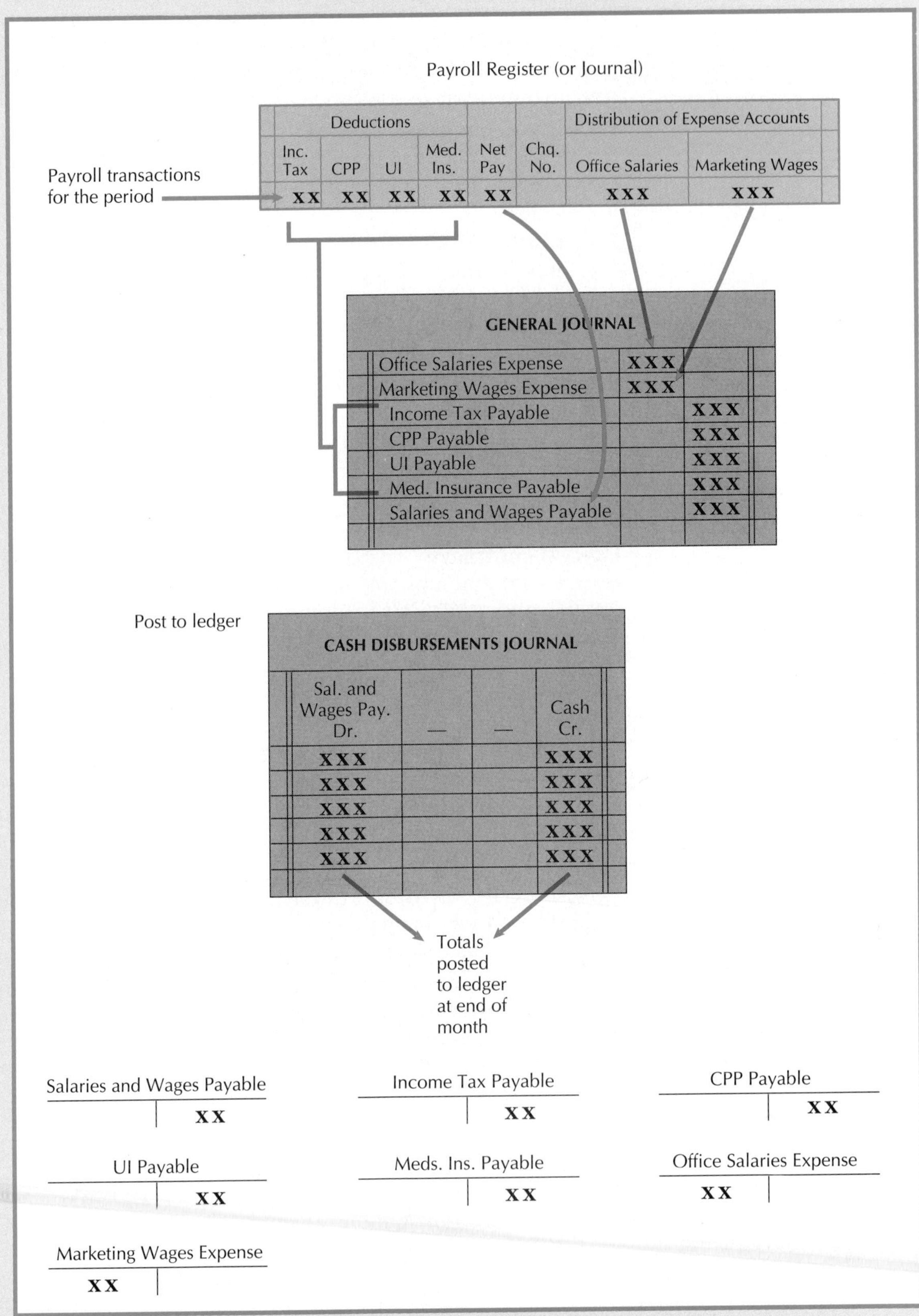

QUESTIONS, EXERCISES, AND PROBLEMS

Discussion Questions

1. Explain how overtime is usually calculated.
2. Define and state the purpose of completing a T4 Supplementary.
3. Usually, claiming more allowances on a TD1 results in receiving more money per paycheque. Please comment.
4. All payroll registers must be special journals. True or false?
5. Define and state the purpose of the Canada or the Quebec Pension Plan.
6. The employer doesn't have to contribute to the Canada Pension Plan. Agree or disagree?
7. Explain how federal and provincial income tax withholdings are determined.
8. What is a calendar year?
9. Define the purpose of an income tax deduction.
10. What purposes does the employee earnings record serve?
11. Explain the differences in determining CPP and UI deductions.
12. Draw a diagram showing how the following relate: (a) weekly payroll; (b) payroll register; (c) individual earnings; (d) journal entries; (e) cash disbursements journal.
13. If you earned $80,000 this year, you would pay more CPP than your brother, who earned $60,000. Agree or disagree? Explain.

Mini Exercises

(The forms you need are on page 7-2 of the *Study Guide and Working Papers*.)

Calculating Gross Earnings

1. Calculate the total wages earned (assume an overtime rate of time-and-a-half over 40 hours):

Employee	*Hourly Rate*	*No. of Hours Worked*
A. Dawn Slowic	$10	37
B. Jill Jones	12	50

CPP & UI

2. Pete Martin, married claiming code 1, has cumulative earnings before this weekly pay period of $41,500. Assuming he is paid $1,200 this week, what will his deduction be for CPP and UI?

Net Pay

3. Calculate Pete's net pay from question 2 above. Income tax is $410 and health insurance is $40.

Payroll Register

4. From the following identify:
   1. Total of gross pay—comes from distribution of expense accounts
   2. A deduction

3. Net pay

____ **A.** Office Salaries Expense and Wages Expense

____ **B.** CPP Payable

____ **C.** UI Payable

____ **D.** Federal Income Tax Payable

____ **E.** Medical Insurance Payable

____ **F.** Salaries and Wages Payable

Payroll Account

5. From the following indicate if the title is:

1. An asset
2. A liability
3. An expense
4. Appears in the income statement
5. Appears on the balance sheet

____ **A.** CPP Payable

____ **B.** Office Salaries Expense

____ **C.** Federal Income Tax Payable

____ **D.** UI Payable

____ **E.** Salaries and Wages Payable

Exercises

1. Calculate the total wages earned for each employee (assume an overtime rate of time-and-a-half over 40 hours):

Calculating wages with overtime.

Employee	*Hourly Rate*	*Hours Worked*
Jean Knott	$11.20	36
Abe Janzen	13.00	44
Mike Toth	14.00	46

2. Compute the net pay for each employee for the first week of February, using the tables in the text.

Calculating net pay.

Employee	*Status*	*Net Claim Code*	*This Week's Pay*
Abe Smith	Married	4	$610
May Cheung	Single	1	420

The only deductions are for income tax, CPP, and UI.

3. Complete the table.

Categorizing accounts.

	Category	*Dr./Cr.*	*Account Appears on Which Financial Rept.*
CPP Payable			
Income Tax Payable			
Medical Insurance Payable			
Wages and Salaries Payable			
Office Salaries Expense			
Marketing Wages Expense			

Payroll register and the journal entry.

4. The following weekly payroll journal entry was prepared by Moore Co. Could you explain which columns of the payroll register the data have come from?

			Dr.	Cr.
Jan.	7	Shop Expense	6 000 00	
		Factory Wages Expense	4 000 00	
		CPP Payable		715 00
		Income Tax Payable		2 700 00
		Union Dues Payable		210 00
		Salaries and Wages Payable		6 375 00

Paying the payroll.

5. From Exercise 4, prepare an entry to pay the payroll from the cash disbursements journal given the following (on January 9):

Employee	*Employee's Net Pay*	*Cheque No.*
Bill Bloss	$2,800	111
Joe Ring	1,200	112
Sally Field	2,375	113

(Use the same headings for the cash disbursements journal that we have used in the chapter.)

Group A Problems

7A-1. From the following information, please complete the chart for gross earnings for the week. (Assume an overtime rate of time-and-a-half over 40 hours.)

Calculating gross earnings with overtime.

Employee	*Hourly Rate*	*No. of Hours Worked*	*Gross Earnings*
Fred Bebe	$ 9.00	42	
Jill Johns	10.50	44	
Dave Paul	11.00	36	
Marsha Royal	13.50	50	

7A-2. March Company has five salaried employees. Your task is to record the following information into a payroll register for the last week of March.

Completing a payroll register.

Employee	*Dept.*	*Net Claim Code*	*Weekly Salary*
Mary Quill	Sales	4	$680
Joe Doane	Sales	2	375
Nora Frye	Office	1	910
Joe Tobert	Office	1	545
Paul Albert	Sales	3	420

Assume that each employee contributes $10 per week for union dues.

7A-3. The bookkeeper for Flynn Co. gathered the following data from employee earnings records as well as daily time cards. Your task is (1) to complete a payroll register on November 8 and (2) to journalize the appropriate entry to record the payroll.

Completing a payroll register and journalizing the payroll entry.

Employee	Net Claim Code	Daily Time M	T	W	T	F	Hourly Rate	Dept.	Cum. CPP Before This Payroll
Trish Smith	1	6	4	8	10	7	$12	Sales	$878.10
Bob Run	4	9	9	10	9	4	9	Office	412.30
Art Angel	2	8	10	7	10	10	15	Sales	893.20
Faye Miller	3	8	8	6	8	8	7	Office	289.60

Assumptions

1. Income tax, CPP, and UIC are from tables in the end of this chapter (See Appendixes 7-1 to 7-3).
2. Each employee contributes $10 per week for health insurance.
3. Overtime is paid at a rate of time-and-a-half over 40 hours per week, or 8 hours in any given day.

7A-4. John Wood, an accountant, has gathered the following data for you.

Completing a payroll register, journalizing, posting, and recording the payment of net pay.

Employee	Net Claim Code	Salary	Chq. No.	Cum. CPP Before This Payroll	Dept.
Robyn Boyn	5	$630	47	$406.10	Factory
EstherAllen	1	840	48	510.80	Office
Jenny Roe	3	920	49	709.80	Factory
Brian Sullivan	4	960	50	887.30	Office

Assumptions

1. Income tax is calculated from tables in the text.
2. Union dues are $8 per week.
3. Medical coverage is $14 per week (except for Brian, whose wife pays the family premium).

Required

1. Prepare a payroll register on December 5.
2. Journalize and post the payroll entry.
3. Record the payment of the payroll on December 7 to each employee.

Group B Problems

7B-1. From the following information, complete the chart for gross earnings for the week. (Assume an overtime rate of time-and-a-half over 40 hours.)

Calculating gross earnings with overtime.

	Hourly Rate	No. of Hours Worked	Gross Earnings
Fred Bebe	$ 9.00	41	
Jill Johns	10.50	45	
Dave Paul	12.00	35	
D. Marsha Royal	14.00	54	

Completing the payroll register.

7B-2. March Company has five salaried employees. Your task is to record the following information into a payroll register for the last week of March.

Employee	*Dept.*	*Net Claim Code*	*Weekly Salary*
Mary Quill	Sales	4	$730
Joe Doane	Sales	3	410
Nora Frye	Office	2	935
Joe Tobert	Office	2	530
Paul Albert	Sales	1	380

Assume that each employee contributes $15 per week for union dues.

Completing the payroll register and journalizing the payroll entry.

7B-3. The bookkeeper for Flynn Co. gathered the following data from employee earnings records as well as daily time cards. Your task is (1) to complete a payroll register on November 8 and (2) to journalize the appropriate entry to record the payroll.

	Net Claim	*Daily Time*					*Hourly*		*Cum. CPP Before This*
Employee	*Code*	*M*	*T*	*W*	*T*	*F*	*Rate*	*Dept.*	*Payroll*
Trish Smith	2	7	5	8	10	8	$14	Sales	$881.40
Bob Run	1	9	10	9	9	6	11	Office	415.90
Art Angel	4	8	10	10	8	9	13	Sales	893.20
Faye Miller	1	8	7	8	9	8	9	Office	307.50

Assumptions

1. Income tax, CPP, and UI are from tables at the end of this chapter. (See Appendixes 7-1 to 7-3.)
2. Each employee contributes $8 per week for health insurance.
3. Overtime is paid at a rate of time-and-a-half over 40 hours per week or over 8 hours in any day.

Payroll register completed, journalizing, posting, and paying the payroll.

7B-4. John Wood, an accountant, has gathered the following data for you.

Employee	*Net Claim Code*	*Salary*	*Chq. No.*	*Cum. CPP Before This Payroll*	*Dept.*
Robyn Boyn	4	$580	57	$518.43	Factory
Esther Allen	1	840	58	652.37	Office
Jenny Roe	1	770	59	871.35	Office
Brian Sullivan	2	920	60	893.20	Factory

Assumptions

1. Income tax is calculated from tables in the text.
2. Union dues are $9 per week.
3. Medical coverage is $10 per week (except for Brian, whose wife pays the family premium).

Required

1. Prepare a payroll register on December 5.
2. Journalize and post the payroll entry.
3. Record the payment of the payroll on December 7 to each employee.

Group C Problems

Calculating gross earning with overtime.

7C-1. From the following data, calculate the gross earnings for each of the five employees who are entitled to time-and-a-half for any hours exceeding 40 for the week or 8 in any given day.

Employee	*M*	*T*	*W*	*T*	*F*	*S*	*Total Hours*	*Hourly Rate*
A. Fern Tobin	6	8	8	8	8	4	42	$13.00
B. Paul Ng	5	7	7	8	7	7	41	14.00
C. Mike Wells	8	6	8	10	8	—	40	11.00
D. Amy Blair	9	4	8	8	7	8	44	15.00
E. Tim Cardinal	8	6	7	14	8	6	49	13.00

Completing the payroll register.

7C-2. The employees mentioned in Problem 7C-1 work for the Waylon Corporation Ltd. Complete a payroll register for the second week of February using the gross earnings you obtained in answering 7C-1. Assume the following additional information:

Employee	*Net Claim Code*	*Union Dues*	*Medical Plan*
A	1	$14	$28.00
B	4	14	44.00
C	1	14	28.00
D	3	14	44.00
E	3	14	44.00

Completing the payroll register (alternative problem).

7C-3. (Alternative to 7C-2.) Assume the following gross earnings for the employees of Waylon Corporation Ltd. for the third week of February. Other information remains the same as in 7C-2. Complete the payroll register for the third week of February.

Employee	*Gross Earnings*
A	$458.00
B	542.00
C	467.00
D	731.00
E	592.00

Recording the payroll entry.

7C-4. Refer to the payroll register you completed in 7C-2. Prepare the journal entry necessary to record the payroll for the second week of February.

Recording the payroll entry (alternative problem).

7C-5. (Alternative to 7C-4.) Refer to the payroll register you completed in 7C-3. Prepare the journal entry necessary to record the payroll for the third week of February.

Completing the payroll register and journalizing the payroll entry.

7C-6. The payroll clerk for the Marlin Company Ltd. has assembled the following data for the company's five employees, before suddenly becoming quite ill. You have been approached to complete the payroll register so that the employees can receive their cheques in a timely fashion. You must (1) complete the payroll register for the week ending October 20 and (2) prepare the entry necessary to record the payroll. Hours in excess of 40 in any given week are paid at time-and-a-half.

Employee	Net Claim Code	Daily Time M	T	W	T	F	S	Rate	Dept.	CPP To Date	Union Dues	Medical
Bert Monk	1	—	8	8	10	12	6	$15.00	Sales	$879.40	$8	$22
Pam Leung	3	9	—	6	10	7	8	13.00	Sales	684.10	8	40
Candy Sallis	1	8	9	8	7	8	6	11.50	Admin.	486.70	8	22
John Frank	6	8	8	8	8	8	—	17.00	Admin.	227.40	8	40
Kevin Ames	2	8	8	7	12	8	8	1,400.00*	Mgr.	893.20	-	40

* Weekly salary.

Comprehensive payroll problem—completing payroll registers, journalizing payrolls, and recording cheques issued.

7C-7. Elliot Engineering Inc. is a consulting firm which employs 4 professional staff, 2 casual clerks, and you as office manager (accountant). Everyone except the clerks is paid a weekly salary. The clerks are paid an hourly rate and receive time-and-a-half for hours worked in excess of 8 per day or 40 per week. Using the information below, complete the payroll register for the week ending August 21, make the necessary entry to record the payroll for that week, and record the issuance of cheques to each employee. Daily hours for the clerks are shown at the end.

Employee	Net Claim Code	Rate or Salary	Life Ins.	Disab.	Med.	Donations	CPP to Date	Chq. No.
Karen Brown	4	$1,510.00	$19	$32	$30.00	$25.00	$893.20	574
Jesus Alvarez	1	1,370.00	12	28	30.00	15.00	869.21	575
May Kemp	2	1,190.00	10	24	18.00	10.00	833.07	576
Dal Harper	1	1,240.00	8	25	30.00	10.00	484.37	577
Taj Singh	3	15.00	—	—	18.00	—	245.23	578
Roy Macy	1	12.00	—	—	30.00	5.00	428.64	579
Yourself	1	825.00	6	18	18.00	5.00	548.75	580

Hourly employees worked:

	M	T	W	T	F	S	Total
Taj Singh	8	7	8	10	4	8	45
Roy Macy	10	8	11	7	6	—	42

Hourly workers receive 1.5 × rate for more than 40 hours in a week, or more than 8 hours in any given day.

REAL WORLD APPLICATIONS

7R-1.

Small Co., a proprietorship, has two employees, Jim Roy and Janice Alter. The owner of Small Co. is Bert Ryan. During the current pay period, Jim has worked 48 hours and Janice 56. The reason for these extra hours is that both Jim and Janice worked their regular 40-hour work week, plus Jim worked 8 extra hours on Sunday while Janice worked 8 extra hours on Saturday as well as Sunday. Their contract with Small Co. is that they are each paid an hourly rate of $8 per hour with all hours over 40 per week to be at time-and-a-half and double time on Sunday. Bert the owner feels he is also entitled to a salary, since he works many hours. He plans to pay himself $425 per week.

As the accountant of Small Co., could you calculate the gross pay for Jim and Janice and offer some advice to Bert regarding his salary?

7R-2.

Marcy Moore recently moved to your city from another large Canadian centre. She was employed as an engineer by a large oil company and was rather well paid. She now works as a senior engineer for a newly established consulting firm. As she moved in October, Marcy had contributed the yearly maximum CPP premiums of $893.20 while employed at the oil company, and feels it is unfair of her new employer to continue to deduct CPP from her salary. She has heard that you are taking an accounting course, and has asked you for your opinion.

What advice can you give her?

make the call

Critical Thinking/Ethical Case

7R-3.

Russ Todd works for a delicatessen. As the bookkeeper Russ has been asked by the owner to keep two separate books for sales tax. The owner has asked Todd to hire someone on the weekends to punch in false tapes that can be submitted to the province. These tapes would show low sales and thus less liability for sales tax payments. You make the call. Write down your specific recommendations to Russ.

ACCOUNTING RECALL

A CUMULATIVE APPROACH

THIS EXAM REVIEWS CHAPTERS 1 THROUGH 7

Your *Study Guide and Working Papers* have forms to complete this exam, as well as worked-out solutions. The page references next to each question identify what page to turn back to if you answer the question incorrectly.

PART I Vocabulary Review

Match the terms to the appropriate definition or phrase.

Page Ref.		
(262)	1. Total earnings columns	A. Gross pay less deductions
(231)	2. Petty cash	B. Records gross payroll
(266)	3. T4 slip	C. A pension plan for most employees
(263)	4. Tax deductions	D. An asset
(266)	5. Calendar year	E. National insurance plan
(258)	6. TD1 form	F. Found in tables by province
(255)	7. UI	G. Basis for determining tax deductions
(263)	8. Net pay	H. An annual summary of payroll amounts
(266)	9. Employee earnings record	I. January 1 to December 31
(255)	10. CPP	J. Updated each pay period

PART II True or False (Accounting Theory)

(256) 11. A biweekly pay period results in 24 payrolls each year.

(264) 12. A payroll register is considered a special journal.

(262) 13. The total earnings column of a payroll register shows earnings that are subject to income tax.

(264) 14. Wages and Salaries Payable records gross pay.

(266) 15. The employee earnings record is updated from the payroll register.

PART III Application Problem (7-23)

Amy Jacobs earns $76,000.00 per year. Assuming a CPP rate of 2.8 percent, and an annual exemption of $3,500.00, calculate the amount of CPP Amy will contribute by way of payroll deductions if the maximum contribution limit salary is $35,400.00.

Employee Payroll Deductions (Extracted): Income Tax, CPP, UIC

Appendix 7-1—Ontario Tax Tables

Ontario
Tax Deductions
Weekly (52 pay periods a year)

Ontario
Retenues d'impôt
Hebdomadaire (52 périodes de paie par année)

Pay / Rémunération		If the employee's claim code from the TD1 form is / Si le code de demande de l'employé selon le formulaire TD1 est										
		0	1	2	3	4	5	6	7	8	9	10
From / De	Less than / Moins que	Deduct from each pay / Retenez sur chaque paie										
237.-	241.	62.15	28.20	24.05	15.20	4.70						
241.-	245.	63.20	29.20	25.05	16.75	5.40	.05					
245.-	249.	64.25	30.25	26.10	17.75	6.05	.70					
249.-	253.	65.25	31.30	27.10	18.80	6.70	1.35					
253.-	257.	66.30	32.30	28.15	19.85	7.95	2.05					
257.-	261.	67.35	33.35	29.20	20.85	9.75	2.70					
261.-	265.	68.35	34.40	30.20	21.90	11.50	3.35					
265.-	269.	69.40	35.40	31.25	22.95	13.30	4.00					
269.-	273.	70.40	36.45	32.30	23.95	15.05	4.65					
273.-	277.	71.45	37.45	33.30	25.00	16.65	5.35					
277.-	281.	72.50	38.50	34.35	26.00	17.70	6.00	.65				
281.-	285.	73.50	39.55	35.40	27.05	18.70	6.65	1.35				
285.-	289.	74.55	40.55	36.40	28.10	19.75	7.85	2.00				
289.-	293.	75.60	41.60	37.45	29.10	20.80	9.60	2.65				
293.-	297.	76.60	42.65	38.45	30.15	21.80	11.40	3.30				
297.-	301.	77.65	43.65	39.50	31.20	22.85	13.15	3.95				
301.-	305.	78.70	44.70	40.55	32.20	23.90	14.95	4.65				
305.-	309.	79.70	45.75	41.55	33.25	24.90	16.60	5.30				
309.-	313.	80.75	46.75	42.60	34.30	25.95	17.60	5.95	.60			
313.-	317.	81.75	47.80	43.65	35.30	27.00	18.65	6.60	1.30			
317.-	321.	82.80	48.80	44.65	36.35	28.00	19.70	7.70	1.95			
321.-	325.	83.85	49.85	45.70	37.35	29.05	20.70	9.50	2.60			
325.-	329.	84.85	50.90	46.75	38.40	30.05	21.75	11.25	3.25			
329.-	333.	85.90	51.90	47.75	39.45	31.10	22.80	13.05	3.90			
333.-	337.	86.95	52.95	48.80	40.45	32.15	23.80	14.80	4.60			
337.-	341.	87.95	54.00	49.80	41.50	33.15	24.85	16.50	5.25			
341.-	345.	89.00	55.00	50.85	42.55	34.20	25.85	17.55	5.90	.60		
345.-	349.	90.05	56.05	51.90	43.55	35.25	26.90	18.60	6.55	1.25		
349.-	353.	91.05	57.10	52.90	44.60	36.25	27.95	19.60	7.60	1.90		
353.-	357.	92.10	58.10	53.95	45.65	37.30	28.95	20.65	9.40	2.55		
357.-	361.	93.10	59.15	55.00	46.65	38.35	30.00	21.70	11.15	3.20		
361.-	365.	94.15	60.20	56.00	47.70	39.35	31.05	22.70	12.95	3.90		
365.-	369.	95.20	61.20	57.05	48.70	40.40	32.05	23.75	14.70	4.55		
369.-	373.	96.20	62.25	58.10	49.75	41.40	33.10	24.80	16.45	5.20		
373.-	377.	97.25	63.25	59.10	50.80	42.45	34.15	25.80	17.50	5.85	.55	
377.-	381.	98.30	64.30	60.15	51.80	43.50	35.15	26.85	18.50	6.50	1.20	
381.-	385.	99.30	65.35	61.15	52.85	44.50	36.20	27.85	19.55	7.50	1.85	
385.-	389.	100.35	66.35	62.20	53.90	45.55	37.20	28.90	20.60	9.25	2.50	
389.-	393.	101.40	67.40	63.25	54.90	46.60	38.25	29.95	21.60	11.05	3.20	
393.-	397.	102.40	68.45	64.25	55.95	47.60	39.30	30.95	22.65	12.80	3.85	
397.-	401.	103.45	69.45	65.30	57.00	48.65	40.30	32.00	23.70	14.60	4.50	
401.-	405.	104.45	70.50	66.35	58.00	49.70	41.35	33.05	24.70	16.35	5.15	
405.-	409.	105.50	71.55	67.35	59.05	50.70	42.40	34.05	25.75	17.40	5.80	.50
409.-	413.	106.55	72.55	68.40	60.05	51.75	43.40	35.10	26.75	18.45	6.50	1.15
413.-	417.	107.55	73.60	69.45	61.10	52.75	44.45	36.15	27.80	19.50	7.35	1.80
417.-	421.	108.60	74.60	70.45	62.15	53.80	45.50	[illegible]	[illegible]	[illegible]	[illegible]	[illegible]
421.-	425.	109.65	75.65	71.50	63.15	54.85	46.50	38.20	29.85	21.55	10.90	3.15
425.-	429.	110.65	76.70	72.50	64.20	55.85	47.55	39.20	30.90	22.55	12.70	3.80
429.-	433.	111.70	77.70	73.55	65.25	56.90	48.60	40.25	31.95	23.60	14.45	4.45
433.-	437.	112.75	78.75	74.60	66.25	57.95	49.60	41.30	32.95	24.65	16.25	5.10
437.-	441.	113.75	79.80	75.60	67.30	58.95	50.65	42.30	34.00	25.65	17.35	5.75
441.-	445.	114.80	80.80	76.65	68.35	60.00	51.65	43.35	35.05	26.70	18.40	6.45
445.-	449.	115.80	81.85	77.70	69.35	61.05	52.70	44.40	36.05	27.75	19.40	7.25
449.-	453.	116.85	82.90	78.70	70.40	62.05	53.75	45.40	37.10	28.75	20.45	9.00
453.-	457.	117.90	83.90	79.75	71.40	63.10	54.75	46.45	38.10	29.80	21.45	10.80

D-2 **This table is available on diskette (TOD). Vous pouvez obtenir cette table sur disquette (TSD).**

Ontario
Tax Deductions
Weekly (52 pay periods a year)

Ontario
Retenues d'impôt
Hebdomadaire (52 périodes de paie par année)

Pay / Rémunération		If the employee's claim code from the TD1 form is / Si le code de demande de l'employé selon le formulaire TD1 est										
From / De	Less than / Moins que	0	1	2	3	4	5	6	7	8	9	10
		Deduct from each pay / Retenez sur chaque paie										
457.-	465.	119.45	85.45	81.30	72.95	64.65	56.30	48.00	39.65	31.35	23.00	13.45
465.-	473.	121.50	87.50	83.35	75.05	66.70	58.40	50.05	41.75	33.40	25.10	16.75
473.-	481.	123.55	89.60	85.40	77.10	68.75	60.45	52.10	43.80	35.45	27.15	18.80
481.-	489.	125.65	91.65	87.50	79.15	70.85	62.50	54.20	45.85	37.55	29.20	20.90
489.-	497.	127.70	93.70	89.55	81.25	72.90	64.55	56.25	47.90	39.60	31.30	22.95
497.-	505.	129.75	95.75	91.60	83.30	74.95	66.65	58.30	50.00	41.65	33.35	25.00
505.-	513.	131.80	97.85	93.70	85.35	77.00	68.70	60.40	52.05	43.75	35.40	27.05
513.-	521.	133.90	99.90	95.75	87.40	79.10	70.75	62.45	54.10	45.80	37.45	29.15
521.-	529.	135.95	101.95	97.80	89.50	81.15	72.80	64.50	56.20	47.85	39.55	31.20
529.-	537.	138.00	104.05	99.85	91.55	83.20	74.90	66.55	58.25	49.90	41.60	33.25
537.-	545.	140.05	106.10	101.95	93.60	85.30	76.95	68.65	60.30	52.00	43.65	35.35
545.-	553.	142.15	108.15	104.00	95.65	87.35	79.00	70.70	62.35	54.05	45.70	37.40
553.-	561.	144.20	110.20	106.05	97.75	89.40	81.10	72.75	64.45	56.10	47.80	39.45
561.-	569.	146.25	112.30	108.10	99.80	91.45	83.15	74.80	66.50	58.15	49.85	41.50
569.-	577.	148.90	114.90	110.75	102.45	94.10	85.80	77.45	69.15	60.80	52.50	44.15
577.-	585.	152.15	118.15	114.00	105.65	97.35	89.00	80.70	72.35	64.05	55.70	47.40
585.-	593.	155.35	121.35	117.20	108.90	100.55	92.25	83.90	75.60	67.25	58.95	50.60
593.-	601.	158.55	124.60	120.45	112.10	103.80	95.45	87.15	78.80	70.50	62.15	53.85
601.-	609.	161.80	127.80	123.65	115.35	107.00	98.65	90.35	82.05	73.70	65.40	57.05
609.-	617.	165.00	131.05	126.90	118.55	110.20	101.90	93.60	85.25	76.95	68.60	60.25
617.-	625.	168.25	134.25	130.10	121.80	113.45	105.10	96.80	88.50	80.15	71.85	63.50
625.-	633.	171.45	137.50	133.30	125.00	116.65	108.35	100.00	91.70	83.35	75.05	66.70
633.-	641.	174.70	140.70	136.55	128.20	119.90	111.55	103.25	94.90	86.60	78.25	69.95
641.-	649.	177.90	143.95	139.75	131.45	123.10	114.80	106.45	98.15	89.80	81.50	73.15
649.-	657.	181.15	147.15	143.00	134.65	126.35	118.00	109.70	101.35	93.05	84.70	76.40
657.-	665.	184.35	150.40	146.20	137.90	129.55	121.25	112.90	104.60	96.25	87.95	79.60
665.-	673.	187.60	153.60	149.45	141.10	132.80	124.45	116.15	107.80	99.50	91.15	82.85
673.-	681.	190.80	156.80	152.65	144.35	136.00	127.70	119.35	111.05	102.70	94.40	86.05
681.-	689.	194.05	160.10	155.90	147.60	139.25	130.95	122.60	114.30	105.95	97.65	89.30
689.-	697.	197.35	163.35	159.20	150.90	142.55	134.20	125.90	117.55	109.25	100.95	92.60
697.-	705.	200.65	166.65	162.50	154.15	145.85	137.50	129.20	120.85	112.55	104.20	95.90
705.-	713.	203.90	169.95	165.75	157.45	149.10	140.80	132.45	124.15	115.80	107.50	99.15
713.-	721.	207.20	173.20	169.05	160.75	152.40	144.05	135.75	127.45	119.10	110.80	102.45
721.-	729.	210.50	176.50	172.35	164.00	155.70	147.35	139.05	130.70	122.40	114.05	105.75
729.-	737.	213.75	179.80	175.60	167.30	158.95	150.65	142.30	134.00	125.65	117.35	109.00
737.-	745.	217.05	183.05	178.90	170.60	162.25	153.95	145.60	137.30	128.95	120.65	112.30
745.-	753.	220.35	186.35	182.20	173.85	165.55	157.20	148.90	140.55	132.25	123.90	115.60
753.-	761.	223.65	189.70	185.55	177.20	168.90	160.55	152.25	143.90	135.60	127.25	118.90
761.-	769.	227.00	193.05	188.90	180.55	172.20	163.90	155.60	147.25	138.95	130.60	122.25
769.-	777.	230.35	196.40	192.25	183.90	175.55	167.25	158.95	150.60	142.30	133.95	125.60
777.-	785.	233.70	199.75	195.60	187.25	178.90	170.60	162.25	153.95	145.65	137.30	128.95
785.-	793.	237.05	203.10	198.90	190.60	182.25	173.95	165.60	157.30	148.95	140.65	132.30
793.-	801.	240.40	206.45	202.25	193.95	185.60	177.30	168.95	160.65	152.30	144.00	135.65
801.-	809.	243.75	209.80	205.60	197.30	188.95	180.65	172.30	164.00	155.65	147.35	139.00
809.-	817.	247.10	213.15	208.95	200.65	192.30	184.00	175.65	167.35	159.00	150.70	142.35
817.-	825.	250.45	216.50	212.30	204.00	195.65	187.35	179.00	170.70	162.35	154.05	145.70
825.-	833.	253.80	219.85	215.65	207.35	199.00	190.70	182.35	174.05	165.70	157.40	149.05
833.-	841.	257.15	223.20	219.00	210.70	202.35	194.05	185.70	177.40	169.05	160.75	152.40
841.-	849.	260.50	226.55	222.35	214.05	205.70	197.40	189.05	180.75	172.40	164.10	155.75
849.-	857.	263.85	229.90	225.70	217.40	209.05	200.75	192.40	184.10	175.75	167.45	159.10
857.-	865.	267.20	233.20	229.05	220.75	212.40	204.10	195.75	187.45	179.10	170.80	162.45
865.-	873.	270.55	236.55	232.40	224.10	215.75	207.45	199.10	190.80	182.45	174.15	165.80
873.-	881.	273.90	239.90	235.75	227.45	219.10	210.80	202.45	194.15	185.80	177.50	169.15
881.-	889.	277.25	243.25	239.10	230.80	222.45	214.15	205.80	197.50	189.15	180.85	172.50
889.-	897.	280.60	246.60	242.45	234.15	225.80	217.50	209.15	200.85	192.50	184.20	175.85

This table is available on diskette (TOD). Vous pouvez obtenir cette table sur disquette (TSD).

D-3

Ontario

Tax Deductions

Weekly (52 pay periods a year)

Ontario

Retenues d'impôt

Hebdomadaire (52 périodes de paie par année)

Pay / Rémunération		If the employee's claim code from the TD1 form is / Si le code de demande de l'employé selon le formulaire TD1 est										
		0	1	2	3	4	5	6	7	8	9	10
From / De	Less than / Moins que	Deduct from each pay / Retenez sur chaque paie										
897.-	909.	284.80	250.80	246.65	238.30	230.00	221.65	213.35	205.00	196.70	188.35	180.05
909.-	921.	289.80	255.85	251.65	243.35	235.00	226.70	218.35	210.05	201.70	193.40	185.05
921.-	933.	294.90	260.85	256.70	248.35	240.05	231.70	223.40	215.05	206.75	198.40	190.10
933.-	945.	300.30	265.90	261.70	253.40	245.05	236.75	228.40	220.10	211.75	203.45	195.10
945.-	957.	305.70	270.90	266.75	258.40	250.10	241.75	233.45	225.10	216.80	208.45	200.15
957.-	969.	311.10	275.90	271.75	263.45	255.10	246.80	238.45	230.15	221.80	213.50	205.15
969.-	981.	316.45	280.95	276.80	268.45	260.15	251.80	243.50	235.15	226.85	218.50	210.20
981.-	993.	321.85	285.95	281.80	273.50	265.15	256.85	248.50	240.20	231.85	223.55	215.20
993.-	1005.	327.25	291.00	286.85	278.50	270.20	261.85	253.55	245.20	236.90	228.55	220.20
1005.-	1017.	332.60	296.20	291.85	283.55	275.20	266.85	258.55	250.25	241.90	233.60	225.25
1017.-	1029.	338.00	301.55	297.10	288.55	280.20	271.90	263.60	255.25	246.95	238.60	230.25
1029.-	1041.	343.40	306.95	302.50	293.60	285.25	276.90	268.60	260.25	251.95	243.65	235.30
1041.-	1053.	348.75	312.35	307.90	298.95	290.25	281.95	273.60	265.30	256.95	248.65	240.30
1053.-	1065.	354.15	317.75	313.25	304.35	295.40	286.95	278.65	270.30	262.00	253.65	245.35
1065.-	1077.	359.55	323.10	318.65	309.75	300.80	292.00	283.65	275.35	267.00	258.70	250.35
1077.-	1089.	364.95	328.50	324.05	315.10	306.20	297.25	288.70	280.35	272.05	263.70	255.40
1089.-	1101.	370.30	333.90	329.40	320.50	311.55	302.65	293.70	285.40	277.05	268.75	260.40
1101.-	1113.	375.70	339.25	334.80	325.90	316.95	308.05	299.10	290.40	282.10	273.75	265.45
1113.-	1125.	381.10	344.65	340.20	331.25	322.35	313.40	304.50	295.55	287.10	278.80	270.45
1125.-	1137.	386.45	350.05	345.60	336.65	327.75	318.80	309.90	300.95	292.15	283.80	275.50
1137.-	1149.	392.10	355.70	351.25	342.30	333.40	324.45	315.55	306.60	297.70	289.10	280.75
1149.-	1161.	398.25	361.70	357.25	348.30	339.40	330.45	321.55	312.60	303.70	294.75	286.35
1161.-	1173.	404.45	367.70	363.25	354.30	345.40	336.45	327.55	318.60	309.70	300.75	291.95
1173.-	1185.	410.60	373.70	369.25	360.35	351.40	342.45	333.55	324.65	315.70	306.80	297.85
1185.-	1197.	416.80	379.70	375.25	366.35	357.40	348.50	339.55	330.65	321.70	312.80	303.85
1197.-	1209.	423.00	385.75	381.25	372.35	363.40	354.50	345.55	336.65	327.70	318.80	309.85
1209.-	1221.	429.15	391.75	387.25	378.35	369.40	360.50	351.55	342.65	333.70	324.80	315.85
1221.-	1233.	435.35	397.85	393.30	384.35	375.40	366.50	357.60	348.65	339.75	330.80	321.85
1233.-	1245.	441.65	404.05	399.45	390.35	381.45	372.50	363.60	354.65	345.75	336.80	327.90
1245.-	1257.	448.00	410.20	405.65	396.45	387.45	378.50	369.60	360.65	351.75	342.80	333.90
1257.-	1269.	454.40	416.40	411.80	402.60	393.45	384.50	375.60	366.65	357.75	348.80	339.90
1269.-	1281.	460.80	422.60	418.00	408.80	399.60	390.50	381.60	372.70	363.75	354.85	345.90
1281.-	1293.	467.15	428.75	424.15	415.00	405.80	396.60	387.60	378.70	369.75	360.85	351.90
1293.-	1305.	473.55	434.95	430.35	421.15	412.00	402.80	393.60	384.70	375.75	366.85	357.90
1305.-	1317.	479.95	441.20	436.55	427.35	418.15	408.95	399.80	390.70	381.75	372.85	363.90
1317.-	1329.	486.30	447.60	442.85	433.55	424.35	415.15	405.95	396.80	387.80	378.85	369.90
1329.-	1341.	492.70	454.00	449.25	439.75	430.50	421.35	412.15	402.95	393.80	384.85	375.95
1341.-	1353.	499.10	460.35	455.65	446.15	436.70	427.50	418.35	409.15	399.95	390.85	381.95
1353.-	1365.	505.45	466.75	462.00	452.55	443.05	433.70	424.50	415.35	406.15	396.95	387.95
1365.-	1377.	511.85	473.15	468.40	458.90	449.40	439.95	430.70	421.50	412.35	403.15	393.95
1377.-	1389.	518.20	479.50	474.80	465.30	455.80	446.30	436.85	427.70	418.50	409.35	400.15
1389.-	1401.	524.60	485.90	481.15	471.70	462.20	452.70	443.20	433.85	424.70	415.50	406.30
1401.-	1413.	531.00	492.30	487.55	478.05	468.55	459.10	449.60	440.10	430.85	421.70	412.50
1413.-	1425.	537.35	498.65	493.90	484.45	474.95	465.45	456.00	446.50	437.05	427.85	418.70
1425.-	1437.	543.75	505.05	500.30	490.80	481.35	471.85	462.35	452.90	443.40	434.05	424.85
1437.-	1449.	550.15	511.45	506.70	497.20	487.70	478.25	468.75	459.25	449.80	440.30	431.05
1449.-	1461.	556.50	517.80	513.05	503.60	494.10	484.60	475.15	465.65	456.15	446.70	437.20
1461.-	1473.	562.90	524.20	519.45	509.95	500.50	491.00	481.50	472.05	462.55	453.05	443.60
1473.-	1485.	569.30	530.55	525.85	516.35	506.85	497.40	487.90	478.40	468.95	459.45	449.95
1485.-	1497.	575.65	536.95	532.20	522.75	513.25	503.75	494.30	484.80	475.30	465.85	456.35
1497.-	1509.	582.05	543.35	538.60	529.10	519.65	510.15	500.65	491.20	481.70	472.20	462.75
1509.-	1521.	588.45	549.70	545.00	535.50	526.00	516.55	507.05	497.55	488.10	478.60	469.10
1521.-	1533.	594.80	556.10	551.35	541.90	532.40	522.90	513.45	503.95	494.45	485.00	475.50
1533.-	1545.	601.20	562.50	557.75	548.25	538.80	529.30	519.80	510.35	500.85	491.35	481.85
1545.-	1557.	607.60	568.85	564.15	554.65	545.15	535.65	526.20	516.70	507.25	497.75	488.25

D-4 **This table is available on diskette (TOD). Vous pouvez obtenir cette table sur disquette (TSD).**

Simulated Canada Pension Plan Contributions

Weekly (52 Pay periods a year)

Students are advised to use this table for classroom purposes only. Although accurate, it has fewer categories of pay amounts than the real table.

Pay			Pay			Pay			Pay			Pay		
From	To	CPP	From	To	CPP	From	To	CPP	From	To	CPP	From	To	CPP
- ~	67.30	-	134.01 ~	135.00	1.88	206.01 ~	207.00	3.90	278.01 ~	279.00	5.91	350.01 ~	351.00	7.93
67.31 ~	67.83	0.01	135.01 ~	136.00	1.91	207.01 ~	208.00	3.93	279.01 ~	280.00	5.94	351.01 ~	352.00	7.96
67.84 ~	68.19	0.02	136.01 ~	137.00	1.94	208.01 ~	209.00	3.95	280.01 ~	281.00	5.97	352.01 ~	353.00	7.99
68.20 ~	68.54	0.03	137.01 ~	138.00	1.97	209.01 ~	210.00	3.98	281.01 ~	282.00	6.00	353.01 ~	354.00	8.01
68.55 ~	68.90	0.04	138.01 ~	139.00	1.99	210.01 ~	211.00	4.01	282.01 ~	283.00	6.03	354.01 ~	355.00	8.04
68.91 ~	69.26	0.05	139.01 ~	140.00	2.02	211.01 ~	212.00	4.04	283.01 ~	284.00	6.05	355.01 ~	356.00	8.07
69.27 ~	69.62	0.06	140.01 ~	141.00	2.05	212.01 ~	213.00	4.07	284.01 ~	285.00	6.08	356.01 ~	357.00	8.10
69.63 ~	69.99	0.07	141.01 ~	142.00	2.08	213.01 ~	214.00	4.09	285.01 ~	286.00	6.11	357.01 ~	358.00	8.13
70.00 ~	71.00	0.09	142.01 ~	143.00	2.11	214.01 ~	215.00	4.12	286.01 ~	287.00	6.14	358.01 ~	359.00	8.15
71.01 ~	72.00	0.12	143.01 ~	144.00	2.13	215.01 ~	216.00	4.15	287.01 ~	288.00	6.17	359.01 ~	360.00	8.18
72.01 ~	73.00	0.15	144.01 ~	145.00	2.16	216.01 ~	217.00	4.18	288.01 ~	289.00	6.19	360.01 ~	361.00	8.21
73.01 ~	74.00	0.17	145.01 ~	146.00	2.19	217.01 ~	218.00	4.21	289.01 ~	290.00	6.22	361.01 ~	362.00	8.24
74.01 ~	75.00	0.20	146.01 ~	147.00	2.22	218.01 ~	219.00	4.23	290.01 ~	291.00	6.25	362.01 ~	363.00	8.27
75.01 ~	76.00	0.23	147.01 ~	148.00	2.25	219.01 ~	220.00	4.26	291.01 ~	292.00	6.28	363.01 ~	364.00	8.29
76.01 ~	77.00	0.26	148.01 ~	149.00	2.27	220.01 ~	221.00	4.29	292.01 ~	293.00	6.31	364.01 ~	365.00	8.32
77.01 ~	78.00	0.29	149.01 ~	150.00	2.30	221.01 ~	222.00	4.32	293.01 ~	294.00	6.33	365.01 ~	366.00	8.35
78.01 ~	79.00	0.31	150.01 ~	151.00	2.33	222.01 ~	223.00	4.35	294.01 ~	295.00	6.36	366.01 ~	367.00	8.38
79.01 ~	80.00	0.34	151.01 ~	152.00	2.36	223.01 ~	224.00	4.37	295.01 ~	296.00	6.39	367.01 ~	368.00	8.41
80.01 ~	81.00	0.37	152.01 ~	153.00	2.39	224.01 ~	225.00	4.40	296.01 ~	297.00	6.42	368.01 ~	369.00	8.43
81.01 ~	82.00	0.40	153.01 ~	154.00	2.41	225.01 ~	226.00	4.43	297.01 ~	298.00	6.45	369.01 ~	370.00	8.46
82.01 ~	83.00	0.43	154.01 ~	155.00	2.44	226.01 ~	227.00	4.46	298.01 ~	299.00	6.47	370.01 ~	371.00	8.49
83.01 ~	84.00	0.45	155.01 ~	156.00	2.47	227.01 ~	228.00	4.49	299.01 ~	300.00	6.50	371.01 ~	372.00	8.52
84.01 ~	85.00	0.48	156.01 ~	157.00	2.50	228.01 ~	229.00	4.51	300.01 ~	301.00	6.53	372.01 ~	373.00	8.55
85.01 ~	86.00	0.51	157.01 ~	158.00	2.53	229.01 ~	230.00	4.54	301.01 ~	302.00	6.56	373.01 ~	374.00	8.57
86.01 ~	87.00	0.54	158.01 ~	159.00	2.55	230.01 ~	231.00	4.57	302.01 ~	303.00	6.59	374.01 ~	375.00	8.60
87.01 ~	88.00	0.57	159.01 ~	160.00	2.58	231.01 ~	232.00	4.60	303.01 ~	304.00	6.61	375.01 ~	376.00	8.63
88.01 ~	89.00	0.59	160.01 ~	161.00	2.61	232.01 ~	233.00	4.63	304.01 ~	305.00	6.64	376.01 ~	377.00	8.66
89.01 ~	90.00	0.62	161.01 ~	162.00	2.64	233.01 ~	234.00	4.65	305.01 ~	306.00	6.67	377.01 ~	378.00	8.69
90.01 ~	91.00	0.65	162.01 ~	163.00	2.67	234.01 ~	235.00	4.68	306.01 ~	307.00	6.70	378.01 ~	379.00	8.71
91.01 ~	92.00	0.68	163.01 ~	164.00	2.69	235.01 ~	236.00	4.71	307.01 ~	308.00	6.73	379.01 ~	380.00	8.74
92.01 ~	93.00	0.71	164.01 ~	165.00	2.72	236.01 ~	237.00	4.74	308.01 ~	309.00	6.75	380.01 ~	381.00	8.77
93.01 ~	94.00	0.73	165.01 ~	166.00	2.75	237.01 ~	238.00	4.77	309.01 ~	310.00	6.78	381.01 ~	382.00	8.80
94.01 ~	95.00	0.76	166.01 ~	167.00	2.78	238.01 ~	239.00	4.79	310.01 ~	311.00	6.81	382.01 ~	383.00	8.83
95.01 ~	96.00	0.79	167.01 ~	168.00	2.81	239.01 ~	240.00	4.82	311.01 ~	312.00	6.84	383.01 ~	384.00	8.85
96.01 ~	97.00	0.82	168.01 ~	169.00	2.83	240.01 ~	241.00	4.85	312.01 ~	313.00	6.87	384.01 ~	385.00	8.88
97.01 ~	98.00	0.85	169.01 ~	170.00	2.86	241.01 ~	242.00	4.88	313.01 ~	314.00	6.89	385.01 ~	386.00	8.91
98.01 ~	99.00	0.87	170.01 ~	171.00	2.89	242.01 ~	243.00	4.91	314.01 ~	315.00	6.92	386.01 ~	387.00	8.94
99.01 ~	100.00	0.90	171.01 ~	172.00	2.92	243.01 ~	244.00	4.93	315.01 ~	316.00	6.95	387.01 ~	388.00	8.97
100.01 ~	101.00	0.93	172.01 ~	173.00	2.95	244.01 ~	245.00	4.96	316.01 ~	317.00	6.98	388.01 ~	389.00	8.99
101.01 ~	102.00	0.96	173.01 ~	174.00	2.97	245.01 ~	246.00	4.99	317.01 ~	318.00	7.01	389.01 ~	390.00	9.02
102.01 ~	103.00	0.99	174.01 ~	175.00	3.00	246.01 ~	247.00	5.02	318.01 ~	319.00	7.03	390.01 ~	391.00	9.05
103.01 ~	104.00	1.01	175.01 ~	176.00	3.03	247.01 ~	248.00	5.05	319.01 ~	320.00	7.06	391.01 ~	392.00	9.08
104.01 ~	105.00	1.04	176.01 ~	177.00	3.06	248.01 ~	249.00	5.07	320.01 ~	321.00	7.09	392.01 ~	393.00	9.11
105.01 ~	106.00	1.07	177.01 ~	178.00	3.09	249.01 ~	250.00	5.10	321.01 ~	322.00	7.12	393.01 ~	394.00	9.13
106.01 ~	107.00	1.10	178.01 ~	179.00	3.11	250.01 ~	251.00	5.13	322.01 ~	323.00	7.15	394.01 ~	395.00	9.16
107.01 ~	108.00	1.13	179.01 ~	180.00	3.14	251.01 ~	252.00	5.16	323.01 ~	324.00	7.17	395.01 ~	396.00	9.19
108.01 ~	109.00	1.15	180.01 ~	181.00	3.17	252.01 ~	253.00	5.19	324.01 ~	325.00	7.20	396.01 ~	397.00	9.22
109.01 ~	110.00	1.18	181.01 ~	182.00	3.20	253.01 ~	254.00	5.21	325.01 ~	326.00	7.23	397.01 ~	398.00	9.25
110.01 ~	111.00	1.21	182.01 ~	183.00	3.23	254.01 ~	255.00	5.24	326.01 ~	327.00	7.26	398.01 ~	399.00	9.27
111.01 ~	112.00	1.24	183.01 ~	184.00	3.25	255.01 ~	256.00	5.27	327.01 ~	328.00	7.29	399.01 ~	400.00	9.30
112.01 ~	113.00	1.27	184.01 ~	185.00	3.28	256.01 ~	257.00	5.30	328.01 ~	329.00	7.31	400.01 ~	401.00	9.33
113.01 ~	114.00	1.29	185.01 ~	186.00	3.31	257.01 ~	258.00	5.33	329.01 ~	330.00	7.34	401.01 ~	402.00	9.36
114.01 ~	115.00	1.32	186.01 ~	187.00	3.34	258.01 ~	259.00	5.35	330.01 ~	331.00	7.37	402.01 ~	403.00	9.39
115.01 ~	116.00	1.35	187.01 ~	188.00	3.37	259.01 ~	260.00	5.38	331.01 ~	332.00	7.40	403.01 ~	404.00	9.41
116.01 ~	117.00	1.38	188.01 ~	189.00	3.39	260.01 ~	261.00	5.41	332.01 ~	333.00	7.43	404.01 ~	405.00	9.44
117.01 ~	118.00	1.41	189.01 ~	190.00	3.42	261.01 ~	262.00	5.44	333.01 ~	334.00	7.45	405.01 ~	406.00	9.47
118.01 ~	119.00	1.43	190.01 ~	191.00	3.45	262.01 ~	263.00	5.47	334.01 ~	335.00	7.48	406.01 ~	407.00	9.50
119.01 ~	120.00	1.46	191.01 ~	192.00	3.48	263.01 ~	264.00	5.49	335.01 ~	336.00	7.51	407.01 ~	408.00	9.53
120.01 ~	121.00	1.49	192.01 ~	193.00	3.51	264.01 ~	265.00	5.52	336.01 ~	337.00	7.54	408.01 ~	409.00	9.55
121.01 ~	122.00	1.52	193.01 ~	194.00	3.53	265.01 ~	266.00	5.55	337.01 ~	338.00	7.57	409.01 ~	410.00	9.58
122.01 ~	123.00	1.55	194.01 ~	195.00	3.56	266.01 ~	267.00	5.58	338.01 ~	339.00	7.59	410.01 ~	411.00	9.61
123.01 ~	124.00	1.57	195.01 ~	196.00	3.59	267.01 ~	268.00	5.61	339.01 ~	340.00	7.62	411.01 ~	412.00	9.64
124.01 ~	125.00	1.60	196.01 ~	197.00	3.62	268.01 ~	269.00	5.63	340.01 ~	341.00	7.65	412.01 ~	413.00	9.67
125.01 ~	126.00	1.63	197.01 ~	198.00	3.65	269.01 ~	270.00	5.66	341.01 ~	342.00	7.68	413.01 ~	414.00	9.69
126.01 ~	127.00	1.66	198.01 ~	199.00	3.67	270.01 ~	271.00	5.69	342.01 ~	343.00	7.71	414.01 ~	415.00	9.72
127.01 ~	128.00	1.69	199.01 ~	200.00	3.70	271.01 ~	272.00	5.72	343.01 ~	344.00	7.73	415.01 ~	416.00	9.75
128.01 ~	129.00	1.71	200.01 ~	201.00	3.73	272.01 ~	273.00	5.75	344.01 ~	345.00	7.76	416.01 ~	417.00	9.78
129.01 ~	130.00	1.74	201.01 ~	202.00	3.76	273.01 ~	274.00	5.77	345.01 ~	346.00	7.79	417.01 ~	418.00	9.81
130.01 ~	131.00	1.77	202.01 ~	203.00	3.79	274.01 ~	275.00	5.80	346.01 ~	347.00	7.82	418.01 ~	419.00	9.83
131.01 ~	132.00	1.80	203.01 ~	204.00	3.81	275.01 ~	276.00	5.83	347.01 ~	348.00	7.85	419.01 ~	420.00	9.86
132.01 ~	133.00	1.83	204.01 ~	205.00	3.84	276.01 ~	277.00	5.86	348.01 ~	349.00	7.87	420.01 ~	421.00	9.89
133.01 ~	134.00	1.85	205.01 ~	206.00	3.87	277.01 ~	278.00	5.89	349.01 ~	350.00	7.90	421.01 ~	422.00	9.92

Simulated Canada Pension Plan Contributions

Weekly (52 Pay periods a year)

Students are advised to use this table for classroom purposes only. Although accurate, it has fewer categories of pay amounts than the real table.

Pay			Pay			Pay			Pay			Pay		
From	To	CPP	From	To	CPP	From	To	CPP	From	To	CPP	From	To	CPP
422.01	423.00	9.95	495.01	496.00	11.99	636.01	638.00	15.95	782.01	784.00	20.04	1,120.01	1,125.00	29.55
423.01	424.00	9.97	496.01	497.00	12.02	638.01	640.00	16.01	784.01	786.00	20.10	1,125.01	1,130.00	29.69
424.01	425.00	10.00	497.01	498.00	12.05	640.01	642.00	16.06	786.01	788.00	20.15	1,130.01	1,135.00	29.83
425.01	426.00	10.03	498.01	499.00	12.07	642.01	644.00	16.12	788.01	790.00	20.21	1,135.01	1,140.00	29.97
426.01	427.00	10.06	499.01	500.00	12.10	644.01	646.00	16.18	790.01	792.00	20.26	1,140.01	1,145.00	30.11
427.01	428.00	10.09	500.01	502.00	12.14	646.01	648.00	16.23	792.01	794.00	20.32	1,145.01	1,150.00	30.25
428.01	429.00	10.11	502.01	504.00	12.20	648.01	650.00	16.29	794.01	796.00	20.38	1,150.01	1,155.00	30.39
429.01	430.00	10.14	504.01	506.00	12.26	650.01	652.00	16.34	796.01	798.00	20.43	1,155.01	1,160.00	30.53
430.01	431.00	10.17	506.01	508.00	12.31	652.01	654.00	16.40	798.01	800.00	20.49	1,160.01	1,165.00	30.67
431.01	432.00	10.20	508.01	510.00	12.37	654.01	656.00	16.46	800.01	805.00	20.59	1,165.01	1,170.00	30.81
432.01	433.00	10.23	510.01	512.00	12.42	656.01	658.00	16.51	805.01	810.00	20.73	1,170.01	1,175.00	30.95
433.01	434.00	10.25	512.01	514.00	12.48	658.01	660.00	16.57	810.01	815.00	20.87	1,175.01	1,180.00	31.09
434.01	435.00	10.28	514.01	516.00	12.54	660.01	662.00	16.62	815.01	820.00	21.01	1,180.01	1,185.00	31.23
435.01	436.00	10.31	516.01	518.00	12.59	662.01	664.00	16.68	820.01	825.00	21.15	1,185.01	1,190.00	31.37
436.01	437.00	10.34	518.01	520.00	12.65	664.01	666.00	16.74	825.01	830.00	21.29	1,190.01	1,195.00	31.51
437.01	438.00	10.37	520.01	522.00	12.70	666.01	668.00	16.79	830.01	835.00	21.43	1,195.01	1,200.00	31.65
438.01	439.00	10.39	522.01	524.00	12.76	668.01	670.00	16.85	835.01	840.00	21.57	1,200.01	1,205.00	31.79
439.01	440.00	10.42	524.01	526.00	12.82	670.01	672.00	16.90	840.01	845.00	21.71	1,205.01	1,210.00	31.93
440.01	441.00	10.45	526.01	528.00	12.87	672.01	674.00	16.96	845.01	850.00	21.85	1,210.01	1,215.00	32.07
441.01	442.00	10.48	528.01	530.00	12.93	674.01	676.00	17.02	850.01	855.00	21.99	1,215.01	1,220.00	32.21
442.01	443.00	10.51	530.01	532.00	12.98	676.01	678.00	17.07	855.01	860.00	22.13	1,220.01	1,225.00	32.35
443.01	444.00	10.53	532.01	534.00	13.04	678.01	680.00	17.13	860.01	865.00	22.27	1,225.01	1,230.00	32.49
444.01	445.00	10.56	534.01	536.00	13.10	680.01	682.00	17.18	865.01	870.00	22.41	1,230.01	1,235.00	32.63
445.01	446.00	10.59	536.01	538.00	13.15	682.01	684.00	17.24	870.01	875.00	22.55	1,235.01	1,240.00	32.77
446.01	447.00	10.62	538.01	540.00	13.21	684.01	686.00	17.30	875.01	880.00	22.69	1,240.01	1,245.00	32.91
447.01	448.00	10.65	540.01	542.00	13.26	686.01	688.00	17.35	880.01	885.00	22.83	1,245.01	1,250.00	33.05
448.01	449.00	10.67	542.01	544.00	13.32	688.01	690.00	17.41	885.01	890.00	22.97	1,250.01	1,255.00	33.19
449.01	450.00	10.70	544.01	546.00	13.38	690.01	692.00	17.46	890.01	895.00	23.11	1,255.01	1,260.00	33.33
450.01	451.00	10.73	546.01	548.00	13.43	692.01	694.00	17.52	895.01	900.00	23.25	1,260.01	1,265.00	33.47
451.01	452.00	10.76	548.01	550.00	13.49	694.01	696.00	17.58	900.01	905.00	23.39	1,265.01	1,270.00	33.61
452.01	453.00	10.79	550.01	552.00	13.54	696.01	698.00	17.63	905.01	910.00	23.53	1,270.01	1,275.00	33.75
453.01	454.00	10.81	552.01	554.00	13.60	698.01	700.00	17.69	910.01	915.00	23.67	1,275.01	1,280.00	33.89
454.01	455.00	10.84	554.01	556.00	13.66	700.01	702.00	17.74	915.01	920.00	23.81	1,280.01	1,285.00	34.03
455.01	456.00	10.87	556.01	558.00	13.71	702.01	704.00	17.80	920.01	925.00	23.95	1,285.01	1,290.00	34.17
456.01	457.00	10.90	558.01	560.00	13.77	704.01	706.00	17.86	925.01	930.00	24.09	1,290.01	1,295.00	34.31
457.01	458.00	10.93	560.01	562.00	13.82	706.01	708.00	17.91	930.01	935.00	24.23	1,295.01	1,300.00	34.45
458.01	459.00	10.95	562.01	564.00	13.88	708.01	710.00	17.97	935.01	940.00	24.37	1,300.01	1,305.00	34.59
459.01	460.00	10.98	564.01	566.00	13.94	710.01	712.00	18.02	940.01	945.00	24.51	1,305.01	1,310.00	34.73
460.01	461.00	11.01	566.01	568.00	13.99	712.01	714.00	18.08	945.01	950.00	24.65	1,310.01	1,315.00	34.87
461.01	462.00	11.04	568.01	570.00	14.05	714.01	716.00	18.14	950.01	955.00	24.79	1,315.01	1,320.00	35.01
462.01	463.00	11.07	570.01	572.00	14.10	716.01	718.00	18.19	955.01	960.00	24.93	1,320.01	1,325.00	35.15
463.01	464.00	11.09	572.01	574.00	14.16	718.01	720.00	18.25	960.01	965.00	25.07	1,325.01	1,330.00	35.29
464.01	465.00	11.12	574.01	576.00	14.22	720.01	722.00	18.30	965.01	970.00	25.21	1,330.01	1,335.00	35.43
465.01	466.00	11.15	576.01	578.00	14.27	722.01	724.00	18.36	970.01	975.00	25.35	1,335.01	1,340.00	35.57
466.01	467.00	11.18	578.01	580.00	14.33	724.01	726.00	18.42	975.01	980.00	25.49	1,340.01	1,345.00	35.71
467.01	468.00	11.21	580.01	582.00	14.38	726.01	728.00	18.47	980.01	985.00	25.63	1,345.01	1,350.00	35.85
468.01	469.00	11.23	582.01	584.00	14.44	728.01	730.00	18.53	985.01	990.00	25.77	1,350.01	1,355.00	35.99
469.01	470.00	11.26	584.01	586.00	14.50	730.01	732.00	18.58	990.01	995.00	25.91	1,355.01	1,360.00	36.13
470.01	471.00	11.29	586.01	588.00	14.55	732.01	734.00	18.64	995.01	1,000.00	26.05	1,360.01	1,365.00	36.27
471.01	472.00	11.32	588.01	590.00	14.61	734.01	736.00	18.70	1,000.01	1,005.00	26.19	1,365.01	1,370.00	36.41
472.01	473.00	11.35	590.01	592.00	14.66	736.01	738.00	18.75	1,005.01	1,010.00	26.33	1,370.01	1,375.00	36.55
473.01	474.00	11.37	592.01	594.00	14.72	738.01	740.00	18.81	1,010.01	1,015.00	26.47	1,375.01	1,380.00	36.69
474.01	475.00	11.40	594.01	596.00	14.78	740.01	742.00	18.86	1,015.01	1,020.00	26.61	1,380.01	1,385.00	36.83
475.01	476.00	11.43	596.01	598.00	14.83	742.01	744.00	18.92	1,020.01	1,025.00	26.75	1,385.01	1,390.00	36.97
476.01	477.00	11.46	598.01	600.00	14.89	744.01	746.00	18.98	1,025.01	1,030.00	26.89	1,390.01	1,395.00	37.11
477.01	478.00	11.49	600.01	602.00	14.94	746.01	748.00	19.03	1,030.01	1,035.00	27.03	1,395.01	1,400.00	37.25
478.01	479.00	11.51	602.01	604.00	15.00	748.01	750.00	19.09	1,035.01	1,040.00	27.17	1,400.01	1,405.00	37.39
479.01	480.00	11.54	604.01	606.00	15.06	750.01	752.00	19.14	1,040.01	1,045.00	27.31	1,405.01	1,410.00	37.53
480.01	481.00	11.57	606.01	608.00	15.11	752.01	754.00	19.20	1,045.01	1,050.00	27.45	1,410.01	1,415.00	37.67
481.01	482.00	11.60	608.01	610.00	15.17	754.01	756.00	19.26	1,050.01	1,055.00	27.59	1,415.01	1,420.00	37.81
482.01	483.00	11.63	610.01	612.00	15.22	756.01	758.00	19.31	1,055.01	1,060.00	27.73	1,420.01	1,425.00	37.95
483.01	484.00	11.65	612.01	614.00	15.28	758.01	760.00	19.37	1,060.01	1,065.00	27.87	1,425.01	1,430.00	38.09
484.01	485.00	11.68	614.01	616.00	15.34	760.01	762.00	19.42	1,065.01	1,070.00	28.01	1,430.01	1,435.00	38.23
485.01	486.00	11.71	616.01	618.00	15.39	762.01	764.00	19.48	1,070.01	1,075.00	28.15	1,435.01	1,440.00	38.37
486.01	487.00	11.74	618.01	620.00	15.45	764.01	766.00	19.54	1,075.01	1,080.00	28.29	1,440.01	1,445.00	38.51
487.01	488.00	11.77	620.01	622.00	15.50	766.01	768.00	19.59	1,080.01	1,085.00	28.43	1,445.01	1,450.00	38.65
488.01	489.00	11.79	622.01	624.00	15.56	768.01	770.00	19.65	1,085.01	1,090.00	28.57	1,450.01	1,455.00	38.79
489.01	490.00	11.82	624.01	626.00	15.62	770.01	772.00	19.70	1,090.01	1,095.00	28.71	1,455.01	1,460.00	38.93
490.01	491.00	11.85	626.01	628.00	15.67	772.01	774.00	19.76	1,095.01	1,100.00	28.85	1,460.01	1,465.00	39.07
491.01	492.00	11.88	628.01	630.00	15.73	774.01	776.00	19.82	1,100.01	1,105.00	28.99	1,465.01	1,470.00	39.21
492.01	493.00	11.91	630.01	632.00	15.78	776.01	778.00	19.87	1,105.01	1,110.00	29.13	1,470.01	1,475.00	39.35
493.01	494.00	11.93	632.01	634.00	15.84	778.01	780.00	19.93	1,110.01	1,115.00	29.27	1,475.01	1,480.00	39.49
494.01	495.00	11.96	634.01	636.00	15.90	780.01	782.00	19.98	1,115.01	1,120.00	29.41	1,480.01	1,485.00	39.63

Appendix 7-3—Unemployment Insurance Premium Calculations

Note to students: The calculation of UI premiums is rather straightforward. You simply multiply the amount of the gross pay for any period (weekly, monthly, etc.) by the current rate, which, as this book is being written, is 2.95 percent. So, for example, if a person makes $700 in a week, the UI premium is:

$$\$700 \times 0.0295 = \$20.65$$

If, instead, the person earned $2,400 in a month, the premium would be:

$$\$2,400 \times 0.0295 = \$70.80$$

Remember that there is a maximum for UI, which is currently $39,000 per year. This means that you cannot deduct more than a certain amount from any employee in any given pay period. These maximums are:

Weekly	$22.13	($39,000 ÷ 52 × 0.0295)
Biweekly	$44.25	($39,000 ÷ 26 × 0.0295)
Semimonthly	$47.94	($39,000 ÷ 24 × 0.0295)
Monthly	$95.88	($39,000 ÷ 12 ×0.0295)

Because of the simplicity of the UI premium calculation, the tables have not been reproduced here. They are available both in the tax tables supplied by Revenue Canada and on diskette from that source. (Your instructor may supply you with the necessary tables, which could be more up to date than these appendixes.)

Additional note to students: Please read the earlier comment on pages 257 and 260 regarding upcoming changes to Canada's UI system. These changes will alter the calculation of UI to a dramatic extent. Your instructor will be kept informed of these important changes by material to be published in the *Instructor's Resource Manual.*

THE EMPLOYER'S TAX RESPONSIBILITIES

8

PRINCIPLES AND PROCEDURES

Chapter Objectives

- How to calculate and record the employer's expenses associated with payroll. (p. 289)
- How employers remit and record their employees' deductions to Revenue Canada. (p. 291)
- Employers' annual responsibilities for filing the T4 Summary form. (p. 301)

In the previous chapter we examined how ABC Company Ltd. calculates its weekly payroll and maintains a record of each employee's earnings. In Canada, employers must remit monthly to the government the totals deducted from their employees in the previous month. Certain employers (those who have more than $15,000 to remit monthly) must send in their withholdings more often. In the balance of this chapter we will assume a smaller employer who remits monthly.

An important fact in our country is that employers share the total cost of CPP and UI. Their share of these payments is considered an expense of doing business and is accounted for as such. In this chapter we will examine how this expense is calculated and illustrate the forms that need to be completed (and sent to the government) as part of the payroll process. We will also examine the accounting procedures which must be followed.

LEARNING UNIT 8-1

Employer's Expenses Associated with Payroll

If you take over another employer's business, you must still obtain a new identification number (unless the business is a corporation).

Employers must apply for a remittance number in order to handle their responsibilities for payroll correctly. A special form called a Request for a Business Number must be submitted which asks the employer to answer several questions about the business' operations. *An example of page one of this form **RC1(E)** is shown in Figure 8-1. Once this form is processed, the employer is issued a permanent unique identification number. This number is used to record correctly the amounts of money sent (we often say **remitted**) to the government each month (or more often in the case of larger employers). It is also used for GST remittances and other purposes.

The actual amount sent to the government each month (or more often) depends on three deductions taken from employees' wages:

1. Income tax.
2. Canada (or Quebec) Pension Plan.
3. Unemployment insurance.

A simple formula can be used to ensure that the correct figure is remitted each period:

Notice that the income tax amount is sent by the employer, but is not an expense, as the employees are paying it.

Income tax deducted × 1.0	=	XXX.XX
CPP deducted × 2.0	=	XXX.XX
UI deducted × 2.4	=	XXX.XX
Total	=	$XXX.XX

*The same form is also used to obtain a Business Number for GST purposes and others as well.

Revenue Canada / Revenu Canada

RC1(E) Rev. 94

REQUEST FOR A BUSINESS NUMBER (BN)

Complete this form if you have a new business and you need to apply for a Business Number (BN). If you are a sole proprietor with more than one business, your BN will apply to all your businesses. **Note: All businesses have to complete Parts A and F. All corporations have to provide a copy of the certificate of incorporation/amalgamation.** Please check the box(es) for the types of BN accounts that you need.

☐ GST account (complete Part B)
☐ Payroll (source) deductions account (complete Part C)
☐ Import/export account (complete Part D)
☐ Corporate income tax account (complete Part E)

For more information, see the pamphlet titled *The Business Number and Your Revenue Canada Accounts.*

Part A

A1 Identification of business (For a corporation, enter the name and address of the head office.)

Name (For individuals or partnerships, also enter first and last names in A2 below.)

Operating, trade, or partnership name (if different from name): If you have more than one business or if your business operates under more than one name, enter the name(s) here. If you need more space, attach a list.

Business address

Postal/zip code

Mailing address (if different from business address) c/o

Address

Postal/zip code

Name and address of business's financial institution

Contact person (If you choose to name a contact for your account, please see page 8 of our pamphlet for information.)

First name | Last name

Title | Telephone number ( ) | Fax number ( )

Language ☐ English ☐ French

A2 Legal status (Check the box(es) that apply to you and enter the information requested. If you need more space, please attach a list.)

☐ **Individual (sole proprietor)** In the space below, enter the name (if not provided above), address, and social insurance number of the owner.
☐ **Partnership** In the space below, enter the name, address, and social insurance number of each partner.
☐ **Corporation** In the space below, enter the name, address, and social insurance number of each corporation director.
☐ **Other** (specify) ____________ In the space below, enter the name, address, and social insurance number of each officer.

☐ Individual ☐ Partner ☐ Director ☐ Officer	First name	Last name	Social insurance number	Telephone number ( )
	Home address			Postal/zip code
☐ Partner ☐ Director ☐ Officer	First name	Last name	Social insurance number	Telephone number ( )
	Home address			Postal/zip code
☐ Partner ☐ Director ☐ Officer	First name	Last name	Social insurance number	Telephone number ( )
	Home address			Postal/zip code

A3 Major business activity

Describe your major business activity: ____________

Specify up to three main products that you mine, manufacture, or sell, or services you provide or contract. Also, please estimate the percentage of revenue that each product or service represents.

____________ ______%
____________ ______%
____________ ______%

A4 Requestor information (Complete this area if you are registering for a BN on behalf of a client. If you want an agent to register on your behalf, please see page 9 of our pamphlet for more information.)

Your name (please print) | Your company's name (please print) | Year Month Day

Ce formulaire existe aussi en français.

FIGURE 8-1 Request for a Business Number

We will soon see how this formula works in more detail. Before we look at the details, however, a word of caution: the employer should ensure that the required remittance is made by the due date (usually the 15th day of the month following the payroll deductions). Failure to remit on time usually results in a penalty of 10 percent of the amount due over $500.00. This penalty is harsh and should be avoided. Not only is the amount high, but it is not deductible as a business expense for tax purposes.

How to calculate employer's remittance

Income Tax

Some provinces levy higher tax rates than others.

Remember that all employees pay an amount of income tax based upon their level of earnings. We saw in Chapter 7 that the ABC Company Ltd. deducted income tax from each employee's earnings. This amount must now be sent to the government. Notice that the amount sent is exactly the same as the amount deducted, since the employer does not contribute to the employee's tax. This part of the required remittance is therefore quite simple: each month employers must send in the exact amount of income tax deducted from employees in the previous month. In our simple formula that is why we multiply by 1.0—the result is exactly the amount deducted.

Canada (Quebec) Pension Plan

Every employee also contributes an amount every pay period to CPP (at least until the maximum is reached). In Canada, the employer must match the employee's contribution to CPP. This means that the amount of CPP remitted is exactly double the amount deducted. In our simple formula, that is why we multiply by 2.0—the result is double the amount deducted.

If an employee commences a job with a new employer part-way through a calendar year, the deduction of CPP continues without regard to the CPP already paid while employed by the former company. If the employee pays more than the yearly maximum, then a refund of CPP contributions can be claimed by the individual when he or she files an income tax return for the year. The employer's share is not refundable and cannot be recovered.

Unemployment Insurance

Recall that employees contribute an amount every pay period for unemployment insurance. Employers also contribute to UI by paying an amount which is 140 percent of the deductions made from employees. The effect is that the employer must remit 2.4 times the amount deducted from the employees. In our simple formula, that is why we multiply by 2.4—1.0 for the employees' deduction, plus 1.4 for the employer's share.

In Chapter 7, the employer made the following entry for the payroll in the first week in March:

	GENERAL JOURNAL			
Date	Account Titles and Description	PR	Dr.	Cr.
	Management Salaries Expense		800 00	
	Sales Wages Expense		720 00	
	Wages Expense		1 273 00	
	Income Taxes Payable			519 95
	CPP Payable			66 89
	UI Payable			80 93
	Medical Plan Payable			52 00
	Charitable Contributions Payable			12 00
	Salaries and Wages Payable			2 061 23
	To record payroll for the first week in March			

ABC Company Ltd. must now make the following additional entry to record its liability correctly:

	GENERAL JOURNAL			
Date	Account Titles and Description	PR	Dr.	Cr.
	Employee Benefits Expense		180 19	
	CPP Payable (1× 66.89)			66 89
	UI Payable (1.4 × 80.93)			113 30
	To record employer portion of CPP and			
	UI for week 1, March			

Note: This expense — employee benefits expense — is also known by many different names—payroll taxes expense, for example. Some employers separate it into UI and CPP portions, but this is not usually necessary.

After the above entry is posted, the following T accounts would be changed as shown:

Employee Benefits Expense		CPP Payable		UI Payable	
180.19*			66.89**		80.93**
			66.89*		113.30*
Expense on the Income Statement		Liability on the Balance Sheet		Liability on the Balance Sheet	

* New entries made above.

** Original entries from Chapter 7.

As a final note, students should be aware that employers sometimes share, or pay entirely for, the cost of other employee benefits, such as extended health care, long-term disability insurance, and dental plans. These costs would also be recorded by journal entry at the same time CPP and UI are recorded; however, these are some of the more intricate aspects of payroll and we will not deal with them in detail in this text.

LEARNING UNIT 8-1 REVIEW

AT THIS POINT you should be able to

- Explain one purpose of form RC1(E). (p. 289)
- Calculate the employer's share of CPP and UI. (p. 289)
- Explain when employee deductions must be remitted. (p. 291)
- Journalize the employer's employee benefits expense. (p. 292)
- Post the above journal entry to appropriate ledger accounts (p. 292)

SELF-REVIEW QUIZ 8-1

Given the following journal entry for the payroll totals for the second week in March, prepare the entry to record ABC Company Ltd.'s portion of CPP and UI:

GENERAL JOURNAL

Date		Account Titles and Description	PR	Dr.	Cr.
		Salaries and Wages Expense		2805 00	
		Income Taxes Payable			522 80
		CPP Payable			67 04
		UI Payable			82 75
		Medical Plan Payable			52 00
		Charitable Contributions Payable			12 00
		Salaries and Wages Payable			2068 41
		To record payroll for the week 2 in March			

Solution to Self-Review Quiz 8-1

GENERAL JOURNAL

Date		Account Titles and Description	PR	Dr.	Cr.
		Employee Benefits Expense		182 89	
		CPP Payable (1 × 60.98)			67 04
		UI Payable (1.4 × 82.50)			115 85
		To record employer portion of CPP and			
		UI for week 2, March			

LEARNING UNIT 8-2

Completing the Monthly Remittance Form

Income tax × 1
+ CPP × 2
+ UI × 2.4 = Amount
CPP × 1
+ UI × 1.4 = Employer's expense

Smaller employers are required to remit the total amounts due in respect to their payrolls each month by the 15th of the following month. Payment may be made at most financial institutions in Canada or a cheque can be mailed as long as it reaches the government by the 15th of the month.

We have already seen the ABC Company Ltd.'s entries for the first week in March. Let us assume the following payroll data for the second, third, and fourth weeks:

GENERAL JOURNAL

Date	Account Titles and Description	Post. Ref.	Dr.	Cr.
	Salaries and Wages Expense		2805 00	
	Income Taxes Payable			522 80
	CPP Payable			67 04
	UI Payable			82 75
	Medical Plan Payable			52 00
	Charitable Contributions Payable			12 00
	Salaries and Wages Payable			2068 41
	To record payroll for the week 2, March*			

GENERAL JOURNAL

Date	Account Titles and Description	Post. Ref.	Dr.	Cr.
	Salaries and Wages Expense		2781 00	
	Income Taxes Payable			508 20
	CPP Payable			66 34
	UI Payable			82 03
	Medical Plan Payable			52 00
	Charitable Contributions Payable			12 00
	Salaries and Wages Payable			2060 43
	To record payroll for week 3, March—new data			

GENERAL JOURNAL

Date	Account Titles and Description	Post. Ref.	Dr.	Cr.
	Salaries and Wages Expense		2856 00	
	Income Taxes Payable			532 40
	CPP Payable			69 40
	UI Payable			84 25
	Medical Plan Payable			52 00
	Charitable Contributions Payable			12 00
	Salaries and Wages Payable			2105 95
	To record payroll for week 4, March—new data			

* See Self-Review Quiz 8-1.

GENERAL JOURNAL

Date		Account Titles and Description	Post. Ref.	Dr.	Cr.
		Employee Benefits Expense		18289	
		CPP Payable			6704
		UI Payable			11585
		To record employer portion of CPP and			
		UI for the second week of March*			

GENERAL JOURNAL

Date		Account Titles and Description	Post. Ref.	Dr.	Cr.
		Employee Benefits Expense		18118	
		CPP Payable			6634
		UI Payable			11484
		To record employer portion of CPP and			
		UI for the third week of March—new data			

GENERAL JOURNAL

Date		Account Titles and Description	Post. Ref.	Dr.	Cr.
		Employee Benefits Expense		18735	
		CPP Payable			6940
		UI Payable			11795
		To record employer portion of CPP and			
		UI for the fourth week of March—new data			

* See Self-Review Quiz 8-1.

After posting, the relevant liability T-accounts would appear as shown:

	Income Taxes Payable	CPP Payable	UI Payable
Week 1: Employees	519.95*	66.89*	80.93*
Employer		66.89**	113.30**
Week 2: Employees	522.80*	67.04*	82.75*
Employer		67.04**	115.85**
Week 3: Employees	508.20*	66.34*	82.03*
Employer		66.34**	114.84**
Week 4: Employees	532.40*	69.40*	84.25*
Employer		69.40**	117.95**
Balance (March)	2083.35	539.34	791.90

* Original payroll entry.
** Benefits entry.

Since these liability accounts contain the total amounts due, ABC Company Ltd. can complete the required **Remittance Form (PD7A)** as shown in Figure 8-2.

ABC Company Ltd. will issue a cheque for $3,414.59 dated April 15, payable to the **Receiver General for Canada**. This cheque will be entered in the **cash disbursements journal** in April. When this cheque is entered, the following accounts will be affected:

GENERAL JOURNAL

Date		Account Titles and Description	Post. Ref.	Dr.	Cr.
		Income Taxes Payable		2083 35	
		CPP Payable		539 34	
		UI Payable		791 90	
		Cash			3414 59
		To record payment of withholdings			

After these amounts are posted, the liability accounts will appear as shown:

	Income Taxes Payable (Dr.)	Income Taxes Payable (Cr.)	CPP Payable (Dr.)	CPP Payable (Cr.)	UI Payable (Dr.)	UI Payable (Cr.)
		519.95		66.89		80.93
				66.89		113.30
		522.80		67.04		82.75
				67.04		115.85
		508.20		66.34		82.03
				66.34		114.84
		532.40		69.40		84.25
				69.40		117.95
Balance (March)		2083.35		539.34		791.90
April 15 cheque	2083.35		539.34		791.90	
Balance		0.00		0.00		0.00

Remember that by April 15 there will be two new weekly payrolls (in April) to contend with, so the ledger accounts will not appear exactly as shown above. The amount payable at the end of any month, however, should be accurate when all postings have been made.

Students will recall that employers sometimes pay part or all of the cost of other benefits. These costs are not sent to the Receiver General; instead, they are remitted (usually monthly) to the provincial health care plan and/or private insurance companies which provide the benefits. These details of payroll are handled in a manner similar to the remittance to the Receiver General and are not dealt with further in this text.

Revenue Canada Customs, Excise and Taxation | Revenu Canada Accise, Douanes et Impôt

STATEMENT OF ACCOUNT PD7A Rev.92

1 Account number XXX 12345 6 Employer name ABC COMPANY LTD 013547

Statement of account as of 23 Mar 19XX Transactions processed after this date will appear on the next statement		Amount paid	Amount owing	You can make your payment where you bank or to:
		19XX		Taxation Centre
	Present balance	9,547.20CR		WINNIPEG R3C 3P8

• IMPORTANT - SEE REVERSE •

EXPLANATION OF CHANGES

Date	Description			Amount
22 Mar	Payment	Feb 19XX	Date Recd 15 Mar 19XX	3,146.20CR

Indicate remittance information in this area for your records

CPP contributions	UI premiums	Tax deductions	Current payment	Gross monthly payroll	No. of empl. - last period
539.34	791.90	2,083.35	3,414.59	11,235.00	6

2 Account number XXX 12345 6 Employer name ABC COMPANY LTD PD7A Rev.92

Thank you for your payment.
Please use part 3 to make your next remittance or explain on the back of part 2 why you will not be remitting.

PIERRE GRAVELLE, QC
DEPUTY MINISTER, DEPARTMENT OF NATIONAL REVENUE, TAXATION

3 Revenue Canada Customs, Excise and Taxation | Revenu Canada Accise, Douanes et Impôt

REMITTANCE FORM FOR CURRENT SOURCE DEDUCTIONS PD7A Rev.92

6 | Account number XXX 12345 6 | For Taxation use only

ABC COMPANY LTD
123 PINE ROAD
ANY CITY, PR C1B 1A1

Amount of payment ▷ 3 4 1 4 5 9

If your payment is not for the period indicated, please enter the correct period here ▷ Year Month

Gross monthly payroll ▷ 1 1 2 3 5 0 0

Number of employees in last pay period ▷ 6

⑆0 2000⑈ 1171⑆ 96

FIGURE 8-2 Remittance Form
Section 1 shows the remittance form, which is filled out and sent to the Receiver General. Section 2 shows the statement returned to the employer from the bank which has deposited the remittance.

ACCOUNTING ENTRIES - EXPLANATIONS

AMOUNT PAID: payments of Canada Pension Plan contributions, Unemployment Insurance premiums and income tax (net of adjustments) for the year indicated.

AMOUNT OWING: unpaid assessments of Canada Pension Plan contributions, Unemployment Insurance premiums and income tax plus assessed amounts of penalties and interest outstanding.

GROSS MONTHLY PAYROLL: all remuneration before any deductions. It includes regular wages, commissions, overtime pay, paid leave, taxable benefits and allowances, piecework payments, and special payments. It is equivalent to the monthly total of all amounts that would appear in Box 14, "Employment income before deductions" on the T4 slip.

NUMBER OF EMPLOYEES IN LAST PAY PERIOD: the number of people who drew pay during the last pay period in the month. Include anyone for whom you will complete a T4 slip, such as part-time and temporary employees, employees absent with pay, etc. Do not include persons for whom you will not complete a T4 slip, such as occasional employees not part of your payroll, and persons who did not draw pay in the last pay period in the month such as those on unpaid leave.

REMITTING PROCEDURES

We must receive deductions made during the month by the 15th day of the following month. The date of receipt is the date the payment is delivered to the Receiver General (i.e., district taxation office, taxation centre, or a financial institution) and not the date you mailed the payment. Please include your share of Canada Pension Plan contributions and Unemployment Insurance premiums when you remit your employees' deductions.

We will apply penalties for late or deficient remittance (other than for wilful delay or deficiency) on amounts over $500. Interest will also be charged.

If there was a name / address change during the month, complete the change of address area of the envelope containing your statement and return with part 3 below.

ENQUIRIES

For clarification, additional information, or assistance in completing the form or using the Payroll Deductions Tables, you should contact your district taxation office. The phone numbers and addresses of all district taxation offices are listed in these tables and the government listings in your telephone book. Please quote your account number on all correspondence.

AMOUNT OF PAYMENT ▶ [ ]

Revenue Canada Customs, Excise and Taxation — Revenu Canada Accise, Douanes et Impôt

If you will not be making a remittance during the month, please enter an explanation below and return it in the preaddressed envelope provided.

☐ Business permanently discontinued — Date ceased ▶

Year	Month	Day

• NOTE: If you permanently discontinued or sold your business, you must file an information "T4 type" return within 30 days of the date of the change.

☐ No employees subject to deductions or business temporarily discontinued — Date you expect to have employees subject to deductions ▶

Year	Month	Day

☐ Other reason: ______________________________

____

____

____

Employer or designate (please print) ____________ Position ____________ Telephone number ____________ Date ____________

Form authorized by the Minister of National Revenue

PAYMENT

You can make your payment at a financial institution by completing parts 1 and 3 of this remittance form and presenting them with your payment. Part 1 will be returned to you as a receipt.

You can also pay at your district office or mail your cheque or money order to your taxation centre. Make your remittance payable to the Receiver General and enclose part 3 of this remittance form. **Do not mail cash.**

FINANCIAL INSTITUTION'S STAMP HERE

FIGURE 8-2 (cont.)

LEARNING UNIT 8-2 REVIEW

AT THIS POINT you should be able to

- Explain the balances in the following ledger accounts before the monthly remittance to the Receiver General is made. (p. 295)
  - **a.** Income tax payable
  - **b.** CPP payable
  - **c.** UI payable
- Complete form PD7A for a typical company. (p. 297)
- Issue and record the cheque which would accompany form PD7A. (p. 296)
- Explain how the balances in the ledger accounts listed in (a) to (c) above would change after posting the remittance cheque. (p. 296)

SELF-REVIEW QUIZ 8-2

Given the two semimonthly payrolls summarized by journal entry below, answer the following:

1. What journal entries would be made to record the employer's share of CPP and UI for the month?
2. Post the original entries and the entries you suggested in question 1 to the T accounts shown. (Not all T accounts are shown; please ignore the ones not shown.)
3. What amount would the employer remit to the Receiver General by the 15th of the following month?

Here are the semimonthly journal entries:

GENERAL JOURNAL

Date		Account Titles and Description	Post. Ref.	Dr.	Cr.
		Sales Salaries		2850 00	
		Office Salaries		3240 00	
		Income Taxes Payable			1560 00
		CPP Payable			112 40
		UI Payable			177 30
		Salaries and Wages Payable			4240 30
		To record payroll data for the first half			
		of the month			

GENERAL JOURNAL					
Date		Account Titles and Description	Post. Ref.	Dr.	Cr.
		Sales Salaries		2850 00	
		Office Salaries		3175 00	
		Income Taxes Payable			1445 00
		CPP Payable			111 80
		UI Payable			176 60
		Salaries and Wages Payable			4291 60
		To record payroll data for the second half of the month			

Here are the T accounts to use in question 2 of the Self-Review Quiz (opening balances are ignored):

Income Tax Payable	CPP Payable	UI Payable

Solutions to Self-Review Quiz 8-2

1.

GENERAL JOURNAL					
Date		Account Titles and Description	Post. Ref.	Dr.	Cr.
		Employee Benefits Expense		360 62	
		CPP Payable			112 40
		UI Payable (176.60 × 1.4)			248 22
		To record benefits expense for the first half of the month			

GENERAL JOURNAL					
Date		Account Titles and Description	Post. Ref.	Dr.	Cr.
		Employee Benefits Expense		359 04	
		CPP Payable			111 80
		UI Payable (176.60 × 1.4)			247 24
		To record benefits expense for the second half of the month			

2. Your T accounts should appear as follows:

Income Tax Payable		CPP Payable		UI Payable	
	1,560.00		112.40		177.30
	1,445.00		112.40		248.22
	3,005.00 Bal.		111.80		176.60
			111.80		247.24
			448.40 Bal.		849.36 Bal.

3. The employer would remit $4,302.76, calculated as follows:

Income Tax Payable (bal.)	$3,005.00
CPP Payable (bal.)	448.40
UI Payable (bal.)	849.36
	$4,302.76

LEARNING UNIT 8-3

Employer's Annual T4-T4A Summary

Careful, accurate work helps ensure that the filing of the T4-T4A Summary is not an unpleasant task.

Every year, employers are required to file an annual return called a **T4-T4A Summary** (see Figure 8-3). This return summarizes the information provided to employees on their **T4** forms (see Chapter 7, Figure 7-5).

It is important to note that this form is completed for a calendar year. Even if the fiscal year ends on September 30, the T4-T4A Summary must be filed for the calendar year (January 1 to December 31). The deadline for submitting this form to both the government and to employees is February 28 each year for the calendar year ended the previous December 31.

The completion of this form can be a difficult task, because any errors made during the year in completing the payroll register, and any errors made in preparing the employees' individual T4 slips, will be discovered in this final step. The totals shown for CPP, UI, and income tax must also agree with the totals remitted according to the monthly PD7A form (see Figure 8-2).

It is not unusual to find intelligent, hard-working, successful employers who find this aspect of payroll processing to be very difficult. Some computer firms selling payroll software are successful because they promise employers relief from the manual balancing procedures each February 28. In actual fact, the task is not too difficult—provided the payroll register is completed with neatness and accuracy and all subsequent steps are done with care.

Revenue Canada / Revenu Canada

1995

Complete this return using the instructions in the *Employers' Guide to Payroll Deductions - Basic Information.*

Vous devez remplir cette déclaration selon les instructions du *Guide de l'employeur – Retenues sur la paie : Renseignements de base.*

T4 SUMMARY / SOMMAIRE

SUMMARY OF REMUNERATION PAID (For the year ending December 31, 1995)

SOMMAIRE DE LA RÉMUNÉRATION PAYÉE (Pour l'année se terminant le 31 décembre 1995)

0505 44111

Copy / Copie **1**

If you file your T4 return on tape or diskette, you do not need to complete this form. For more information see the guide called *Computer Specifications for Data Filed on Magnetic Media.*

Si vous produisez votre déclaration T4 sur disquette ou sur bande, vous n'avez pas à remplir ce formulaire. Pour plus de renseignements, consultez le guide intitulé *Spécifications informatiques pour données produites sur support magnétique.*

Important Employer's name and account number has to be the same as on your PD7A remittance form. **You have to file the T4 Summary on or before February 29, 1996.**

Le nom et le numéro de compte de l'employeur doivent être les mêmes que ceux qui figurent sur le formulaire de versement PD7A. **Vous devez produire la déclaration T4 *Sommaire* au plus tard le 29 février 1996.**

Account number / Numéro de compte: XXX 12345 6

Tax centre / Centre fiscal — TSO code / Code du BSF

Name and address of employer / Nom et adresse de l'employeur:

ABC Company Ltd
123 Pine Road
Any City, Province
C1B 1A1

T4 Supplementary slips totals — For returns with over 300 T4 slips, please see instructions in the *Employers' Guide to Payroll Deductions - Basic Information* about the breakdown of large returns.

Totaux des feuillets T4 *Supplémentaire* — Pour les déclarations renfermant plus de 300 feuillets T4, consultez le *Guide de l'employeur – Retenues sur la paie : Renseignements de base* pour la répartition des déclarations volumineuses.

Item		Box	Amount
Total number of T4 slips filed	Nombre total de feuillets T4 produits	88	10
Employment income before deductions	Revenus d'emploi avant retenues	14	155,670.50
Registered pension plan contributions	Cotisations à un régime de pension agréé	20	
Pension adjustment	Facteur d'équivalence	52	
UI insurable earnings	Gains assurables d'AC	24	
Employee's CPP contributions	Cotisations de l'employé au RPC	16	3,492.50
Employer's CPP contributions	Cotisations de l'employeur au RPC	27	3,492.50
Employee's UI premiums	Cotisations de l'employé à l'AC	18	4,514.20
Employer's UI premiums	Cotisations de l'employeur à l'AC	19	6,319.88
Income tax deducted	Impôt sur le revenu retenu	22	26,007.70

Of the total number at left, indicate how many T4 slips are for employees whose addresses are in the U.S.A. / Du total inscrit à gauche, indiquez le nombre de feuillets T4 émis pour des employés dont l'adresse est aux É.-U.

Departmental use only / Réservé au Ministère

	Box	Amount
Total deductions reported (16 + 27 + 18 + 19 + 22) / Total des retenues déclarées (16 + 27 + 18 + 19 + 22)	80	43,826.78
Minus: remittances – Moins : versements	82	43,826.78
Difference – Différence		

We do not charge or refund a difference of less than $2. / Nous n'exigeons et ne remboursons pas une différence inférieure à 2 $.

Overpayment / Paiement en trop 84 — * Balance due / Solde à payer 86

* If you have not paid the total deductions reported, include the balance with this completed return. You may have to pay a penalty for late payment if you have any balance owing. / Si vous n'avez pas payé le montant total des retenues déclarées, veuillez joindre le solde à payer, à cette déclaration. Tout solde à payer est assujetti à une pénalité pour paiement tardif.

Amount enclosed / Somme jointe

Revenue Canada - issued registration number(s) for RPP or DPSP – Numéro(s) d'agrément émis par Revenu Canada pour le ou les RPA ou RPDB: 71, 72, 73

Canadian-controlled private corporations or unincorporated employers: Enter the SIN of the proprietor(s) or principal owner(s). / Sociétés privées sous contrôle canadien ou employeurs non constitués : Inscrivez le NAS du ou des propriétaires. 74, 75

Person to contact about this return – Personne avec qui communiquer au sujet de cette déclaration: 76 ELAINE (First name – Prénom) DUMONT (Surname – Nom de famille)

Telephone number – Numéro de téléphone: 78 900 (Area code – Indicatif régional) 123 4567

Certification - Attestation

I, / Je, ELAINE DUMONT (Name and surname (in capital letters) - Nom et prénom (en lettres majuscules)), certify that the information given in this T4 return (T4 Summary and related T4 Supplementary slips) is, to the best of my knowledge, correct and complete. / atteste que les renseignements fournis dans cette déclaration T4 (la déclaration T4 *Sommaire* et les feuillets T4 *Supplémentaire* connexes) sont, à ma connaissance, exacts et complets.

February 22, 19XY (Date) — Elaine Dumont (Signature of authorized person - Signature de la personne autorisée) — Manager (Position or office - Titre ou poste)

For departmental use only: please do not write in this area - Réservé au Ministère : N'écrivez rien ici

Transfer / Transfert: 90 — 1 Last to current / Précédente à courante; 2 No action / Aucune mesure; 3 Other / Autre

Pro Forma: 91 — 1 No / Non; 2 Yes / Oui

93 Date; 94 A; B

Memo – Note

Late-filing penalty / Pénalité pour production tardive

Prepared by - Établi par — Date

	Code 2	Correspond.	Inc.	TPC – CCT	Dressed – MAP	Rev. – Rév.	No Accounts – Aucun n°
Initials – Initiales							
Date							

* Keep the working copy of this form for your records.
* Send copies 1 and 2 of this form and copy 1 of the related T4 Supplementary slips to the appropriate tax centre address shown on the back of this form.

Privacy Act personal information bank number RCT/P-PU-005

* Conservez le brouillon de ce formulaire dans vos dossiers.
* Envoyez les copies 1 et 2 de ce formulaire ainsi que la copie 1 des feuillets T4 *Supplémentaire* connexes au centre fiscal approprié, dont l'adresse figure au verso de ce formulaire.

Loi sur la protection des renseignements personnels, fichier numéro RCT/P-PU-005

FIGURE 8-3
Summary of Remuneration Paid

In Figure 8-3, the figures were obtained from the individual employee earnings records as summarized below:

*Refer to Chapter 7, Figure 7-5 and Figure 7-7.

AT THIS POINT you should be able to

- Describe the process of filing an annual T4-T4A Summary. (p. 293)

Employee Name	Total Wages	Deductions		
		Income Tax	CPP	UI
Janet Johnson*	$ 20,910.00	4,086.60	487.48	616.85
Peter Black	20,875.00	4,000.50	486.50	615.81
John Chernochan	19,462.00	2,050.10	446.94	574.13
Tony Chui	22,147.00	4,156.20	552.12	653.34
Beth Madora	18,256.50	2,647.60	413.16	538.57
Elaine Dumont	38,400.00	7,425.00	893.20	1,132.80
Other Casual Employees (total)	15,620.00	1,560.45	243.10	382.70
Totals	$155,670.50	25,926.45	3,492.50	4,514.20

- Illustrate the completion of the T4-T4A Summary. (p. 294)

LEARNING UNIT 8-3 REVIEW

SELF-REVIEW QUIZ 8-3

Respond true or false to the following:

1. A T4-T4A Summary must be filed each year by February 28.
2. A T4-T4A Summary is sent to each employee by February 28 each year.
3. The completion of the T4-T4A forms can be a difficult task.
4. The total of the individual amounts on all T4-T4A Supplementary forms must equal the totals on the T4-T4A Summary.

Solutions to Self-Review Quiz 8-3

1. True **2.** False **3.** True **4.** True

Chapter Review

SUMMARY OF KEY POINTS

Learning Unit 8-1

1. The employer's remittance to the Receiver General includes (a) income tax (employees' share only), (b) CPP (both employees' and employer's share), and (c) UI (again both employees' and employer's share).
2. The payroll tax expense is made up of both CPP (same amount as deducted from employees) and UI (1.4 times the amount deducted from employees).
3. Journal entries are made to record the payroll and then to record the employer's share of CPP and UI.
4. Employers sometimes share, or pay entirely for, the cost of other employee benefits (health care, insurance, etc.). These costs would also be recorded by journal entry at the same time as CPP and UI.

Learning Unit 8-2

1. Employers must complete form PD7A and submit it with their remittance to the Receiver General for Canada by the 15th day of the month following the month in which the salary payment was made. (Larger employers remit more often.)
2. A significant penalty is paid by any employer remitting after the due date.
3. Employers sometimes pay part or all of the cost of health care, insurance plans, etc., on behalf of their employees. These costs are not sent to the Receiver General; instead, they are remitted (usually monthly) to the provincial health care plan and/or private companies which provide the benefits.

Learning Unit 8-3

1. Once every year, by February 28, employers must file an annual T4-T4A Summary (for the previous calendar year) with the federal government.
2. On or before the same date, each employee must be given a copy of his or her individual earnings summary (T4-T4A Supplementary) form. This form summarizes all relevant payroll information for each employee for the previous calendar year.
3. Unless care is taken in preparing the payroll records throughout the year, the completion of the T4-T4A forms can be a challenging task.

KEY TERMS

Employer identification number A number given by the federal government which uniquely identifies each employer who is required to forward deductions made from employees. Used to keep track of the exact remittance each employer sends on behalf of its employees.

Monthly remittance form (PD7A) A form used to identify the employer and the amounts of money sent to the Receiver General for Canada periodically on behalf of employees.

Remittance formula A formula which can be used to double-check the amount of money being sent in each month on behalf of the employees. Computed as:

Income tax deducted × 1.0	=	XXX.XX
CPP deducted × 2.0	=	XX.XX
UI deducted × 2.4	=	XX.XX
Total		XXX.XX

T4-T4A Summary A form sent to the federal government once each year showing the totals of income tax, CPP, and UI deducted from all employees during the last calendar year. The totals on this form must agree exactly with the totals submitted on the various T4-T4A Supplementary forms described below.

T4-T4A Supplementary A form given to each employee by February 28 every year which gives the total of wages earned, income tax, CPP, and UI deducted, and other similar information for the past calendar year. Total of all T4-T4A Supplementary slips must agree with the totals reported on the T4-T4A Summary. (See above.)

Blueprint of the Tax Calendar

A Sampling of Dates Involving Employer's Tax Responsibilities

January 15 (and the 15th of each month)	PD7A form	Remit the monthly amount to the Receiver General for Canada. Remember the formula: 1 × tax deducted + 2 × CPP deducted + 2.4 × UI deducted = Total amount to be remitted
February 28	T-4 and T-4A forms	Complete these forms and send or deliver them to all persons employed during the year.
February 28	T-4 Summary	Send this form, together with copies of the individual T-4 or T-4A forms, to the government. The totals on this form must match the sum of all individual T-4 and T-4A slips, and, as well, must agree with the employer's accounting records.

Certain other forms may be required throughout the year, although they are not subject to an exact timetable:

	RC1 form	Every employer needs to obtain a permanent number which permits the government to keep an accurate record of funds remitted. Since this number is permanent, employers will only need to submit this form once.

(Cont.)

Record of Employment	Whenever an employee ceases his or her employment, this form must be completed and a copy given to the former employee within one week. A copy goes to the the government to assiss in the fair and efficient administration of the Unemployment Insurance Act.

QUESTIONS, EXERCISES, AND PROBLEMS

Discussion Questions

1. What makes up employee benefits expense?
2. All employers must remit their payroll deductions once a month (by the 15th of the following month). Please comment.
3. The only payroll-related costs borne by employers are CPP and UI. Please comment.
4. An RC1 form must be submitted annually by all employers. True or false?
5. Why could failure to remit employees' deductions on time be costly?
6. Each employer doubles the amount of income tax deducted from employees each month when remitting to the Receiver General for Canada. True or false?
7. Which of the following accurately summarizes the correct formula for determining the monthly remittance to the Receiver General? (IT = income tax.)
   a. (2 × IT) + (2.4 × CPP) + (2 × UI)
   b. (1 × IT) + (2 × CPP) + (2.4 × UI)
   c. (1 × IT) + (2.4 × CPP) + (2 × UI)
   d. (2 × IT) + (2 × CPP) + (2.4 × UI)
8. A remittance form (PD7A) must be sent to the federal government once every pay period. True or false?
9. Why do some computer firms do good business selling payroll software to employers?
10. Employers must complete their T4-T4A Summaries no later than two months after the end of their fiscal year. True or false?

Mini Exercises

1. The Fisher Company had two employees for the week ended July 23. On the basis of the following information, prepare a general journal entry to record the employee benefits expense for the employee benefits expense for that payroll.

		Deductions			
Employee	*Salary*	*IT*	*CPP*	*UI*	*Net Pay*
Brett Pym	900	250	25	27	598
Carmen Flynn	1000	300	28	30	642

2. Assume that the Fisher Company (see above) had 5 payrolls in the month of July, all identical to the one shown above. What amount would the company send to the Receiver General in August to meet its legal obligation for payroll remittance?

3. For the payroll week ending on September 30 (the 39th payroll period of the year), the 3 employees shown below had gross earnings as indicated. Each was employed at the same salary since January 1:

Beth Hudson	$1,000
John Wong	925
Ida Hastings	850

Without using tables, compute the amount of CPP and UI to be deducted from each employee for payroll number 39.

4. Fred Blake has agreed to work for the Cummings Foundation at a total annual salary of $42,000. He is uncertain whether he should be paid biweekly or semimonthly, and has asked for your assistance. Calculate the typical deductions for CPP and UI that must be taken from Fred's salary under either alternative. Will the choice affect the total UI or CPP Fred pays during the year?

Exercises

Recording employee benefits expense.

1. From the following information, prepare a general journal entry to record the employee benefits expense for Jones Company for the weekly payroll of July 9:

		Deductions			
Employee	*Total Salary*	*Tax*	*CPP*	*UI*	*Net Pay*
Troy Ness	900	210	23	22	645
Jay Young	600	150	15	18	417
Tim Wyatt	800	190	20	22	568

Recording employee benefits expense.

2. From the following information, prepare a general journal entry to record the employee benefits expense for Windsor Company for the monthly payroll for July:

		Deductions			
Employee	*Total Salary*	*Tax*	*CPP*	*UI*	*Net Pay*
Bert Lamont	2,500	509	62	74	1,855
Joan Quan	2,300	450	56	68	1,726
Mark Totem	1,700	290	39	50	1,321
Jean Dzurko	1,800	318	42	53	1,387

Remittance calculation.

3. What amount will the Windsor Company send to the Receiver General in the month of August (for July payroll)? See Exercise 2 above.

Recording payroll tax expense, stage 1.

4. For the first two weeks of March, the Star Company had payroll details as shown below:

				Deductions			
Employee	*Hours*	*Rate*	*Total Pay*	*Tax*	*CPP*	*UI*	*Net Pay*
Pam Tifford	80	16	1,280	282	32	38	928
Isaac Gold	70	17	1,190	250	30	35	875
Bob Boudreau	80	14	1,120	221	28	33	838

Prepare the general journal entry to record the employee benefits expense for the two-week period.

Recording employee benefits expense, stage 2.

5. For the last two weeks in March, the Star Company had payroll details as shown below:

Employee	*Hours*	*Rate*	*Total Pay*	*Deductions*			*Net Pay*
				Tax	*CPP*	*UI*	
Pam Tifford	75	16	1,200	256	30	35	879
Isaac Gold	85	17	1,445	353	37	43	1,012
Jim Francis	80	14	1,120	220	28	33	839

Prepare the general journal entry to record the employee benefits expense for the last two-week period.

Calculating a remittance—multiple periods.

6. There are only four payroll weeks in March. Calculate the total remittance that Star Company would make to the Receiver General in the month of April based on its March payroll activities. Refer to Exercises 4 and 5 above.

Group A Problems

8A-1. The payroll register for Rice Company is summarized below for the month of April:

Employee	*Total Salary*	*Deductions*					*Net Pay*	*Chq. No.*
		Tax	*CPP*	*UI*	*Med-ical*	*Union Dues*		
Brae Roberts	2,700	591	67	80	22	21	1,919	474
Robin Capp	2,600	550	65	77	44	21	1,843	475
Ashley Tropp	2,200	424	53	65	44	21	1,593	476
Ishma Blumen	2,300	450	56	68	44	21	1,661	477

Recording employee benefits expense and subsequent entries.

The union dues are remitted to the treasurer of the union by the 10th day of the next month. Rice Company matches its employees' contributions to the medical plan. Assume that the information in the above table has been recorded as cheques 474–477 were issued.

Required

a. Record the company's benefits expense assuming no such entry was made when cheques 474–477 were recorded.

b. In May, the Rice Company issued the following three cheques:

1. May 10, 19XX, to the Employees' Union, cheque no. 495.
2. May 15, 19XX, to the Receiver General, cheque no. 502.
3. May 20, 19XX, to the Provincial Health Care Insurance Company, cheque no. 531.

How much was each cheque for?

c. What journal entries would be made to record the three cheques in **b** above?

Recording employee benefits expense and subsequent calculations.

8A-2. Pebbles Inc. recorded the following details in its payroll journal for March:

Employee	*Total Salary*	*Deductions*						*Net Pay*	*Chq. No.*
		Tax	*CPP*	*UI*	*LTD*	*Med-ical*	*Union Dues*		
Fred Jones	2,700	591	67	80	29	20	28	1,885	716
Marsha Thom	2,300	449	56	68	46	40	28	1,613	717
Brendan May	2,400	476	59	71	46	20	28	1,700	718
Joyce Fisher	2,200	624	53	65	29	-	28	1,401	719
Pat Smith	1,900	346	45	56	29	20	28	1,376	720

Union dues are remitted by the end of the following month to the employees' union treasurer. Employees pay 100 percent of the long term disability (LTD). Pebbles Inc. matches its employees' contributions to the medical plan and remits by the 20th of the following month.

Required

a. Assume that there was no employee benefits expense recognized as the payroll register was recorded. Give the general journal entry necessary to record this employee benefits expense for March.

b. List the cheques, together with their amounts and dates, which Pebbles Inc. would issue in April in respect of the above payroll data.

8A-3. The Candy Co. pays its workers twice each month. Data for the two pay periods in June is shown below:

First half of June:

				Deductions						
Employee	*Hours*	*Rate*	*Total Pay*	*Tax*	*CPP*	*UI*	*Union*	*Chari-table*	*Net Pay*	*Chq. No.*
Amy Wynott	90	15	1,350	296	34	40	14	10	956	312
Jim Elliot	95	14	1,330	282	33	39	14	10	952	313
Bren Stairs	85	13	1,105	213	27	33	14	10	808	314
Gwen Holtz	92	14	1,288	267	32	38	14	10	927	315

Second half of June:

				Deductions						
Employee	*Hours*	*Rate*	*Total Pay*	*Tax*	*CPP*	*UI*	*Union*	*Chari-table*	*Net Pay*	*Chq. No.*
Amy Wynott	94	15	1,410	318	35	42	14	10	991	387
Jim Elliot	95	14	1,330	282	33	39	14	10	952	388
Bren Stairs	90	13	1,170	232	29	35	14	10	850	389
Gwen Holtz	96	15	1,440	333	36	42	14	10	1,005	390

Recording employee benefits expense—a more comprehensive example.

Union dues must be remitted to the union treasurer by the 15th of the following month. Candy Co. matches the employees' charitable contributions on a 2-to-1 basis. Donations are mailed to World Hunger Relief semiannually. Deductions from all employees to May 31 this year have totalled $425. A cheque will be sent for the first half of the year on July 5, 19XX.

Required

a. Assuming that the payroll register has been posted, but no entries have been made for employee benefits expense for June, make the two journal entries that are necessary to record this expense for Candy Co. for June.

b. Give details of the various cheques which will be issued in July based on Candy Co.'s payroll activities for the year so far.

8A-4. The Ripcord Parachute Club employs three people and pays them on a weekly basis. Payroll data for the four weeks in February is given below:

Week 1—February

Employee	*Sal.*	*Deductions* *Tax*	*CPP*	*UI*	*LTD*	*Pen.*	*Med.*	*Net Pay*	*Chq. No.*
Phil Rawlins	700	167	18	21	15	38	16	425	205
Janet Fox	700	162	18	21	15	35	10	439	206
Wey Card	800	206	20	22	15	41	16	480	207

Week 2—February

Employee	*Sal.*	*Deductions* *Tax*	*CPP*	*UI*	*LTD*	*Pen.*	*Med.*	*Net Pay*	*Chq. No.*
Phil Rawlins	800	206	20	22	15	41	16	480	216
Janet Fox	700	162	18	21	15	35	10	439	217
Wey Card	800	206	20	22	15	41	16	480	218

Week 3—February

Employee	*Sal.*	*Deductions* *Tax*	*CPP*	*UI*	*LTD*	*Pen.*	*Med.*	*Net Pay*	*Chq. No.*
Phil Rawlins	800	206	20	22	15	41	16	480	221
Janet Fox	700	162	18	21	15	35	10	439	222
Wey Card	800	206	20	22	15	44	16	477	223

Week 4—February

Employee	*Sal.*	*Deductions* *Tax*	*CPP*	*UI*	*LTD*	*Pen.*	*Med.*	*Net Pay*	*Chq. No.*
Phil Rawlins	800	206	20	22	15	41	16	480	244
Janet Fox	700	162	18	21	15	35	10	439	245
Wey Card	850	226	22	22	15	47	16	502	246

Assumptions

Employees pay 100 percent of the cost of long term disability (LTD). Employees contribute just over 5 percent of their salary to the pension plan; the employer contributes 6 percent of the employees' salary to the plan. Medical cost is split 50/50 by employees and employer. All payroll-related deductions are paid on the 15th of March.

Required

Recording employee benefits expense—multiple periods.

a. In recording the payroll journal in February the bookkeeper for the Ripcord Parachute Club did not record any expense for employee benefits. Give the four journal entries which should be made for the month to record this expense.

Posting routine entries for a monthly period.

b. Post the entries from the payroll journal and the entries in **a** above to the T accounts shown below. (You may ignore the accounts which are not shown.)

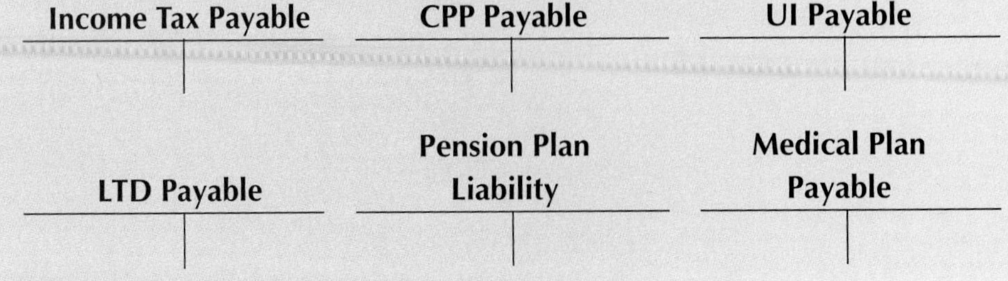

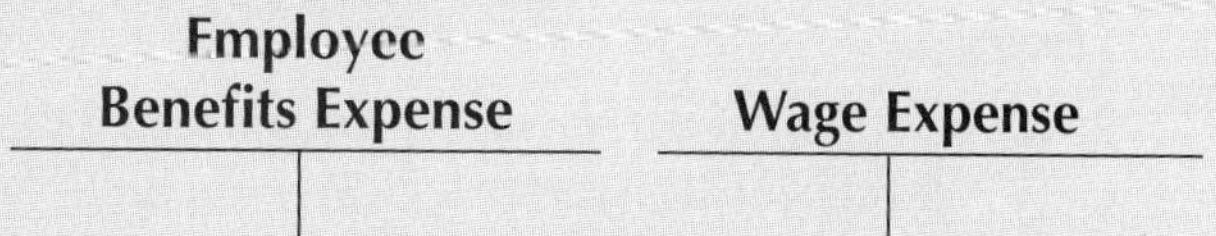

Calculating remittances.

c. List the cheques and the amounts of the cheques which will be issued on March 15 for the February payroll.

Group B Problems

8B-1. The payroll register for Rice Company is summarized below for the month of April:

		Deductions						
Employee	*Total Salary*	*Tax*	*CPP*	*UI*	*Med-ical*	*Union Dues*	*Net Pay*	*Chq. No.*
Brae Roberts	2,800	720	70	83	24	23	1,880	662
Robin Capp	2,700	600	67	80	48	23	1,882	663
Ashley Tropp	2,300	525	56	68	48	23	1,580	664
Ishma Blumen	2,400	510	59	71	48	23	1,689	665

Recording employee benefits expense and subsequent entries.

The union dues are remitted to the treasurer of the union by the 10th day of the next month. Rice Company matches its employees' contributions to the medical plan. Assume that the information in the above table has been recorded as cheques 662-665 were issued.

Required

a. Record the company's benefits expense assuming no such entry was made when cheques 662-665 were recorded.

b. In May, Rice Company issued the following three cheques:

1. May 10, 19XX, to the Employees' Union, cheque no. 681.
2. May 15, 19XX, to the Receiver General, cheque no. 698.
3. May 20, 19XX, to the Provincial Health Care Insurance Company, cheque no. 713.

How much was each cheque for?

c. What entries would be made to record the three cheques in **b** above?

8B-2. Pebbles Inc. recorded the following details in its payroll journal for March:

		Deductions							
Employee	*Total Salary*	*Tax*	*CPP*	*UI*	*LTD*	*Med-ical*	*Union Dues*	*Net Pay*	*Chq. No.*
Fred Jones	2,800	735	70	83	25	22	30	1,835	833
Marsha Thom	2,400	540	59	71	48	44	30	1,608	834
Brendan May	2,500	620	62	74	25	22	30	1,667	835
Joyce Fisher	2,300	510	56	68	48	44	30	1,544	836
Pat Smith	2,000	410	48	59	25	22	30	1,406	837

Recording employee benefits expense and subsequent calculations.

Union dues are remitted by the end of the following month to the employees' union treasurer. Employees pay 100 percent of the long term disability (LTD). Pebbles Inc. matches its employees' contributions to the medical plan and remits by the 20th of the following month.

Required

a. Assume that there was no employees' benefit expense recognized as the payroll register was recorded. Give the general journal entry necessary to record this employee benefits expense for March.

b. List the cheques, together with their amounts and dates, which Pebbles Inc. would issue in April in respect of the above payroll data.

8B-3. The Candy Co. pays its workers twice each month. Data for the two pay periods in June is shown below:

First half of June:

				Deductions						
Employee	*Hours*	*Rate*	*Total Pay*	*Tax*	*CPP*	*UI*	*Union*	*Charitable*	*Net Pay*	*Chq. No.*
Amy Wynott	85	16	1,360	325	34	40	18	6	937	318
Jim Elliot	100	14	1,400	350	35	41	18	6	950	319
Bren Stairs	85	13	1,105	215	27	33	18	6	806	320
Gwen Holtz	92	14	1,288	320	32	38	18	6	874	321

Second half of June:

				Deductions						
Employee	*Hours*	*Rate*	*Total Pay*	*Tax*	*CPP*	*UI*	*Union*	*Charitable*	*Net Pay*	*Chq. No.*
Amy Wynott	99	16	1,584	385	40	47	18	6	1,088	343
Jim Elliot	95	14	1,330	320	33	39	18	6	914	344
Bren Stairs	96	13	1,248	265	31	37	18	6	891	345
Gwen Holtz	88	15	1,320	330	33	39	18	6	894	346

Recording employee benefits expense—a more comprehensive example.

Union dues must be remitted to the union treasurer by the 15th of the following month. Candy Co. matches the employees' charitable contributions on a 2-to-1 basis. Donations are mailed to World Hunger Relief semiannually. Deductions from all employees to May 31 this year have totalled $280. A cheque will be sent for the first half of the year on July 5, 19XX.

Required

a. Assuming that the payroll register has been posted, but no entries have been made for employee benefits expense for June, make the two journal entries that are necessary to record this expense for Candy Co. for June.

b. Give details of the various cheques which will be issued in July based on Candy Co.'s payroll activities for the year so far.

8B-4. The Ripcord Parachute Club employs three people and pays them on a weekly basis. Payroll data for the four weeks in February are given below:

Week 1—February

		Deductions							
Employee	*Sal.*	*Tax*	*CPP*	*UI*	*LTD*	*Pen.*	*Med.*	*Net Pay*	*Chq. No.*
Phil Rawlins	850	220	22	22	12	44	18	512	318
Janet Fox	800	190	21	22	12	41	12	502	319
Wey Card	900	245	24	22	12	46	18	533	320

Week 2—February

Employee	*Sal.*	*Deductions*						*Net*	*Chq.*
		Tax	*CPP*	*UI*	*LTD*	*Pen.*	*Med.*	*Pay*	*No.*
Phil Rawlins	900	235	24	22	12	46	18	543	334
Janet Fox	800	190	21	22	12	41	12	502	335
Wey Card	900	245	24	22	12	46	18	533	336

Week 3—February

Employee	*Sal.*	*Deductions*						*Net*	*Chq.*
		Tax	*CPP*	*UI*	*LTD*	*Pen.*	*Med.*	*Pay*	*No.*
Phil Rawlins	900	235	24	22	12	46	18	543	356
Janet Fox	800	190	21	22	12	41	12	502	357
Wey Card	900	245	24	22	12	46	18	533	358

Week 4—February

Employee	*Sal.*	*Deductions*						*Net*	*Chq.*
		Tax	*CPP*	*UI*	*LTD*	*Pen.*	*Med.*	*Pay*	*No.*
Phil Rawlins	900	235	24	22	12	46	18	543	377
Janet Fox	800	190	21	22	12	41	12	502	378
Wey Card	950	265	25	22	12	49	18	559	379

Assumptions

Employees pay 100 percent of the cost of long term disability (LTD). Employees contribute just over 5 percent of their salary to the pension plan; the employer contributes 6 percent of the employees' salary to the plan. Medical cost is split 50/50 by employees and employer. All payroll-related deductions are paid on the 15th of March.

Required

Recording employee benefits expense—multiple periods.

a. In recording the payroll journal in February, the bookkeeper for the Ripcord Parachute Club did not record any expense for employee benefits. Give the four journal entries which should be made for the month to record this expense.

Posting routing entries for a monthly period.

b. Post the entries from the payroll journal and the entries in **a** above to the T accounts shown below. (You may ignore the accounts which are not shown.)

Income Tax Payable	CPP Payable	UI Payable

LTD Payable	Pension Plan Liability	Medical Plan Payable

Employee Benefits Expense	Wage Expense

c. List the cheques and the amounts of the cheques which will be issued on March 15 for the February payroll.

Group C Problems

8C-1. The payroll register for Mission Hardware Ltd. for the month of May is shown below:

		Deductions						Net	Chq.
Employee	*Salary*	*IT*	*CPP*	*UI*	*Health*	*LTD*	*Union*	*Pay*	*No.*
Cliff Moore	2,300	450	56	68	25	35	24	1,642	514
Mary Watt	1,950	360	46	58	42	30	24	1,390	515
Kyle George	1,800	318	42	53	25	31	24	1,307	516
Verna Chau	2,400	476	59	71	42	37	24	1,691	517
Roy Verhagen	1,800	300	42	53	42	27	24	1,312	518
	10,250	1,904	245	303	176	160	120	7,342	

Recording benefits expense and computing and entering cheques issued re payroll.

Union dues must be submitted to the treasurer of the union by the 20th day of the next month. Mission matches the employees' contributions to the long term disability plan and the total must be sent to the insurance company by the 10th of each month following the payroll. Assume that all payroll information except for benefits has been recorded as the cheques 514–518 were issued.

Required

a. Record Mission's benefits expense for the month of May.

b. In June, Mission issued the following 3 cheques:

1. Cheque 543, June 10, to ABC Insurance Company for the LTD.
2. Cheque 551, June 15, to the Receiver General for Canada for employee deductions.
3. Cheque 567, June 15, to the Hardware Employees Union, Local 471, for union dues.

How much was each cheque for?

c. What entry would be made in the general journal to record each cheque in **b** above?

8C-2. Counterpoint Counselling Inc. recorded the following details in its Professional Payroll Journal for July:

		Deductions							Net	Chq.
						Life	Assn.			
Employee	*Salary*	*IT*	*CPP*	*UI*	*Char.*	*Ins.*	*Dues*	*Health*	*Pay*	*No.*
Paula Amer	3,950	1,094	102	96	50	40	42	78	2,448	582
Mike Stern	4,400	1,292	115	96	60	45	42	78	2,672	583
Pat McIvor	3,680	982	100	96	50	40	42	46	2,324	584
Debbie Chan	4,850	1,502	128	96	70	50	42	78	2,884	585
Boris Helsin	4,700	1,432	123	96	70	50	42	46	2,841	586
Ken George	4,000	1,116	104	96	50	40	42	78	2,474	587
	25,580	7,418	672	576	350	265	252	404	15,643	

Counterpoint matches the charitable donation of each employee and forwards the total on the 25th of each month to the Canadian Centre for Counselling Research. Association dues are sent to the Provincial Counsellors Society on the 20th of each month. Life insurance premiums are remitted to ABCD Insurance Company Ltd. by the 20th day of the following month. Health

Recording benefits expense and liabilities; calculating dates and amounts of cheques to be issued.

insurance premiums are remitted to the Provincial Health Care Organization by the 15th of the next month, at the same time as the employee deductions are sent to the Receiver General for Canada.

Required

a. Give the general journal entry necessary to complete the recording of this payroll assuming no entry was made for benefits or related expenses when the payroll was recorded.

b. List the cheques along with their amounts and dates which Counterpoint would issue in the month of August, in respect of this payroll.

8C-3. Refer to Problem 7C-2.

Recording benefits expense and liabilities.

Required

a. Give the general journal entry necessary to recognize all payroll benefits expense arising from that payroll, given the entry you made in Chapter 7.

8C-4. Refer to Problem 7C-3.

Recording benefits expense and liabilities.

Required

a. Give the general journal entry necessary to recognize all payroll benefits expenses arising from that payroll, given the entry you made in Chapter 7.

8C-5. Munchkin Bakery Ltd. pays its employees every two weeks (26 pay periods per year). There are two pay periods in the month of March, and details of each follow:

March 12 Payroll

		Deductions					*Net*	*Chq.*
Employee	*Salary*	*IT*	*CPP*	*UI*	*Health*	*Union*	*Pay*	*No.*
Clara Worth	1,700	402	44	44	22	8	1,180	358
Reg Holbert	1,025	196	25	30	22	8	759	359
Amos Troy	1,150	230	28	34	38	8	812	360
Del Swiftl	975	183	24	29	38	8	693	361
Pam Knott	1,210	256	30	36	22	8	858	362
Totals	6,060	1,267	151	173	142	40	4,324	

March 26 Payroll

		Deductions					*Net*	*Chq.*
Employee	*Salary*	*IT*	*CPP*	*UI*	*Health*	*Union*	*Pay*	*No.*
Clara Worth	1,700	402	44	44	22	8	1,180	386
Reg Holbert	1,050	204	26	31	22	8	764	387
Amos Troy	1,100	217	27	32	38	8	778	388
Del Swiftl	1,025	196	25	30	38	8	728	389
Pam Knott	1,246	269	31	37	22	8	879	390
Totals	6,121	1,288	153	174	142	40	4,329	

Union dues must be remitted to the union treasurer by the 28th of the following month, while health premiums are matched by Munchkin and remitted to the provincial treasurer by the 10th of the month following. A cheque is sent to the Receiver General by the 15th of each following month as well.

Recording benefits expense and related liabilities for two pay periods, plus calculating details of payroll benefits cheques to be issued.

Required

a. Assuming that the payroll register has been journalized but no other related entries made, prepare the two journal entries necessary to record the benefits expense for March.

b. Give the details of all cheques which Munchkin will issue in April with respect to payroll.

Recording benefits expense and related liabilities for five pay periods in a month, plus calculating details of payroll benefits cheques to be issued.

8C-6. The Grierson Auto Repair Company pays each of its employees weekly each Friday. During the month of May there were five pay periods, which are detailed below. (Note that employees pay 100 percent of the cost of health and dental plans.)

Week 1

		Deductions							
Employee	*Weekly Earnings*	*IT*	*CPP*	*UI*	*Union Dues*	*Health Plan*	*Dental Plan*	*Net Pay*	*Chq. No.*
Hal Martinez	740.00	153.95	18.72	21.83	7.00	13.20	9.75	515.55	1475
Morna James	785.00	198.90	20.12	22.13	7.00	9.20	9.75	517.90	1476
LeRoy Black	866.00	224.10	22.36	22.13	7.00	9.20	9.75	571.46	1477
Peter Tsui	900.00	213.35	23.20	22.13	7.00	13.20	9.75	611.37	1478
Wendy Abrahms	725.00	172.35	18.44	21.39	7.00	13.20	9.75	482.87	1479
Weekly Totals	4,016.00	962.65	102.84	109.61	35.00	58.00	48.75	2,699.15	

Week 2

		Deductions							
Employee	*Weekly Earnings*	*IT*	*CPP*	*UI*	*Union Dues*	*Health Plan*	*Dental Plan*	*Net Pay*	*Chq. No.*
Hal Martinez	718.00	144.05	18.16	21.18	7.00	13.20	9.75	504.66	1512
Morna James	738.00	178.90	18.72	21.77	7.00	9.20	9.75	492.66	1513
LeRoy Black	884.00	230.80	22.92	22.13	7.00	9.20	9.75	582.20	1514
Peter Tsui	892.00	209.15	23.20	22.13	7.00	13.20	9.75	607.57	1515
Wendy Abrahms	705.00	165.75	17.88	20.80	7.00	13.20	9.75	470.62	1516
Weekly Totals	3,937.00	928.65	100.88	108.01	35.00	58.00	48.75	2,657.71	

Week 3

		Deductions							
Employee	*Weekly Earnings*	*IT*	*CPP*	*UI*	*Union Dues*	*Health Plan*	*Dental Plan*	*Net Pay*	*Chq. No.*
Hal Martinez	765.00	163.90	19.56	22.13	7.00	13.20	9.75	529.46	1577
Morna James	714.00	169.05	18.16	21.06	7.00	9.20	9.75	479.78	1578
LeRoy Black	832.00	207.35	21.52	22.13	7.00	9.20	9.75	555.05	1579
Peter Tsui	916.00	218.35	23.76	22.13	7.00	13.20	9.75	621.81	1580
Wendy Abrahms	725.00	172.35	18.44	21.39	7.00	13.20	9.75	482.87	1581
Weekly Totals	3,952.00	931.00	101.44	108.84	35.00	58.00	48.75	2,668.97	

Week 4

Employee	Weekly Earnings	IT	CPP	UI	Union Dues	Health Plan	Dental Plan	Net Pay	Chq. No.
		Deductions							
Hal Martinez	810.00	184.00	20.68	22.13	7.00	13.20	10.50	552.49	1604
Morna James	736.00	175.60	18.72	21.71	7.00	9.20	10.50	493.27	1605
LeRoy Black	884.00	230.80	22.92	22.13	7.00	9.20	10.50	581.45	1606
Peter Tsui	815.00	175.65	20.96	22.13	7.00	13.20	10.50	565.56	1607
Wendy Abrahms	725.00	172.35	18.42	21.39	7.00	13.20	10.50	482.14	1608
Weekly Totals	3,970.00	938.40	101.70	109.49	35.00	58.00	52.50	2,674.91	

Week 5

Employee	Weekly Earnings	IT	CPP	UI	Union Dues	Health Plan	Dental Plan	Net Pay	Chq. No.
		Deductions							
Hal Martinez	731.00	150.65	18.44	21.56	7.00	13.20	10.50	509.65	1638
Morna James	714.00	169.05	18.16	21.06	7.00	9.20	10.50	479.03	1639
LeRoy Black	866.00	224.10	22.36	22.13	7.00	9.20	10.50	570.71	1640
Peter Tsui	904.00	213.35	23.48	22.13	7.00	13.20	10.50	614.34	1641
Wendy Abrahms	725.00	172.35	18.44	21.39	7.00	13.20	10.50	482.12	1642
Weekly Totals	3,940.00	929.50	100.88	108.27	35.00	58.00	52.50	2,655.85	

Required

a. Assuming that the payroll register has been journalized but no other related entries made, prepare the five journal entries necessary to record the benefits expense for May, 19XX.

b. Give the details of all cheques which Grierson will issue in June, 19XX with respect to payroll.

Real World Applications

8R-1.

The Tidy Tax Return Co. employs 50 extra people for the period February 1 through April 30 each year in order to process a large volume of tax returns. Each employee receives $10 per hour and works 40 hours a week (for 14 weeks). Early in May, all 50 additional workers are laid off.

A personnel service has offered to supply the needed 50 workers at a cost of $12 per hour. The managers of Tidy Tax Return Co. are not sure whether to accept the new offer.

Please prepare a memo to the management outlining the advantages of using the personnel service bureau and also the advantage of continuing with the present arrangement. Do not restrict your answer to financial considerations only.

Critical Thinking/Ethical Case

8R-2.
Abby Ross works in the Payroll Department for Lange Co. as a junior accountant. Abby also is going to school for an advanced degree in accounting. After work each day she uses the company's photocopy machine to make extra copies of her assignments. Should she be photocopying personal material on a company machine? You make the call. Write down your specific recommendations to Abby.

ACCOUNTING RECALL
A CUMULATIVE APPROACH

THIS EXAM REVIEWS CHAPTERS 1 THROUGH 8

Your *Study Guide and Working Papers* has forms to complete this exam, as well as worked-out solutions. The page references next to each question identify what page to turn back to if you answer the question incorrectly.

PART I Vocabulary Review

Match the terms to the appropriate definition or phrase.

Page Ref.

(297) 1. PD7A
(292) 2. Payroll tax expense
(130) 3. Mixed account
(260) 4. Union dues
(80) 5. Fiscal year
(302) 6. T4-T4A Summary
(226) 7. Bank reconciliation
(267) 8. Record of employment
(260) 9. Medical plan payable
(290) 10. RC1(E)

A. A liability account
B. Form used to obtain a Business Number
C. Agrees two differing amounts
D. Rarely an expense
E. Form sent with remittance
F. Employer's share of deductions
G. Any 52-week period
H. Filled out only when an employee leaves or is fired
I. Part balance sheet and part income statement
J. Form summarizing calendar year events in the payroll

PART II True or False (Accounting Theory)

(291) 11. Income tax deductions are part of the payroll tax expense.
(291) 12. Remittances are sent to the Receiver General each quarter.
(257) 13. Employees often must pay more income tax than has been deducted from their paycheques.

(266) 14. Employers are required by law to file a record of employment form for each employee annually.

(290) 15. Each employer must obtain a unique identification number from the federal government to permit employees deductions to be tracked accurately.

PART III Applications Problem

From the following information, calculate the employer's tax expense for the month of March. The employer has agreed to match the employees dollar for dollar for amounts deducted for charitable purposes:

Employee	*Monthly Salary*	*Net Claim Code*	*Charitable*	*Union Dues*
F. Shields	2,900	4	25	16
B. Chan	1,950	1	14	16
K. Gold	3,500	2	35	—

MINI PRACTICE SET

Pete's Market

Completing Payroll Requirements

This Mini Practice Set will aid in putting the piece of payroll together. In this project, you are the bookkeeper and will have the responsibility of recording payroll in the payroll register, paying the payroll, recording the employer's tax responsibilities, and making payment of the Receiver General requirements.

Pete's Market, owned by Pete Reel, is located at 33 Riel Drive, Your Town, Alberta T5C 1L2. His Business Number is 12345 6789 RC. The following are the employees of Pete's Market along with their salary, exemptions, etc.

Weekly Salaries

Date	*Name*	*Net Claim Code*	*Weekly Salary*
Oct. 4, 1999	Fred Flynn	1	$900
Oct. 11, 1999	Fred Flynn	1	900
Oct. 18, 1999	Fred Flynn	1	950
Oct. 25, 1999	Fred Flynn	1	950

Note: Fred Flynn receives a salary increase Oct. 18, 1999.

Oct. 4, 1999	Mary Jones	1	$850
Oct. 11, 1999	Mary Jones	1	850
Oct. 18, 1999	Mary Jones	1	850
Oct. 25, 1999	Mary Jones	4	850

Note: On October 11, 1999, Mary reaches her CPP maximum of $893.20. Deduct only $2.31 CPP for Mary in that payroll, then no further CPP in October.

Oct. 4, 1999	Lilly Vron	1	$700
Oct. 11, 1999	Lilly Vron	1	700
Oct. 18, 1999	Lilly Vron	1	700
Oct. 25, 1999	Lilly Vron	1	700

Source deductions payable at September 30, 1999 (employer portion already recorded):

CPP Payable	*UI Payable*	*Income Taxes Payable*
$503.68	$623.12	$2,427.52

Using the general journal and payroll register provided, complete the following for the month of October 1999:

1999

Oct. 4 Complete payroll register for October 4 payroll, journal payroll entry, and journalize entry for employer's CPP and UI expense.

4 Transfer cash for October 4 payroll net pay from operating account to payroll account.

11 Process payroll (follow same procedures as for October 4 payroll above.)

11 Transfer cash for October 11 payroll net pay from operating account to payroll account.

15 Pay Receiver General for prior month's source deductions payable.

18 Process payroll for October 18. Note change in Fred Flynn's salary.

18 Transfer cash for October 18 payroll net pay from operating account to payroll account.

25 Process payroll for October 25.

25 Transfer cash for October 25 payroll net pay from operating account to payroll account.

Computerized Accounting Application for Pete's Market Mini Practice Set (Chapter 8)

Completing Payroll and Miscellaneous Other Requirements

Before starting on this assignment, read and complete the tasks discussed in Parts A, B, and F of Appendix B at the end of this book and complete the Computer Workshop assignments for Chapter 3, Chapter 4, and the Valdex Realty Mini Practice Set (Chapter 5).

Pete's Market, owned by Pete Reel, is located at 33 Riel Drive, Your Town, Alberta T5C 1L2. His Business No. is 12345 6789 RC. The data set for CA-Simply Accounting for Windows packaged with this text uses the 1996 federal and provincial tax laws, and these are calculated automatically by the program. If your version of the program uses a different set of tax laws, your figures may vary a bit from the figures provided; but they should be reasonably similar. Some settings will use ACCPAC Plus software, in which case you should follow the directions of your instructor, using the data set which is also provided on the diskette accompanying the text.

The Payroll Journal in CA-Simply Accounting for Windows is designed to work with the General Ledger module in an integrated fashion. When transactions are recorded in the Payroll Journal, the program automatically updates the Payroll Register, records the journal entry, and posts all accounts affected in the general ledger. The following are the employees of Pete's Market and their weekly wages for the month of October.

	Fred Flynn	*Mary Jones*	*Lilly Vron*
Oct. 4	900	850	700
Oct. 11	900	850	700
Oct. 18	950	850	700
Oct. 25	950	850	700

The net claim code for all employees is 1, except that Mary Jones changes to code 4 on October 25 (you will need to make this change). The personal exemption is $6,456 for code 1 and $11,202 for code 4.

On October 18, Fred Flynn received a raise of $50 per week. Mary will reach the maximum CPP contribution for the year as outlined by Revenue Canada during the month, and you will need to manage this situation correctly. The maximum CPP payable in the current year is $893.20.

Here is the trial balance for Pete's Market as at 30/09/99 provided in the data set:

1010	Operating Account	$30,785.80	—
1020	Payroll Account	568.68	—
1050	GST Paid	3,897.12	—
1110	Computer Equipment	3,500.00	—
1210	Furniture and Fixtures	2,750.00	—
2010	Accounts Payable		2,086.50
2270	UI Payable		623.12
2280	CPP Payable		503.68
2290	Income Taxes Payable		2,427.52

2395	GST Collected		9,601.56
2450	Loan Payable		950.00
3600	Pete Reel, Capital		10,000.00
4005	Sales		158,403.94
5040	Purchases	66,713.95	—
5520	Accounting and Legal	825.00	—
5530	Advertising	387.24	—
5535	Bank Charges and Interest	35.00	—
5545	Office	200.00	—
5555	Telephone	242.04	—
5560	Wages	69,600.00	—
5565	UI Expense	2,523.73	—
5570	CPP Expense	1,792.76	—
5585	Courses	775.00	—
	Totals	$184,596.32	$184,596.32

1. Start Windows; insert your Student Data Files disk into drive A or B; then double-click on the CA-Simply Accounting icon. The CA-Simply Accounting Open File dialogue box will appear.
2. Enter one of the following paths into the **Open File name** text box:
   - A:\PETE:ASC (if you are storing your student data files on the disk in drive A).
   - B:\PETE:ASC (if you are storing your student data files on the disk in drive B).
3. Click on the **OK** button; enter "10/04/99" into the **Using date for this session** text box; then click on the **OK** button. The Company Window for Pete will appear.
4. Click on the Company Window Setup Menu; then click on Company Information. The Company Information dialogue box will appear. Insert your name in place of the text "Name" in the **Name** text box. Click on the **OK** button to return to the Company Window.
5. Double-click on the Payroll Journal icon. The Payroll Journal dialogue box will appear.
6. Click on the arrow button to the right of the **To the Order of** text box. Click on Fred Flynn's name; then press the TAB key.
7. Accept the default cheque number; click the **TAB** key, enter date, again click on the **TAB** key; click on the **Salary** text box; enter "900"; then press the **TAB** key. This completes the data you need to enter into the Payroll Journal dialogue box to record the payroll journal entry for Fred Flynn's October 4 weekly payroll. Your screen should look like this:

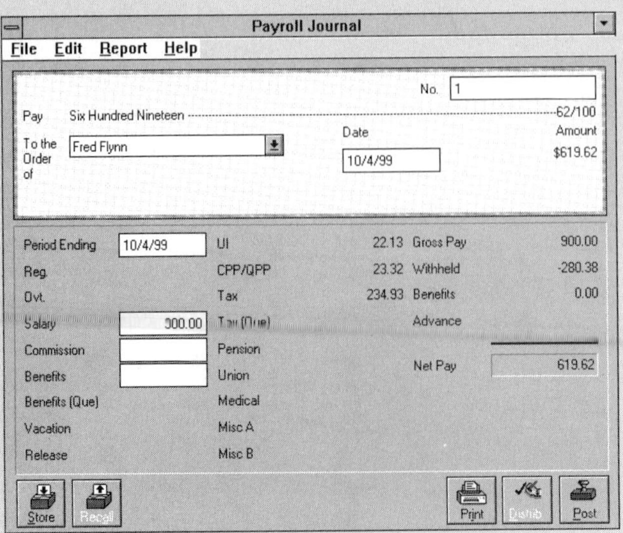

Payroll Journal

File Edit Report Help

No. 1

Pay Six Hundred Nineteen ---- 62/100

Date

Amount

To the Order of Fred Flynn

10/4/99

$619.62

Period Ending	10/4/99	UI	22.13	Gross Pay	900.00
Reg.		CPP/QPP	23.32	Withheld	-280.38
Ovt.		Tax	234.93	Benefits	0.00
Salary	900.00	Tax (Que)		Advance	
Commission		Pension			
Benefits		Union		Net Pay	619.62
Benefits (Que)		Medical			
Vacation		Misc A			
Release		Misc B			

Store Recall Print Distrib Post

8. Before posting this transaction, you need to verify that the transaction data are correct by reviewing the payroll journal entry. To review the entry, click on the Payroll Journal Report menu; then click on Display Payroll Journal Entry. The journal entry representing the data you have recorded in the Payroll Journal dialogue box is displayed.

9. Note that the program has combined the journal entry to record and pay the payroll with the journal entry to record the employer's payroll tax expenses into a single compound journal entry. Also note that the program uses three individual payroll tax expense accounts (CPP, UI, and Tax Expense) in place of a single Payroll Tax Expense account. Review the payroll entry for accuracy, noting any errors.

10. Close the Payroll Journal Entry window by double-clicking on the control menu box. If you have made an error, use the following editing techniques to correct it:

Editing a Payroll Journal Entry

- Move to the text box that contains the error by pressing either the TAB key to move forward through each text box or the SHIFT and TAB keys together to move to a previous text box. This will highlight the selected text box information so that you can change it. Alternatively, you can use the mouse to point to a text box and drag through the incorrect information to highlight it.
- Type the correct information; then press the TAB key to enter it.
- If you have associated the transaction with an incorrect employee, reselect the correct employee from the employee list display after clicking on the arrow button to the right of the **To the order of** text box.
- To discard an entry and start over, double-click on the control menu box. Click on the **Yes** button in response to the question "Are you sure you want to discard this journal entry?"
- Review the journal entry for accuracy after editing corrections.
- **It is important to note that the only way to edit a payroll journal entry after it is posted is to reverse the entry and input the correct entry.** To correct payroll journal entries posted in error, see Part C of Appendix B.

11. After verifying that the payroll journal entry is correct, click on the **Post** button to post this transaction. A blank Payroll Journal dialogue box is displayed, ready for additional Payroll Journal transactions to be recorded.

12. Record the October 4 payroll journal for Mary Jones and Lilly Vron in a manner similar to your recording of Fred Flynn. Close the Payroll Journal.

13. Using the General Journal, record a transfer to the payroll bank account from the general bank account for the exact amount of the net pay for the three employees determined in the payroll entries you just completed. You may find it handy to view or print the payroll journal to assist you with this task. Date this entry 10/04/99 (so there is no need to adjust the Using Date) and accept the default cheque number presented by the program.

14. Click on the Company Window Maintenance menu; then click on Advance Using Date. Enter "10/10/99" into the **New using date** text box; then click on the **OK** button.

15. Using the General Journal, record the following transactions:

    Before entering these, create a new account Office Supplies (number 1040). Make this a right account so it will add in with other current asset accounts.

    Oct. 9 Paid for office supplies, $202 to T&G Office Supplies Co. Use cheque number 43 for the general account.

    Oct. 10 Purchased on account products from Market Distributions, $2,165.

16. Click on the Company Window Maintenance menu; then click on Advance Using Date. Enter "10/11/99" into the **New using date** text box; then click on the **OK** button.

17. Record the October 11 payroll for Fred Flynn, Mary Jones, and Lilly Vron. Close the Payroll Journal.

18. Using the General Journal, record a transfer to the payroll bank account from the general bank account for the exact amount of the net pay for the three employees you determined in the October 11 payroll entries just completed.

19. Advance **Using Date** to 10/13/99. Record the following general journal entry after setting up the new account described:

Oct. 13 Pete Reel withdraws $3,000 from the business general account for personal use. Use the default cheque number. You must set up a new account in the ledger to handle this withdrawal. Use account number 3710. See Appendix A if assistance is needed in setting up accounts.

20. Advance **Using Date** to 10/15/99. Record the following general journal entry:

Oct. 15 Record the compound journal entry for the payment of source deductions to Receiver General for Canada from last month's payroll. The figures you need are on the trial balance (see above). Accept the default cheque number for the general bank account.

21. Advance **Using Date** to 10/17/99. Record the following general journal entry:

Oct. 17 Purchased a new office desk from Office Warehouse on account, $450. Use a logical cheque number.

22. Close the General Journal. At the Company Window, click on Maintenance; then advance **Using Date** to 10/18/99.

    Note that Fred Flynn's salary increased from $900 to $950. You will need to make this change before recording the October 18 payroll. From the Company Window, click on **Employee Ledger** and change the salary per pay period from $900 to $950.

23. Record the October 18 payroll for Fred Flynn, Mary Jones, and Lilly Vron.

24. After you have posted the payroll journal entries, double-click on the control menu box to close the Payroll Journal dialogue box. This will restore the Company Window screen.

25. Using the General Journal, record a transfer to the payroll bank account from the general bank account for the exact amount of the net pay for the three employees you determined in the October 18 payroll entries just completed.

26. Change the **Using Date** to 10/25/99 and record the 10/25/99 payroll journal entries for Fred Flynn and Lilly Vron.

    Note that Mary Jones' net claim code changed from 1 to 4. To make this change double-click on her **Employee Ledger** from the Company Window and enter "11,202" as her total claim amount in the **Federal Claim** box. Record Mary Jones' payroll for 10/25/99.

    Notice also that the program automatically adjusted Mary's CPP deduction toward the end of October. Since she reached the maximum for the year ($893.20 as this book is written), no additional deduction is necessary after this point is reached.

    Remember to transfer funds to the Payroll bank account.

27. Click on the Company Window Report menu, then click on Employee. The Employee Report Options dialogue box will appear. Click on the **Employee Summary** option button; click on the **Select All** button; then click **OK**. From the **File** menu option, select **Print** to print the report. Close this window and open the general journal.

28. Using the General Journal, and a Using Date of 10/31/99, record the following transactions (use logical cheque numbers in all cases):

Oct. 26 Payment to JR Accounting Services, $625.

Oct. 27 Payment to Campus Telephone, $82.15.

Oct. 30 Deposit to general account. Sales for the month were $8,878.50.

29. Record the accrued salaries payable ($2000) as of October 31, 1999. You will need to create a new account (Accrued Salaries Payable, number 2398) before making this adjusting entry in the General Journal as of 10/31/99. If you need help in creating a new account, see Appendix A.

30. The program can display and print separate Journal Reports that list transactions recorded in a specific journal (General, Purchases, Payments, Sales, Receipts, Payroll, Transfers, or Adjustments). The program can also generate a single General Journal Report that lists transactions recorded in all journals. To display or print such a report, check the **All ledger entries** checkbox.

31. Print the following reports:

 a. Employee Summary (Select All).

 b. General Journal (By posting date, All ledger entries, Start 10/1/99, finish 10/31/99).

 c. Trial Balance as of 10/31/99.

 d. Financial statements (if required by your instructor).

32. Review your printed reports. If you have made an error in a posted journal entry, see Part C of Appendix B for information on how to correct the error.

33. Click on the Company Window File menu; click on Save As; then enter one of the following new file names into the **Save file as** text box:

 - A:\PETEOCT.ASC (if you are storing your student data files on the disk in drive A).
 - B:\PETEOCT.ASC (if you are storing your student data files on the disk in drive B).

34. Click on the Save button. Note that the company name in the Company Window has changed from Pete to Peteoct. Click on the Company Window File menu again; then click on Save As. Enter one of the following new file names into the **Save file as** text box:

 - A:\PETE.ASC (if you are storing your student data files on the disk in drive A).
 - B:\PETE.ASC (if you are storing your student data files on the disk in drive B).

35. Click on the **Save** button. Click on the **Yes** button in response to the question "Replace existing data files with the same name?" Note that the company name in the Company Window has changed back from Peteoct to Pete.

36. You now have two sets of company data files for Pete's Market on your Student Data Files disk. The current data is stored under the file name PETE.ASC. The October backup data is stored under the file name PETEOCT.ASC.

SPECIAL JOURNALS

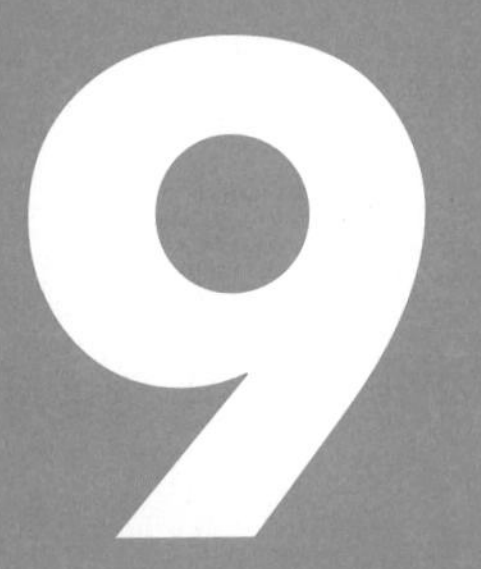

SALES AND

CASH

RECEIPTS

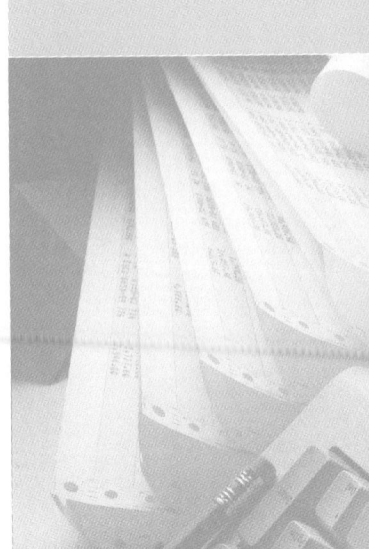

Chapter Objectives

- Journalizing sales on account in a sales journal. (p. 327)
- Posting from a sales journal to the general ledger. (p. 333)
- Recording to the accounts receivable ledger from a sales journal. (p. 331)
- Preparing, journalizing, recording, and posting a credit memorandum. (p. 336)
- Recording PST and GST in the sales journal as well as with a credit memorandum. (pp. 335–338)
- Journalizing and posting transactions using cash receipts journal, as well as recording to the accounts receivable ledger. (pp. 341–345)
- Preparing a schedule of accounts receivable. (p. 350)

In Chapters 9 and 10 we will take a look at how merchandise companies operate. Chapter 9 focuses on sellers of goods; Chapter 10 discusses buyers. Let's first look at Chou's Toy Shop to get an overview of merchandise terms and journal entries. After that, we will take an in-depth look at how Art's Wholesale Clothing Company keeps its books.

LEARNING UNIT 9-1

Chou's Toy Shop: Seller's View of a Merchandise Company

Chou's Toy Shop is a **retailer.** It buys toys, games, bikes, etc., from manufacturers and **wholesalers** and resells these goods (or **merchandise**) to its customers. The shelving, display cases, and so on are called "fixtures" or "equipment." These items are not for resale.

Gross sales

Gross sales: revenue earned from sale of merchandise to customers.

Each cash or charge sale made at Chou's Toy Shop is rung up at the cash register. Suppose the shop had $3,000 in sales on July 18. Of that amount, $1,800 were cash sales and $1,200 were charges. This is how the account that recorded those sales would look:

Sales (Gross)	
Dr.	Cr.
	3,000 ← Revenue account with a credit balance

This account is a revenue account with a credit balance and will be found on the income statement. Here is the journal entry for the day. ***Note:*** We will talk about provincial sales tax later.

Accounts Affected	Category	↑↓	Rules	T Account Update
Cash	Asset	↑	Dr.	Cash: Dr. 1,800
Accounts Receivable	Asset	↑	Dr.	Accounts Receivable: Dr. 1,200
Sales	Revenue	↑	Cr.	Sales: Cr. 3,000

Date		Account	PR	Dr.	Cr.
July	18	Cash		1800 00	
		Accounts Receivable		1200 00	
		Sales			3000 00
		Sales for July 18			

SALES RETURNS AND ALLOWANCES

It would be great for Chou if all the customers were completely satisfied, but that rarely is the case. On July 19, Michelle Reese brought back a doll she bought on account for $50. She told Chou that the doll was defective and she wanted either a price reduction or a new doll. They agreed on a $10 price reduction. Michelle now owes Chou $40. The account called **Sales Returns and Allowances** would record this information.

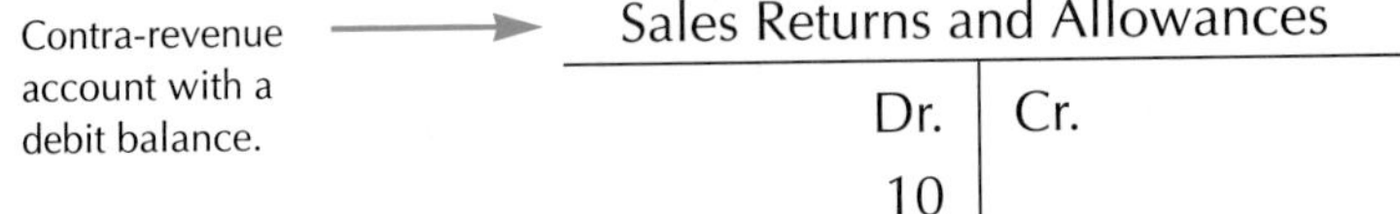

This account is a contra-revenue account with a debit balance. It will be recorded on the income statement. This is how the journal entry would look:

Accounts Affected	Category	↑ ↓	Rules	T Account Update
Sales Returns and Allowances	**Contra-revenue**	↑	**Dr.**	**Sales Ret. & Allow.** Dr. | Cr. 10 |
Accounts Receivable, Michelle Reese	**Asset**	↓	**Cr.**	**Accounts Receivable** Dr. | Cr. 1,200 | 10

Look at how the sales returns and allowances increase.

Date		Account	PR	Dr.	Cr.
July	19	Sales Returns and Allowances		10 00	
		Accounts Receivable, Michelle Reese			10 00
		Issued credit memorandum			

SALES DISCOUNT

Chou gives a 2 percent **sales discount** to customers who pay their bills early. He wants his customers to know about this policy, so he posted the following sign at the cash register:

Sales Discount Policy

2/10, n/30	2% discount is allowed off price of bill if paid within the first 10 days or full amount is due within 30 days.
n/10, EOM	No discount, full amount of bill is due within 10 days after the end of the month.

Note the **discount period** is the time when a discount is granted. The discount period is less time than the **credit period,** which is the length of time allowed to pay back the amount owed on the bill.

If Michelle pays her $40 bill early she will get an $0.80 discount. This is the account that records this information:

Contra-revenue account with a debit balance. → Sales Discount

Dr.	Cr.
0.80	

This is how Michelle's discount is calculated:

$$0.02 \times \$40 = \$0.80$$

Michelle pays her bill on July 24. She is entitled to the discount because she paid her bill within 10 days. Let's look at how Chou would record this on the company's books.

Gross sales
− Sales discount
− SRA
= Net sales

Accounts Affected	Category	↑↓	Rules	T Account Update
Cash	Asset	↑	Dr.	Cash Dr. | Cr. 39.20 |
Sales Discount	Contra-revenue	↑	Dr.	Sales Discount Dr. | Cr. 0.80 |
Accounts Receivable	Asset	↓	Cr.	Accounts Receivable Dr. | Cr. 1,200 | 10 | 40

July	24	Cash		39 20	
		Sales Discount		80	
		Accounts Receivable, Michelle Reese			40 00

Although Michelle pays $39.20, her Accounts Receivable is credited for the full amount, $40.

In the examples so far we have not shown any transactions with provincial sales tax. Let's look at how Chou would record monthly sales if provincial sales tax were charged.

Provincial Sales Tax Payable

None of the examples shown above show provincial sales tax. Still, like it or not, Chou must collect that tax from his customers and send it to the province. Sales tax represents a liability to Chou's business.

Assume that Chou's business is located in a province that charges a 5 percent sales tax. Remember, Chou's sales on July 18 were $3,000. Chou must figure out the provincial sales tax on the sales. For this purpose, let's assume that there were only two sales on that date: the cash sale ($1,800) and the charge sale ($1,200).

The provincial sales tax on the cash sale is calculated as follows:

$$\$1,800 \times 0.05 = \$90 \text{ tax}$$

$$\$1,800 + \$90 \text{ tax} = \$1,890 \text{ cash}$$

Here is how the provincial sales tax on the charge sale is computed:

$\$1,200 \times 0.05 = \$60$ tax $+ \$1,200$ charge $= \$1,260$ Accounts Receivable

This is how it would be recorded:

Accounts Affected	Category	↑↓	Rules	T Account Update
Cash	Asset	↑	Dr.	Cash: Dr. 1,890 | Cr.
Accounts Receivable	Asset	↑	Dr.	Accounts Receivable: Dr. 1,260 | Cr.
Sales Tax Payable	Liability	↑	Cr.	Sales Tax Payable: Dr. | Cr. 150*
Sales	Revenue	↑	Cr.	Sales: Dr. | Cr. 3,000

*$3,000 × 0.05 = $150 sales tax payable.

In a later unit in this chapter, we will show you how to record a credit memorandum with sales tax. Notice that in either case (cash or credit) it is the customer who pays the provincial sales tax, not Chou's business.

LEARNING UNIT 9-1 REVIEW

AT THIS POINT you should be able to

- Explain the purpose of a contra-revenue account. (p. 328)
- Define, journalize, and explain gross sales, sales returns and allowances, and sales discounts. (pp. 327–329)
- Journalize an entry for sales tax payable. (p. 330)

SELF-REVIEW QUIZ 9-1

(The forms you need can be found on page 9-1 of the *Study Guide and Working Papers.*)

Which of the following statements are false?

1. Sales Returns and Allowances is a contra-asset account.
2. Sales Discount has a normal balance of a debit.
3. Sales Tax Payable is a liability.
4. Sales Discount is a contra-asset.
5. Credit terms are standard in all industries.

Solution to Self-Review Quiz 9-1

Numbers 1, 4, and 5 are false.

LEARNING UNIT 9-2

The Sales Journal and Accounts Receivable Subsidary Ledger

Special Journals

Now let's examine how Art's Wholesale Clothing Company keeps its books. Art's business conducts many transactions. The following partial general journal shows the journal entries Art's must make for these sales on account transactions.

ART'S WHOLESALE CLOTHING COMPANY GENERAL LEDGER					
April	3	Accounts Receivable, Hal's		800 00	
		Sales			800 00
		Sales on account			
	6	Accounts Receivable, Bevans		1600 00	
		Sales			1600 00
		Sales on account			
	18	Accounts Receivable, Roe		2000 00	
		Sales			2000 00
		Sales on account			

This method is not very efficient. However, if Art's Wholesale Clothing Company kept a **special journal** for each type of transaction conducted, the number of postings and recordings required for each transaction would be reduced. After carefully looking at the situation with his accountant, Art has decided to use the following special journals:

For a discussion of recording of credit cards in special journals see appendix.

Special Journal Type	*What It Records*	
Sales journal	Sale of merchandise on account	Covered in this chapter
Cash receipts journal	Receiving cash from any source	Covered in this chapter
Purchases journal	Buying merchandise or other items on account	Covered in next chapter
Cash payments journal (cash disbursement journal)	Payment of cash for any purpose	Covered in next chapter

Subsidiary Ledgers

In the same way Art's Wholesale Clothing Company needs more than just a general journal, the business needs more than just a general ledger. For example, so far in this text, the only title we have used for recording amounts owed to the seller has been Accounts Receivable. Art could have replaced the Accounts Receivable title in the general ledger with the following list of customers who owe him money:

- Accounts Receivable, Bevans Company.
- Accounts Receivable, Hal's Clothing.
- Accounts Receivable, Mel's Department Store.
- Accounts Receivable, Roe Company.

As you can see, this would not be manageable if Art had 1,000 credit customers. To solve this problem, Art sets up a separate **accounts receivable subsidiary ledger.** Such a special ledger, often simply called a **subsidiary ledger,** contains a single type of account, such as "on account" customers. A page is opened for each customer and they are arranged alphabetically.

The diagram in Figure 9-1 shows how the accounts receivable subsidiary ledger fits in with the general ledger. To clarify the difference in updating the general ledger versus the subsidiary ledger we will *post* to the general ledger and *record* to the subsidiary ledger. The word "post" refers to information that is moved from the journal to the general ledger; the word "record" refers to information that is transferred from the journal into the individual customer's account in the subsidiary ledger.

The general ledger is *not* in the same book as the accounts receivable subsidiary ledger.

The accounts receivable subsidiary ledger, or any other subsidiary ledger, can be in the form of a card file, a binder notebook, or computer tapes or disks. It probably will not have page numbers. The accounts receivable subsidiary ledger is organized alphabetically by customer name and address; new customers can be added and inactive customers deleted.

Proving: At the end of the month, the sum of the accounts receivable subsidiary ledger will equal the ending balance in accounts receivable, the controlling account in the general ledger.

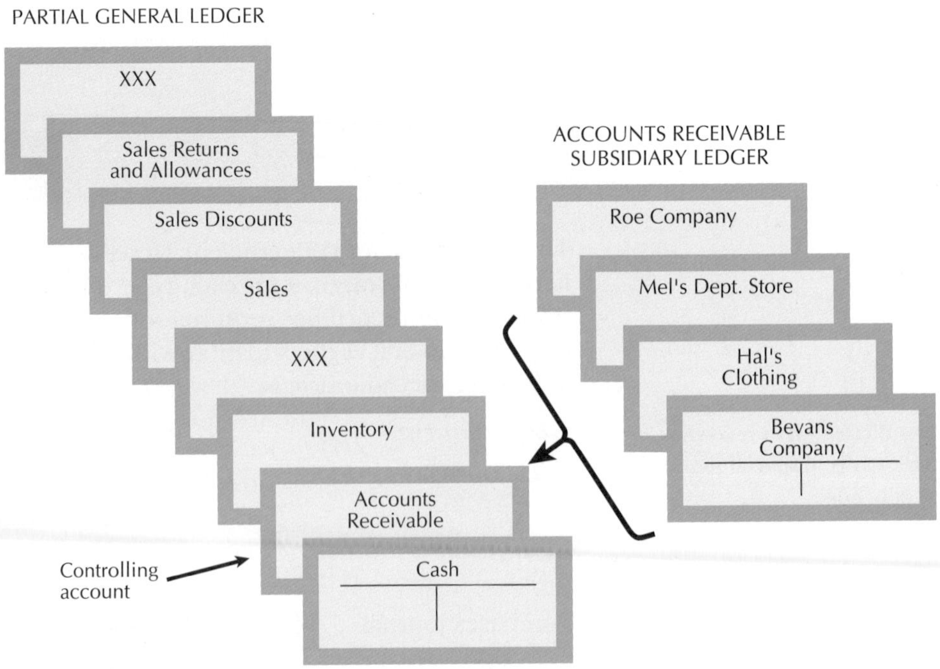

FIGURE 9-1
Partial General Ledger of Art's Wholesale Clothing Company and Accounts Receivable Subsidiary Ledger

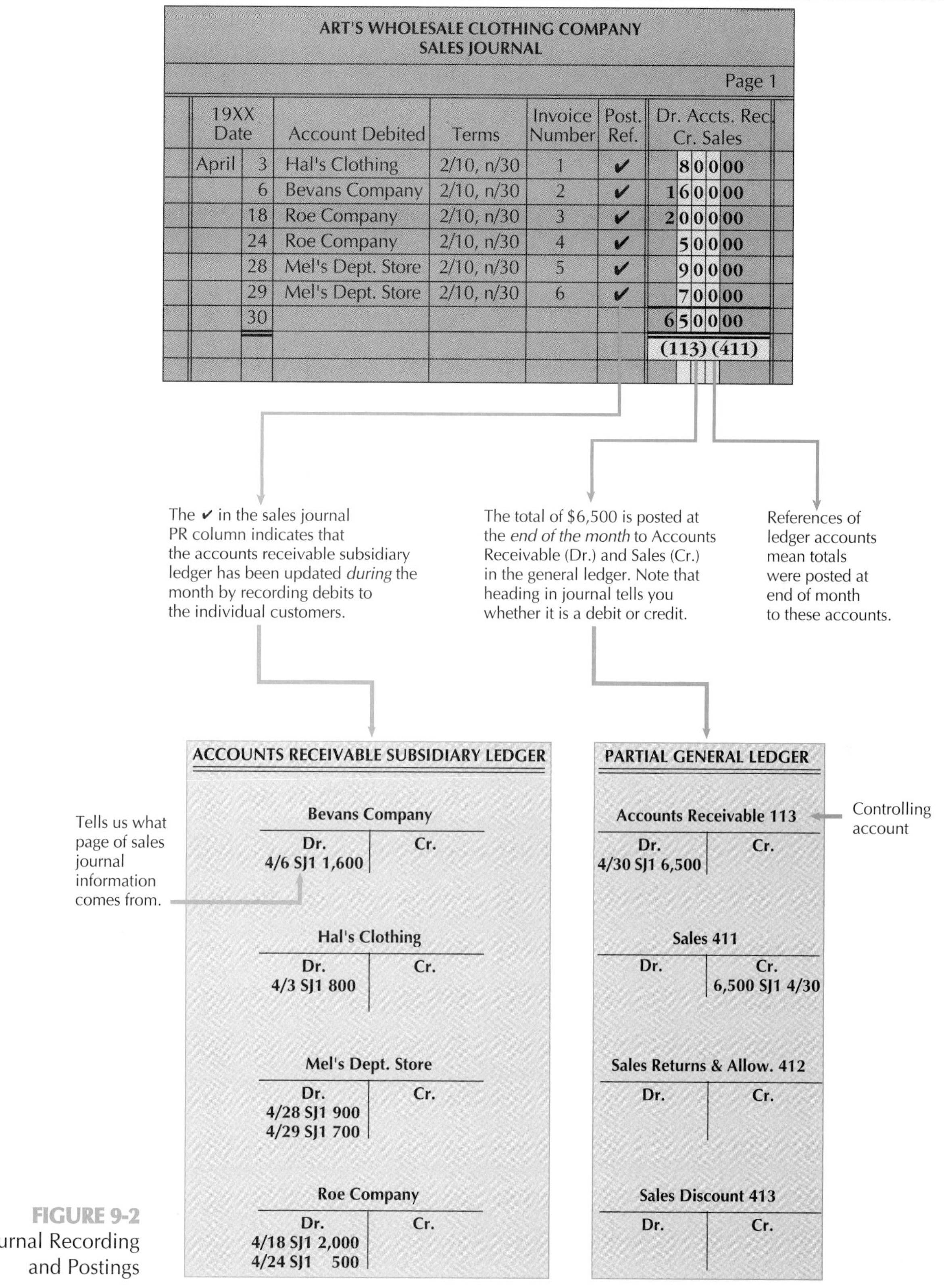

ART'S WHOLESALE CLOTHING COMPANY SALES JOURNAL						
						Page 1
19XX Date		Account Debited	Terms	Invoice Number	Post. Ref.	Dr. Accts. Rec. Cr. Sales
April	3	Hal's Clothing	2/10, n/30	1	✔	80000
	6	Bevans Company	2/10, n/30	2	✔	160000
	18	Roe Company	2/10, n/30	3	✔	200000
	24	Roe Company	2/10, n/30	4	✔	50000
	28	Mel's Dept. Store	2/10, n/30	5	✔	90000
	29	Mel's Dept. Store	2/10, n/30	6	✔	70000
	30					650000
						(113) (411)

The ✔ in the sales journal PR column indicates that the accounts receivable subsidiary ledger has been updated *during* the month by recording debits to the individual customers.
The total of $6,500 is posted at the *end of the month* to Accounts Receivable (Dr.) and Sales (Cr.) in the general ledger. Note that heading in journal tells you whether it is a debit or credit.
References of ledger accounts mean totals were posted at end of month to these accounts.
ACCOUNTS RECEIVABLE SUBSIDIARY LEDGER
Tells us what page of sales journal information comes from.
Bevans Company
Dr. Cr.
4/6 SJ1 1,600
Hal's Clothing
Dr. Cr.
4/3 SJ1 800
Mel's Dept. Store
Dr. Cr.
4/28 SJ1 900
4/29 SJ1 700
Roe Company
Dr. Cr.
4/18 SJ1 2,000
4/24 SJ1 500
PARTIAL GENERAL LEDGER
Accounts Receivable 113
Controlling account
Dr. Cr.
4/30 SJ1 6,500
Sales 411
Dr. Cr.
6,500 SJ1 4/30
Sales Returns & Allow. 412
Dr. Cr.
Sales Discount 413
Dr. Cr.

FIGURE 9-2
Sales Journal Recording and Postings

When using an accounts receivable subsidiary ledger, the title Accounts Receivable in the general ledger is called the **controlling account,** since it summarizes or controls the accounts receivable subsidiary ledger. At the end of the month the total of the individual accounts in the accounts receivable ledger must equal the ending balance in Accounts Receivable in the general ledger.

Art's Wholesale Clothing Company will use the following subsidiary ledgers:

Accounts receivable subsidiary ledger	Records money owed by credit customers	Covered in this chapter
Accounts payable subsidiary ledger	Records money owed to creditors	Covered in next chapter

Let's now look closer at the sales journal, general ledger, and subsidiary ledger for Art's Wholesale Clothing Company to see how transactions are updated in the special journal as well as posted and recorded to specific titles.

THE SALES JOURNAL

The **sales journal** for Art's Wholesale Clothing Company records all sales made on account to customers. Figure 9-2 shows the sales journal at the end of the first month in operation, along with the recordings to the accounts receivable ledger and posting to the general ledger. Keep in mind that the reason the balances in the accounts receivable subsidiary ledger are *debit* balances is that the customers listed *owe* Art's Wholesale money.

Look at the first transaction listed in the sales journal. It shows that on April 3 Art's Wholesale Clothing Company sold merchandise on account to Hal's Clothing for $800. The bill or **sales invoice** for this sale is shown in Figure 9-3 below.

Recording to the accounts receivable subsidiary ledger occurs daily.

Hal's Clothing	
Dr.	Cr.
4/3 SJ1	
800	

✓ means accounts receivable ledger has been updated.

Recording from the Sales Journal to the Accounts Receivable Subsidiary Ledger

As shown on the first line of the sales journal in Figure 9-2, the information on the invoice is recorded in the sales journal. However, *the PR column is left blank.* As soon as possible we now update the accounts receivable subsidiary ledger. To do this, we pull out the Hal's Clothing file card and update it: the debit side must show the $800 he owes Art along with the date (April 3) and page of the sales journal (p. 1). Once that is done, place a √ in the posting-reference column of the sales journal. Thus, we know Hal's outstanding balance at any moment in time. We do

FIGURE 9-3 Sales Invoice

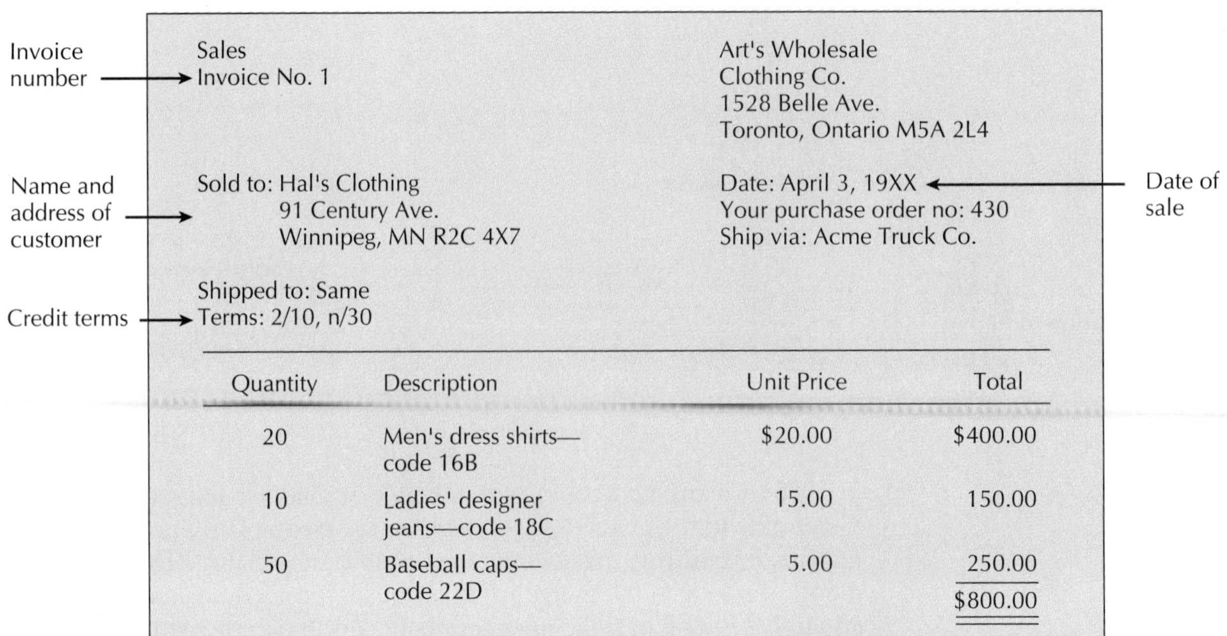

Sales
Invoice No. 1

Art's Wholesale
Clothing Co.
1528 Belle Ave.
Toronto, Ontario M5A 2L4

Sold to: Hal's Clothing
91 Century Ave.
Winnipeg, MN R2C 4X7

Date: April 3, 19XX
Your purchase order no: 430
Ship via: Acme Truck Co.

Shipped to: Same
Terms: 2/10, n/30

Quantity	Description	Unit Price	Total
20	Men's dress shirts—code 16B	$20.00	$400.00
10	Ladies' designer jeans—code 18C	15.00	150.00
50	Baseball caps—code 22D	5.00	250.00
			$800.00

not have to go through all the invoices. Note how the sales journal only needs one line instead of the three lines that would have been required in a general journal.

Posting at End of Month from the Sales Journal to the General Ledger

Recording to the general ledger occurs at end of month.

Accts. Rec. 113	
Dr.	Cr.
4/30 SJ1	
6,500	

Sales 411	
Dr.	Cr.
	6,500 SJ1
	4/30

The sales journal is totaled ($6,500) at the end of the month. Looking back at page 319, you can see that the heading of Art's sales journal is a debit to accounts receivable and a credit to sales. Therefore, at the end of the month the $6,500 total is posted to Accounts Receivable (debit) *and* to Sales (credit) in the general ledger. In the general ledger we record the date (4/30), the initials of the journal (SJ), the page of the sales journal (1), and appropriate debit or credit ($6,500). Once the account in the general ledger is updated, we place below the totals in the sales journal the account numbers to which the information was posted (in this case accounts 113 and 411).

Provincial Sales Tax

Art's Wholesale Clothing Company does not have to deal with provincial sales tax because it sells goods wholesale.

However, if Art's was a retail company, it would have to collect and remit provincial sales tax.

Let's look at how Munroe Menswear Company, a retailer, handles provincial sales tax on a sale made to Jones Company. Figure 9-4 shows Munroe's Sales Journal.

Sales Tax Payable	
	XXX

A liability in general ledger.

Also, a new account, **Provincial Sales Tax Payable,** must be created. That account is a liability account in the general ledger with a credit balance. The customer owes Munroe the sale amount plus the tax.

Keep in mind that if sales discounts are available, they are not normally calculated on the sales tax. The discount is on the selling price less any returns before the tax. For example, if Jones receives a 2 percent discount, he pays the following:

	$5,250	Total owed (tax is $250)
$5,000 × 0.02 = $100 savings →	− 100	Savings (discount)
	$5,150	Amount paid

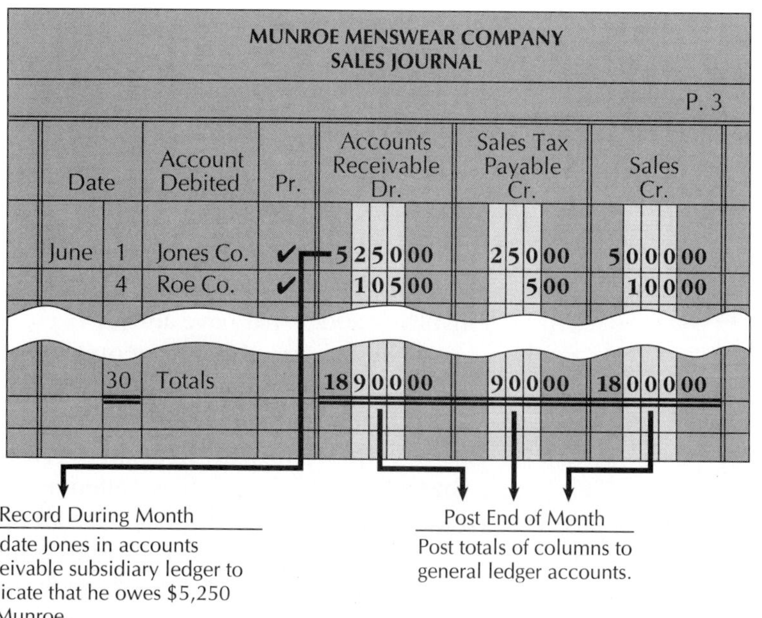

MUNROE MENSWEAR COMPANY
SALES JOURNAL

P. 3

Date		Account Debited	Pr.	Accounts Receivable Dr.	Sales Tax Payable Cr.	Sales Cr.
June	1	Jones Co.	✔	525000	25000	500000
	4	Roe Co.	✔	10500	500	10000
	30	Totals		1890000	90000	1800000

Record During Month
Update Jones in accounts receivable subsidiary ledger to indicate that he owes $5,250 to Munroe.
Post End of Month
Post totals of columns to general ledger accounts.

FIGURE 9-4
Munroe Sales Journal

LEARNING UNIT 9-2 REVIEW

AT THIS POINT you should be able to

- Define and state the purposes of special journals. (p. 331)
- Define and state the purposes of the accounts receivable subsidiary ledger. (p. 332)
- Define and state the purpose of the controlling account, Accounts Receivable. (p. 333)
- Journalize, record, or post sales on account to a sales journal and its related accounts receivable and general ledgers. (p. 333)

SELF-REVIEW QUIZ 9-2

(The forms you need are on page 9-1 of the *Study Guide and Working Papers.*)
Which of the following statements are false?

1. Special journals completely replace the general journal.
2. Special journals aid the division of labour.
3. The subsidiary ledger makes the general ledger less manageable.
4. The subsidiary ledger is separate from the general ledger.
5. The controlling account is located in the accounts receivable subsidiary ledger.
6. The total(s) of a sales journal are posted to the general ledger at the end of the month.
7. The accounts receivable subsidiary ledger is arranged in alphabetical order.
8. Transactions recorded into a sales journal are recorded only weekly to the accounts receivable subsidiary ledger.

Solution to Self-Review Quiz 9-2

Numbers 1, 3, 5, and 8 are false.

LEARNING UNIT 9-3

The Credit Memorandum

At the beginning of this chapter we introduced the Sales Returns and Allowances account. Merchandising businesses often use this account to handle transactions involving goods that have already been sold. For example, if a customer returns the goods he has bought, his account will be credited for the amount charged for the goods returned; if a customer gets an allowance because the goods he purchased were damaged, his account will be credited for the amount of the allowance. In both of these examples, the company's net sales revenue decreases. That is why the account is called a contra-revenue account: the sales revenue decreases and its normal balance is a debit.

A credit memorandum *reduces* accounts receivable.

Companies usually handle sales returns and allowances by means of a **credit memorandum.** Credit memoranda inform customers that the amount of the goods returned or the amount allowed for damaged goods has been subtracted (credited) from the customer's ongoing account with the company.

End result is that Bevan owes Art's Wholesale less money.

Art's Wholesale Clothing Co.
1528 Belle Ave.
Toronto, ON M5A 2L4

Credit
Memorandum No. 1
Date: April 12

Credit to: Bevans Company
110 Aster Rd.
Amherst, NS B4H 3A5

We credit your account as follows:
Merchandise returned 60 model 8B men's dress gloves—$600

FIGURE 9-5
Credit Memorandum

Remember, no provincial sales tax was involved because Art's is a wholesale company.

Sales Returns and Allowances	
Dr.	Cr.
+	–

A contra-revenue account.

A sample credit memorandum from Art's Wholesale Clothing Company appears in Figure 9-5. It shows that on April 12 credit memo no. 1 was issued to Bevans Company for defective merchandise that had been returned. (Figure 9-2 shows that Art's Wholesale Clothing Company sold Bevans Company $1,600 of merchandise on April 6.)

Let's assume that Art's Wholesale has high-quality goods and does not expect many sales returns and allowances. On this assumption, no special journal for sales returns and allowances will be needed. Instead, any returns and allowances will be recorded in the general journal, and all postings and recordings will be done when journalized. Let's look at a transaction analysis chart before we journalize, record, and post this transaction.

Note that the Sales Returns and Allowances account is increasing, which in turn reduces sales revenue and reduces amount owed by customer (accounts receivable).

Accounts Affected	Category	↑↓	Rules
Sales Returns and Allowances	**Contra-revenue account**	↑	**Dr.**
Accounts Receivable, Bevans Co.	**Asset**	↓	**Cr.**

JOURNALIZING, RECORDING, AND POSTING THE CREDIT MEMORANDUM

The credit memorandum results in two postings to the general ledger and one recording to the accounts receivable subsidiary ledger (see Figure 9-6).

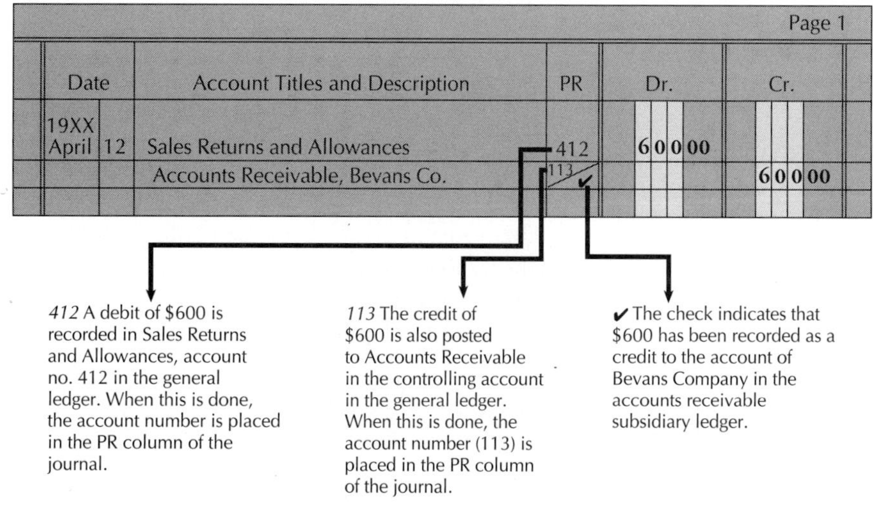

Page 1

Date		Account Titles and Description	PR	Dr.	Cr.
19XX April	12	Sales Returns and Allowances	412	600 00	
		Accounts Receivable, Bevans Co.	113/✓		600 00

412 A debit of $600 is recorded in Sales Returns and Allowances, account no. 412 in the general ledger. When this is done, the account number is placed in the PR column of the journal.
113 The credit of $600 is also posted to Accounts Receivable in the controlling account in the general ledger. When this is done, the account number (113) is placed in the PR column of the journal.
✔ The check indicates that $600 has been recorded as a credit to the account of Bevans Company in the accounts receivable subsidiary ledger.

FIGURE 9-6
Postings and Recordings for the Credit Memorandum

Remember, sales discounts are *not* taken on returns.

Note in the PR column next to Accounts Receivable, Bevans Co., that there is a diagonal line with the account number 113 above and a √ below. This is to show that the amount of $600 has been credited to Accounts Receivable in the controlling account in the general ledger *and* credited to the account of Bevans Company in the accounts receivable subsidiary ledger.

If the accountant for Art's Wholesale Clothing Company decided to develop a special journal for sales allowances and returns, the entry for a credit memorandum such as the one we've been discussing would look like this:

SALES RETURNS AND ALLOWANCES JOURNAL

Date		Credit Memo No.	Account Credited	PR	Sales Ret. and Allow. — Dr. Accts. Rec. — Cr.
19XX April	12	1	Bevans Company	✔	600 00

THE CREDIT MEMORANDUM WITH PROVINCIAL SALES TAX (PST)

Figure 9-4 shows the sales journal for Munroe Menswear Company. Remember, since Munroe is a retail company, its customers must pay provincial sales tax. Let's assume that on June 8 Roe returns $50 worth of the $100 of merchandise he bought earlier in the month. Let's analyze and journalize the credit memo that Munroe issued. Keep in mind that the customer is no longer responsible for paying for either the returned merchandise or the tax on it.

Accounts Affected	Category	↑↓	Rules	T Account Update
Sales Returns and Allowances	Contra-revenue	↑	Dr.	Sales Ret. & Allow.: Dr. 50 / Cr.
Provincial Sales Tax Payable ($5 tax on $100) ($2.50 tax on $50)	Liability	↓	Dr.	Provincial Sales Tax Payable: Dr. 2.50 / Cr.
Accounts Receivable, Roe	Asset	↓	Cr.	Accts. Rec.: Dr. / Cr. 52.50; Roe Co.: Dr. 105 / Cr. 52.50

Date		Account	Dr.	Cr.
June	8	Sales Returns and Allowances	50 00	
		Provincial Sales Tax Payable	2 50	
		Accounts Receivable, Roe Co.		52 50
		Received credit memo		

This journal entry requires three postings to the general ledger and one recording to Roe in the accounts receivable subsidiary ledger. Note that since Roe returned half of his merchandise he was able to reduce what he pays for provincial sales tax by half (from $5 to $2.50).

LEARNING UNIT 9-3 REVIEW

AT THIS POINT you should be able to

- Explain Provincial Sales Tax Payable in relation to Sales Discount. (p. 338)
- Explain, journalize, post, and record a credit memorandum with or without provincial sales tax. (pp. 337–338)

SELF-REVIEW QUIZ 9-3

(The forms you need are on pages 9-1 to 9-3 of the *Study Guide and Working Papers.*)

Journalize the following transactions into the sales journal or general journal for Moss Co. Record to the accounts receivable subsidiary ledger and post to general ledger accounts as appropriate. Use the same journal headings that we used for Art's Wholesale Clothing Company. (All sales carry credit terms of 2/10, n/30.) There is no tax.

19XX

May 1 Sold merchandise on account to Jane Company, invoice no. 1, $600.
5 Sold merchandise on account to Ralph Company, invoice no. 2, $2,500.
20 Issued credit memo no. 1 to Jane Company for $200 due to defective merchandise returned.

Solution to Self-Review Quiz 9-3

MOSS COMPANY
SALES JOURNAL

Page 1

Date		Account Debited	Terms	Invoice No.	Post. Ref.	Dr. Accts. Rec. Cr. Sales
19XX May	1	Jane Company	2/10, n/30	1	✓	600 00
	5	Ralph Company	2/10, n/30	2	✓	2 500 00
	31					3 100 00
						(112) (411)

Note: Total of accounts receivable subsidiary ledger $400 + $2,500 does indeed equal the balance in the controlling account, accounts receivable $2,900 at end of month, in the general ledger.

MOSS COMPANY
GENERAL JOURNAL

Page 1

Date		Account Titles and Description	PR	Dr.	Cr.
19XX May	20	Sales Ret. and Allowances	412	200 00	
		Accts. Rec., Jane Company	112/✓		200 00
		Issued credit memo #1			

PARTIAL GENERAL LEDGER

Accounts Receivable — Acct. No. 112

Date 19XX		Explanation	Post. Ref.	Debit	Credit	Dr. or Cr.	Balance
May	20		GJ1		200 00	Cr.	200 00
	31		GJ2	3100 00		Dr.	2900 00

Controlling Account

Note the unusual balance of $200 (Cr.) because of the return. Why? Because total of sales journal is not posted until end of month.

Sales — Acct. No. 411

Date 19XX		Explanation	Post. Ref.	Debit	Credit	Dr. or Cr.	Balance
May	31		SJ1		3100 00	Cr.	3100 00

Sales Returns and Allowances — Acct. No. 412

Date 19XX		Explanation	Post. Ref.	Debit	Credit	Dr. or Cr.	Balance
May	20		GJ1	200 00		Dr.	200 00

ACCOUNTS RECEIVABLE LEDGER

NAME Jane Company
ADDRESS 1218 Broadview Ave., Toronto ON

Date 19XX		Explanation	Post. Ref.	Debit	Credit	Dr. Balance
May	1		SJ1	600 00		600 00
	20		GJ1		200 00	400 00

Customers owe Moss money and thus have a debit balance.

NAME Ralph Company
ADDRESS 1300 Marine Drive, West Vancouver BC

Date 19XX		Explanation	Post. Ref.	Debit	Credit	Dr. Balance
May	5		SJ1	2500 00		2500 00

LEARNING UNIT 9-4

How Companies Record the Goods and Services Tax

On January 1, 1991, Canadians faced a new tax on the majority of the goods and services they purchased—the **Goods and Services Tax (GST)**. This new tax is calculated at 7 percent on almost every item purchased or service consumed. There are a few exceptions, for example, food and financial services. This learning unit is not intended to provide a complete discussion of the details of the GST. Rather it will illustrate the basics of accounting for the tax, which will apply to most businesses in Canada.

Similarities and differences between PST and GST.

Before illustrating the normal accounting treatment of the GST, notice that there are both similarities and differences between the GST and provincial sales taxes (covered in Learning Unit 9-3). Like the provincial sales tax (PST), the GST is added to the total of each invoice prepared for a customer. And, like the PST, the GST must be remitted to the appropriate taxing authority periodically.

However, there are also a few notable differences:

1. GST applies to services as well as goods (for example, a lawyer will add 7 percent to each invoice for professional services).
2. GST applies at all levels in the economy—not just the retail level as in the case of PST.
3. GST is paid by businesses to their suppliers as well as collected by them from their customers. The difference between the tax collected and tax paid is the amount sent to the federal government each period.
4. GST might result in a business receiving a refund in some periods. Since GST is payable on large asset purchases (a delivery van, for example), a business may claim this amount against the GST they owe. In the long run if a business is successful, it should remit more GST than it receives as a refund; however in a particular period it may be eligible to receive a refund.

GST COLLECTED ON SALES

To illustrate the basic accounting treatment for **GST collected**, we will refer to an example you have already seen. Figure 9-3 (sales invoice) showed what an invoice would look like before GST. Figure 9-7 shows the same invoice with GST added.

Sales
Invoice No. 1

Art's Wholesale
Clothing Co.
1528 Belle Ave.
Toronto, Ontario M5A 2L4

Sold to: Hal's Clothing
91 Century Ave.
Winnipeg, MN R2C 4X7

Date: April 3, 19XX
Your purchase order no: 430
Ship via: Acme Truck Co.

Shipped to: Same
Terms: 2/10, n/30

Quantity	Description	Unit Price	Total
20	Men's dress shirts—code 16B	$20.00	$400.00
10	Ladies' designer jeans—code 18C	15.00	150.00
50	Baseball caps—code 22D	5.00	250.00
		Subtotal	$800.00
	Add:	GST	56.00
		TOTAL	$856.00

GST reg. no. 109309799

FIGURE 9-7
Sales Invoice with GST

NOTE: There are more similarities than differences with the bookkeeping procedures described previously.

You should notice two things about this invoice. First, the GST is added at 7 percent of the total price of the goods. Second, the invoice shows a GST registration number. Each business in Canada (except very small ones) must obtain a number from the federal government and show it on their invoices.

This invoice is recorded in the sales journal of Art's Wholesale Clothing Company. The main difference is that now the bookkeeping task is made slightly longer because of the need to keep track of the GST. Figure 9-2 showed the sales journal before GST. Figure 9-8 shows how this new invoice (and some others not illustrated individually) are recorded with GST. Posting to the various ledger accounts is also illustrated.

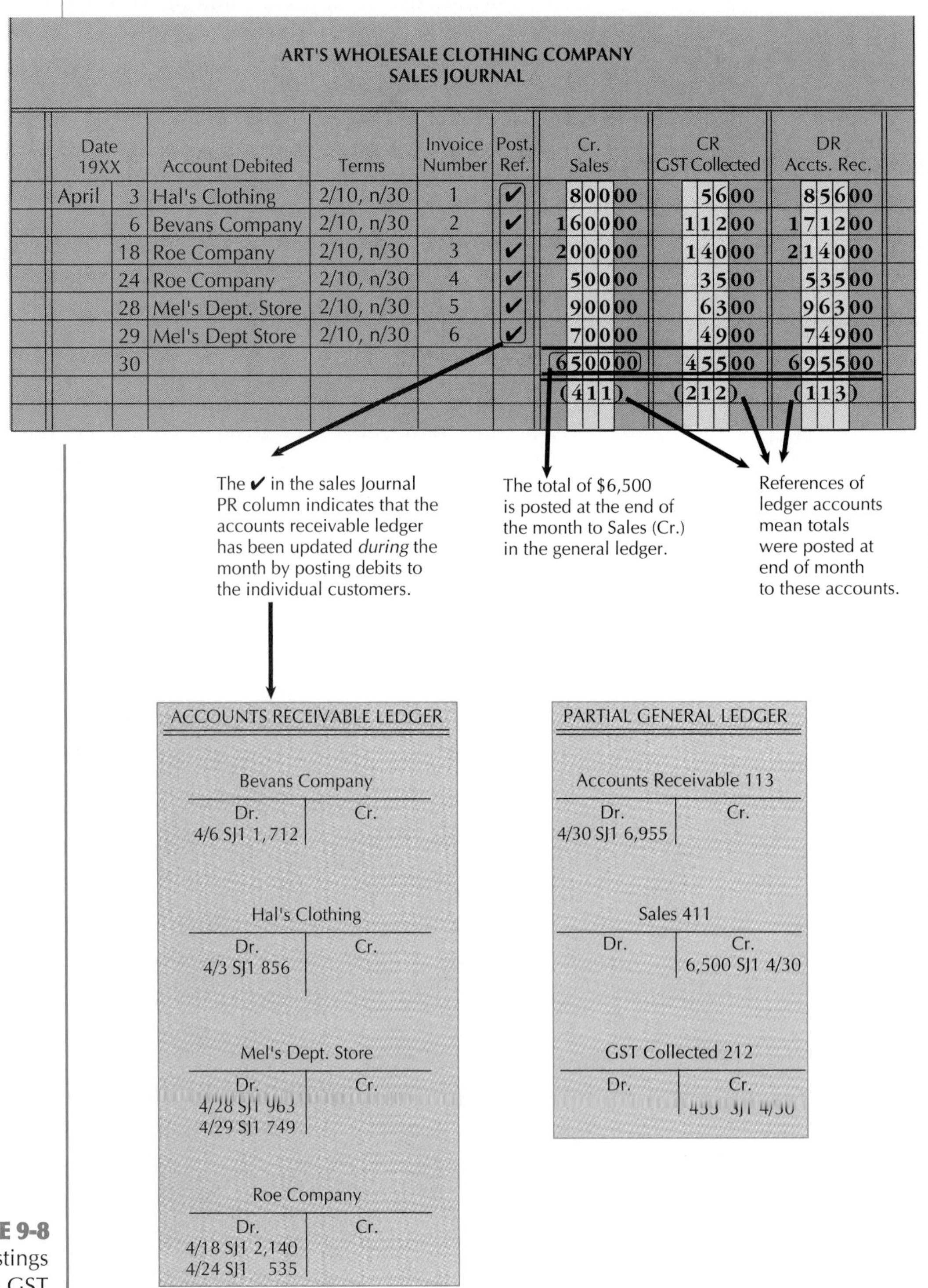

ART'S WHOLESALE CLOTHING COMPANY
SALES JOURNAL

Date 19XX		Account Debited	Terms	Invoice Number	Post. Ref.	Cr. Sales	CR GST Collected	DR Accts. Rec.
April	3	Hal's Clothing	2/10, n/30	1	✔	800 00	56 00	856 00
	6	Bevans Company	2/10, n/30	2	✔	1600 00	112 00	1712 00
	18	Roe Company	2/10, n/30	3	✔	2000 00	140 00	2140 00
	24	Roe Company	2/10, n/30	4	✔	500 00	35 00	535 00
	28	Mel's Dept. Store	2/10, n/30	5	✔	900 00	63 00	963 00
	29	Mel's Dept Store	2/10, n/30	6	✔	700 00	49 00	749 00
	30					6500 00	455 00	6955 00
						(411)	(212)	(113)

FIGURE 9-8
Sales Journal and Postings with GST

The total invoice amounts are posted during the month to the individual customers' accounts in the accounts receivable ledger. This process is identical to the pre-GST method except that the totals are 7 percent higher.

At the end of the month instead of posting a single amount as *both* a credit (to Sales) and a debit (to Accounts Receivable), there are three totals to post. A new account is now required—GST collected—#212. This is a liability account in the general ledger with a credit balance. Notice that the totals of the two credits (Sales and GST) equal the single debit (Accounts Receivable).

GST AND THE CREDIT MEMORANDUM

The credit memorandum with GST is very similar to an invoice with GST except that the amounts are opposite in meaning and effect, and often smaller.

As you already know, occasionally a business finds it necessary to issue to a customer a credit memorandum (often called a credit note). The pre-GST form of a credit memorandum is shown in Figure 9-5. The new form of credit memorandum is shown in Figure 9-9.

As before, we will assume that the volume of credit notes is low and that Art's Wholesale uses the general journal to record these. The journal entry will appear as shown in Figure 9-10.

Art's Wholesale
Clothing Co.
1528 Belle Ave.
Toronto, ON M5A 2L4

Credit
Memorandum No. 1
Date: April 12

Credit to: Bevans Company
110 Aster Rd.
Amherst, NS B4H 3A5

We credit your account as follows:

Merchandise returned 60 model 8B men's dress gloves—	$600.00
Plus GST	42.00
Total Credit	$642.00

GST reg. no. 109309799

FIGURE 9-9
Credit Memorandum with GST

ART'S WHOLESALE CLOTHING CO.
GENERAL JOURNAL

Page 1

Date		Account Titles and Descriptions	PR	Debit	Credit
19XX April	12	GST Collected	212	42 00	
		Sales Returns and Allowances	412	600 00	
		Accounts Receivable, Bevans Co.	113/✓		642 00

212 A debit of $42 is recorded in the GST Collected account 212 in the general ledger. When this is done, the account number is placed in the PR column of the journal.

412 A debit of $600 is recorded in Sales Returns and Allowances, account no. 412 in the general ledger. When this is done, the account number is placed in the PR column of the journal.

113 The credit of $642 is also posted to Accounts Receivable in the controlling account in the general ledger. When this is done, the account number (113) is placed in the PR column of the journal, above the /.

✓ The check indicates that $642 has been posted as a credit to the account of Bevans Company in the accounts receivable ledger.

FIGURE 9-10
Postings for the Credit Memorandum with GST

Remember that the $42 debit posting will reduce the amount of GST owing to the federal government and must be taken into account when preparing a cheque for the amount owing at period-end. The customer, Bevans Company, now receives a credit totalling $642. This includes the extra 7 percent for GST. Since the original invoice included this 7 percent tax as an addition, it is proper that any refund for returned or damaged goods also include the 7 percent tax. The amount owing to Art's Clothing by Bevans Company is reduced by $642.

PROVINCIAL SALES TAX WITH GST

When a sale is made to a customer at the retail level, provincial sales tax is often added to the invoice (there are exceptions which vary somewhat from province to province). Since January 1, 1991, it is also necessary to add GST to these invoices. A typical invoice in a province with a 9 percent provincial sales tax might look like the following:

Munroe Menswear Company
147 Main Street
Saskatoon, Saskatchewan
S8A 2G7

To: Jones Company
228 Market Street
Saskatoon, Saskatchewan
S8J 2P2

Invoice # 1420
June 01, 19XX

10 Company Blazers with logo @ $150.00 each		$1,500.00
	PST @ 9%	135.00
		1,635.00
	GST @ 7%	105.00
	Total	$1,740.00

GST reg.no. 142716491

FIGURE 9-11
Sales Invoice with PST and GST

SALES INVOICE WITH PST AND GST

The Munroe Menswear Company would record this invoice along with other invoices for June, 19XX, in their sales journal. This recording and posting process is illustrated in Figure 9-12. Note that, apart from the addition of one more column (for the GST), this is similar to the illustration shown in Figure 9-8.

Be aware that in some provinces, the PST is added after the GST. Although the math is changed a bit, the rest of the process remains as shown in Figure 9-12.

Also worthy of repetition is the point that if sales discounts are available, they are usually taken on the *sales amount only*, not the GST or PST. If Jones Co. receives a 2 percent discount on invoice no. 1420 (see Figure 9-11), they would pay the following amount:

No sales discount is taken on GST or PST amounts because the monies are collected on behalf of the government.

Original sales amount of invoice no. 1420	$1,500
Less: 2% Discount	30
	1,470
Plus: PST as originally computed	135
Plus: GST as originally computed	105
Amount paid	$1,710

New tax harmonization regulation agreed to by the Atlantic Provinces will simplify this recording process. A single tax of 15 percent will replace both the GST and PST in these four provinces.

FIGURE 9-12
Munroe's Sales Journal with GST

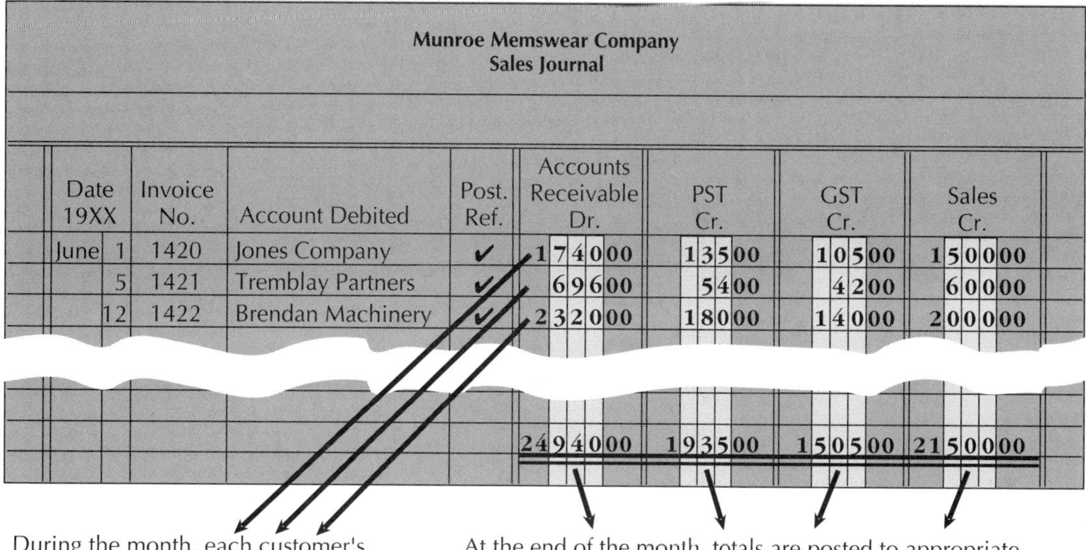

Munroe Memswear Company
Sales Journal

Date 19XX		Invoice No.	Account Debited	Post. Ref.	Accounts Receivable Dr.	PST Cr.	GST Cr.	Sales Cr.
June	1	1420	Jones Company	✓	1 740 00	135 00	105 00	1 500 00
	5	1421	Tremblay Partners	✓	696 00	54 00	42 00	600 00
	12	1422	Brendan Machinery	✓	2 320 00	180 00	140 00	2 000 00
					24 940 00	1 935 00	1 505 00	21 500 00

During the month, each customer's account in the accounts receivable ledger is posted to update the amount they owe. Note that these figures include the PST and GST.

At the end of the month, totals are posted to appropriate accounts in the general ledger. Note that Dr. total to Accounts Receivable ($24,940) equals 3 Cr. postings to PST, GST and Sales ($1935 + 1505 + 21,500 = $24,940).

Credit Memorandum with PST and GST

Let us assume that Jones Co. receives permission to return part of the goods billed on invoice no.1420 (Figure 9-11). This results in a credit memo (or credit note) being prepared by Munroe Menswear Company. This credit memo would appear as shown in Figure 9-13.

This credit memo would be recorded by Munroe Company in their general journal (unless there was a large number of returns, in which case a special journal could be used). The entry to record credit note no. 104 is as shown in Figure 9-14.

This entry is posted in a similar fashion to the entry in Figure 9-10. The only change is that there is also a posting of a debit to PST payable (account number 210) as well as to GST collected (account number 212).

The credit memorandum with PST and GST is very similar to an invoice with PST and GST except that the amounts are opposite in meaning and effect, and often smaller.

Munroe Menswear Company
147 Main Street
Saskatoon, Saskatchewan
S8A 2G7

To: Jones Company
228 Market Street
Saskatoon, Saskatchewan
S8J 2P2

Credit Memo # 104
July 15, 19XX

Returned 2 Blazers—Ref. Invoice 1420, June 1, 19XX @ $150.00 each

	$300.00
PST @ 9%	27.00
	327.00
GST @ 7%	21.00
Total	$348.00

GST reg.no. 142716491

FIGURE 9-13
Credit Memo with PST and GST

FIGURE 9-14
Recording Credit Memo with PST and GST

MUNROE MENSWEAR COMPANY
GENERAL JOURNAL

Page 1

Date		Account Titles and Descriptions	PR	Debit	Credit
19XX July	15	Sales Returns and Allowances	412	300 00	
		GST Collected	212	21 00	
		PST Payable	410	27 00	
		Accounts Receivable, Jones Co.	113/✔		348 00
		To record credit memo number 104			

LEARNING UNIT 9-4 REVIEW

AT THE POINT you should be able to

1. Explain the basics of GST added to sales invoices in Canada. (p. 341)
2. Explain, journalize, and post an invoice which includes both GST and PST. (pp. 344-345)
3. Explain, journalize, and post a credit memorandum which includes both GST and PST. (pp. 345-346)

SELF-REVIEW QUIZ 9-4

Journalize the following transactions into the sales journal or the general journal for Moss Company. Post to the accounts receivable and general ledger accounts as appropriate. Use the same journal headings and general ledger account numbers that were used in Figures 9-12 and 9-14.

19XX

May 1 Sold merchandise to Jane Company, invoice no. 101—$400 plus PST $36 plus GST $28—total $464.00. Terms 2/10, n/30.

5 Sold merchandise to Ralph Company, invoice no. 102—$3000 plus PST $270 plus GST $210—total $3,480.00. Terms 2/10, n/30.

21 Issued credit memorandum to Ralph Company, CM #4—$500 plus PST $45 plus GST $35—total $580.00. Reason—defective goods.

Solution to Self-Review Quiz 9-4

MOSS COMPANY
SALES JOURNAL

Page 1

Date 19XX		Account Debited	Invoice Number	Post. Ref.	Dr. Accts. Rec.	Cr. PST	Cr. GST Collected	Cr. Sales
May	1	Jane Company	101	✔	464 00	36 00	28 00	400 00
	5	Ralph Company	102	✔	3480 00	270 00	210 00	3000 00
					3944 00	306 00	238 00	3400 00

MOSS COMPANY GENERAL JOURNAL					
Date		Account Titles and Descriptions	PR	Debit	Credit
19XX May	21	Sales Returns and Allowances	412	500 00	
		GST Collected	212	35 00	
		PST Payable	210	45 00	
		Accounts Receivable, Ralph Co.	112/✔		580 00
		To record credit memo no. 4			

LEARNING UNIT 9-5

Cash Receipts Journal and Schedule of Accounts Receivable

Besides the sales journal, another special journal often used in a merchandising operation is the cash receipts journal. The **cash receipts journal** records the receipt of cash (or cheques) from any source. The number of columns a cash receipts journal will have depends on how frequently certain types of transactions occur. For example, in the cash receipts journal for Art's Wholesale the accountant has developed the headings shown in Figure 9-15. Note that a column for GST (on cash sales only) has been included. GST on credit sales is recorded in the sales journal as already described. Below each heading is a description of the purpose of each column and when to update the accounts receivable ledger as well as general ledger.

FIGURE 9-15 Cash Receipts Journal with GST

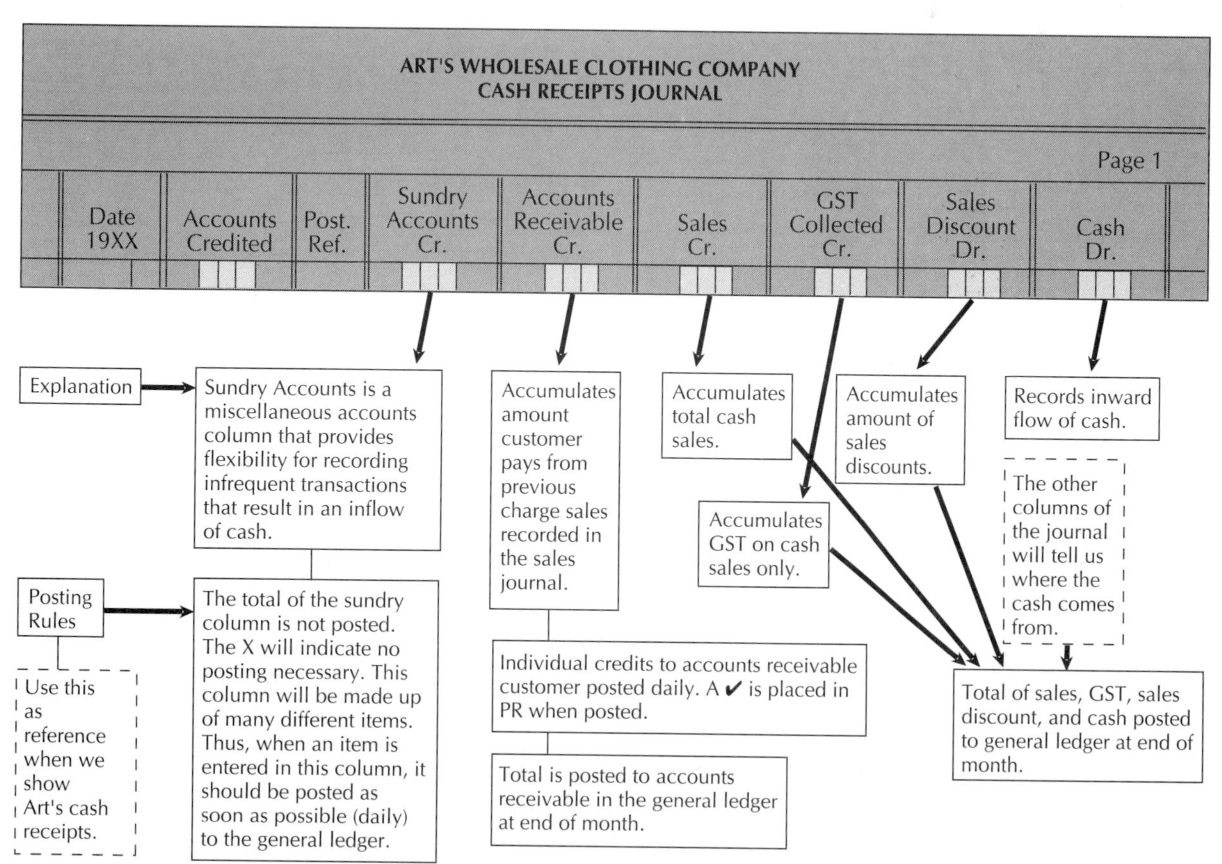

The following transactions occurred in April for Art's Wholesale and affected the cash receipts journal:

19XX

April	1	Art Newner invested $8,000 in the business.
	4	Received cheque from Hal's Clothing for payment of invoice no. 1 less discount.
	15	Cash sales for first half of April, $900 plus GST.
	16	Received cheque from Bevans Company in settlement of invoice no. 2 less returns and discount.
	22	Received cheque from Roe Company for payment of invoice no. 3 less discount.
	27	Sold store equipment, $500.
	30	Cash sales for second half of April, $1,200 plus GST.

The diagram in Figure 9-16 shows the cash receipts journal for the end of April along with the recordings to the accounts receivable ledger and posting to the general ledger. Study the diagram; we will review it in a moment.

JOURNALIZING, RECORDING, AND POSTING FROM THE CASH RECEIPTS JOURNAL

On April 4 Art's Wholesale received a cheque from Hal's Clothing for payment of invoice no. 1 less discount. Remember, it was in the sales journal that this transaction was first recorded (Figure 9-8). At that time we updated the accounts receivable ledger, indicating that Hal's Clothing owed Art $856. Since Hal's Clothing is paying within the 10-day discount period, Art's Wholesale offers a $16 sales discount ($800 × 0.02). (Remember, all credit sales carried terms of 2/10, n/30.)

Now, when payment is received, Art's Wholesale updates the cash receipts journal (see p. 349) by entering the date (April 4), cash debit of $840, sales discount debit of $16, credit to accounts receivable of $856, and which account name (Hal's Clothing) is to be credited. The terms of sale indicate that Hal's Clothing is entitled to the discount and no longer owes Art's Wholesale the $856 balance. *As soon as this line is entered into the cash receipts journal, Art's Wholesale will update the ledger account of Hal's Clothing.* Note in the accounts receivable ledger of Hal's Clothing how the date (April 4), posting reference (CRJ1), and credit amount ($856) are recorded. The balance in the accounts receivable ledger is zero. The last step of this transaction is to go back to the cash receipts journal and put a √ in the posting reference column.

The last step is to put a checkmark in the PR of the cash receipts journal to show the accounts receivable ledger is up to date.

In studying this cash receipts journal, note that:

1. All totals of cash receipts journal *except* sundry were posted to the general ledger at the end of the month.
2. Art Newner, Capital, and Store Equipment were posted to the general ledger when entered in the sundry column. It is assumed that the equipment account had a beginning balance of $4,000 in the general ledger. There is no GST on the owner's capital contribution.
3. The cash sales were not posted when entered (thus the X to show no posting is needed). The sales and cash totals are posted at the end of the month.
4. A √ means information was recorded daily to the accounts receivable ledger.
5. The Accounts Credited column describes each transaction.

We can prove the accuracy of recording transactions of the cash receipts journal by totalling the columns with debit balances and the columns with credit balances. This process, called **crossfooting**, is done before the totals are posted. Also, if a bookkeeper were using more than one page for the cash receipts journal, the balances on the bottom of one page would be brought forward to the top of the next page. This verifying of totals would result in less work when trying to find journalizing or posting errors at a later date. Let's see how to crossfoot the cash receipts journal of Art's Wholesale (Figure 9-16).

Proving the cash receipts journal.

Debit Columns	=	**Credit Columns**
Cash + Sales Discount	=	**Accounts Receivable + Sales + Sundry + GST**
$14,772 + $76	=	**$4,066 + $2,100 + $8,500 + $182**
$14,848	=	**$14,848**

Now let's take a moment to see what PST would look like in the cash receipts journal of a business that would need to record sales tax as well as GST. A typical cash receipts journal might look as follows:

CASH RECEIPTS JOURNAL

Page 1

Date 19XX	Accounts Credited	PR	Sales Tax Payable Cr.	Sundry Cr.	GST Cr.	Sales Cr.	Accounts Receivable Cr.	Sales Discount Dr.	Cash Dr.

The total of sales tax payable would be posted to Sales Tax Payable in the general ledger at the end of the month.

The total of the sales tax as a result of cash sales would be posted to Sales Tax Payable in the general ledger at the end of the month. It represents a liability of the merchant to forward the tax to the provincial government. Remember, no cash discounts are taken on the sales tax (or GST).

Now let's prove the accounts receivable ledger to the controlling account—Accounts Receivable—at the end of April for Art's Wholesale Clothing Company.

FIGURE 9-16 Cash Receipts Journal and Posting with GST

CASH RECEIPTS JOURNAL

Page 1

Date 19XX		Accounts Credited	PR	Sundry Accounts Cr.	Accounts Receivable Cr.	Sales Cr.	GST Collected Cr.	Sales Discount Dr.	Cash Dr.
April	1	Art Newner, Capital	311	8 000 00					8 000 00
	4	Hal's Clothing	✔		856 00			16 00	840 00
	15	Cash Sales	✗			900 00	63 00		963 00
	16	Bevans Company	✔		1 070 00			20 00	1 050 00
	22	Roe Company	✔		2 140 00			40 00	2 100 00
	27	Store Equipment	121	500 00			35 00		535 00
	30	Cash Sales	✗			1 200 00	84 00		1 284 00
	30			8 500 00	4 066 00	2 100 00	182 00	76 00	14 772 00
				(X)	(113)	(411)	(212)	(413)	(111)

Total not posted. Totals posted to general ledger at end of month.

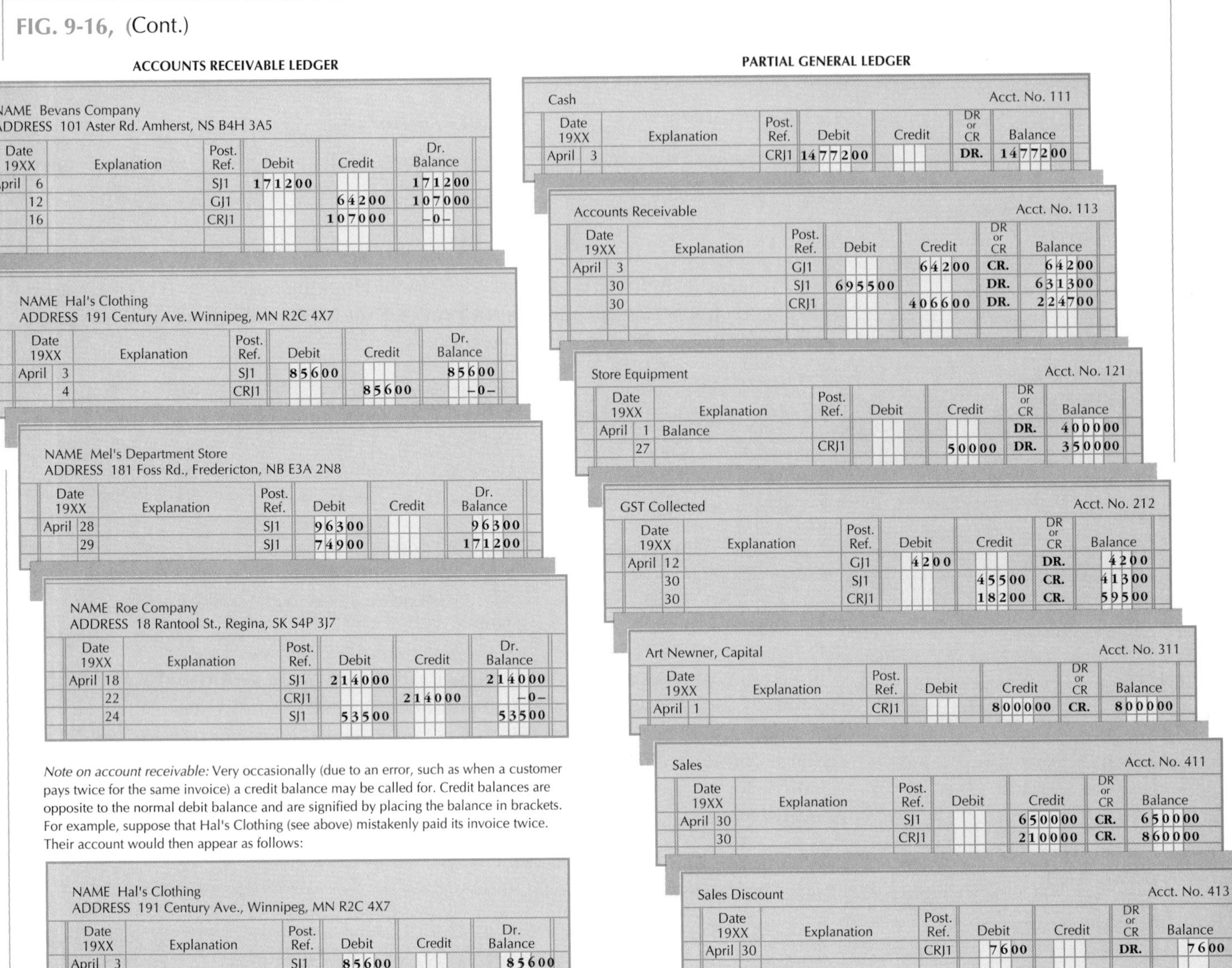

FIG. 9-16, (Cont.)

ACCOUNTS RECEIVABLE LEDGER

NAME Bevans Company
ADDRESS 101 Aster Rd. Amherst, NS B4H 3A5

Date 19XX		Explanation	Post. Ref.	Debit	Credit	Dr. Balance
April	6		SJ1	1712 00		1712 00
	12		GJ1		642 00	1070 00
	16		CRJ1		1070 00	–0–

NAME Hal's Clothing
ADDRESS 191 Century Ave. Winnipeg, MN R2C 4X7

Date 19XX		Explanation	Post. Ref.	Debit	Credit	Dr. Balance
April	3		SJ1	856 00		856 00
	4		CRJ1		856 00	–0–

NAME Mel's Department Store
ADDRESS 181 Foss Rd., Fredericton, NB E3A 2N8

Date 19XX		Explanation	Post. Ref.	Debit	Credit	Dr. Balance
April	28		SJ1	963 00		963 00
	29		SJ1	749 00		1712 00

NAME Roe Company
ADDRESS 18 Rantool St., Regina, SK S4P 3J7

Date 19XX		Explanation	Post. Ref.	Debit	Credit	Dr. Balance
April	18		SJ1	2140 00		2140 00
	22		CRJ1		2140 00	–0–
	24		SJ1	535 00		535 00

Note on account receivable: Very occasionally (due to an error, such as when a customer pays twice for the same invoice) a credit balance may be called for. Credit balances are opposite to the normal debit balance and are signified by placing the balance in brackets. For example, suppose that Hal's Clothing (see above) mistakenly paid its invoice twice. Their account would then appear as follows:

NAME Hal's Clothing
ADDRESS 191 Century Ave., Winnipeg, MN R2C 4X7

Date 19XX		Explanation	Post. Ref.	Debit	Credit	Dr. Balance
April	3		SJ1	856 00		856 00
	4		CRJ1		856 00	–0–
	10		CRJ1		856 00	(856 00)

PARTIAL GENERAL LEDGER

Cash — Acct. No. 111

Date 19XX		Explanation	Post. Ref.	Debit	Credit	DR or CR	Balance
April	3		CRJ1	14772 00		DR.	14772 00

Accounts Receivable — Acct. No. 113

Date 19XX		Explanation	Post. Ref.	Debit	Credit	DR or CR	Balance
April	3		GJ1		642 00	CR.	642 00
	30		SJ1	6955 00		DR.	6313 00
	30		CRJ1		4066 00	DR.	2247 00

Store Equipment — Acct. No. 121

Date 19XX		Explanation	Post. Ref.	Debit	Credit	DR or CR	Balance
April	1	Balance				DR.	4000 00
	27		CRJ1		500 00	DR.	3500 00

GST Collected — Acct. No. 212

Date 19XX		Explanation	Post. Ref.	Debit	Credit	DR or CR	Balance
April	12		GJ1	42 00		DR.	42 00
	30		SJ1		455 00	CR.	413 00
	30		CRJ1		182 00	CR.	595 00

Art Newner, Capital — Acct. No. 311

Date 19XX		Explanation	Post. Ref.	Debit	Credit	DR or CR	Balance
April	1		CRJ1		8000 00	CR.	8000 00

Sales — Acct. No. 411

Date 19XX		Explanation	Post. Ref.	Debit	Credit	DR or CR	Balance
April	30		SJ1		6500 00	CR.	6500 00
	30		CRJ1		2100 00	CR.	8600 00

Sales Discount — Acct. No. 413

Date 19XX		Explanation	Post. Ref.	Debit	Credit	DR or CR	Balance
April	30		CRJ1	76 00		DR.	76 00

SCHEDULE OF ACCOUNTS RECEIVABLE

Schedule is listed in alphabetical order.

From Figure 9-16 let's list the customers that have an ending balance in the accounts receivable ledger of Art's Wholesale. This listing is called a **schedule of accounts receivable**. The balance of the controlling account, Accounts Receivable ($2,247), in the general ledger (p. 335) does indeed equal the sum of the individual customer balances in the accounts receivable ledger ($2,247). The schedule of accounts receivable can help forecast potential cash inflows as well as possible credit and collection decisions.

Art's Wholesale Clothing Company
Schedule of Accounts Receivable
April 30, 19XX

Mel's Dept. Store	$1,712.00
Roe Company	535.00
Total Accounts Receivable	$2,247.00

LEARNING UNIT 9-5 REVIEW

AT THIS POINT you should be able to

1. Journalize, record, and post transactions with or without sales tax using a cash receipts journal. (pp. 349–350)
2. Prepare a schedule of accounts receivable. (p. 350)

SELF-REVIEW QUIZ 9-5

Journalize, crossfoot, record, and post when appropriate the following transactions into the cash receipts journal of Moore Co. Use the same headings as for Art's Wholesale.

Accounts Receivable Ledger

Name	*Balance*	*Invoice No.*
Irene Welch	$535	1
Chantel Simard	214	2

Partial General Ledger

Account	*Acct. No.*	*Balance*
Cash	110	$600
Accounts Receivable	120	749
Store Equipment	130	600
GST Collected	212	49
Sales	410	700
Sales Discount	420	—

19XX

May 1 Received cheque from Irene Welch for invoice no. 1 less 2 percent discount.

8 Cash sales collected, $400 plus GST of $28.

15 Received cheque from Chantel Simard for invoice no. 2 less 2 percent discount.

19 Sold store equipment at cost, $300 (assume no GST).

Solution to Self-Review Quiz 9-5

MOORE COMPANY
CASH RECEIPTS JOURNAL

Page 1

Date 19XX		Accounts Credited	PR	Sundry Accounts Cr.	Accounts Receivable Cr.	Sales Cr.	GST Collected Cr.	Sales Discount Dr.	Cash Dr.
April	1	Irene Welch	✔		53500			1000	52500
	8	Cash Sales	✗			40000	2800		42800
	15	Chantel Simard	✔		21400			400	21000
	19	Store Equipment	130	30000					30000
	31			30000	74900	40000	2800	1400	146300
				(X)	(120)	(410)	(212)	(420)	(110)

Crossfooting: $1,477.00 = $1,477.00

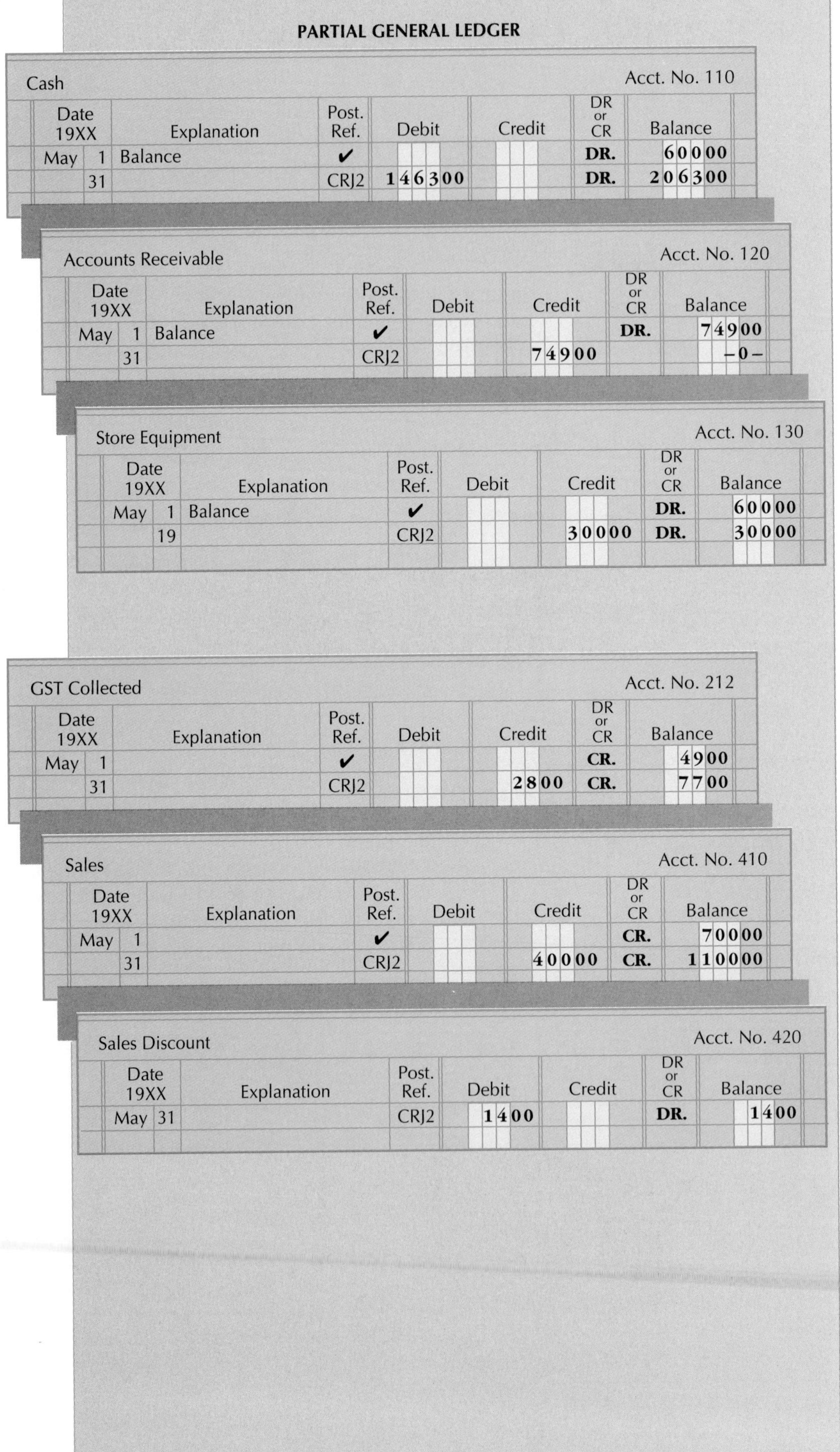

PARTIAL GENERAL LEDGER

Cash — Acct. No. 110

Date 19XX		Explanation	Post. Ref.	Debit	Credit	DR or CR	Balance
May	1	Balance	✔			DR.	600 00
	31		CRJ2	1463 00		DR.	2063 00

Accounts Receivable — Acct. No. 120

Date 19XX		Explanation	Post. Ref.	Debit	Credit	DR or CR	Balance
May	1	Balance	✔			DR.	749 00
	31		CRJ2		749 00		–0–

Store Equipment — Acct. No. 130

Date 19XX		Explanation	Post. Ref.	Debit	Credit	DR or CR	Balance
May	1	Balance	✔			DR.	600 00
	19		CRJ2		300 00	DR.	300 00

GST Collected — Acct. No. 212

Date 19XX		Explanation	Post. Ref.	Debit	Credit	DR or CR	Balance
May	1		✔			CR.	49 00
	31		CRJ2		28 00	CR.	77 00

Sales — Acct. No. 410

Date 19XX		Explanation	Post. Ref.	Debit	Credit	DR or CR	Balance
May	1		✔			CR.	700 00
	31		CRJ2		400 00	CR.	1100 00

Sales Discount — Acct. No. 420

Date 19XX		Explanation	Post. Ref.	Debit	Credit	DR or CR	Balance
May	31		CRJ2	14 00		DR.	14 00

ACCOUNTS RECEIVABLE LEDGER

NAME Irene Welch
ADDRESS 10 Rong Rd., Timmins, ON P4N 4M3

Date 19XX		Explanation	Post. Ref.	Debit	Credit	Dr. Balance
May	1	Balance	✔			535 00
	1		CRJ2		535 00	–0–

NAME Chantel Simard
ADDRESS 9017 Robitaille Rd., Montreal PQ H1K 4R3

Date 19XX		Explanation	Post. Ref.	Debit	Credit	Dr. Balance
May	1	Balance	✔			214 00
	15		CRJ2		214 00	–0–

Chapter Review

Comprehensive Demonstration Problem with Solution Tips

(The forms you need are on pages 9-8 to 9-10 of the *Study Guide and Working Papers.*)

a. Journalize, record, and post as needed, the following transactions to the sales, cash receipts, and general journal. All terms are 2/10, n/30.

b. Prepare a schedule of accounts receivable.

Ignore GST and PST.

Solution Tips to Journalizing

	19XX		
CRJ	July	1	Walter Lantz invested $2,000 into the business.
SJ		1	Sold merchandise on account to Panda Co., invoice no. 1—$300.
SJ		2	Sold merchandise on account to Buzzard Co., invoice no. 2—$600.
CRJ		3	Cash sale—$400.
GJ		9	Issued credit memorandum no. 1 to Panda Co. for defective merchandise—$100.
CRJ		10	Received cheque from Panda Co. for invoice no. 1 less returns and discount.
CRJ		16	Cash sale—$500.
SJ		19	Sold merchandise on account to Panda Co.—$550, invoice no. 3.

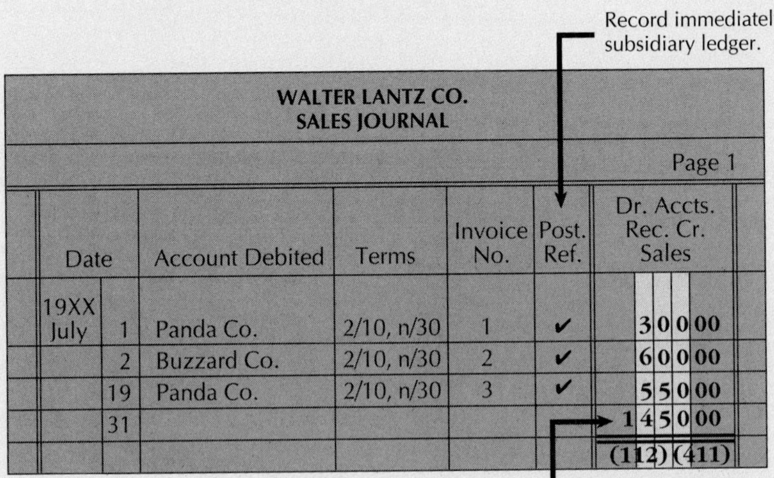
Record immediately to subsidiary ledger.
Total posted at end of month to general ledger accounts.

WALTER LANTZ CO.
SALES JOURNAL

Page 1

Date		Account Debited	Terms	Invoice No.	Post. Ref.	Dr. Accts. Rec. Cr. Sales
19XX July	1	Panda Co.	2/10, n/30	1	✔	300 00
	2	Buzzard Co.	2/10, n/30	2	✔	600 00
	19	Panda Co.	2/10, n/30	3	✔	550 00
	31					1 450 00
						(112) (411)

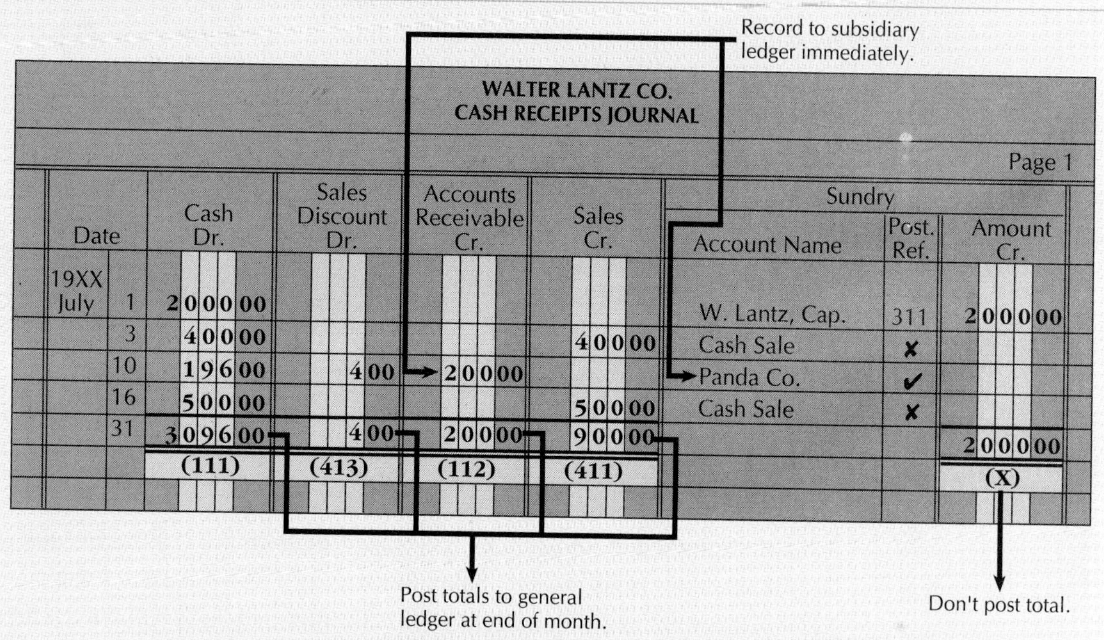

WALTER LANTZ CO.
CASH RECEIPTS JOURNAL

Page 1

Date		Cash Dr.	Sales Discount Dr.	Accounts Receivable Cr.	Sales Cr.	Sundry Account Name	Post. Ref.	Amount Cr.
19XX July	1	2000 00				W. Lantz, Cap.	311	2000 00
	3	400 00			400 00	Cash Sale	✗	
	10	196 00	4 00	200 00		Panda Co.	✓	
	16	500 00			500 00	Cash Sale	✗	
	31	3096 00	4 00	200 00	900 00			2000 00
		(111)	(413)	(112)	(411)			(X)

Record to subsidiary ledger immediately.
Post totals to general ledger at end of month.
Don't post total.

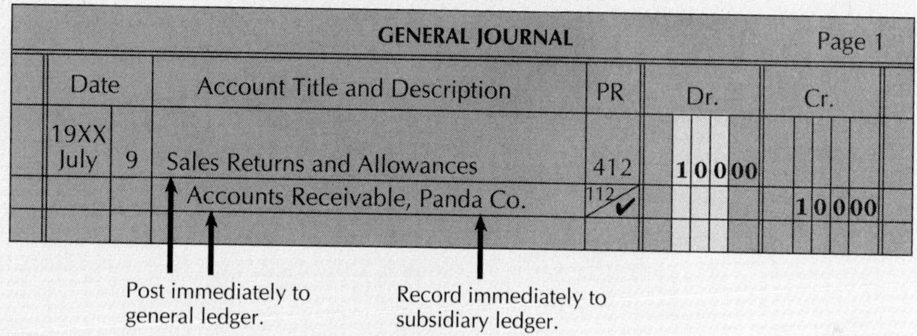

GENERAL JOURNAL

Page 1

Date		Account Title and Description	PR	Dr.	Cr.
19XX July	9	Sales Returns and Allowances	412	100 00	
		Accounts Receivable, Panda Co.	112/✓		100 00

Post immediately to general ledger.
Record immediately to subsidiary ledger.

Accounts receivable subsidiary ledger is usually a debit balance.

Accounts Receivable Subsidiary Ledger

Buzzard Co.

Date		PR	Debit	Credit	Dr. Balance
19XX July	2	SJ1	600 00		600 00

Panda Co.

Date		PR	Debit	Credit	Dr. Balance
19XX July	1	SJ1	300 00		300 00
	9	GJ1		100 00	200 00
	10	CRJ1		200 00	
	19	SJ1	550 00		550 00

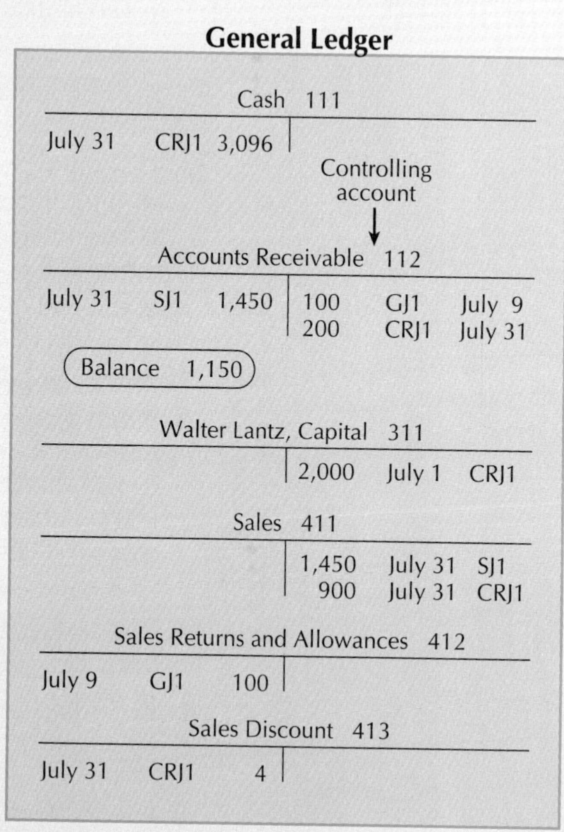

General Ledger

Cash 111

Dr.	Cr.
July 31 CRJ1 3,096	

Controlling account

Accounts Receivable 112

Dr.	Cr.
July 31 SJ1 1,450	100 GJ1 July 9
	200 CRJ1 July 31

Balance 1,150

Walter Lantz, Capital 311

Dr.	Cr.
	2,000 July 1 CRJ1

Sales 411

Dr.	Cr.
	1,450 July 31 SJ1
	900 July 31 CRJ1

Sales Returns and Allowances 412

Dr.	Cr.
July 9 GJ1 100	

Sales Discount 413

Dr.	Cr.
July 31 CRJ1 4	

The controlling account at end of the month equals the sum of the accounts receivable subsidiary ledger.

LANTZ CO. SCHEDULE OF ACCOUNTS RECEIVABLE JULY 31, 19XX	
Buzzard Co.	$ 600 00
Panda Co.	550 00
Total Accounts Receivable	$1150 00

Summary of Key Points

Learning Unit 9-1

1. Sales Returns and Allowances and Sales Discount are contra-revenue accounts.
2. Net Sales = Gross Sales − Sales Returns and Allowances − Sales Discounts.
3. Discounts are not taken on sales tax, freight, or goods returned. The discount period is shorter than the credit period.

Learning Unit 9-2

1. A general journal is still used with special journals.
2. A sales journal records sales on account.
3. The accounts receivable subsidiary ledger, organized in alphabetical order, is not in the same book as Accounts Receivable, the controlling account in the general ledger.
4. At the end of the month the total of all customers' ending balances in the accounts receivable subsidiary ledger should be equal to the ending balance in Accounts Receivable, the controlling account in the general ledger.

Learning Unit 9-3

1. The √ in the posting-reference column of the sales journal means a customer's account in the accounts receivable ledger (or the accounts receivable subsidiary ledger) (on the debit side) has been updated (or recorded) during the month.
2. At the end of the month the totals of the sales journal are posted to general ledger accounts.
3. Provincial Sales Tax Payable is a liability found in the general ledger.
4. When a credit memorandum is issued, the result is that Sales Returns and Allowances is increasing, and Accounts Receivable is decreasing. When we record this in a general journal we assume that all parts of the transaction will be posted to the general ledger and recorded in the subsidiary ledger when the entry is journalized.

Learning Unit 9-4

1. Recording GST in the sales journal requires the addition of one new column. Other procedures are not changed.

2. Often both PST and GST will appear on the same invoice. Recording this in the sales journal requires the use of two extra columns but again the basic procedures are little changed.
3. When a sales discount is allowed, it is taken on the pre-PST and pre-GST amount only, not on the total invoice.
4. Recording a credit memorandum with PST and GST requires an extra line in the general journal for each. The credit to the customer's account includes the invoice amount plus PST and GST.

Learning Unit 9-5

1. The cash receipts journal records receipt of cash from any source.
2. The Sundry column records the credit part of a transaction that does not occur frequently. Never post the *total* of sundry. Post items in sundry column to the general ledger when entered.
3. A √ in the posting reference column of the cash receipts journal means that the accounts receivable ledger (or the accounts receivable subsidiary ledger) has been updated (recorded) with a credit.
4. An X in the cash receipts journal posting-reference column means no posting was necessary, since the totals of these columns will be posted at the end of the month.
5. Crossfooting means proving that the total of debits and the total of credits are equal in the special journal, thus verifying the accuracy of recording.
6. A schedule of accounts receivable is a listing of the ending balances of customers in the accounts receivable subsidiary ledger. This total should be the same balance as found in the controlling account, Accounts Receivable, in the general ledger.

Key terms

Accounts receivable subsidiary ledger A book or file that contains the individual records of amounts owed by various credit customers, usually in alphabetical order.

Cash receipts journal A special journal that records all transactions involving the receipt of cash from any source.

Controlling account—Accounts Receivable The Accounts Receivable account in the general ledger, after postings are complete, shows the total amount of money owed to a firm. This figure is broken down in the accounts receivable ledger, where it indicates specifically who owes the money.

Credit memorandum A piece of paper sent by the seller to a customer who has returned merchandise previously purchased on credit. The credit memorandum indicates to the customer that the seller is reducing the amount owed by the customer.

Credit period Length of time allowed for payment of goods sold on account.

Crossfooting The process of proving that the total debit columns of a special journal are equal to the total credit columns of a special journal.

Discount period Period that is shorter than credit period in which a customer can take a cash discount to encourage early payment of bills.

Goods and Services Tax (GST) A new "value added" tax introduced in Canada in 1991. It is added to most sales of goods and services. Currently calculated at 7 percent.

Gross sales The revenue earned from sale of merchandise to customers.

GST collected account The amount collected from customers and due to be sent to the federal government. It is a liability account with a credit balance. See also the next chapter for a fuller explanation of the net amount payable.

Harmonized tax A new 15 percent tax agreed to by the Atlantic Provinces. Will replace both the PST and GST.

Merchandise Goods brought into a store for resale to customers.

Net sales Gross sales less sales returns and allowances less sales discounts.

Provincial Sales Tax (PST) Payable account An account in the general ledger that accumulates the amount of provincial sales tax owed. It has a credit balance.

Retailers Buy goods from wholesalers or manufacturers for resale to customers.

Sales discount Contra-revenue account that records cash discounts granted to customers for payments made within a specific period of time.

Sales invoice A bill sent to customer(s) reflecting a sale, usually on credit.

Sales journal A special journal used to record only sales made on account. May have multiple colums if GST or PST is involved.

Sales Returns and Allowances Contra-revenue account that records price adjustments and allowances granted on merchandise that is defective and has been returned.

Schedule of accounts receivable A list of the customers, in alphabetical order, that have an outstanding balance in the accounts receivable subsidiary ledger. This total should be equal to the balance of the Accounts Receivable controlling account in the general ledger at the end of the month.

Special journal A journal used to record similar groups of transactions. *Example:* the sales journal, which records all sales on account.

Subsidiary ledger A ledger that contains accounts of a single type. *Example:* the accounts receivable subsidiary ledger, which records all customers that purchase goods on account.

Sundry Miscellaneous accounts column(s) in a special journal, which records part of transactions that do not occur too often.

Wholesalers Those who buy goods from suppliers and manufacturers for sale to retailers.

Blueprint of Sales and Cash Receipts Journals

Summary of How to Post and Record Single-Column Sales Journal

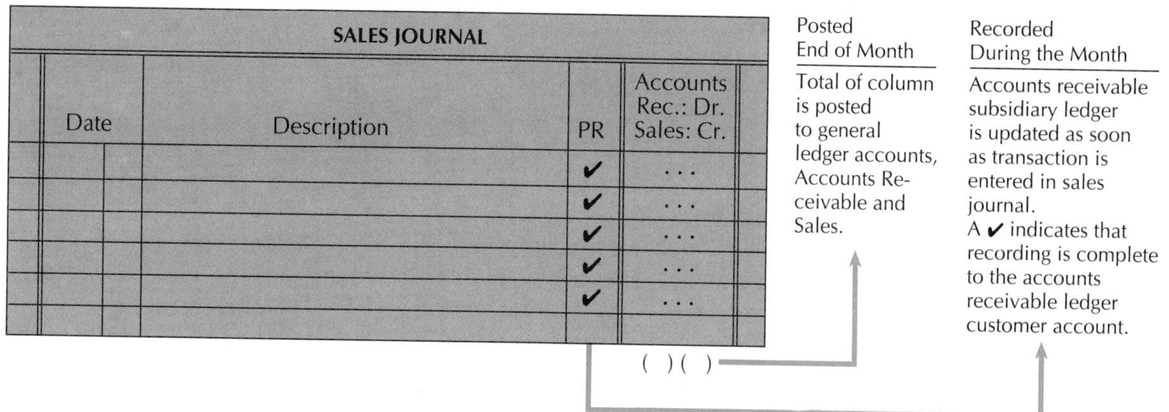

SALES JOURNAL
Date
Description
PR
Accounts Rec.: Dr. Sales: Cr.
( )( )
Posted End of Month
Total of column is posted to general ledger accounts, Accounts Receivable and Sales.
Recorded During the Month
Accounts receivable subsidiary ledger is updated as soon as transaction is entered in sales journal.
A ✔ indicates that recording is complete to the accounts receivable ledger customer account.

Multicolumn Sales Journal

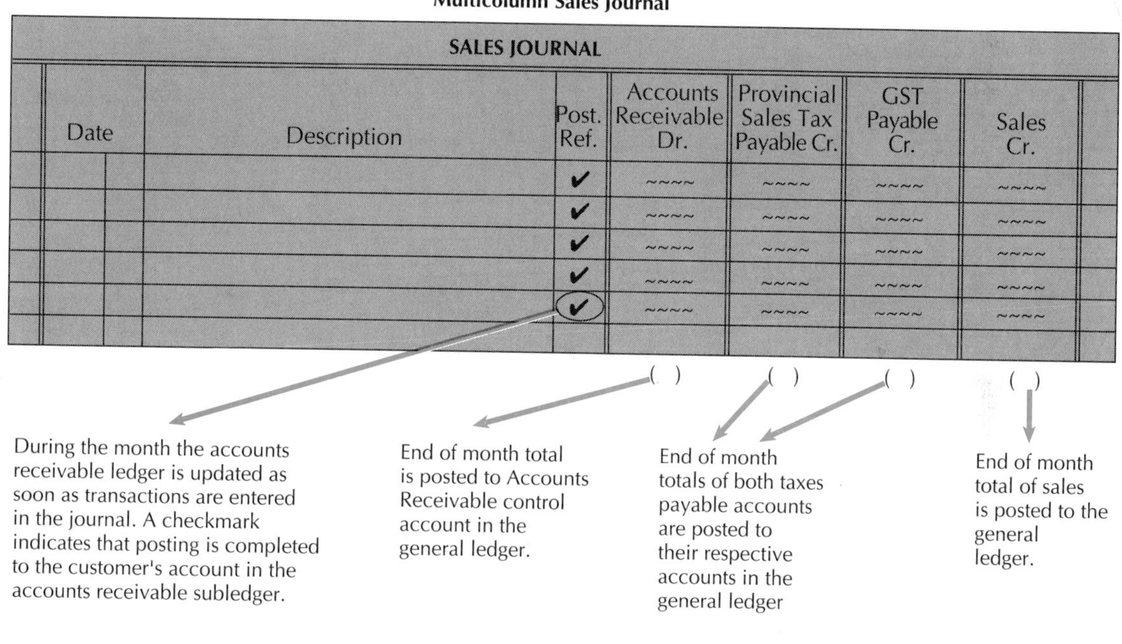

SALES JOURNAL
Date
Description
Post. Ref.
Accounts Receivable Dr.
Provincial Sales Tax Payable Cr.
GST Payable Cr.
Sales Cr.
During the month the accounts receivable ledger is updated as soon as transactions are entered in the journal. A checkmark indicates that posting is completed to the customer's account in the accounts receivable subledger.
End of month total is posted to Accounts Receivable control account in the general ledger.
End of month totals of both taxes payable accounts are posted to their respective accounts in the general ledger
End of month total of sales is posted to the general ledger.

Recording a Credit Memo Without Sales Tax or GST in a General Journal

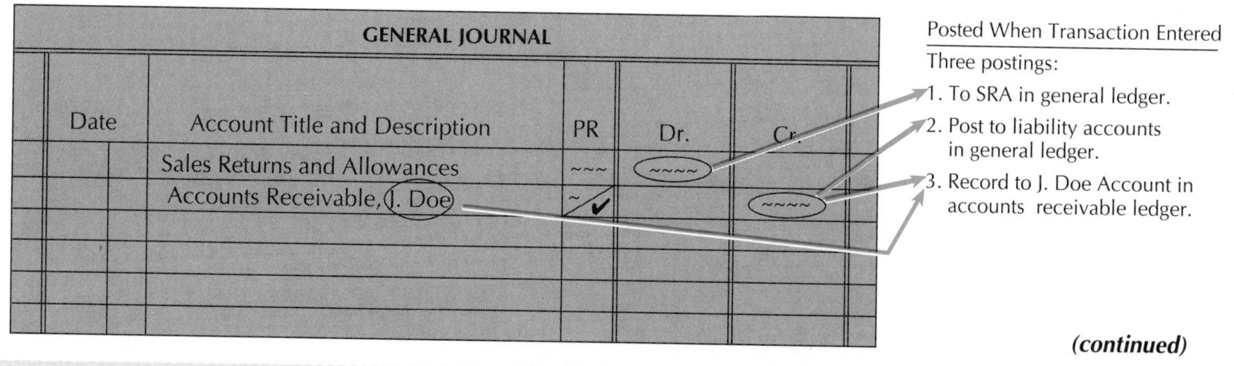

(continued)

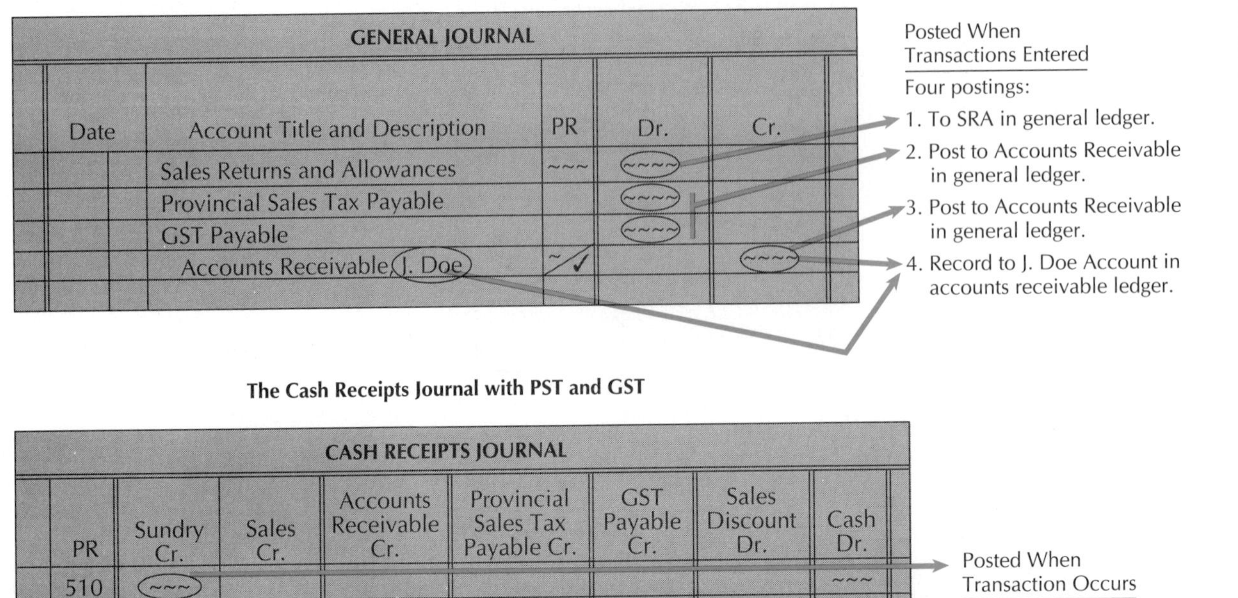

Recording a Credit Memo with Sales Tax and GST in a General Journal
GENERAL JOURNAL
Date
Account Title and Description
PR
Dr.
Cr.
Sales Returns and Allowances
Provincial Sales Tax Payable
GST Payable
Accounts Receivable J. Doe
Posted When Transactions Entered
Four postings:
1. To SRA in general ledger.
2. Post to Accounts Receivable in general ledger.
3. Post to Accounts Receivable in general ledger.
4. Record to J. Doe Account in accounts receivable ledger.
The Cash Receipts Journal with PST and GST
CASH RECEIPTS JOURNAL
PR
Sundry Cr.
Sales Cr.
Accounts Receivable Cr.
Provincial Sales Tax Payable Cr.
GST Payable Cr.
Sales Discount Dr.
Cash Dr.
510
(X)
( )
Posted When Transaction Occurs
Posted to general ledger account when transaction is entered. In this case it was account no. 510.
Posted During the Month
These individual amounts are posted during the month to the accounts receivable subledger. When they are posted, a checkmark is placed in the PR column of the cash receipts journal.
Posted at End of Month
These totals are posted to the general ledger accounts at the end of the month.
No posting needed during month, since totals of sales, GST, PST, and cash are posted at end of month.
Total of the Sundry column is never posted. The individual amounts making up the total are posted as the month progresses.

Questions, Exercises, and Problems

Discussion Questions

1. Explain the purpose of a contra-revenue account.
2. What is the normal balance of sales discount?
3. Give two examples of contra-revenue accounts.
4. What is the difference between a discount period and a credit period?
5. Explain the terms (a) 2/10, n/30; (b) n/10, EOM.
6. If special journals are used, what purpose will a general journal serve?
7. Compare and contrast the controlling account Accounts Receivable to the accounts receivable subsidiary ledger.
8. Why is the accounts receivable subsidiary ledger organized in alphabetical order?
9. When is a sales journal used?
10. What is an invoice? What purpose does it serve?

11. Why is provincial sales tax a liability to the business?
12. Sales discounts are taken on sales tax. Agree or disagree and tell why.
13. When a seller issues a credit memorandum (assume no provincial sales tax), what accounts will be affected?
14. Explain the function of a cash receipts journal.
15. When is the sundry column of the cash receipts journal posted?
16. Explain the purpose of a schedule of accounts receivable.

Mini Exercises

(The forms you need are on pages 9-12 and 9-13 of the *Study Guide and Working Papers.*)

Overview

1. Complete the following table for Sales, Sales Returns and Allowances, and Sales Discounts.

	Category	↑ ↓	Temporary or Permanent

Calculating Net Sales

2. Given the following, calculate net sales:

Gross sales	$20
Sales returns and allowances	2
Sales discounts	1
Beginning inventory	4

Sales Journal and General Journal

3. Match the following to the three journal entries (more than one number can be used).

1. Journalized into sales journal.
2. Record immediately to subsidiary ledger.
3. Post totals from sales journal at end of month to general journal.
4. Journalized in general journal.
5. Record and post immediately to subsidiary and general ledger.

a. ____ Sold merchandise on account to Ree Co., invoice no. 1—$50.

b. ____ Sold merchandise on account to Flynn Co., invoice no. 2—$100.

c. ____ Issued credit memorandum no. 1 to Flynn Co. for defective merchandise—$25.

Credit Memorandum

4. Draw a transactional analysis box for the following credit memorandum: Issued credit memorandum to Bob Corp. for defective merchandise—$50.

Sales and Cash Receipts Journal

5. Match the following to the four journal entries (a number can be used more than once).

> 1. Journalized into sales journal.
> 2. Journalized into cash receipts journal.
> 3. Record immediately to subsidiary ledger.
> 4. Totals of special journals will be posted at end of month (except Sundry column).
> 5. Post to general ledger immediately.
> 6. Journalize into general journal.

a. ____ Sold merchandise on account to Ally Co., invoice no. 10—$40.

b. ____ Received cheque from Moore Co.—$100 less 2 percent discount.

c. ____ Cash Sales—$100.

d. ____ Issued credit memorandum no. 2 to Ally Co. for defective merchandise—$20.

6. From the following, prepare a schedule of accounts receivable for Blue Co., for May 31, 19XX.

Accounts Receivable Subsidiary Ledger

Bon Co.

Dr.		Cr.	
5/6 SJ1	100		

Peke Co.

Dr.		Cr.	
5/20 SJ1	30	5/27 CRJ1	10

Green Co.

Dr.		Cr.	
5/9 SJ1	10		

General Ledger

Accounts Receivable

Dr.		Cr.	
5/31 SJ1	140	5/31 CRJ1	10

Exercises

(The forms you need are on pages 9-14 to 9-16 of the *Study Guide and Working Papers.*)

Recording to accounts receivable ledger and posting to general ledger.

9-1. From the following sales journal, record to the accounts receivable subsidiary ledger and post to the general ledger accounts as appropriate.

SALES JOURNAL

P. 1

Date		Account Debited	Invoice No.	PR	Dr. Accts. Receivable Cr. Sales
19XX April	18	Kevin Stone Co.	1		400 00
	19	Bill Valley Co.	2		600 00

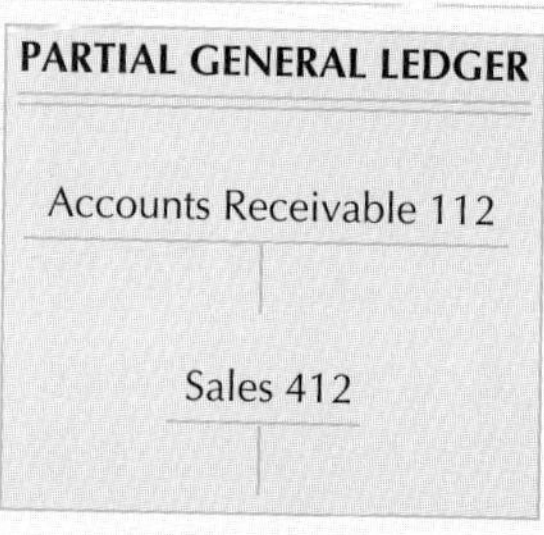

Journalizing, recording, and posting that includes credit memorandum.

9-2. Journalize, record, and post when appropriate the following transactions into the sales journal (same heading as Exercise 9-1) and general journal (p. 1) (all sales carry terms of 2/10, n/30):

19XX
May 16 Sold merchandise on account to Ronald Co., invoice no. 1, $1,000.
18 Sold merchandise on account to Bass Co., invoice no. 2, $1,700.
20 Issued credit memorandum no. 1 to Bass Co. for defective merchandise, $700.

Use the following account numbers: Accounts Receivable, 112; Sales, 411; Sales Returns and Allowances, 412.

Journalizing transaction into cash receipts journal.

9-3. From Exercise 9-2, journalize in the cash receipts journal the receipt of a cheque from Ronald Co. for payment of invoice no. 1 on May 24. Use the same headings as for Walter Lantz Co. (on p. 355).

Journalizing, recording, and posting sales and cash receipts journal; schedule of accounts receivable.

9-4. From the following transactions for Edna Co., when appropriate, journalize, record, post, and prepare a schedule of accounts receivable. Use the same journal headings (all p. 1) and chart of accounts (use Edna Cares, Capital) that Art's Wholesale Clothing used in the text. You will have to set up your own accounts receivable subsidiary ledger and partial general ledger as needed. All sales terms are 2/10, n/30.

19XX
June 1 Edna Cares invested $3,000 in the business.
1 Sold merchandise on account to Boston Co., invoice no. 1, $700.
2 Sold merchandise on account to Gary Co., invoice no. 2, $900.
3 Cash sale, $200.
8 Issued credit memorandum no. 1 to Boston for defective merchandise, $200.
10 Received cheque from Boston for invoice no. 1 less returns and discount.
15 Cash sale, $400.
18 Sold merchandise on account to Boston Co., invoice no. 3, $600.

9-5. From the following facts calculate what Ann Frost must pay Blue Co. for the purchase of a dining room set. Sale terms are 2/10, n/30.

a. Sales ticket price before tax, $4,000—dated April 5.

b. Provincial sales tax, 8 percent, GST, 7 percent.

c. Returned one defective chair for credit of $400 before any taxes on April 8.

d. Paid bill on April 13.

9-6. Peter Rockford purchased eight stereo speakers from Waverly Electronics for his restaurant. The price before any taxes was $400.00 each. Terms were 2/10, n/30 and PST of 10 percent was added to the total before GST of 7 percent was included. What amount will Rockford pay, given the following:

a. Sale was dated June 11, 19XX.

b. Returned two speakers due to defective sound on June 15, 19XX.

c. Credit of $400 each plus all applicable taxes was received on June 15.

d. .Full payment was made on June 20, 19XX.

Group A Problems

(The forms you need are on pages 9-17 to 9-39 of the *Study Guide and Working Papers.*)

Multicolumn journal: journalizing and posting to general journal and recording to accounts receivable subsidiary ledger and preparing a schedule of accounts receivable.

9A-1. Jill Blue has opened Max Co., a wholesale grocery and pizza company. The following transactions occurred in June:

19XX

June 1 Sold grocery merchandise to Joe Kase Co. on account, $400, invoice no. 1.

4 Sold pizza merchandise to Sue Moore Co. on account, $600, invoice no. 2.

8 Sold grocery merchandise to Long Co. on account, $700, invoice no. 3.

10 Issued credit memorandum no. 1 to Joe Kase for $150 of grocery merchandise returned due to spoilage.

15 Sold pizza merchandise to Sue Moore Co. on account, $160, invoice no. 4.

19 Sold grocery merchandise to Long Co. on account, $300, invoice no. 5.

25 Sold pizza merchandise to Joe Kase Co. on account, $1,200, invoice no. 6.

Required

1. Journalize the transactions in the appropriate journals.

2. Record to the accounts receivable subsidiary ledger and post to general ledger as appropriate.

3. Prepare a schedule of accounts receivable.

Multicolumn sales journal: Use of sales tax; journalizing and posting to general ledger and recording to accounts receivable subsidiary ledger; and preparing a schedule of accounts receivable.

9A-2. The following transactions of Ted's Auto Supply occurred in November (your working papers have balances as of November 1 for certain general ledger and accounts receivable ledger accounts):

19XX

Nov. 1 Sold auto parts merchandise to R. Volan on account, $1,000, invoice no. 60, plus 5 percent PST.

5 Sold auto parts merchandise to J. Seth on account, $800, invoice no. 61, plus 5 percent PST.

8 Sold auto parts merchandise to Lance Corner on account, $9,000, invoice no. 62, plus 5 percent PST.

10 Issued credit memorandum no. 12 to R. Volan for $500 for defective auto parts merchandise returned from November 1 transaction. (Be careful to record the reduction in sales tax payable as well.)

12 Sold auto parts merchandise to J. Seth on account, $600, invoice no. 63, plus 5 percent PST.

Required

1. Journalize the transactions in the appropriate journals.
2. Record to the accounts receivable subsidiary ledger and post to general ledger as appropriate.
3. Prepare a schedule of accounts receivable.

Comprehensive problem: Recording transactions into sales, cash receipts, and general journals; recording to accounts receivable subsidiary ledger and posting to general ledger; preparing a schedule of accounts receivable.

No GST or PST.

9A-3. Mark Peaker owns Peaker's Sneaker Shop. (In your working papers balances as of May 1 are provided for the accounts receivable and general ledger accounts.) The following transactions occurred in May:

19XX

May 1 Mark Peaker invested an additional $12,000 in the sneaker store.

3 Sold $700 of merchandise on account to B. Dale, sales ticket no. 60, terms 1/10, n/30.

4 Sold $500 of merchandise on account to Ron Lester, sales ticket no. 61, terms 1/10, n/30.

9 Sold $200 of merchandise on account to Jim Zon, sales ticket no. 62, terms 1/10, n/30.

10 Received cash from B. Dale in payment of May 3 transaction, sales ticket no. 60, less discount.

20 Sold $3,000 of merchandise on account to Pam Pry, sales ticket no. 63, terms 1/10, n/30.

22 Received cash payment from Ron Lester in payment of May 4 transaction, sales ticket no. 61.

23 Collected cash sales, $3,000.

24 Issued credit memorandum no. 1 to Pam Pry for $2,000 of merchandise returned from May 20 sales on account.

26 Received cash from Pam Pry in payment of May 20, sales ticket no. 63. (Don't forget about the credit memo and discount.)

28 Collected cash sales, $7,000.

30 Sold sneaker rack equipment for $300 cash. (Beware.)

30 Sold merchandise priced at $4,000, on account to Ron Lester, sales ticket no. 64, terms 1/10, n/30.

31 Issued credit memorandum no. 2 to Ron Lester for $700 of merchandise returned from May 30 transaction, sales ticket no. 64.

Required

1. Journalize the transactions.
2. Record to the accounts receivable subsidiary ledger and post to general ledger as needed.
3. Prepare a schedule of accounts receivable.

Comprehensive problem: Using PST in recording transactions into sales, cash receipts, and general journals; recording to accounts receivable subsidiary ledger and posting to general ledger; crossfooting and preparing a schedule of accounts receivable.

9A-4. Bill Murray opened Bill's Cosmetic Market on April 1. There is a 6 percent provincial sales tax (PST) on all cosmetic sales. Bill offers no sales discounts. The following transactions occurred in April:

19XX

April 1 Bill Murray invested $8,000 in the Cosmetic Market from his personal savings account.

5 From the cash register tapes, lipstick cash sales were $5,000 plus PST.

5 From the cash register tapes, eye shadow cash sales were $2,000 plus PST.

8 Sold lipstick on account to Alice Koy Co., $300, sales ticket no. 1, plus PST.

9 Sold eye shadow on account to Marika Sanchez Co., $1,000, sales ticket no. 2, plus PST.

15 Issued credit memorandum no. 1 to Alice Koy Co. for $150 for lipstick returned. (Be sure to reduce PST payable for Bill.)

19 Marika Sanchez Co. paid half the amount owed from sales ticket no. 2, dated April 9.

21 Sold lipstick on account to Jeff Tong Co., $300, sales ticket no. 3, plus PST.

24 Sold eye shadow on account to Rusty Neal Co., $800, sales ticket no. 4, plus PST.

25 Issued credit memorandum no. 2 to Jeff Tong Co. for $200 for lipstick returned from sales ticket no. 3, dated April 21.

29 Cash sales taken from the cash register tape showed:
1. Lipstick — $1,000 + $60 PST collected.
2. Eye shadow — $3,000 + $180 PST collected.

29 Sold lipstick on account to Marika Sanchez Co., $400, sales ticket no. 5, plus PST.

30 Received payment from Marika Sanchez Co. of sales ticket no. 5, dated April 29.

Required

1. Journalize the above in the sales journal, cash receipts journal, or general journal.
2. Record to the accounts receivable subsidiary ledger and post to general ledger when appropriate.
3. Prepare a schedule of accounts receivable for the end of April.

Comprehensive problem: Using PST and GST in recording transactions into sales, cash receipts, and general journals; recording to accounts receivable and posting to general ledger; crossfooting and preparing a schedule of accounts receivable.

9A-5. Mary Parker owns Parker's SCUBA Shop. (In your working papers balances as of April 1 are provided for the accounts receivable and general ledger accounts.) In Mary's province it is necessary to add PST of 8 percent and GST of 7 percent to arrive at the final invoice amount. The following transactions occurred in April:

19XX

April 1 Mary Parker invested an additional $17,000 in the business.

3 Sold $500 of merchandise on account to J. Simpson, sales ticket no. 614, terms 2/10, n/30.

4 Sold $1,200 of merchandise on account to R. Langley, sales ticket no. 615, terms 2/10, n/30.

9 Sold $300 of merchandise on account to J. Fellowes, sales ticket no. 616, terms 2/10, n/30.

10 Received cash from J. Simpson in payment of April 3 transaction, sales ticket no. 614, less discount.

20 Sold $2,000 of merchandise on account to Phyllis Leung, sales ticket no. 617, terms 2/10, n/30.

22 Received cash payment from R. Langley in payment of April 4 transaction, sales ticket no. 615.

23 Collected cash sales, $1,600 plus necessary taxes.

24 Issued credit memorandum no. 101 to Phyllis Leung for $500 of merchandise returned from April 20 sales on account.

25 Received payment from Roland doncaster of the amount due from previous month,, $907.15.

26 Received cash from Phyllis Leung in payment of April 20 sales ticket no. 617. (Don't forget about the credit memo, all taxes, and discount.)

28 Collected cash sales, $4,000 plus necessary taxes.

29 Sold merchandise priced at $3,000, on account to Roland Doncaster, sales ticket no. 618, terms 2/10, n/30.

30 Issued credit memorandum no. 102 to Roland Doncaster for $800 of merchandise returned from April 29 transaction, sales ticket no. 618.

Required

1. Journalize the transactions.
2. Record to the accounts receivable ledger and post to general ledger as needed.
3. Prepare a schedule of accounts receivable.

Group B Problems

(The forms you need are on pages 9-17 to 9-39 of the *Study Guide and Working Papers.*)

Multicolumn journal: Journalizing and posting to general ledger and recording to accounts receivable subsidiary ledger and preparing a schedule of accounts receivable.

9B-1. The following transactions occurred for Max Co. for the month of June:

19XX

June 1 Sold grocery merchandise to Joe Kase Co. on account, $800, invoice no. 1.

4 Sold pizza merchandise to Sue Moore Co. on account, $550, invoice no. 2.

8 Sold grocery merchandise to Long Co. on account, $900, invoice no. 3.

10 Issued credit memorandum no. 1 to Joe Kase for $160 of grocery merchandise returned due to spoilage.

15 Sold pizza merchandise to Sue Moore Co. on account, $700, invoice no. 4.

19 Sold grocery merchandise to Long Co. on account, $250, invoice no. 5.

Required

1. Journalize the transactions in the appropriate journals.
2. Record to the accounts receivable subsidiary ledger and post to general ledger as appropriate.
3. Prepare a schedule of accounts receivable.

Multicolumn sales journal: Use of sales tax; journalizing and posting to general ledger and recording to accounts receivable subsidiary ledger; preparing a schedule of accounts receivable.

9B-2. In November the following transactions occurred for Ted's Auto Supply (your working papers have balances as of November 1 for certain general ledger and accounts receivable ledger accounts):

19XX

Nov. 1 Sold merchandise to R. Volan on account, $4,000, invoice no. 70, plus 5 percent PST.

5 Sold merchandise to J. Seth on account, $1,600, invoice no. 71, plus 5 percent PST.

8 Sold merchandise to Lance Corner on account, $15,000, invoice no. 72, plus 5 percent PST.

10 Issued credit memorandum no. 14 to R. Volan for $2,000 for defective merchandise returned from November 1 transaction. (Be careful to record the reduction in PST payable as well.)

12 Sold merchandise to J. Seth on account, $1,400, invoice no. 73, plus 5 percent PST.

Required

1. Journalize the transactions in the appropriate journals.
2. Record to the accounts receivable subsidiary ledger and post to general ledger as appropriate.
3. Prepare a schedule of accounts receivable.

9B-3. (In your working papers all the beginning balances needed are provided for the accounts receivable subsidiary and general ledger.) The following transactions occurred for Peaker's Sneaker Shop:

Comprehensive problem: Recording transactions into sales, cash receipts, and general journals; recording to accounts receivable subsidiary ledger and posting to general ledger; preparing a schedule of accounts receivable.

No GST or PST.

19XX

May 1 Mark Parker invested an additional $14,000 in the sneaker store.

3 Sold $2,000 of merchandise on account to B. Dale, sales ticket no. 60, terms 1/10, n/30.

4 Sold $900 of merchandise on account to Ron Lester, sales ticket no. 61, terms 1/10, n/30.

9 Sold $600 of merchandise on account to Jim Zon, sales ticket no. 62, terms 1/10, n/30.

10 Received cash from B. Dale in payment of May 3 transaction, sales ticket no. 60, less discount.

20 Sold $4,000 of merchandise on account to Pam Pry, sales ticket no. 63, terms 1/10, n/30.

22 Received cash payment from Ron Lester in payment of May 4 transaction, sales ticket no. 61.

23 Collected cash sales, $6,000.

24 Issued credit memorandum no. 1 to Pam Pry for $500 of merchandise returned from May 20 sales on account.

26 Received cash from Pam Pry in payment of May 20 sales ticket no. 63. (Don't forget about the credit memo and discount.)

28 Collected cash sales, $12,000.

30 Sold sneaker rack equipment for $200 cash. (Beware.)

30 Sold $6,000 of merchandise on account to Ron Lester, sales ticket no. 64, terms 1/10, n/30.

31 Issued credit memorandum no. 2 to Ron Lester for $800 of merchandise returned from May 30 transaction, sales ticket no. 64.

Required

1. Journalize the transactions in the appropriate journals.
2. Record and post as appropriate.
3. Prepare a schedule of accounts receivable.

Comprehensive problem: Using sales tax in recording transactions into sales, cash receipts, and general journals; recording to accounts receivable subsidiary ledger and posting to general ledger; preparing a schedule of accounts receivable.

9B-4. Bill's Cosmetic Market began operating in April. There is a 6 percent provincial sales tax (PST) on all cosmetic sales. Bill offers no discounts. The following transactions occurred in April:

19XX

April 1 Bill Murray invested $10,000 in the Cosmetic Market from his personal account.

5 From the cash register tapes, lipstick cash sales were $5,000 plus PST.

5 From the cash register tapes, eye shadow cash sales were $3,000 plus PST.

8 Sold lipstick on account to Alice Koy Co., $400, sales ticket no. 1, plus PST.

9 Sold eye shadow on account to Marika Sanchez Co., $900, sales ticket no. 2, plus PST.

15 Issued credit memorandum no. 1 to Alice Koy Co. for lipstick returned, $200. (Be sure to reduce PST payable for Bill.)

19 Marika Sanchez Co. paid half the amount owed from sales ticket no. 2, dated April 9.

21 Sold lipstick on account to Jeff Tong Co., $600 sales ticket no. 3, plus PST.

24 Sold eye shadow on account to Rusty Neal Co., $1,000, sales ticket no. 4, plus PST.

25 Issued credit memorandum no. 2 to Jeff Tong Co. for $300, for lipstick returned from sales ticket no. 3, dated April 21.

29 Cash sales taken from the cash register tape showed:

1. Lipstick — $4,000 + $240 PST collected.

2. Eye shadow — $2,000 + $120 PST collected.

29 Sold lipstick on account to Marika Sanchez Co., $700, sales ticket no. 5 plus PST.

30 Received payment from Marika Sanchez Co. of sales ticket no. 5, dated April 29.

Required

1. Journalize, record, and post as appropriate.

2. Prepare a schedule of accounts receivable for the end of April.

Comprehensive problem: Using PST and GST in recording transactions into sales, cash receipts, and general journals; recording to accounts receivable and posting to general ledger; and preparing a schedule of accounts receivable.

9B-5. Mary Parker owns Parker's SCUBA Shop. (In your working papers, balances as of April 1 are provided for the accounts receivable and general ledger accounts.) In Mary's province it is necessary to add PST of 9 percent and GST of 7 percent to the sales total to arrive at the final invoice amount. This means that PST of $90 and GST of $70 would be added to an invoice for $1,000. The following transactions occurred in April:

19XX

April 1 Mary Parker invested an additional $13,000 in the business.

3 Sold $800 of merchandise on account to J. Simpson, sales ticket no. 614, terms 2/10, n/30.

4 Sold $1,600 of merchandise on account to R. Langley, sales ticket no. 615, terms 2/10, n/30.

9 Sold $600 of merchandise on account to J. Fellowes, sales ticket no. 616, terms 2/10, n/30.

10 Received cash from J. Simpson in payment of April 3 transaction, sales ticket no. 614, less discount.

20 Sold $3,000 of merchandise on account to Phyllis Leung, sales ticket no. 617, terms 2/10, n/30.

22 Received cash payment from R. Langley in payment of April 4 transaction, sales ticket no. 615.

23 Collected cash sales, $2,500 plus necessary taxes.

24 Issued credit memorandum no. 101 to Phyllis Leung for $900 of merchandise returned from April 20 sales on account.

25 Received payment from Roland Doncaster of the amount due from previous month, $907.15.

26 Received cash from Phyllis Leung in payment of April 20 sales ticket no. 617. (Don't forget the credit memo, all taxes and discount.)

28 Collected cash sales, $3,200 plus necessary taxes.

29 Sold merchandise priced at $4,000, on account to Roland Doncaster, sales ticket no. 618, terms 2/10, n/30.

30 Issued credit memorandum no. 102 to Roland Doncaster for $1,000 of merchandise returned from April 29 transaction, sales ticket no. 618.

Required

1. Journalize the transactions.

2. Record to the accounts receivable ledger and post to general ledger as needed.

3. Prepare a schedule of accounts receivable.

Group C Problems

Multicolumn column journal: Journalizing and posting to general ledger and recording to accounts receivable ledger and preparing a schedule of accounts receivable.

9C-1. The following transactions occurred for Lodge Co. for the month of July:

19XX

July	1	Sold upholstery merchandise to Joan Timkins Co. on account, $1,500, invoice no. 115. Terms net 30 days.
	4	Sold carpet merchandise to Chris Cowan Co. on account, $825, invoice no. 116. Terms net 30 days.
	8	Sold upholstery merchandise to Cross & Co. on account, $1,950, invoice no. 117. Terms net 30 days.
	10	Issued credit memorandum no. 1 to Joan Timkins Co. for $300 of merchandise returned due to faulty colouring match.
	15	Sold carpet merchandise to Chris Cowan Co. on account, $925, invoice no. 118. Terms net 30 days.
	19	Sold upholstery merchandise to Cross & Co. on account, $730, invoice no. 119. Terms net 30 days.
	24	Sold carpet merchandise to Joan Timkins Co. on account, $2,025, invoice no. 120. Terms net 30 days.

Required

1. Journalize the transactions in the appropriate journals.
2. Record to the accounts receivable ledger and post to general ledger as appropriate.
3. Prepare a schedule of accounts receivable.

Multicolumn sales journal: Use of sales tax; journalizing and posting to general ledger and recording to accounts receivable ledger; and preparing a schedule of accounts receivable.

9C-2. In September the following transactions occurred for Forrest Equipment Supply (your working papers have balances as of September 1 for certain general ledger and accounts receivable ledger accounts):

19XX

Sept.	1	Sold merchandise to Ray Fortuna on account, $9,500, invoice no. 703, plus 9 percent PST.
	5	Sold merchandise to Wilma Jorge on account, $3,000, invoice no. 704, plus 9 percent PST.
	8	Sold merchandise to Cassie Ho on account, $15,800, invoice no. 705, plus 9 percent PST.
	10	Issued credit memorandum no. 14 to Ray Fortuna for $1,200 for defective merchandise returned from September 1 transaction. (Be careful to record the reduction in PST payable as well.)
	12	Sold merchandise to Wilma Jorge on account, $3,650, invoice no. 706, plus 9 percent PST.

Required

1. Journalize the transactions in the appropriate journals.
2. Record to the accounts receivable ledger and post to general ledger as appropriate.
3. Prepare a schedule of accounts receivable.

Comprehensive Problem: Recording transactions into sales, cash receipts, and general journals; recording to accounts receivable and posting to general ledger; preparing a schedule of accounts receivable. No PST or GST.

9C-3. (In your working papers all the beginning balances needed are provided for the accounts receivable and general ledger.) The following transactions occurred for Inner City Sausage Supply Co.:

19XX

Sept. 1 Karen Blum, owner invested an additional $18,000 in the business.

3 Sold $1,850 of merchandise on account to Petra's Meat Market, sales ticket no. 460, terms 1/10, n/30.

4 Sold $825 of merchandise on account to Chapman's Deli, sales ticket no. 461, terms 1/10, n/30.

8 Sold $930 of merchandise on account to Valemont Variety Meats Co, sales ticket no. 462, terms 1/10, n/30.

12 Received cash from Petra's Meat Market in payment of September 3 transaction, sales ticket no. 460, less discount.

21 Sold $1,500 of merchandise on account to Discount Meats, sales ticket no. 463, terms 1/10, n/30.

22 Received cash payment from Chapman's Deli in payment of September transaction, sales ticket no. 461.

23 Collected cash sale, $638.

24 Issued credit memorandum no. 101 to Discount Meats for $300 of merchandise returned from September 21 sales on account.

26 Received cash from Discount Meats in payment of September 21 sales ticket no. 463. (Don't forget about the credit memo and discount.)

27 Collected cash sales, $813.

28 Sold meat cooling equipment for $900 cash. (Beware.)

29 Sold $1,420 of merchandise on account to Chapman's Deli, sales ticket no. 464, terms 1/10, n/30.

30 Issued credit memorandum no. 102 to Chapman's Deli for $420 of merchandise returned from September 29 transaction, sales ticket no. 464.

Required

1. Journalize the transactions in the appropriate journals.
2. Record and post as appropriate.
3. Prepare a schedule of accounts receivable.

Comprehensive problem: Using sales tax in recording transactions into sales, cash receipts, and general journals; recording to accounts receivable and posting to general ledger; and preparing a schedule of accounts receivable.PST, but no GST.

9C-4. Roye's Communication Sales Co. began operating in August. There is an 8 percent provincial sales tax on all sales. Royce's offers no discounts (all terms are net 30 days). The following transactions occurred in August:

19XX

Aug. 1 Royce Lamoureux invested $32,000 in Communication Sales Co. from his personal account.

5 From the cash register tapes, cellular cash sales were $5,400 plus PST.

5 From the cash register tapes, radio cash sales were $8,150 plus PST.

8 Sold cellular equipment on account to Kelly's Real Estate Co., $4,260, sales ticket no. 201, plus PST.

9 Sold radio equipment on account to Well's Hotshot Service Co., $3,100, sales ticket no. 202, plus PST.

15 Issued credit memorandum no. 1 to Kelly's Real Estate Co. for cellular equipment returned, $800. (Be sure to reduce PST payable.)

19 Well's Hotshot Service Co. paid half the amount owed from sales ticket no. 2, dated August 9.
20 Sold cellular equipment on account to Mountain Explorations Co., $5,770 sales ticket no. 203, plus PST.
21 Received proceeds of loan from the Small Business Development Bank $50,000.
24 Sold radio equipment on account to Walkin's Safety Supply Co., $5,820. Sales ticket no. 204, plus PST.
25 Issued credit memorandum no. 2 to Mountain Explorations Co. for $1,420, for equipment returned from sales ticket no. 203, dated August 20.PST was also credited.
27 Received payment of net amount due from Kelly's Real Estate Co. as per sales ticket no. 201 less the credit allowed.
29 Cash sales taken from the cash register tape showed:
(1) cellular—$8,400 + $588 PST collected.
(2) radio—$7,600 + $532 PST collected.
29 Sold cellular equipment on account to Well's Hotshot Service Co., $4,150 sales ticket no. 205, plus PST.
30 Received payment from Well's Hotshot Service Co. of sales ticket no. 202, dated August 9.

Required

1. Journalize, record, and post as appropriate.
2. Prepare a schedule of accounts receivable for the end of August.

Comprehensive problem: Using PST and GST in recording transactions into sales, cash receipts, and general journals; recording to accounts receivable and posting to general ledger; and preparing a schedule of accounts receivable.

9C-5. Martha Worth owns Rarity Collectibles Shop. (In your working papers balances as of January 1 are provided for the accounts receivable and general ledger accounts.) In this province it is necessary to add PST of 8 percent and GST of 7 percent to the sales total to arrive at the final invoice amount. This means that PST of $8 and GST of $7 would be added to each invoice for $100. The following transactions occurred in January:

19XX
Jan. 1 Martha Worth invested $34,000 in the business.
3 Sold $2,600 of merchandise on account to Starcraft Reproductions, sales ticket no. 344, terms 2/10, n/30.
4 Sold $3,200 of merchandise on account to Burgess Fancys, sales ticket no. 345, terms 2/10, n/30.
9 Sold $3,800 of merchandise on account to Hard-To-Find Co., sales ticket no. 346, terms 2/10, n/30.
10 Received cash from Starcraft Reproductions in payment of January 3 transaction, sales ticket no. 344, less discount.
20 Sold $2,480 of merchandise on account to Georgina's Collections, sales ticket no. 347, terms 2/10, n/30.
22 Received cash payment from Burgess Fancys in payment of January 4 transaction, sales ticket no. 345.
23 Collected cash sales, $4,125 plus necessary taxes.
24 Issued credit memorandum no. 10 to Georgina's Collections for $500 of merchandise returned from January 20 sales on account.
26 Received cash from Georgina's Collections in payment of January 20 sales ticket no. 347. (Don't forget about the credit memo, all taxes, and discount.)
28 Collected cash sales, $4,720 plus necessary taxes.

29 Sold merchandise priced at $5,000, on account to Perfect Sales Co., sales ticket no. 348, terms 2/10, n/30.

30 Issued credit memorandum no. 11 to Perfect Sales Co. for $1,200 of merchandise returned from January 29 transaction, sales ticket no. 348.

Required

1. Journalize the transactions.
2. Record to the accounts receivable ledger and post to general ledger as needed.
3. Prepare a schedule of accounts receivable.

Real World Applications

9R-1.

Ronald Howard has been hired by Green Company to help reconstruct the sales journal, general journal, and cash receipts journal, which were recently destroyed in a fire. The owner of Green has supplied him with the following data. Please ignore dates, invoice numbers, etc., and enter the entries into the reconstructed sales journal, general journal, and cash receipts journal. What written recommendation should Ron make so reconstruction will not be needed in the future?

Accounts Receivable Subsidiary Ledger

P. Bond

Debit		Credit
Bal.	100	150 CRJ
SJ	150	Entitled to 2 percent discount

M. Raff

Debit		Credit
Bal.	200	
SJ	100	

J. Smooth

Debit		Credit
Bal.	300	1,000 GJ
SJ	2,000	1,000 CRJ ←
SJ	1,000	500 GJ
		Entitled to 1 percent discount (refers to 1,000 CRJ)

R. Venner

Debit		Credit
Bal.	200	400 CRJ
SJ	400	

Partial General Ledger

Cash

Debit		Credit
Bal.	12,737	

Accounts Receivable

Debit		Credit
Bal.	800	1,000 GJ
SJ	3,650	500 GJ
		1,550 CRJ

Shelving Equipment

Debit		Credit
Bal.	200	200 CRJ

M. Rang, Capital

Debit	Credit	
	1,000	Bal.
	5,000	(Additional investment this month)

Sales

Debit	Credit	
	800	Bal.
	6,000	CRJ ← 5,000 and 1,000
	3,650	SJ

Sales Discount

Debit		Credit
CRJ	13	

Sales Returns and Allowances		
GJ	1,000	
GJ	500	

9R-2.
The bookkeeper of Floore Company records credit sales in a sales journal and returns in a general journal. The bookkeeper did the following:

1. Recorded an $18 credit sale as $180 in the sales journal.
2. Correctly recorded a $40 sale in the sales journal but posted it to B. Blue's account as $400 in the accounts receivable ledger.
3. Made an additional error in determining the balance of J. B. Window Co. in the accounts receivable ledger.
4. Posted a sales return that was recorded in the general journal to the Sales Returns and Allowance account and the Accounts Receivable account but forgot to record it to the B. Katz Co.
5. Added the total of the sales column incorrectly.
6. Posted a sales return to the Accounts Receivable account but not to the Sales Returns and Allowances account. Accounts receivable ledger was recorded correctly.

Could you inform the bookkeeper in writing as to when each error will be discovered?

make the call

Critical Thinking/Ethical Case

9R-3.
Amy Jak is the National Sales Manager of Rowe Co. In order to get sales up to the projection for the old year, Amy asked the accountant to put the first two weeks of sales in January back into December. Amy told the accountant that this secret would only be between them. Should Amy move the new sales into the old sales year? You make the call. Write down your specific recommendations to Amy.

ACCOUNTING RECALL

A CUMULATIVE APPROACH

THIS EXAM REVIEWS CHAPTERS 1 THROUGH 9

Your *Study Guide and Working Papers* has forms (pp. 9-66 and 9-67) to complete this exam, as well as worked-out solutions. The page references next to each question identify what page to turn back to if you answer the question incorrectly.

PART I Vocabulary Review

Match the terms to the appropriate definition or phrase.

Page Ref.

(332) 1. Accounts receivable subsidiary ledger
(347) 2. Sundry
(265) 3. Medical plan payable
(191) 4. Closing
(226) 5. Deposit in transit
(328) 6. Sales returns and allowances
(333) 7. Controlling account
(334) 8. Sales journal
(347) 9. Cash receipts journal
(328) 10. Sales discount

A. The results of a cash discount
B. Records sales on account
C. A contra-revenue account
D. Clears temporary accounts
E. In alphabetical order
F. Miscellaneous
G. Records receipt of cash
H. A liability
I. Deposits not received by the bank
J. Accounts receivable

PART II True or False (Accounting Theory)

(232) 11. Petty cash is a liability.

(333) 12. The controlling account balance at end of month will equal the sum of the subsidiary ledger.

(337) 13. Issuing a credit memo results in sales returns and allowances decreasing.

(257) 14. CPP is always an equal deduction every month.

(333) 15. A $\surd$ means the controlling account has been updated.

PART III Applications Problem

Record the following transactions into the cash receipts journal for Lang Co. Record and post as appropriate.

19XX

June	1	Received cheque from Al Aoy for invoice no. 1 less 5 percent discount.
	7	Cash sales collected, $400.
	17	Received cheque from Alice Barr for invoice no. 2 less 5 percent discount.
	21	Sold store equipment at cost, $400.

Given

Accounts Receivable Subsidiary Ledger

Al Aoy	$ 600	Invoice no. 1
Alice Barr	1,000	Invoice no. 2

Partial General Ledger

	Account No.	Balance
Cash	110	$ 500
Accounts receivable	120	1,600
Store equipment	130	1,400
Sales	410	900
Sales discount	420	—

SPECIAL JOURNALS

10

PURCHASES AND CASH PAYMENTS

Chapter Objectives

- Calculating cost of goods sold. (p. 372)
- Journalizing transactions in a purchases journal. (p. 384)
- Posting from a purchases journal to the accounts payable ledger and the general ledger. (p. 384)
- Recording from the purchases journal to the accounts payable ledger. (p. 378)
- Journalizing transactions which include GST, then recording and posting same. (pp. 394-397)
- Preparing, journalizing, recording, and posting a debit memorandum both with and without GST. (pp. 384-385 and 396-398)
- Journalizing, recording, and posting transactions using a cash payments journal both with and without GST. (pp. 388-391 and 398-400)
- Preparing a schedule of accounts payable. (pp. 391, 401)

Chapter 9 focussed on the sellers in merchandise companies. This chapter will look at the buyers. Many of the concepts and rules related to special journals will carry over to this chapter.

LEARNING UNIT 10-1

Chou's Toy Shop: Buyer's View of a Merchandise Company

Purchases

The account that records the cost of merchandise Chou brings into his toy store for resale to customers is called **Purchases.** Suppose that Chou buys $4,000 worth of Barbie dolls on account from Mattel Manufacturing on July 6. The Purchases account records all merchandise bought for resale. Here's how this would be recorded if special journals were not used.

Purchases is a cost.

The rules work just as if they were an expense.

Purchases	
Dr.	Cr.
4,000	

This account has a debit balance and is classified as a cost. Purchases represent costs that are directly related to bringing merchandise into the store for resale to customers. The July 6 entry would be analyzed and journalized as follows:

If Chou's purchased a new display case for the store, it would not show up in the Purchases account. The case is considered equipment that is not for resale to customers.

Accounts Affected	Category	↑ ↓	Rules	T Account Update
Purchases	Cost	↑	Dr.	Purchases: Dr. 4,000 | Cr.
Accounts Payable, Mattel	Liability	↑	Cr.	Accts. Payable: Dr. | Cr. 4,000; Mattel: 4,000

Date		Account	Dr.	Cr.
July	6	Purchases	400000	
		Accounts Payable, Mattel		400000
		Purchases on account		

Keep in mind wc would have to record a liability to Mattel in the accounts payable subsidiary ledger. We will talk about the subsidiary ledger in Learning Unit 10-2.

PURCHASES RETURNS AND ALLOWANCES

Chou noticed that some of the dolls he received were not as ordered, and he notified the manufacturer of this fact. On July 9, Mattel issued a debit memorandum* indicating that Chou would get a $500 reduction from the original selling price. Chou then agreed to keep the dolls. The account that records a decrease to a buyer's cost is a contra-expense account called **Purchases Returns and Allowances.** The account lowers the cost of purchases.

Purchases Returns and Allowances	
Dr.	Cr.
	500

← Normal balance is a credit.

Let's analyze this reduction to cost and prepare a general journal entry.

Accounts Affected	Category	↑ ↓	Rules	T Account Update
Accounts Payable, Mattel	Liability	↓	Dr.	Accts. Payable: Dr. 500 / Cr. 4,000; Mattel: Dr. 500 / Cr. 4,000
Purchases Returns and Allowances	Contra-expense	↑	Cr.	Purchases Ret. & Allow.: Dr. / Cr. 500

Date		Account	Dr.	Cr.
July	9	Accounts Payable, Mattel	500 00	
		Purchases Returns and Allowances		500 00
		Received debit memorandum		

When posted to general ledger accounts as well as recording to Mattel in the accounts payable subsidiary ledger, the records show that Chou's Toy Shop owes $500 less.

PURCHASES DISCOUNT

Remember, for Mattel this is a sales discount, while for Chou this is a purchases discount.

Now let's look at the analysis and journal entry when Chou pays Mattel. Mattel offers a 2 percent cash discount if the invoice is paid within 10 days. To take advantage of this cash discount, Chou sent a company cheque to Mattel on July 15. The discount is taken after the allowance.

$4,000
− 500 allowance
$3,500 × 0.02 = $70 purchases discount

Remember: Purchases were a debit, purchases discounts are credits.

The account that records this discount is called **Purchases Discount.** It, too, is a contra-expense account because it lowers the cost of purchases.

Purchases Discount	
Dr.	Cr.
	70

← Normal balance is a credit.

*Technically, Mattel would issue a **credit** memorandum. This is explained later in the chapter.

Let's analyze and prepare a general journal entry:

Accounts Affected	Category	↑ ↓	Rules	T Account Update
Accounts Payable, Mattel	Liability	↓	Dr.	Accts. Payable: Dr. 500, 3,500 | Cr. 4,000; Mattel: 500, 3,500 | 4,000
Purchases Discount	Contra-expense	↑	Cr.	Purchases Discounts: Dr. | Cr. 70
Cash	Asset	↓	Cr.	Cash: Dr. | Cr. 3,430

July	15	Accounts Payable, Mattel	3 5 0 0 00	
		Purchases Discount		7 0 00
		Cash		3 4 3 0 00
		Paid Mattel bal. owed		

After the journal entry is posted and recorded to Mattel, the result will show that Chou saved $70 and totally paid what his company owed to Mattel. The actual—or net—cost of his purchase is $3,430, calculated as follows:

Purchases	$4,000
- Purchases Returns and Allowances	500
- Purchases Discounts	70
= Net Purchases	$3,430

Seller pays freight to point of destination.

Freight charges are not taken into consideration in calculating net purchases. Still, they are very important. If the seller is responsible for paying the shipping cost until the goods reach their destination, the freight charges are **F.O.B. destination.** For example, if a seller located in Winnipeg sold goods F.O.B. destination to a buyer in Edmonton, the seller would have to pay the cost of shipping the goods to the buyer.

If the buyer is responsible for paying the shipping costs, the freight charges are **F.O.B. shipping point.** In this situation, the seller sometimes will prepay the freight charges as a matter of convenience and will add it to the invoice of the purchaser.

Example

Bill amount ($800 + $80 prepaid freight)	$880
Less 5 percent cash discount (0.05 × $800)	40
Amount to be paid by buyer	$840

Purchases discounts are not taken on freight.

When does title change to goods shipped?

If the seller ships goods F.O.B. shipping point, legal ownership (title) passes to the buyer *when the goods are shipped.* If goods are shipped by the seller F.O.B. destination, title will change *when goods have reached their destination.*

LEARNING UNIT 10-1 REVIEW

AT THIS POINT you should be able to

- Explain and calculate purchases, purchases returns and allowances, and purchases discounts. (pp. 378 and 379)
- Calculate net purchases. (p. 380)
- Explain why purchases discounts are not taken on freight. (p. 380)
- Compare and contrast F.O.B. destination with F.O.B. shipping point. (p. 380)

SELF-REVIEW QUIZ 10-1

(The forms you need can be found on page 10-1 of the *Study Guide and Working Papers.*)

Which of the following statements are false?

1. Net Purchases = Purchases − Purchases Returns and Allowances − Purchases Discount.
2. Purchases is a contra-cost.
3. F.O.B. destination means the seller covers shipping cost and retains title until goods reach their destination.
4. Purchases discounts are not taken on freight.
5. Purchases Discount is a contra-cost account.

Solution to Self-Review Quiz 10-1

Number 2 is false.

LEARNING UNIT 10-2

Steps Taken in Purchasing Merchandise and Recording Purchases

Merchandising companies must take specific steps when they purchase goods for resale. Let's look at the steps Art's Wholesale Clothing Company took when it ordered goods from Abby Blake Company on April 1.

STEPS TAKEN BY ART'S WHOLESALE WHEN ORDERING GOODS

Step 1: Prepare a Purchase Requisition at Art's Wholesale

Authorized personnel initiate purchase requisition.

The inventory clerk notes a low inventory level of ladies' jackets for resale, so he sends a **purchase requisition** to the purchasing department. A duplicate copy is sent to the accounting department. A third copy remains with the department that initiated the request, to be used as a check on the purchasing department.

Step 2: Purchasing Department of Art's Wholesale Prepares a Purchase Order

After checking various price lists and suppliers' catalogues, the purchasing department fills out a form called a **purchase order.** This form gives Abby Blake

Purchase Order No. 1
Art's Wholesale Clothing Company
1528 Belle Ave.
Toronto, Ontario M5A 2L4

Purchased From: Abby Blake Company
12 Foster Road
Quebec City, PQ G1M 4H3

Date: April 1, 19XX
Shipped VIA: Freight truck
Terms: 2/10, n/60
FOB: Quebec City

Quantity	Description	Unit Price	Total
100	Ladies' Jackets Code 14-0	$50	$5,000

Art's Wholesale
By: Bill Joy

Purchase order number must appear on all invoices.

FIGURE 10-1
Purchase Order

Four copies of purchase order: (1) (original) to supplier, (2) to accounting department, (3) remains with department that initiated purchase requisition, (4) to file of purchasing department.

Company the authority to ship the ladies' jackets ordered by Art's Wholesale Clothing Company (see Figure 10-1).

Step 3: Sales Invoice Prepared by Abby Blake Company

Abby Blake Company receives the purchase order and prepares a sales invoice. The sales invoice for the seller is the **purchase invoice** for the buyer. A sales invoice is shown in Figure 10-2.

The invoice shows that the goods will be shipped F.O.B. Quebec City. This means that Art's Wholesale Clothing Company is responsible for paying the shipping costs.

The sales invoice also shows a freight charge. This means that Abby Blake prepaid the shipping costs as a matter of convenience. Art's will repay the freight charges when it pays the invoice.

Step 4: Receiving the Goods

When goods are received, Art's Wholesale inspects the shipment and completes a **receiving report.** The receiving report verifies that the exact merchandise that was ordered was received in good condition.

Sales Invoice No. 228
Abby Blake Company
12 Foster Road
Quebec City, PQ G1M 4H3

Sold to: Art's Wholesale
Clothing Co.
1528 Belle Ave.
Toronto, ON
M5A 2L4FOB:

Date: April 3, 19XX
Shipped VIA: Freight truck
Terms: 2/10, n/60
Your Order No.:1
FOB: Quebec City

Quantity	Description	Unit Price	Total
100	Ladies' Jackets Code 14-0 Freight	$50	$5,000 50 $5,050

FIGURE 10-2
Sales Invoice

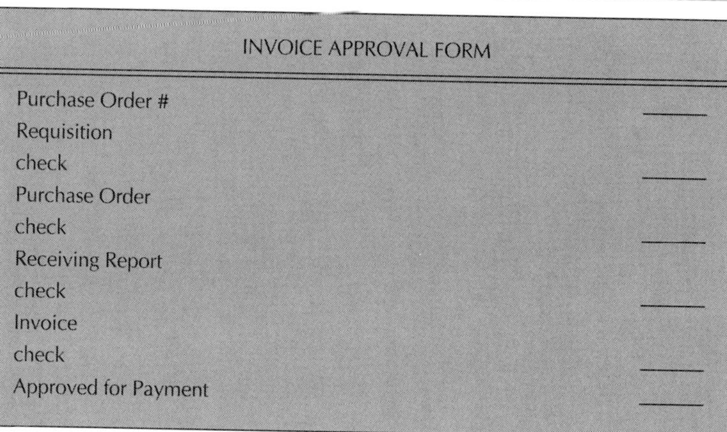

INVOICE APPROVAL FORM

Purchase Order #	____
Requisition check	____
Purchase Order check	____
Receiving Report check	____
Invoice check	____
Approved for Payment	____

FIGURE 10-3
Invoice Approval Form

Step 5: Verifying the Numbers

Before the invoice is approved for recording and payment, the accounting department must check the purchase order, invoice, and receiving report to make sure that all are in agreement and that no steps have been omitted. The form used for checking and approval is an **invoice approval form** (see Figure 10-3).

Keep in mind that Art's Wholesale Clothing Company does not record this purchase until the *invoice is approved for recording and payment.* However, Abby Blake Company records this transaction in its records when the sales invoice is prepared.

THE PURCHASES JOURNAL AND ACCOUNTS PAYABLE SUBSIDIARY LEDGER

Let's look at how Art's Wholesale Clothing Company journalizes, posts, and records to the accounts payable subsidiary ledger. We will also look at the **purchases journal,** a multicolumn special journal Art's uses to record the buying of merchandise or other items on account, and the **accounts payable subsidiary ledger**, an alphabetical list of the amounts owed to creditors from purchases on account.

For example, on April 3 Art's Wholesale Clothing Company records in its purchases journal the following:

- Date: April 3, 19XX.
- Account Credited: Abby Blake Company.
- Date of Invoice: April 3.
- Invoice Number: 228.
- Terms: 2/10, n/60.
- Accounts payable: $5,050; Purchases: $5,000; Freight-In, $50.

See Figure 10-4 for complete purchases journal.

As soon as the information is journalized in the purchases journal (see Figure 10-4), you should:

1. Record to Abby Blake Co. in the accounts payable subsidiary ledger to indicate that the amount owed is now $5,050. When this is complete, place a √ in the PR column of the purchases journal.
2. Post to Freight-In, account no. 514, in the general ledger right away. When this is complete, record the 514 in the PR column under Sundry in the purchases journal.

Note that the normal balance in the accounts payable subsidiary ledger is a credit.

The posting and recording rules are similar to those in the previous chapter, but here we are looking at the buyer rather than at the seller.

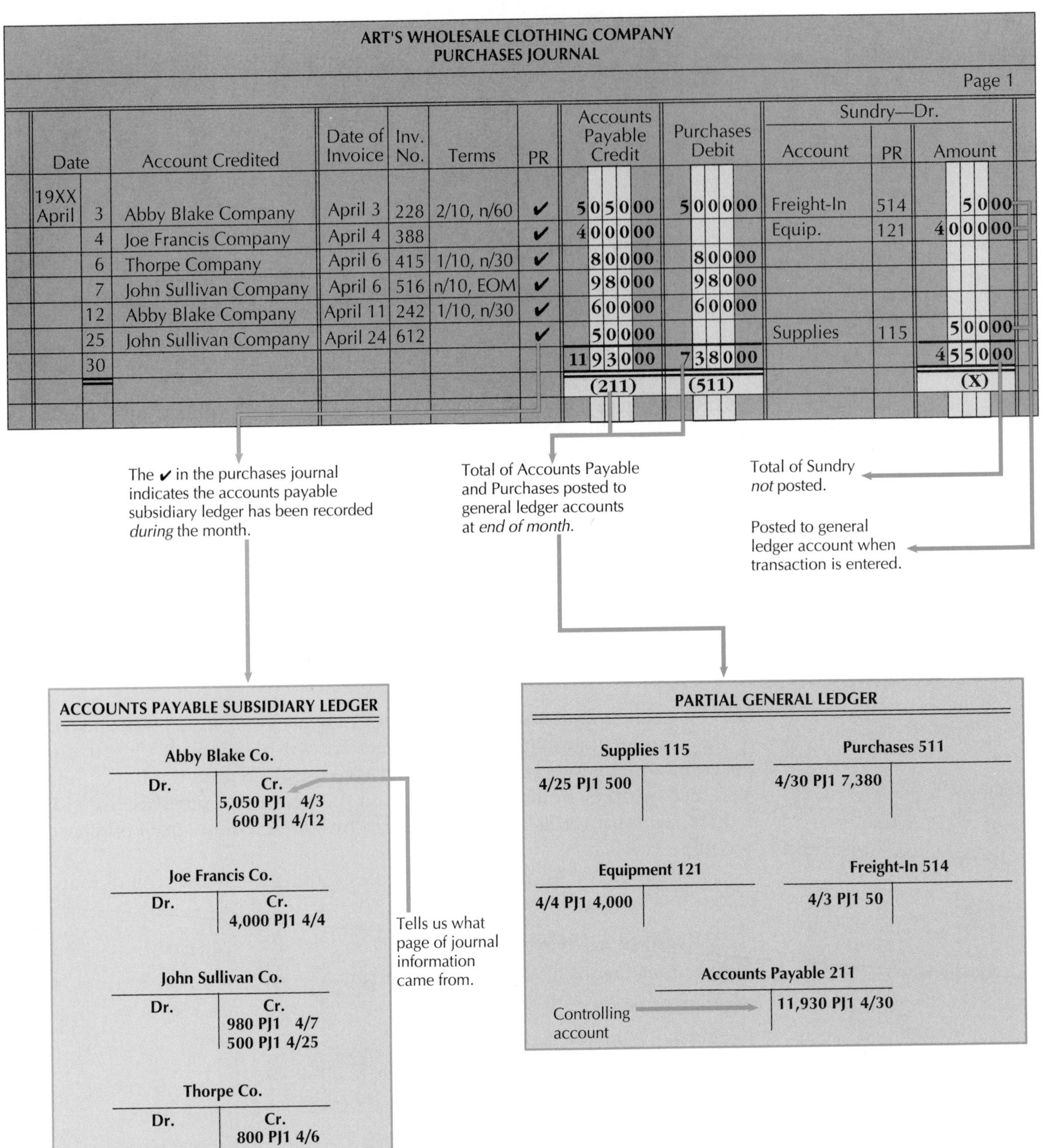

ART'S WHOLESALE CLOTHING COMPANY
PURCHASES JOURNAL

Page 1

Date		Account Credited	Date of Invoice	Inv. No.	Terms	PR	Accounts Payable Credit	Purchases Debit	Sundry—Dr. Account	Sundry—Dr. PR	Sundry—Dr. Amount
19XX April	3	Abby Blake Company	April 3	228	2/10, n/60	✔	5050 00	5000 00	Freight-In	514	50 00
	4	Joe Francis Company	April 4	388		✔	4000 00		Equip.	121	4000 00
	6	Thorpe Company	April 6	415	1/10, n/30	✔	800 00	800 00			
	7	John Sullivan Company	April 6	516	n/10, EOM	✔	980 00	980 00			
	12	Abby Blake Company	April 11	242	1/10, n/30	✔	600 00	600 00			
	25	John Sullivan Company	April 24	612		✔	500 00		Supplies	115	500 00
	30						11930 00	7380 00			4550 00
							(211)	(511)			(X)

FIGURE 10-4 Purchases Journal

THE DEBIT MEMORANDUM

In Chapter 9, Art's Wholesale Clothing Company had to handle returned goods as a seller. It did this by issuing credit memoranda to customers who returned goods or received an allowance on the price. In this chapter, Art's must handle returns as a buyer. It does this by using debit memoranda. A **debit memorandum** is a piece of paper issued by a customer to a seller that indicates that a return or allowance has occurred.

A debit memo shows that Art's does not owe as much money as was indicated in the company's purchases journal.

Debit Memorandum			No. 1
Art's Wholesale Clothing Company 1528 Belle Ave. Toronto, ON M5A 2L4			
To: Thorpe Company 3 Access Road Fredericton, NB E3B 4T3			April 9, 19XX
WE DEBIT your account as follows:			
Quantity		Unit Cost	Total
20	Men's Hats Code 827—defective brims	$10	$200

FIGURE 10-5
Debit Memorandum

Suppose that on April 6 Art's Wholesale had purchased men's hats for $800 from Thorpe Company (see Figure 10-4). On April 9, 20 hats valued at $200 were found to have defective brims. Art's issued a debit memorandum to Thorpe Company, as shown in Figure 10-5. At some point in the future, Thorpe will issue Art's a credit memorandum. Let's look at how Art's Wholesale Clothing Company handles such a transaction in its accounting records.

Journalizing and Posting the Debit Memo

First, let's look at a transactional analysis chart.

Result of debit memo: debits or reduces Accounts Payable. On seller's books, accounts affected would include Sales Returns and Allowances and Accounts Receivable.

Accounts Affected	Category	↑ ↓	Rules
Accounts Payable	Liability	↓	Dr.
Purchases Returns and Allowances	Contra-expense	↑	Cr.

Next, let's examine the journal entry for the debit memorandum:

Purchases Returns and Allowances	
Dr.	Cr.
+	–

A contra-cost-of-goods-sold account.

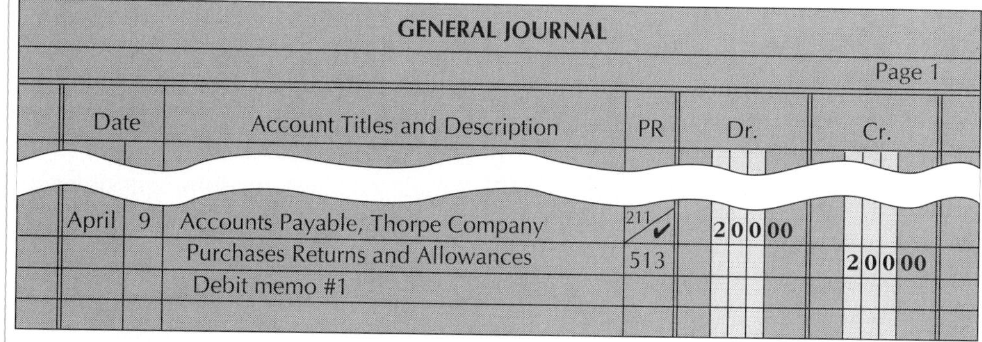

GENERAL JOURNAL — Page 1

Date		Account Titles and Description	PR	Dr.	Cr.
April	9	Accounts Payable, Thorpe Company	211/✔	200 00	
		Purchases Returns and Allowances	513		200 00
		Debit memo #1			

The two postings and one recording are:

1. 211—Post to Accounts Payable as a debit in the general ledger account no. 211. When this is done, place in the PR column the account number, 211, above the diagonal on the same line as Accounts Payable in the journal.
2. √—Record to Thorpe Co. in the accounts payable subsidiary ledger to show that Art's doesn't owe Thorpe as much money. When this is done, place a √ in the journal in the PR column below the diagonal line on the same line as Accounts Payable in the journal.

3. 513—Post to Purchases Returns and Allowances as a credit in the general ledger (account no. 513). When this is done, place the account number, 513, in the posting reference column of the journal on the same line as Purchases Returns and Allowances. (If equipment was returned that was not merchandise for resale, we would credit Equipment and not Purchases Returns and Allowances.)

LEARNING UNIT 10-2 REVIEW

AT THIS POINT you should be able to

- Explain the relationship between a purchase requisition, a purchase order, and a purchase invoice. (pp. 381 and 382)
- Explain why a typical invoice approval form may be used. (p. 383)
- Journalize transactions into a purchases journal. (p. 384)
- Explain how to record the accounts payable subsidiary ledger and post to the general ledger from a purchases journal. (p. 384)
- Explain a debit memorandum and be able to journalize an entry resulting from its issuance. (p. 385)

SELF-REVIEW QUIZ 10-2

(The forms you need are on pages 10-2 to 10-4 of the *Study Guide and Working Papers.*)

Journalize the following transactions into the purchases journal or general journal for Munroe Co. Record to accounts payable subsidiary ledger and post to general ledger accounts as appropriate. Use the same journal headings we used for Art's Wholesale Clothing Company.

19XX		
May	5	Bought merchandise on account from Flynn Co., invoice no. 512, dated May 6, terms 1/10, n/30, $900.
	7	Bought merchandise from John Butler Company, invoice no. 403, dated May 7, terms n/10 EOM, $1,000.
	13	Issued debit memo no. 1 to Flynn Co. for merchandise returned, $300, from invoice no. 512.
	17	Purchased $400 of equipment on account from John Butler Company, invoice no. 413, dated May 18.

Solution to Self-Review Quiz 10-2

MUNROE CO.
PURCHASES JOURNAL

Page 2

Date		Account Credited	Date of Invoice	Inv. No.	Terms	PR	Accounts Payable Credit	Purchases Debit	Sundry—Dr. Account	PR	Amount
19XX May	5	Flynn Co.	May 6	512	1/10, n/30	✔	90000	90000			
	7	John Butler	May 7	403	n/10, EOM	✔	100000	100000			
	17	John Butler	May 18	413		✔	40000		Equip.	121	40000
	31						230000	190000			40000
							(212)	(512)			(X)

MUNROE CO.
GENERAL JOURNAL

Page 1

Date		Account Titles and Description	PR	Dr.	Cr.
19XX May	13	Accounts Payable, Flynn Co.	212/✔	30000	
		Purchases Returns and Allowances	513		30000
		Debit memo #1			

ACCOUNTS PAYABLE SUBSIDIARY LEDGER
JOHN BUTLER COMPANY
18 REED RD.
WINNIPEG, MB R2B 8G6

Date 19XX		Explanation	Post. Ref.	Debit	Credit	CR. Balance
May	7		PJ2		100000	100000
	17		PJ2		4000	140000

FLYNN COMPANY
15 FOSS AVE.
QUEBEC CITY, PQ G1L 2W4

Date 19XX		Explanation	Post. Ref.	Debit	Credit	CR. Balance
May	5		PJ2		90000	90000
	13		GJ1	30000		60000

PARTIAL GENERAL LEDGER

Equipment — Acct. No. 121

Date 19XX		Explanation	Post. Ref.	Debit	Credit	DR or CR	Balance
May	17		PJ2	40000		DR.	40000

Accounts Payable — Acct. No. 212

Date 19XX		Explanation	Post. Ref.	Debit	Credit	DR or CR	Balance
May	13		GJ2	30000		DR.	30000
	31		PJ2		230000	CR.	200000

Purchases — Acct. No. 512

Date 19XX		Explanation	Post. Ref.	Debit	Credit	DR or CR	Balance
May	31		PJ2	190000		DR.	190000

Purchases Returns and Allowances — Acct. No. 513

Date 19XX		Explanation	Post. Ref.	Debit	Credit	DR or CR	Balance
May	13		GJ1		30000	CR.	30000

LEARNING UNIT 10-3

The Cash Payments Journal and Schedule of Accounts Payable

Art's Wholesale Clothing Company will record all payments made by cheque in a **cash payments journal.** (Also called a *cash disbursements journal*). In many ways, the structure of this journal resembles that of the cash receipts journal discussed in Chapter 9. Now, however, we are looking at the outward flow of cash instead of the inward flow.

Art's conducted the following cash transactions in April:

19XX

April 2 Issued cheque no. 1 to Pete Blum for insurance paid in advance, $900.

7 Issued cheque no. 2 to Joe Francis Company in payment of its April 5 invoice no. 388.

9 Issued cheque no. 3 to Rick Flo Co. for merchandise purchased for cash, $800.

12 Issued cheque no. 4 to Thorpe Company in payment of its April 6 invoice no. 414 less the return and discount.

28 Issued cheque no. 5, $700, for salaries paid.

The diagram in Figure 10-6 shows the cash payments journal for the end of April along with the recordings to the accounts payable subsidiary ledger and postings to the general ledger. Study the diagram; we will review it in a moment.

FIGURE 10-6
Cash Payments Journal Recording and Posting

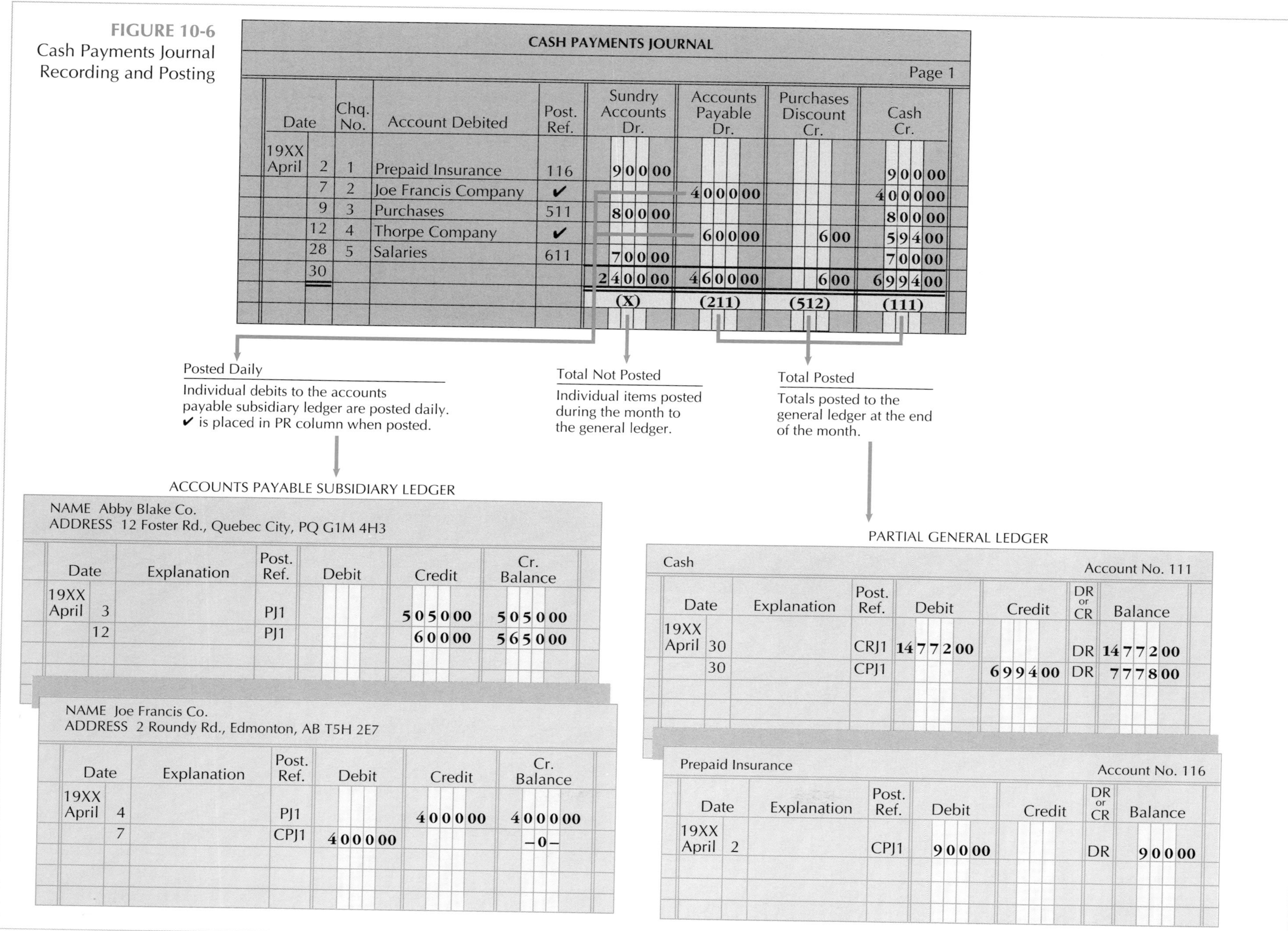

CASH PAYMENTS JOURNAL — Page 1

Date	Chq. No.	Account Debited	Post. Ref.	Sundry Accounts Dr.	Accounts Payable Dr.	Purchases Discount Cr.	Cash Cr.
19XX April 2	1	Prepaid Insurance	116	900 00			900 00
7	2	Joe Francis Company	✔		4 000 00		4 000 00
9	3	Purchases	511	800 00			800 00
12	4	Thorpe Company	✔		600 00	6 00	594 00
28	5	Salaries	611	700 00			700 00
30				2 400 00	4 600 00	6 00	6 994 00
				(X)	(211)	(512)	(111)

Posted Daily
Individual debits to the accounts payable subsidiary ledger are posted daily. ✔ is placed in PR column when posted.
Total Not Posted
Individual items posted during the month to the general ledger.
Total Posted
Totals posted to the general ledger at the end of the month.
ACCOUNTS PAYABLE SUBSIDIARY LEDGER
PARTIAL GENERAL LEDGER

ACCOUNTS PAYABLE SUBSIDIARY LEDGER

NAME Abby Blake Co.
ADDRESS 12 Foster Rd., Quebec City, PQ G1M 4H3

Date	Explanation	Post. Ref.	Debit	Credit	Cr. Balance
19XX April 3		PJ1		5 050 00	5 050 00
12		PJ1		600 00	5 650 00

NAME Joe Francis Co.
ADDRESS 2 Roundy Rd., Edmonton, AB T5H 2E7

Date	Explanation	Post. Ref.	Debit	Credit	Cr. Balance
19XX April 4		PJ1		4 000 00	4 000 00
7		CPJ1	4 000 00		–0–

PARTIAL GENERAL LEDGER

Cash — Account No. 111

Date	Explanation	Post. Ref.	Debit	Credit	DR or CR	Balance
19XX April 30		CRJ1	14 772 00		DR	14 772 00
30		CPJ1		6 994 00	DR	7 778 00

Prepaid Insurance — Account No. 116

Date	Explanation	Post. Ref.	Debit	Credit	DR or CR	Balance
19XX April 2		CPJ1	900 00		DR	900 00

FIG. 10-6, (cont.)

NAME John Sullivan Co.
ADDRESS 18 Print St. Regina, SK S4P 2A6

Date		Explanation	Post. Ref.	Debit	Credit	Cr. Balance
19XX April	7		PJ1		980 00	980 00
	25		PJ1		500 00	1 480 00

NAME Thorpe Co.
ADDRESS 3 Access Rd., Fredericton, NB E3B 4T3

Date		Explanation	Post. Ref.	Debit	Credit	Cr. Balance
19XX April	6		PJ1		800 00	800 00
	9		GJ1	200 00		600 00
	12		CPJ1	600 00		–0–

Note on accounts payable balance: Very occasionally (perhaps due to the return of defective goods after they have been paid for) a debit balance may be called for in accounts payable. Debit balances are opposite to the normal credit balance and are signified by placing the balance in brackets. For example, suppose we get a credit note from Joe Francis Co. for $400 after we have paid off their account completely. Their account would then appear as follows:

NAME Joe Francis Co.
ADDRESS 2 Roundy Rd., Edmonton, AB T5H 2E7

Date		Explanation	Post. Ref.	Debit	Credit	Cr. Balance
19XX April	4		PJ1		4 000 00	4 000 00
	7		CPJ1	4 000 00		–0–
	14		GJ4	400 00		(400 00)

Controlling Account

Accounts Payable — Account No. 211

Date		Explanation	Post. Ref.	Debit	Credit	DR or CR	Balance
19XX April	9		GJ1	200 00		DR	200 00
	30		PJ1		11 930 00	CR	11 730 00
	30		CPJ1	4 600 00		CR	7 130 00

Purchases — Account No. 511

Date		Explanation	Post. Ref.	Debit	Credit	DR or CR	Balance
19XX April	9		CPJ1	800 00		DR	800 00
	30		PJ1	7 380 00		DR	8 180 00

Purchases Discount — Account No. 512

Date		Explanation	Post. Ref.	Debit	Credit	DR or CR	Balance
19XX April	30		CPJ1		6 00	CR	6 00

Salaries Expense — Account No. 611

Date		Explanation	Post. Ref.	Debit	Credit	DR or CR	Balance
19XX April	28		CPJ1	700 00		DR	700 00

Posting and recording rules for this journal are similar to those for the cash receipts journal in Chapter 9.

JOURNALIZING, POSTING, AND RECORDING FROM THE CASH PAYMENTS JOURNAL TO THE ACCOUNTS PAYABLE SUBSIDIARY LEDGER AND THE GENERAL LEDGER

Figure 10-6 shows how Art's Wholesale Clothing Company recorded the payment of cash on April 12 to Thorpe Company. The purchases journal shows that Art's purchased $800 of merchandise from Thorpe on account on April 6. The amount Art's owes is discounted 1 percent. The amount owed ($800 – $200 returns) is recorded in the accounts payable subsidiary ledger as soon as the entry is made in the cash payments journal. The payment reduces the balance to Thorpe to zero. Art's Wholesale Clothing Company receives a $6 purchases discount.

As explained in Chapter 9, Sundry is a miscellaneous accounts column that provides flexibility for reporting infrequent transactions that result in an outflow of cash.

At the end of the month the totals of the Cash, Purchases Discount, and Accounts Payable accounts are posted to the general ledger. The total of Sundry is *not* posted. The accounts Prepaid Insurance, Purchases, and Salaries Expense are posted to the general ledger at the time the entry is put in the journal.

The cash payments journal of Art's Wholesale Clothing Company can be crossfooted as follows:

Remember, there is no discount on sales tax or freight.

Debit Columns = Credit Columns

Sundry + Accounts Payable = Purchases Discounts + Cash

$2,400 + $4,600 = $6 + $6,994

$7,000 = $7,000

Schedule of Accounts Payable

Now let's prove that the sum of the accounts payable subsidiary ledger at the end of the month is equal to the controlling account, Accounts Payable, at the end of April for Art's Wholesale Clothing Company. To do this, creditors with an ending balance in Art's accounts payable subsidiary ledger must be listed in the schedule of accounts payable (see Figure 10-7). At the end of the month the total owed ($7,130) in Accounts Payable, the **controlling account** in the general ledger should equal the sum owed the individual creditors that are listed on the schedule of accounts payable. If it doesn't, the journalizing, posting, and recording must be checked to ensure that they are complete. Also, the balances of each title should be checked.

Trade Discounts

Trade discounts are reductions from the purchase price. Usually, they are given to customers who buy items to resell or to use to produce other salable goods.

Amount of Trade Discount = List Price – Net Price

ART'S WHOLESALE CLOTHING COMPANY
SCHEDULE OF ACCOUNTS PAYABLE
APRIL 30, 19XX

Abby Blake Co.	$5 6 5 0 00
John Sullivan Co.	1 4 8 0 00
Total Accounts Payable	$7 1 3 0 00

FIGURE 10-7
Schedule of Accounts Payable

Different trade discounts are available to different classes of customers. Often, trade discounts are listed in catalogues that contain the list price and the amount of trade discount available. Such catalogues usually are updated by discount sheets.

Trade discounts have *no relationship* to whether a customer is paying a bill early. Trade discounts and list prices are not shown in the accounts of either the

Trade discounts are not reflected on the books.

purchaser or the seller. Cash discounts are not taken on the amount of trade discount.

For example, look at the following:

- List price, $800.
- 30 percent Trade discount.
- 5 percent Cash discount.
- *Thus:* Invoice cost of $560 ($800 − $240) less the cash discount of $28 ($560 × 0.05) results in a final cost of $532 if the cash discount is taken.

The purchaser as well as the seller would record the invoice amount at $560.

LEARNING UNIT 10-3 REVIEW

AT THIS POINT you should be able to

- Journalize, post, and record transactions utilizing a cash payments journal. (p. 389)
- Prepare a schedule of accounts payable. (p. 391)
- Compare and contrast a cash discount to a trade discount. (p. 392)

SELF-REVIEW QUIZ 10-3

(The forms you need are on pages 10-4 and 10-5 of the *Study Guide and Working Papers.*)

Given the following information, journalize, crossfoot, and when appropriate record and post the transactions of Melissa Company. Use the same headings as used for Art's Wholesale. All purchases discounts are 2/12, n/30. The cash payments journal is page 2.

Accounts Payable Subsidiary Ledger

Name	*Balance*	*Invoice No.*
Bob Finkelstein	$300	488
Al Jeep	200	410

Partial General Ledger

Account No.	*Balance*
Cash 110	$700
Accounts Payable 210	500
Purchases Discount 511	—
Advertising Expense 610	—

19XX

June 1 Issued cheque no. 15 to Al Jeep in payment of its May 25 invoice no. 410 less purchases discount.

8 Issued cheque no. 16 to Moss Advertising Co. to pay advertising bill due, $75, no discount.

9 Issued cheque no. 17 to Bob Finkelstein in payment of its May 28 invoice no. 488 less purchases discount.

Solution to Self-Review Quiz 10-3

MELISSA COMPANY
CASH PAYMENTS JOURNAL

Page 2

Date		Ck. No.	Account Debited	Post. Ref.	Sundry Accounts Dr.	Accounts Payable Dr.	Purchases Discount Cr.	Cash Cr.
19XX June	1	15	Al Jeep	✔		200 00	4 00	196 00
	8	16	Advertising Expense	610	75 00			75 00
	9	17	Bob Finkelstein	✔		300 00	6 00	294 00
					75 00	500 00	10 00	565 00
					(X)	(210)	(511)	(110)

$75 + $500 = $10 + $565
$575 = $575

ACCOUNTS PAYABLE SUBSIDIARY LEDGER

NAME Bob Finkelstein
ADDRESS 112 Flying Highway, Montreal, PQ H1K 2H7

Date		Explanation	Post. Ref.	Debit	Credit	Cr. Balance
19XX June	1	Balance	✔			300 00
	9		CPJ2	300 00		–0–

NAME Al Jeep
ADDRESS 118 Wang Rd., London, ON N5X 2Y3

Date		Explanation	Post. Ref.	Debit	Credit	Cr. Balance
19XX June	1	Balance	✔			200 00
	1		CPJ2	200 00		–0–

PARTIAL GENERAL LEDGER

Cash — Acct. No. 110

Date 19XX		Explanation	Post. Ref.	Debit	Credit	DR or CR	Balance
June	1	Balance	✔			DR	700 00
	30		CPJ2		565 00	DR	135 00

Accounts Payable — Acct. No. 210 ← Controlling account

Date 19XX		Explanation	Post. Ref.	Debit	Credit	DR or CR	Balance
June	1	Balance	✔			CR	500 00
	30		CPJ2	500 00			–0–

Purchases Discount — Acct. No. 511

Date 19XX		Explanation	Post. Ref.	Debit	Credit	DR or CR	Balance
June	30		CPJ2		10 00	CR	10 00

Advertising Expense — Acct. No. 610

Date 19XX		Explanation	Post. Ref.	Debit	Credit	DR or CR	Balance
June	8		CPJ2	75 00		DR	75 00

LEARNING UNIT 10-4

GST Paid on Purchases

OVERVIEW

In the previous chapter we learned that GST collected on sales needs to be sent to the government periodically. No surprises here—this is very similar to PST. However, the GST is what we refer to as a value-added tax. Without getting overly technical, each business in effect adds a net tax to the "improvement" in value it adds to the goods and/or services it provides or sells. If a company buys some merchandise (to resell) for $1,000 and actually sells it for $1,500, then the GST is applicable only to the $500 difference.

While that is true, the tax works in the following manner:

Companies remit the net difference between the GST they collect on sales and the GST they pay on purchases.

- First, the business charges the 7 percent on the selling price of $1,500. This would amount to $105 (7% × $1,500) (covered in Chapter 9).
- Second, the business pays the 7 percent tax on the $1,000 merchandise purchased. This amounts to $70 (7% × $1,000) (covered in this chapter).
- Finally, the tax sent to the federal government is only $35 (7% × $500) because the business gets a refund for the tax it paid on the purchase.

Summary

Tax collected on sale of merchandise: 7% × $1,500.00 =	$105
Tax paid on purchase of merchandise: 7% × $1,000.00 =	$70
Net tax to be remitted	$35

Businesses do not keep separate track of GST on each item of inventory they sell, of course. However, the above example makes it plain that companies must keep track of the total GST they pay so they can claim a refund when they calculate the GST they must periodically send to the federal government.

This learning unit details the accounting tasks which must be handled properly to accurately record GST.

RECORDING PURCHASES WITH GST

Note: Recording purchases with GST is very similar to recording purchases with no GST—just one extra column is needed.

In the above learning units we discussed purchases and cash payments without GST. In Figure 10-1 a typical purchase order is illustrated. Many companies have not changed their purchase orders to include GST since it is now the law for GST to be included even if the purchase order says nothing. Other companies may refer to the fact that the specified price does not include GST. They expect that 7 percent GST will be added. Still other companies specify and calculate the GST. These companies would produce a purchase order which would look like the one shown below in Figure 10-8.

When the supplier fills the purchase order, an invoice will be prepared which includes GST. In Figure 10-2 a sales invoice before GST was illustrated. The same sales invoice incorporating GST is shown in Figure 10-9. Note that GST is charged on the shipping charges as well as the amount charged for the goods.

This invoice (and others) is recorded by the purchaser in a manner similar to that for the original example shown earlier in this chapter (see Figure 10-4). The major change is that now the purchases journal has one additional column — **Prepaid GST.** Figure 10-9 shows how the purchases journal would appear with GST included.

A more technically correct term for the refund a company receives for the GST it pays is – Input Tax Credit. Do not be confused by the use of the word *Credit;* these GST amounts are debits in a formal bookkeeping sense. This is logical since GST on purchases is considered an asset. However, it is sometimes treated as a contra-liability since it offsets the GST payable on sales made.

Purchase Order No. 1
Art's Wholesale Clothing Co.
1528 Belle Ave.
Toronto, Ontario M5A 2L4

Purchased From: Abby Blake Company
12 Foster Road
Quebec City, PQ G1M 4H3

Date: April 1, 19XX
Shipped VIA: Freight truck
Terms: 2/10, n/60
FOB: Quebec City

Quantity	Description	Unit Price	Total
100	Ladies' Jackets Code 14-0	$50	$5,000.00
		Add GST	350.00
		Total Price Before Shipping	$5,350.00

Purchase order number must appear on all invoices.

Art's Wholesale
By: Bill Joy

FIGURE 10-8
Purchase Order with GST

Sales Invoice No. 228
Abby Blake Company
12 Foster Road
Quebec City, PQ G1M 4H3

Sold to: Art's Wholesale
Clothing Co.
1528 Belle Ave.
Toronto, ON
M5A 2L4

Date: April 3, 19XX
Shipped VIA: Freight truck
Terms: 2/10, n/60
Your Order No: 1
FOB: Quebec City

Quantity	Description	Unit Price	Total
100	Ladies' Jackets Code 14-0	$50	$5,000.00
	Freight		50.00
	Sub-total		$5,050.00
	GST		353.50
	Total		$5,403.50
	GST Reg. No. 142714982		

FIGURE 10-9
Sales Invoice with GST

Note the following while you review Figure 10-10:

1. GST is paid on equipment purchases as well as on purchases of goods for resale.
2. A different account (number 125) is used to record GST on purchases than was used to record sales (recall account number 212 was used in Chapter 9 for recording GST on sales). While not absolutely required, this procedure can make the preparation of the periodic governmental returns less of a burden.
3. The basic operation of the purchases journal is much the same as before. Crossfooting reveals that the addition of a GST column has not disturbed the equality of debits (7,380 + 4,550 + 835.10 = 12,765.10) and credits (12,765.10).
4. The amounts posted to the accounts payable ledger are posted at the same time and in the same way as previously. The amounts are now higher, of course, as they include GST at 7 percent.

While this is being written, the four Atlantic Provinces have agreed in principle to a combined PST and GST to be called the harmonized tax. When details become available, they will be covered in the *Instructor's Resource Guide* so that all students can be informed of the bookkeeping and accounting implications of the new tax.

THE DEBIT MEMORANDUM

A debit memorandum with GST is very similar to a supplier's invoice with GST except that the amounts are opposite in meaning and effect, and often smaller.

As already discussed, from time to time purchased goods are returned to suppliers due to insufficient quality, defective manufacturing, and the like. We have seen an example of a debit memorandum which is prepared when goods are returned (refer to Figure 10-5). When GST is charged on the original purchase, it must also be added to the debit memorandum as shown in Figure 10-11 below.

Recording this debit memorandum is usually done in the general journal, although a specialized journal could be used if a large number of debit memos were common in a given business. Art's Wholesale Clothing Company would record the debit memorandum (illustrated in Figure 10-11) in their general journal (see Figure 10-12).

The four postings are:

1. 211 — Post to Accounts Payable as a debit in the general ledger account no. 211. When this is done, place in the PR column the account number, 211, above the diagonal on the same line as Accounts Payable.
2. √ — Post to Thorpe Co. in the accounts payable ledger to show we don't owe Thorpe as much money. When this is done place a √ in the journal in the PR column below the diagonal line on the same line as Accounts Payable.
3. 513 — Post to Purchases Returns and Allowances as a credit in the general ledger (account no. 513). When this is done, place the account number, 513, in

FIGURE 10-10 Purchases Journal with GST

ART'S WHOLESALE CLOTHING COMPANY
PURCHASES JOURNAL

Page 1

Date			Date of Invoice	Inv. No.	Terms	PR	Accounts Payable Credit	Purchases Debit	Prepaid GST Dr.	Sundry—Dr. Account Name	Post. Ref.	Amount
19XX April	3	Abby Blake Company	April 03	228	2/10, n/60	✔	5 403 50	5 000 00	353 50	Freight-In		50 00
	4	Joe Francis Company	April 05	388		✔	4 280 00		280 00	Equip.		4 000 00
	6	Thorpe Company	April 06	415	1/10, n/30	✔	856 00	800 00	56 00			
	7	John Sullivan Company	April 06	516	n/10, EOM	✔	1 048 60	980 00	68 60			
	12	Abby Blake Company	April 13	242	1/10, n/30	✔	642 00	600 00	42 00			
	25	John Sullivan Company	April 26	612		✔	535 00		35 00	Supplies		500 00
	30						12 765 10	7 380 00	835 10			4 550 00
							(211)	(511)	(125)			(X)

The ✔ in the posting reference column indicates the accounts payable ledger has been updated during the month.

Total Accounts Payable, Prepaid GST, and Purchases posted to general ledger accounts at end of month.

Posted to general ledger account when transaction is entered.

Total of Sundry not posted—the individual items are posted instead.

ACCOUNTS PAYABLE LEDGER

Tells us what page of journal information came from.

Abby Blake Co.

Dr.	Cr.
	5,403.50 PJ1 4/3
	642.00 PJ1 4/12

Joe Francis Co.

Dr.	Cr.
	4,280.00 PJ1 4/4

John Sullivan Co.

Dr.	Cr.
	1,048.60 PJ1 4/7
	535.00 PJ1 4/25

Thorpe Co.

Dr.	Cr.
	856.00 PJ1 4/6

PARTIAL GENERAL LEDGER

Supplies 115

Dr.	Cr.
4/25 PJ1 500.00	

Purchases 511

Dr.	Cr.
4/30 PJ1 7,380.00	

Equipment 121

Dr.	Cr.
4/4 PJ1 4,000.00	

Freight-In 514

Dr.	Cr.
4/4 PJ1 50.00	

GST Prepaid 125

Dr.	Cr.
4/30 PJ1 835.10	

Accounts Payable 211

Dr.	Cr.
	12,765.10 PJ1 4/30

Debit Memorandum			Page 1

Art's Wholesale
Clothing Co.
1528 Belle Ave.
Toronto, Ontario M5A 2L4

To: Thorpe Company
3 Access Road
Fredericton, NB E3B 4T3

WE DEBIT your account as follows:

Quantity		Unit Cost	Total
20	Men's Hats Code 827—defective brims	$10.00	$200.00
	Add GST @ 7%		14.00
	Total Adjustment		$214.00

FIGURE 10-11
Debit Memorandum with GST

GENERAL JOURNAL

Page 1

Date		Account Titles and Description	PR	Dr.	Cr.
19XX April	9	Accounts Payable, Thorpe Company	211/✔	214 00	
		Purchases, Returns and Allowances	513		200 00
		GST Prepaid	125		14 00
		To record debit memo #1			

FIGURE 10-12
Posting the Debit Memo with GST

the posting reference column of the journal on the same line as Purchases Returns and Allowances (if equipment was returned that was not merchandise for resale, we would credit Equipment and not Purchases Returns and Allowances).

4. 125 — Post to GST Prepaid as a credit. This acts to increase the amount of GST owed to the federal government because it decreases the amount which is claimable to offset the liability recorded in account 212 (see Chapter 9 for details of this account).

The Cash Payments Journal

Note that, even though the CPJ has a column for GST, it is never used when paying a regular suppliers. The GST on these purchases is recorded when the original entries are made in the Purchases Journal. Do not record the GST on these purchases twice!

The addition of GST does not alter the fact that Art's Wholesale will record all payments made by cash (or most likely by cheque) in a cash payments journal. However, as you probably suspect, this journal now has one column more than the original illustration which is shown in Figure 10-6.

Trace the following cash disbursements through the revised Figure 10-13 on pages 399 and 400. The following (revised) transactions affected the cash disbursements journal:

April 2 Issued cheque no. 1 to Pete Blum for insurance paid in advance, $900.
7 Issued cheque no. 2 to Joe Francis Company in payment of its April 5 invoice No. 388.
9 Issued cheque no. 3 to Flo Co. for merchandise purchased for cash $800 plus GST $56. Total $856.
12 Issued cheque no. 4 to Thorpe Company in payment of its April 6 invoice no. 414 less the return and discount.
28 Issued cheque no. 5, $700 salaries paid.

In tracing the cash payments to the payments journal, a few points may be of interest:

1. There is no GST on the insurance payment of $900. Insurance premiums are classified as financial services and no GST is paid on these.

FIGURE 10-13 Cash Payments Journal and Posting with GST

CASH PAYMENTS JOURNAL

Page 1

Date		Chq. No.	Account Debited	Post. Ref.	Sundry Accounts Dr.	Accounts Payable Dr.	Purchases Dr.	GST Prepaid Dr.	Purchases Discount Cr.	Cash Cr.
19XX April	2	1	Pete Blum, Insurance	116	900 00					900 00
	7	2	Joe Francis Company	✔		4280 00				4280 00
	9	3	Flo Co., Cash Purchases				800 00	56 00		856 00
	12	4	Thorpe Company	✔		642 00			6 00	636 00
	28	5	Salaries	611	700 00					700 00
					1600 00	4922 00	800 00	56 00	6 00	7372 00
					(X)	(211)	(512)	(125)	(513)	(111)

Total not posted.

Total posted to general ledger at end of month.

ACCOUNTS PAYABLE LEDGER

NAME Abby Blake Co.
ADDRESS 12 Foster Rd., Quebec City, PQ G1M 4H3

Date		Explanation	Post. Ref.	Debit	Credit	Cr. Balance
19XX April	3		PJ1		5403 50	5403 50
	12		PJ1		642 00	6045 50

NAME Joe Francis Co.
ADDRESS 2 Roundy Rd., Edmonton, AB T5H 2E7

Date		Explanation	Post. Ref.	Debit	Credit	Cr. Balance
19XX April	4		PJ1		4280 00	4280 00
	7		CPJ1	4280 00		–0–

PARTIAL GENERAL LEDGER

Cash — Acct. No. 111

Date 19XX		Explanation	Post. Ref.	Debit	Credit	DR or CR	Balance
April	30		CRJ1	14772 00		DR	14772 00
	30		CPJ1		7372 00	DR	7400 00

Prepaid Insurance — Acct. No. 116

Date 19XX		Explanation	Post. Ref.	Debit	Credit	DR or CR	Balance
April	2		CPJ1	900 00		DR	900 00

FIG. 10-13, (cont.)

NAME John Sullivan Co.
ADDRESS 18 Print St., Regina, SA S4P 2A6

Date		Explanation	Post. Ref.	Debit	Credit	Cr. Balance
19XX April	7		PJ1		1048 60	1048 60
	25		PJ1		535 00	1583 60

NAME Thorpe Company
ADDRESS 3 Access Rd., Fredericton, NB E3B 4T3

Date		Explanation	Post. Ref.	Debit	Credit	Cr. Balance
19XX April	6		PJ1		856 00	856 00
	9		GJ1	214 00		642 00
	12		CPJ1	642 00		–0–

Note on accounts payable balance: Very occasionally (due, perhaps to the return of defective goods after they have been paid for) a debit balance may be called for on accounts payable. Debit balances are opposite to the normal credit balance and are signified by placing the balance in brackets. For example, suppose we get a credit note from Joe Francis Co. for $428.00 after we have paid off their account completely. Their account would then appear as follows:

NAME Joe Francis Co.
ADDRESS 2 Roundy Rd., Edmonton, AB T5H 2E7

Date		Explanation	Post. Ref.	Debit	Credit	Cr. Balance
19XX April	4		PJ1		4280 00	4280 00
	7		CPJ1	4280 00		–0–
	14		GJ4	428 00		(428 00)

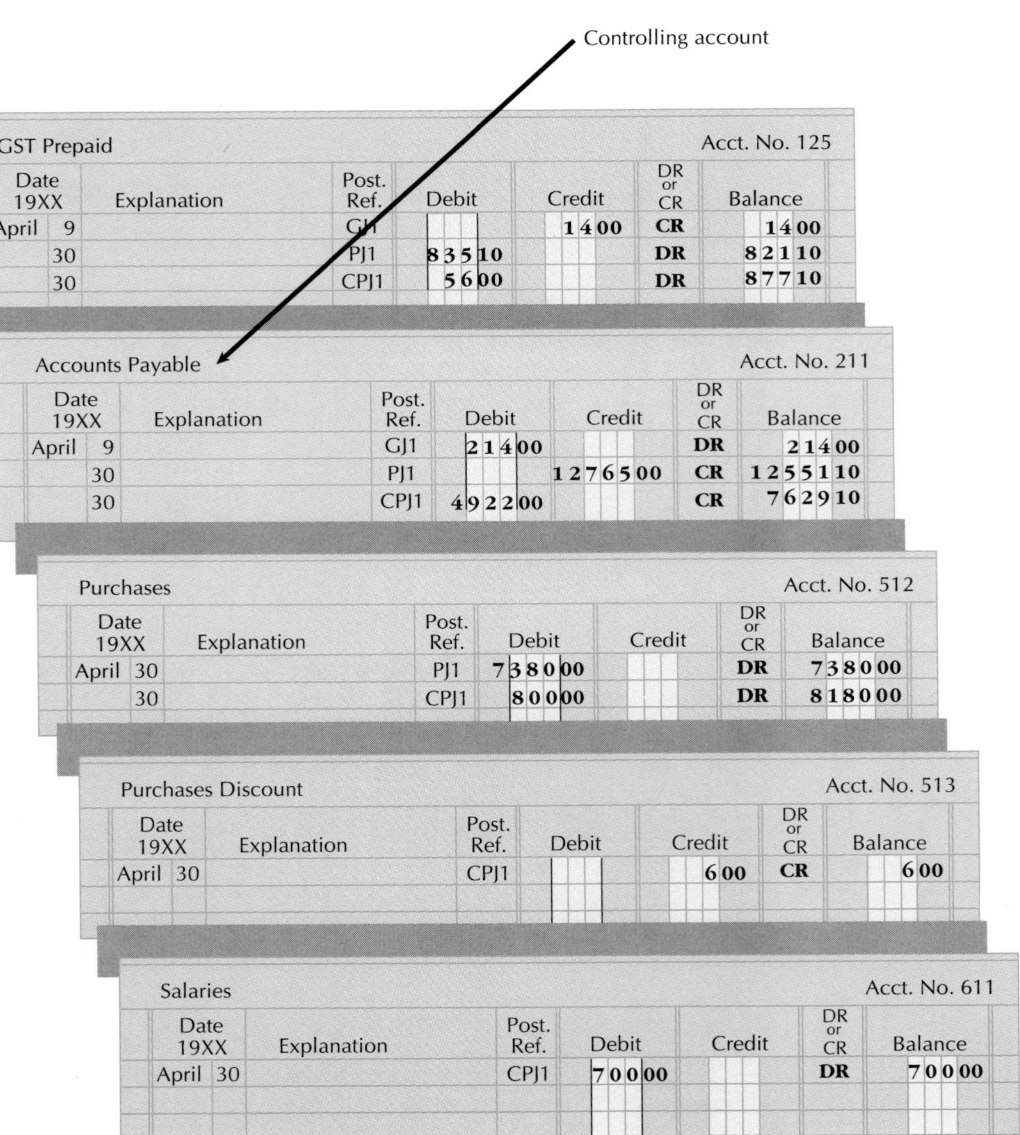

GST Prepaid — Acct. No. 125

Date 19XX		Explanation	Post. Ref.	Debit	Credit	DR or CR	Balance
April	9		GJ1		14 00	CR	14 00
	30		PJ1	835 10		DR	821 10
	30		CPJ1	56 00		DR	877 10

Accounts Payable — Acct. No. 211

Date 19XX		Explanation	Post. Ref.	Debit	Credit	DR or CR	Balance
April	9		GJ1	214 00		DR	214 00
	30		PJ1		12765 00	CR	12551 10
	30		CPJ1	4922 00		CR	7629 10

Purchases — Acct. No. 512

Date 19XX		Explanation	Post. Ref.	Debit	Credit	DR or CR	Balance
April	30		PJ1	7380 00		DR	7380 00
	30		CPJ1	800 00		DR	8180 00

Purchases Discount — Acct. No. 513

Date 19XX		Explanation	Post. Ref.	Debit	Credit	DR or CR	Balance
April	30		CPJ1		6 00	CR	6 00

Salaries — Acct. No. 611

Date 19XX		Explanation	Post. Ref.	Debit	Credit	DR or CR	Balance
April	30		CPJ1	700 00		DR	700 00

2. Similarly, no GST is paid on salaries of $700 on April 28.
3. GST does not affect the $6 purchase discount allowed when payment is made to the Thorpe Company on April 12. This discount is calculated only on the $600 (net) purchase, not on the $642 which is the total amount payable due to the extra 7 percent GST. The actual amount paid is $636, because the $642 is reduced by $6 due to the allowed purchase discount.

Schedule of Accounts Journal

Notice that from Figure 10-13 it is not difficult to prepare a schedule of accounts payable at month-end. This schedule would look like:

Art's Wholesale Clothing Company
Schedule of Accounts Payable
April 30, 19XX

Abby Blake Co.	$6,045.50
John Sullivan Co.	1,583.60
Total Accounts Payable	$7,629.10

If you refer again to Figure 10-13 you can see that $7,629.10 is exactly the balance in account 211—Accounts Payable. Hence, the subsidiary ledger accounts are in agreement with the controlling account in the general ledger. As always, if the total of the individual accounts in the accounts payable ledger does not agree with the control account, it will be necessary to double-check all postings and the mathematical computations of balances in each supplier's account to find the difference. Also, be sure that any entries made in the general journal are posted to the general ledger accounts.

LEARNING UNIT 10-4 REVIEW

AT THIS POINT you should be able to

- Describe the nature of the GST. (p. 394)
- Record the GST on purchases. (p. 395)
- Record the GST on returned purchasess. (p. 396)
- Record the GST on other cash disbursements. (p. 398)
- Prepare a schedule of accounts payable at period-end. (p. 401)

SELF-REVIEW QUIZ 10-4

Journalize the following transactions into the purchases journal (page 2) or general journal (page 1) for Munroe Co. Post or record to accounts payable ledger and general ledger accounts as appropriate. Use the same journal headings we used for Art's Wholesale Clothing Company.

19XX

May 5 Bought merchandise on account from Flynn Co., invoice no. 5121, dated May 6, terms 1/10, n/30 plus GST $63. Total $963.

7 Bought merchandise from John Butler Company, invoice no. 403, dated May 7, terms n/10, EOM, $1,000 plus GST $70. Total $1,070.

13 Issued debit memo no. 1 to Flynn Co. for merchandise returned, $300, from invoice No. 512, plus GST $21. Total $321.

17 Purchased $400 of equipment on account from John Butler Company, invoice no. 413, dated May 18, plus GST $28. Total $428.

Solution to Self-Review Quiz 10-4

MUNROE CO.
PURCHASES JOURNAL

Page 2

Date			Date of Invoice	Inv. No.	Terms	PR	Accounts Payable Credit	Purchases Debit	GST Prepaid Debit	Sundry—Dr. Account Name	Post. Ref.	Amount
19XX May	5	Flynn Co.	May 6	5121	1/10, n/30	✔	963 00	900 00	63 00			
	7	John Butler Co.	May 7	403	n/10, EOM	✔	1070 00	1000 00	70 00			
	17	John Butler Co.	May 18	413		✔	428 00		28 00	Equipment	121	400 00
	31						2461 00	1900 00	161 00			400 00
							(212)	(512)	(125)			(X)

MUNROE CO.
GENERAL JOURNAL

Page 1

Date		Account Titles and Description	PR	Dr.	Cr.
19XX May	13	Accounts Payable, Flynn Company	212/✔	321 00	
		Purchases Returns and Allowances	513		300 00
		GST Prepaid	125		21 00

Chapter Review

COMPREHENSIVE DEMONSTRATION PROBLEM WITH SOLUTION TIPS

(The forms you need are on pages 10-8 to 10-10 of the *Study Guide and Working Papers.*)

Record the following transactions into special or general journals. Record and post as appropriate.

Note: All credit sales are 2/10, n/30. All merchandise purchased on account has 3/10, n/30 credit terms.

Solution Tips to Journalizing

	19XX		
CRJ	March	1	J. Ling invested $2,000 into the business.
SJ		1	Sold merchandise on account to Balder Co., $500, invoice no. 1.
PJ		2	Purchased merchandise on account from Case Co., $500.
CRJ		4	Sold $2,000 of merchandise for cash.
CPJ		6	Paid Case Co. for previous purchases on account, cheque no. 1.
SJ		8	Sold merchandise on account to Lewis Co., $1,000, invoice no. 2.
CRJ		10	Received payment from Balder for invoice no. 1.
GJ		12	Issued a credit memorandum to Lewis Co. for $200 for faulty merchandise.
CRJ		14	Received payment from Lewis Co.
PJ		16	Purchased merchandise on account from Noone Co., $1,000.
PJ		17	Purchased equipment on account from Case Co., $300.
GJ		18	Issued a debit memorandum to Noone Co. for $500 for defective merchandise.
CPJ		20	Paid salaries, $300, cheque no. 2.
CPJ		24	Paid Noone balance owed, cheque no. 3.

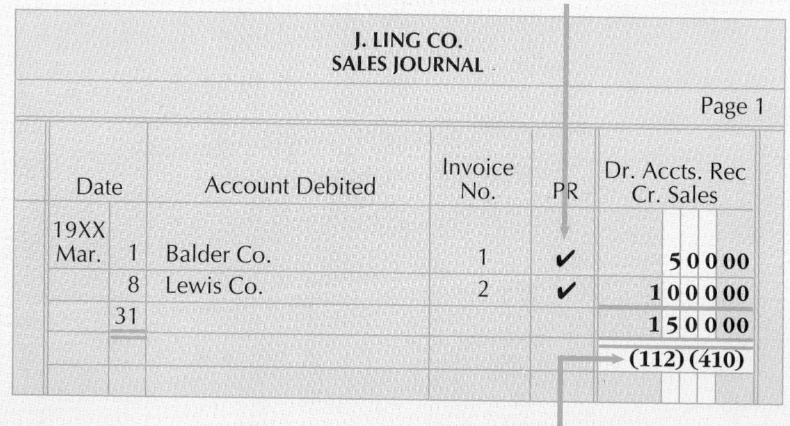
Record accounts receivable subsidiary ledger immediately.
Total posted at end of month to these accounts.

J. LING CO.
SALES JOURNAL

Page 1

Date		Account Debited	Invoice No.	PR	Dr. Accts. Rec Cr. Sales
19XX Mar.	1	Balder Co.	1	✔	50000
	8	Lewis Co.	2	✔	100000
	31				150000
					(112) (410)

GENERAL JOURNAL					Page 1
Date		Account Titles and Description	PR	Dr.	Cr.
19XX Mar.	12	Sales Returns and Allowances	420	200 00	
		Accounts Receivable, Lewis Co.	112/✓		200 00
		Issued credit memo			
	18	Accounts Payable, Noone Co.	210/✓	500 00	
		Purchases Returns and Allowances	520		500 00
		Issued debit memo			

Record and post immediately to subsidiary and the general ledger.

ACCOUNTS RECEIVABLE SUBSIDIARY LEDGER

Balder Company

Date	PR	Dr.	Cr.	Dr. Bal.
19XX 3/1	SJ1	500		500
3/10	CRJ1		500	—

Lewis Company

Date	PR	Dr.	Cr.	Dr. Bal.
19XX 3/8	SJ1	1,000		1,000
3/12	GJ1		200	800
3/14	CPJ1		800	—

ACCOUNTS PAYABLE SUBSIDIARY LEDGER

Case Company

Date	PR	Dr.	Cr.	Cr. Bal.
19XX 3/2	PJ1		500	
3/6	CPJ1	500		—
3/17	PJ1		300	300

Noone Company

Date	PR	Dr.	Cr.	Cr. Bal.
19XX 3/16	PJ1		1,000	1,000
3/18	GJ1	500		500
3/24	CPJ1	500		—

GENERAL LEDGER

Cash 111

Dr.	Cr.
3/31 CRJ1 5,274	1,270 3/31 CPJ1
Balance 4,004	

Sales 410

Dr.	Cr.
	1,500 3/31 SJ1
	2,000 3/31 CRJ1
	3,500 Balance

Accounts Receivable 112

Dr.	Cr.
3/31 SJ1 1,500	200 3/12 GJ1
	1,300 3/31 CRJ1

Sales Returns & Allowances 420

Dr.	Cr.
3/12 GJ1 200	

Equipment 116

Dr.	Cr.
3/17 PJ1 300	

Sales Discount 430

Dr.	Cr.
3/31 CRJ1 26	

Accounts Payable 210

Dr.	Cr.
3/18 GJ1 500	1,800 3/31 PJ1
3/31 CPJ1 1,000	
	300 Balance

Purchases 510

Dr.	Cr.
3/31 PJ1 1,500	

J. Ling, Capital 310	
	2,000 3/1 CRJ1

Purchases Ret. and Allow. 520	
	500 3/18 GJ1

Purchases Discount 530	
	30 3/31 CPJ1

Salaries Expense 610	
3/20 CPJ1 300	

Summary of Solution Tips

Chapter 9—Seller	*Chapter 10—Buyer*
Sales journal	Purchases journal
Cash receipts journal	Cash payments journal
Accounts receivable subsidiary ledger	Accounts payable subsidiary ledger
Sales (Cr.)	Purchases (Dr.)
Sales Returns and Allowances (Dr.)	Purchase Returns and Allowances (Cr.)
Sales Discounts (Dr.)	Purchases Discounts (Cr.)
Accounts Receivable (Dr.)	Accounts Payable (Cr.)
Issue a credit memo	Receive a credit memo
or	*or*
Receive a debit memo	Issue a debit memo
Schedule of accounts receivable	Schedule of accounts payable

When Do I Do What? — A Step-by-Step Walk-Through of This Comprehensive Demonstration Problem

Transaction *What to Do Step by Step*

19XX

March 1 *Money Received:* Record in cash receipts journal. Post immediately to J. Ling, Capital, since it is in Sundry.

1 *Sale on Account:* Record in sales journal. Record immediately to Balder Co., in Accounts Receivable Subsidiary Ledger. Place a ✓ in PR column of sales journal when subsidiary is updated.

2 *Buy Merchandise on Account:* Record in purchases journal. Record to Case Co. immediately in the accounts payable subsidiary ledger.

4 *Money In:* Record in cash receipts journal. No posting needed (put an X in PR column.)

6 *Money Out:* Record in cash payments journal. Save $15, which is a Purchases Discount. Record immediately to Case Co. in accounts payable subsidiary ledger (the full amount of $500).

8 *Sales on Account:* Record in sales journal. Update immediately to Lewis in accounts receivable subsidiary ledger.

10 *Money In:* Record in cash receipts journal. Since Balder pays within 10 days, they get a $10 discount. Record immediately to Balder in the accounts receivable subsidiary ledger, the full amount.

12 *Returns:* Record in general journal. Seller issues credit memo resulting in higher sales returns and customers owing less. All postings and recordings are done immediately.

14 *Money In:* Record in cash receipts journal:

$$\$1{,}000 - \$200 \text{ returns} = \$800 \times 0.02 = \$16 \text{ discount}$$

Record immediately the $800 to Lewis in the accounts receivable subsidiary ledger.

16 *Buy Now, Pay Later:* Record in purchases journal. Record immediately to Noone Co. in the accounts payable subsidiary ledger.

17 *Buy Now, Pay Later:* Record in purchases journal in Sundry. This is not merchandise for resale. Record and post immediately.

18 *Returns:* Record in general journal. Buyer issues a debit memo reducing their accounts payable due to Purchases Return and Allowances. Post and record immediately.

20 *Salaries:* Record in cash payments journal, Sundry column. No posting till end of month.

24 *Money Out:* Record in cash payments journal. Save 3 percent — $15, a Purchases Discount. Record immediately to Accounts Payable Subsidiary Ledger that you reduce Noone by $500.

At End of Month: Post totals (except Sundry) of special journal to the general ledger.

Note: In this problem at end of month (1) Accounts Receivable in the general ledger, the controlling account, has a zero balance, as does each title in the accounts receivable subsidiary ledger. (2) The balance in Accounts Payable (the controlling account) is $300. In the accounts payable subsidiary ledger, we owe Case $300. The sum of the subsidiary does equal the balance in the controlling account at the end of the month.

Summary of Key Points

Learning Unit 10-1

1. Purchases are merchandise for resale. It is a cost.
2. Purchases Returns and Allowances and Purchases Discount are contra-cost.
3. "F.O.B. shipping point" means that the purchaser of the goods is responsible for covering the shipping costs. If the terms were "F.O.B. destination," the seller would be responsible for covering the shipping costs until the goods reached their destination.
4. Purchases discounts are not taken on freight.

Learning Unit 10-2

1. The steps for buying merchandise from a company may include:
   - **a.** The requesting department prepares a purchase requisition.
   - **b.** The purchasing department prepares a purchase order.
   - **c.** Seller receives the order and prepares a sales invoice (a purchase invoice for the buyer).
   - **d.** Buyer receives the goods and prepares a receiving report.
   - **e.** Accounting department verifies and approves the invoice for payment.
2. The purchases journal records the buying of merchandise or other items on account.
3. The accounts payable subsidiary ledger, organized in alphabetical order, is not in the same book as Accounts Payable, the controlling account in the general ledger.

4. At the end of the month the total of all creditors' ending balances in the accounts payable subsidiary ledger should equal the ending balance in Accounts Payable, the controlling account in the general ledger.
5. A debit memorandum (issued by the buyer) indicates that the amount owed from a previous purchase is being reduced because some goods were defective or not up to a specific standard and thus were returned or an allowance requested. On receiving the debit memorandum, the seller will issue a credit memorandum.

Learning Unit 10-3

1. All payments by cheque are recorded in the cash payments journal.
2. At the end of the month, the schedule of accounts payable, a list of ending amounts owed individual creditors, should equal the ending balance in Accounts Payable, the controlling account in the general ledger.
3. Trade discounts are deductions off the list price that have nothing to do with early payments (cash discounts). Invoice amounts are recorded after the trade discount is deducted. Cash discounts are not taken on trade discounts.

Learning Unit 10-4

1. GST is paid on most purchases of goods and services in Canada. It is very important for businesses to keep proper track of the GST they pay because they get to deduct this from the GST otherwise payable on their own sales.
2. A separate column is added to the purchases journal and to the cash payments journal to record the GST on things purchased either on account or for cash.
3. When a debit note is received for a purchase return or allowance, the GST is always added to the total. When the debit note is recorded in the general journal, the GST amount is credited to the same account used to track the GST amounts paid for the period. This operates to increase the amount owed to the federal government. Other postings are done in the same way as described earlier.

KEY TERMS

Accounts payable subsidiary ledger A book or file that contains in alphabetical order the name of the creditor and amount owed from purchases on account.

Cash payments journal (cash disbursements journal) A special journal that records all transactions involving payment by cheque.

Controlling account The account in the general ledger that summarizes or controls a subsidiary ledger. *Example:* The Accounts Payable account in the general ledger is the controlling account for the accounts payable subsidiary ledger. After postings are complete, it shows the total amount owed from purchases made on account.

Debit memorandum A memo issued by a purchaser to a seller, indicating that some Purchases Returns and Allowances have occurred and therefore the purchaser now owes less money on account.

F.O.B. "Free on board," which means without shipping charge to the buyer up to a specified location. The seller bears the cost up to the specified location and the buyer bears the cost from that location to the actual destination.

F.O.B. destination *Seller* pays or is responsible for the cost of freight to purchaser's location or destination.

F.O.B. shipping point *Purchaser* pays or is responsible for the shipping costs from seller's shipping point to purchaser's location.

Invoice approval form The accounting department uses this form in checking the invoice and finally approving it for recording and payment.

Prepaid GST An asset account used to accumulate the GST paid (or payable) to suppliers on goods or services purchased. It is an asset because it can be deducted from the amount otherwise payable to the federal government.

Purchases Merchandise for resale. It is a cost.

Purchases Discount A contra-cost account in the general ledger that records discounts offered by suppliers of merchandise for prompt payment of purchases by buyers.

Purchase invoice The seller's sales invoice, which is sent to the purchaser.

Purchases journal A multicolumn special journal that records the buying of merchandise or other items on account.

Purchase order A form used in business to place an order for the buying of goods from a seller.

Purchase requisition A form used within a business by the requesting department asking the purchasing department of the business to buy specific goods.

Purchases Returns and Allowances A contra-cost account in the ledger that records the amount of defective or unacceptable merchandise returned to suppliers and/or price reductions given for defective items.

Receiving report A business form used to notify purchasing and accounting of the ordered goods received along with the quantities and specific condition of the goods.

Blueprint of Purchases and Cash Payments Journals

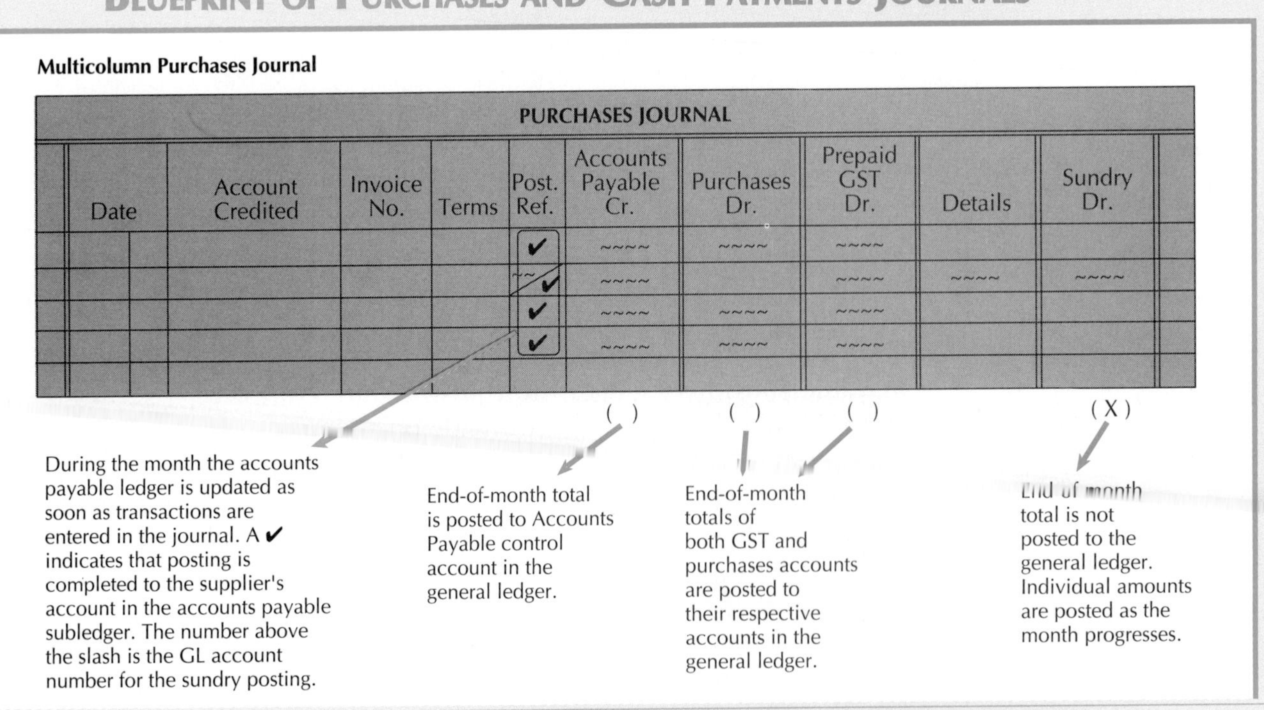

Multicolumn Purchases Journal
PURCHASES JOURNAL
Date
Account Credited
Invoice No.
Terms
Post. Ref.
Accounts Payable Cr.
Purchases Dr.
Prepaid GST Dr.
Details
Sundry Dr.
( )
( )
( )
(X)
During the month the accounts payable ledger is updated as soon as transactions are entered in the journal. A ✔ indicates that posting is completed to the supplier's account in the accounts payable subledger. The number above the slash is the GL account number for the sundry posting.
End-of-month total is posted to Accounts Payable control account in the general ledger.
End-of-month totals of both GST and purchases accounts are posted to their respective accounts in the general ledger.
End of month total is not posted to the general ledger. Individual amounts are posted as the month progresses.

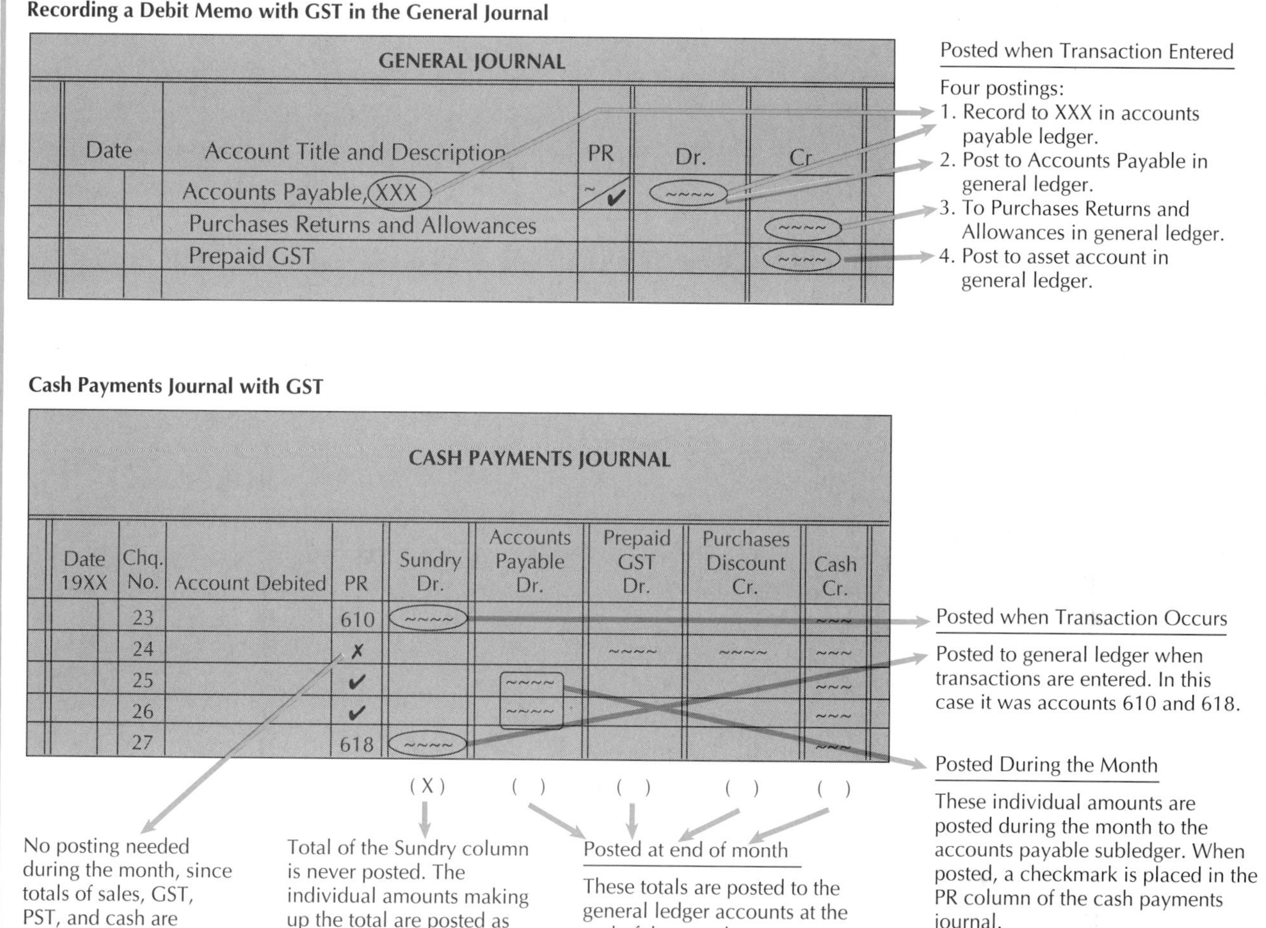

Recording a Debit Memo with GST in the General Journal
GENERAL JOURNAL
Date
Account Title and Description
PR
Dr.
Cr.
Accounts Payable, XXX
Purchases Returns and Allowances
Prepaid GST
Posted when Transaction Entered
Four postings:
1. Record to XXX in accounts payable ledger.
2. Post to Accounts Payable in general ledger.
3. To Purchases Returns and Allowances in general ledger.
4. Post to asset account in general ledger.
Cash Payments Journal with GST
CASH PAYMENTS JOURNAL
Date 19XX
Chq. No.
Account Debited
PR
Sundry Dr.
Accounts Payable Dr.
Prepaid GST Dr.
Purchases Discount Cr.
Cash Cr.
23
610
24
25
26
27
618
(X)
( )
Posted when Transaction Occurs
Posted to general ledger when transactions are entered. In this case it was accounts 610 and 618.
Posted During the Month
These individual amounts are posted during the month to the accounts payable subledger. When posted, a checkmark is placed in the PR column of the cash payments journal.
No posting needed during the month, since totals of sales, GST, PST, and cash are posted at end of month.
Total of the Sundry column is never posted. The individual amounts making up the total are posted as the month progresses.
Posted at end of month
These totals are posted to the general ledger accounts at the end of the month.

QUESTIONS, EXERCISES, AND PROBLEMS

Discussion Questions

1. Explain how net purchases is calculated.
2. What is the normal balance of Purchases Discount?
3. What is a contra-cost?
4. Explain the difference between F.O.B. shipping point and F.O.B. destination.
5. F.O.B. destination means that title to the goods will switch to the buyer when goods are shipped. Agree or disagree. Why?
6. What is the normal balance of each creditor in the accounts payable subsidiary ledger?
7. Why doesn't the balance of the controlling account, Accounts Payable, equal the sum of the accounts payable subsidiary ledger during the month?
8. What is the relationship between a purchase requisition and a purchase order?
9. What purpose could a typical invoice approval form serve?
10. Explain the difference between merchandise and equipment.

11. Why would the purchaser issue a debit memorandum?
12. Explain the relationship between a purchases journal and a cash payments journal.
13. Explain why a trade discount is not a cash discount.
14. State why it is so important for firms to keep track of the GST they pay each period.
15. Why does GST on a debit note act to increase the net amount of GST payable?

Mini Exercises

(The forms you need are on page 10-12 of the *Study Guide and Working Papers.*)

Overview

1. Complete the following table:

To the Seller		To the Buyer
Sales	↔	**a.** ________
Sales Returns and Allowances	↔	**b.** ________
Sales Discount	↔	**c.** ________
Sales journal	↔	**d.** ________
Cash receipts journal	↔	**e.** ________
Credit memorandum	↔	**f.** ________
Schedule of Accounts Receivable	↔	**g.** ________
Accounts Receivable Subsidiary Ledger	↔	**h.** ________

2. Complete the following table:

Accounts Affected	Category	↑	↓	Temporary or Permanent
Purchases				
Purchases Returns and Allowances				
Purchases Discount				

Calculating Net Purchases

3. Calculate Net Purchases from the following: Purchases, $6; Purchases Returns and Allowances, $2; Purchases Discounts, $1.

Purchases Journal, General Journal, Recording and Posting

4. Match the following to the three journal entries (more than one number can be used).
   1. Journalized into purchases journal.
   2. Record immediately to subsidiary ledger.
   3. Post totals from purchases journal (except Sundry total) at end of month to general ledger.
   4. Journalized in general journal.
   5. Record and post immediately to subsidiary and general ledger.

   a. Bought merchandise on account from Also Co., invoice no. 12, $20.
   b. Bought equipment on account from Jone Co., invoice no. 13, $40.
   c. Issued debit memo no. 1 to Also Co. for merchandise returned, $4, from invoice no. 12.

Recording Transactions in Special Journals

5. Indicate in which journal each transaction will be journalized:

1. SJ　　**4.** CPJ
2. PJ　　**5.** GJ
3. CRJ

—— **a.** Issued credit memo no. 2, $13.
—— **b.** Cash sales, $20.
—— **c.** Received cheque from Blue Co., $50 less 3 percent discount.
—— **d.** Bought merchandise on account from Mel Co., $35, 1/10, n/30, invoice no. 20.
—— **e.** Cash purchase, $15.
—— **f.** Issued debit memo to Mel Co., $15 for merchandise returned from invoice no. 20.

6. From the following prepare a schedule of accounts payable for AVE Co. for May 31, 19XX:

Accounts Payable Subsidiary Ledger

Rowe Co.

			5/7	PJ1	60

Bloss Co.

5/25	CPJ1	10	5/20	PJ1	50

General Ledger

Accounts Payable

5/31	CPJ	10	5/31	PJ1	110

Exercises

(The forms you need are on pages 10-13 and 10-14 of the *Study Guide and Working Papers*.)

10-1. From the accompanying purchases journal, record to the accounts payable subsidiary ledger and post to general ledger accounts as appropriate.

Page 1

Date		Account Credited	Date of Invoice	Terms	Post. Ref.	Accounts Payable Credit	Purchases Debit	Sundry—Dr. Account	PR	Amount
19XX June	3	Barr Co.	May 3	1/10, n/30		600 00	600 00			
	4	Jess Co.	May 4	n/10, EOM		900 00	900 00			
	8	Rey Co.	May 8			400 00		Equipment		400 00

Recording to the accounts payable subsidiary ledger and posting to the general ledger from a purchases journal.

Partial Accounts Payable Subsidiary Ledger　　**Partial General Ledger**

Journalizing, recording, and posting a debit memorandum.

10-2. On July 10, 19XX, Aster Co. issued debit memorandum no. 1 for $400 to Reel Co. for merchandise returned from invoice no. 312. Your task is to journalize, record, and post this transaction as appropriate. Use the same account numbers as found in the text for Art's Wholesale Clothing Company. The general journal is page 1.

Journalizing, recording, and posting a cash payments journal.

10-3. Journalize, record, and post when appropriate the following transactions into the cash payments journal (p. 2) for Morgan's Clothing. Use the same headings as found in the text (p. 375). All purchases discounts are 2/10, n/30.

Accounts Payable Subsidiary Ledger

Name	*Balance*	*Invoice No.*
A. James	$1,000	522
B. Foss	400	488
J. Ranch	900	562
B. Swanson	100	821

Partial General Ledger

Account	*Balance*
Cash 110	$3,000
Accounts Payable 210	2,400
Purchases Discount 511	
Advertising Expense 610	

19XX

April 1 Issued cheque no. 20 to A. James Company in payment of its March 28 invoice no. 522.

8 Issued cheque no. 21 to Flott Advertising in payment of its advertising bill, $100, no discount.

15 Issued cheque no. 22 to B. Foss in payment of its March 25 invoice no. 488.

Schedule of accounts payable.

10-4. From Exercise 10-3, prepare a schedule of accounts payable and verify that the total of the schedule equals the amount in the controlling account.

F.O.B. destination.

10-5. Record the following transaction in a transaction analysis chart for the buyer: Bought merchandise for $9,000 on account. Shipping terms were F.O.B. destination. The cost of shipping was $500.

Trade and cash discounts.

10-6. Angie Rase bought merchandise with a list price of $4,000. Angie was entitled to a 30 percent trade discount, as well as a 3 percent cash discount. What was Angie's actual cost of buying this merchandise after the cash discount?

Group A Problems

Journalizing, recording, and posting a purchases journal.

10A-1. (GST not involved in this problem.) Judy Clark recently opened a sporting goods shop. As the bookkeeper of her shop, journalize, record, and post when appropriate the following transactions (account numbers are: Store Supplies, 115; Store Equipment, 121; Accounts Payable, 210; Purchases, 510):

19XX

June 4 Bought merchandise on account from Aster Co., invoice no. 442, dated June 4, terms 2/10, n/30; $900.

5 Bought store equipment from Norton Co., invoice no. 502, dated June 5; $4,000.

8 Bought merchandise on account from Rolo Co., invoice no. 401, dated June 7; terms 2/10, n/30; $1,400.

14 Bought store supplies on account from Aster Co., invoice no. 519, dated June 14; $900.

10A-2. Mabel's Natural Food Store uses a purchases journal (p. 10) and a general journal (p. 2) to record the following transactions (continued from April):

Journalizing, recording, and posting a purchases journal as well as recording a debit memorandum and preparing a schedule of accounts payable.

19XX

May 8 Purchased merchandise on account from Aton Co., invoice no. 400, dated May 7, terms 2/10, n/60; $600 plus GST.

10 Purchased merchandise on account from Broward Co., invoice no. 120, dated May 10, terms 2/10, n/60; $1,200 plus GST.

12 Purchased store supplies on account from Midden Co., invoice no. 510, dated May 12, $500 plus GST.

14 Issued debit memo no. 8 to Aton Co. for merchandise returned, $400 (plus GST) from invoice no. 400.

17 Purchased office equipment on account from Relar Co., invoice no. 810, dated May 17, $560 plus GST.

24 Purchased additional store supplies on account from Midden Co., invoice no. 516, dated May 23, terms 2/10, n/30; $650 plus GST.

The food store has decided to keep a separate column for the purchases of supplies in the purchases journal which also has a separate column for GST.

Required

1. Journalize the transactions.
2. Post and record as appropriate.
3. Prepare a schedule of accounts payable.

Accounts Payable Ledger

Name	*Balance*
Aton Co.	$ 428
Broward Co.	642
Midden Co.	1,284
Relar Co.	535

Partial General Ledger

Account	*Number*	*Balance*
Store Supplies	110	$ —
Prepaid GST	112	498
Office Equipment	120	—
Accounts Payable	210	2,889
Purchases	510	16,000
Purchases Returns and Allowances	512	—

Journalizing, recording, and posting a cash payments journal with GST; preparing a schedule of accounts payable.

10A-3. Wendy Jones operates a wholesale computer centre. All transactions requiring the payment of cash are recorded in the cash payments journal (p. 5). The account balances as of May 1, 19XX, are as follows:

Accounts Payable Ledger

Name	*Balance*	*GST Included*
Alvin Co.	$1,284	$84
Henry Co.	642	42
Soy Co.	856	56
Xon Co.	1,498	98

Partial General Ledger

Account	*Number*	*Balance*
Cash	110	$17,000
Prepaid GST	132	965
Delivery Truck	150	—
Accounts Payable	210	4,280
Computer Purchases	510	—
Computer Purchases Discount	511	—
Rent Expense	610	—
Utilities Expense	620	—

Required

1. Journalize the following transactions.
2. Record to the accounts payable ledger and post to general ledger as appropriate.
3. Prepare a schedule of accounts payable.

19XX

May 1 Paid half the amount owed Henry Co. from previous purchases of computers on account, less a 2 percent purchases discount, cheque no. 21.

3 Bought a delivery truck for $8,000 cash plus GST of $560, cheque no. 22, payable to Bill Ring Co.

6 Bought computer merchandise from Lectro Co., cheque no. 23, $2,900, plus GST.

18 Bought additional computer merchandise from Pulse Co., cheque no. 24, $800, plus GST.

24 Paid Xon Co. the amount owed less a 2 percent purchases discount, cheque no. 25.

28 Paid rent expense to King's Realty Trust, cheque no. 26, $2,000, plus GST.

29 Paid utilities expense to Stone Utility Co., cheque no. 27, $300, plus GST.

30 Paid half the amount owed Soy Co., no discount, cheque no. 28.

Comprehensive review problem with GST: All special journals and the general journal; schedule of accounts payable and accounts receivable.

10A-4. Abby Ellen owns Abby's Toy House. As her newly hired accountant, your task is to

1. Journalize the transactions for the month of March.
2. Record to subsidiary ledgers and post to general ledger as appropri ate.
3. Total, rule, and crossfoot the journals.
4. Prepare a schedule of accounts receivable and a schedule of accounts payable.

The following is the partial chart of accounts for Abby's Toy House:

Assets	**Revenue**
110 Cash	410 Toy Sales
112 Accounts Receivable	412 Sales Returns and Allowances
114 Prepaid Rent	414 Sales Discounts
116 Prepaid GST	
121 Delivery Truck	**Cost of Goods**
	510 Toy Purchases
Liabilities	512 Purchases Returns and Allowances
210 Accounts Payable	514 Purchases Discount
218 GST Payable	
	Expenses
Owner's Equity	610 Salaries Expense
310 A. Ellen, Capital	612 Cleaning Expense

19XX

March 1 Abby Ellen invested $8,000 in the toy store.

1 Paid three months' rent in advance, cheque no. 1, $3,000, plus GST.

1 Purchased merchandise from Earl Miller Company on account, $4,000, plus GST. Invoice no. 410, dated March 1, terms 2/10, n/30.

3 Sold merchandise to Bill Burton on account, $1,000, plus GST. Invoice no. 1, terms 2/10, n/30.

6 Sold merchandise to Jim Rex on account, $700, plus GST. Invoice no. 2, terms 2/10, n/30.

8 Purchased merchandise from Earl Miller Co. on account, $1,200, plus GST. Invoice no. 415, dated March 7, terms 2/10, n/30.

9 Sold merchandise to Bill Burton on account, $600, plus GST. Invoice no. 3, terms 2/10, n/30.

9 Paid cleaning service $300, plus GST. Cheque no. 2.

10 Jim Rex returned merchandise that cost $300 (before GST) to Abby's Toy House. Abby issued credit memorandum no. 1 to Jim Rex for $300, plus GST.

10 Purchased merchandise from Minnie Katz on account, $4,000, plus GST. Invoice no. 311, dated March 10, terms 1/15, n/60.

12 Paid Earl Miller Co. invoice no. 410, dated March 2, cheque no. 3.

13 Sold $1,300 (plus GST) of toy merchandise for cash.

13 Paid salaries, $600, cheque no. 4.

14 Returned merchandise to Minnie Katz in the amount of $1,000, plus GST. Abby's Toy House issued debit memorandum no. 1 to Minnie Katz.

15 Sold merchandise for cash $4,000, plus GST.

16 Received payment from Jim Rex, invoice no. 2 (less returned merchandise), less discount.

16 Bill Burton paid invoice no. 1.

16 Sold toy merchandise to Amy Rose on account, $4,000, plus GST. Invoice no. 4, terms 2/10, n/30.

20 Purchased delivery truck on account from Sam Katz Garage, $3,000, plus GST. Invoice no. 111, dated March 20 (no discount).

22 Sold to Bill Burton merchandise on account, $900, plus GST. Invoice no. 5, terms 2/10, n/30.

23 Paid Minnie Katz balance owed, cheque no. 5.

24 Sold toy merchandise on account to Amy Rose, $1,100, plus GST. Invoice no. 6, terms 2/10, n/30.

25 Purchased toy merchandise, $600, plus GST. Cheque no. 6.

26 Purchased toy merchandise from Woody Smith on account, $4,800, plus GST. Invoice no. 211, dated March 26, terms 2/10, n/30.
28 Bill Burton paid invoice no. 5, dated March 22.
28 Amy Rose paid invoice no. 6, dated March 24.
28 Abby invested an additional $5,000 in the business.
28 Purchased merchandise from Earl Miller Co., $1,400, plus GST. Invoice no. 436, dated March 27, terms 2/10, n/30.
30 Paid Earl Miller Co. invoice no. 436, cheque no. 7.
30 Sold merchandise to Bonnie Flow Company on account, $3,000, plus GST. Invoice no. 7, terms 2/10, n/30.

Group B Problems

Journalizing, recording, and posting a purchases journal.

10B-1. (GST not involved in this problem.) From the following transactions of Judy Clark's sporting goods shop, journalize in the purchases journal and record and post as appropriate:

19XX
June 4 Bought merchandise on account from Rolo Co., invoice No. 400, dated June 4, terms 2/10, n/30; $1,800.
5 Bought store equipment from Norton Co., invoice No. 518, dated June 4; $6,000.
8 Bought merchandise on account from Aster Co., invoice No. 411, dated June 8, terms 2/10, n/30; $400.
14 Bought store supplies on account from Aster Co., invoice No. 415, dated June 13, $1,200.

Journalizing, recording, and posting a purchases journal with GST as well as recording the issuing of a debit memorandum and preparing a schedule of accounts payable.

10B-2. As the accountant of Mabel's Natural Food Store (1) journalize the following transactions into the purchases (p. 10) or general journal (p. 2), (2) record and post as appropriate, and (3) prepare a schedule of accounts payable. Beginning balances are in your working papers.

19XX
May 8 Purchased merchandise on account from Broward Co., invoice no. 420, dated May 7, terms 2/10, n/60; $500, plus GST.
10 Purchased merchandise on account from Aton Co., invoice no. 400, dated May 10, terms 2/10, n/60; $900, plus GST.
12 Purchased store supplies on account from Midden Co., invoice no. 510, dated May 12, $700, plus GST.
14 Issued debit memo no. 7 to Aton Co. for merchandise returned,.$400, plus GST. (From invoice no. 400.)
17 Purchased office equipment on account from Relar Co., invoice no. 810, dated May 17, $750, plus GST.
24 Purchased additional store supplies on account from Midden Co., invoice no. 516, dated May 23, $850, plus GST.

Journalizing, recording, and posting a cash payments journal with GST. Preparing a schedule of accounts payable.

10B-3. Wendy Jones has hired you as her bookkeeper to record the following transactions in the cash payments journal. She would like you to record and post as appropriate and supply her with a schedule of accounts payable. (Beginning balances are in your workbook or Problem 10A-3.)

19XX
May 1 Bought a delivery truck for $8,000 cash, plus GST. Cheque no. 21, payable to Randy Rosse Co.
3 Paid half the amount owed Henry Co. from previous purchases of computer merchandise on account, less a 5 percent purchases discount, cheque no. 22.

6 Bought computer merchandise from Jane Co. for $900 cash, plus GST. Cheque no. 23.
18 Bought additional computer merchandise from Jane Co., cheque no. 24, $1,000, plus GST.
24 Paid Xon Co. the amount owed less a 5 percent purchases discount, cheque no. 25.
28 Paid rent expense to Regan Realty Trust, cheque no. 26, $3,000, plus GST.
29 Paid half the amount owed Soy Co., no discount, cheque no. 27.
30 Paid utilities expense to County Utility, cheque no. 28, $425, plus GST.

Comprehensive review problem with GST: All special journals and the general journal; schedule of accounts payable and accounts receivable.

10B-4. As the new accountant for Abby's Toy House, your task is to

1. Journalize the transactions for the month of March.
2. Record to subsidiary ledgers and post to the general ledger as appropriate.
3. Total, rule, and crossfoot the journals.
4. Prepare a schedule of accounts receivable and a schedule of accounts payable.

(Use the same chart of accounts as in Problem 10A-4. Your workbook has all the forms you need to complete this problem.)

19XX
March 1 Abby invested $4,000 in the new toy store.
1 Paid two months' rent in advance, cheque no. 1, $1,000, plus GST.
1 Purchased merchandise from Earl Miller Company, invoice no. 410, dated March 1, terms 2/10, n/30; $6,000, plus GST.
3 Sold merchandise to Bill Burton on account, $1,600, plus GST. Invoice no. 1, terms 2/10, n/30.
6 Sold merchandise to Jim Rex on account, $800, plus GST. Invoice no. 2, terms 2/10, n/30.
8 Purchased merchandise from Earl Miller Company, $800, plus GST. Invoice no. 415, dated March 7, terms 2/10, n/30.
9 Sold merchandise to Bill Burton on account, $700, plus GST. Invoice no. 3, terms 2/10, n/30.
9 Paid cleaning service, $400, plus GST. Cheque no. 2.
10 Jim Rex returned merchandise that cost $200 (plus GST) to Abby. Abby issued credit memorandum no. 1 to Jim Rex for $200, plus GST.
10 Purchased merchandise from Minnie Katz, $7,000, plus GST. Invoice no. 311, dated March 10, terms 1/15, n/60.
12 Paid Earl Miller Co. invoice no. 410, dated March 1, cheque no. 3.
13 Sold $1,500 (plus GST) of toy merchandise for cash.
13 Paid salaries, $700, cheque no. 4.
14 Returned merchandise to Minnie Katz in the amount of $500, plus GST. Abby issued debit memorandum No. 1 to Minnie Katz.
15 Sold merchandise for cash, $4,800, plus GST.
16 Received payment from Jim Rex for invoice no. 2 (less returned merchandise) less discount.
16 Bill Burton paid invoice No. 1.
16 Sold toy merchandise to Amy Rose on account, $6,000, plus GST. Invoice no. 4, terms 2/10, n/30.
20 Purchased delivery truck on account from Sam Katz Garage, $2,500, plus GST. Invoice no. 111, dated March 20 (no discount).
22 Sold to Bill Burton merchandise on account, $2,000, plus GST. Invoice no. 5, terms 2/10, n/30.
23 Paid Minnie Katz balance owed, cheque no. 5.

24 Sold toy merchandise on account to Amy Rose, \$2,000, plus GST. Invoice no. 6, terms 2/10, n/30.
25 Purchased toy merchandise, \$800, plus GST. Cheque no. 6.
26 Purchased toy merchandise from Woody Smith on account, \$5,900, plus GST. Invoice No. 211, dated March 25, terms 2/10, n/30.
28 Bill Burton paid invoice no. 5, dated March 22.
28 Amy Rose paid invoice no. 6, dated March 24.
28 Abby invested an additional \$3,000 in the business.
28 Purchased merchandise from Earl Miller Co., \$4,200, plus GST. Invoice no. 436, dated March 27, terms 2/10, n/30.
30 Paid Earl Miller Co. invoice no. 436, cheque no. 7.
30 Sold merchandise to Bonnie Flow Company on account, \$3,200, plus GST. Invoice no. 7, terms 2/10, n/30.

Group C Problems

Journalizing, recording, and posting a purchases journal.

10C-1. (GST not involved in this problem.) Barb Wells recently opened an imported foods store. As the bookkeeper of her store, journalize, record, and post when appropriate the following transactions (account numbers are: Store Supplies, 115; Store Equipment, 141; Accounts Payable, 210; Purchases, 510):

19XX

May 4 Bought merchandise on account from Convey Co., invoice no. 751, dated May 5, terms 2/10, n/30; \$715.
5 Bought store equipment from Reliable Co., invoice no. 1202, dated May 6; \$5,180.
8 Bought merchandise on account from Brendan Co., invoice no. 401, dated May 9; terms 1/10, n/30; \$1,740.
14 Bought store supplies on account from Convey Co., invoice no. 823 dated May 14; \$785.

Journalizing, recording, and posting a purchases journal with GST as well as recording the issuing of a debit memorandum and preparing a schedule of accounts payable.

10C-2. Farber's Fabric Co. uses a purchases journal (p. 21) and a general journal (p. 32) to record the following transactions (continued from July) the GST rate is 7 percent:

19XX

August 3 Purchased fabric for resale from European Import Fabrics Co., invoice no. 653, dated August 2, terms net 15 days; \$1,362 plus GST.
8 Purchased merchandise on account from Eddyn Co., invoice no. 250, dated August 9, terms 2/10, n/60; \$920 plus GST.
10 Purchased merchandise on account from Forward Co., invoice no. 1124, dated August 11, terms 1/10, n/60; \$1,626 plus GST.
12 Purchased store supplies on account from Lavoy Co., invoice no. 712, dated August 13, \$2,680 plus GST.
14 Issued debit memo no. 8 to Eddyn Co. for merchandise returned, \$160 (plus GST), from invoice no. 250.
17 Purchased office equipment on account from Reliant Co., invoice No. 873, dated August 18, \$1,610 plus GST.
24 Purchased additional store supplies on account from Lavoy Co., invoice No. 816, dated August 25, terms 2/10, n/30; \$725 plus GST.
29 Purchased fabric for resale from European Import Fabrics Co., invoice no. 713, dated August 27, terms net 15 days; \$2,740 plus GST.

The fabric store has decided to keep a separate column for the purchases of supplies in the purchases journal and also has a separate column for GST.

Required

1. Journalize the transactions.
2. Post and record as appropriate.
3. Prepare a schedule of accounts payable.

Accounts Payable Ledger

Name	*Balance*
Eddyn Co.	$ 856
European Import	3,267
Forward Co.	1,672
Reliant Co.	2,773
Lavoy Co.	535

Partial General Ledger

Account	*Number*	*Balance*
Store Supplies	130	$ —
Prepaid GST	142	2,873
Office Equipment	180	—
Accounts Payable	220	9,103
Purchases	500	86,340
Purchases Returns and Allowances	510	1,374

Journalizing, recording, and posting a cash payments journal with GST. Preparing a schedule of accounts payable.

10C-3. Jim Stokes owns and operates a wholesale welding supplies company. All transactions requiring the payment of cash are recorded in the cash payments journal (p. 45).The account balances as of May 1, 19XX, are as follows:

Accounts Payable Ledger

Name	*Balance*	*GST Included*
Dominion Gases Co.	$1,482.20	$ 96.97
Vertal Rod Co.	2,480.42	162.27
Marker Gloves Co.	1,847.48	120.86
Glover Gauges Co.	881.71	57.68
Prism Accessories Co.	3,942.86	257.94

Partial General Ledger

Account	*Number*	*Balance*
Cash	100	$22,941.18
Prepaid GST	145	2,421.14*
Delivery Truck	170	—
Accounts Payable	200	10,634.67
Welding Purchases	500	56,422.29
Welding Purchases Discount	510	506.20
Rent Expense	670	3,730.00
Utilities Expense	690	1,204.66

*Will not agree with the amounts included in the accounts payable balances.

Required

1. Journalize the following transactions.
2. Record to the accounts payable ledger and post to general ledger as appropriate.
3. Prepare a schedule of accounts payable.

19XX

May 1 Paid half the amount owed Dominion Gases Co. from previous purchases on account, less a 2 percent purchases discount, cheque no. 464.

3 Bought a delivery truck for $21,400 cash plus GST of $1,498, cheque no. 465, payable to City Truck Sales Co.

5 Paid the amount owing to Glover Gauges Co, cheque no. 466.

6 Bought welding merchandise (cash purchase) from Vericon Canada Co., cheque no. 467, $1,846, plus GST.

14 Paid the balance due to Prism Accessories Co. after deducting a 5 percent discount as per usual terms for this company, cheque no. 468.

18 Bought additional welding merchandise (cash purchase) from Pulse Co., cheque no. 469, $525 plus GST.

24 Paid Marker Gloves Co. the amount owed less a 2 percent purchases discount, cheque no. 470.

28 Paid rent expense to Abbott Properties Co., cheque no. 471, $1,720 plus GST.

29 Paid utilities expense to Stoney Plain Utility Co., cheque no. 472, $364 plus GST.

30 Paid $900.00 to Vertal Rod Co., no discount, cheque no. 473.

Comprehensive review problem with GST: All special journals and the general journal; schedule of accounts payable and accounts receivable.

10C-4. Bill Cardinal runs Cardinal's Book Shop. As his newly hired accountant, your task is to

1. Journalize the transactions for the month of October.
2. Record to subsidiary ledgers and post to general ledger as appropriate.
3. Total, rule, and crossfoot the journals.
4. Prepare a schedule of accounts receivable and a schedule of accounts payable as of October 31.

The following is the partial chart of accounts for Cardinal's Book Shop:

Assets

110 Cash
120 Accounts Receivable
135 Prepaid Rent
138 Prepaid GST
180 Delivery Truck

Liabilities

210 Accounts Payable
218 GST Payable

Owner's Equity

310 B. Cardinal, Capital

Revenue

410 Book Sales
412 Sales Returns and Allowances
414 Sales Discounts

Cost of goods

510 Book Purchases
512 Purchases Returns and Allowances
514 Purchases Discount

Expenses

615 Cleaning Expense
650 Salaries Expense

19XX

Oct. 1 Bill Cardinal invested $24,000 in the bookstore.

1 Paid three months' rent in advance, cheque no. 121, $2,700 plus GST.

1 Purchased merchandise from Milligan Book Company on account, $4,270 plus GST. Invoice no. 1240, dated October 2, terms 2/10, n/30.

3 Sold merchandise to First City Library on account, $2,465 plus GST. Invoice no. 781, terms 2/10, n/30.

6 Sold merchandise to District College on account, $3,160 plus GST. Invoice no. 782, terms 2/10, n/30.

8 Purchased merchandise from Milligan Book Co. on account, $2,940 plus GST. Invoice no. 415, dated October 9, terms 2/10, n/30.

9 Sold merchandise to First City Library on account, $1,856 plus GST. Invoice no. 783, terms 2/10, n/30.

9 Paid cleaning service $280 plus GST. Cheque no. 122.

10 District College returned merchandise that cost $312 (before GST) to Cardinal's Book Shop. Cardinal issued credit memorandum no. 1 to District College for $312 plus GST.

10 Purchased merchandise from Winnipeg Book Supply on account, $1,852 plus GST. Invoice no. 311, dated October 11, terms 1/15, n/60.

12 Paid Milligan Book Co. invoice no. 410, dated October 2, cheque no. 123.

13 Sold $1,420 (plus GST) of book merchandise for cash.

13 Paid salaries, $920, cheque no. 124.

14 Returned merchandise to Winnipeg Book Supply in the amount of $362 plus GST. Cardinal's Book Shop issued debit memorandum no. 1 to Winnipeg Book Supply.

15 Sold merchandise for cash $1,047 plus GST.

16 Received payment from District College, invoice no. 782 (less returned merchandise), less discount.

16 First City Library paid invoice no. 781.

16 Sold book merchandise to Rural Bookmobile Co. on account, $2,484 plus GST. Invoice no. 784, terms 2/10, n/30.

20 Purchased delivery truck on account from Suburban Auto Sales Co., $18,600 plus GST. Invoice no. 111, dated October 21 (no discount).

22 Sold to First City Library merchandise on account, $2,694 plus GST. Invoice no. 785, terms 2/10, n/30.

23 Paid Winnipeg Book Supply balance owed, cheque no. 125.

24 Sold book merchandise on account to Rural Bookmobile Co., $2,412 plus GST. Invoice no. 786, terms 2/10, n/30.

25 Purchased used book merchandise for cash, $3,200 plus GST. Cheque no. 126.

26 Purchased book merchandise from Smithsonian Book Co. on account, $5,820 plus GST. Invoice no. 211, dated October 27, terms 2/10, n/30.

27 Sold merchandise for cash, $940 plus GST.

28 First City Library paid invoice no. 785, dated October 22.

28 Rural Bookmobile Co. paid invoice no. 786, dated October 24.

28 Bill invested an additional $12,000 in the business.

28 Purchased merchandise from Milligan Book Co., $3,120 plus GST. Invoice no. 436, dated October 29, terms 2/10, n/30.

30 Paid Milligan Book Co. invoice no. 436, cheque no. 127.

30 Sold merchandise to Flower & Company on account, $3,126 plus GST. Invoice no. 787, terms 2/10, n/30.

Real World Applications

Hint: $R = \frac{I}{PT}$

10R-1.

Angie Co. bought merchandise for $1,000 with credit terms of 2/10, n/30. Owing to the bookkeeper's incompetence, the 2 percent cash discount was missed. The bookkeeper told Pete Angie, the owner, not to get excited. After all, it was a $20 discount that was missed—not hundreds of dollars. Could you act as Mr. Angie's assistant and show the bookkeeper that his $20 represents a sizeable equivalent interest cost? In your calculation assume a 360-day year. Make some written recommendations so that this will not happen again.

10R-2.

Jeff Ryan completed an Accounting I course and was recently hired as the bookkeeper of Spring Co. The special journals have not been posted, nor are "Dr." and "Cr." used on the column headings. Please assist Jeff by marking the Dr. and Cr. headings as well as setting up and posting to the general ledger and recording to the subsidiary ledger. (Only post or record the amounts, since no chart of accounts is provided.) Make some written recommendations on how a new computer system may lessen the need for posting.

SALES JOURNAL

Account	PR	
Blue Co.		480000
Jon Co.		560000
Roff Co.		640000
Totals		1680000

PURCHASES JOURNAL

Account	PR	
Ralph Co.		400000
Sos Co.		600000
Jingle Co.		800000
Totals		1800000

GENERAL JOURNAL

Sales Returns and Allowances		160000	
Accounts Receivable, Jon Co.			160000
Customer returned merchandise			
Accounts Payable, Jingle Co.		80000	
Purchases Returns and Allowances			80000
Returned defective merchandise			

CASH RECEIPTS JOURNAL*

Cash Dr.	Sales Discount Dr.	Accounts Receivable Cr.	Sales Cr.	Sundry—Dr. Account Name	PR	Amount Cr.
470400	9600	480000		Blue Co.		
196000	4000	200000		Jon Co.		
500000			500000	Sales		
2000000				Notes Payable		2000000
313600	6400	320000		Roff Co.		
460000			460000	Sales		
3940000	20000	1000000	960000	Totals		2000000

* Note: This company's set of columns differs from that shown in the chapter.

CASH PAYMENTS JOURNAL

Account	PR	Sundry	Accounts Payable	Purchases Discount	Cash
Sos Co.			300000	6000	294000
Salaries Expense		260000			260000
Jingle Co.			400000	8000	392000
Salaries Expense		260000			260000
Totals		520000	700000	14000	1206000

make the call

Critical Thinking/Ethical Case

10R-3.

Spring Co. bought merchandise from All Co. with terms 2/10, n/30. Joanne Ring, the bookkeeper, forgot to pay the bill within the first 10 days. She went to Mel Ryan, Head Accountant, who told her to backdate the cheque so it looked like the bill was paid within the discount period. Joanne told Mel that she thought they could get away with it. Should Joanne and Mel backdate the cheque to take advantage of the discount? You make the call. Write down your specific recommendations to Joanne.

ACCOUNTING RECALL

A CUMULATIVE APPROACH

THIS EXAM REVIEWS CHAPTERS 1 THROUGH 10

Your *Study Guide and Working Papers* has forms (pp. 10-56 and 10-57) to complete this exam, as well as worked-out solutions. The page references next to each question identify what page to turn back to if you answer the question incorrectly.

PART I Vocabulary Review

Match the terms to the appropriate definition or phrase.

Page Ref.

(227) 1. Cheques outstanding
(380) 2. F.O.B. destination
(384) 3. Purchases journal
(333) 4. Sales journal
(379) 5. Purchases Discount
(336) 6. Credit memorandum
(297) 7. PD7A

A. A contra-cost account
B. Issued by a buyer to the seller
C. Special journal that records buying on account
D. Sales on account
E. Seller pays cost of freight
F. Form completed monthly for income tax, CPP, and UI

(384) 8. Debit memorandum	G. Merchandise for resale
(388) 9. Cash payments journal	H. Payment by cheque
(378)10. Purchases	I. Issued by seller
	J. Cheques not yet processed by the bank

PART II True or False (Accounting Theory)

(336)11. Issuing a credit memo results in seller increasing its purchases returns and allowances.

(379)12. Purchases discounts have a normal balance of a debit.

(257)13. UI and CPP have different rates.

(383)14. Each creditor in the accounts payable subsidiary ledger usually has a debit balance.

(232)15. Petty cash is an asset that will only be debited with establishment or when raising to a higher amount.

PART III Applications Problem

Journalize, record, and post as appropriate the following transactions. All purchases discounts are 2/10, n/30. Ignore GST.

19XX

July 1 Issued cheque no. 12 to Sue Willige in payment of June 25 invoice no. 415 less purchases discount.

8 Issued cheque no. 13 to Roland Co. to pay selling expense due $90, no discount.

9 Issued cheque no. 14 to Ralph Smol in payment of June 30 invoice no. 417 less purchases discount.

Accounts Payable Subsidiary Ledger

Name	*Balance*	*Invoice No.*
Ralph Smol	$400	417
Sue Willige	300	415

Partial General Ledger

Account No.	*Balance*
Cash 110	$1,600
Accounts Payable 210	700
Purchases Discount 511	—
Selling Expense 610	—

COMPUTER WORKSHOP

Computerized Accounting Application for Chapter 10

PART A: Recording Transactions in the Sales, Receipts, Purchases, and Payments Journals

PART B: Computerized Accounting Instructions for Abby's Toy House (Problem 10A-4)

Before starting on this assignment, read and complete the tasks discussed in Parts A, B, and F of Appendix B at the back of this book and complete the Computerized Accounting Application assignments for Chapter 3, Chapter 4, the Valdez Realty Mini Practice Set (Chapter 5) and the Pete's Market Mini Practice Set (Chapter 8). If you are using ACCPAC Plus software, follow the instructions given by your instructor.

PART A: Recording Transactions in the Sales, Receipts, Purchases, and Payments Journals

What to Record in a Computerized Sales or Receipts Journal

The Sales and Receipts Journals in the CA-Simply Accounting for Windows program are designed to work with the Receivables and General Ledgers modules in an integrated fashion. When transactions are recorded in the sales and receipts journals, the program automatically posts the customer's account in the accounts receivable subsidiary ledger, records the journal entry, and posts all accounts affected in the general ledger. However, the type of transactions recorded in the sales and receipts journals in the CA-Simply Accounting for Windows computerized system differ from the types of transactions recorded in these journals in a manual accounting system. An explanation of the differences appears in the following chart:

Name of Computerized Journal	Types of Transactions Recorded in Computerized Journal
Sales journal	Sales of merchandise on account
	Sales returns and allowances (credit memos)
	Sales discounts
Receipts journal	Cash receipts from credit customers
General journal	Cash receipts from all sources other than credit customers

Computerized Schedule of Accounts Receivable

A Customer Aged Detail report (the computerized version of a schedule of accounts receivable) for The Mars Company appears below (terms of 2/10, n/30 are offered to all credit customers of The Mars Company):

The Mars Company: Customer Aged Detail As at 3/1/99

			Total	*Current*	*31 to 60*	*61 to 90*	*91+*
John Dunbar							
909	2/25/99	Invoice	500.00	500.00	—	—	—
Kevin Tucker							
911	2/26/99	Invoice	550.00	550.00	—	—	—
			1,050.00	1,050.00	—	—	—

What to Record in a Computerized Purchases or Payments Journal

The purchases and payments journals in the CA-Simply Accounting for Windows program are also designed to work with the payables and general ledgers modules in an integrated fashion. When transactions are recorded in the purchases and payments journals, the program automatically posts the vendor's account in the accounts payable subsidiary ledger, records the journal entry, and posts all accounts affected in the general ledger. However, the type of transactions recorded in the purchases and payments journals in the CA-Simply Accounting for Windows computerized system differ from the types of transactions recorded in these journals in a manual accounting system. An explanation of the differences appears in the following chart:

Name of Computerized Journal	Types of Transactions Recorded in Computerized Journal
Purchases journal	Purchases of merchandise and other items on account
	Purchase returns and allowances (debit memos)
	Purchases discount
Payments journal	Cash payments to credit vendors
General journal	Cash payments for all purposes other than payments to credit vendors

Computerized Schedule of Accounts Payable

A Vendor Aged Detail report (the computerized version of a schedule of accounts payable) for The Mars Company appears below:

The Mars Company: Vendor Aged Detail As at 3/1/99

			Total	*Current*	*31 to 60*	*61 to 90*	*91+*
Laurie Snyder							
567	2/27/99	Invoice	435.00	435.00	—	—	—
Pat Young							
789	2/25/99	Invoice	112.00	112.00	—	—	—
			547.00	547.00	—	—	—

Open the Company Data Files

1. Start Windows; insert your Student Data Files disk into disk drive A or B; then double-click on the CA-Simply Accounting icon. The CA-Simply Accounting-Open File dialogue box will appear.
2. Enter one of the following paths into the **Open file name** text box:
   - A:\MARS.ASC (if you are storing your student data files on the disk in drive A).
   - B:\MARS.ASC (if you are storing your student data files on the disk in drive B).
3. Click on the **Open** button; enter "3/31/99" into the **Using date for this session** text box; then click on the **OK** button. Click on the **OK** button in response to the message "The date entered is more than one week past your previous **Using** date of 3/1/99." The Company Window for Mars will appear.

Add Your Name to the Company Name

4. Click on the Company Window Setup menu; then click on Company Information. The Company Information dialogue box will appear. Insert your name in place of the text "Your Name" in the **Name** text box. Click on the **OK** button to return to the Company Window.

How to Record a Sale on Account

5. On March 1, 1999, sold merchandise to Kevin Tucker on account, $800, invoice no. 913, terms 2/10, n/30. Double-click on the Sales Journal icon to open the Sales Journal dialogue box. Note that the program automatically offers **Invoice** 913 as the invoice number for this transaction through the program's automatic invoice numbering feature. Click on the arrow button to the right of the **Sold to** text box to display a list of customers; then click on Kevin Tucker. Highlight the **Date** text box; enter 3/1/99; then press the TAB key until the insertion point is positioned in the **Amount** text box. Enter 800; then press the TAB key. The flashing insertion point will move to the **Acct**

text box. Press the ENTER key to display the Select Account dialogue box; then select 4110 Sales. Your screen should look like this:

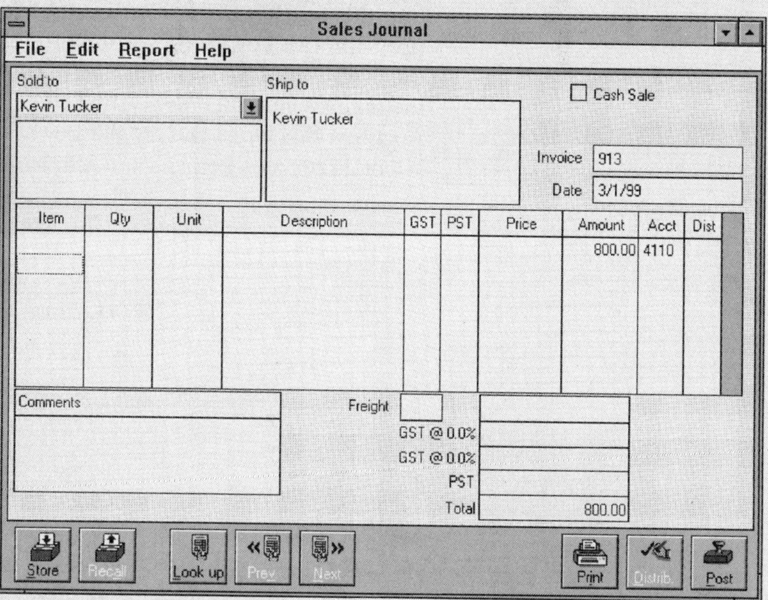

How to Review a Sales Journal Entry

6. Before posting this transaction, you need to verify that the transaction data are correct by reviewing the journal entry. To review the entry, click on the Sales Journal Report menu; then click on Display Sales Journal Entry. The journal entry representing the data you have recorded in the Sales Journal dialogue box is displayed. Review the journal entry for accuracy noting any errors. Note that the program has automatically debited the accounts receivable account through its integration feature.

How to Edit a Sales or Purchases Journal Entry Prior to Posting

7. Close the Sales Journal Entry window by double-clicking on the control menu box. If you have made an error, use the following editing techniques to correct the error:

Editing a Sales or Purchases Journal Entry

- Move to the text box that contains the error by either pressing the TAB key to move forward through each text box or the SHIFT and TAB keys together to move to a previous text box. This will highlight the selected text box information so that you can change it. Alternatively, you can use the mouse to point to a text box and drag through the incorrect information to highlight it.
- Type the correct information; then press the TAB key to enter it.
- If you have associated the transaction with an the incorrect customer or vendor, reselect the correct customer or vendor from the customer or vendor list display after clicking on the arrow button to the right of the **Sold to** text box (customers) or **Purchased from** text box (vendors).
- If you have associated a transaction with an incorrect account, double-click on the incorrect account; then select the correct account from the Select Account dialogue box. This will replace the incorrect account with the correct account.
- To discard an entry and start over, double-click on the control menu box. Click on the **Yes** button in response to the question "Are you sure you want to discard this journal entry?"
- Review the journal entry for accuracy after any editing corrections.
- **It is important to note that the only way to edit a journal entry after it is posted is to reverse the entry and enter the correct journal entry.** To correct journal entries posted in error, see Part C of Appendix B at the back of this book.

How to Post a Sales Journal Entry

8. After verifying that the journal entry is correct, click on the **Post** button to post this transaction. A blank Sales Journal dialogue box is displayed, ready for additional Sales Journal transactions to be recorded.

senting the data you have recorded in the Receipts Journal dialogue box is displayed. Review the journal entry for accuracy noting any errors. Note that the program has automatically debited the cash account and credited the accounts receivable account through its integration feature.

How to Edit a Receipts or Payments Journal Entry Prior to Posting

20. Close the Receipts Journal Entry window by double-clicking on the control menu box. If you have made an error, use the following editing techniques to correct the error:

Editing a Receipts or Payments Journal Entry

- Move to the text box that contains the error by either pressing the TAB key to move forward through each text box or the SHIFT and TAB keys together to move to a previous text box. This will highlight the selected text box information so that you can change it. Alternatively, you can use the mouse to point to a text box and drag through the incorrect information to highlight it.
- Type the correct information; then press the TAB key to enter it.
- If you have associated the transaction with an the incorrect customer or vendor, reselect the correct customer or vendor from the customer or vendor list display after clicking on the arrow button to the right of the **From** text box (customers) or **To the order of** text box (vendors). You will be asked to confirm that you want to discard the current transaction. Click on the **Yes** button to discard the incorrect entry and display the outstanding invoices for the correct customer or vendor.
- To discard an entry and start over, double-click on the control menu box. Click on the **Yes** button in response to the question "Are you sure you want to discard this journal entry?"
- Review the journal entry for accuracy after any editing corrections.
- **It is important to note that the only way to edit a journal entry after it is posted is to reverse the entry and enter the correct journal entry.** To correct journal entries posted in error, see Part C of the Appendix B at the back of this book.

How to Post a Receipts Journal Entry

21. After verifying that the journal entry is correct, click on the **Post** button to post this transaction. A blank Receipts Journal dialogue box is displayed, ready for additional Receipts Journal transactions to be recorded. Close the Receipts Journal dialogue box.

How to Record a Purchase on Account

22. On March 15, 1999, purchased merchandise from Pat Young on account, $275, invoice no. 796, terms 3/15, n/30. Double-click on the Purchases Journal icon to open the Purchases Journal dialog box. Click on the arrow button to the right of the **Purchased from** text box; then click on Pat Young. Click on the **Invoice** text box; enter 796; then press the TAB key. Enter 3/15/99 into the **Date** text box; then press the TAB key until the insertion point is positioned in the **Amount** text box. Enter 275; then press the TAB key. The flashing insertion point will move to the **Acct** text box. Press the ENTER key to display the Select Account dialogue box; then select 5100 Purchases. Your screen should look like this:

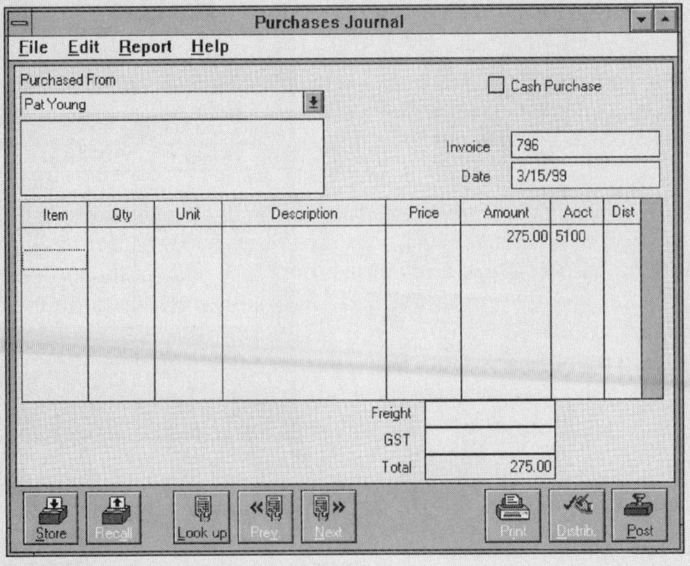

Purchases Journal
File Edit Report Help
Purchased From: Pat Young
Cash Purchase
Invoice: 796
Date: 3/15/99

Item	Qty	Unit	Description	Price	Amount	Acct	Dist
					275.00	5100	

Freight
GST
Total 275.00

Store | Recall | Look up | Prev | Next | Print | Distrib. | Post

How to Review a Purchases Journal Entry

23. Before posting this transaction, you need to verify that the transaction data are correct by reviewing the journal entry. To review the entry, click on the Purchases Journal Report menu; then click on Display Purchases Journal Entry. The journal entry representing the data you have recorded in the Purchases Journal dialogue box is displayed. Review the journal entry for accuracy noting any errors. Note that the program has automatically credited the accounts payable account through its integration feature.

24. Close the Purchases Journal Entry window; then make any editing corrections required.

How to Post a Purchases Journal Entry

25. After verifying that the journal entry is correct, click on the **Post** button to post this transaction. A blank Purchases Journal dialogue box is displayed, ready for additional Purchases Journal transactions to be recorded.

How to Record a Debit Memo

26. On March 17, 1999, returned merchandise to Pat Young in the amount of $75. Issued debit memorandum no. 27. Click on the arrow button to the right of the **Purchased from** text box; then click on Pat Young. Click on the **Invoice** text box; enter "Dm 27"; then press the TAB key. Enter "3/17/99" into the **Date** text box; then press the TAB key until the insertion point is positioned in the **Amount** text box. Enter "– 75" (don't forget the minus sign!); then press the TAB key. The flashing insertion point will move to the **Acct** text box. Press the ENTER key to display the Select Account dialogue box; then select 5120 Purchase Returns and Allowances. Your screen should look like this:

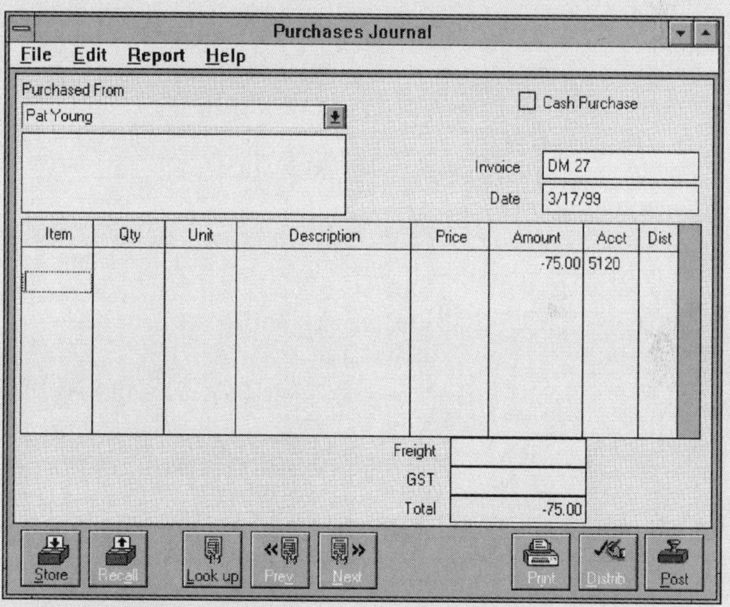

Review the Entry

27. Click on the Purchases Journal Report menu; then click on Display Purchases Journal Entry. Review the journal entry for accuracy noting any errors. Note that the program has automatically debited the accounts payable account through its integration feature.

28. Close the Purchases Journal Entry window; then make any editing corrections required.

Post the Entry

29. After verifying that the journal entry is correct, click on the **Post** button to post this transaction. A blank Purchases Journal dialogue box is displayed, ready for additional Purchases Journal transactions to be recorded.

How to Record a Purchases Discount

30. On March 25, 1999, issued cheque no. 437 to Pat Young in the amount of $194 in payment of invoice no. 796 ($275), dated March 15, less debit memorandum no. 27 ($75), less 3 percent discount ($6). Two steps are required to record purchase discounts in CA-Simply Accounting for Windows. First, the amount of the discount is recorded as a negative invoice in the purchases journal. Second, the amount of the negative invoice is taken into consideration when the payment of the original invoice is recorded in the payments journal.

31. Click on the arrow button to the right of the **Purchased from** text box; then click on Pat Young. Click on the **Invoice** text box; enter "D796" (the "D" indicates that this is a purchase discount related to invoice no. 796); then press the TAB key. Enter "3/25/99" into the **Date** text box; then press the TAB key until the insertion point is positioned in the **Amount** text box. Enter "– 6" (don't forget the minus sign!); then press the TAB key. The flashing insertion point will move to the **Acct** text box. Press the ENTER key to display the Select Account dialogue box; then select 5140 Purchases Discount. Your screen should look like this:

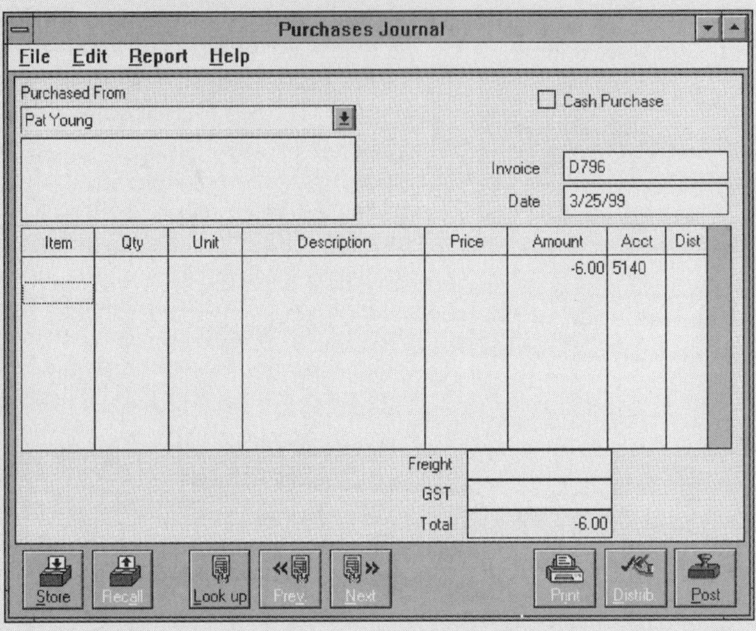

Review the Entry

32. Click on the Purchases Journal Report menu; then click on Display Purchases Journal Entry. Review the journal entry for accuracy noting any errors. Note that the program has automatically debited the accounts payable account through its integration feature.

33. Close the Purchases Journal Entry window; then make any editing corrections required.

Post the Entry

34. After verifying that the journal entry is correct, click on the **Post** button to post this transaction; then close the Purchases Journal dialogue box by double-clicking on the control menu box.

How to Record a Cash Payment to a Credit Vendor

35. Open the Payments Journal dialogue box by double-clicking on the Payments Journal icon. Click on the arrow button to the right of the **To the order of** text box; click on Pat Young; then press the TAB key. Enter "437" into the **No.** text box; then press the TAB key. (The program has offered a default cheque **No.** of 435 which is the next cheque number in the program's automatic cheque numbering sequence. However, since certain cash payments are recorded in the general journal and the cheques used are not recorded in the payments journal, the cheque **No.** needs to be advanced to the next cheque number in The Mars Company's chequebook.) Enter "3/25/99" into the **Date** text box; then press the TAB key. The 112.00 amount for invoice no. 789 will be highlighted. Press the DELETE key; then press the TAB key. The Mars Company is not paying invoice no. 789. The 275.00 amount for invoice no. 796 will be highlighted. Press the TAB key three times to accept 275.00, – 75.00, and – 6.00 in the **Payment Amt.** text box. Your screen should look like this:

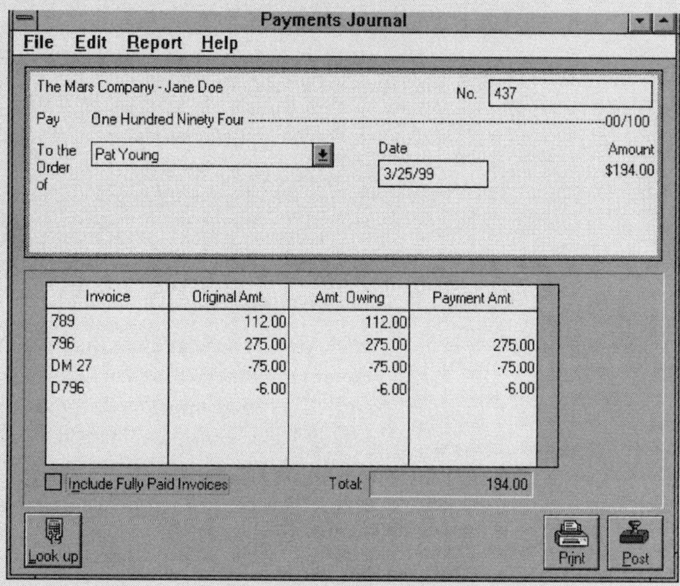

How to Review a Payments Journal Entry

36. Before posting this transaction, you need to verify that the transaction data are correct by reviewing the journal entry. To review the entry, click on the Payments Journal Report menu; then click on Display Payments Journal Entry. The journal entry representing the data you have recorded in the Payments Journal dialogue box is displayed. Review the journal entry for accuracy noting any errors. Note that the program has automatically debited the accounts payable account and credited the cash account through its integration feature.

37. Close the Payments Journal Entry window; then make any editing corrections required.

How to Post a Payments Journal Entry

38. After verifying that the journal entry is correct, click on the **Post** button to post this transaction. A blank Payments Journal dialogue box is displayed, ready for additional Payments Journal transactions to be recorded. Close the Payments Journal dialogue box.

How to Display and Print a Customer Aged Detail Report

39. Click on the Company Window Report menu; then click on Customer Aged. The Customer Aged Report Options dialogue box will appear asking you to define the information you want displayed. Click on the **Detail** option button, click on the **Select All** button; then click on the **OK** button. Click on the Customer Aged Detail File menu; then click on Print to print the report.

How to Display and Print a Vendor Aged Detail Report

40. Close the Customer Aged Detail window; click on the Company Window Report menu; then click on Vendor Aged. The Vendor Aged Report Options dialogue box will appear asking you to define the information you want displayed. Click on the **Detail** option button, click on the **Select All** button; then click on the **OK** button. Click on the Vendor Aged Detail File menu; then click on Print to print the report.

Print Reports

41. Close the Vendor Aged Detail window, then print the following reports:
    - **a.** General journal (By posting date, All ledger entries, Start: 3/1/99, Finish: 3/31/99).
    - **b.** General ledger report (Start: 3/1/99, Finish: 3/31/99, Select All).

    Note that by checking the **All ledger entries** checkbox in the General Journal Options dialogue box, all transactions recorded in the Sales, Receipts, Purchases, and Payments Journals are reflected in the General Journal report.

Review your printed reports. If you have made an error in a posted journal entry, see Part C of Appendix B for information on how to correct the error.

Exist from the Program

42. Click on the Company Window File menu; then click on Exit to end the current work session and return to your Windows desktop.

Complete the Report Transmittal

43. Complete The Mars Company Report Transmittal located in Appendix A of your *Study Guide and Working Papers.*

PART B: Computerized Accounting Instructions for Abby's Toy House (Problem 10A-4)

Open the Company Data Files

1. Start Windows; insert your Student Data Files disk into disk drive A or B; then double-click on the CA-Simply Accounting icon. The CA-Simply Accounting-Open File dialogue box will appear.
2. Enter one of the following paths into the **Open file name** text box:
   - A:\ABBY.ASC (if you are storing your student data files on the disk in drive A).
   - B:\ABBY.ASC (IF YOU ARE STORING YOUR STUDENT DATA FILES ON THE DISK IN DRIVE B).
3. Click on the **Open** button; enter "3/31/99" into the **Using date for this session** text box; then click on the **OK** button. Click on the **OK** button in response to the message "The date entered is more than one week past your previous **Using** date of 3/1/99." The Company Window for Abby will appear.

Add your Name to the Company Name

4. Click on the Company Window Setup menu; then click on Company Information. The Company Information dialogue box will appear. Insert your name in place of the text "Your Name" in the **Name** text box. Click on the **OK** button to return to the Company Window.

Record Transactions

5. Record the following transactions using the General, Sales, Receipts, Purchases, and Payments Journals:

1999

March	1	Abby Ellen invested $8,000 in the toy store.
	1	Paid three months' rent in advance, cheque no. 1, $3,000 plus GST.
	2	Purchased merchandise from Earl Miller Company on account, $4,000 plus GST, invoice no. 410, terms 2/10, n/30.
	3	Sold merchandise to Bill Burton on account, $1,000 plus GST, invoice no. 1, terms 2/10 n/30.
	6	Sold merchandise to Jim Rex on account, $700 plus GST, invoice no. 2, terms 2/10 n/30.
	9	Purchased merchandise from Earl Miller Co. on account, $1,200 plus GST, invoice no. 415, terms 2/10, n/30.
	9	Sold merchandise to Bill Burton on account, $600 plus GST, invoice no. 3, terms 2/10, n/30.
	9	Paid cleaning service $300 plus GST, cheque no. 2.
	10	Jim Rex returned merchandise that cost $300 (plus GST) to Abby's Toy House. Abby issued credit memorandum no. 1 to Jim Rex for $321.
	11	Purchased merchandise from Minnie Katz on account, $4,000 plus GST, invoice no. 311, terms 1/15, n/60.
	12	Issued cheque no. 3 to Earl Miller Co. in the amount of $4,200 in payment of invoice no. 410 ($4,280), dated March 2, less 2 percent discount ($80). (*Reminder:* A purchases discount is recorded in two steps.)
	13	Sold $1,300 of toy merchandise for cash. (*Reminder:* Cash sales are recorded in the general journal.) Add GST.
	13	Paid salaries, $600, cheque no. 4.
	14	Returned merchandise to Minnie Katz in the amount of $1,000 plus GST; Abby's Toy House issued debit memorandum no. 1 to Minnie Katz.
	15	Sold merchandise for $4,000 cash plus GST. (*Reminder:* Cash sales are recorded in the general journal.)
	16	Received cheque no. 9823 from Jim Rex in the amount of $420 in payment of invoice no. 2 ($749), dated March 6, less credit memorandum no. 1 ($321), less 2 percent discount ($8). (*Reminder:* A sales discount is recorded in two steps.)
	16	Received cheque no. 4589 from Bill Burton in the amount of $1,070 in payment of invoice no. 1, dated March 3.
	16	Sold toy merchandise to Amy Rose on account, $4,000 plus GST, invoice no. 4, terms 2/10, n/30.
	21	Purchased delivery truck on account from Sam Katz Garage, $3,000 plus GST, invoice no. 111, (no discount). (*Reminder:* Purchases of merchandise and

other items on account are recorded in the purchases journal.)

22 Sold to Bill Burton merchandise on account, $900 plus GST, invoice no. 5, terms 2/10, n/30.

23 Issued cheque no. 5 to Minnie Katz in the amount of $3,180 in payment of invoice no. 311 ($4,280), dated March 11, less debit memorandum no. 1 ($1,070), less 1 percent discount ($30). (*Reminder:* A purchases discount is recorded in two steps.)

24 Sold toy merchandise on account to Amy Rose, $1,100 plus GST, invoice no. 6, terms 2/10, n/30.

25 Purchased toy merchandise, $600 plus GST, cheque no. 6. (*Reminder:* Cash purchases are recorded in the general journal.)

27 Purchased toy merchandise from Woody Smith on account, $4,800 plus GST, invoice no. 211, terms 2/10, n/30.

28 Received cheque no. 4598 from Bill Burton in the amount of $945 in payment of invoice no. 5 ($963), dated March 22, less 2 percent discount ($18). (*Reminder:* A sales discount is recorded in two steps.)

28 Received cheque no. 3217 from Amy Rose in the amount of $1155 in payment of invoice no. 6, dated March 24, less 2 percent discount ($22). (*Reminder:* A sales discount is recorded in two steps.)

28 Abby invested an additional $5,000 in the business.

29 Purchased merchandise from Earl Miller Co., $1,400 plus GST, invoice no. 436, terms 2/10, n/30.

30 Issued cheque no. 7 to the Earl Miller Co. in the amount of $1,470 in payment of invoice no. 436 ($1,498), dated March 29, less 2 percent discount ($28). (*Reminder:* A purchases discount is recorded in two steps.)

30 Sold merchandise to Bonnie Flow Company on account, $3,000 plus GST, invoice no. 7, terms 2/10, n/30.

Print Reports

6. Print the following reports:
   - **a.** Customer Aged report (Detail, Select All).
   - **b.** Vendor Aged report (Detail, Select All).
   - **c.** General journal (By posting date, All ledger entries, Start: 3/1/99, Finish: 3/31/99).
   - **d.** General ledger report (Start: 3/1/99, Finish: 3/31/99, Select All).

   Review your printed reports. If you have made an error in a posted journal entry, see Part C of Appendix B at the back of this book for information on how to correct the error.

Exit from the Program

7. Click on the Company Window File menu; then click on Exit to end the current work session and return to your Windows desktop.

Complete the Report Transmittal

8. Complete The Abby's Toy House Report Transmittal located in Appendix A of your *Study Guide and Working Papers.*

THE SYNOPTIC (COMBINED) JOURNAL

11

Chapter Objectives

- Defining methods of accounting: accrual basis, cash basis, and modified cash basis. (p. 437)
- Recording, journalizing, and posting transactions for a synoptic journal of a professional service company using a modified cash basis of accounting. (p. 438)
- Recording, journalizing, and posting transactions for a synoptic journal of a merchandise company using the accrual basis of accounting. (p. 444)

In the first ten chapters of this text we have used general journals and special journals in recording business transactions. Over the years many students have asked how to set up journals for starting their own small business. They have felt that the general journals were too simple and the special journals were too detailed. In dealing with this topic, the chapter is broken down into two Units:

- Learning Unit 11-1 Journal for a dentist, Dr. Gail Walensa—a professional service company that uses a modified cash system.
- Learning Unit 11-2 Synoptic journal for Art's Wholesale Clothing Company—a merchandise company that uses an accrual approach.

From these two presentations, students should be able to take accounting theory and procedures and apply them to their own business recordkeeping needs.

Before we start the first unit, however, we need to talk about the difference between the cash basis of accounting and the accrual basis of accounting.

Accrual accounting:
- **Earned revenue.**
- **Incurred expenses.**

In the chapters so far we have been using the accrual basis of accounting, which is based on the *matching principle*. The matching principle says that you record revenue when it is earned (not when the money actually comes in), and you record expenses when they are incurred in producing revenue (not when they are paid).

Cash accounting:
- **Cash received.**
- **Cash paid.**

In the cash basis of accounting, revenue is recorded when cash is received, and expenses are recorded when they are paid.

Companies choose the accrual basis because they want to show earned revenue along with the expenses that were incurred to earn that revenue. They can do so with the accrual basis but not always with the cash basis. However, service companies sometimes use the cash basis because it is simpler and more convenient, and provides enough information for the decisions they need to make.

Many service companies will use the cash method if they have no inventories.

Let's look at the difference between accrual and cash bases with the following example: John Mills earned real estate commissions of $100,000, of which he received $60,000 in cash. Expenses were $25,000, of which $10,000 was paid in cash.

Comparison of Cash Basis with Accrual Basis for the Month of July 19XX

Cash Basis		*Accrual Basis*	
Revenue (received)	$60,000	Revenue (earned)	$100,000
Expenses (paid)	10,000	Expenses (incurred)	25,000
Net income	$50,000	Net income	$ 75,000

Note how net income differs according to which system is used. Keep in mind that all revenue and expenses will show up eventually if the cash basis is used, but not in this accounting period.

Now let's look at the recordkeeping needs of a dentist, Dr. Gail Walensa, who wants to use a cash-basis system of accounting because of its simplicity and convenience.

LEARNING UNIT 11-1

Synoptic Journal: A Modified Cash System for a Service Company

Dentists can't charge entire cost of dental equipment to the year it was purchased for cash.

Dr. Walensa's accountant has informed her that keeping strictly to a cash-basis system is difficult to do. The reason is that because of tax regulations, Dr. Walensa's accountant would be distorting financial reports by using a strictly cash system. She feels that the best system for a dentist will be a combination of the cash and accrual methods. This combination is known as the **modified cash basis** or **hybrid** method. Under this method Dr. Walensa will record professional fees only when cash is received and record expenses only when paid in cash. To satisfy the tax department, an adjustment for amounts accrued at year-end is required before financial statements are prepared (not illustrated here). The following exceptions, however, are an attempt to clearly reflect income and minimize distortion of the financial reports:

Only the supplies *used up* are shown as an expense.

1. Long-lived assets (equipment, building, etc.) are treated the same under cash and accrual accounting. This means that the amount paid for equipment in one year may not be treated as expense of just that period; Dr. Walensa will be depreciating or allocating the cost of her dental equipment over a period of years.
2. Insurance premiums and purchases of a large amount of supplies are treated the same under cash and accrual accounting. This means that the amount consumed or used up is shown as an expense in the current year and that the amount on hand is carried over into the next accounting period.

These exceptions require adjusting entries (which we saw before under accrual accounting) when the modified cash basis is used.

Two types of personal services might use a modified cash basis. They are:

1. Professional services—lawyers, doctors, dentists, accountants, and so on.
2. Business services—real estate, insurance, software support, and so on.

CHART OF ACCOUNTS

The chart of accounts for Dr. Walensa is provided in Figure 11-1. Note that, unlike a chart of accounts on the accrual basis, there are no categories for Accounts Receivable, Accounts Payable, or Salaries Payable (these are added at year-end by the accountant). This chart of accounts does have titles for handling the exceptions (for example, Accumulated Depreciation, Prepaid Insurance, etc.). There is no supplies account under assets, since Dr. Walensa is not buying a large amount of supplies, and thus all can be shown as Dental Supplies Expense without distorting the financial reports.

The transactions that occurred for the month of November are listed on p. 439. We will show you the recording of these transactions in the **synoptic journal** (or **combined journal**)—a special journal that will replace the general journal and save journalizing and posting labour. The synoptic journal has the same basic features as other special journals that we introduced in Chapters 9 and 10. Remember, each business will design the headings of the synoptic journal to fit its individual needs. Often it is not unusual to find such journals with a total of 24 columns, or even more—although we will be keeping things at a more manageable size in this textbook. Accounts that are used most often are the ones that should have a special column. This will save time when journalizing and posting.

Another important point is that, to keep things simple, GST is not included in the earlier examples in this text, but is covered at the end of Learning Unit 11-2.

FIGURE 11-1
Chart of Accounts

Dr. Walensa
Chart of Accounts

Assets
111 Cash
113 Petty Cash Fund
131 Prepaid Insurance
141 Office Furniture
142 Accum. Dep., Office Furniture
151 Dental Equipment
152 Accum. Dep., Dental Equipment
161 Auto
162 Accum. Dep., Auto

Liabilities
211 Due to Receiver General
212 Other Payroll Deds. Payable
213 Notes Payable

Owner's Equity
311 G. Walensa, Capital
312 G. Walensa, Withdrawals
313 Income Summary

Revenue
411 Professional Fees

Expenses
511 Automobile Expense
512 Rent Expense
513 Salaries Expense
514 Telephone Expense
515 Dep. Exp., Office Furniture
516 Dep. Exp., Dental Equipment
517 Dep. Exp., Auto
518 Miscellaneous Expense
519 Insurance Expense
520 Dental Supplies Expense
521 Payroll Tax Expense

Transactions for Dr. Walensa

Example of a modified cash system.

19XX

Nov. 1 Paid $700 office rent for November, cheque no. 61.
1 Received cheques for $3,000 from patients for dental work.
4 Paid telephone bill, $80, cheque no. 62.
4 Issued cheque no. 63 to Bill Blan Insurance Agency for premium on insurance for three years, $900.
8 Purchased dental supplies from Roe Suppliers, $450, cheque no. 64.
8 Received cheques from patients, $1,600.
8 Calculated current cash balance.
11 Issued cheque no. 65 to Moe Gas for automobile expenses charged during October, $280.
11 Dr. Walensa withdrew $500 for personal use, cheque no. 66.
14 Issued cheque no. 67 to V. P. Suppliers Company for dental supplies charged during October, $650.
15 Paid office salaries for the period November 1 to November 15, $3,000, cheque no. 68.
15 Cash receipts from patients totalled $2,800 for the week.
15 Calculated current cash balance.
19 Collected $800 from insurance companies for patients' accounts.
21 Purchased dental supplies from J. Labs, $500, cheque no. 69.
22 Cash receipts for the week totalled $2,900.
22 Calculated current cash balance.
27 Issued cheque no. 70 for charitable contributions, $300.
27 Purchased dental supplies from J. Labs, $300, cheque no. 71.

28 Received cheques from patients' insurance companies totalling $3,300.
29 Paid office salaries for the period November 15 to November 30, $2,250, cheque no. 72.
30 Calculated current cash balance and crossfooted journal.

Recording Transactions in the Synoptic Journal

The synoptic journal for Dr. Walensa is shown in Figure 11-2. Note that the bank balance can be calculated at any time. For example, in the explanation column, note the beginning balance of $9,500. On November 8 the current balance was calculated as follows:

Beg. balance	$ 9,500	
+ Deposits	4,600	
- Cheques written	2,130	
Ending balance	$11,970	(Recorded in explanation column)

As we saw with special journals before, this synoptic journal is proved in the following way:

Proving the journal.

	Dr.	*Cr.*
Cash	$14,400	$ 9,910
Sundry	8,010	
Professional Fees		14,400
Dental Sup. Exp.	1,900	
	$24,310	$24,310

Posting the Synoptic Journal

Memorandum records can be used in a modified cash system.

Since this is a modified cash system, there are no subsidiary ledgers for accounts receivable or accounts payable. Companies using a modified cash basis may keep information about any receivables or payables in an informal memorandum record until cash is received or paid. During the month, items entered into the Sundry column can be updated in the general ledger. At the end of the month the totals of Cash, Professional Fees, and Dental Supplies Expense would be posted to the general ledger. The account numbers are shown at the bottom of the columns of the synoptic journal to show that the totals were posted. The X means that no posting is necessary. The total of the Sundry column is not posted, because the various items making up the total are posted individually.

Recording Payroll Deductions and Employer's Tax Expense

Back in Chapters 7 and 8 we studied payroll, with the payroll register recording gross pay, deductions, and net pay. From the payroll register a general journal entry is prepared to record the payroll. We also discussed using a general journal to record the employer's payroll tax expense before it is paid (for CPP and UI). The recordkeeping involved in paying an employee will be quite similar in a synoptic journal using the cash-basis method, but recording the employer's payroll tax expense will change.

Why? In the cash-basis method of accounting the owner's share of CPP as well as UI will not be recorded until it is paid. Under accrual accounting we recorded them when incurred, not when paid.

DR. WALENSA
SYNOPTIC JOURNAL

Month: November

Cash Deposits Dr.	Cheques Cr.	Chq. No.	Date 19XX		Explanation		PR	Sundry Dr.	Sundry Cr.	Professional Fees Cr.	Dental Supplies Expense Dr.
					Cash balance	*9,500*					
	700 00	61	Nov.	1	Rent Expense		512	700 00			
3000 00				1	Professional Fees		✗			3000 00	
	80 00	62		4	Telephone Expense		514	80 00			
	900 00	63		4	Prepaid Insurance		131	900 00			
	450 00	64		7	Roe Supplies		✗				450 00
1600 00				8	Professional Fees	*11,970*	✗			1600 00	
	280 00	65		11	Auto Expense		511	280 00			
	500 00	66		11	G. Walensa, Withdr.		312	500 00			
	650 00	67		14	V.P. Suppliers		✗				650 00
	3000 00	68		15	Salaries Expense		513	3000 00			
2800 00				15	Professional Fees	*10,340*	✗			2800 00	
800 00				19	Professional Fees		✗			800 00	
	500 00	69		21	J. Labs		✗				500 00
2900 00				22	Professional Fees	*13,540*	✗			2900 00	
	300 00	70		27	Miscellaneous Expense		518	300 00			
	300 00	71		27	J. Labs		✗				300 00
3300 00				28	Professional Fees		✗			3300 00	
	2250 00	72		29	Salaries Expense	*13,990*	513	2250 00			
14400 00	9910 00							8010 00		14400 00	1900 00
(111)	(111)							(X)		(411)	(520)

$24,310 = $24,310

FIGURE 11-2 The Synoptic Journal

Let's look at the partially completed synoptic journal on p. 443 and explain each entry. For simplicity we are ignoring the remittance requirements and monthly reports that we covered in the payroll chapters.

A. Bill Smith's gross salary of $500 is recorded as a salary expense, and the deductions for income tax, CPP, and UI are listed as liabilities until the employer makes the remittance. Note that the cheque is written for $375 (net pay). The same procedure is followed for Joe Ring.

B. On June 9 the remittance to the Receiver General is assumed made. This means the employer pays the CPP and UI for the employees as well as the matching share along with the income tax deducted from the employees' paycheques.

Note: The payroll tax expense is now being recorded for the employer's share of CPP and UI, since it is now being *paid*. Note that the cheque amount is for $264.80, which includes the following:

Inc. tax payable	140.00
CPP payable	24.00
Payroll tax expense — CPP	24.00
UI payable	32.00
Payroll tax expense — UI ($32.00 × 1.4)	44.80
	264.80

The end result is to reduce the liabilities owed as well as record the employer's share of CPP and UI as payroll tax expense. When the remittance is actually made to the Receiver General for Canada, the following entry is made in the Synoptic:

	Dr.	*Cr.*
Income tax payable	XXX.XX	
CPP payable	XX.XX	
UI payable	XX.XX	
Payroll tax expense	XX.XX	
Cash		XXX.XX

In summary, sometimes companies will record the expense portion of CPP and UI when the *payroll* is paid, instead of when the remittance is made. If this is the case, then when the remittance is made, the Synoptic will record this entry:

	Dr.	*Cr.*
Income tax payable	XXX.XX	
CPP payable	XX.XX	
UI payable	XX.XX	
Cash		XXX.XX

LEARNING UNIT 11-1 REVIEW

AT THIS POINT you should be able to

- Explain the modified cash basis of accounting. (p. 437)
- Journalize transactions into a synoptic journal. (pp. 439 and 440)
- Calculate the current bank balance of a synoptic journal. (p. 439)
- Prove a synoptic journal. (p. 439)
- Explain how to record payroll as well as payroll tax expense into a synoptic journal. (pp. 439 to 442)

SELF-REVIEW QUIZ 11-1

Answer true or false to the following:

1. A modified cash system will only have one exception, long-lived assets, in the adjustment process.
2. A cash-basis system in a chart of accounts usually has titles for Due to Receiver General and Payroll Deductions Payable.
3. Headings of synoptic journals can be modified to meet the needs of the user.
4. The cash balance can easily be updated in a synoptic journal.
5. Payroll tax expense will be recorded when the remittance is made to the Receiver General.

Solution to Self-Review Quiz 11-1

1. False **2.** False **3.** True **4.** True **5.** True

SYNOPTIC JOURNAL

	Royal Bank							Sundry				Payroll Deductions		
	Deposits Dr.	Cheques Cr.	Chq. No.	Date 19XX		Account or Explanation	PR	Dr.	Cr.	Professional Fees Cr.	Salary Expense Dr.	Income Tax Payable Cr.	CPP Payable Cr.	UI Payable Cr.
(A)		375 00	33	May	5	Bill Smith	✗				500 00	90 00	15 00	20 00
		229 00	34		5	Joe Ring	✗				300 00	50 00	9 00	12 00
(B)		264 80	50	June	9	Receiver General								
						Tax Payable	211	140 00						
						CPP Payable	212	24 00						
						UI Payable	213	32 00						
						Payroll Tax Exp	521	68 80*						

*Calculated as [($24 ×1) + ($32×1.4)]

LEARNING UNIT 11-2

Synoptic Journal for Art's Wholesale Clothing Company

Back in Chapters 9 and 10 we developed the sales journal, cash receipts journal, purchases journal, cash payments journal, and general journal for Art's Wholesale Clothing Company. Many small businesses that are concerned with saving journalizing, recording, and posting labour, however, are not concerned about division of labor (having a bookkeeper working on each special journal), since they have only one bookkeeper. Such businesses may want the advantages provided by special journals but would like to reduce the number of journals needed. This unit will develop a synoptic journal, a book of original entry, that dispenses with the special journals, yet gains their advantages in journalizing, recording, and posting for a company that uses an accrual accounting approach. (In order to focus on the basics of the synoptic journal, payroll details are not described at this point.)

Our goal in this unit is to place all the special journals for Art's Wholesale into the following synoptic journal:

SYNOPTIC JOURNAL

Month: April — Page 1

Date	Explanation	Cheque No.	PR	Sundry		Cash		Accts. Rec.		Accts. Pay.		Sales Cr.	Sales Disc. Dr.	Pur. Dr.	Pur. Disc. Cr.
				Dr.	Cr.	Dr.	Cr.	Dr.	Cr.	Dr.	Cr.				

Note that since Art's business uses *accrual* accounting, we now have columns for accounts receivable and accounts payable.

If Art decided to use the synoptic journal, he and the accountant would go over the chart of accounts. They would be concerned with setting up columns in the synoptic journal for accounts in which transactions would occur frequently. On the basis of their analysis, Art and the accountant agreed to set up the following special columns in a synoptic journal.

- **Cash Dr.** This column records increases in cash.
- **Cash Cr.** This column records decreases in cash.
- **Accounts Receivable Dr.** This column records amounts owed from sales on account.
- **Accounts Receivable Cr.** This column records amounts paid by customers from past sales on account.
- **Accounts Payable Dr.** This column reflects amounts paid to creditors.
- **Accounts Payable Cr.** This column reflects amounts owed to creditors.
- **Sales Cr.** This column records all sales made for cash or on account.
- **Sales Discount Dr.** This column records the amounts of discounts taken by customers.
- **Purchases Dr.** All purchases of merchandise for resale are recorded in this column.
- **Purchases Discount Cr.** This column records the amounts of discounts Art receives by paying for purchases before the discount period expires.
- **Sundry Dr., Cr.** These two columns record transactions that do not occur very frequently. If a transaction occurs and no special columns are set up to record part or all of it, it can be recorded in the sundry columns.

Figure 11-3 shows the completed synoptic journal for the month of April for Art's Wholesale Clothing Company (we will go over the recordings and postings in a moment).

Checking the accuracy of the synoptic journal.

The synoptic journal can be proved as follows:

Account Title	Dr.	Cr.
Sundry	$ 6750.00	$ 8700.00
Cash	14324.00	6994.00
Accounts Receivable	6500.00	4400.00
Accounts Payable	4800.00	11930.00
Sales		8600.00
Sales Discount	76.00	
Purchases	8180.00	
Purchases Discount		6.00
Totals	$40630.00	$40630.00

Recording and Posting the Synoptic Journal

The recording and posting rules we learned for Art's special journals will hold true for the synoptic journal. Here are some key points:

1. ✓ Record to accounts receivable or accounts payable subsidiary ledgers daily.
2. **Sundry** Update the general ledger account on a daily basis. Use the ledger account number as a posting reference.
3. **X** in the PR column indicates no posting, since the total is posted at the end of the month. An X below the total means that the total of the column is not posted.

End of Month

SJ1 (Synoptic Journal, page 1) will be placed in PR of ledger account, where information from journal is updated in ledger.

The total of each column (except Sundry) will be posted to the general ledger at the end of the month. Note that the account number from the ledger is placed at the bottom of the column in the synoptic journal, indicating that the total was posted to that account.

Note the following when a synoptic journal is used:

1. Charge *and* cash sales are recorded in the sales column.
2. Purchases returns, sales returns, etc., are recorded in sundry, since no general journal is used with a synoptic journal.
3. Adjusting and closing entries will be recorded in the sundry columns.

Adjusting and closing entries could be recorded in the Sundry columns of a synoptic journal.

Whether Art's Wholesale uses a synoptic journal or a set of special journals, the schedule of accounts receivable and accounts payable will be the same, as will the trial balance.

To sum up, the synoptic journal is an option for small businesses that do not have many transactions. Lawyers, doctors, dentists, and other professionals may use a synoptic journal, which may be modified in many ways to suit their individual needs.

As the business grows, the volume of transactions may increase, possibly creating the need for more-specialized journals or a computerized set of records rather than just the synoptic journal. For example, if a company adds bookkeepers to its accounting department, management must be prepared to provide a system of dividing the work to be done. This division of labour may play an important part in determining the types of special journals that are needed.

It is possible to use an electronic spreadsheet running on a computer to "build" a synoptic journal in computer form. This idea is workable but of doubtful value since a variety of low cost full-featured accounting programs are available. Many small businesses use Simply Accounting for Windows (illustrated throughout this text).

ART'S WHOLESALE CLOTHING COMPANY
SYNOPTIC JOURNAL

Date		Explanation	Chq. No.	PR	Sundry Dr.	Sundry Cr.	Cash Dr.	Cash Cr.
19XX Apr.	1	Art Newner, Cap.		311		8,000.00	8,000.00	
	2	Prepaid Ins.	1	116	900.00			900.00
	3	Hal's Clothing		✓				
	3	Freight-In, Abby Blake		514/✓	50.00			
	4	Equip., Joe Francis		121/✓	4,000.00			
	4	Hal's Clothing		✓			784.00	
	6	Thorpe Co.		✓				
	6	Bevans Co.		✓				
	7	J. Francis Co.	2	✓				4,000.00
	7	J. Sullivan Co.		✓				
	9	Purchases	3	✗				800.00
	9	Pur. R&A, Thorpe Co.		514/✓		200.00		
	12	Thorpe Co.	4	✓				594.00
	12	Sales R&A, Bevans Co.		412/✓	600.00			
	12	Abby Blake Co.		✓				
	15	Cash Sales		✗			900.00	
	16	Bevans Co.		✓			980.00	
	18	Roe Co.		✓				
	22	Roe Co.		✓			1,960.00	
	24	Roe Co.		✓				
	25	Sup., J. Sullivan		115/✓	500.00			
	27	Store Equip.		121		500.00	500.00	
	28	Salaries Expense	5	611	700.00			700.00
	28	Mel's Dept. Store		✓				
	29	Mel's Dept. Store		✓				
	30	Cash Sales		✗			1,200.00	
		Totals			6,750.00	8,700.00	14,324.00	6,994.00
					(X)	(X)	(111)	(111)

FIGURE 11-3 Synoptic Journal Completed

Before stating the objectives of this unit, let's look at a sample of how a synoptic journal might look if it included Provincial Sales Tax Payable and GST. See Figure 11-4. Notice that at the end of the month we will still post to the general ledger the totals of Accounts Receivable, Sales, Sales Tax Payable, and GST Payable. Keep in mind that Sales Tax Payable and GST Payable are liabilities shown on the balance sheet. Also bear in mind that the principles of recording PST and GST have not changed at all from Chapters 9 and 10 where we covered them in detail. The main difference is that now we are including both collections and remittances in the same journal.

Another point worth stressing is that in the modern business world there is less need to study the large synoptic journal with a lot of intensity. If a large synoptic journal is necessary due to complex transactions (or a large volume of these) a computer plus some inexpensive software is perhaps a better solution. Remember that a knowledge of manual bookkeeping and accounting procedures means that a computerized system can be more useful and efficient.

Month: April

Accounts Receivable Dr.	Accounts Receivable Cr.	Accounts Payable Dr.	Accounts Payable Cr.	Sales Cr.	Sales Discount Dr.	Purchases Dr.	Purchases Discount Cr.
800 00				800 00			
			5050 00			5000 00	
			4000 00				
	800 00				16 00		
			800 00			800 00	
1600 00				1600 00			
		4000 00					
			980 00			980 00	
						800 00	
		200 00					
		600 00					6 00
	600 00						
			600 00			600 00	
				900 00			
	1000 00				20 00		
2000 00				2000 00			
	2000 00				40 00		
500 00				500 00			
			500 00				
900 00				900 00			
700 00				700 00			
				1200 00			
6500 00	4400 00	4800 00	11930 00	8600 00	76 00	8180 00	6 00
(113)	(113)	(211)	(211)	(411)	(413)	(511)	(512)

If a retail company has many sales returns and allowances as well as purchases, the following synoptic journal heading could be designed.

SYNOPTIC JOURNAL

Page 1

Cash and sundry would be located here.	Accts. Rec. Dr.	Accts. Rec. Cr.	Sales Cr.	Sales R&A Dr.	Accts. Pay. Dr.	Accts. Pay. Cr.	Sales Tax Payable Cr.	Pur. Dr.	Sup. Dr.	Office Equip. Dr.

SYNOPTIC JOURNAL

Date 19XX		Explanation	Chq. No.	PR	Sundry Dr.	Sundry Cr.	Cash Dr.	Cash Cr.	Accounts Receivable Dr.	Accounts Receivable Cr.
May	1	Bill Jones		✔					116 00	
May	3	Alice Smith		✔					464 00	
May	5	Alice Smith—Pmt. = 2%	376	✔			456 00			464 00
May	7	Birchmount Co.		✔						
May	9	Cooper & Co.		✔						
May	18	Cooper & Co.—Pmt. = 2%		✔				6300 00		
		Month-end totals					456 00	6300 00	580 00	464 00

Recorded immediately to the accounts receivable or accounts payable ledgers

Totals posted at the end of the month to the general ledger

Month-end totals

FIGURE 11-4 Synoptic Journal with Sales Tax and GST

LEARNING UNIT 11-2 REVIEW

AT THIS POINT you should be able to

- Journalize transactions into the synoptic journal for a merchandise company. (pp. 443 to 445)
- Explain how to record and post the synoptic journal. (p. 446)
- Compare special journals (cash payments, receipts, etc.) and the synoptic journal. (p. 446)
- Explain how sales tax and GST could be recorded in a synoptic journal. (p. 447)

SELF-REVIEW QUIZ 11-2

On the basis of the synoptic journal presented in this unit, classify each statement as true or false.

1. Synoptic journals are less efficient than other types of special journals.

Month: April

Accounts Payable Dr.	Accounts Payable Cr.	GST Dr.	GST Cr.	Sales Cr.	Sales Discount Dr.	Purchases Dr.	Purchases Discount Cr.	Sales Tax Cr.
			7 00	100 00				9 00
			28 00	400 00				36 00
					8 00			
	1177 00	77 00				1100 00		
	6420 00	420 00				6000 00		
6420 00							120 00	
6420 00	7597 00	497 00	35 00	500 00	8 00	7100 00	120 00	45 00

2. The total of the Cash column is posted daily.
3. The total of the Sundry column is not posted.
4. The total of the Sales column is not posted.
5. All synoptic journals have the same headings.
6. Synoptic journals cannot be proved.
7. Subsidiary ledgers are posted from the cash column.
8. The synoptic journals is used for large companies.
9. A dentist could use a synoptic journal.
10. A lawyer will always use a synoptic journal.

Solution to Self-Review Quiz 11-2

1. False
2. False
3. True
4. False
5. False
6. False
7. False
8. False
9. True
10. False

Chapter Review

Summary of key points

Learning Unit 11-1

1. A company with inventory will not use the cash method.
2. The modified cash system is used because federal and provincial requirements make a strictly cash-basis system difficult to implement without distorting financial reports.
3. The modified cash system will require adjustments for depreciation, insurance premiums, and large amounts of supplies purchased. Adjustments often will be recorded in the Sundry columns of the synoptic journal and additional adjustments can be made at year-end.

RUTH RAMOS

ASSISTANT DIRECTOR FISCAL OPERATIONS, CONTROLLER

HEAD START, MAJOR NOT-FOR-PROFIT ORGANIZATION

Ruth Ramos started out as a secretary/bookkeeper and quickly discovered that she preferred working with numbers. When she was hired as a secretary at Head Start, a nonprofit child development program, it was not long before she took on bookkeeping duties, relying on her previous job experience.

As Ruth took on more responsibilities, she felt the need to have a solid academic background in accounting. "I decided to take my job seriously and go back to school," she says. Her employer offered tuition reimbursement for job-related courses so she began taking bookkeeping and accounting courses.

"Getting a background in accounting has been enormously helpful," she says. "The College Accounting course gave me a more thorough understanding of the theory, and helped me to learn the language of accounting."

Ruth is now Assistant Director for Fiscal Operations, Controller for a major Head Start operation. Her responsibilities include preparing budget proposals for million dollar programs. She is also responsible for day-to-day cost analysis, payroll, general ledger and journal, trial balances, and monthly financial statements. She prepares for outside audits and supervises a staff of seven bookkeepers.

"My courses helped me to understand how to read budgets and how to prepare them," she says. "The first time I had to work with outside auditors, I was scared stiff. But now I feel confident. I know my stuff, and the auditors have been impressed with my knowledge."

"Going back to school was the best decision I ever made," Ruth says. "The courses gave me confidence in my job and gave me the confidence to continue my education."

4. No accounts for accounts payable or accounts receivable are used in the chart of accounts for a modified cash system. Companies use memoranda to keep track of receivables or payables until money is received or paid.
5. The bank balance (cash balance) can be determined at any time when a synoptic journal is used.
6. A synoptic journal can be proved by listing debits and credits.
7. The payroll tax expense for the employer using a cash-basis system is recorded when the remittance is made. In the cash-basis system no *liability* accounts exist for Due to Receiver General or other payroll taxes payable; you record them when *paid* as part of Payroll Tax Expense.

Learning Unit 11-2

1. A synoptic journal for Art's Wholesale replaces the individual special journals (SJ, CRJ, PJ, CPJ, GJ).
2. Many small companies use a synoptic journal.
3. A synoptic journal on an accrual basis uses columns for accounts receivable and accounts payable. Subsidiary ledgers will be recorded during the month. The total of the sundry columns is not posted.
4. Adjusting and closing entries will be recorded in the sundry columns.

Key terms

Accrual accounting synoptic journal A special journal that combines the features of the sales, cash payments, cash receipts, purchases, and general journals.

Modified-cash-basis method (hybrid) The accounting method that records revenue when cash is received, and expenses when they are paid. Adjustments to long-lived assets, as well as insurance premiums and amounts of supplies on hand, are required by provincial and federal laws so that financial reports will not be distorted.

Synoptic (combined) journal A special journal that combines the features of the sales, cash payments, cash receipts, purchases, and sometimes general journals.

Questions, exercises, and problems

Discussion Questions

1. All companies with inventory must use the cash basis of accounting. Agree or disagree.
2. Why does the strictly cash basis tend to distort financial reports?
3. List three adjustments that may result in a modified cash system.
4. Explain how a company can change its method of accounting.
5. A modified cash system has an accounts receivable as well as accounts payable ledger. Agree or disagree. Please support your answer.

Blueprint of a Typical Chart of Accounts for a Lawyer Using a Modified Cash Basis (Including Payroll)

	Assets		
No Accounts Receivable account	Royal Bank	111	
	Petty Cash	112	
	Office Supplies	113	
	Prepaid Insurance	114	
	Office Equip.	115	
	Accum. Dep., Office Equip.	116	
	Automobiles	117	
	Accum. Dep., Auto	118	
	Liabilities		
No Accounts Payable account	Income Tax Payable	211	
	CPP Payable	212	
	UI Payable	213	
	Notes Payable	214	
	Owner's Equity		
	J. Smith, Capital	311	
	J. Smith, Withdrawals	312	
	Income Summary	313	
Only recorded when cash received ←	**Revenue**		
	Professional Fees	411	
	Expenses		
	Dep. Exp., Office Equip.	511	For adjustments so financial reports will not be distorted (511–514)
	Dep. Exp., Auto	512	
	Insurance Expense	513	
	Office Supplies Expense	514	
	Dues	515	
	Postage	516	
	Payroll Tax Expense	517	→ Records the tax expense for employer when the CPP, UI, and income tax is remitted
	Rent Expense	518	
	Salary Expense	519	
	Telephone Expense	520	
	Miscellaneous Expense	521	

6. Explain how a cash balance can be calculated during the month when using a synoptic journal.

7. How is a synoptic journal proved?

8. Explain why there are no accounts for Due to Receiver General or other payroll taxes payable in the chart of accounts in the cash basis.

9. What purpose would an informal memorandum serve when dealing with accounts payable and accounts receivable in a modified cash system?

10. Explain when the Payroll Tax Expense account will be updated in a modified cash system.

11. Explain how a synoptic journal for an accrual-basis company will aid in reducing the number of special journals needed.

12. "If a company is expanding, a synoptic journal could be efficient." Please respond.

Mini Exercises

(The forms you need are on page 11-3 of the *Study Guide and Working Papers.*)

Accounts Needing Adjustment

1. Which of the following titles may require adjusting entries using modified cash basis?

	Yes	*No*
Cash	______	______
Accounts Receivable	______	______
Equipment	______	______
Supplies	______	______
Accounts Payable	______	______
Salaries Payable	______	______
Accumulated Depreciation	______	______
Prepaid Insurance	______	______

Payment of Payroll

2. Mel Blanc uses a modified-cash-basis system. His company's payroll records show deductions for income tax $280, CPP $36, and UI $46. Please record the necessary entry in the sundry columns of the synoptic journal. (Only the sundry columns are shown.)

Combined Journal Headings

3. Match the following partial list of column headings of Pete Moore's synoptic journal to the statements below. Use only one number for each letter.

1. Cash	Cr.
2. Accounts Payable	Cr.
3. Sales Discounts	Dr.
4. Sundry	Dr./Cr.
5. Sales	Cr.

______ **a.** Reflects amounts owed to creditors.

______ **b.** Records the amounts of discounts taken by customers.

______ **c.** Records transactions that do not occur very often.

______ **d.** Records sales made for cash or on account.

______ **e.** Records decreases in cash.

Recording to Subsidiary Ledgers

4. Indicate which of the following transactions would result in a recording to a subsidiary ledger. The company uses a synoptic journal with an accrual accounting approach.

a. Pete Daving invests $20,000 into the business.

b. Sold $300 of merchandise to French Co. on account.

c. Cash sales $200.

d. Received half the amount owed by French from sales on account in **b**.

Exercises

Identifying adjustment titles for a modified cash system.

1. In a modified cash system, which of the following titles may need adjustments?

- Cash
- Supplies
- Prepaid Insurance
- Equipment
- Notes Payable
- A. Swan, Capital
- A. Swan, Withdrawals
- Commission Sales
- Salary Expense

Posting a synoptic journal using the accrual approach.

2. Avon Company uses a synoptic journal with the following headings:

Sundry	Dr./Cr.
Accounts Receivable	Dr./Cr.
Accounts Payable	Dr./Cr.
Commission Sales	Cr.
Salary Expense	Dr.
Cash	Dr./Cr.

a. How can the balance of cash be determined at any point in the month?

b. Which column total will not be posted?

c. Do you think Avon Company has subsidiary ledgers? Please explain.

d. Which columns will be used to record the payment of advertising expense?

Preparing a chart of accounts for a modified cash system.

3. Listed below are the accounts used by Dr. Jonson, who keeps his records on a strictly cash basis. As his accountant, which titles do you think could be added to use a modified cash system? Assume that a large amount of supplies is bought.

Cash; Notes Payable; L. Jonson, Capital; L. Jonson, Withdrawals; Professional Fees; Auto Expense; Rent Expense; Office Furniture Expense; Insurance Expense; Medical Supplies Expense.

Explaining postings of a synoptic journal for a modified cash basis.

4. Using the headings of the synoptic journal for Dr. Walensa (Figure 11-2), indicate when postings would occur.

19XX

May	3	Al Henson invested $4,000 in the dental business.
	8	Paid three months' insurance premiums, $1,200.
	15	Received cheques from patients, $900.
	19	Paid office salaries, $500.

Explaining recordings and postings of a synoptic journal using an accrual approach.

5. Using the headings of the synoptic journal for Art's Wholesale (Figure 11-3), indicate when recordings and postings would occur.

19XX

May	2	Joe Davis invested $12,000 in the business.
	5	Bought $600 of merchandise for cash.
	8	Cash sale, $600.
	19	Received $400 less a 3 percent discount from Alvie Corp. from past sale on account.

Group A Problems

Journalizing transactions of a modified cash system in a synoptic journal.

11A-1. Peter Lovejoy, M.D., uses the following chart of accounts:

Chart of Accounts

Assets
111 Alberta Bank
113 Petty Cash
114 Prepaid Insurance
115 Medical Supplies
121 Medical Equipment
122 Accumulated Depreciation, Medical Equipment
123 Office Furniture
124 Accumulated Depreciation, Office Furniture
125 Auto
126 Accumulated Depreciation, Auto

Liabilities
211 Notes Payable

Owner's Equity
311 P. Lovejoy, Capital
312 P. Lovejoy, Withdrawals
313 Income Summary

Revenue
411 Professional Fees

Expenses
511 Rent Expense
512 Donation Expense
513 Salaries Expense
514 Medical Supplies Expense
515 Depreciation Expense, Medical Equipment
516 Depreciation Expense, Office Furniture
517 Depreciation Expense, Automobile
518 Insurance Expense
519 Telephone Expense
610 Cleaning Expense
611 Miscellaneous Expense

The headings of the synoptic journal are as follows:

Page 1

Date	Explanation	PR	Sundry		Medical Supplies Dr.	Dr. Lovejoy, Withdrawals Dr.	Cleaning Expense Dr.	Prof. Fees Cr.	Chq. No.	Alberta Bank	
			Dr.	Cr.						Dr.	Cr.

From the transactions listed below:

1. Journalize them in the synoptic journal.
2. Prove the synoptic journal.

Transactions

19XX

May 1 Dr. Lovejoy deposited $6,000 in the practice.
3 Paid rent for the month to Foster Realty, $800, cheque no. 1.
8 Bought medical equipment from Ace Supply Co., $1,500, cheque no. 2.
12 Bought medical supplies from Lone Co., $700, cheque no. 3.
15 Received cash from patients, $2,800.
18 Bought additional medical supplies from Lone Co., $1,200, cheque no. 4.

19 Dr. Lovejoy withdrew $600 for personal use, cheque no. 5.
21 Paid Al's Janitorial Service, $300, cheque no. 6.
24 Received cash from patients, $1,900.
25 Paid for postage stamps, $40 (miscellaneous expense), cheque no. 7.
27 Paid salaries for month, $1,400, cheque no. 8.
28 Paid Al's Janitorial Service, $400, cheque no. 9.
29 Dr. Lovejoy withdrew $400 for personal use, cheque no. 10.

11A-2. The following is the chart of accounts of Dr. Fox, M.D.:

Journalizing transactions of a modified cash system into a synoptic journal with headings for payroll deductions as well as recording payroll tax expense.

Chart of Accounts

Assets
111 Bank of Regina
112 Prepaid Insurance
113 Medical Supplies
122 Accumulated Depreciation, Office Equipment

Liabilities
211 Due to Receiver General
212 Other Payroll Taxes Payable

Owner's Equity
311 Al Fox, Capital
312 Al Fox, Withdrawals
313 Income Summary

Revenue
411 Professional Fees

Expenses
511 Rent Expense
512 Medical Supplies Expense
513 Salaries Expense
514 Payroll Tax Expense
515 Telephone Expense
516 Depreciation Expense, Office Equipment
517 Insurance Expense
518 Cleaning Expense
519 Miscellaneous Expense

The headings of Dr. Fox's synoptic journal are as follows:

Date	Explanation	PR	Bank of Regina		Chq. No.	Prof. Fees Cr.	Sal. Exp. Dr.	Payroll Deductions			Med. Sup. Dr.	Sundry	
			Dr.	Cr.				Income Tax Payable Cr.	CPP Payable Cr.	UI Payable Cr.		Dr.	Cr.

From the transactions listed below:

1. Journalize them in the synoptic journal (beginning balances are provided in the working papers).
2. Prove the synoptic journal.

Transactions

19XX

May 1 Received $3,000 from patients.
3 Issued cheque no. 480 to Lane Drug for medical supplies, $600.
5 Issued cheque no. 481 to A. Realty to pay three months' insurance premiums, $1,200.
9 Received cheques from patients, $2,000.
12 Issued the following payroll cheques to his staff:

Employee	*Chq. No.*	*Gross Pay*	*IT*	*CPP*	*UI*	*Net Pay*
Abby Slat	482	$ 700	$140	$18	$21	$ 521
Jane Reeves	483	600	120	16	18	446
Bob Swan	484	500	100	14	15	371
		$1,800	$360	$48	$54	$1,338

18 Issued cheque no. 485 to Lane Drug for medical supplies, $400.
25 Dr. Fox withdrew $700 for personal use, cheque no. 486.
28 Dr. Fox made the necessary remittance to the Receiver General from payroll of May 12, cheque no. 487. (Don't forget Dr. Fox's share of CPP and UI.)

Journalizing and proving synoptic journal, recording transactions using an accrual basis of accounting.

11A-3. Debra Clark, a recent graduate of a medical school, has decided to open her own office. Based on the advice of her accountant, she will use a synoptic journal. The following is the chart of accounts for Dr. Clark's office:

Chart of Accounts

Assets
111 Cash
112 Accounts Receivable
113 Prepaid Insurance
121 Office Equipment

Liabilities
211 Accounts Payable

Owner's Equity
311 D. Clark, Capital
312 Income Summary

Revenue
411 Medical Fees

Expenses
511 Telephone Expense
512 Cleaning Expense
513 Utilities Expense

The headings of Dr. Clark's synoptic journal are:

SYNOPTIC JOURNAL													
						Month							Page 1
				Sundry		Cash		Accts. Rec.		Accts. Pay.		Office Equip.	Medical Fees
Date	Explanation	Chq. No.	PR	Dr.	Cr.	Dr.	Cr.	Dr.	Cr.	Dr.	Cr.	Dr.	Cr.

Required

1. Record the following transactions in the synoptic journal. Complete the PR column as if you were recording and posting.
2. Prove the synoptic journal.

19XX

July 1 Debra Clark invested $7,000 cash and $4,000 of office equipment in the practice.
1 Paid insurance on the office for one year in advance, $1,700, cheque no. 1.
9 Purchased office equipment on account from Smith Stationery Co., $400.

12 Purchased office equipment on account from Vole Stationery Co., $700.
18 Completed vaccination of each schoolchild at Salem Elementary School, $3,000 on account.
18 Received $900 cash for medical fees earned.
19 Performed a complete examination for Alvin Ray's son, $75 on account.
20 Paid Smith Stationery one-half the amount owed from July 9 transaction, cheque no. 2.
26 Paid telephone bill, $90, cheque no. 3.
27 Paid utilities, $170, cheque no. 4.
28 Paid Toby Cleaning Co. for cleaning service performed, $100, cheque no. 5.
29 Paid one-half the amount owed Vole Stationery Company from July 12 transaction, cheque no. 6.

11A-4. (GST at 7 percent and PST at 9 percent [not cumulative] are involved in this problem.) Buzzy Sullivan opened a dry cleaning store that also sold accessories. The following is the chart of accounts for Buzzy's Cleaning Company.

Journalizing, recording, and posting synoptic journal used to record transactions utilizing accrual basis of accounting.

Chart of Accounts

Assets
111 Cash
112 Accounts Receivable
113 Prepaid Insurance
115 Prepaid GST
121 Cleaning Equipment

Liabilities
211 Accounts Payable
212 Note Payable
215 GST Collected
217 PST Payable

Owner's Equity
311 B. Sullivan, Capital
312 Income Summary

Revenue
411 Cleaning Sales
412 Sales Discount
413 Accessory Sales

Cost of Goods Sold
511 Purchases
512 Purchases Returns and Allowances
513 Purchases Discounts

Expenses
611 Utilities Expense
612 Advertising Expense
613 Cleaning Supplies Expense

Here are the transactions for the month of January:

19XX

Jan. 2 Buzzy Sullivan invested $8,000 cash in the business.
8 Paid a five-year insurance policy in advance, $1,500 (no taxes), cheque no. 1.
10 Purchased merchandise on account from Role Company, $900, plus GST.
12 Cleaned shirts for cash, $650, plus PST and GST.
15 Cleaned suits on account for Pete Daley, $200, plus PST and GST.
17 Purchased cleaning equipment on account from Ral Co., $900, plus GST.
20 Borrowed $6,000 from National Bank.
21 Cleaned shirts for Pete Daley for $50, plus PST and GST on account.
24 Received entire payment from Pete Daley for January 15 transaction less a 2 percent discount.

25 Purchased merchandise on account from Bomb Co., $250, plus GST.
26 Cleaned slacks on account for Alice Small, $15, plus PST and GST.
27 Paid amount due to Role Company less a 2 percent discount for January 10 transaction, cheque no. 2.
28 Returned $100 of cleaning equipment to Ral Company for faulty workmanship. (Remember the GST.)
29 Paid Bomb Company the amount due on the January 25 purchase less a 10 percent discount, cheque no. 3.
30 Cash sales, $800, plus PST and GST.
30 Received amount due from Alice Small on the January 26 transaction, less a 20 percent sales discount.

Required

1. Set up accounts in the general ledger (some accounts may not be used in January).
2. Set up accounts in the accounts payable and accounts receivable ledgers as needed.
3. Journalize the above transactions.
4. Record to the accounts payable and accounts receivable ledger as appropriate.
5. Post to the general ledger as appropriate.
6. Prove the sum of the subsidiary ledgers equal to the controlling accounts.
7. Prove the synoptic journal.

The headings of the synoptic journal of Buzzy's Cleaning Company will be as follows:

BUZZY'S CLEANING COMPANY
SYNOPTIC JOURNAL

Date	Explanation	Chq. No.	PR	Sundry		Cash		Accts. Rec.		Accts. Pay.		GST		Clean. Revenue	Sales Disc.	Pur.	Pur. Disc.	9% Sales Tax
				Dr.	Cr.	Dr.	Cr.	Dr.	Cr.	Dr.	Cr.	Dr.	Cr.	Cr.	Dr.	Dr.	Cr.	Cr.

Group B Problems

11B-1. Using the chart of accounts of Dr. Lovejoy from Problem 11A-1, record the following transactions in the synoptic journal and then prove the journal:

Journalizing transactions of a modified cash system into a synoptic journal.

19XX

May 1 Dr. Lovejoy deposited $9,000 in the practice.
3 Paid rent for the month to Jane Jones Realty, $700, cheque no. 1.
8 Bought medical supplies from Able Co., $750, cheque no. 2.
12 Bought medical equipment from Jane's Supply, $4,000, cheque no. 3.
15 Received cash from patients, $3,000.
18 Bought additional medical supplies from Able Co., $910, cheque no. 4.
19 Dr. Lovejoy withdrew $790 for personal use, cheque no. 5.
21 Paid Ron's Janitorial Service, $500, cheque no. 6.
24 Received cash from patients, $3,400.
25 Paid for postage stamps, $30 (miscellaneous expense), cheque no. 7.
27 Paid salaries for month, $1,600, cheque no. 8.

28 Paid Ron's Janitorial Service, $300, cheque no. 9.
29 Dr. Lovejoy withdrew $300 for personal use, cheque no. 10.

11B-2. Using the chart of accounts for Dr. Fox from Problem 11A-2, record the following transactions in the synoptic journal and then prove the journal. (Beginning balances are in your working papers.)

Journalizing transactions of a modified cash system into a synoptic journal with headings for payroll deductions, and recording payroll tax expenses.

19XX

May 1 Received $4,000 from patients.
3 Issued cheque no. 563 to Lane Drug for medical supplies, $700.
5 Issued cheque no. 564 to J. Realty to pay three months' insurance premiums, $900.
9 Received cheques from patients, $3,000.
12 Issued the following payroll cheques:

Employee	*Chq. No.*	*Gross Pay*	*IT*	*CPP*	*UI*	*Net Pay*
Abby Slat	565	$ 900	$210	$25	$27	$ 638
Jane Reeves	566	800	190	22	24	564
Bob Swan	567	600	130	15	18	437
		$2,300	$530	$62	$69	$1,639

18 Issued cheque no. 568 to Lane Drug for medical supplies, $900.
25 Dr. Fox withdrew $400 for personal use, cheque no. 569.
28 Dr. Fox sent cheque to Receiver General relating to payroll of May 12, cheque no. 570. (Don't forget Dr. Fox's share of CPP and UI.)

11B-3. Using the chart of accounts of Debra Clark from Problem 11A-3, journalize the following transactions and prove the synoptic journal. Fill in the PR column as if you were actually recording and posting to the ledger.

Journalizing, recording, and posting synoptic journal used to record transactions utilizing the accrual basis of accounting.

19XX

July 1 Debra Clark invested $6,000 cash and $4,000 of office equipment in the practice.
1 Paid insurance on the office for one year in advance, $1,200, cheque no. 1.
9 Purchased office equipment on account from Smith Stationery Co., $1,400.
12 Completed physical examinations on each schoolchild at Simcoe Elementary School, $2,000 on account.
18 Received $700 cash for medical fees earned.
19 Performed a complete examination for Alvin Ray's son, $200 on account.
20 Paid Smith Stationery one-half the amount owed from July 9 transaction, cheque no. 2.
26 Paid telephone bill, $95, cheque no. 3.
27 Paid utilities, $60, cheque no. 4.
28 Paid Toby Cleaning Co. for cleaning service performed, $75, cheque no. 5.

11B-4. (GST at 7 percent and PST at 8 percent [not cumulative] are involved in this problem.) Buzzy Sullivan opened a dry cleaning store that also sold accessories. The chart of accounts and synoptic journal headings for Buzzy's Cleaning Company are given in Problem 11A-4. Here are the transactions for the month of January:

19XX

Jan. 2 Buzzy Sullivan invested $6,000 cash in the business.
8 Paid for a five-year company insurance policy in advance, $1,200, cheque no. 101 (no GST or PST).
10 Purchased merchandise on account from Role Company, $700, plus GST.
12 Cleaned shirts for cash, $950, plus GST and PST.
15 Cleaned suits on account for Pete Daley, $500, plus GST and PST.
17 Purchased cleaning equipment on account from Ral Co., $600, plus GST.
20 Borrowed $4,000 from National Bank.
21 Cleaned shirts on account for P. Daley, $50, plus GST and PST.
24 Received entire payment from P. Daley less a 2 percent discount from January 15 transaction.
25 Purchased merchandise on account from Bomb Company, $90, plus GST.
26 Cleaned silk blouse on account for Alice Small, $20, plus GST and PST.
27 Paid Role Company the amount due (less a 2 percent discount) for merchandise that was purchased on January 10, cheque no. 102.
28 Returned $200 of cleaning equipment to Ral Company for faulty workmanship. (Remember the GST.)
29 Paid Bomb Company the amount due (less a 10 percent discount) on the purchases made on account on January 25, cheque no. 103.
30 Cash sales, $700, plus GST and PST.

Your task is to journalize, record, post, and prove the synoptic journal for the cleaning company. See Problem 11A-4 for detailed requirements.

Group C Problems

Journalizing transactions of a modified cash system into a synoptic journal.

11C-1. Using a chart of accounts similar to that for Problem 11A-1, record the following transactions for Carla Walgee, Physiotherapist, in her synoptic journal, and then prove the journal:

19XX

May 1 Ms. Walgee deposited $18,000 in the practice.
3 Paid rent for the month to Abby Glenn Realty, $800, cheque no. 341.
8 Bought supplies from Perkins Co., $680, cheque no. 342.
12 Bought exercise equipment from Atlas Supply, $6,800, cheque no. 343.
15 Received cash from patients, $4,550.
18 Bought additional supplies from Perkins Co., $920, cheque no. 344.
19 Ms. Walgee withdrew $900 for personal use, cheque no. 345.
21 Paid Rockford Janitorial Service, $420, cheque no. 346.
24 Received cash from patients, $3,850.
25 Paid for postage stamps, $75 (miscellaneous expense), cheque no. 347.
27 Paid salary to Brenda Curtis for month, $1,820, cheque no. 348.
28 Paid Rockford Janitorial Service, $420, cheque no. 349.
29 Ms. Walgee withdrew another $900 for personal use, cheque no. 350.

Journalizing transactions of a modified cash system into a synoptic journal with headings for payroll deductions, and recording payroll tax expenses.

11C-2. Using a chart of accounts similar to that for Problem 11A-2, record the following transactions for Sandy Williams, Dentist, in the synoptic journal, and then prove the journal. (Beginning balances are given in your working papers.)

19XX

June 1 Received $4,820 from patients.

3 Issued cheque no. 230 to Walkins Drug for dental supplies, $780.

5 Issued cheque no. 231 to Game Agencies to pay six months' insurance premiums, $2,400.

9 Received cheques from patients, $3,910.

12 Issued the following payroll cheques:

Employee	*Chq. No.*	*Gross Pay*	*IT*	*CPP*	*UI*	*Net Pay*
Ted Forth	232	$ 800	$165	$23	$ 24	$ 588
Carol Hahn	233	900	183	25	27	665
Ed Birch	234	700	146	19	21	514
Kim Shaw	235	1,100	245	31	33	791
		$3,500	$739	$98	$105	$2,558

18 Issued cheque no. 236 to Walkins Drug for dental supplies, $1,340.

25 Dr. Williams withdrew $2,400 for personal use, cheque no. 237.

26 Issued the following payroll cheques:

Employee	*Chq. No.*	*Gross Pay*	*IT*	*CPP*	*UI*	*Net Pay*
Ted Forth	238	$ 850	$175	$24	$ 25	$ 626
Carol Hahn	239	900	183	25	27	665
Ed Birch	240	700	146	19	21	514
Kim Shaw	241	1,100	245	31	33	791
		$3,550	$749	$99	$106	$2,596

28 Dr. Williams sent the remittance cheque to the Receiver General for the payrolls of June 12 and 26, cheque no. 242. (Don't forget Dr. Williams's share of CPP and UI.)

11C-3. Using a chart of accounts similar to that for Problem 11A-3, journalize the following transactions for Sammy Wong, Optometrist, and prove the synoptic journal. Fill in the PR column as if you were actually recording and posting to the ledger.

Journalizing, recording, and posting synoptic journal used to record transactions utilizing accrual basis of accounting.

19XX

April 1 Dr. Wong invested $12,000 cash and $32,000 of optical equipment in the practice.

1 Paid insurance premium for one year in advance, $2,870, cheque no. 761.

8 Purchased office equipment on account from Adobe Stationery Co., $4,170.

12 Completed optical examinations on each schoolchild at Eastside Elementary School, $4,120 on account.

18 Received $2,850 cash for professional fees earned.

19 Performed a complete optical examination for Ms. Rachel Flemming, a famous film star, $400 on account.

20 Paid Adobe Stationery one-half the amount owed from April 8 transaction, cheque no. 762.

26 Paid telephone bill, $87, cheque no. 766.

27 Paid utilities, $140, cheque no. 764.

28 Paid Neally Cleaning Co. for services performed, $350, cheque no. 765.

30 Received first payment from Eastside Elementary School, $2,000.

11C-4. (GST at 7 percent and PST at 6 percent [not cumulative] are involved in this problem.) Freda Schragge opened an appliance repair shop that also sold accessories. The chart of accounts for her shop is shown below. Here are the transactions for the month of October:

19XX

Oct.	1	Freda Schragge invested $25,000 cash in the business.
	8	Paid First City Agency Co. for a three-year insurance policy in advance, $1,120, cheque no. 101 (no GST or PST).
	10	Purchased merchandise on account from Colter & Co., $1,680, plus GST.
	12	Repaired appliances for five customers for cash, $670, plus GST and PST.
	13	Sold accessories for cash, $650, plus GST and PST.
	15	Repaired appliances on account for Vince Lombardi, $940, plus GST and PST.
	16	Freda withdrew $700 for personal expenses, cheque no. 102.
	17	Purchased repair equipment on account from Sattrap Co., $7,000, plus GST.
	20	Borrowed $10,000 from National Bank.
	21	Repaired appliances on account for Vince Lombardi, $280, plus GST and PST.
	22	Sold accessories for cash, $920, plus GST and PST.
	24	Received payment from Vince Lombardi for October 15 transaction less a 2 percent discount.
	25	Purchased merchandise on account from Apex Company, $840, plus GST.
	26	Cleaned stove on account for J. Fresnel, $80, plus GST and PST.
	27	Paid Colter & Co. for merchandise purchased on October 10 less a 2 percent discount, cheque no. 103.
	28	Returned $200 of repair equipment to Sattrap Co. due to faulty workmanship. (Remember the GST.)
	29	Paid Apex Company the amount owed (less a 5 percent discount) on the purchases made on account on October 25, cheque no. 104.
	30	Repairs made for cash, $620, plus GST and PST.

Chart of Accounts

Assets
111 Cash
112 Accounts Receivable
113 Prepaid Insurance
115 Prepaid GST
121 Repair Equipment

Liabilities
211 Accounts Payable
212 Note Payable
215 GST Collected
217 PST Payable

Owner's Equity
311 F. Schragge, Capital
312 F. Schragge, Withdrawals
315 Income Summary

Revenue
411 Appliance Sales
412 Appliance Sales Discount
413 Repair Revenue

Cost of Goods Sold
511 Purchases
512 Purchases Returns and Allowances
513 Purchases Discounts

Expenses
611 Utilities Expense
612 Advertising Expense
613 Supplies Expense

The headings for the synoptic journal should look like this:

FREDA'S APPLIANCE REPAIR AND SALES SYNOPTIC JOURNAL																		
Date	Explanation	Chq. No.	PR	Sundry		Cash		Accts. Rec.		Accts. Pay.		GST Paid/Coll.	Repairs Revenue	Appl. Sales	Sales Disc.	Pur.	Pur. Disc.	Sales Tax Payable
				Dr.	Cr.	Dr.	Cr.	Dr.	Cr.	Dr.	Cr.	(Dr.) or Cr.	Cr.	Cr.	Dr.	Dr.	Cr.	Cr.

Your task is to journalize, record, post, and prove the business's synoptic journal for October 19XX.

Real World Applications

11R-1.
Jeff Smith has been running his business on a strictly cash basis. At a party over the weekend he met an accountant who told him that his business should use a modified cash system. Jeff has brought you his chart of accounts so that you may revise it as well as lay out a synoptic journal. Using the following chart of accounts for Jeff Smith, design a synoptic journal for him. Allow columns for payroll deductions.

Chart of Accounts

Assets
111 Cash
113 Petty Cash

Liabilities
211 Notes Payable

Owner's Equity
311 J. Smith, Capital
312 J. Smith, Withdrawals
313 Income Summary

Revenue
411 Professional Fees

Expenses
511 Insurance Expense
512 Furniture Expense
514 Medical Equipment Expense
515 Medical Supplies Expense
516 Salary Expense
517 Telephone Expense
518 Miscellaneous Expense

11R-2.
Margie Henley is about to open a dry cleaning shop. She has hired you to design a synoptic journal for her shop. It will definitely be a small business with a limited number of transactions that are not too complicated. After analyzing Margie's company, you develop the following chart of accounts:

1. Cash
2. Accounts Receivable
3. Equipment
4. Accounts Payable
5. Cleaning Sales
6. Wage Expense
7. Supplies Expense
8. Miscellaneous Expense

Margie has asked you to provide her, as soon as possible, with a justification for your design of the parts of the synoptic journal. Be prepared to support the synoptic journal you present to her. Label all headings of the journal in terms of debits and credits. What titles are missing from the chart of accounts?

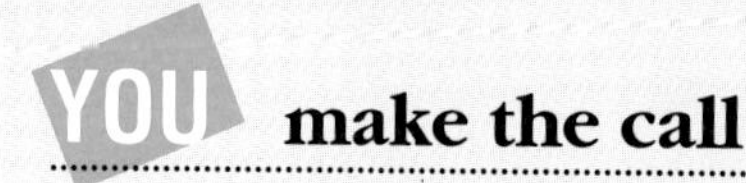

Critical Thinking/Ethical Case

11R-3.

Angel Shower, the bookkeeper of Aster Co., also collects the payment of invoices by customers. Angel noticed that Rume Co. paid the April 10 invoice twice. Angel, who is in need of extra cash, does not plan to inform Rume Co. of the double payment. Do you agree with Angel's decision? You make the call. Write down your specific recommendations to Angel.

ACCOUNTING RECALL

A CUMULATIVE APPROACH

THIS EXAM REVIEWS CHAPTERS 1 THROUGH 11

Your *Study Guide and Working Papers* has forms to complete this exam, as well as worked-out solutions. The page references next to each question identify what page to turn back to if you answer the question incorrectly.

PART I Vocabulary Review

Match the terms to the appropriate definition or phrase.

Page Ref.		
(438)	1. Hybrid	A. A special journal
(444)	2. Sundry	B. Amounts deducted from employees plus employer's share of CPP and UI
(445)	3. X	C. Records revenue when cash is received
(437)	4. Accrual accounting	D. Accounts payable
(445)	5. √	E. Verification
(289)	6. Due to Receiver General for Canada	F. No posting
		G. Record to subsidiary
(292)	7. Payroll tax expense	H. Records revenue when earned
(333)	8. Controlling account	I. Miscellaneous
(445)	9. Crossfoot	J. CPP + UI (employer's share)
(438)	10. Synoptic journal	

PART II True or False (Accounting Theory)

(332) 11. We post to subsidiary ledgers and record to general ledgers.

(444) 12. Small businesses could use synoptic journals.

(445) 13. Adjusting entries would be recorded in the Sundry columns of a special journal.

(446) 14. Sales Tax Payable has a normal balance of a debit.

(446) 15. The total of Accounts Receivable is posted to the subsidiary ledger.

PART III Applications Problem

Assuming a modified-cash-basis combined journal, indicate when postings would occur.

May 9 Pete Saley invests $3,000 in business.
14 Paid two months' insurance premiums, $1,400.
21 Received cheques from customers, $800.
24 Paid office salaries, $600.

PREPARING A WORKSHEET FOR A MERCHANDISE COMPANY

12

Chapter Objectives

- ◆ **Figuring adjustments for merchandise inventory, unearned rent, supplies used, insurance expired, depreciation expense, and salaries accrued. (pp. 468–470)**
- ◆ **Preparing a worksheet for a merchandise company. (p. 472)**

In Chapters 9 and 10 we discussed the special journals and subsidiary ledgers of a merchandise company, and in Chapters 7 and 8 we looked at payroll recordkeeping practices and procedures. Now our attention will shift to recording adjustments and completing a worksheet for a merchandise company. Learning Unit 12-1 will introduce two new adjustments that we have not yet discussed, Merchandise Inventory and Unearned Rent. Learning Unit 12-2 will show how to complete the worksheet with these new adjustments.

LEARNING UNIT 12-1

Adjustments for Merchandise Inventory and Unearned Rent

An important item in a merchandise company work sheet and financial records is *Merchandise Inventory*. This means the goods that a company has available to sell to customers. There are several ways of keeping track of the cost of goods sold and quantity of inventory that a company has on hand. In Chapter 16 we will discuss the **perpetual inventory system**, which is used by companies with low-volume sales and high unit prices, and in which the record of inventory is continually updated throughout the year. Most such companies use a computer to keep track of their inventory records.

In this chapter we will discuss the **periodic inventory system**, in which the balance in inventory is updated only at the end of the accounting period. This system is used by smaller companies which sell a variety of merchandise with low unit prices. The number of companies using this system of accounting for inventory is still significant but is declining. This is because of the increasing availability of computers and software which together encourage the use of the more useful and informative perpetual system.

Let's take as an example the merchandise inventory of Art's Wholesale Clothing Company. Let's assume Art's Wholesale started the year with $19,000 worth of merchandise; this is called **beginning merchandise inventory** or simply **beginning inventory**. During the period, the cost of beginning inventory does not change; instead, all purchases of merchandise are recorded in the Purchases account. During the period $52,000 worth of merchandise was purchased and recorded in the Purchases account.

At the end of the period, the company takes a physical count of the merchandise in stock; this amount is called **ending merchandise inventory** or simply **ending inventory** and is calculated on an inventory sheet as shown in Figure 12-1.

Cost of goods sold:
Beginning inventory
+ Net purchases
– Ending inventory
= Cost of goods sold

This $4,000, which is the ending inventory for this period, will be the beginning inventory for the next period.

When the income statement is prepared, the cost of goods sold section will require two distinct numbers for inventory. The beginning inventory adds to the cost of goods sold, while the ending inventory is subtracted from the cost of

FIGURE 12-1
Ending Inventory Sheet

ART'S WHOLESALE CLOTHING COMPANY
ENDING INVENTORY SHEET
AS OF DECEMBER 31, 19X2

Amount	Explanation	Unit Cost	Total
20	Ladies' Jackets code 14-0	$50	$1,000
10	Men's Hats code 327	10	100
90	Men's Shirts code 423	10	900
100	Ladies' Blouses code 481	20	2,000
			$4,000

Counted by ______ Checked and priced by ______

goods sold. Remember that the two figures for beginning and ending inventory were calculated months apart. Thus they cannot merely be combined to come up with one inventory figure; that would not be accurate.

Adjustment for Merchandise Inventory

First adjustment transfers amount in beginning inventory from Merchandise Inventory to Income Summary.

Adjusting the Merchandise Inventory account is a two-step process because we want to keep both beginning inventory and ending inventory amounts separate; we cannot simply combine them. So the first step deals with beginning merchandise inventory.

Note that Income Summary has no normal balance of debit or credit.

Given: Beginning Inventory, $19,000 Our first adjustment removes that amount from the asset account (Merchandise Inventory) and transfers it to Income Summary. We do this by crediting Merchandise Inventory for $19,000 and debiting Income Summary for the same amount. This is shown below in T account form and on a transaction analysis chart:

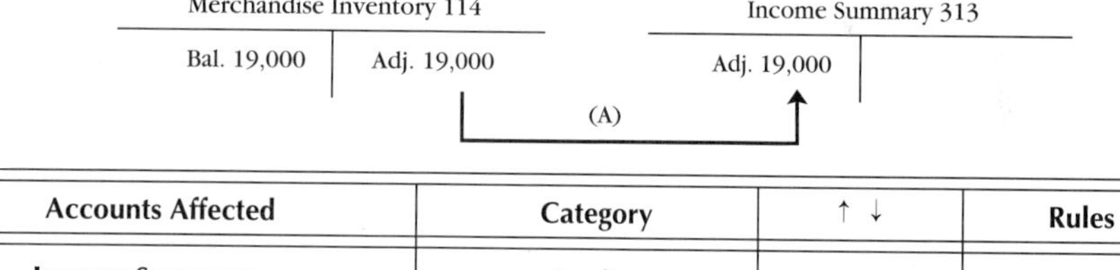

Accounts Affected	Category	↑ ↓	Rules
Income Summary	Equity		Dr.
Merchandise Inventory	Asset	↓	Cr.

(The adjusting entries would be entered first on the worksheet and then formally recorded in the general journal.)

Second adjustment updates inventory account with a figure for ending inventory.

The second step is to enter the amount of ending inventory ($4,000) in the Merchandise Inventory account. This is done to record the amount of goods on hand at the end of the period as an asset, and to subtract this amount from the cost of goods sold (since we have not sold this inventory yet). To do this we debit Merchandise Inventory for $4,000 and credit Income Summary for the same amount. This is shown below in T account form and on a transaction analysis chart:

Merchandise Inventory 114	
Bal. 19,000 Adj. 4,000	Adj. 19,000

Income Summary 313	
Adj. 19,000	Adj. 4,000

(B)

Accounts Affected	Category	↑ ↓	Rules
Merchandise Inventory	Asset	↑	Dr.
Income Summary	Equity		Cr.

Let's look at how this process or method of recording merchandise inventory is reflected in the balance sheet and income statement (see Figure 12-2). Note that the $19,000 of beginning inventory is assumed sold and is shown on the income statement as part of the cost of goods sold. The ending inventory of $4,000 has not been sold and so is subtracted from the cost of goods sold on the income statement. The ending inventory for this period becomes the next period's beginning inventory. When the income statement is prepared, we will need a figure for beginning inventory as well as a figure for ending inventory.

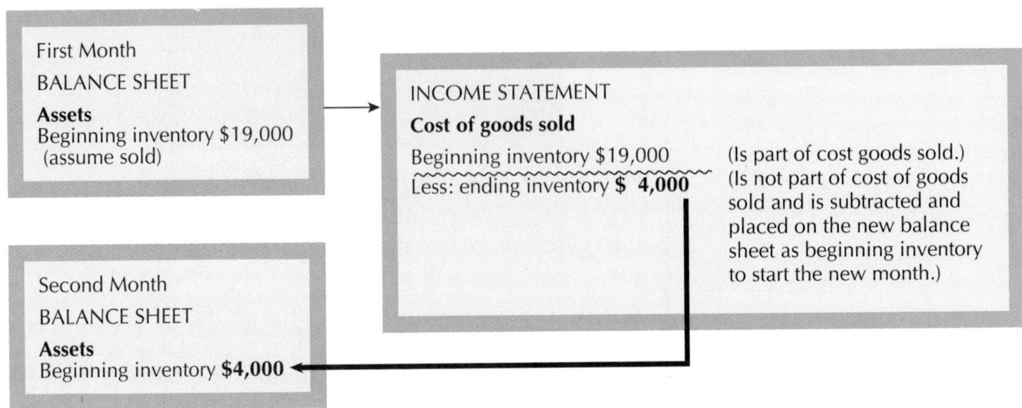

FIGURE 12-2 Recording Inventory on the Balance Sheet and Income Statement

The second adjustment we will discuss in this unit concerns an account that we have never dealt with before, Unearned Rent.

ADJUSTMENT FOR UNEARNED RENT

A new account we have not seen before is a liability called Unearned Rent. This account records the amount collected for rent before the service has been provided (renting the space). For example, Art's Wholesale is subletting some unneeded space to Jesse Company for $200 per month. Jesse Company sends Art a cheque for $600 for three months' rent paid in advance. This unearned rent ($600) is also often called Rent Received in Advance. Regardless of the actual name, it is a liability on the balance sheet because Art's Wholesale owes Jesse Company three months' worth of occupancy.

Received cash for renting space in future.

Cash	A	↑	Dr.
Unearned Rent	Liab.	↑	Cr.

When Art's Wholesale fulfills a portion of the rental agreement (when Jesse Company has been in the space for a period of time), this liability account will be reduced and the account called Rental Income will be increased, because Art's Wholesale will have earned the rent. Rental Income is another type of revenue for Art's Wholesale, in addition to its revenue earned from sales of merchandise.

The adjustment when rental income is earned:

Unearned Rent	Liab.	↓	Dr.
Rental Income	Other Rev.	↑	Cr.

There are other types of unearned revenue besides unearned rent—examples would be subscriptions for magazines, legal fees collected before the work is performed, insurance, and so on. The key point is that revenue, under accrual accounting, is recognized when it is *earned*, whether money is received then or not. Here Art's Wholesale collected cash in advance for a service that it has not performed as yet. Thus a liability called Unearned Rent is the result. Art's Wholesale may have the cash, but no Rental Income is recorded until it is *earned*.

In the next unit we will show how to record the adjustment to Rental Income when the worksheet is completed.

LEARNING UNIT 12-1 REVIEW

AT THIS POINT you should be able to

- Define the periodic method of inventory accounting. (p. 468)
- Explain why beginning and ending inventory are two separate figures in the cost of goods sold section on the income statement. (p. 469)
- Show how to calculate a figure for ending inventory. (p. 469)
- Explain why unearned rent is a liability account. (p. 470)

SELF-REVIEW QUIZ 12-1

Given the following, prepare the two adjusting entries for Merchandise Inventory on 12/31/XX:

Merchandise Inventory, 1/1/XX	$ 6,000
Purchases	9,000
Merchandise Inventory, 12/31/XX	5,000
Cost of Goods Sold	10,000
Unearned Magazine Subscriptions	8,000

Solution to Self-Review Quiz 12-1

Dec.	31	Income Summary	6 0 0 0 00	
		Merchandise Inventory		6 0 0 0 00
	31	Merchandise Inventory	5 0 0 0 00	
		Income Summary		5 0 0 0 00
		To record opening and closing inventories		

LEARNING UNIT 12-2
Completing the Worksheet

In this unit we will prepare a worksheet for Art's Wholesale Clothing Company. For convenience we reproduce the company's chart of accounts in Figure 12-3.

Figure 12-4 shows the trial balance that was prepared on December 31, 19XX, from the general ledger of Art's Wholesale. (*Note:* It is recorded directly on the first two columns of the worksheet).

In looking at the trial balance we see many new titles that have appeared since we completed a trial balance for a service company back in Chapter 5. Let's look specifically at these new titles in the summary in Table 12-1.

FIGURE 12-3
Art's Wholesale Clothing Company Chart of Accounts

Chart of Accounts

Assets 100–199
111 Cash
112 Petty Cash
113 Accounts Receivable
114 Merchandise Inventory
115 Supplies
116 Prepaid Insurance
121 Store Equipment
122 Accum. Depreciation, Store Equipment

Liabilities 200–299
211 Accounts Payable
212 Salary Payable
213 Income Tax Payable
214 CPP Payable
215 UI Payable
218 Unearned Rent
220 Mortgage Payable

Owner's Equity 300–399
311 Art Newner, Capital
312 Art Newner, Withdrawals
313 Income Summary

Revenue 400–499
411 Sales
412 Sales Returns and Allowances
413 Sales Discount
414 Rental Income

Cost of Goods Sold 500–599
511 Purchases
512 Purchases Discount
513 Purchases Returns and Allowances
514 Freight-In

Expenses 600–699
611 Salary Expense
612 Payroll Tax Expense
613 Depreciation Expense, Store Equipment
614 Supplies Expense
615 Insurance Expense
616 Postage Expense
617 Miscellaneous Expense
618 Interest Expense
619 Cleaning Expense
620 Delivery Expense

FIGURE 12-4
Trial Balance Section of the Worksheet

	Trial Balance	
	Dr.	Cr.
Cash	12920 00	
Petty Cash	100 00	
Accounts Receivable	14500 00	
Merchandise Inventory	19000 00	
Supplies	800 00	
Prepaid Insurance	900 00	
Store Equipment	4000 00	
Accum. Dep., Store Equipment		400 00
Accounts Payable		17900 00
Income Tax Payable		1240 00
CPP Payable		260 00
UI Payable		200 00
Unearned Rent		600 00
Mortgage Payable		2320 00
Art Newner, Capital		7905 00
Art Newner, Withdrawals	8600 00	
Income Summary		
Sales		95000 00
Sales Returns and Allowances	950 00	
Sales Discount	670 00	
Purchases	52000 00	
Purchases Discount		860 00
Purchases Returns and Allowances		680 00
Freight-In	450 00	
Salary Expense	11700 00	
Payroll Tax Expense	420 00	
Postage Expense	25 00	
Miscellaneous Expense	30 00	
Interest Expense	300 00	
	127365 00	127365 00

TABLE 12-1 SUMMARY OF NEW ACCOUNT TITLES

Title	Category	Report (s) Found On:	Normal Balance	Temporary/ Permanent
Petty Cash	Asset	Balance sheet	Dr.	Permanent
Merchandise Inventory* (Beginning)	Asset	Balance sheet from prior period	Dr.	Permanent
	Cost of goods sold	Income statement of current period		
Income Tax Payable	Liability	Balance sheet	Cr.	Permanent
CPP Payable	Liability	Balance sheet	Cr.	Permanent
UI Payable	Liability	Balance sheet	Cr.	Permanent
Unearned Rent **	Liability	Balance sheet	Cr.	Permanent
Mortgage Payable	Liability	Balance sheet	Cr.	Permanent
Sales	Revenue	Income statement	Cr.	Temporary
Sales Returns and Allowances	Revenue (contra)	Income statement	Dr.	Temporary
Sales Discount	Revenue (contra)	Income statement	Dr.	Temporary
Purchases	Expense	Income statement	Dr.	Temporary
Purchases Discount	Expense (contra)	Income statement	Cr.	Temporary
Purchases Returns and Allowances	Expense (contra)	Income statement	Cr.	Temporary
Freight-In	Expense	Income statement	Dr.	Temporary
Payroll Tax Expense	Expense	Income statement	Dr.	Temporary
Postage Expense	Expense	Income statement	Dr.	Temporary
Interest Expense	Expense	Income statement	Dr.	Temporary

*The ending inventory of current period is a contra-cost-of-goods-sold on the income statement and will be an asset on the balance sheet for next period.

**Referred to as Unearned Revenue.

Note the following:

1. **Mortgage Payable** is a liability account that records the increases and decreases in the amount of debt owed on a mortgage. We will discuss this more in the next chapter, when financial reports are prepared.
2. **Interest Expense** represents a nonoperating expense for Art's Wholesale and thus is categorized as "other expense." The interest would be a regular expense if it were incurred for business purposes. We will also be looking at this in the next chapter.
3. **Unearned Revenue** is a liability account that records receipt of payment for goods and services in advance of delivery. Unearned Rent is a particular example of this general type of account.

We have already discussed Adjustments A and B (p. 469), which make up the two-step process involved in adjusting Merchandise Inventory at the end of the accounting period. Now we will go on to show T accounts and transaction analysis charts for some more adjustments that need to be made at this point in a merchandise firm, just as they do in a service company.

Adjustment C: Rental Income Earned by Art's Wholesale, $200 A month ago, Cash was increased by $600, as was a liability, Unearned Rent. Art's Wholesale received payment in advance but had not earned the rental income. Now, since $200 has been earned, the liability is reduced and Rental Income can be recorded for the $200.

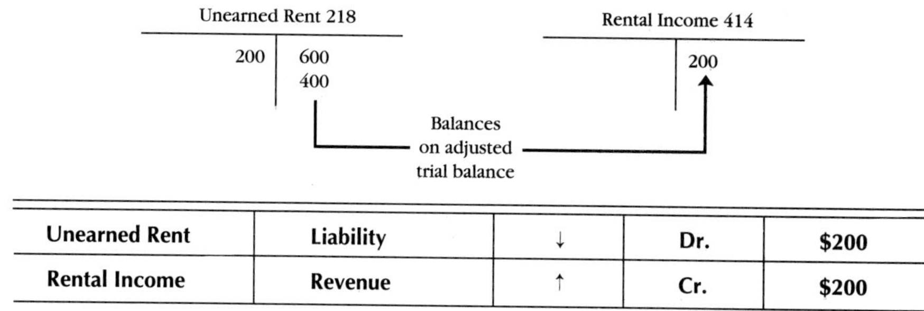

Unearned Rent	Liability	↓	Dr.	$200
Rental Income	Revenue	↑	Cr.	$200

Adjustment D: Supplies on Hand, $300 $500 worth of supplies has been used up; thus there is a need to increase Supplies Expense and decrease the asset Supplies.

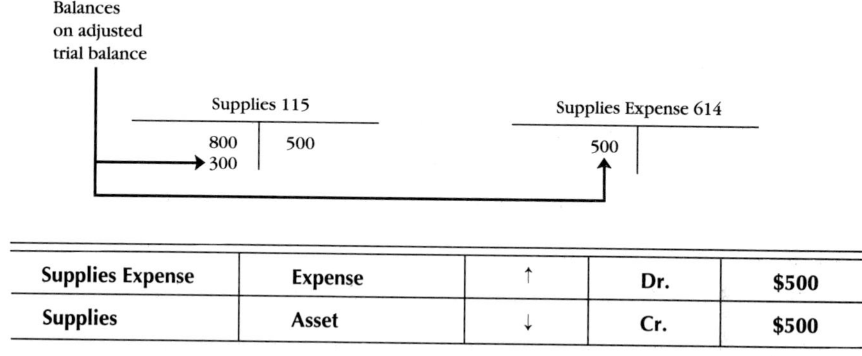

Supplies Expense	Expense	↑	Dr.	$500
Supplies	Asset	↓	Cr.	$500

Adjustment E: Insurance Expired, $300 Since insurance has expired by $300, Insurance Expense is increased by $300 and the asset Prepaid Insurance is decreased by $300.

Balances
on adjusted
trial balance

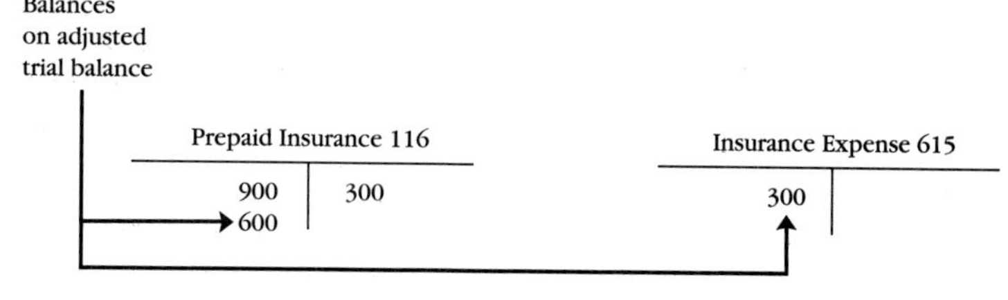

Insurance Expense	Expense	↑	Dr.	$300
Prepaid Insurance	Asset	↓	Cr.	$300

Adjustment F: Depreciation Expense, $50 When depreciation is taken, depreciation expense and accumulated depreciation are both increased by $50. Note that the cost of the store equipment remains the same.

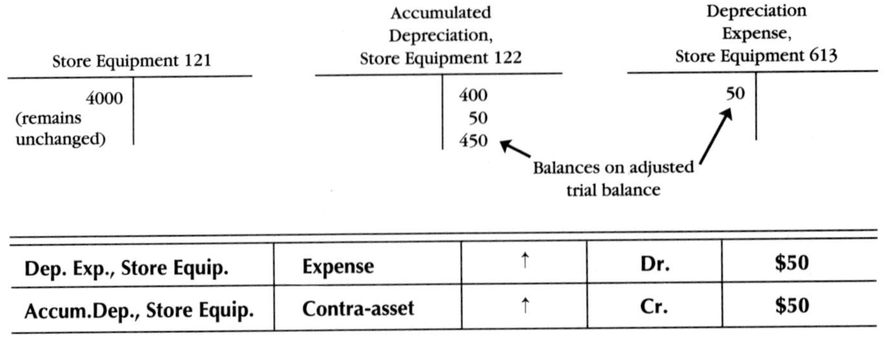

Dep. Exp., Store Equip.	Expense	↑	Dr.	$50
Accum.Dep., Store Equip.	Contra-asset	↑	Cr.	$50

Adjustment G: Salaries Accrued, $600 The $600 in Salaries Accrued causes an increase in Salaries Expense and Salaries Payable.

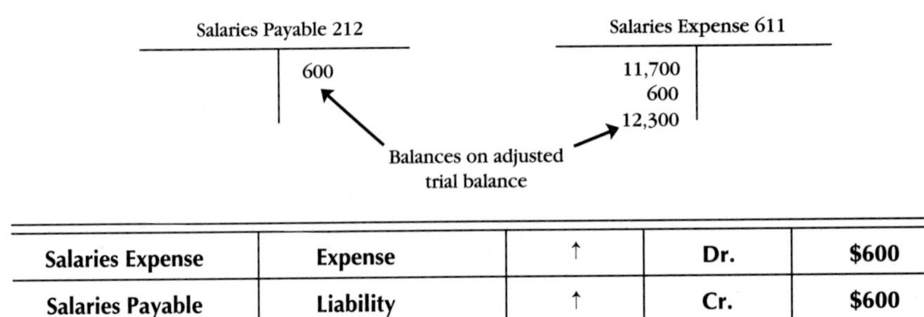

Salaries Expense	Expense	↑	Dr.	$600
Salaries Payable	Liability	↑	Cr.	$600

Figure 12-5 shows the worksheet with the adjustments and adjusted trial balance column filled out. Note that the adjustment numbers in Income Summary from beginning and ending inventory are also carried over to the adjusted trial balance and are *not* combined.

The next step in completing the worksheet is to fill out the income statement columns from the adjusted trial balance, as shown in Figure 12-6.

The next step in completing the worksheet is to fill out the balance sheet columns (Figure 12-7). Note how only ending inventory is carried over to the balance sheet from the adjusted trial balance column. Take time also to look at the placement of the payroll tax liabilities as well as Unearned Rent on the worksheet.

Figure 12-8 is the completed worksheet.

FIGURE 12-5 Worksheet with Three Columns Completed

	Trial Balance		Adjustments		Adjusted Trial Balance	
	Dr.	Cr.	Dr.	Cr.	Dr.	Cr.
Cash	12920 00				12920 00	
Petty Cash	100 00				100 00	
Accounts Receivable	14500 00				14500 00	
Merchandise Inventory	19000 00		(B) 4000 00	(A) 19000 00	4000 00	
Supplies	800 00			(D) 500 00	300 00	
Prepaid Insurance	900 00			(E) 300 00	600 00	
Store Equipment	4000 00				4000 00	
Accum. Dep., Store Equipment		400 00		(F) 50 00		450 00
Accounts Payable		17900 00				17900 00
Income Tax Payable		1240 00				1240 00
CPP Payable		260 00				260 00
UI Payable		200 00				200 00
Unearned Rent		600 00	(C) 200 00			400 00
Mortgage Payable		2320 00				2320 00
Art Newner, Capital		7905 00				7905 00
Art Newner, Withdrawals	8600 00				8600 00	
Income Summary			(A) 19000 00	(B) 4000 00	19000 00	4000 00
Sales		95000 00				95000 00
Sales Returns and Allowances	950 00				950 00	
Sales Discount	670 00				670 00	
Purchases	52000 00				52000 00	
Purchases Discount		860 00				860 00
Purchases Returns and Allowances		680 00				680 00
Freight-In	450 00				450 00	
Salary Expense	11700 00		(G) 600 00		12300 00	
Payroll Tax Expense	420 00				420 00	
Postage Expense	25 00				25 00	
Miscellaneous Expense	30 00				30 00	
Interest Expense	300 00				300 00	
	127365 00	127365 00				
Rental Income				(C) 200 00		200 00
Supplies Expense			(D) 500 00		500 00	
Insurance Expense			(E) 300 00		300 00	
Depreciation Expense, Store Equip.			(F) 50 00		50 00	
Salary Payable				(G) 600 00		600 00
			24650 00	24650 00	132015 00	132015 00

FIGURE 12-6 Income Statement Section of the Worksheet

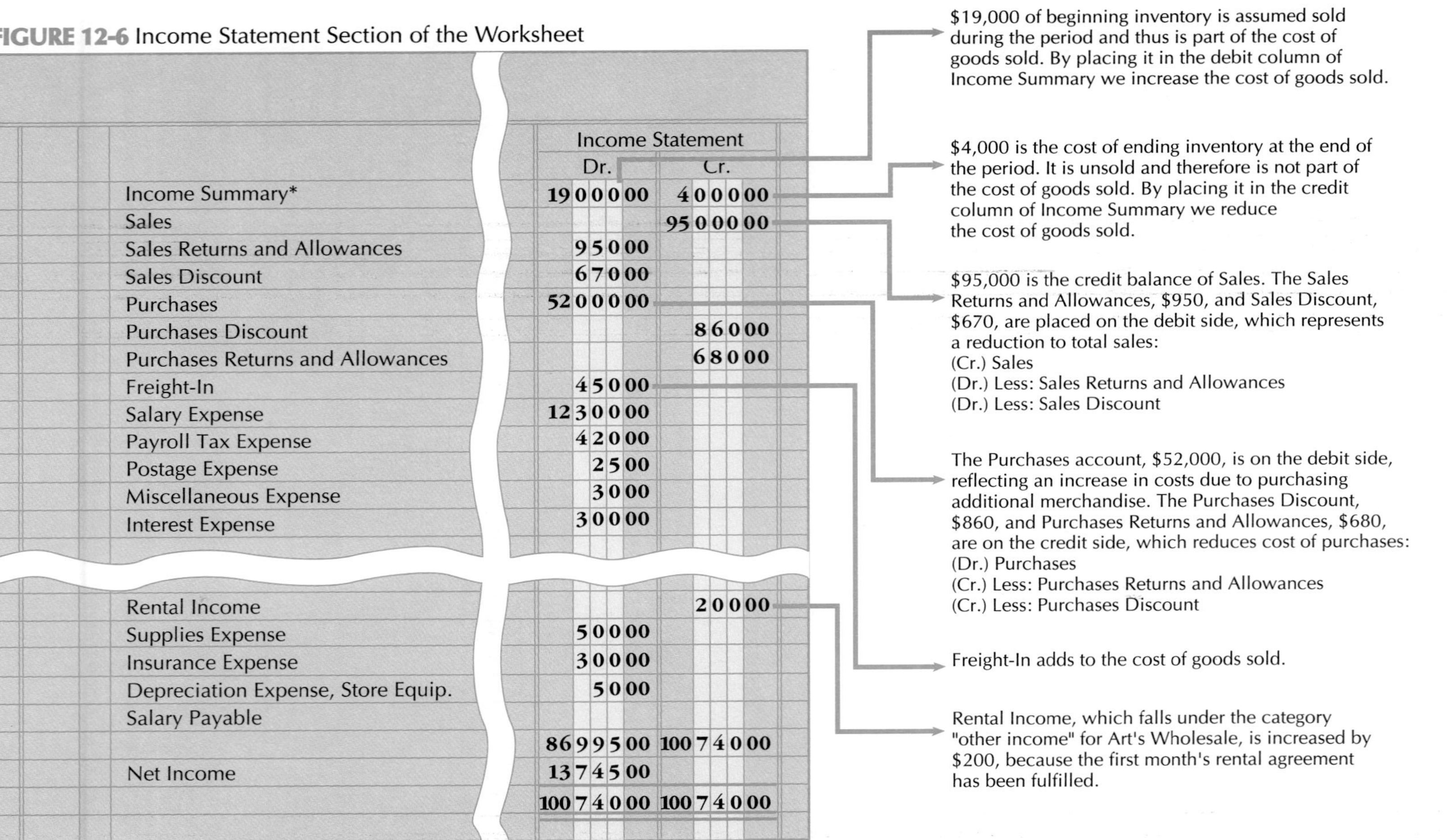

	Income Statement Dr.	Income Statement Cr.
Income Summary*	19 000 00	4 000 00
Sales		95 000 00
Sales Returns and Allowances	950 00	
Sales Discount	670 00	
Purchases	52 000 00	
Purchases Discount		860 00
Purchases Returns and Allowances		680 00
Freight-In	450 00	
Salary Expense	12 300 00	
Payroll Tax Expense	420 00	
Postage Expense	25 00	
Miscellaneous Expense	30 00	
Interest Expense	300 00	
Rental Income		200 00
Supplies Expense	500 00	
Insurance Expense	300 00	
Depreciation Expense, Store Equip.	50 00	
Salary Payable		
	86 995 00	100 740 00
Net Income	13 745 00	
	100 740 00	100 740 00

$19,000 of beginning inventory is assumed sold during the period and thus is part of the cost of goods sold. By placing it in the debit column of Income Summary we increase the cost of goods sold.
$4,000 is the cost of ending inventory at the end of the period. It is unsold and therefore is not part of the cost of goods sold. By placing it in the credit column of Income Summary we reduce the cost of goods sold.
$95,000 is the credit balance of Sales. The Sales Returns and Allowances, $950, and Sales Discount, $670, are placed on the debit side, which represents a reduction to total sales:
(Cr.) Sales
(Dr.) Less: Sales Returns and Allowances
(Dr.) Less: Sales Discount
The Purchases account, $52,000, is on the debit side, reflecting an increase in costs due to purchasing additional merchandise. The Purchases Discount, $860, and Purchases Returns and Allowances, $680, are on the credit side, which reduces cost of purchases:
(Dr.) Purchases
(Cr.) Less: Purchases Returns and Allowances
(Cr.) Less: Purchases Discount
Freight-In adds to the cost of goods sold.
Rental Income, which falls under the category "other income" for Art's Wholesale, is increased by $200, because the first month's rental agreement has been fulfilled.

*Remember, we do not combine the $19,000 and $4,000 in Income Summary. When we prepare the cost of goods sold section for the formal financial report, we will need both a beginning and an ending figure for inventory.

FIGURE 12-7 Balance Sheet Section of the Worksheet

	Balance Sheet Dr.	Balance Sheet Cr.
Cash	12920 00	
Petty Cash	100 00	
Accounts Receivable	14500 00	
Merchandise Inventory	4000 00	
Supplies	300 00	
Prepaid Insurance	600 00	
Store Equipment	4000 00	
Accum. Dep., Store Equipment		450 00
Accounts Payable		17900 00
Income Tax Payable		1240 00
CPP Payable		260 00
UI Payable		200 00
Unearned Rent		400 00
Mortgage Payable		2320 00
Art Newner, Capital		7905 00
Art Newner, Withdrawals	8600 00	
Rental Income		
Supplies Expense		
Insurance Expense		
Depreciation Expense, Store Equip.		
Salary Payable		600 00
	45020 00	31275 00
Net Income		13745 00
	45020 00	45020 00

This ending inventory, $4,000, now becomes the beginning inventory of Art to begin on January 1. When this beginning inventory is sold, it will be part of the cost of goods sold.

$400 of unearned rent (a liability) still exists.

Note how net income of $13,745 is added to the credit column of the balance sheet.

FIGURE 12-8 Completed Worksheet

Worksheet for Year Ended December 31, 19X2

	Trial Balance		Adjustments		Adjusted Trial Balance		Income Statement		Balance Sheet	
	Dr.	Cr.	Dr.	Cr.	Dr.	Cr.	Dr.	Cr.	Dr.	Cr.
Cash	12920 00				12920 00				12920 00	
Petty Cash	100 00				100 00				100 00	
Accounts Receivable	14500 00		(B)	(A)	14500 00				14500 00	
Merchandise Inventory	19000 00		4000 00	19000 00	4000 00				4000 00	
Supplies	800 00			(D) 500 00	300 00				300 00	
Prepaid Insurance	900 00			(E) 300 00	600 00				600 00	
Store Equipment	4000 00				4000 00				4000 00	
Accum. Dep., Store Equipment		400 00		(F) 50 00		450 00				450 00
Accounts Payable		17900 00				17900 00				17900 00
Income Tax Payable		1240 00				1240 00				1240 00
CPP Payable		260 00				260 00				260 00
UI Payable		200 00				200 00				200 00
Unearned Rent		600 00	(C) 200 00			400 00				400 00
Mortgage Payable		2320 00				2320 00				2320 00
Art Newner, Capital		7905 00				7905 00				7905 00
Art Newner, Withdrawals	8600 00		(A)	(B)	8600 00				8600 00	
Income Summary			19000 00	4000 00	19000 00	4000 00	19000 00	4000 00		
Sales		95000 00				95000 00		95000 00		
Sales Returns and Allowances	950 00				950 00		950 00			
Sales Discount	670 00				670 00		670 00			
Purchases	52000 00				52000 00		52000 00			
Purchases Discount		860 00				860 00		860 00		
Purchases Returns and Allowances		680 00				680 00		680 00		
Freight-In	450 00				450 00		450 00			
Salary Expense	11700 00		(G) 600 00		12300 00		12300 00			
Payroll Tax Expense	420 00				420 00		420 00			
Postage Expense	25 00				25 00		25 00			
Miscellaneous Expense	30 00				30 00		30 00			
Interest Expense	300 00				300 00		300 00			
	127365 00	127365 00								
Rental Income				(C) 200 00		200 00		200 00		
Supplies Expense			(D) 500 00		500 00		500 00			
Insurance Expense			(E) 300 00		300 00		300 00			
Depreciation Expense, Store Equip.			(F) 50 00		50 00		50 00			
Salary Payable				(G) 600 00		600 00				600 00
			24650 00	24650 00	132015 00	132015 00	86995 00	100740 00	45020 00	31275 00
Net Income							13745 00			13745 00
							100740 00	100740 00	45020 00	45020 00

LEARNING UNIT 12-2 REVIEW

AT THIS POINT you should be able to

- Complete adjustments for a merchandise company. (pp. 475–476)
- Complete a worksheet. (pp. 476–480)

SELF-REVIEW QUIZ 12-2

From the trial balance shown here, complete a worksheet for Ray Company. Additional data includes: (a and b) On December 31, 19XX, ending inventory was calculated as $200; (c) storage fees earned, $516; (d) rent expired, $100; (e) depreciation expense, office equipment, $60; (f) salaries accrued, $200.

Account Titles	Trial Balance Dr.	Trial Balance Cr.
Cash	248600	
Merchandise Inventory	82400	
Prepaid Rent	115200	
Prepaid Insurance	6000	
Office Equipment	216000	
Accumulated Depreciation, Office Equipment		56000
Unearned Storage Fees		251600
Accounts Payable		10000
B. Ray, Capital		193200
Income Summary	—	—
Sales		1104000
Sales Returns and Allowances	54600	
Sales Discount	21600	
Purchases	525600	
Purchases Returns and Allowances		16800
Purchases Discount		10200
Salaries Expense	201600	
Insurance Expense	139200	
Utilities Expense	9600	
Plumbing Expense	21400	
	1641800	1641800

Solution to Self-Review Quiz 12-2

Solution is shown on the following page.

RAY COMPANY
WORKSHEET
FOR YEAR ENDED DECEMBER 31, 19XX

Account Titles	Trial Balance Dr.	Trial Balance Cr.	Adjustments Dr.	Adjustments Cr.	Adjusted Trial Balance Dr.	Adjusted Trial Balance Cr.	Income Statement Dr.	Income Statement Cr.	Balance Sheet Dr.	Balance Sheet Cr.
Cash	2486 00				2486 00				2486 00	
Merchandise Inventory	824 00		(B) 200 00	(A) 824 00	200 00				200 00	
Prepaid Rent	1152 00			(D) 100 00	1052 00				1052 00	
Prepaid Insurance	60 00				60 00				60 00	
Office Equipment	2160 00				2160 00				2160 00	
Accum. Dep., Store Equipment		560 00		(E) 60 00		620 00				620 00
Unearned Storage Fees		2516 00	(C) 516 00			2000 00				2000 00
Accounts Payable		100 00				100 00				100 00
B. Ray, Capita		1932 00				1932 00				1932 00
Income Summary			(A) 824 00	(B) 200 00	824 00	200 00	824 00	200 00		
Sales		11040 00				11040 00		11040 00		
Sales Returns and Allowances	546 00				546 00		546 00			
Sales Discount	216 00				216 00		216 00			
Purchases	5256 00				5256 00		5256 00			
Purchases Returns and Allowances		168 00				168 00		168 00		
Purchases Discount		102 00				102 00		102 00		
Salaries Expense	2016 00		(F) 200 00		2216 00		2216 00			
Insurance Expense	1392 00				1392 00		1392 00			
Utilities Expense	96 00				96 00		96 00			
Plumbing Expense	214 00				214 00		214 00			
	16418 00	16418 00								
Storage Fees Earned				(C) 516 00		516 00		516 00		
Rent Expense			(D) 100 00		100 00		100 00			
Depreciation Expense, Equipment			(E) 60 00		60 00		60 00			
Salaries Payable				(F) 200 00		200 00				200 00
			1900 00	1900 00	16878 00	16878 00	10920 00	12026 00	5958 00	4852 00
Net Income							1106 00			1106 00
							12026 00	12026 00	5958 00	5958 00

Chapter Review

Summary of key points

Learning Unit 12-1

1. The periodic inventory system updates the record of goods on hand only at the *end* of the accounting period. This system is used by companies with a variety of merchandise with low unit prices.
2. In the periodic inventory system, additional purchases of merchandise during the accounting period will be recorded in the Purchases account. The amount in beginning inventory will remain unchanged during the accounting period. At the end of the period a new figure for ending inventory will be calculated.
3. Beginning inventory at the end of the accounting period is added to the cost of goods sold, while ending inventory is deducted from cost of goods sold.
4. The perpetual inventory system keeps a continuous record of inventory. It is used by companies with low volume and high unit prices, and often utilizes a computer system.
5. Unearned Revenue is a liability account that accumulates revenue that has not been earned yet, although the cash has been received. It represents a liability to the seller until the service or product is performed or delivered.

Learning Unit 12-2

1. Two important adjustments in the accounting for a merchandise company deal with the Merchandise Inventory account and with the Unearned Revenue account (unearned rent).
2. Figures for beginning and ending inventory on the Income Summary line on the worksheet are never combined; they are also carried over separately to the adjusted trial balance and income statement columns of the worksheet. On the balance sheet column the figure for ending inventory becomes the beginning inventory figure for the new accounting period.
3. When a company delivers goods or services for which it has been paid in advance, an adjustment is made to reduce the liability account Unearned Revenue and to increase a revenue account.

Key terms

Beginning merchandise inventory (beginning inventory) The cost of goods on hand in a company at the beginning of an accounting period.

Ending merchandise inventory (ending inventory) The cost of goods that remain unsold at the end of the accounting period. It is an asset on the balance sheet.

Mortgage Payable A liability account showing the amount owed on a mortgage.

Periodic inventory system An inventory system that, at the end of each accounting period, calculates the cost of the unsold goods on hand by taking the cost of each unit times the number of units of each product on hand.

Perpetual inventory system An inventory system that keeps continual track of each type of inventory by recording units on hand at beginning, units sold, and the current balance after each sale or purchase.

Unearned Revenue A liability account that records receipt of payment for goods or services in advance of delivery. When the goods or services are delivered, an adjustment is made to reduce Unearned Revenue and increase earned revenue. (The example we used in this chapter is Unearned Rent.)

BLUEPRINT OF A WORKSHEET FOR A MERCHANDISE COMPANY

Account Titles	Adjustments		Adjusted Trial Balance		Income Statement		Balance Sheet	
	Dr.	Cr.	Dr.	Cr.	Dr.	Cr.	Dr.	Cr.
Cash			X				X	
Petty Cash			X				X	
Accounts Receivable			X				X	
Merchandise Inventory	X-E	X-B	X-E				X-E	
Supplies			X				X	
Equipment			X				X	
Accum. Dep., Store Equipment				X				X
Accounts Payable				X				X
Income Tax Payable				X				X
CPP Payable				X				X
UI Payable				X				X
Unearned Sales				X				X
Mortgage Payable				X				X
A. Flynn, Capital				X				X
A. Flynn, Withdrawals			X				X	
Income Summary*	X-B	X-E	X-B	X-E	X-B	X-E		
Sales				X		X		
Sales Returns and Allow.			X		X			
Sales Discount			X		X			
Purchases			X		X			
Purchases Ret. and Allow.				X		X		
Purchases Discount				X		X		
Freight-In			X		X			
Salaries Expense			X		X			
Payroll Tax Expense			X		X			
Insurance Expense			X		X			
Depreciation Expense			X		X			
Salaries Payable				X				X
Rental Income				X		X		

*Note that the figures for beginning inventory (X-B) and ending inventory (X-E) are never combined on the Income Summary line of the worksheet. When the formal income statement is prepared, two distinct figures for inventory will be used to explain and calculate cost of goods sold. Beginning inventory adds to cost of goods sold; ending inventory reduces cost of goods sold.

QUESTIONS, EXERCISES, AND PROBLEMS

Discussion Questions

1. When would a company consider using a periodic inventory system?
2. What is the function of the Purchases account?
3. A low-volume, high-unit-price inventory requires a company to use a periodic inventory system. Accept or reject, and support your answer.
4. Explain why Unearned Revenue is a liability account.
5. In a periodic system of inventory, the balance of beginning inventory will remain unchanged during the period. True or false?
6. What is the purpose of an inventory sheet?
7. Why do many Unearned Revenue accounts have to be adjusted?
8. Explain why figures for beginning and ending inventory are not combined on the Income Summary line of the worksheet.

Mini Exercises

(The forms you need are on page 12-3 of the *Study Guide and Working Papers.*)

Adjustment for Merchandise Inventory

1. Given the following, journalize the adjusting entries for merchandise inventory. Note ending inventory has a balance of $12,000.

Merchandise Inventory 114	
20,000	

Income Summary 313	

Adjustment for Unearned Fees

2. a. Given the following, journalize the adjusting entry. By December 31, $300 of the unearned dog walking fees were earned.

Unearned Dog Walking Fees 225	
	650 12/1/XX

Earned Dog Walking Fees 441	
	4,000 12/1/XX

   b. What is the category of unearned dog walking fees?

Worksheet

3. Match the following:

   1. Located on the Income Statement debit column of the worksheet
   2. Located on the Income Statement credit column of the worksheet
   3. Located on the Balance Sheet debit column of the worksheet
   4. Located on the Balance Sheet credit column of the worksheet

   _____ a. Ending Merchandise Inventory
   _____ b. Unearned Rent
   _____ c. Sales Discount
   _____ d. Purchases
   _____ e. Rental Income
   _____ f. Petty Cash

Merchandise Inventory Adjustment on Worksheet

4. Adjustment column of a worksheet:

Merchandise Inventory	(A)	(B)
Income Summary	(B)	(A)

Explain what the letters A and B represent. Why are the letters A and B never combined?

Income Summary on the Worksheet

5.

	Adj.		ATB		Income Statement	
	Dr.	Cr.	Dr.	Cr.	Dr.	Cr.
Income Summary	A	B	C	D	E	F

Given a figure of Beginning Inventory of $500 and a $700 figure for Ending Inventory, place these numbers on the Income Summary line of this partial worksheet.

Exercises

Categorizing account titles.

12-1. Indicate the normal balance and category of each of the following accounts:

a. Purchases Returns and Allowances
b. Merchandise Inventory (beginning of period)
c. Freight-In
d. Payroll Tax Expense
e. Purchases Discount
f. Sales Discount
g. CPP Payable
h. Unearned Revenue

Calculating net sales, cost of goods sold, gross profit, and net income.

12-2. From the following, calculate **a.** net sales, **b.** cost of goods sold, **c.** gross profit, and **d.** net income:
Data Sales, $22,000; Sales Discount, $500; Sales Returns and Allowances, $250; Beginning Inventory, $650; Net Purchases, $13,200; Ending Inventory, $510; Operating Expenses, $3,600.

Unearned revenue.

12-3. Allan Co. had the following balances on December 31, 19XX:

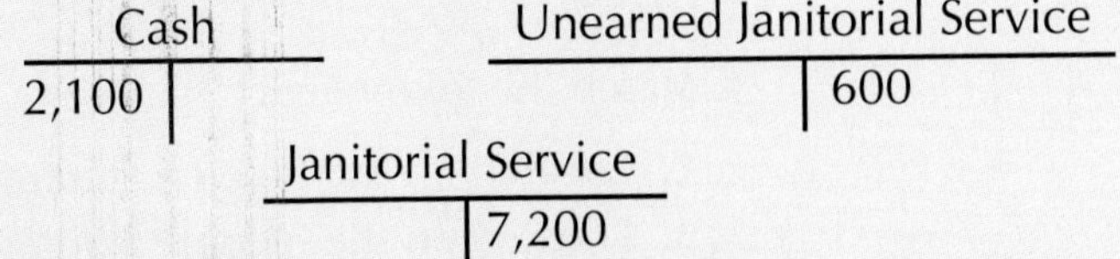

The accountant for Allan has asked you to make an adjustment, since $400 of janitorial services has just been performed for customers who had paid in advance. Construct a transaction analysis chart.

Calculating cost of goods sold.

12-4. Lesan Co. purchased merchandise costing $400,000. Calculate the cost of goods sold under the following different situations:

a. Beginning inventory $40,000 and no ending inventory.
b. Beginning inventory $50,000 and a $60,000 ending inventory.
c. No beginning inventory and a $30,000 ending inventory.

Preparing a worksheet.

12-5. Prepare a worksheet from the following information:

(A and B) Merchandise Inventory—ending	13
(C) Store Supplies on hand	4
(D) Depreciation on Store Equipment	4
(E) Accrued Salaries	2

MOORE CO.
TRIAL BALANCE
DECEMBER 31, 19XX

	Dr.	Cr.
Cash	8 00	
Accounts Receivable	5 00	
Merchandise Inventory	11 00	
Store Supplies	10 00	
Store Equipment	20 00	
Accumulated Depreciation, Store Equipment		6 00
Accounts Payable		5 00
J. Moore, Capital		34 00
Income Summary	—	—
Sales		64 00
Sales Returns and Allowances	9 00	
Purchases	23 00	
Purchases Discount		3 00
Freight-In	3 00	
Salaries Expense	10 00	
Advertising Expense	13 00	
Totals	112 00	112 00

Group A Problems

Calculating net sales, cost of goods sold, gross profit, and net income.

12A-1. On the basis of the accounts listed below, calculate:

a. Net sales
b. Cost of goods sold
c. Gross profit
d. Net income

Accounts Payable	$2,200
Operating Expenses	1,490
J. Jensen, Capital	8,200
Purchases	4,250
Freight-In	60
Ending Merchandise Inventory, Dec. 31, 19XX	1,240
Sales	9,210
Accounts Receivable	1,389
Cash	656
Purchases Discount	132
Sales Returns and Allowances	185
Beg. Merchandise Inventory, Jan. 1, 19XX	1,560
Purchases Returns and Allowances	247
Sales Discount	352

Comprehensive problem: Completing a worksheet for a merchandise company.

12A-2. From the following trial balance, complete a worksheet for Jim's Hardware.

JIM'S HARDWARE TRIAL BALANCE DECEMBER 31, 19XX		
	Dr.	Cr.
Cash	78600	
Accounts Receivable	115200	
Merchandise Inventory	60000	
Prepaid Insurance	68400	
Store Equipment	216000	
Accumulated Depreciation, Store Equipment		66000
Accounts Payable		51600
Jim Spool, Capital		163200
Income Summary	—	—
Hardware Sales		1104000
Hardware Sales Returns and Allowances	54600	
Hardware Sales Discount	21600	
Purchases	525600	
Purchases Discount		16800
Purchases Returns and Allowances		10200
Wages Expense	171600	
Rent Expense	79200	
Telephone Expense	11400	
Miscellaneous Expense	9600	
	1411800	1411800

Assumptions

A. **and** B. Ending inventory on Dec. 31 is calculated at $415.
C. Insurance expired, $220.
D. Depreciation on store equipment, $75.
E. Accrued wages, $112.

Comprehensive problem: Completing a worksheet.

12A-3. The owner of Waltz Company has asked you to prepare a worksheet from the following trial balance and additional data:

WALTZ COMPANY TRIAL BALANCE DECEMBER 31, 19XX		
	Dr.	Cr.
Cash	540800	
Petty Cash	24000	
Accounts Receivable	251200	
Beginning Merchandise Inventory, Jan. 1	509200	
Prepaid Rent	61600	
Office Supplies	94400	
Office Equipment	928000	
Accumulated Depreciation, Office Equipment		760000
Accounts Payable		596400
K. Waltz, Capital		547600
K. Waltz, Withdrawals	480000	
Income Summary	—	—
Sales		5248400
Sales Returns and Allowances	9600	
Sales Discount	240000	
Purchases	2931600	
Purchases Discount		1600
Purchases Returns and Allowances		34800
Office Salaries Expense	740800	
Insurance Expense	240000	
Advertising Expense	80000	
Utilities Expense	57600	
	7188800	7188800

Additional Data

A. **and** B. Ending merchandise inventory on December 31, $2,140.
C. Office supplies used up, $345.
D. Rent expired $214.
E. Depreciation expense on office equipment, $485.
F. Office salaries earned but not paid, $280.

Comprehensive problem: Completing a worksheet with payroll and unearned revenue.

12A-4. From the following trial balance and additional data, complete the worksheet for Ron's Wholesale Clothing Company.

RON'S WHOLESALE CLOTHING COMPANY
TRIAL BALANCE
DECEMBER 31, 19XX

	Dr.	Cr.
Cash	4460 00	
Petty Cash	300 00	
Accounts Receivable	7500 00	
Merchandise Inventory	9000 00	
Supplies	1000 00	
Prepaid Insurance	850 00	
Store Equipment	2500 00	
Accumulated Depreciation, Store Equipment		1500 00
Accounts Payable		10635 00
Income Tax Payable		1060 00
CPP Payable		108 00
UI Payable		150 00
Unearned Storage Fees		357 00
Ron Win, Capital		12500 00
Ron Win, Withdrawals	4300 00	
Income Summary	—	—
Sales		45000 00
Sales Returns and Allowances	1475 00	
Sales Discount	1335 00	
Purchases	26000 00	
Purchases Discount		550 00
Purchases Returns and Allowances		400 00
Freight-In	225 00	
Salaries Expense	12000 00	
Payroll Tax Expense	420 00	
Interest Expense	895 00	
	72260 00	72260 00

Additional Data

A. **and** B. Ending merchandise inventory on December 31, $7,200.

C. Supplies on hand, $380.

D. Insurance expired, $560.

E. Depreciation on store equipment, $425.

F. Storage fees earned, $154.

Group B Problems

Calculating net sales, cost of goods sold, gross profit, and net income.

12B-1. From the following accounts, calculate **a.** net sales, **b.** cost of goods sold, **c.** gross profit, **d.** net income.

Sales Discount	$ 452
Purchases Returns and Allowances	64
Beginning Merchandise Inventory, Jan. 1, 19XX	79
Sales Returns and Allowances	191
Purchases Discounts	42
Cash	3,895
Accounts Receivable	441
Sales	3,950
Ending Merchandise Inventory, Dec. 31, 19XX	75
Freight-In	41
Purchases	1,152
R. Roland, Capital	1,950
Operating Expenses	895
Accounts Payable	129

Comprehensive problem: Completing a worksheet for a merchandise company.

12B-2. As the accountant for Jim's Hardware, you have been asked to complete a worksheet from the following trial balance as well as additional data.

JIM'S HARDWARE
TRIAL BALANCE
DECEMBER 31, 19XX

	Dr.	Cr.
Cash	960 00	
Accounts Receivable	1600 00	
Merchandise Inventory	736 00	
Prepaid Insurance	1112 00	
Store Equipment	3200 00	
Accumulated Depreciation, Store Equipment		1680 00
Accounts Payable		1408 00
J. Spool, Capital		2576 00
Income Summary	—	—
Hardware Sales		14800 00
Hardware Sales Returns and Allowances	728 00	
Hardware Sales Discount	688 00	
Purchases	7088 00	
Purchases Discounts		240 00
Purchases Returns and Allowances		248 00
Wages Expense	2304 00	
Rent Expense	1840 00	
Telephone Expense	552 00	
Miscellaneous Expense	144 00	
	20952 00	20952 00

Additional Data

A. **and** B. Cost of ending inventory on December 31, $392.

C. Insurance expired, $240.

D. Depreciation on store equipment, $100.

E. Accrued wages, $250.

Comprehensive problem: Completing a worksheet.

12B-3. From the following, complete a worksheet for Waltz Company.

WALTZ COMPANY
TRIAL BALANCE
DECEMBER 31, 19XX

	Dr.	Cr.
Cash	380000	
Petty Cash	10000	
Accounts Receivable	340000	
Merchandise Inventory	520400	
Prepaid Rent	120000	
Office Supplies	136000	
Office Equipment	968000	
Accumulated Depreciation, Office Equipment		404000
Accounts Payable		796400
K. Waltz, Capital		547600
K. Waltz, Withdrawals	500000	
Income Summary	—	—
Sales		5246200
Sales Returns and Allowances	11600	
Sales Discount	220000	
Purchases	2929600	
Purchases Discounts		120800
Purchases Returns and Allowances		135000
Office Salaries Expense	740800	
Insurance Expense	220000	
Advertising Expense	80000	
Utilities Expense	73600	
	7250000	7250000

Additional Data

A. **and** B. Ending merchandise inventory on December 31, $2,840.

C. Office supplies on hand, $390.

D. Rent expired, $300.

E. Depreciation expense on office equipment, $325.

F. Salaries accrued, $295.

Comprehensive problem: Completing a worksheet with payroll and unearned revenue.

12B-4. From the following trial balance and additional data, complete the worksheet for Ron's Wholesale Clothing Company.

RON'S WHOLESALE CLOTHING COMPANY
TRIAL BALANCE
DECEMBER 31, 19XX

	Dr.	Cr.
Cash	260000	
Petty Cash	3000	
Accounts Receivable	300000	
Beginning Merchandise Inventory, Jan. 1	360000	
Supplies	27000	
Prepaid Insurance	18000	
Store Equipment	100000	
Accumulated Depreciation, Store Equipment		49600
Accounts Payable		459000
Income Tax Payable		59000
CPP Payable		7400
UI Payable		10000
Unearned Storage Fees		35000
Ron Win, Capital		273400
Ron Win, Withdrawals	180000	
Income Summary	—	—
Sales		1940000
Sales Returns and Allowances	56000	
Sales Discount	48000	
Purchases	860000	
Purchases Discount		24000
Purchases Returns and Allowances		16000
Freight-In	10000	
Salaries Expense	600000	
Payroll Tax Expense	19400	
Interest Expense	32000	
	2873400	2873400

Additional Data

A. **and** B. Ending merchandise inventory on December 31, $4,800.
C. Supplies on hand, $78.
D. Insurance expired, $72.
E. Depreciation on store equipment, $95.
F. Storage fees earned, $130.

Group C Problems

Calculating net sales, cost of goods sold, gross profit, and net income.

12C-1. On the basis of on the accounts listed below, calculate:

a. Net sales

b. Cost of goods sold

c. Gross profit

d. Net income

Accounts Payable	$ 3,800
Operating Expenses	1,150
P. Juarez, Capital	12,460
Purchases	6,785
Freight-In	157
Ending Merchandise Inventory, Dec. 31, 19XX	1,670
Sales	13,730
Accounts Receivable	2,675
Cash	1.456
Purchases Discount	262
Sales Returns and Allowances	315
Beg. Merchandise Inventory, Jan. 1, 19XX	1,940
Purchases Returns and Allowances	466
Sales Discount	376

Comprehensive problem: Completing a worksheet for a merchandise company.

12C-2. From the following trial balance and additional data, complete a worksheet for Corocan Tile Company.

Additional Data

A. **and** B. Ending merchandise inventory on October 31, $9,462.

C. Supplies on hand, $427.70.

D. Insurance expired, $246.72.

E. Depreciation on equipment, $916.

F. Advertising bill received, $500 plus GST of $35.00.

COROCAN TILE COMPANY
TRIAL BALANCE
OCTOBER 31, 19XX

	Dr.	Cr.
Cash	171040	
Petty Cash	20000	
Accounts Receivable	431670	
Beginning Merchandise Inventory, Nov. 1	1346700	
Supplies	73300	
Prepaid Insurance	91400	
GST Prepaid	74852	
Tile Cutting Equipment	782000	
Accumulated Depreciation, Equipment		146600
Accounts Payable		1678240
GST Collected		167358
Income Tax Payable		177100
CPP Payable		24620
UI Payable		37380
Winnie Corocan, Capital		639544
Winnie Corocan, Withdrawals	633800	
Income Summary	—	—
Sales		6935628
Sales Returns and Allowances	138824	
Sales Discounts	71542	
Purchases	4277264	
Purchases Discount		88230
Purchase Returns and Allowances		51286
Freight-In	42570	
Salaries Expense	1587000	
Payroll Taxes Expense	142600	
Interest Expense	61424	
	9945986	9945986

Comprehensive problem: Completing a worksheet.

12C-3. The owner of Chapel Antique Clock Company has asked you to prepare a worksheet from the following trial balance:

CHAPEL ANTIQUE CLOCK COMPANY TRIAL BALANCE MAY 31, 19XX		
	Dr.	Cr.
Cash	76240	
Petty Cash	15000	
Accounts Receivable	271596	
Beginning Clock Inventory, June 1	1076642	
Repair Supplies	62430	
Prepaid Insurance	75376	
GST Prepaid	69614	
Clock Repair Equipment	430000	
Accumulated Depreciation, Repair Equipment		124890
Accounts Payable		868692
GST Collected		91247
Income Tax Payable		115540
CPP Payable		16770
UI Payable		27860
Mike Patel, Capital		556609
Mike Patel, Withdrawals	438000	
Income Summary	—	—
Sales		5724518
Sales Returns and Allowances	26710	
Sales Discounts	17642	
Purchases	3148892	
Purchases Discount		27744
Purchase Returns and Allowances		51286
Freight-In	9631	
Salaries Expense	1347500	
Payroll Taxes Expense	127640	
Advertising Expense	72168	
Rent Expense	278800	
Utilities Expense	61275	
	7605156	7605156

Additional Data

A. **and** B. Ending clock inventory on May 31, $11,281.17.

C. Supplies used during period, $219.40.

D. Insurance expired, $491.16.

E. Depreciation on equipment, $716.16.

F. Advertising bill received, $300 plus GST of $21.

Comprehensive problem: Completing a worksheet with payroll and unearned revenue.

12C-4. From the following trial balance and additional data, complete the worksheet for Gwendolyn's Archery Sales Company.

GWENDOLYN'S ARCHERY SALES COMPANY TRIAL BALANCE APRIL 30, 19XX		
	Dr.	Cr.
Cash	246793	
Petty Cash	7500	
Accounts Receivable	76482	
Beginning Merchandise Inventory, May 1	1736844	
Supplies on Hand	89626	
Prepaid Insurance	115820	
GST Prepaid	145876	
Equipment	897500	
Accumulated Depreciation, Equipment		576214
Accounts Payable		2147950
GST Collected		244470
Income Tax Payable		97470
CPP Payable		13250
UI Payable		17832
Gwen Sterling, Capital		1137306
Gwen Sterling, Withdrawals	845000	
Income Summary	—	—
Sales		7842276
Sales Returns and Allowances	46713	
Sales Discounts	47238	
Purchases	5638158	
Purchases Discount		78240
Purchase Returns and Allowances		132837
Freight-In	37682	
Salaries Expense	1476280	
Payroll Taxes Expense	156623	
Advertising Expense	257284	
Rent Expense	372000	
Utilities Expense	94426	
	12287845	12287845

Additional Data

A. **and** B. Ending merchandise inventory on April 30, $24,718.13.

C. Supplies on hand at end of April, $476.39.

D. Insurance expired, $622.96.

E. Depreciation on equipment, $817.90.

F. Utilities bill received, $110 plus GST of $7.70.

REAL WORLD APPLICATIONS

12R-1.

Kim Andrews prepared the following income statement on a cash basis for Ed Sloan, M.D.:

ED SLOAN, M.D.
INCOME STATEMENT
FOR YEAR ENDED DECEMBER 31, 19X2

Professional Fees Earned	5000000
Expenses	1800000
Net Income	3200000

Ed Sloan has requested information from Kim as to what his professional fees earned would be under the accrual-basis system of accounting. Kim has asked you to provide Dr. Sloan with this information, basing it on the following facts that Kim ignored in the original preparation of the financial report:

	19X1	*19X2*
Accrued Professional Fees	$4,200	$5,300
Unearned Professional Fees	6,200	4,250

12R-2.

Abby Jay is having a difficult time understanding the relationship of sales, cost of goods sold, gross profit, and net income for a merchandise company. As the accounting lab tutor, you have been asked to sit down with Abby and explain how to calculate the missing amounts in each situation listed below. Keep in mind that each situation is a distinct and separate business problem.

	Sales	Beg. Inv.	Purchases	End. Inv.	Cost of Goods Sold	Gross Profit	Expense	Net Income or Loss
Sit. 1	320,000	200,000	160,000	?	260,000	?	80,000	?
Sit. 2	380,000	140,000	?	180,000	200,000	?	100,000	80,000
Sit. 3	480,000	200,000	?	160,000	?	220,000	140,000	80,000
Sit. 4	?	160,000	280,000	140,000	?	160,000	140,000	?
Sit. 5	440,000	160,000	260,000	?	240,000	?	100,000	?
Sit. 6	280,000	120,000	?	140,000	160,000	?	?	40,000
Sit. 7	?	160,000	200,000	120,000	?	160,000	?	–20,000
Sit. 8	320,000	?	200,000	140,000	?	120,000	?	40,000

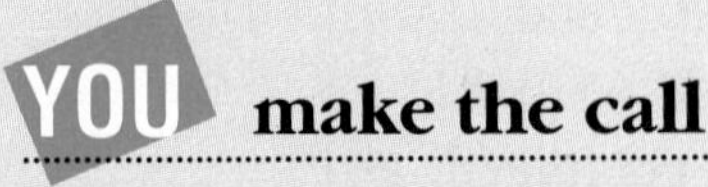

make the call

Critical Thinking/Ethical Case

12R-3.

Jim Heary is the custodian of petty cash. Jim, who is short of personal cash, decided to pay his home electrical and phone bill from petty cash. He plans to pay it back next month. Do you feel Jim should do this? You make the call. Write down your specific recommendations to Jim.

ACCOUNTING RECALL

A CUMULATIVE APPROACH

THIS EXAM REVIEWS CHAPTERS 1 THROUGH 12

Your *Study Guide and Working Papers* has forms to complete this exam, as well as worked-out solutions. The page references next to each question identify what page to turn back to if you answer the question incorrectly.

PART I Vocabulary Review

Match the terms to the appropriate definition or phrase.

Page Ref.

(474) 1. Interest expense
(474) 2. Sales return and allowance
(468) 3. Ending merchandise inventory
(476) 4. Accumulated depreciation
(469) 5. Income summary
(470) 6. Rental income
(474) 7. Unearned revenue
(474) 8. Purchases
(174) 9. Closing
(468) 10. Perpetual inventory

A. A liability
B. Cost of goods sold
C. Continual track
D. Contra-asset
E. Non-operating expense
F. New figure for capital
G. Subtracted from cost of goods sold
H. Other income
I. Contra-revenue account
J. Used in adjusting merchandise inventory

PART II True or False (Accounting Theory)

(470) 11. Unearned rent is an asset.
(468) 12. Beginning and ending inventory are combined on the worksheet.
(468) 13. Ending inventory is added to cost of goods sold.
(291) 14. Due to Receiver General for Canada is a liability that includes only amounts deducted from employees.
(174) 15. The normal balance of income summary is a debit.

PART III Applications Problem

From the following trial balance and adjustment data complete a worksheet for Bill's Antique Shop for year ended December 31, 19XX.

TRIAL BALANCE		
	Dr.	Cr.
Cash	4 1 0 0 00	
Accounts Receivable	23 8 0 0 00	
Merchandise Inventory	20 0 0 0 00	
Prepaid Insurance	6 0 0 00	
Equipment	18 0 0 0 00	
Accumulated Depreciation, Equipment		1 0 0 0 00
Unearned Rent		5 0 0 00
Accounts Payable		11 0 0 0 00
B. J. Jensen, Capital		50 0 0 0 00
B. J. Jensen, Withdrawals	15 0 0 0 00	
Income Summary	—	—
Sales		279 0 0 0 00
Sales Returns and Allowances	3 0 0 0 00	
Sales Discount	4 5 0 0 00	
Purchases	180 0 0 0 00	
Purchases Returns and Allowances		1 5 0 0 00
Purchases Discount		3 5 0 0 00
Freight-In	2 5 0 0 00	
Salaries Expense	45 0 0 0 00	
Advertising Expense	10 0 0 0 00	
Rent Expense	12 0 0 0 00	
Utility Expense	8 0 0 0 00	
	346 5 0 0 00	346 5 0 0 00

Adjustment Data

A. **and** B. Ending merchandise inventory, December 31, 19XX, $24,000.

C. Insurance expense, $200.

D. Depreciation, $1,000.

E. Salaries owed, $500.

F. Rent earned, $100.

COMPLETION OF THE ACCOUNTING CYCLE FOR A MERCHANDISE COMPANY

13

LEARNING UNIT 13-1:
Preparing Financial Reports

The Income Statement
- Revenue Section
- Cost of Goods Sold Section
- Gross Profit
- Operating Expenses Section
- Other Income (or Other Revenue) Section
- Other Expenses Section

Statement of Owner's Equity
The Balance Sheet

LEARNING UNIT 13-1 REVIEW

LEARNING UNIT 13-2:
Journalizing and Posting Adjusting and Closing Entries; Preparing the Post-Closing Trial Balance

Journalizing and Posting Adjusting Entries
Journalizing and Posting Closing Entries
The Post-Closing Trial Balance

LEARNING UNIT 13-2 REVIEW

LEARNING UNIT 13-3:
Reversing Entries

LEARNING UNIT 13-3 REVIEW

CHAPTER REVIEW

- Summary of Key Points
- Key Terms
- Blueprint of Financial Reports
- Questions, Exercises, and Problems
- Real World Applications
- You Make the Call: Critical Thinking/Ethical Case

ACCOUNTING RECALL

MINI PRACTICE SET

COMPUTER WORKSHOP

Chapter Objectives

- Preparing financial reports for a merchandise company. (pp. 502–508)
- Recording adjusting and closing entries. (pp. 509–512)
- Preparing a post-closing trial balance. (pp. 512–515)
- Dealing with reversing entries. (pp. 515–517)

In Chapter 12 we covered adjustments and completing a worksheet for a merchandise company. In this chapter we will discuss the steps involved in completing the accounting cycle for a merchandise company: preparing financial reports, journalizing and posting adjusting and closing entries, preparing a post-closing trial balance, and reversing entries. First we will deal with preparing financial reports at the close of the accounting cycle.

LEARNING UNIT 13-1

Preparing Financial Reports

As we discussed in Chapter 5, when we were dealing with a service company rather than a merchandise company, the three financial reports can be prepared from the worksheet. Let's begin by looking at how Art's Wholesale Clothing Company prepares the income statement.

THE INCOME STATEMENT

See Chapters 9 and 10 for a review of terms such as net sales, cost of goods sold, and operating expenses.

Art is interested in knowing how well his business performed for the year ended December 31, 19XX. What were its net sales? Were there many returns of goods from dissatisfied customers? What was the cost of the goods brought into the store vs. the selling price received? How many goods were returned to suppliers? What is the cost of the goods that have not been sold? What was the cost of the Freight-In? The income statement in Figure 13-1 is prepared from the income statement columns of the worksheet. (Review it first, and then we will explain each section of the income statement and where on the worksheet the information came from.)

Note that there are no debit or credit columns on the formal income statement — the inside columns on financial reports are used for subtotalling, not for debit and credit.

Note how the income statement is broken down into several sections. Remembering the sections can help you make sense of the statement and set it up correctly on your own. Basically what it presents is this:

Net Sales
– Cost of Goods Sold
= Gross Profit
– Operating Expenses
= Net Income from Operations
+ Other Income
– Other Expenses
= Net Income

ART'S WHOLESALE CLOTHING COMPANY
PARTIAL WORKSHEET
FOR YEAR ENDED DECEMBER 31, 19X2

	Income Statement Dr.	Income Statement Cr.
Income Summary	1900000	400000
Sales		9500000
Sales Returns and Allowances	95000	
Sales Discount	67000	
Purchases	5200000	
Purchases Discount		86000
Purchases Returns and Allowances		68000
Freight-In	45000	
Salaries Expense	1230000	
Payroll Tax Expense	42000	
Postage Expense	2500	
Miscellaneous Expense	3000	
Interest Expense	30000	
Rental Income		20000
Supplies Expense	50000	
Insurance Expense	30000	
Depreciation Expense, Store Equip.	5000	
Salaries Payable		
	8699500	10074000
Net Income	1374500	
	10074000	10074000

ART'S WHOLESALE CLOTHING COMPANY
INCOME STATEMENT
FOR YEAR ENDED DECEMBER 31, 19X2

Revenue:				
Gross Sales				$9500000
Less: Sales Ret. and Allow.			$ 95000	
Sales Discount			67000	162000
Net Sales				9338000
Cost of Goods Sold:				
Merchandise Inventory, 1/1/X2			1900000	
Purchases		$5200000		
Less: Pur. Discount	$ 86000			
Pur. Ret. and Allow.	68000	154000		
Net Purchases		5046000		
Add: Freight-In		45000		
Net Cost of Purchases			5091000	
Cost of Goods Available for Sale			6991000	
Less: Merch. Inv., 12/31/X2			400000	
Cost of Goods Sold				6591000
Gross Profit				2747000
Operating Expenses:				
Salaries Expense			1230000	
Payroll Tax Expense			42000	
Dep. Exp., Store Equip.			5000	
Supplies Expense			50000	
Insurance Expense			30000	
Postage Expense			2500	
Miscellaneous Expense			3000	
Total Operating Expenses				1362500
Net Income from Operations				1384500
Other Income:				
Rental Income			20000	
Other Expenses:				
Interest Expense			30000	10000
Net Income				$1374500

FIGURE 13-1
Partial Work Sheet and Income Statement

Let's take these sections one at a time and see where the figures come from on the worksheet.

Revenue Section

Sales
– Sales Ret. & Allow.
– Sales Discount
= Net Sales

Net Sales The first major category of the income statement shows net sales. The figure here of $93,380 is *not* found on the worksheet—the accountant must take the individual amounts for gross sales, sales returns and allowances, and sales discount found on the worksheet and *combine* them to arrive at a figure for net sales. Thus, although the worksheet has the individual components, it is not until the formal income statement that these individual amounts are summarized in one figure for net sales.

Cost of Goods Sold Section

Beg. Inventory
+ Net Cost of Purchases
– Ending Inventory
= Cost of Goods Sold

On the worksheet we separate figures for Merchandise Inventory. The $19,000 represents the beginning inventory of the period, while the $4,000, calculated from an inventory sheet, is the ending inventory. Note on the financial report how the cost of goods sold section uses two separate figures for inventory. Remember that in the periodic system goods brought in during the accounting period are added to the Purchases account, not to the Merchandise Inventory account.

Note that the following numbers are not found on the worksheet but are shown on the formal income statement (they are combined by the accountant in preparing the income statement):

- **Net Purchases:** $50,460 (Purchases - Purchases Discount - Purchases Returns and Allowances)
- **Net Cost of Purchases:** $50,910 (Net Purchases + Freight-In)
- **Cost of Goods Available for Sale:** $69,910 (Beginning Inventory + Net Cost of Purchases)
- **Cost of Goods Sold:** $65,910 (Cost of Goods Available for Sale - Ending Inventory)

Gross Profit

Net Sales
– Cost of Goods Sold
= Gross Profit

The figure for gross profit ($27,470) is arrived at by subtracting cost of goods sold from net sales ($93,380 - $65,910). The gross profit figure of $27,470 is not found by itself on the worksheet, but, like others we have discussed, is calculated by the accountant from separate figures on the worksheet.

Operating Expenses Section

The total of the operating expenses does not appear on its own on the worksheet; to get this figure of $13,625 the accountant adds up all the expenses on the worksheet that resulted from doing business.

Many companies break expenses down into those directly related to the selling activity of the company (**selling expenses**) and those related to administrative or office activity (**administrative expenses** or **general expenses**). Here's a sample list broken down into these two categories:

Operating Expenses

Selling Expenses:	*Administrative Expenses:*
Sales Salaries Expense	Rent Expense
Delivery Expense	Office Salaries Expense
Advertising Expense	Utilities Expense

Depreciation Expense,
Store Equipment
Insurance Expense
Total Selling Expenses

Supplies Expense
Depreciation Expense, Office
Equipment
Total Administrative Expenses

Other Income (or Other Revenue) Section

This section will record any revenue other than revenue from sales. For example, Art's Wholesale makes a profit from subletting a portion of a building and earning rental income of $200, and that income goes in this section.

Other Expenses Section

This section will record nonoperating expenses—those not related to the main operating activities of the business. For example, Art's Wholesale has paid or owes $300 interest on money it has borrowed.

STATEMENT OF OWNER'S EQUITY

Statement of owner's equity is the same for a merchandise business as for a service firm.

The information used to complete the statement of owner's equity comes from the balance sheet columns of the worksheet. Keep in mind the capital account in the ledger should be checked to see if any additional investments have occurred during the period. Note in the following diagram how the worksheet aids in this. The ending figure of $13,050 for Art Newner, Capital, will be carried over to the balance sheet, which is the final report we will look at in this chapter.

Any additional investment by owner would be added to his or her beginning capital amount. The illustration at the right does not show this, however.

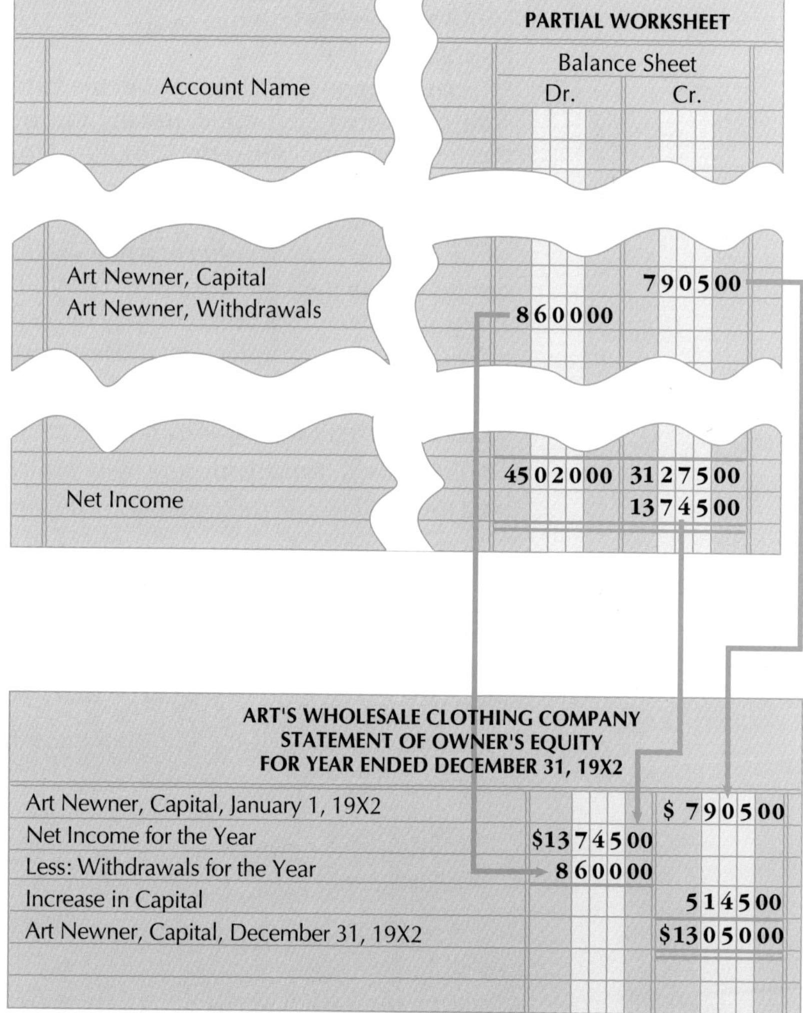

ART'S WHOLESALE CLOTHING COMPANY
STATEMENT OF OWNER'S EQUITY
FOR YEAR ENDED DECEMBER 31, 19X2

Art Newner, Capital, January 1, 19X2		$ 790500
Net Income for the Year	$1374500	
Less: Withdrawals for the Year	860000	
Increase in Capital		514500
Art Newner, Capital, December 31, 19X2		$1305000

THE BALANCE SHEET

The diagram in Figure 13-2 shows how a worksheet is used to aid in the preparation of the balance sheet. The following is called a **classified balance sheet** because assets and liabilities are broken down into more detail.

Let's look at each of the categories on the classified balance sheet in turn.

Current assets are defined as cash and assets that will be converted into cash or used up during the normal operating cycle of the company or one year, whichever is longer. (Think of the **operating cycle** as the time period it takes a company to buy and sell merchandise and then collect accounts receivable.)

Accountants list current assets in order of how easily they can be converted into cash (this is called *liquidity*). In most cases Accounts Receivable can be turned into cash more quickly than Merchandise Inventory—for example, it can be quite difficult to sell an outdated computer in a computer store, or to sell last year's model car this year.

Capital assets are long-lived assets used in the production or sale of goods or services. Art's Wholesale has only one fixed asset, store equipment; other capital assets could include buildings and land. The assets are usually listed in order of how long they will last; the shortest-lived assets are listed first. Land would always be the last asset listed (and land is never depreciated). Note that we still show the cost of the asset less its accumulated depreciation.

Current liabilities are the debts or obligations of Art's Wholesale that must be paid within one year or one operating cycle. The order of listing accounts in this section is not always the same—many times companies will list their liabilities in the order that they expect to pay them off. Note that the current portion of the mortgage, $320 (that portion due within one year), is listed before Accounts Payable.

Mortgage Payable:
$2,320
– 320 current portion
$2,000 long-term

Long-term liabilities are debts or obligations not due and payable for a comparatively long period, usually for more than one year. For Art's Wholesale there is only one long-term liability—Mortgage Payable. The long-term portion of the mortgage is listed here; the current portion, due within one year, is listed under Current Liabilities.

The current portion of a long-term liability is the amount of principal to be repaid next year. Do not include any interest to be paid next year.

A classified balance sheet (when examined along with the Income Statement) can provide management, owners, creditors, and suppliers with more information about the company's ability to pay debts, both current and long-term, as well as provide a more complete financial picture of the firm. Some of the following questions might also be answered or raised:

1. Is inventory turning over quickly enough?
2. Is the owner receiving a proper return on his or her investment?
3. How efficient is the collections department?

LEARNING UNIT 13-1 REVIEW

AT THIS POINT you should be able to

- Prepare a detailed income statement from the worksheet. (pp. 502–504)
- Explain the difference between selling and administrative expenses. (p. 504)
- Explain which columns of the worksheet are used in preparing a statement of owner's equity. (p. 505)
- Prepare a classified balance sheet from a worksheet. (p. 506)
- Explain as well as compare current assets with plant and equipment. (p. 506)
- Using Mortgage Payable as an example, explain the difference between current and long-term liabilities. (p. 506)

ART'S WHOLESALE CLOTHING COMPANY
WORKSHEET
FOR YEAR ENDED DECEMBER 31, 19X2

	Balance Sheet Dr.	Balance Sheet Cr.
Cash	12920 00	
Petty Cash	100 00	
Accounts Receivable	14500 00	
Merchandise Inventory	4000 00	
Supplies	300 00	
Prepaid Insurance	600 00	
Store Equipment	4000 00	
Accum. Dep., Store Equipment		450 00
Accounts Payable		17900 00
Income Tax Payable		1240 00
CPP Payable		260 00
UI Payable		200 00
Unearned Rent		400 00
Mortgage Payable		2320 00
Art Newner, Capital		7905 00
Salaries Payable		600 00
	45020 00	31275 00
Net Income		13745 00
	45020 00	45020 00

Note: The figure of $13,050 for Art Newner, Capital, comes from the statement of owner's equity.

ART'S WHOLESALE CLOTHING COMPANY
CLASSIFIED BALANCE SHEET
FOR YEAR ENDED DECEMBER 31, 19X2

Assets		
Current Assets:		
Cash	$12920 00	
Petty Cash	100 00	
Accounts Receivable	14500 00	
Merchandise Inventory	4000 00	
Supplies	300 00	
Prepaid Insurance	600 00	
Total Current Assets		$32420 00
Capital Assets:		
Store Equipment	4000 00	
Less: Accum. Dep.	450 00	3550 00
Total Assets		$35970 00
Liabilities		
Current Liabilities:		
Mortgage Payable (current portion)	$ 320 00	
Accounts Payable	17900 00	
Income Tax Payable	1240 00	
CPP Payable	260 00	
UI Payable	200 00	
Salary Payable	600 00	
Unearned Rent	400 00	
Total Current Liabilities		$20920 00
Long-Term Liabilities		
Mortgage Payable		2000 00
Total Liabilities		22920 00
Owner's Equity		
Art Newner, Capital, December 31, 19X2		13050 00
Total Liabilities and Owner's Equity		$35970 00

FIGURE 13-2
Partial Worksheet and Balance Sheet

SELF-REVIEW QUIZ 13-1

Using the worksheet from Self-Review Quiz 12-2, prepare in proper form (1) an income statement, (2) a statement of owner's equity, (3) a classified balance sheet for Ray Company.

Solution to Self-Review Quiz 13-1

1.

RAY COMPANY
INCOME STATEMENT
FOR YEAR ENDED DECEMBER 31, 19XX

Revenue:				
Sales				$11040 00
Less: Sales Ret. and Allow.			$ 546 00	
Sales Discount			216 00	762 00
Net Sales				10278 00
Cost of Goods Sold:				
Merchandise Inventory, 1/1/XX			824 00	
Purchases		$5256 00		
Less: Pur. Ret. and Allow.	$ 168 00			
Purchases Discount	102 00	270 00		
Net Purchases			4986 00	
Cost of Goods Available for Sale			5810 00	
Less: Merchandise Inv., 12/31/XX			200 00	
Cost of Goods Sold				5610 00
Gross Profit				4668 00
Operating Expenses:				
Salaries Expense		2216 00		
Insurance Expense		1392 00		
Utilities Expense		96 00		
Plumbing Expense		214 00		
Rent Expense		100 00		
Depreciation Exp., Equip.		60 00		
Total Operating Expenses				4078 00
Net Income from Operations				$ 590 00
Other Income:				
Storage Fees				516 00
Net Income				$ 1106 00

2.

RAY COMPANY
STATEMENT OF OWNER'S EQUITY
FOR YEAR ENDED DECEMBER 31, 19XX

B. Ray, Capital, 1/1/XX	$ 1932 00
Net Income for the Year	1106 00
B. Ray, Capital, 12/31/XX	$ 3038 00

3.

RAY COMPANY
BALANCE SHEET
DECEMBER 31, 19XX

Assets		
Current Assets:		
Cash	$ 2 4 8 6 00	
Merchandise Inventory	2 0 0 00	
Prepaid Rent	1 0 5 2 00	
Prepaid Insurance	6 0 00	
Total Current Assets		$ 3 7 9 8 00
Capital Assets:		
Office Equipment	$ 2 1 6 0 00	
Less: Accumulated Depreciation	6 2 0 00	1 5 4 0 00
Total Assets		$ 5 3 3 8 00
Liabilities		
Current Liabilities:		
Accounts Payable	$ 1 0 0 00	
Salaries Payable	2 0 0 00	
Unearned Storage Fees	2 0 0 0 00	
Total Liabilities		$ 2 3 0 0 00
Owner's Equity		
B. Ray, Capital, December 31, 19XX		3 0 3 8 00
Total Liabilities and Owner's Equity		$ 5 3 3 8 00

LEARNING UNIT 13-2

Journalizing and Posting Adjusting and Closing Entries; Preparing the Post-Closing Trial Balance

JOURNALIZING AND POSTING ADJUSTING ENTRIES

From the worksheet of Art's Wholesale, repeated here in Figure 13-3 for your convenience, the adjusting entries can be journalized from the adjustments column and posted to the ledger. Keep in mind that the adjustments have been recorded only on the worksheet, not in the ledger—at this point the ledger still contains only unadjusted amounts.

FIGURE 13-3 Completed Worksheet

ART'S WHOLESALE CLOTHING CO.
WORKSHEET
FOR YEAR ENDED DECEMBER 31, 19X2

	Trial Balance		Adjustments		Adjusted Trial Bal.		Income Statement		Balance Sheet	
	Dr.	Cr.	Dr.	Cr.	Dr.	Cr.	Dr.	Cr.	Dr.	Cr.
Cash	12920 00				12920 00				12920 00	
Petty Cash	100 00				100 00				100 00	
Accounts Receivable	14500 00				14500 00				14500 00	
Merchandise Inventory	19000 00		(B) 4000 00	(A) 19000 00	4000 00				4000 00	
Supplies	800 00			(D) 500 00	300 00				300 00	
Prepaid Insurance	900 00			(E) 300 00	600 00				600 00	
Store Equipment	4000 00				4000 00				4000 00	
Accum. Dep., Store Equipment		400 00		(F) 50 00		450 00				450 00
Accounts Payable		17900 00				17900 00				17900 00
Income Tax Payable		1240 00				1240 00				1240 00
CPP Payable		260 00				260 00				260 00
UI Payable		200 00				200 00				200 00
Unearned Rent		600 00	(C) 200 00			400 00				400 00
Mortgage Payable		2320 00				2320 00				2320 00
Art Newner, Capital		7905 00				7905 00				7905 00
Art Newner, Withdrawals	8600 00				8600 00				8600 00	
Income Summary			(A) 19000 00	(B) 4000 00	19000 00	4000 00	19000 00	4000 00		
Sales		95000 00				95000 00		95000 00		
Sales Returns and Allowances	950 00				950 00		950 00			
Sales Discount	670 00				670 00		670 00			
Purchases	52000 00				52000 00		52000 00			
Purchases Discount		860 00				860 00		860 00		
Purchases Returns and Allowances		680 00				680 00		680 00		
Freight-In	450 00				450 00		450 00			
Salary Expense	11700 00		(G) 600 00		12300 00		12300 00			
Payroll Tax Expense	420 00				420 00		420 00			
Postage Expense	25 00				25 00		25 00			
Miscellaneous Expense	30 00				30 00		30 00			
Interest Expense	300 00				300 00		300 00			
	127365 00	127365 00								
Rental Income				(C) 200 00		200 00		200 00		
Supplies Expense			(D) 500 00		500 00		500 00			
Insurance Expense			(E) 300 00		300 00		300 00			
Depreciation Expense, Store Equip.			(F) 50 00		50 00		50 00			
Salary Payable				(G) 600 00		600 00				600 00
			24650 00	24650 00	132015 00	132015 00	86995 00	100740 00	45020 00	31275 00
Net Income							13745 00			13745 00
							100740 00	100740 00	45020 00	45020 00

The journalized and posted adjusting entries are shown below. Note that the liability Unearned Rent is reduced by $200 and Rental Income has increased by $200.

ART'S WHOLESALE CLOTHING CO.
GENERAL JOURNAL

Page 2

Date 19X2		Account Titles and Description	PR	Dr.	Cr.
		Adjusting Entries			
Dec.	31	Income Summary	313	1900000	
		Merchandise Inventory	114		1900000
		Transferred beginning inventory			
		to Income Summary			
	31	Merchandise Inventory	114	400000	
		Income Summary	313		400000
		Records cost of ending inventory			
	31	Unearned Rent	218	20000	
		Rental Income	414		20000
		Rental income earned			
	31	Supplies Expense	614	50000	
		Supplies	115		50000
		Supplies consumed			
	31	Insurance Expense	615	30000	
		Prepaid Insurance	116		30000
		Insurance expired			
	31	Dep. Exp., Store Equipment	613	5000	
		Acc. Dep., Store Equipment	122		5000
		Depreciation on equipment			
	31	SalaryExpense	611	60000	
		SalaryPayable	212		60000
		Accrued salary			

Partial Ledger

Merchandise Inventory 114

Dr.	Cr.
19,000	19,000
4,000	

Accum. Dep., Store Equipment 122

Dr.	Cr.
	400
	50

Income Summary 313

Dr.	Cr.
19,000	4,000

Dep. Expense, Store Equip. 613

Dr.	Cr.
50	

Supplies 115

Dr.	Cr.
800	500

Salary Payable 212

Dr.	Cr.
	600

Supplies Expense 614

Dr.	Cr.
500	

Salary Exp. 611

Dr.	Cr.
11,700	
600	

Prepaid Insurance 116

Dr.	Cr.
900	300

Unearned Rent 218

Dr.	Cr.
200	600

Insurance Expense 615

Dr.	Cr.
300	

Rental Income 414

Dr.	Cr.
	200

JOURNALIZING AND POSTING CLOSING ENTRIES

Back in Chapter 5 we discussed the closing process for a service company. The goals of closing have not changed. They are to clear all temporary accounts in the ledger to zero and update capital in the ledger to its latest balance. A merchandise company will also use the worksheet and the following steps to complete the closing process:

1. Close all balances on the income statement credit column of the worksheet *except* Income Summary by Debits and credit the total to the Income Summary account.
2. Close all balances on the income statement debit column of the worksheet *except* Income Summary by Credits and debit the total to the Income Summary account.
3. Transfer the balance of the Income Summary account to the Capital account.
4. Transfer the balance of the owner's Withdrawal account to the Capital account.

Let's look now at the journalized closing entries in Figure 13-4.

When these entries are posted, all the temporary accounts will have zero balances in the ledger, and the Capital account will be updated with a new balance.

Let's take a moment to look at the Income Summary account in T account form:

Income Summary 313

		Dr.	Cr.	
	Adj.	19,000	4,000	Adj.
	Clos.	67,995	96,740	Clos.
		86,995	100,740	
Net income →	Clos.	13,745		

Note that Income Summary before the closing process contains the adjustments for Merchandise Inventory. Sometimes accountants include the inventory adjustments as part of the closing. This is not illustrated in this text; *it is not very important which procedure is used*, just that it is made accurately. The end result is that the net income of $13,745 is closed to the Capital account.

THE POST-CLOSING TRIAL BALANCE

The post-closing trial balance (often referred to as an opening trial balance) shown on p. 514 is prepared from the general ledger. Note first that all temporary accounts have been closed and thus are not shown on this post-closing trial balance. Note also that the ending inventory figure of the last accounting period, $4,000, becomes the beginning inventory figure on Jan. 1, 19X3.

Notice that the adjustments to inventory are not included in these closing entries, although some accountants do include them here.

ART'S WHOLESALE CLOTHING CO.
GENERAL JOURNAL

Page 2

Date		Account Titles and Description	PR	Dr.	Cr.
19XX		Closing Entries			
Dec.	31	Sales	411	95 000 00	
		Rental Income	414	200 00	
		Purchases Income	512	860 00	
		Purchases Ret. and Allow.	513	680 00	
		Income Summary	313		96 740 00
		Transfers credit account balances			
		on income statement column of			
		worksheet to Income Summary			
	31	Income Summary	313	67 995 00	
		Sales Returns and Allowances	412		950 00
		Sales Discount	413		670 00
		Purchases	511		52 000 00
		Freight-In	514		450 00
		Salaries Expense	611		12 300 00
		Payroll Tax Expense	612		420 00
		Postage Expense	616		25 00
		Miscellaneous Expense	617		30 00
		Interest Expense	618		300 00
		Supplies Expense	614		500 00
		Insurance Expense	615		300 00
		Depreciation Expense, Store Equip.	613		50 00
		Transfers all expenses, and			
		reductions to Sales are			
		closed to Income Summary			
	31	Income Summary	313	13 745 00	
		A. Newner, Capital	311		13 745 00
		Transfer of net income to			
		Capital from Income Summary			
	31	A. Newner, Capital	311	8 600 00	
		A. Newner, Withdrawals	312		8 600 00
		Closes withdrawals to			
		Capital account			

FIGURE 13-4
General Journal

ART'S WHOLESALE CLOTHING COMPANY
POST-CLOSING TRIAL BALANCE
DECEMBER 31, 19X2

	Dr.	Cr.
Cash	1292000	
Petty Cash	10000	
Accounts Receivable	1450000	
Merchandise Inventory	400000	
Supplies	30000	
Prepaid Insurance	60000	
Store Equipment	400000	
Accum. Depreciation, Store Equipment		45000
Accounts Payable		1790000
Income Tax Payable		124000
CPP Payable		26000
UI Payable		20000
Salary Payable		60000
Unearned Rent		40000
Mortgage Payable		232000
Art Newner, Capital		1305000
	3642000	3642000

LEARNING UNIT 13-2 REVIEW

AT THIS POINT you should be able to

- Journalize and post adjusting entries for a merchandise company. (pp. 509–511)
- Explain the relationship of the worksheet to the adjusting and closing process. (p. 509)
- Complete the closing process for a merchandise company. (p. 512)
- Prepare a post-closing trial balance and explain why ending Merchandise Inventory is not a temporary account. (p. 512)

SELF-REVIEW QUIZ 13-2

Using the worksheet from Self-Review Quiz 12-2, journalize the closing entries.

Solution to Self-Review Quiz 13-2

Page 2

Date		Account Titles and Description	PR	Dr.	Cr.
		Closing			
Dec.	31	Sales		110400	
		Storage Fees Earned		51600	
		Purchases Returns and Allowances		16800	
		Purchases Discount		10200	
		Income Summary			1182600
	31	Income Summary		1009600	
		Sales Returns and Allowances			54600
		Sales Discount			21600
		Purchases			525600
		Salaries Expense			221600
		Insurance Expense			139200
		Utilities Expense			9600
		Plumbing Expense			21400
		Rent Expense			10000
		Depreciation Exp., Equipment			6000
	31	Income Summary		110600	
		B. Ray, Capital			110600

LEARNING UNIT 13-3

Reversing Entries

Reversing entries are not mandatory.

Now that we have completed the accounting cycle for Art's Wholesale Clothing Company, let's look at an optional way of handling some adjusting entries—it is called reversing entries. **Reversing entries** are general journal entries that are the opposite of adjusting entries. Reversing entries help reduce potential errors and simplify the recordkeeping process. Let's look at how Art's bookkeeper handles a reversing entry for salaries at the end of the year (see Figure 13-5).

Note that the permanent account Salaries Payable carries over to the new accounting period a $600 balance. *Remember:* The $600 was an expense of the prior year.

On January 8 of the new year the payroll to be paid is $2,000. If the optional reversing entry is *not* used, the bookkeeper makes the following journal entry:

		Account	PR	Dr.	Cr.
		Salaries Payable		60000	
		Salaries Expense		140000	
		Cash			200000

Sal. Exp.	
1,400	

Sal. Pay.	
600	600

Cash	
	2,000

To do this the bookkeeper has to refer to the adjustment on December 31 to determine how much of the salary of $2,000 is indeed a new salary expense and what portion was shown in the old year although not paid. It is easy to see how errors can result if the bookkeeper pays the payroll but forgets about the adjustment in the previous year. In this way reversing entries can help avoid errors.

Figure 13-6 shows the steps the bookkeeper would take if reversing entries were used. Note that steps 1 and 2 are the same whether the accountant uses reversing entries or not.

FIGURE 13-5 Reversing Entries

Adjusting Journal Entry

T Account Update

(1)
On December 31 after adjusting entries were journalized and posted for $600 of salaries incurred but not paid

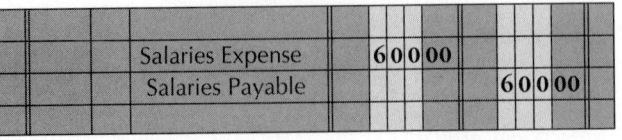

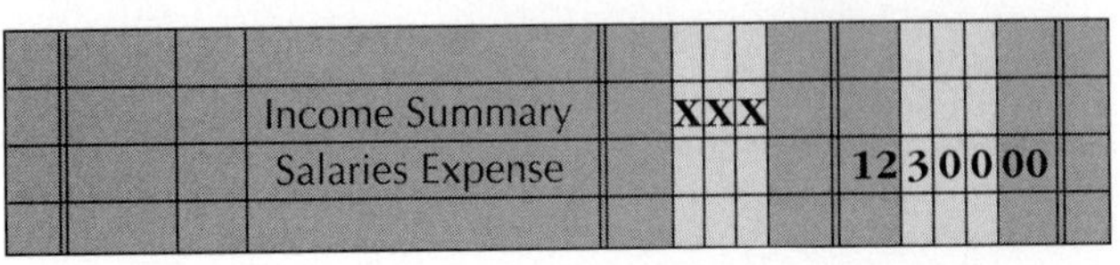

Date		Account	Dr.	Cr.
		Salaries Expense	60000	
		Salaries Payable		60000

Salaries Exp.		Salaries Pay.	
11,700			600
600			

(2)
On January 1 after closing entries have been journalized and posted

Date		Account	Dr.	Cr.
		Income Summary	XXX	
		Salaries Expense		1230000

Salaries Exp.		Salaries Pay.	
11,700			600
600	12,300		
Bal. –0–			

Note that the balance of Salaries Expense is indeed only $1,400, the *true* expense in the new year. Reversing results in switching the adjustment the first day of the new period. Also note that each of the accounts ends up with the same balance no matter which method is chosen. However, using reversing entry for salaries allows the accountant to make the normal entry when it is time to pay salaries.

FIGURE 13-6 Reversing Entries

(1)
On December 31 adjustment for salary was recorded

Salaries Exp.		Salaries Pay.	
11,700			600
600			

(2)
Closing entry on December 31

Salaries Exp.		Salaries Pay.	
11,700	12,300		600
600			

(3)
On January 1 (first day of the following fiscal period) reverse adjusting entry was made for salary on December 31. (This means "flipping" adjustment.)

Date		Account	Dr.	Cr.
Jan.	1	Salaries Payable	60000	
		Salaries Expense		60000

Salaries Exp.		Salaries Pay.	
	600	600	600

By doing this the liability is reduced to zero. We know it will be paid in this new period but the salaries expense has a credit balance of $600 until the payroll is paid. When the payroll of $2,000 is paid, the following happens:

(4)
Paid payroll $2,000

Date		Account	Dr.	Cr.
Jan.	1	Salaries Expense	200000	
		Cash		200000

Salaries Exp.		Cash	
2,000	600		2,000

One should be careful with reversing entries, since not all adjustments can be reversed. Here is a list of the types of adjustments that can be reversed:

1. When there is an increase in an asset account (no previous balance).
   Example: Interest Receivable
   Interest Income
   (Interest earned but not collected; we will cover this in later chapters.)
2. When there is an increase in a liability account (no previous balance).
   Example: Wages Expense
   Wages Payable

Except in the case of businesses in their first year of operation, accounts such as Accumulated Depreciation or Inventory will have previous balances and thus will *not* be reversed. As we progress in the course, we will take time to review whether reversing takes place or not.

The increasing use of computers in accounting has changed the role and purpose of reversing entries somewhat. Most accounting software packages allow users to establish recurring entries which can be entered into the accounting records more or less automatically each month. Also, many accounting programs permit a given entry to be automatically reversed in the next period by simply checking a box on a screen.

In this text we are continuing to illustrate reversing entries as being done manually. Students are encouraged to discover what features are present in the software they are using (or have access to) which modify the nature, purpose, and usefulness of reversing entries.

LEARNING UNIT 13-3 REVIEW

AT THIS POINT you should be able to

- Explain the purpose of reversing entries. (p. 515)
- Complete a reversing entry. (pp. 515–516)
- Explain when reversing entries can be used. (p. 517)

SELF-REVIEW QUIZ 13-3

Explain which of the following situations could be reversed:

1.

Supplies Exp.	
200	

Supplies	
800	200

2.

Wages Exp.	
3,000	
200	

Wages Payable	
	200

3.

Sales	
	4,000
	50

Unearned Sales	
50	200

Solution to Self-Review Quiz 13-3

1. Not reversed—asset Supplies is decreasing, not increasing.
2. Reversed—liability is increasing and no previous balance exists.
3. Not reversed—liability is decreasing and a previous balance exists.

Chapter Review

Summary of key points

Learning Unit 13-1

1. The formal income statement can be prepared from the income statement columns of the worksheet.
2. There are no debit or credit columns on the formal income statement.
3. The cost of goods sold section has a figure for beginning inventory and a separate figure for ending inventory.
4. Operating expenses could be broken down into selling and administrative expenses.
5. The ending figure for capital is not found on the worksheet. It comes from the statement of owner's equity.
6. A classified balance sheet breaks assets down into current and capital. Liabilities are broken down into current and long-term.

Learning Unit 13-2

1. The information for journalizing, adjusting, and closing entries can be obtained from the worksheet.
2. In the closing process all temporary accounts will be zero and the capital account is brought up to its new balance.
3. Inventory is not a temporary account. The ending inventory, along with other permanent accounts, will be listed in the post-closing trial balance.

Learning Unit 13-3

1. Reversing entries are optional and could aid in reducing potential errors and simplify the recordkeeping process.
2. The reversing entry "flips" the adjustment on the first day of new fiscal period. Thus, the bookkeeper need not look back at what happened in the old year when recording the current year's transactions.
3. Reversing entries are only used if (a) assets are increasing and have no previous balance, (b) liabilities are increasing and have no previous balance.

Key terms

Administrative expenses (general expenses) Expenses such as general office expenses that are incurred indirectly in the selling of goods.

Capital assets Long-lived assets such as buildings or land that are used in the production or sale of goods or services.

Classified balance sheet A balance sheet that categorizes assets as current or capital and groups liabilities as current or long-term.

Current assets Assets that can be converted into cash or used within one year or the normal operating cycle of the business, whichever is longer

Current liabilities Obligations that will come due within one year or within the operating cycle, whichever is longer.

Long-term liabilities Obligations that are not due or payable for a long time, usually for more than a year.

Operating cycle Average time it takes to buy and sell merchandise and then collect accounts receivable.

Other expenses These are nonoperating expenses that do not relate to the main operating activities of the business; they appear in a separate section on the income statement. One example given in the text is Interest Expense—interest owed on money borrowed by the company.

Other income This includes any revenue other than revenue from sales and appears in a separate section on the income statement. Examples would be Rental Income and Storage Fees.

Reversing entries Year-end optional bookkeeping technique in which certain adjusting entries are reversed or switched on the first day of the new accounting period so that transactions in the new period can be recorded without referring to prior adjusting entries.

Selling expenses Expenses directly related to the sale of goods.

BLUEPRINT OF FINANCIAL REPORTS

(1) INCOME STATEMENT

Revenue:				
Sales				$ XXX
Less: Sales Ret. and Allow.			$ XXX	
Sales Discount			XXX	XXX
Net Sales				$ XXXX
Cost of Goods Sold:				
Merchandise Inventory, 1/1/XX			$ XXX	
Purchases		$XXX		
Less: Pur. Ret. and Allow.	$XXX			
Purchases Discount	XXX	XXX		
Net Purchases		XXX		
Add: Freight-In		XXX		
Net Cost of Purchases			XXX	
Cost of Goods Avail. for Sale			$XXXX	
Less: Merch. Inv., 12/31/XX			XXX	
Cost of Goods Sold				XXXX
Gross Profit				$XXXX
Operating Expenses:				
∼∼∼∼∼∼∼∼			$XXX	
∼∼∼∼∼∼∼∼			XXX	
∼∼∼∼∼∼∼∼			XXX	
Total Operating Expenses				XXX
Net Income from Operations				$ XXX
Other Income:				
Rental Income			$ XXX	
Storage Fees Income			XXX	
Total Other Income			$ XXX	$ XXX
Other Expenses:				
Interest Expense			XXX	XXX
Net Income:				$ XXX

(cont.)

(2) STATEMENT OF OWNER'S EQUITY

Beginning Capital		$XXX
Additional Investments		XXX
Total Investment		$XXX
Net Income*	$XXX	
Less: Withdrawals	XXX	
Increase (Decrease) in Capital		XXX
Ending Capital		$XXX

*From the income statement.

(3) BALANCE SHEET

Assets			
Current Assets:			
Cash		$ XXXX	
Acccounts Receivable		XXXX	
Merchandise Inventory		XXXX	
Prepaid Insurance		XXX	
Total Current Assets			$ XXXX
Capital Assets:			
Store Equipment	$XXXX		
Less: Accumulated Depreciation	XXX	$XXXX	
Office Equipment	$XXXX		
Less: Accumulated Depreciation	XXX	XXXX	
Total Capital Assets			XXXX
Total Assets			$XXXX

Liabilities			
Current Liabilities:			
Accounts Payable		$XXX	
Salaries Payable		XXX	
Income Taxes Payable		XXX	
Unearned Revenue		XX	
Mortgage Payable (current portion)		XX	
Total Current Liabilities			$ XXX
Long-Term Liabilities			
Mortgage Payable			$ XXX
Total Liabilities			$XXXX
Owner's Equity			
Capital*			XXXX
Total Liabilities and Owner's Equity			$XXXX

* From statement of owner's equity.

QUESTIONS, EXERCISES, AND PROBLEMS

Discussion Questions

1. Which columns of the worksheet aid in the preparation of the income statement?
2. Explain the components of cost of goods sold.
3. Explain how operating expenses can be broken down into different categories.
4. What is the difference between current assets and capital assets?
5. What is an operating cycle?
6. Why journalize adjusting entries after the formal reports have been prepared?
7. Explain the steps of closing for a merchandise company.
8. Temporary accounts could appear on a post-closing trial balance. Agree or disagree.
9. What is the purpose of using reversing entries? Are they mandatory? When should they be used?

Mini Exercises

(The forms you need are on page 13-7 of the *Study Guide and Working Papers.*)

Calculate Net Sales

1. From the following calculate net sales:

Purchases	$ 50
Gross Sales	100
Sales Returns and Allowances	5
Sales Discount	2
Operating Expenses	12

Calculate Cost of Goods Sold

2. Calculate cost of goods sold:

Freight-In	$ 5
Beginning Inventory	20
Ending Inventory	15
Net Purchases	50

Calculate Gross Profit and Net Income

3. Using Mini Exercises 1 and 2, calculate:
   - **a.** Gross profit
   - **b.** Net income or net loss

Classification of Accounts

4. Match the following categories to each account listed below:

1. Current assets
2. Capital assets
3. Current liabilities
4. Long-term liabilities

____ **a.** Merchandise Inventory
____ **b.** Unearned Rent
____ **c.** Prepaid Insurance
____ **d.** CPP Payable
____ **e.** Store Equipment
____ **f.** Mortgage Payable (Not Current)
____ **g.** Income Tax Payable
____ **h.** Accumulated Depreciation
____ **i.** UI Payable
____ **j.** Petty Cash

Reversing Entries

5. a. On January 1 prepare a reversing entry. On January 8, journalize the entry to record the paying of salary expense, $900.

b. What will be the balance in Salary Expense on January 8 (after posting)?

December 31

Salary Expense			Salaries Payable	
	900	1,200 closing		300 Adj.
Adj.	300			

Exercises

Preparing cost of goods sold section.

13-1. From the following accounts, prepare a cost of goods sold section in proper form: Freight-In, $300; Merchandise Inventory, 12/31/X1, $5,000; Purchases Discount, $900; Merchandise Inventory, 12/1/X1, $4,000; Purchases, $58,000; Purchases Returns and Allowances, $1,100.

Categorizing and classifying account titles.

13-2. Give the category, the classification, and the report(s) on which each of the following appears (for example: **Cash**—asset, current asset, balance sheet):

a. Salaries Payable
b. Accounts Payable
c. Mortgage Payable
d. Unearned Legal Fees
e. Income Tax Payable
f. Office Equipment
g. Land

Journalizing closing entries.

13-3. From the following partial worksheet, journalize the closing entries of December 31 for A. Slow Co.

A. SLOW CO.
WORKSHEET
FOR YEAR ENDED DECEMBER 31, 19XX

Account Titles	Income Statement Dr.	Income Statement Cr.	Balance Sheet Dr.	Balance Sheet Cr.
Cash			193 00	
Merch. Inventory			450 00	
Prepaid Advertising			561 00	
Prepaid Insurance			30 00	
Office Equipment			1080 00	
Accum. Dep., Office Equip.				210 00
Accounts Payable				258 00
A. Slow, Capital				966 00
Income Summary	362 00	450 00		
Sales		5520 00		
Sales Returns and Allowances	223 00			
Sales Discount	108 00			
Purchases	2628 00			
Purchases Returns and Allow.		34 00		
Purchases Discount		51 00		
Salaries Expense	1083 00			
Insurance Expense	696 00			
Utilities Expense	48 00			
Plumbing Expense	57 00			
Advertising Expense	15 00			
Dep. Expenses, Office Equip.	30 00			
Salaries Payable				75 00
	5250 00	6055 00	2314 00	1509 00
Net Income	805 00			805 00
	6055 00	6055 00	2314 00	2314 00

Preparing partially completed balance sheet.

13-4. From the worksheet in Exercise 3, prepare the assets section of a classified balance sheet.

Reversing entry.

13-5. On December 31, 19X1, $300 of salaries has been accrued. (Salaries before accrued amount totalled $26,000.) The next payroll to be paid will be on February 3, 19X2, for $6,000. Do the following:

a. Journalize and post the adjusting entry (use T accounts).

b. Journalize and post the reversing entry on January 1.

c. Journalize and post the payment of the payroll. Cash has a balance of $15,000 before the payment of payroll on February 3.

Group A Problems

Preparing an income statement from a worksheet.

13A-1. Prepare a formal income statement from the following partial worksheet for Porter's Pants Co.

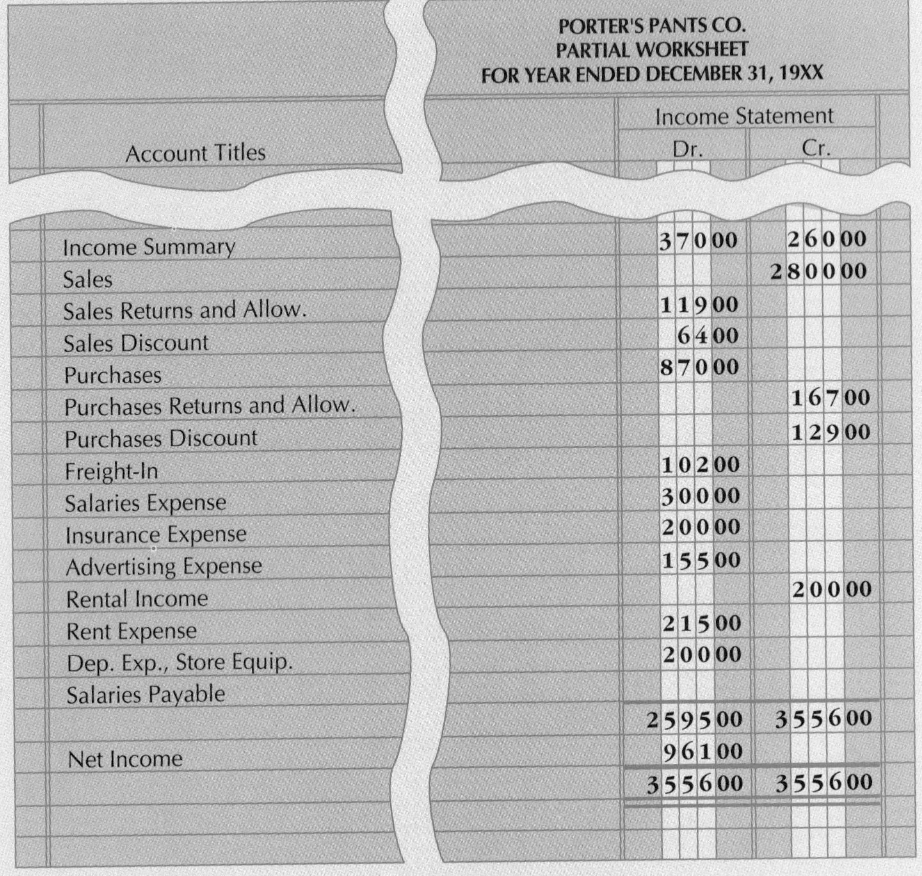

PORTER'S PANTS CO.
PARTIAL WORKSHEET
FOR YEAR ENDED DECEMBER 31, 19XX

Account Titles	Income Statement Dr.	Income Statement Cr.
Income Summary	370 00	260 00
Sales		2800 00
Sales Returns and Allow.	119 00	
Sales Discount	64 00	
Purchases	870 00	
Purchases Returns and Allow.		167 00
Purchases Discount		129 00
Freight-In	102 00	
Salaries Expense	300 00	
Insurance Expense	200 00	
Advertising Expense	155 00	
Rental Income		200 00
Rent Expense	215 00	
Dep. Exp., Store Equip.	200 00	
Salaries Payable		
	2595 00	3556 00
Net Income	961 00	
	3556 00	3556 00

13A-2. Prepare a statement of owner's equity and a classified balance sheet from the worksheet for James Company (pp. 13-11 and 13-12). *Note:* Of the Mortgage Payable, $200 is due within one year.

Completion of worksheet: preparation of financial reports; journalizing adjusting and closing entries.

13A-3. **a.** Complete the worksheet for Jay's Supplies (p. 13-13).

b. Prepare an income statement, a statement of owner's equity, and a classified balance sheet. *Note:* The amount of the mortgage due the first year is $800.

c. Journalize the adjusting and closing entries.

Comprehensive problem: Worksheet preparation: preparing financial reports; journalizing and posting adjusting and closing entries; preparing a post-closing trial balance; journalizing reversing entry

13A-4. Using the ledger balances and additional data shown on the next two pages, do the following for Callahan Lumber for the year ended December 31, 19XX:

1. Prepare the worksheet.
2. Prepare the income statement, statement of owner's equity, and balance sheet.
3. Journalize and post adjusting and closing entries. (Be sure to put beginning balances in the ledger first.)
4. Prepare a post-closing trial balance.
5. Journalize the reversing entry for wages.

Preparing statement of owner's equity and a classified balance sheet from a worksheet.

JAMES COMPANY
WORKSHEET
FOR YEAR ENDED DECEMBER 31, 19XX

Account Titles	Balance Sheet Dr.	Balance Sheet Cr.
Cash	850000	
Petty Cash	9000	
Accounts Receivable	135000	
Merchandise Inv.	400000	
Supplies	32500	
Prepaid Insurance	50000	
Store Equipment	280000	
Accum. Dep., Store Eq.		70000
Automobile	170000	
Accum. Dep., Auto		22500
Accounts Payable		280000
Taxes Payable		240000
Unearned Rent		850000
Mortgage Payable		45000
H. James, Capital		740000
H. James, Withdr.	10000	
Salaries Payable		60000
	1936500	2307500
Net Loss	371000	
	2307500	2307500

Additional Data (for Problem 13A-4)

Acct. No.		
110	Cash	$1 ,680
111	Accounts Receivable	960
112	Merchandise Inventory	4,550
113	Lumber Supplies	269
114	Prepaid Insurance	218
121	Lumber Equipment	3,000
122	Accum. Dep., Lumber Equipment	490
220	Accounts Payable	1,160
221	Wages Payable	
330	J. Callahan, Capital	7,352
331	J. Callahan, Withdrawals	3,000
332	Income Summary	—
440	Sales	22,800
441	Sales Returns and Allowances	200
550	Purchases	14,800
551	Purchases Discount	285
552	Purchases Returns and Allowances	300
660	Wages Expense	2,480
661	Advertising Expense	400
662	Rent Expense	830
663	Dep. Expense, Lumber Equipment	
664	Lumber Supplies Expense	
665	Insurance Expense	

JAY'S SUPPLIES
WORKSHEET
FOR YEAR ENDED DECEMBER 31, 19XX

Account Titles	Trial Balance Dr.	Trial Balance Cr.	Adjustments Dr.	Adjustments Cr.
Cash	200000			
Accounts Receivable	300000			
Merch. Inv., 1/1/XX	1100000		(B) 1040000	1100000 (A)
Prepaid Insurance	188000			50000 (E)
Equipment	340000			
Accum. Dep., Equipment		108000		40000 (D)
Accounts Payable		508000		
Unearned Training Fees		212000	(C) 32000	
Mortgage Payable		120000		
P. Jay, Capital		1056000		
P. Jay, Withdrawals	428000			
Income Summary			(A) 1100000	1040000 (B)
Sales		9580000		
Sales Returns and Allow.	320000			
Sales Discount	260000			
Purchases	6360000			
Purchases Returns and Allow.		1360000		
Purchases Discount		320000		
Freight-In	268000			
Advertising Expense	1140000			
Rent Expense	1000000			
Salaries Expense	1360000			
	13264000	13264000		
Training Fees Earned				32000 (C)
Dep. Exp., Equipment			(D) 40000	
Insurance Expense			(E) 50000	
			2262000	2262000

Additional Data (for Problem 13A-4)

a. and **b.** Merchandise inventory, December 31	$5,420
c. Lumber supplies on hand, December 31	110
d. Insurance expired	120
e. Depreciation for the year	300
f. Accrued wages on December 31	125

Group B Problems

Preparing an income statement from a worksheet.

13B-1. From the partial worksheet shown below, prepare a formal income statement.

PORTER'S PANTS CO.
PARTIAL WORKSHEET
FOR YEAR ENDED DECEMBER 31, 19XX

Account Titles	Income Statement Dr.	Income Statement Cr.
Income Summary	300 00	295 00
Sales		4100 00
Sales Ret. and Allow.	145 00	
Sales Disc.	175 00	
Purchases	2000 00	
Purchases Ret. and Allow.		175 00
Purchases Disc.		85 00
Freight-In	50 00	
Salaries Expense	360 00	
Insurance Expense	275 00	
Advertising Expense	165 00	
Rental Income		230 00
Rent Expense	225 00	
Dep. Exp., Store Equip.	115 00	
Salaries Payable		
	3810 00	4885 00
Net Income	1075 00	
	4885 00	4885 00

Preparing a statement of owner's equity and a classified balance sheet from a worksheet.

13B-2. From the worksheet shown on page 528, complete

a. Statement of owner's equity

b. Classified balance sheet

Note: Of the Mortgage Payable, $3,000 is due within one year.

Completing the worksheet; preparing financial reports; journalizing adjusting and closing entries.

13B-3. From the partial worksheet shown on page 529, your task is to

1. Complete the worksheet.
2. Prepare the income statement, statement of owner's equity, and classified balance sheet. The amount of the mortgage due the first year is $800.
3. Journalize the adjusting and closing entries.

JAMES COMPANY
WORKSHEET
FOR YEAR ENDED DECEMBER 31, 19XX

Account Titles	Balance Sheet Dr.	Balance Sheet Cr.
Cash	250000	
Petty Cash	5000	
Accts. Rec.	130000	
Merch. Inv.	425000	
Supplies	34400	
Prepaid Ins.	60000	
Store Equip.	1800000	
Accum. Dep., Store Eq.		75000
Automobile	250000	
Accum. Dep., Auto		50000
Accts. Pay.		345000
Taxes Pay.		210000
Unearned Rent		1100000
Mortgage Pay.		800000
H. James, Capital		1050000
H. James, Withdr.	400000	
Salaries Payable		10000
	3354400	3640000
Net Loss	285600	
	3640000	3640000

Comprehensive problem: Worksheet preparation; preparing financial reports, journalizing and posting adjusting and closing entries; preparing a post-closing trial balance; journalizing reversing entry.

13B-4. From the following ledger balances and additional data, do the following:

1. Prepare the worksheet.
2. Prepare the income statement, statement of owner's equity, and balance sheet.
3. Journalize and post adjusting and closing entries. (Be sure to put beginning balances in the ledger first.)
4. Prepare a post-closing trial balance.
5. Journalize the reversing entry for wages.

Acct. No.		
110	Cash	$1,140
111	Accounts Receivable	1,270
112	Merchandise Inventory	5,600
113	Lumber Supplies	260
114	Prepaid Insurance	117
121	Lumber Equipment	2,600
122	Accum. Dep., Lumber Equipment	340
220	Accounts Payable	1,330
221	Wages Payable	
330	J. Callahan, Capital	7,562
331	J. Callahan, Withdrawals	3,500
332	Income Summary	—
440	Sales	23,000
441	Sales Returns and Allowances	400
550	Purchases	14,700
551	Purchases Discount	440

JAY'S SUPPLIES
WORKSHEET
FOR YEAR ENDED DECEMBER 31, 19XX

Account Titles	Trial Balance Dr.	Trial Balance Cr.	Adjustments Dr.	Adjustments Cr.
Cash	3000 00			
Accounts Receivable	3000 00			
Merch. Inventory, 1/1/XX	11700 00		(B) 8000 00	11700 00 (A)
Prepaid Insurance	1000 00			350 00 (E)
Equipment	5000 00			
Accum. Dep., Equipment		1900 00		500 00 (D)
Accounts Payable		2100 00		
Unearned Training Fees		1450 00	(C) 400 00	
Mortgage Payable		2400 00		
P. Jay, Capital		27750 00		
P. Jay, Withdrawals	4000 00			
Income Summary			(A) 11700 00	8000 00 (B)
Sales		100800 00		
Sales Returns and Allow.	4100 00			
Sales Discount	2800 00			
Purchases	70000 00			
Purchases Returns and Allow.		2000 00		
Purchases Discount		1400 00		
Freight-In	2700 00			
Advertising Expense	8000 00			
Rent Expense	8500 00			
Salaries Expense	16000 00			
	139800 00	139800 00		
Training Fees Earned				400 00 (C)
Dep. Exp., Equipment			(D) 500 00	
Insurance Expense			(E) 350 00	
			20950 00	20950 00

552	Purchases Returns and Allowances	545
660	Wages Expense	2,390
661	Advertising Expense	400
662	Rent Expense	840
663	Dep. Exp., Lumber Equipment	
664	Lumber Supplies Expense	
665	Insurance Expense	

Additional Data

a. and **b.** Merchandise inventory, December 31	$4,700
c. Lumber supplies on hand, December 31	80
d. Insurance expired	70
e. Depreciation for the year	460
f. Accrued wages on December 31	165

Group C Problems

13C-1. From the partial worksheet shown below, prepare a formal income statement for Kate's Pie and Kite Shop.

KATE'S PIE AND KITE SHOP PARTIAL WORKSHEET FOR THE YEAR ENDED SEPTEMBER 30, 19XX		
	Income Statement	
Account Titles	Dr.	Cr.
Income Summary	425782	547726
Sales		5356825
Sales Returns and Allowances	83450	
Sales Discount	34475	
Purchases	2145834	
Purchases Returns and Allowances		55830
Purchases Discount		23876
Freight-In	47158	
Advertising Expense	135250	
Cleaning Expense	240000	
Depreciation Expense, Equipment	87500	
Insurance Expenses	36875	
Rental Income		180000
Rent Expense	720000	
Salaries Expense	1145860	
Utilities Expense	254260	
Salaries Expense		
	5356444	6164257
Net Income	807813	
	6164257	6164257

13C-2. From the partial worksheet of Castell Ceramics Co. shown on p. 523, complete

a. Statement of owner's equity

b. Classified balance sheet

Note: Of the Mortgage Payable, $1,800 is due within one year.

13C-3. From the partial worksheet of Mikolaski Modern Design Company, shown on page 524, your task is to

1. Complete the worksheet.
2. Prepare the income statement, statement of owner's equity, and classified balance sheet. The amount of the mortgage due the first year is $3,600.
3. Journalize the adjusting and closing entries.

CASTELL CERAMICS CO.
PARTIAL WORKSHEET
FOR YEAR ENDED AUGUST 31, 19XX

Account Titles	Balance Sheet	
	Dr.	Cr.
Petty Cash	75 00	
Cash	11538 62	
Accounts Receivable	18976 30	
Merchandise Inventory	22766 28	
Supplies on Hand	1268 75	
Prepaid Insurance	875 40	
Prepaid GST	2137 64	
Cutting Equipment	18760 00	
Accum. Dep., Cutting Equip.		7250 00
Delivery Van	21875 00	
Accum. Dep., Delivery Van		4780 00
Accounts Payable		27648 36
GST Collected		2874 62
Unearned Rent		1750 00
Chattel Mortgage Payable, Van		15742 37
B. Castell, Capital		42675 98
B. Castell, Withdrawals	14670 00	
Salaries Payable		860 00
Net Income		9361 66
	112942 99	112942 99

13C-4. From the following ledger balances of Brennan Sales Co. as of December 31, 19XX, and the additional data, do the following:

1. Prepare the worksheet.
2. Prepare the income statement, statement of owner's equity, and balance sheet.
3. Journalize and post adjusting and closing entries. (Be sure to put beginning balances in the ledger first.)
4. Prepare a post-closing trial balance.
5. Journalize the reversing entry for wages.

Acct. No.		
1100	Cash	$ 720
1110	Accounts Receivable	1,620
1120	Merchandise Inventory	5,910
1130	Supplies on Hand	430
1140	Prepaid Insurance	238
1150	Prepaid GST	647
1210	Equipment	8,500
1220	Accum. Dep., Equipment	1,640
2200	Accounts Payable	1,660
2210	Wages Payable	
2220	GST Collected	897

MIKOLASKI MODERN DESIGN COMPANY
WORKSHEET
FOR YEAR ENDED NOVEMBER 30, 19XX

Account Titles	Trial Balance Dr.	Trial Balance Cr.	Adjustments Dr.	Adjustments Cr.
Cash in Bank	346578			
Petty Cash	5000			
Accounts Receivable	1157520			
Merch. Inventory, Dec. 1, 19XX	1647922		(B)2567244	1647922 (A)
Prepaid Insurance	76585			25775 (E)
Prepaid GST	165345			
Equipment	2157500			
Accum. Depreciation, Equipment		1476240		135760 (D)
Building	2870000			
Accum. Depreciation, Building		2165370		64782 (D)
Accounts Payable		840000		
Mortgage Payable		1144652		
Unearned Rent		240000	(C)80000	
GST Collected		216785		
L. Mikolaski, Capital		3242022		
L. Mikolaski, Withdrawals	1645000			
Income Summary			(A)1647922	2567244 (B)
Sales		7732756		
Sales Discounts and Returns	35892			
Purchases	4264904			
Purchases Returns and Allowances		45572		
Purchases Discount		57622		
Freight-In	63288			
Advertising Expense	124500			
Cleaning Expense	260560			
Repair Expense	87620			
Salaries Expense	2157560			
Utilities Expense	95245			
	17161019	17161019		
Rental Income Earned				80000 (C)
Dep. Exp., on Equip. and Building			(D)200542	
Insurance Expense			(E) 25775	
			4521483	4521483

3300	W. Brennan, Capital	12,012
3310	W. Brennan, Withdrawals	4,700
3320	Income Summary	—
4400	Sales	31,000
4410	Sales Returns and Allowances	630
5500	Purchases	18,400
5510	Purchases Discount	730
5520	Purchases Returns and Allowances	276
6600	Wages Expense	4,530
6610	Advertising Expense	690
6620	Rent Expense	1,200
6630	Dep. Exp., Equipment	
6640	Supplies Expense	
6650	Insurance Expense	

Additional Data

a. and **b.**	Merchandise inventory, December 31	$4,875
c.	Supplies on hand, December 31	190
d.	Insurance expired	68
e.	Depreciation for the year	750
f.	Accrued wages on December 31	395
g.	Advertising bill received — due next year (add Prepaid GST of $14)	200

REAL WORLD APPLICATIONS

13R-1.

Chan Company recently had most of its records destroyed in a fire. The information for 19XX was discovered by the bookkeeper.

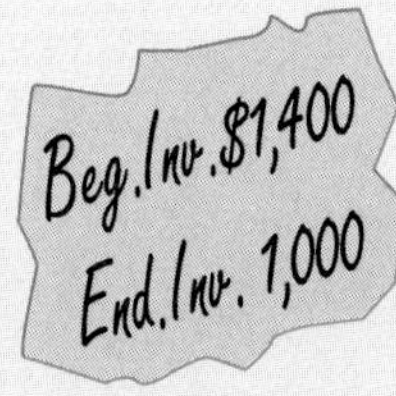

CHAN CORP.
GENERAL JOURNAL

Page 2

19XX Date		Description	PR	Dr.	Cr.
Dec.	31	Income Summary	312	3630 00	
		Sales Returns and Allowances	420		140 00
		Sales Discount	430		30 00
		Purchases	500		2400 00
		Delivery Expense	600		90 00
		Salaries Expense	610		840 00
		Rent Expense	620		30 00
		Office Supplies Expense	630		50 00
		Advertising Expense	640		10 00
		Dep. Exp., Store Equipment	650		40 00
	31	Sales	410	5542 00	
		Purchases Discount	510	120 00	
		Purchases Returns and Allowances	520	100 00	
		Income Summary	312		5762 00
	31	Income Summary	312	1732 00	
		J. Chan, Capital	310		1732 00

Please assist the bookkeeper in reconstructing an income statement for 19XX.

13R-2.

Hope Lang, a junior accountant, has the December 31, 19XX, trial balance of Gregot Company sitting on her desk. Attached is a memo from her supervisor requesting that a classified balance sheet be prepared. Hope gathers the following data:

1. A physical inventory at December 31 showed $80,000 on hand.
2. Office supplies on hand was $600.
3. Insurance unexpired was $750.
4. Depreciation (straight-line) is based on a 25-year life.

Using the following trial balance of Gregot Co., assist Hope with this project. *Hint:* Ending figure for capital is $115,850.

GREGOT COMPANY TRIAL BALANCE DECEMBER 31, 19XX		
	Dr.	Cr.
Cash	11000 00	
Accounts Receivable	38000 00	
Inventory, Jan. 1	80000 00	
Prepaid Insurance	2000 00	
Office Supplies	1000 00	
Land	17500 00	
Building	50000 00	
Accumulated Depreciation, Building		10000 00
Notes Payable		40000 00
Accounts Payable		30000 00
G. Gregot, Capital		98400 00
G. Gregot, Withdrawals	13000 00	
Income Summary	—	
Retail Sales		329000 00
Sales Returns and Allowances	21000 00	—
Sales Discount	8000 00	
Purchases	215500 00	
Purchases Returns and Allowances		11600 00
Purchases Discount		4000 00
Transportation-In	5000 00	
Advertising Expense	2500 00	
Wage Expense	55000 00	
Utilities Expense	3500 00	
	523000 00	523000 00

make the call

Critical Thinking/Ethical Case

13R-3.

Janet Flynn, owner of Reel Company, plans to apply for a bank loan at Canadian National Bank. Since the company has a lot of debt on its balance sheet, Janet does not plan to show the loan officer the balance sheet. She plans only to bring the income statement. Do you feel this is a sound financial move by Janet? You make the call. Write down your specific recommendations to Janet.

ACCOUNTING RECALL

A CUMULATIVE APPROACH

THIS EXAM REVIEWS CHAPTERS 1 THROUGH 13

Your *Study Guide and Working Papers* has forms to complete this exam, as well as worked-out solutions. The page references next to each question identify what page to turn back to if you answer the question incorrectly.

PART I Vocabulary Review

Match the terms to the appropriate definition or phrase.

Page Ref.	Term		Definition
(506)	1. Current asset	A.	General expenses
(506)	2. Current liabilities	B.	Contra-asset
(379)	3. Purchases discount	C.	Converted into cash or used within one year
(174)	4. Income summary	D.	Contra-cost-of-goods-sold
(504)	5. Administrative expenses	E.	Land
(133)	6. Accumulated depreciation	F.	Mortgage payable
(504)	7. Net sales	G.	Optional bookkeeping
(506)	8. Capital assets	H.	A temporary account used only at period-end.
(506)	9. Long-term liability	I.	Sales–SRA–SD
(515)	10. Reversing entries	J.	Due within one year

PART II True or False (Accounting Theory)

(502)11. There are debit and credit columns on the formal reports.

(515)12. Reversing entries are the same as adjusting entries.

(517)13. All adjustments should be reversed.

(506)14. Equipment is a current asset.

(504)15. Administrative expenses are directly incurred in the selling of goods.

PART III Applications Problem

From the following worksheet of Bill's Antique Shop for year ended December 31, 19XX, complete the financial reports and journalize the adjusting and closing entries.

BILL'S ANTIQUE SHOP
WORKSHEET

Account Titles	Trial Balance Dr.	Trial Balance Cr.	Adjustments Dr.	Adjustments Cr.	Adjusted Trial Balance Dr.	Adjusted Trial Balance Cr.	Income Statement Dr.	Income Statement Cr.	Balance Sheet Dr.	Balance Sheet Cr.
Cash	4100 00				4100 00				4100 00	
Accounts Receivable	23800 00				23800 00				23800 00	
Merchandise Inventory	20000 00		(B) 24000 00	(A) 20000 00	24000 00				24000 00	
Prepaid Insurance	600 00			(C) 200 00	400 00				400 00	
Equipment	18000 00				18000 00				18000 00	
Accum. Dep., Equipment		1000 00		(D) 1000 00		2000 00				2000 00
Unearned Rent		500 00	(F) 100 00			400 00				400 00
Accounts Payable		11000 00				11000 00				11000 00
B. J. Jensen, Capital		50000 00				50000 00				50000 00
B. J. Jensen, Withdrawals	15000 00				15000 00				15000 00	
Income Summary			(A) 20000 00	(G) 24000 00	20000 00	24000 00	20000 00	24000 00		
Sales		279000 00				279000 00		279000 00		
Sales Returns and Allowances	3000 00				3000 00		3000 00			
Sales Discount	4500 00				4500 00		4500 00			
Purchases	180000 00				180000 00		180000 00			
Purchases Returns and Allowances		1500 00				1500 00		1500 00		
Purchases Discount		3500 00				3500 00		3500 00		
Freight-In	2500 00				2500 00		2500 00			
Salaries Expense	45000 00		(E) 500 00		45500 00		45500 00			
Advertising Expense	10000 00				10000 00		10000 00			
Rent Expense	12000 00				12000 00		12000 00			
Utility Expense	8000 00				8000 00		8000 00			
	346500 00	346500 00								
Insurance Expense			(C) 200 00		200 00		200 00			
Depreciation Expense			(D) 1000 00		1000 00		1000 00			
Salaries Payable				(E) 500 00		500 00				500 00
Rent Earned				(F) 100 00		100 00		100 00		
			45800 00	45800 00	372000 00	372000 00	286700 00	308100 00	85300 00	63900 00
Net Income							21400 00			21400 00
							308100 00	308100 00	85300 00	85300 00

MINI PRACTICE SET

The Corner Dress Shop

This practice set will help you review all the key concepts of the accounting cycle for a merchandise company along with the integration of payroll.

Since you are the bookkeeper of The Corner Dress Shop, we have gathered the following information for you. It will be your task to complete the accounting cycle for March.

The Corner Dress Shop
Post-Closing Trial Balance
February 28, 19XX

Cash	1,774.90	
Petty Cash	50.00	
Accounts Receivable	3,011.00	
Merchandise Inventory	5,600.00	
Supplies on Hand	624.30	
Prepaid Rent	1,800.00	
GST Prepaid	703.42	
Delivery Truck	21,500.00	
Accumulated Depreciation, Truck		8,950.00
Accounts Payable		2,354.00
GST Collected		1,149.27
Income Tax Payable		2047.05
CPP Payable		454.72
UI Payable		562.87
Medical Plan Premiums Payable		112.00
Unearned Rent		800.00
B. Loeb, Capital		18,633.71
Totals	35,063.62	35,063.62

Balances in subsidiary ledgers as of March 1:

*Accounts Receivable **		*Accounts Payable**	
Bing Co.	$2,241.00	Blew Co.	$1,926.00
Gray Co.	—	Jones Co.	428.00
Ronald Co.	770.00	Moe's Garage	—
		Morris Co.	—

*(Includes 7 percent GST.)

Payroll is paid monthly and employee claim codes are unchanged.

The payroll register for January and February is provided. In March, salaries are as follows (all deductions the same unless indicated):

Mel Case	$1,860	New income tax = $242.45. CPP and UI—use same approach as in Chapter 7.
Jane Holl	2,900	
Jackie Moore	4,300	

Required

1. Set up a general ledger, accounts receivable ledger and accounts payable ledger, auxiliary petty cash record, and payroll register. (Be sure to update ledger accounts on the basis of given information in the post-closing trial balance for February 28 before beginning.)
2. Journalize all transactions during March.
3. Prepare the payroll register for March.
4. Update the accounts payable and accounts receivable subsidiary ledgers for March.
5. Post to the general ledger.
6. Prepare a trial balance on a worksheet and complete the worksheet as of March 31, 19XX.
7. Prepare an income statement, statement of owner's equity, and classified balance sheet.
8. Journalize the adjusting and closing entries.
9. Post the adjusting and closing entries to the ledger.
10. Prepare a post-closing trial balance.

The chart of accounts for The Corner Dress Shop is as follows:

Chart of Accounts

Assets
110 Cash
111 Accounts Receivable
112 Petty Cash
114 Merchandise Inventory
116 Prepaid Rent
117 Supplies on Hand
118 GST Prepaid
120 Delivery Truck
121 Accumulated Depreciation, Truck

Liabilities
210 Accounts Payable
212 Salaries Payable
214 Income Tax Payable
216 CPP Payable
218 UI Payable
220 Medical Plan Premium Payable
222 Unearned Rent
228 GST Collected

Owner's Equity
310 B. Loeb, Capital
320 B. Loeb, Withdrawals
330 Income Summary

Revenue
410 Sales
412 Sales Returns and Allowances
414 Sales Discount
416 Rental Income

Cost of Goods Sold
510 Purchases
512 Purchases Returns and Allowances
514 Purchases Discount

Expenses
610 Sales Salaries Expense
611 Office Salaries Expense
612 Payroll Tax Expense
614 Cleaning Expense
616 Depreciation Expense, Truck
618 Rent Expense
620 Postage Expense
622 Supplies Expense
624 Delivery Expense
626 Miscellaneous Expense

PAYROLL REGISTER—JANUARY

Employee	Net Claim Code	Monthly Salary	Cumulative CPP	Income Tax	Deductions				Net Pay	Chq. No.	Expense Accounts	
					CPP	UI	Health	Charitable			Office	Sales
Mel Case	4	1800 00	—	224 20	42 23	53 10	28 00	20 00	1432 47		1800 00	
Jane Holl	1	2900 00	—	649 55	73 03	85 55	42 00	30 00	2019 87			2900 00
Jackie Moore	3	4300 00	—	1173 30	112 10	95 88	42 00	40 00	2836 72			4300 00
Totals		9000 00		2047 05	227 36	234 53	112 00	90 00	6289 06		1800 00	7200 00

PAYROLL REGISTER—FEBRUARY

Employee	Net Claim Code	Monthly Salary	Cumulative CPP	Income Tax	Deductions				Net Pay	Chq. No.	Expense Accounts	
					CPP	UI	Health	Charitable			Office	Sales
Mel Case	4	1800 00	42 23	224 20	42 23	53 10	28 00	20 00	1432 47		1800 00	
Jane Holl	1	2900 00	73 03	649 55	73 03	85 55	42 00	30 00	2019 87			2900 00
Jackie Moore	3	4300 00	112 10	1173 30	112 10	95 88	42 00	40 00	2836 72			4300 00
Totals		9000 00		2047 05	227 36	234 53	112 00	90 00	6289 06		1800 00	7200 00

Transactions

19XX

March 1 Received amount due from Bing, no discount.

2 Purchased merchandise from Morris Company on account, $10,000, plus GST, terms 2/10, n/30.

2 Paid $6 from the petty cash fund for donuts, voucher no. 18 (consider this miscellaneous expense — no GST).

3 Sold merchandise to Ronald Company on account, $7,000, plus GST, invoice no. 51, terms 2/10, n/30.

5 Paid $12.84 from the petty cash fund for postage, voucher no. 19.

6 Sold merchandise to Ronald Company on account, $5,000, plus GST, invoice no. 52, terms 2/10, n/30.

8 Paid $10 from the petty cash fund for first aid emergency, voucher no. 20 (no GST).

9 Purchased merchandise from Morris Company on account, $5,000, plus GST, terms 2/10, n/30.

9 Received amount due from Ronald Co. at February 28 less 2 percent discount.

9 Paid $5 for delivery expense (no GST) from petty cash fund, voucher no. 21.

9 Sold more merchandise to Ronald Company on account, $3,000, plus GST, invoice no. 53, terms 2/10, n/30.

9 Paid cleaning service, $300, plus GST, cheque no. 110.

10 Ronald Company returned merchandise costing $1,000 from invoice no. 52; The Corner Dress Shop issued credit memo No. 10 to Ronald Company for $1,000, plus GST.

11 Purchased merchandise from Jones Company on account, $10,000, plus GST, terms 1/15, n/60.

12 Paid Morris Company invoice dated March 2, cheque no. 111.

13 Sold merchandise for cash, $700, plus GST.

14 Returned merchandise to Jones Company in amount of $2,000; The Corner Dress Shop issued debit memo no. 4 to Jones Company, $2,000, plus GST.

14 Paid $5 from the petty cash fund for delivery expense, voucher no. 22 (no GST).

15 Paid amount due to Receiver General for Canada for February withholdings - cheque no. 112.

15 Sold merchandise for cash, $29,000, plus GST.

15 B. Loeb withdrew $1,000 for her personal account, cheque no. 113.

15 Paid net amount of GST due $445.85, cheque no. 114.

16 Paid amount due to Blew Co. at the end of February, cheque no. 115.

16 Received payment from Ronald Company for invoice no. 52, less discount and less returned merchandise.

16 Ronald Company paid invoice no. 51, $7,490.

16 Sold merchandise to Bing Company on account, $3,200, plus GST, invoice no. 54. terms 2/10, n/30.

21 Purchased another delivery truck on account from Moe's Garage, $17,200, plus GST.

22 Sold merchandise to Ronald Company on account, $4,000, plus GST, invoice no. 55, terms 2/10, n/30.

23 Paid Jones Company the balance owed, cheque no. 116.

24 Sold merchandise to Bing Company, $2,000, plus GST, invoice no. 56, terms 1/10, n/30.

25 Purchased merchandise for cash, $1,000, plus GST, cheque no. 117.

27 Purchased merchandise from Blew Company on account, $6,000, plus GST, terms 2/10, n/30.
27 Paid amount due to Provincial Health Care with respect to February payroll, cheque no. 118.
28 Ronald Company paid invoice no. 55 dated March 22, less discount.
28 Bing Company paid invoice no. 54 dated March 16.
29 Purchased merchandise from Morris Company on account, $9,000, plus GST, terms 2/10, n/30.
30 Sold merchandise to Gray Company on account, $10,000, plus GST, invoice no. 57, terms 2/10, n/30.
30 Issued cheque no. 119 to replenish the petty cash fund.
30 Recorded March payroll in payroll register.
30 Journalized payroll entry (to be paid on 31st).
30 Journalized employer's payroll tax expense.
31 Paid payroll cheques nos. 120, 121, and 122.
31 Remitted total March charitable deductions to World Preventable Disease Foundation, cheque no. 123.

Additional Data

a. and **b.** Ending merchandise inventory, $4,280.

c. During March, rent expired, $600.

d. Trucks depreciated, $480.

e. Rental income earned, $300 (one month's rent from subletting).

COMPUTER WORKSHOP

Computerized Accounting Application for The Corner Dress Shop Mini Practice Set (Chapter 13)

Inventory Adjusting Entries

Before starting on this assignment, read and complete the tasks discussed in Parts A, B, and F of Appendix B at the end of this book and complete the Computerized Accounting Application assignments for Chapter 3, Chapter 4, Valdez Realty Mini Practice Set (Chapter 5), Pete's Market Mini Practice Set (Chapter 8), and Chapter 10.

This practice set will help you review all the key concepts of a merchandise company along with the integration of payroll.

Since you are the bookkeeper of The Corner Dress Shop, we have gathered the following information for you. It will be your task to complete the accounting cycle for March.

The Corner Dress Shop: Trial Balance As at March 1, 1999

	Debits	Credits
Cash	1,774.90	—
Petty Cash	50.00	—
Accounts Receivable	3,011.00	—
Merchandise Inventory	5,600.00	—
Supplies on Hand	624.30	—
Prepaid Rent	1,800.00	—
GST Prepaid	703.42	—
Delivery Truck	21,500.00	—
Accumulated Depreciation, Truck	—	8,950.00
Accounts Payable	—	2,354.00
GST Collected	—	1,149.27
Income Tax Payable	—	2,047.05
CPP Payable	—	454.72
UI Payable	—	562.87
Medical Plan Premiums Payable	—	112.00
Unearned Rent	—	800.00
B. Loeb, Capital	—	18,633.71
Totals	35,063.62	35,063.62

The Corner Dress Shop: Customer Aged Detail As at March 1, 1999

			Total	Current	31 to 60	61 to 90	91 +
Bing Co.							
12	12/31/98	Invoice	2,241	—	2,241	—	—
Ronald Co.							
310	01/15/99	Invoice	770	—	770		

The Corner Dress Shop: Vendor Aged Detail As at March 1, 1999

			Total	Current	31 to 60	61 to 90	91 +
Blew Co.							
510	12/31/98	Invoice	1,926	—	1,926	—	—
Jones Co.							
914	01/24/99	Invoice	428	—	428	—	—

The Corner Dress Shop, owned by Betty Loeb, is located at 1 Milgate Road, Whitby, ON L1N 3H8. Her employer identification number is ABC123456. The data set for CA-Simply Accounting for Windows packaged with this text uses the tax laws in effect on January 1, 1996. Federal income tax, CPP and UI are all calculated automatically by the program.

Open the Company Data Files

1. Start Windows; insert your Student Data Files disk into disk drive A or B; then double-click on the CA-Simply Accounting icon. The CA-Simply Accounting-Open File dialogue box will appear.
2. Enter one of the following paths into the **Open file name** text box:
   - A:\DRESS.ASC (if you are storing your student data files on the disk in drive A).
   - B:\DRESS.ASC (if you are storing your student data files on the disk in drive B).
3. Click on the **Open** button; enter "3/31/99" into the **Using date for this session** text box; then click on the **OK** button. Click on the **OK** button in response to the message " The date entered is more than one week past your previous **Using** date of 3/1/99." The Company Window for Dress will appear.

Add Your Name to the Company Name

4. Click on the Company Window Setup menu; then click on Company Information. The Company Information dialogue box will appear. Insert your name in place of the text "Your Name" in the **Name** text box. Click on the **OK** button to return to the Company Window.

Record March Transactions

5. Record the following transactions* using the general, purchases, payments, sales, receipts, and payroll journals:

Transactions

19XX

March 1 Received amount due from Bing, no discount.

2 Purchased merchandise from Morris Company on account, $10,000, plus GST, terms 2/10, n/30.

2 Paid $6 from petty cash fund for donuts, voucher no. 18 (consider this miscellaneous expense—no GST).

3 Sold merchandise to Ronald Company on account, $7,000, plus GST, invoice no. 51, terms 2/10, n/30.

5 Paid $12.84 (includes $0.84 GST) from the petty cash fund for postage, voucher no. 19.

6 Sold merchandise to Ronald Company on account, $5,000, plus GST, invoice no. 52, terms 2/10, n/30.

8 Paid $10 from the petty cash fund for first aid emergency, voucher no. 20 (no GST).

9 Purchased merchandise from Morris Company on account, $5,000, plus GST, terms 2/10, n/30.

9 Received amount due from Ronald Co. at February 28 less 2 percent discount.

9 Paid $5 for delivery expense (no GST) from petty cash fund, voucher no. 21.

9 Sold more merchandise to Ronald Company on account, $3,000, plus GST, invoice no. 53, terms 2/10, n/30.

9 Paid cleaning service, $300, plus GST, cheque no. 110.

10 Ronald Company returned merchandise costing $1,000 from invoice no. 52; The Corner Dress Shop issued credit memo no. 10 to Ronald Company for $1,000, plus GST.

---

*You will probably find it helpful to print a Chart of Accounts to aid you in entering transactions.

11 Purchased merchandise from Jones Company on account, $10,000, plus GST, terms 1/15, n/60.
12 Paid Morris Company invoice dated March 2, cheque no. 111.
13 Sold merchandise for cash, $700, plus GST.
14 Returned merchandise to Jones Company in amount of $2,000; The Corner Dress Shop issued debit memo no. 4 to Jones Company, $2,000, plus GST.
14 Paid $5 from the petty cash fund for delivery expense, voucher no. 22 (no GST).
15 Paid amount due to Receiver General for Canada for February withholdings—cheque no. 112.
15 Sold merchandise for cash, $29,000, plus GST.
15 B. Loeb withdrew $1,000 for her personal account, cheque no. 113.
15 Paid net amount of GST due at February 28 $484.18, cheque no. 114.
16 Paid amount due to Blew Co. at the end of February, cheque no. 115.
16 Received payment from Ronald Company for invoice no. 52, less discount and less returned merchandise.
16 Ronald Company paid invoice no. 51, $7,490.
16 Sold merchandise to Bing Company on account, $3,200, plus GST, invoice no. 54, terms 2/10, n/30.
21 Purchased another delivery truck on account from Moe's Garage, $17,200, plus GST.
22 Sold merchandise to Ronald Company on account, $4,000, plus GST, invoice no. 55, terms 2/10, n/30.
23 Paid Jones Company the balance owed, cheque no. 116.
24 Sold merchandise to Bing Company, $2,000, plus GST, invoice no. 56, terms 1/10, n/30.
25 Purchased merchandise for cash, $1,000, plus GST, cheque no. 117.
27 Purchased merchandise from Blew Company on account, $6,000, plus GST, terms 2/10, n/30.
27 Paid amount due to Provincial Health Care with respect to February payroll, cheque no. 118.
28 Ronald Company paid invoice no. 55 dated March 22, less discount.
28 Bing Company paid invoice no. 54 dated March 16.
29 Purchased merchandise from Morris Company on account, $9,000, plus GST, terms 2/10, n/30.
30 Sold merchandise to Gray Company on account, $10,000, plus GST, invoice no. 57, terms 2/10, n/30.
30 Issued cheque no. 119 to replenish the petty cash fund.
30 Recorded March payroll in payroll register.
30 Journalized payroll entry (to be paid on 31st).
30 Journalized employer's payroll tax expense.
31 Paid payroll cheques nos. 120, 121, and 122.
31 Remitted total March charitable deducations to World Preventable Disease Foundation, cheque no. 123.

Additional Data

a. and b. Ending merchandise inventory, $4,280.
c. During March, rent expired, $600.
d. Trucks depreciated, $480.
e. Rental income earned, $300 (one month's rent from subletting).

Print Reports

6. Print the following reports:

a. General Journal (By posting date, All ledger entries, Start: 3/1/99, Finish: 3/31/99).
b. Trial Balance As at 3/31/99.
c. Customer Aged report (Detail, Select All).
d. Vendor Aged report (Detail, Select All).
e. Employee Payroll Register 1 (Select All).
f. Payroll reports as necessary.

Review your printed reports. If you have made an error in a posted journal entry, see Part C of the Appendix B at the end of this book for information on how to correct the error.

Record March Adjusting Entries

7. Open the general journal; then record adjusting journal entries on the basis of the following adjustment data:

How to Record Inventory Adjusting Entries

a. and b. Ending inventory, $4,280. The format of the adjusting entries for inventory in a computerized accounting system, and specifically for The Corner Dress Shop, are as follows:

	Debit	*Credit*
5050 Beginning Inventory	$5,600	
1130 Inventory		$5,600
1130 Inventory	$4,280	
5150 Ending Inventory		$4,280

c. During March, rent expired, $600.

d. Trucks depreciated, $480.

e. Rental income earned, $300 (one month's rent from subletting).

Print Reports

8. After you have posted the adjusting journal entries, close the general journal; then print the following reports:

a. General Journal (By posting date, All ledger entries, Start: 3/1/99, Finish: 3/31/99).

b. Trial Balance As at 3/31/99.

c. General Ledger Report (Start: 3/1/99, Finish: 3/31/99, Select All).

d. Income Statement (Start: 3/1/99, Finish: 3/31/99).

e. Balance Sheet As at 3/31/99.

Review your printed reports. If you have made an error in a posted journal entry, see Part C of Appendix B for information on how to correct the error.

Record Entry to Close Withdrawals Account

9. Open the general journal; then record the closing journal entry for Betty Loeb's Withdrawals account.

10. After you have posted the closing entry for Betty Loeb's Withdrawals account, close the General Journal to return to the Company Window.

Make a Backup Copy of March Accounting Records

11. Click on the Company Window File menu; click on Save As; then enter one of the following new file names into the **Save file as** text box:

- A:\DRESSMAR.ASC (if you are storing your student data files on the disk in drive A).
- B:\DRESSMAR.ASC (if you are storing your student data files on the disk in drive B).

12. Click on the **Save** button. Note that the company name in the Company Window has changed from Dress to Dressmar. Click on the Company Window File menu again; then click on Save As. Enter one of the following new file names into the **Save file as** text box:

- A:\DRESS.ASC (if you are storing your student data files on the disk in drive A).
- B:\DRESS.ASC (if you are storing your student data files on the disk in drive B).

13. Click on the **Save** button. Click on the **Yes** button in response to the question "Replace existing data files with the same name?" Note that the company name in the Company Window has changed back from Dressmar to Dress.

14. You now have two sets of company data files for The Corner Dress Shop on your Student Data Files disk. The current data is stored under the file name DRESS.ASC. The backup data is stored under the file name DRESSMAR.ASC.

Advance the Using Date

15. Click on the Company Window Setup menu; then click on Advance Using Date. Enter "4/1/99" into the **New using date** text box; then click on the **OK** button. Click on the **OK** button in response to the warning message. The backup you created using the Save As method will serve as the backup suggested in the warning message.

Print a Post-Closing Trial Balance

16. Print a post-closing trial balance as at 4/1/99.

Exit from the Program

17. Click on the Company Window File menu; then click on Exit to end the current work session and return to your Windows desktop.

Note: If you are using ACCPAC Plus, your instructor will provide details. Note that payroll is a separate module and may not always be available. Accordingly, the data set provided for ACCPAC Plus does not include any payroll files. Process the payroll manually and enter the details into the general ledger module in the normal way.

ACCOUNTING FOR BAD DEBTS

14

Chapter Objectives

- Using the Bad Debts Expense account and the Allowance for Doubtful Accounts account to record bad debts. (p. 548)
- Using the income statement approach and the balance sheet approach to estimate the amount of bad debts expense. (p. 551)
- Preparing an aging of accounts receivable. (p. 553)
- Writing off an account using the Allowance for Doubtful Accounts account. (p. 555)
- Using the direct write-off method. (p. 557)

All companies that sell goods or services on account will eventually have to face the problem of not being able to collect the money owed them. At what point accounts receivable turn into bad debts (or uncollectible accounts), how and what to charge them to, and how to write them off are some of the questions that we will be dealing with in this chapter.

The question of bad debts is important to a company because it affects its credit policy. If a company extends credit too easily, it may end up with too many uncollectible accounts. On the other hand, if the credit policy is too strict, the company will end up losing customers to other firms with easier credit policies—and that could mean a loss in profit just as uncollectible debts do.

In the first learning unit we will look at how bad debts are recorded in the accrual system of accounting.

LEARNING UNIT 14-1

Accrual Accounting and Recording Bad Debts

As we discussed in an earlier chapter, in the accrual system of accounting it is important to match earned revenue with expenses that have been incurred in producing revenue during an accounting period. In other words, in a merchandising firm, for example, it is important to match cost of goods sold with revenue earned by the sale of those goods. And one expense that is incurred as a result of sales on credit or on account is a bad debts expense. The problem is that at the time the sale occurs, one doesn't know whether or not it is going to be uncollectible—one may not know this until much later, possibly a year or so. So how on the books can one match sales with expenses (in this case bad debts expense)?

One way to do this is to estimate at the end of the year what percentage of sales made during that year will turn out to be bad debts. There are several ways of arriving at the percentage, which we will discuss in a later Unit, but at the moment let's say that Abby Ellen Company estimates that 1.6 percent of their sales of $100,000 for the year 19X1 will not be collectible; that means that the company expects not to collect $1,600 of the $100,000 owed them from sales.

To handle this situation we need to introduce two accounts that we haven't dealt with before, Bad Debts Expense and Allowance for Doubtful Accounts. **Bad Debts Expense** is an expense account whose normal balance is a debit; it is a temporary account that is closed to Income Summary at year's end. **Allowance for Doubtful Accounts** is a contra-asset account that accumulates the expected amount of bad debts as of a given date; its normal balance is a credit. It is a permanent account that is *not* closed to Income Summary at the end of the year.

In the case of Abby Ellen Company, which expects to be unable to collect $1,600 of the $100,000 owed them from sales, at the end of the year (19X1) an adjustment is made debiting Bad Debts Expense and crediting Allowance for

Doubtful Accounts for $1,600. This transaction is shown below, along with a transaction analysis chart:

			Dr.	Cr.
Dec.	31	Bad Debt Expense	1 6 0 0 00	
		Allowance for Doubtful Accounts		1 6 0 0 00
		Record estimate of bad debts		

Will go on income statement as an operating expense and eventually be closed to Income Summary.

Will go on balance sheet as a reduction of Accounts Receivable. The normal balance of the allowance account is a credit. It will not be closed at the end of the period.

1 Accounts Affected	2 Category	3 ↑ ↓	4 Rules
Bad Debts Expense	Expenses	↑	Dr.
Allowance for Doubtful Accounts	Contra-Asset	↑	Cr.

Accounts Receivable
− Allowance for Doubtful Accounts
= Net Realizable Value

We will do write-offs in Learning Unit 14-3. This is only an introductory example.

Think of the Allowance for Doubtful Accounts as a reservoir that is filled before bad debts occur. When the customers' bills are declared uncollectible, this reservoir will be drained. Abby Ellen Company estimates that out of its $100,000 of credit sales, $1,600 will prove to be uncollectible, but it does not know at this time which accounts will be uncollectible. The allowance account is subtracted from Accounts Receivable, leaving a **net realizable value** of $98,400. Net realizable value is the amount Abby Ellen Company expects to collect. When an account is written off, the net realizable value doesn't change, because both the Accounts Receivable and the Allowance for Doubtful Accounts are reduced.

Figure 14-1 shows a partial balance sheet to see how the Allowance for Doubtful Accounts relates to Accounts Receivable.

ABBY ELLEN COMPANY
PARTIAL BALANCE SHEET
DECEMBER 31, 19X1

Assets		
Current Assets:		
Cash		$ 51 4 0 0 00
Accounts Receivable	$100 0 0 0 00	
Less: Allowance for Doubtful Accounts	1 6 0 0 00	98 4 0 0 00
Merchandise Inventory		200 0 0 0 00
Total Current Assets		$349 8 0 0 00

FIGURE 14-1
Partial Balance Sheet

At some point a customer's bill must be written off as uncollectible. Let's look at how Abby Ellen Company would write off the account of Jones Moore on June 5, 19X2. (The sale was made to him in 19X1.)

Writing off an account. Note: Bad Debts Expense is not involved.

WRITING OFF AN ACCOUNT DEEMED UNCOLLECTIBLE

Remember, at end of year 19X1 Abby made an adjusting entry increasing Bad Debts Expense (debit) and filling the Allowance for Doubtful Accounts (credit) with the estimate of accounts receivable that would not be collectible.

Now, on June 5, 19X2, Jones Moore's account is deemed to be uncollectible for $200, and the following journal entry is recorded to write off this account:

19X2 June	5	Allowance For Doubtful Accounts	200 00	
		Accounts Receivable, J. Moore		200 00
		Writing off J. Moore account		

The bad debts expense was recorded in the old year when credit sales were earned.

Note that we did *not* debit the account Bad Debts Expense, since the estimate for this account was made on December 31, 19X1 (and applies to that year, not to 19X2). When that estimate was made, we did not know which customers would turn out to be uncollectible and thus we recorded the estimate in the Allowance for Doubtful Accounts. Now that the debt is identified as uncollectible, we *reduce* or drain the Allowance account and reduce the controlling account Accounts Receivable as well as update the accounts receivable ledger. Note that the subsidiary ledger will be credited just as the controlling account is.

LEARNING UNIT 14-1 REVIEW

AT THIS POINT you should be able to

- Define and explain the purpose of Bad Debts Expense and Allowance for Doubtful Accounts. (p. 548)
- Explain why the subsidiary ledger account cannot be updated at the time the Bad Debts Expense is estimated. (p. 549)
- Prepare an adjusting entry for Bad Debts Expense. (p. 549)
- Prepare a partial balance sheet showing the relationship between the Allowance for Doubtful Accounts and Accounts Receivable. (p. 549)
- Explain net realizable value. (p. 549)
- Prepare a journal entry to write off a customer's debt in a year following the sale. (p. 550)

SELF-REVIEW QUIZ 14-1

Respond true or false to the following:

1. The Bad Debts Expense account should be updated only when the customer's debt is declared to be uncollectible.
2. The Allowance for Doubtful Accounts is a contra-asset account on the balance sheet.
3. Bad Debts Expense is part of cost of goods sold.
4. Net Realizable Value equals Accounts Receivable less Allowance for Doubtful Accounts.
5. When a customer's debt is written off as uncollectible, the account Allowance for Doubtful Accounts is credited.

Solutions to Self-Review Quiz 14-1

1. False **2.** True **3.** False **4.** True **5.** False

LEARNING UNIT 14-2

The Allowance Method: Two Approaches to Estimating the Amount of Bad Debts Expense

As we said earlier, at the end of the year a company estimates what percentage of the sales that occurred that year will turn out to be uncollectible accounts, or bad debts. How is this estimate arrived at? In this unit we will look at two approaches to making an annual estimate of Bad Debts Expense. Figure 14-2 presents an overview. Don't memorize it; we will be covering it step by step.

THE INCOME STATEMENT APPROACH

Bad Debts Expense is based on a percentage of the dollar volume of net credit sales on the income statement.

Abby Ellen Company uses the **income statement approach** at the end of the year to calculate how much Bad Debts Expense will be associated with this year's sales. On the basis of the past several years, the company has averaged Bad Debts Expense of 1 percent of net credit sales. From the following facts, let's prepare an adjusting entry to record the Bad Debts Expense that is based on a percentage of net credit sales.

19X4	*Dr.*	*Cr.*
Sales (all credit)		$95,000
Sales Returns and Allowances	$10,000	
Sales Discount	5,000	
Allowance for Doubtful Accounts		100
Accounts Receivable	7,000	

Analysis:

Sales	$95,000
– SRA	10,000
– SD	5,000
Net Credit Sales	$80,000

1 Accounts Affected	2 Category	3 ↑ ↓	4 Rules
Bad Debts Expense	**Operating Expenses**	↑	**Dr.**
Allowance for Doubtful Accounts	**Contra-Asset**	↑	**Cr.**

Dec.	31	Bad Debts Expense	80000	
		Allowance for Doubtful Accounts		80000
		Record estimate of bad debts		
		(0.01 × $80,000)		

Note in this income statement approach that the existing credit balance of $100 in the Allowance account is ignored and, when posted, the Allowance account is as follows:

Allowance for Doubtful Accounts

Dr.	Cr.
	100 → Ignored in Calculating amount of Bad Debts Expense (Balance before adjustment)
	800 → Adjustment
	900 → New Balance

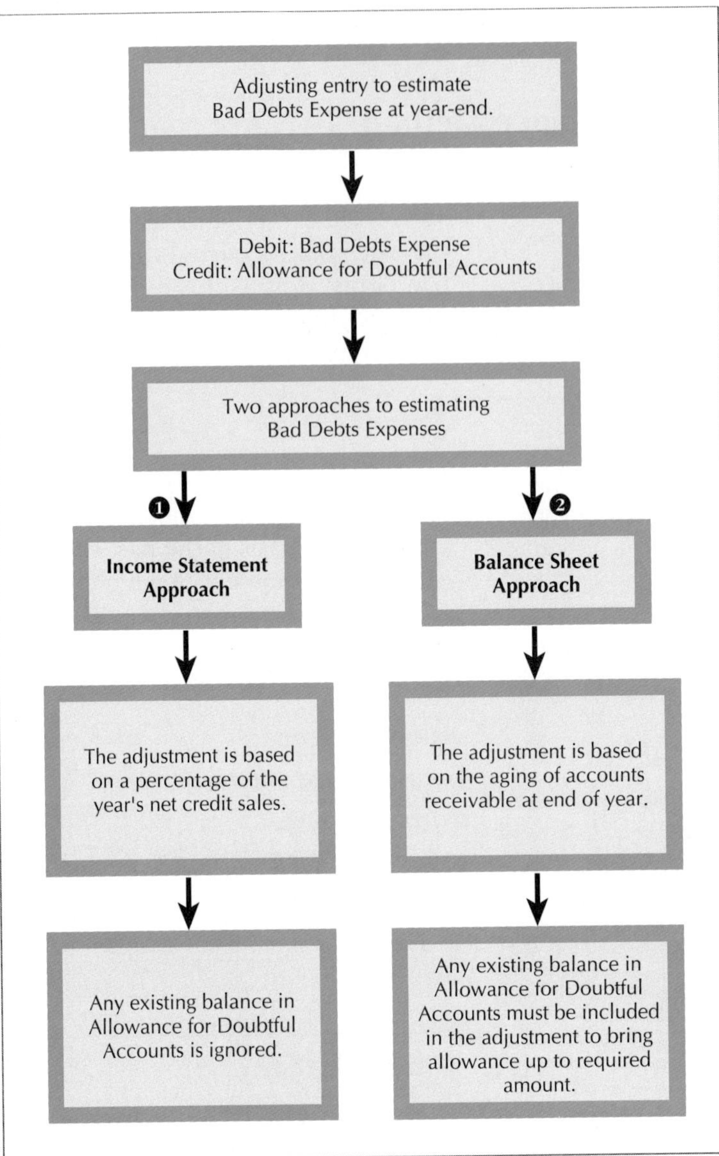

FIGURE 14-2
Two Approaches to Estimating Amount of Bad Debts Expense

Beginning balance in Allowance account represents potential bad debts from previous periods.

Why? The balance in the Allowance for Doubtful Accounts is ignored, since this approach calculates the amount of bad debts expense *for the year* based on a percent of net credit sales. This approach emphasizes the matching requirements of the income statement. The $100 in the Allowance account represents a carry-over of potential bad debts from prior years. Thus, the total of $900 represents total potential uncollectible accounts of several periods of sales. If, over the years, the estimate for Bad Debts Expense has been inaccurate, an adjusting entry can be made in the current year's Bad Debts Expense. If this happens, the company may reevaluate its percentage, and use a higher or lower percentage as necessary.

The Balance Sheet Approach

In the income statement approach, the estimate for the Bad Debts Expense used a percentage of net credit sales from the income statement as the basis for the adjusting entry. The **balance sheet approach**, on the other hand, uses accounts receivable on the balance sheet as its basis in preparing the adjusting entry to estimate bad debts expense. *Keep in mind that the adjusting entry will take into consideration the existing balance in the Allowance for Doubtful Accounts.* (In the income statement approach the balance in the Allowance account was ignored.)

Let's look now at one balance sheet approach—the aging of the accounts receivable.

AGING THE ACCOUNTS RECEIVABLE

Aging classifies uncollected amounts of individual customers according to days past due.

The longer a bill has been due and not paid, the more likely it is that it is not going to be paid. Therefore, one way of estimating the amount of bad debts for the year just past is to look at Accounts Receivable and analyze it according to how many days past due the accounts are. This is called **aging the accounts receivable**. Table 14-1 shows an analysis that the Abby Ellen Company did on December 31, 19X4.

TABLE 14-1 AGING OF ACCOUNTS RECEIVABLE

Name of Customer	Total Balance	Not Yet Due	Days Past Due			
			1–30	31–60	61–90	Over 90
Sarah Elliot	$ 100	$ 100				
Joshua Karras	30			$ 30		
Alan Ledbury	160	160				
John Sullivan	180				$160	$ 20
Sheri Missan	80	80				
Others	6,450	3,260	$2,000	840	40	310
Totals	$7,000	$3,600	$2,000	$870	$200	$330
Percentage of total (rounded to nearest whole number)	100%	51% ($\frac{\$3,600}{\$7,000}$)	29% ($\frac{\$2,000}{\$7,000}$)	12% ($\frac{\$870}{\$7,000}$)	3% ($\frac{\$200}{\$7,000}$)	5% ($\frac{\$330}{\$7,000}$)

Today, with the computer, an analysis of Accounts Receivable can be completed quickly.

Note that 29 percent of the total receivables for Abby Ellen are past due from 1 to 30 days. (This analysis will also provide feedback to the credit department as to how well the current credit policy is working.) Now let's look at how the company will estimate what balance in the Allowance for Doubtful Accounts is required to meet probable bad debts. The schedule shown in Table 14-2 is prepared to assist the company in calculating the needed balance.

TABLE 14-2 BALANCE REQUIRED TO MEET PROBABLE BAD DEBTS

	Amount	Estimated Percentage Considered to be Bad Debts Expense	Amount Needed in Allowance Allowance for Doubtful Accounts to Cover Estimated Bad Debts Expense
Not yet due	$3,600	3	$108 ($3,600 × 0.03)
Days past due			
1–30	2,000	4	80
31–60	870	10	87
61–90	200	20	40
Over 90	330	50	165
Total accounts receivable	$7,000	Total balance required in allowance for doubtful accounts	$480

In this schedule Abby Ellen Company has applied a sliding scale of percentages (3, 4, 10, 20, 50), based on *previous experience*, to the total amount of receivables due in each time period. For example, of the $200 overdue by 61-90 days, 20 percent or $40 will probably never be paid. Looking at this schedule reveals that Abby Ellen Company needs $480 to cover estimated bad debts. *Presently* the balance in the allowance account is $100. Thus, to reach a balance of $480, we must adjust the balance of the account by the following adjusting journal entry:

The balance in the Allowance for Doubtful Accounts is not ignored.

			Dr.	Cr.
19X4 Dec.	31	Bad Debts Expense	380 00	
		Allowance for Doubtful Accounts		380 00
		Record estimate of bad debts		

Bad Debts Expense

Dr.	Cr.
380	

Allowance for Doubtful Accounts

Dr.	Cr.
	100 Beg. Balance
	380 Adj.
	480 New balance in Allowance

The desired balance of $480 is now reached. If the Allowance had a *debit* balance of $100 before the adjustment, the amount of the adjusting entry would be $580 credit to the Allowance to arrive at the $480 balance. Once again, the adjustment *must* consider the *existing balance* in the Allowance account before the adjusting entry is prepared.

Some companies that feel aging is too time-consuming may estimate bad debts on the basis of a percentage of total Accounts Receivable.

LEARNING UNIT 14-2 REVIEW

AT THIS POINT you should be able to

- Explain the two approaches to estimating Bad Debts Expense. (p. 551)
- Explain why the balance in Allowance for Doubtful Accounts is ignored when an adjusting entry for bad debts is prepared in the income statement approach. (p. 551)
- Show how to prepare an aging of accounts receivable. (p. 553)
- Explain how the aging of accounts receivable is used to arrive at the balance required in Allowance for Doubtful Accounts. (p. 553)

SELF-REVIEW QUIZ 14-2

From the following, prepare an adjusting journal entry for Bad Debts Expense for (1) the income statement approach and (2) the balance sheet approach.

Allowance for Doubtful Accounts

Dr.	Cr.
	400

Income Statement Approach

Net Sales: $160,000

1% of Net Sales

Balance Sheet Approach | | *Percentage Considered Bad Debts*

Not yet due:	$4,000	4
Days past due:		
1–30	3,000	5
31–60	400	10
Over 60	5,000	30

Solution to Self-Review Quiz 14-2

				Dr.	Cr.
(1)	Dec.	31	Bad Debts Expense	160000	
			Allowance for Doubtful Accounts		160000
			(0.01 × $160,000)		
(2)		31	Bad Debts Expense	145000	
			Allowance for Doubtful Accounts		145000
			$4,000 × 0.04 = $ 160		
			3,000 × 0.05 = 150		
			400 × 0.10 = 40		
			5,000 × 0.30 = 1,500		
			$1,850		
			Note allowance adjusted:		
			$1,850 – $400 = $1,450		

LEARNING UNIT 14-3

Writing Off Uncollectible Accounts

This Unit will look at two ways to write off uncollectible accounts, one using the Allowance for Doubtful Accounts, the other using the direct write-off method.

WRITING OFF AN ACCOUNT USING THE ALLOWANCE FOR DOUBTFUL ACCOUNTS

Let's assume that on March 18, 19X7, the Abby Ellen Company determines that the account of Jill Sullivan for $900 is uncollectible. (The sale to Jill Sullivan was back in 19X6.) This means that this Accounts Receivable amount should no longer be considered an asset and should be written off. The following journal entry reduces the Allowance for Doubtful Accounts and reduces the Accounts Receivable controlling account as well as the accounts receivable subsidiary ledger.

					Dr.	Cr.
19X7 Mar.	18	Allowance for Doubtful Accounts			90000	
		Accounts Receivable, Jill Sullivan				90000
		Wrote off Sullivan account				

JOYCE THOMAS

SENIOR TAX ANALYST

MUTUAL BENEFIT LIFE INSURANCE COMPANY

Joyce Thomas came to Mutual Benefit Life Insurance Company immediately after high school. She had a bookkeeping background from high school and got a job in the actuarial department. "I found that I enjoyed the work," she says, "but I knew that I would not get very far with just a high school diploma."

Joyce decided to go back to school to get a diploma in accounting. "It was hard work," she says, "but I received a lot of support from my supervisors." Joyce received promotions as she took more courses and demonstrated her abilities in the office. "In some cases," Joyce says, "the accounting courses I took helped me to understand the reasons behind a job I was already doing. In other cases, the courses helped me to get a better job." Since Joyce was allowed to move to different areas within a large accounting department, she was able to see which jobs she preferred.

Joyce is now a Senior Tax Analyst and is working toward a degree in accounting. "Combining work with college courses in accounting was a good decision for me," she says. "I am able to earn money in a field I love while getting a degree to help me further my career."

Note the following key points:

1. This journal entry does *not* affect any expenses. Remember, Bad Debts Expense is *not* affected when an account is finally written off. The estimate for Bad Debts Expense was recorded in the previous year before the bad debt actually occurred.
2. If more than one customer is written off, a compound entry can be used, debiting Allowance for the total and crediting each individual account.
3. The net realizable value of Accounts Receivable is unchanged. Let's prove this:

	Balances Before the Write-off		*Balances After the Write-off*
Accounts Receivable	$12,000	$900 write-off →	$11,100
Less: Allowance for Doubtful Accounts	2,000	$900 drain →	1,100
Estimated realizable value (what to expect to collect)	$10,000	No change →	$10,000

Let's look now at what would happen on the books of Abby Ellen Company if Jill Sullivan in the future should pay part or all of the debt.

Let's assume that Jill Sullivan is able to pay off half of her debt and send a cheque to Abby Ellen Company on February 1, 19X8. (Keep in mind the fact that her account was written off on March 18, 19X7, and the original sale was made in 19X6.) To record this, Abby Ellen Company reverses in part the entry that was made to write off the account in the amount expected to be recovered and records the amount received from Jill. The following are the journal entries to record the recovery of $450 out of the original amount of $900:

Reinstates the account.

Records the amount received.

				Dr.	Cr.
19X8 Feb.	1	Accounts Receivable, Jill Sullivan		450 00	
		Allowances for Doubtful Accounts			450 00
		Restores collectible portion			
	1	Cash		450 00	
		Accounts Receivable, Jill Sullivan			450 00
		Records payment received			

The reason we record both a debit and a credit to Accounts Receivable is that it provides a clear picture of the transactions involving Jill Sullivan. If the company is considering giving credit again to Jill Sullivan, these previous records could be of assistance in determining how much if any credit could be extended. Note how the first entry reinstates the account and the second entry records the cash received. In fact, the second entry would be made in a special journal.

Let's look now at another method of handling Bad Debts Expense, the direct write-off method.

THE DIRECT WRITE-OFF METHOD

The direct write-off method does not fulfill the matching principle.

When a company cannot reasonably estimate its Bad Debts Expense, it may use the **direct write-off method**. Using this method, an account that is determined to be uncollectible would be directly written off to this year's Bad Debts Expense account without regard to when the original sale was made. In this method, the Allowance for Doubtful Accounts is not used, since no adjustment is needed at the end of the year to estimate Bad Debts Expense. Let's replay the Jill Sullivan write-off as well as the recovery so that we can make comparisons between the Allowance for Doubtful Accounts method and the direct write-off method. In the recovery we will see a new account title, "Bad Debts Recovered". Think of it as a revenue account found in the Other Income section of an income statement.

Writing off Jill Sullivan on March 18, 19X7. Note that Allowance account is not used. See p. 556.

				Dr.	Cr.
19X7 Mar.	18	Bad Debts Expense		900 00	
		Accts. Rec., Jill Sullivan			900 00
		Wrote off account			

Recovery of half the amount owed by Jill Sullivan on Feb. 1, 19X8. Note that Bad Debts Recovered replaces Allowance for Doubtful Accounts.

On the balance sheet, Accounts Receivable is recorded at gross. No Allowance account or realizable amount is used.

				Dr.	Cr.
19X8 Feb.	1	Accts. Rec., Jill Sullivan		450 00	
		Bad Debts Recovered			450 00
		Restores collectible portion			
	1	Cash		450 00	
		Accts. Rec., Jill Sullivan			450 00
		Records payment received			

Bad Debts Recovered	Other Revenue	↑	Cr.

In the direct write-off method, when the amount is written off, no Allowance for Doubtful Accounts is used. Rather, the debit is to Bad Debts Expense. On the recovery in years following the sale, instead of crediting the Allowance, the direct method credits **Bad Debts Recovered** (an account in the "Other Revenue" category). This in effect increases the revenue and puts the Accounts Receivable back on the books. If recovery is made in the same year, you just reverse the entry you made to write off the account:

Date		Account	PR	Dr.	Cr.
19X7 May	1	Accounts Receivable, Jill Sullivan		450 00	
		Bad Debts Expense			450 00

INSIGHT INTO INCOME TAX REGULATIONS

For tax purposes the law permits the bad debt reserve method of deducting bad debts. Since the direct write-off method does vary from generally accepted accounting principles, tax law follows the *CICA Handbook* and allows the deduction of an annual reserve.

LEARNING UNIT 14-3 REVIEW

AT THIS POINT you should be able to

- Write off an account using the Allowance for Doubtful Accounts method. (p. 555)
- Explain why net realizable value is unchanged after a write-off is complete. (p. 556)
- Prepare journal entries to recover entire or partial amounts that were once declared uncollectible. (p. 557)
- Explain the direct write-off method and prepare appropriate journal entries for write-off and recovery. (p. 557)

SELF-REVIEW QUIZ 14-3

Respond true or false to the following:

1. When an account is written off using the Allowance for Doubtful Accounts method in a period following the sale, the result is a debit to Bad Debts Expense and a credit to Accounts Receivable.
2. The direct write-off method will sometimes use the Allowance for Doubtful Accounts.
3. When an account is written off (using the Allowance for Doubtful Accounts method), net realizable value is unchanged.
4. Bad Debts Recovered is an asset.
5. A debit balance in the Allowance for Doubtful Accounts indicates that the estimate for Bad Debts Expense was too low.

Solutions to Self-Review Quiz 14-3

1. False **2.** False **3.** True **4.** False **5.** True

Chapter Review

SUMMARY OF KEY POINTS

Learning Unit 14-1

1. If accrual accounting is used, Bad Debts Expense should be recognized in the year the sale was made, even though the actual write-off may not yet have taken place.
2. Bad Debts Expense is an expense found on the income statement.
3. The Allowance for Doubtful Accounts is a contra-asset account found on the balance sheet that accumulates the amount of estimated uncollectibles before they are actually written off.
4. Net realizable value equals Accounts Receivable minus Allowance for Doubtful Accounts.
5. When an account is written off, the Allowance for Doubtful Accounts is debited and Accounts Receivable is credited (along with the subsidiary ledger account).

Learning Unit 14-2

1. The two approaches to estimating Bad Debts Expense are the income statement approach and the balance sheet approach.
2. The income statement approach estimates Bad Debts Expense on the basis of a percentage of net sales. (Some companies use credit sales, some use total sales.) The balance is ignored in the allowance for doubtful accounts when the Bad Debts Expense is estimated from sales of the period.
3. The balance sheet approach estimates the balance required in the Allowance for Doubtful Accounts by aging the accounts receivable. The balance in the Allowance account will have to be adjusted based on the aging of the receivables.

Learning Unit 14-3

After the write-off, net realizable value is unchanged.

1. When an account is written off (using the Allowance account) in years following the sale, the result is to debit Allowance for Doubtful Accounts and credit Accounts Receivable. Do not debit Bad Debts Expense, as it has already been recorded in the year the sale was made.
2. When an uncollectible account has been written off and is now recovered, the entry reverses the original write-off by debiting Accounts Receivable and crediting the Allowance for Doubtful Accounts. Then the cash received is debited and the Accounts Receivable is credited.
3. The direct write-off method will recognize the bad debts expense when the customer account is declared uncollectible. The direct method does *not* use the Allowance for Doubtful Accounts, since no estimate is made for bad debts. This method does not follow the matching principle in the accrual basis of accounting.
4. Bad Debts Recovered is classified as "other revenue" when a customer account is reinstated after being written off in the direct method.

BLUEPRINT SUMMARY OF RECORDING BAD DEBTS EXPENSE, WRITE-OFFS, AND RECOVERY

Situation	Allowance for Doubtful Accounts Method						Direct Write-off Method		
	A. Income Statement Approach			B. Balance Sheet Approach					
Adjusting entry made to record estimated uncollectible accounts.	Bad Debts Expense	XX		Bad Debts Expense	XX		None		
	Allowance for Doubtful Accounts		XX	Allowance for Doubtful Accounts		XX			
	Based on percent of net sales.			Aging of Accounts Receivable					
	Balance in Allowance account			determines amount needed					
	is ignored.			in Allowance account.					
				Balance in Allowance account					
				is adjusted.					
Accts. Receivable is determined to be uncollectible.	Allowance for Doubtful Accounts	XX		Allowance for Doubtful Accounts	XX		Bad Debts Expense	XX	
	Accounts Receivable		XX	Accounts Receivable		XX	Accounts Receivable		XX
Bad debts are recovered.	Accounts Receivable	XX		Accounts Receivable	XX		Accounts Receivable	XX	
	Allowance for Doubtful Accounts		XX	Allowance for Doubtful Accounts		XX	Bad Debts Recovered*		XX
	Cash	XX		Cash	XX		Cash	XX	
	Accounts Receivable		XX	Accounts Receivable		XX	Accounts Receivable		XX
Bal. sheet updated.	Shows net realizable value.			Shows net realizable value.			Does not show net realizable value.		

*Used if recovery is not in the same year as the sale.

KEY TERMS

Aging of accounts receivable The procedure of classifying accounts of individual customers by age group, where age is the number of days elapsed from due date.

Allowance for Doubtful Accounts A contra-asset account that is subtracted from the Accounts Receivable. This account accumulates the *expected* amount of uncollectibles as of a given date.

Bad Debts Expense The operating expense account that estimates the amount of credit sales in a given accounting period that will probably not be collectible when the Allowance method is used. For the direct write-off method, this account would be the actual amount written off.

Bad Debts Recovered When an account receivable has been written off and is recovered, this account, which is in the "Other Revenue" category, is credited in the direct write-off method if the recovery is in a year *following* the write-off.

Balance sheet approach A method used to calculate the amount *required* in Allowance for Doubtful Accounts to cover expected uncollectibles. This method is based on the Accounts Receivable account and the aging process. The balance in the Allowance account will have to be adjusted.

Direct write-off method The method of writing off uncollectibles when they occur, thus not using the Allowance for Doubtful Accounts. This method does not follow the matching principle of accrual accounting.

Income statement approach A method that estimates the amount of Bad Debts Expense that will result on the basis of a percentage of net credit sales for the period. The balance in the Allowance account will be ignored.

Net realizable value The amount (Accounts Receivable—Allowance for Doubtful Accounts) that is expected to be collected.

QUESTIONS, EXERCISES, AND PROBLEMS

Discussion Questions

1. Explain the matching principle in relationship to recording Bad Debts Expense.
2. What is the purpose of the Allowance for Doubtful Accounts?
3. What is net realizable value?
4. When an Account Receivable is written off, Bad Debts Expense must be debited. True or false? Please discuss.
5. Explain why Allowance for Doubtful Accounts is a contra-asset account.
6. Recording Bad Debts Expense is a closing entry. True or false? Defend your position.
7. The income statement approach used to estimate bad debts is based on Accounts Receivable on the balance sheet. Accept or reject. Why?
8. In which approach is the balance of the Allowance for Doubtful Accounts considered when the estimate of Bad Debts Expense is made? Please explain.
9. Why would a company age its accounts receivable?
10. Using the Allowance for Doubtful Accounts method, what journal entries would be made to write off an account as well as later record the recovery of the Accounts Receivable?

11. Why doesn't net realizable value change when an account is written off in the use of the Allowance account?
12. What is the purpose of using a direct write-off method?
13. Explain the purpose of the Bad Debts Recovered account.

Mini Exercises

(The forms you need are on page 14-3 of the *Study Guide and Working Papers.*)

Categorizing Accounts

1. a. Complete the following transactional analysis chart:

Accounts Affected	Category	↓ ↑	Rules of Dr. and Cr.
Bad Debts Expense			
Allowance for Doubtful Accounts			

b. Which financial statement will each title be recorded on?
c. Which account is temporary? Which account is permanent?

Allowance Method

2. Complete the table:

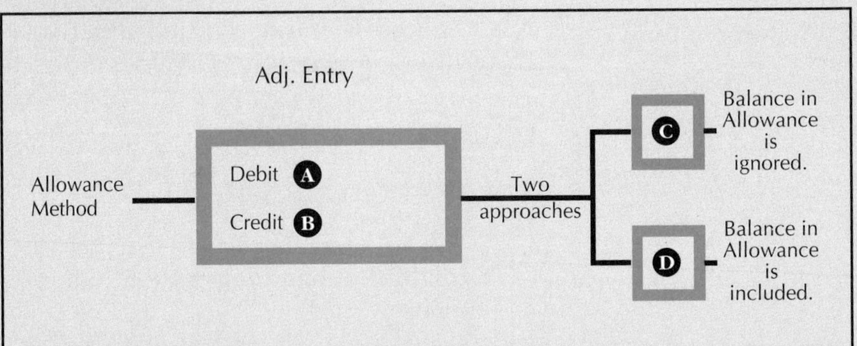

Journalize Adjusting Entries for Income Statement and Balance Sheet Approach

3. Given the balance in the Allowance for Doubtful Accounts of $100 credit. Prepare adjusting entries for Bad Debts based on the following assumptions:
   a. Bad Debts to be 5 percent of Net Credit Sales or $400.
   b. On the basis of Aging of Accounts Receivable, Bad Debts should be $400.

Writing Off Uncollectible Accounts and Reinstatement—Allowance Method

4. Journalize entries for the following situations (assume allowance method):
   Situation 1: Wrote off Bill Allen as a bad debt 2 years after the sale for $50.
   Situation 2: Reinstated Bill Allen who sent in his past due amount.

Writing Off Uncollectible Account and Reinstatement—Direct Write-Off Method

5. Journalize entries for the following situation (assume direct write-off method).

Situation 1: Wrote off Bill Allen as a bad debt two years after the sale of $50.

Situation 2: Reinstated Bill Allen who sent in his past due amount two years after it had been written off.

Exercises

Preparing a partial balance sheet with Allowance for Doubtful Accounts.

14-1. Jetson Co. has requested that you prepare a partial balance sheet on December 31, 19XX, from the following: Cash, $105,000; Petty Cash, $60; Accounts Receivable, $60,000; Bad Debts Expense, $40,000; Allowance for Doubtful Accounts, $12,000; Merchandise Inventory, $18,000.

Calculating Bad Debts Expense by income statement approach.

14-2. Given the following information:

Accounts Receivable		Sales		Sales Returns and Allowances	
30,000			110,000	500	

Allowance for Sales Discount		Doubtful Accounts	
9,500			5,000

journalize the adjusting entry on December 31, 19XX, for Bad Debts Expense, which is estimated to be 4 percent of net sales. The income statement approach is used.

Calculating Bad Debts Expense by balance sheet approach.

14-3. Assuming that in Exercise 2 the balance sheet approach is used, prepare a journalized adjusting entry for Bad Debts Expense. Aging of accounts receivable indicates that an $8,000 balance in the Allowance account will be needed to cover bad debts.

Journalizing adjustment for Bad Debts as well as reinstatement by Allowance method; comparison with direct write-off method.

14-4. The Austin Co., which uses an Allowance for Doubtful Accounts, had the following transactions in 19X5 and 19X6. (Use the income statement approach.)

19X5
Dec. 31 Recorded Bad Debts Expense of $12,000.

19X6
Apr. 3 Wrote off Angie Ring account of $4,000 as uncollectible.
June 4 Wrote off Mike Catuc account of $3,000 as uncollectible.

19X7
Aug. 5 Recovered $500 from Mike Catuc.

a. Journalize the transactions. (They use the income statement approach in estimating bad debts.)

b. Journalize how Austin Co. would record the Mike Catuc bad debt situation if the direct write-off method were used.

Journalizing adjustments for Bad Debts Expense on the basis of (1) percentage of sales, (2) aging of Accounts Receivable with balance of Allowance for Doubtful Accounts, a debit balance.

14-5. Rowe Company had credit sales of $200,000 during 19X7. The balance in the Allowance for Doubtful Accounts is a $1,000 debit balance. Journalize the Bad Debts Expense for December 31 using each of the following methods:

a. Bad Debts Expense is estimated at 0.5 percent of credit sales.

b. The aging of Accounts Receivable indicates that $2,200 will be required in the Allowance account to cover Bad Debts Expense.

Group A Problems

The income statement approach: journalizing Bad Debts Expense and writing accounts off.

14A-1. The Palter Co. has requested that you prepare journal entries from the following (this company uses the Allowance for Doubtful Accounts method based on the income statement approach).

19X7
Dec. 31 Recorded Bad Debts Expense of $11,000.

19X8
Jan. 7 Wrote off Gene Smore's account of $800 as uncollectible.
Mar. 5 Wrote off Paul Jane's account of $600 as uncollectible.
July 8 Recovered $300 from Paul Jane.
Aug. 19 Wrote off Bob Seager's account of $1,300 as uncollectible.
24 Wrote off Jill Neuman's account of $750 as uncollectible.
Nov. 19 Recovered $400 from Bob Seager.

The balance sheet approach: aging analysis and journalizing of Bad Debts Expense.

14A-2. Given the Additional Data in the table below:

a. Prepare on December 31, 19XX, the adjusting journal entry for Bad Debts Expense.

b. Prepare a partial balance sheet on December 31, 19XX, showing how net realizable value is calculated.

c. If the balance in the Allowance for Doubtful Accounts was a $300 debit balance, journalize the adjusting entry for Bad Debts Expense on December 31, 19XX.

Balances: Cash, $30,000; Accounts Receivable, $152,000; Allowance for Doubtful Accounts, $300; Inventory, $12,000.

Additional Data

Alvie Co.
December 31, 19XX

	Amount	*Estimated Percentage Considered to Be Bad Debts Expense*	*Estimated Amount Needed in Allowance for Doubtful Accounts*
Not yet due	$130,000	1	______
0–60	9,000	5	______
61–180	8,000	20	______
Over six months	5,000	40	______
	$152,000		

The direct write-off method.

14A-3. T. J. Rack Company uses the direct write-off method for recording Bad Debts Expense. At the beginning of 19X8, Accounts Receivable has a $119,000 balance. Journalize the following transactions for T. J. Rack:

19X8
Mar. 13 Wrote off S. Rose's account for $1,800.
Apr. 14 Wrote off P. Soy's account for $750.

19X9
Nov. 8 P. Soy paid bad debt of $750 that was written off April 14, 19X8.
Dec. 7 Wrote off J. Miller's account as uncollectible, $285.
12 Wrote off D. Lovejoy's account for $375 due from sales made on account in 19X7.

Journalizing and posting adjustments for Bad Debts Expense and write-offs and recovery based on balance sheet approach; preparation of partial balance sheet.

14A-4. Simon Company completed the following transactions:

19X8

Jan.	9	Sold merchandise on account to Ray's Supply, $1,500.
	15	Wrote off the account of Pete Runnels as uncollectible because of his death, $600.
Mar.	17	Received $400 from Roland Co., whose account had been written off in 19X7. The account was reinstated and the collection recorded.
Apr.	9	Received 10 percent of the $4,000 owed by Lane Drug. The remainder was written off as uncollectible.
June	15	The account of Mel's Garage was reinstated for $1,200. The account was written off three years ago.
Oct.	18	Prepared a compound entry to write the following accounts off as uncollectible: Jane's Diner, $200; Keen Auto, $400; Ralph's Hardware, $600.
Nov.	12	Sold merchandise on account to J. B. Rug, $1,900.
Dec.	31	On the basis of an aging of Accounts Receivable it was estimated that $7,000 will be uncollectible out of a total of $160,000 in Accounts Receivable.
	31	Closed Bad Debts Expense to Income Summary.

Additional Data

	Acct. No.	*Balance*
Allowance for Doubtful Accounts	114	$4,100
Income Summary	312	—
Bad Debts Expense	612	—

Required

1. Journalize the transactions.

2. Post to Allowance for Doubtful Accounts, Income Summary, or Bad Debts Expense as needed. (Be sure to record beginning balance in the Allowance account in your workbook.)

3. Prepare a current assets section of the balance sheet. Ending balances needed: Cash, $13,000; Accounts Receivable, $160,000; Office Supplies, $2,110; Merchandise Inventory, $103,000; Prepaid Rent, $1,250.

Group B Problems

The income statement approach: journalizing Bad Debts Expense and writing accounts off.

14B-1. The Palter Co. has requested that you prepare journal entries from the following (this company uses the Allowance for Doubtful Accounts method based on the income statement approach).

19X7

Dec.	31	Recorded Bad Debts Expense of $14,800.

19X8

Jan.	7	Wrote off Woody Tree's account of $1,200 as uncollectible.
Mar.	5	Wrote off Jim Lantz's account of $600 as uncollectible.
July	8	Recovered $600 from Jim Lantz.
Aug.	19	Wrote off Mabel Hest's account of $750 as uncollectible.
	24	Wrote off Jim O'Reilly's account of $950 as uncollectible.
Nov.	19	Recovered $500 from Mabel Hest.

The balance sheet approach: aging analysis and journalizing of Bad Debts Expense.

14B-2. Given the information below, and assuming the following balances: Cash, $42,000; Accounts Receivable, $173,000; Allowance for Doubtful Accounts, $400; Inventory, $12,000:

a. Prepare on December 31, 19XX, the adjusting journal entry for Bad Debts Expense.

b. Prepare a partial balance sheet on December 31, 19XX, showing how net realizable value is calculated.

c. If the balance in the Allowance for Doubtful Accounts was a $400 debit balance, journalize the adjusting entry for Bad Debts Expense on December 31, 19XX.

Additional Information

Alvie Co.
December 31, 19XX

	Amount	*Estimated Percentage Considered to Be Bad Debts Expense*	*Estimated Amount Needed in Allowance for Doubtful Accounts*
Not yet due	$150,000	2	________
0–60	10,000	6	________
61–180	9,000	20	________
Over six months	4,000	40	________
	$173,000		

The direct write-off method.

14B-3. T. J. Rack Company uses the direct write-off method for recording Bad Debts Expense. At the beginning of 19X8, Accounts Receivable has a $88,000 balance. Journalize the following transactions for T. J. Rack:

19X8
Mar. 13 Wrote off Jill Diamond's account for $1,950.
Apr. 14 Wrote off Buffy Hall's account for $900.

19X9
Nov. 8 Buffy Hall paid debt of $900 that was written off April 14, 19X8.
Dec. 7 Wrote off Joe Francis's account as uncollectible, $880.
12 Wrote off Joe Martin's account for $410 from sales made on account in 19X7.

Journalizing and posting adjustments for Bad Debts Expense and write-offs and recovery based on balance sheet approach; partial balance sheet prepared.

14B-4. Simon Company completed the following transactions:

19X8
Jan. 9 Sold merchandise on account to Lowe's Supply, $1,900.
15 Wrote off the account of Kevin Reese as uncollectible because of his death, $700.
Mar. 17 Received $300 from J. James, whose account had been written off in 19X7. The account was reinstated and the collection recorded.
Apr. 9 Received 20 percent of the $5,000 owed by Long Drug. The remainder was written off as uncollectible.
June 15 The account of Morse's Garage was reinstated for $3,100. The account was written off three years ago.
Oct. 18 Prepared a compound entry to write the following accounts off as uncollectible: Sal's Diner, $800; Ring Auto, $1,300; Neel's Hardware, $800.
Nov. 12 Sold merchandise on account to Able Roy, $1,950.
Dec. 31 On the basis of an aging of Accounts Receivable, it was estimated that $8,000 will be uncollectible out of a total of $170,000 in Accounts Receivable.
31 Closed Bad Debts Expense to Income Summary.

Additional Data

	Acct. No.	*Balance*
Allowance for Doubtful Accounts	114	$3,300
Income Summary	312	—
Bad Debts Expense	612	—

1. Journalize the transactions.
2. Post to Allowance for Doubtful Accounts, Income Summary, or Bad Debts Expense as needed.
3. Prepare a current assets section of the balance sheet. Ending balances needed: Cash, $24,000; Accounts Receivable, $170,000; Office Supplies, $3,000; Merchandise Inventory, $94,000; Prepaid Rent, $1,200.

Group C Problems

The income statement approach: journalizing Bad Debts Expense and writing accounts off.

14C-1. The Samsom Co. has requested that you prepare journal entries from the following (this company uses the Allowance for Doubtful Accounts method based on the income statement approach).

19X7
Dec. 31 Recorded Bad Debts Expense of $9,200.

19X8
Jan. 7 Wrote off Helen Jamison's account of $850 as uncollectible.
Mar. 5 Wrote off Rob Hart's account of $400 as uncollectible.
July 8 Recovered $200 from Rob Hart.
Aug. 19 Wrote off Brian Brisk's account of $1,640 as uncollectible.
24 Wrote off Ellen Watt's account of $525 as uncollectible.
Nov. 19 Recovered $700 from Brian Brisk.

The balance sheet approach: aging analysis and journalizing of Bad Debts Expense.

14C-2. Given the Additional Information presented below:

a. Prepare on December 31, 19X4, the adjusting journal entry for Bad Debts Expense.

b. Prepare a partial balance sheet on December 31, 19X4, showing how net realizable value is calculated.

c. If the balance in the Allowance for Doubtful Accounts was a $500 debit balance, journalize the adjusting entry for Bad Debts Expense on December 31, 19X4.

Additional Information

Dominion Company
December 31, 19X4

	Amount	*Estimated Percentage Considered to Be Bad Debts Expense*	*Estimated Amount Needed in Allowance for Doubtful Accounts*
Not yet due	$76,000	1	______
0–30	12,000	2	______
31–60	8,000	6	______
61–180	4,000	13	______
Over six months	6,000	30	______
	$106,000		

Balances: Cash, $16,400; Accounts Receivable, $106,000; Allowance for Doubtful Accounts, $700; Inventory, $53,700.

The direct write-off method.

14C-3. Camping Equipment Company uses the direct write-off method for recording Bad Debts Expense. At the beginning of 19X5, Accounts Receivable has an $86,700 balance. Journalize the following transactions for the company:

19X5

Mar.	23	Wrote off F. Robichaud's account for $1,280.
Jun.	9	Wrote off K. Cheung's account for $915.

19X6

Aug.	15	K. Cheung paid bad debt of $915 that was written off June 9, 19X5.
Dec.	5	Wrote off S. Lowe's account as uncollectible, $418.
	18	Wrote off R. Patel's account for $316 due from sales made on account in 19X4.

Journalizing and posting adjustments for Bad Debts Expense and write-offs and recovery based on balance sheet approach; partial balance sheet prepared.

14C-4. Prospecting Supply Company completed the following transactions:

19X6

Jan.	8	Sold merchandise on account to May Expeditions, $4,160.
Feb.	19	Wrote off the account of Avery Fischer as uncollectible because of his death, $624.
Mar.	14	Received $600 from Maximum Co., whose account had been written off in 19X5. The account was reinstated and the collection recorded.
Apr.	5	Received 25 percent of the $6,400 owed by Airborne Surveys. The remainder was written off as uncollectible.
July	18	The account of Hallicrafter Explorations was reinstated for $3,000 (amount received). The account was written off three years ago.
Oct.	28	Prepared a compound entry to write the following accounts off as uncollectible: Corbett Co., $275; Quark Co., $654; Lonely Expeditions, $247.
Nov.	17	Sold merchandise on account to Partridge Surveys, $4,280.
Dec.	31	Based on an aging of Accounts Receivable it was estimated that $6,850 will be uncollectible out of a total of $142,000 in Accounts Receivable.
	31	Closed Bad Debts Expense to Income Summary.

Additional Data As of 01/01/19X6:

	Acct. No.	*Balance*
Allowance for Doubtful Accounts	1124	$6,150
Income Summary	3100	—
Bad Debts Expense	6125	—

Required

1. Journalize the transactions.

2. Post to Allowance for Doubtful Accounts, Income Summary, or Bad Debts Expense as needed. (Be sure to record beginning balance in the Allowance account in your workbook.)

3. Prepare a current assets section of the balance sheet. Ending balances needed: Cash, $16,742; Accounts Receivable, $142,000; Office Supplies, $2,630; Merchandise Inventory, $107,000; Prepaid Rent, $3,500; and your calculated balance for the Allowance account.

Real world applications

14R-1.

Joan Rivers, the newly hired bookkeeper of Lyon Company, has until 5 p.m. today to prepare an analysis on December 31 of Accounts Receivable by age as well as record the entry for Bad Debts Expense. Assist Joan, who has found the following invoices and balances scattered on her desk. Terms of all sales are n/30.

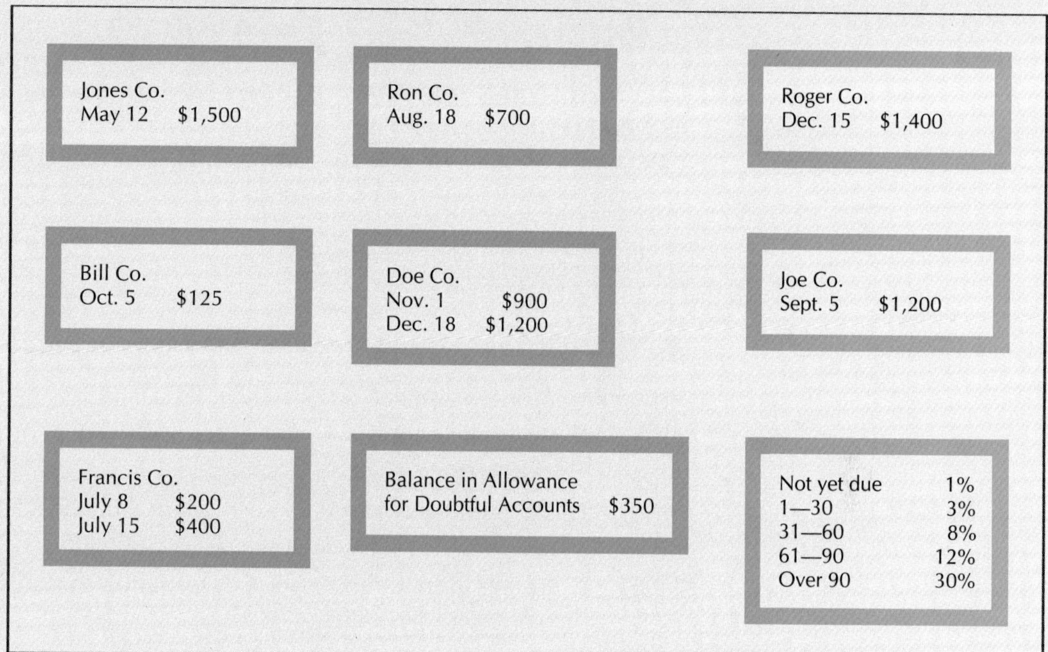
Jones Co.
May 12 $1,500

Ron Co.
Aug. 18 $700

Roger Co.
Dec. 15 $1,400

Bill Co.
Oct. 5 $125

Doe Co.
Nov. 1 $900
Dec. 18 $1,200

Joe Co.
Sept. 5 $1,200

Francis Co.
July 8 $200
July 15 $400

Balance in Allowance for Doubtful Accounts $350

Not yet due	1%
1—30	3%
31—60	8%
61—90	12%
Over 90	30%

14R-2.

TO: *Al Jones* *Sept. 30, 19XX*

FROM: *Peter Flynn, Pres.*

RE: *Bad Debts*

At a party last night a friend of mine told me that we should not be using the direct write-off method. He told me that it doesn't fulfill the matching principle of accounting. Give me your arguments to support or reject this information.

make the call

Critical Thinking/Ethical Case

14R-3.

Pete Sazich, the accountant for Moore Company, feels that all bad debts will be eliminated if credit transactions are done by credit card. He also feels that the cost of the credit cards should be added on to the price of the goods. Pete feels that in the future, the allowance method will be totally eliminated. You make the call. Write a letter stating your opinion regarding this matter to Pete's boss.

ACCOUNTING RECALL

A CUMULATIVE APPROACH

THIS EXAM REVIEWS CHAPTERS 1 THROUGH 14

Your *Study Guide and Working Papers* has forms to complete this exam, as well as worked-out solutions. The page references next to each question identify what page to turn back to if you answer the question incorrectly.

PART I Vocabulary Review

Match the terms to the appropriate definition or phrase.

Page Ref.		
(553)	1. Aging of accounts receivable	A. In alphabetical order
(558)	2. Bad debts recovered	B. Balance in allowance account will have to be adjusted
(468)	3. Ending merchandise inventory	C. Operating expense
(548)	4. Allowance for doubtful accounts	D. Does not use allowance for doubtful accounts
(506)	5. Fixed asset	E. Classifying of accounts
(332)	6. Subsidiary ledgers	F. Land
(549)	7. Net realizable value	G. Contra-asset account
(557)	8. Direct write-off method	H. Other revenue
(552)	9. Balance sheet approach	I. Subtracted from cost of goods sold
(548)	10. Bad debt expense	J. Accounts receivable less allowance for doubtful accounts

PART II True or False (Accounting Theory)

(551) 11. In the income statement approach any existing balance in the allowance for doubtful account is ignored.

(553) 12. The income statement approach is based on aging of accounts receivable.

(557) 13. Allowance for doubtful accounts is used in the direct write-off method.

(548) 14. The allowance for doubtful accounts is listed on the income statement.

(549) 15. A debit to the allowance account will increase it.

PART III Applications Problem

From the following transactions prepare journal entries. (The company uses the allowance for doubtful accounts method based on the income statement approach.)

19X7

Dec.	31	Recorded Bad Debts Expense of $16,000.

19X8

Jan.	8	Wrote off Al Smith's account of $14,000 as uncollectible.
Mar.	9	Wrote off Billie French's account of $700 as uncollectible.
July	15	Recovered $700 from Billie French.
Aug.	6	Wrote off Alice Fall's account of $650 as uncollectible.
Sept.	9	Wrote off Pete Reston's account of $900 as uncollectible.
Nov.	18	Recovered $400 from Alice Fall.

NOTES RECEIVABLE AND NOTES PAYABLE

Chapter Objectives

- ◆ Determining interest calculations and maturity dates on notes. (p. 573)
- ◆ Journalizing entries to record renewal of a note, dishonouring of a note, eventual receipt of payment, and note given in exchange for equipment purchased. (p. 578)
- ◆ Discounting an interest-bearing note receivable and recording a discounted note that has been dishonoured. (p. 583)
- ◆ Handling adjustments for interest expense and interest income. (p. 588)

Notes receivable—asset.
Notes payable—liability.

So far the accounts receivable and accounts payable transactions we have been discussing have not involved formal written promises (a purchase order or a sales receipt is not a formal written promise). In this chapter we will turn to transactions by buyers and sellers that do require formal written promises, also called promissory notes or notes. The notes record amounts owed to a company by others (notes receivable) and amounts the company itself owes (notes payable).

There are a number of reasons why a company uses notes instead of informal promises:

1. To record sales of high-cost items such as farm machinery or construction equipment that have long-term credit periods (usually over 60 days).
2. To give additional time to settle past due accounts.
3. To borrow money from a bank.
4. To collect a fee for the use of one's money over a period of time. This is called **interest**. If one lends money, one gets interest; if one borrows money, one pays interest.
5. To have a stronger legal claim for collecting a past due account. In this case the note acts as formal proof of the transaction.

Before looking at recording notes receivable and notes payable, let's first discuss the structure of a note and how to determine interest calculations and *maturity dates* (when the note comes due).

LEARNING UNIT 15-1

Promissory Notes, Calculations, and Determining Maturity Dates

A **promissory note** (often called simply a **note**) is a written promise by a borrower to pay a certain sum of money to the lender at a fixed future date. The following is a promissory note that Able Company issued to Green Company. Take a moment to look at the structure of the note, shown in Figure 15-1. The following explanation is keyed to the figure:

Think of the payee as the lender.

A. Able Company is borrowing $20,000; this amount is called the **principal.**
B. Money is being borrowed for 60 days.
C. The note is issued on October 2, 19XX.
D. The Green Company is the **payee** to whom the note is payable.
E. The note carries a 12 percent annual interest rate. (Even though the note is for 60 days, interest is stated as a yearly rate.)

FIGURE 15-1
A Promissory Note

$ 20,000 (A) Winnipeg, Manitoba October 2nd 19 XX (C)

sixty days (B) after date we promise to pay

to the order of Green Company (D)

Twenty-thousand and 00/100 Dollars

Payable at Bank of Montreal

Interest Rate 12% per annum (E)

No. 115 Due December 4, 19XX (F)

Able Company (G)

Joe Mack

Treasurer

F. The date the note will come due, December 4, 19XX, is called the **maturity date** and includes three days' grace—a common practice in Canada.

G. Able Company is the **maker**, or the one promising to pay the note plus interest when it comes due.

The maker is often also called the payor or debtor.

Think of the maker (Able Company) as the borrower, who thus calls this obligation a **note payable**. On the other side of the coin the payee (Green Company) views this note as an asset called a **note receivable**. What will be interest expense for Able Company will be interest income for Green Company. Remember, interest expense is classified on the income statement as "other expenses," and interest income is "other income."

Most interest on notes will be paid on maturity date. We will cover exceptions later in the chapter.

How to calculate interest

The formula for calculating the interest on a note is:

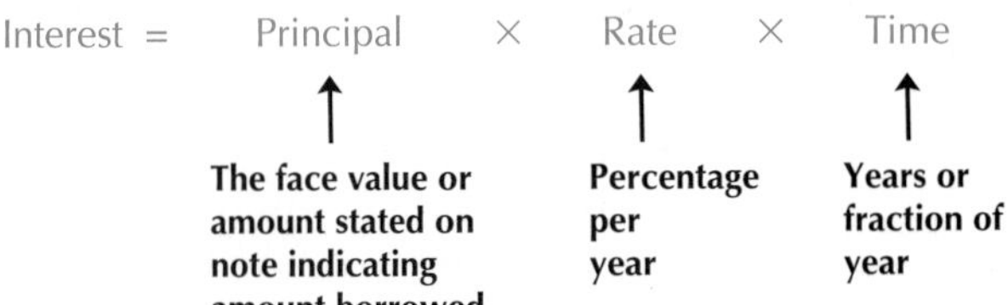

Let's look at some illustrative situations to show specific interest calculation:

◆ **Interest calculated for one year on a $6,000 12 percent note.**

$12\% = 0.12 \text{ or } \frac{12}{100}$

$$I = P \times R \times T$$
$$I = \$6{,}000 \times 0.12 \times 1$$
$$I = \$720$$

◆ **Interest calculated for five months on an $8,000 10 percent note.**

Time is expressed in twelfths of a year; thus, 5 months is $\frac{5}{12}$.

$$I = P \times R \times T$$
$$= \$8{,}000 \times 0.10 \times \frac{5}{12}$$
$$= \$333.33$$

◆ **Interest calculated for exact number of days based on a 365-day year, 60 days at 6 percent on a $4,000 note.** When the note is given in days, the fraction for time is

$$\frac{\text{Exact Number of Days + 3 Days' Grace}}{365}$$

So we have:

$$I = P \times R \times T$$
$$= \$4{,}000 \times 0.06 \times \frac{63}{365}$$
$$= \$41.42$$

◆ **Interest calculated for specific three-month period. $5,000, 8 percent note dated June 1, 19XX.** Time is expressed in terms of three specific months:

June	30 days
July	31 days
August	31 days
Grace period	3 days
Total	95 days

So we have:

$$I = P \times R \times T$$
$$= \$5{,}000 \times 0.08 \times \frac{95}{365}$$
$$= \$104.11$$

A Shortcut: The 6 Percent, 60-Day Method and Its Variations

Common business practice in Canada is to use 365 days, but occasionally 360 days is used as a quick approximation.

Note: Each rate multiplied times the number of days equals 360.

Sometimes to simplify calculation it is assumed that a year has 360 days. When that assumption is made, the interest on any note that is 6 percent for 60 days is always equal to 1 percent of the principal of the note:

$$0.06 \times \frac{60}{360} = 0.01$$

Thus, when the rate times the number of days equals 360, it is equal to 1 per cent, and the interest is calculated by moving the decimal two places to the left.

For example:

$4,000 at 6 percent for 60 days = $40
$481.40 at 6 percent for 60 days = $4.81
$6,000 at 10 percent for 36 days = $60

Saying: "30 days have September, April, June, and November, all the rest have 31, except February alone." February has 28 (29 in a leap year).

How to Determine Maturity Date

By Exact Days

To determine the maturity date of a 90-day note dated June 21, the following could be set up (or you could count on a calendar):

Number of days remaining in June (30 − 21)	9
Days in July	31
Days in August	31
Number of days at end of August	71
Days in September to reach 90	22
Term of note	93

Thus the maturity date of the note is September 22.

Another way to calculate the maturity date is to use a table of days in a year (see Table 15-1).

The original note is dated June 21. Look at the top of the table for June and down the left column to day 21. The point of intersection reveals that June 21 is the 172nd day of the year. If we add 172 and 93 (length of note) we get 265. By searching in the table for 265, we see the date of maturity is September 22.

TABLE 15-1 Days in a Year

Day of Month	Jan.	Feb.*	Mar.	Apr.	May	June	July	Aug.	Sept.	Oct.	Nov.	Dec.	Day of Month
1	1	32	60	91	121	152	182	213	244	274	305	335	1
2	2	33	61	92	122	153	183	214	245	275	306	336	2
3	3	34	62	93	123	154	184	215	246	276	307	337	3
4	4	35	63	94	124	155	185	216	247	277	308	338	4
5	5	36	64	95	125	156	186	217	248	278	309	339	5
6	6	37	65	96	126	157	187	218	249	279	310	340	6
7	7	38	66	97	127	158	188	219	250	280	311	341	7
8	8	39	67	98	128	159	189	220	251	281	312	342	8
9	9	40	68	99	129	160	190	221	252	282	313	343	9
10	10	41	69	100	130	161	191	222	253	283	314	344	10
11	11	42	70	101	131	162	192	223	254	284	315	345	11
12	12	43	71	102	132	163	193	224	255	285	316	346	12
13	13	44	72	103	133	164	194	225	256	286	317	347	13
14	14	45	73	104	134	165	195	226	257	287	318	348	14
15	15	46	74	105	135	166	196	227	258	288	319	349	15
16	16	47	75	106	136	167	197	228	259	289	320	350	16
17	17	48	76	107	137	168	198	229	260	290	321	351	17
18	18	49	77	108	138	169	199	230	261	291	322	352	18
19	19	50	78	109	139	170	200	231	262	292	323	353	19
20	20	51	79	110	140	171	201	232	263	293	324	354	20
21	21	52	80	111	141	172	202	233	264	294	325	355	21
22	22	53	81	112	142	173	203	234	265	295	326	356	22
23	23	54	82	113	143	174	204	235	266	296	327	357	23
24	24	55	83	114	144	175	205	236	267	297	328	358	24
25	25	56	84	115	145	176	206	237	268	298	329	359	25
26	26	57	85	116	146	177	207	238	269	299	330	360	26
27	27	58	86	117	147	178	208	239	270	300	331	361	27
28	28	59	87	118	148	179	209	240	271	301	332	362	28
29	29		88	119	149	180	210	241	272	302	333	363	29
30	30		89	120	150	181	211	242	273	303	334	364	30
31	31		90		151		212	243		304		365	31

* For leap years, February has 29 days, and the number of each day after February 28 is one greater than the number given in the table.

By Number of Months

If the note were expressed in months rather than days, the table or calendar would not be needed. The maturity date could be found by counting the months from the date the note was issued, regardless of number of days in each month. Let's look at several examples:

Date of Note	*Length of Note*	*Maturity Date*
March 31	2 months + 3 days	June 3
April 30	3 months + 3 days	Aug. 3
July 31	2 months + 3 days	Oct. 3

LEARNING UNIT 15-1 REVIEW

AT THIS POINT you should be able to

- Explain the advantages of using notes instead of informal promises. (p. 573)
- Define and explain the structure of a promissory note. (p. 573)
- Calculate interest on notes in days, monthly, or yearly. (pp. 574–575)
- Calculate maturity date by days in the month, by special chart, or by months. (pp. 576–577)

SELF-REVIEW QUIZ 15-1

1. Calculate the interest for the following:

a. $10,000	12%	1 year	(Ignore days of grace)
b. $ 9,000	13%	7 months	(Ignore days of grace)
c. $ 7,000	10%	80 days	(With 3 days of grace)

2. Find the maturity date of an 80-day note dated March 3 by (a) days in each month, (b) using a days-in-a-year chart.
3. Find the maturity date of a note dated March 31, due in 5 months.

Solutions to Self-Review Quiz 15-1

1. **a.** $10,000 × 0.12 × 1 = $1,200
   b. $9,000 × 0.13 × 7/12 = $682.50
   c. $7,000 × 0.10 × 83/365 = $159.18
2. **a.**

Number of days remaining in March (31 - 3)	28
Days in April	30
Number of days at end of April	58
Days in May to reach 83	25
Maturity date—May 25	

   b.

March 3	62 days	
	+83	
	145	May 25

3. March 31, April, May, June, July, August 31 + 3 days = September 3.

LEARNING UNIT 15-2
Recording Notes

We will use general journal entries to keep things simple instead of using special journals.

To understand how notes may be used to extend credit periods as well as to see how a note is paid off, let's look at some illustrative transactions involving Mace Company and Jane Company.

SALE OF MERCHANDISE ON ACCOUNT

On August 1, 19XX, Mace Company sold $6,000 of merchandise on account to Jane Company.

ON BOOKS OF SELLER—MACE COMPANY

			Dr.	Cr.
Aug.	1	Accounts Receivable, Jane Co.	600000	
		Sales		600000
		Sold merchandise on account		

ON BOOKS OF BUYER—JANE COMPANY

			Dr.	Cr.
Aug.	1	Purchases	600000	
		Accounts Payable, Mace Co.		600000
		Purchased merchandise on account		

TIME EXTENSION WITH A NOTE

Notes Receivable is a current asset on the balance sheet.

On September 1, the end of the credit period, Jane Company gave a $6,000, 60-day, 13 percent note to Mace Company to gain additional time to settle the past due account. The following entries would be made on the books of the buyer and the seller.

SELLER—MACE COMPANY

			Dr.	Cr.
Sept.	1	Notes Receivable	600000	
		Accounts Receivable, Jane Co.		600000
		Received 60-day, 13% note for		
		extension of past due account		

BUYER—JANE COMPANY

			Dr.	Cr.
Sept.	1	Accounts Payable, Mace Co.	600000	
		Notes Payable		600000
		Issued 60-day, 13% note for		
		extension of past due account		

Notes Payable is a current liability on the balance sheet.

When this transaction is journalized, both Accounts Receivable and Accounts Payable are reduced. With notes a subsidiary ledger is usually *not* needed, since the file of the notes provides all the information.

Why would Mace accept this note as an extension? Because:

1. The Jane Company doesn't pay, a formal written promise is in hand and is easier to enforce, legally speaking.
2. Interest accumulates on a note.

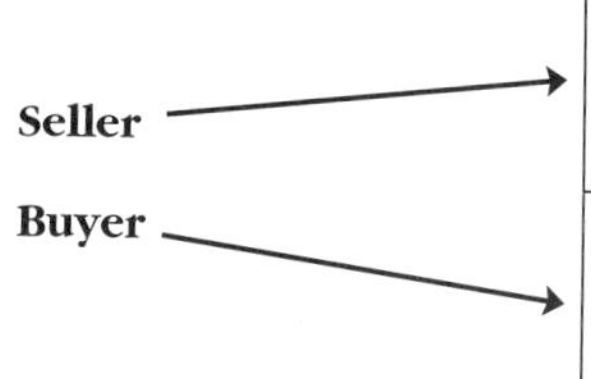

The end result of this transaction is a shifting of assets of Mace Company from Accounts Receivable to Notes Receivable.

For Jane Company the result is a shift in liabilities from Accounts Payable to Notes Payable.

Note due and paid at maturity

Now let's look at the journal entries that will be made if Jane Company pays off the note on November 3.

SELLER—MACE COMPANY

Nov.	3	Cash	6 1 3 4 63	
		Notes Receivable		6 0 0 0 00
		Interest Income		1 3 4 63
		Collected Jane Company note		

[$6,000 x .013 x $\frac{63}{360}$ = $134.63 interest income]

BUYER—JANE COMPANY

Oct.	31	Notes Payable	6 0 0 0 00	
		Interest Expense	1 3 4 63	
		Cash		6 1 3 4 63
		Paid note to Mace Company		

[$6,000 x .013 x $\frac{63}{360}$ = $134.64 interest expense]

It is important to emphasize that the interest is calculated on the maturity date of the note, plus three days' grace, or November 3.

Note renewed at maturity

If Jane Company is unable to pay the $6,134.63 at maturity, it is possible for the company to renew all or part of the note. Let's assume that the company can pay the interest of $134.63 and give another note for 90 days at 13 percent.

The transaction could be recorded as follows on the books of the buyer and the seller:

SELLER—MACE COMPANY

Date		Account	Debit	Credit
Nov.	3	Cash	134 63	
		Notes Receivable (new)	6 000 00	
		Notes Receivable (old)		6 000 00
		Interest Income		134 63
		Interest of old note collected and renewal of note for 90 days		

BUYER—JANE COMPANY

Date		Account	Debit	Credit
Nov.	3	Notes Payable (old)	6 000 00	
		Interest Expense	134 63	
		Notes Payable (new)		6 000 00
		Cash		134 63
		Interest of old note paid and renewal of note recorded		

Notice on the seller's books how the interest is received, the old note is cancelled, and the new note is put on the books.

Now let's look at another alternative, the case in which Jane Company fails to pay the original note at maturity, but the note will *not* be renewed.

DISHONOURED NOTE

If Jane Company fails to pay the **maturity value** (the $6,000 principal plus interest of $134.63) on October 31, the note is said to be **dishonoured**. Another way of saying this is to say that Jane Company has **defaulted** on its note. On Jane's and Mace's books the amounts in Notes Receivable and Notes Payable will then be removed and transferred back to Accounts Receivable and Accounts Payable, because the note has reached the maturity date. At the same time, whether the note is paid or not, the interest expense is due and payable and should be recorded (for Mace Company this is Interest Income and for Jane Company it is Interest Expense).

Let's see what entries will look like if Jane Company first defaults and then finally pays the amount owed on December 1. To keep it simple, no additional charges will be calculated for the extra month Jane Company has taken to pay off the amount owed to Mace Company.

Only unmatured notes are in the Notes Receivable account.

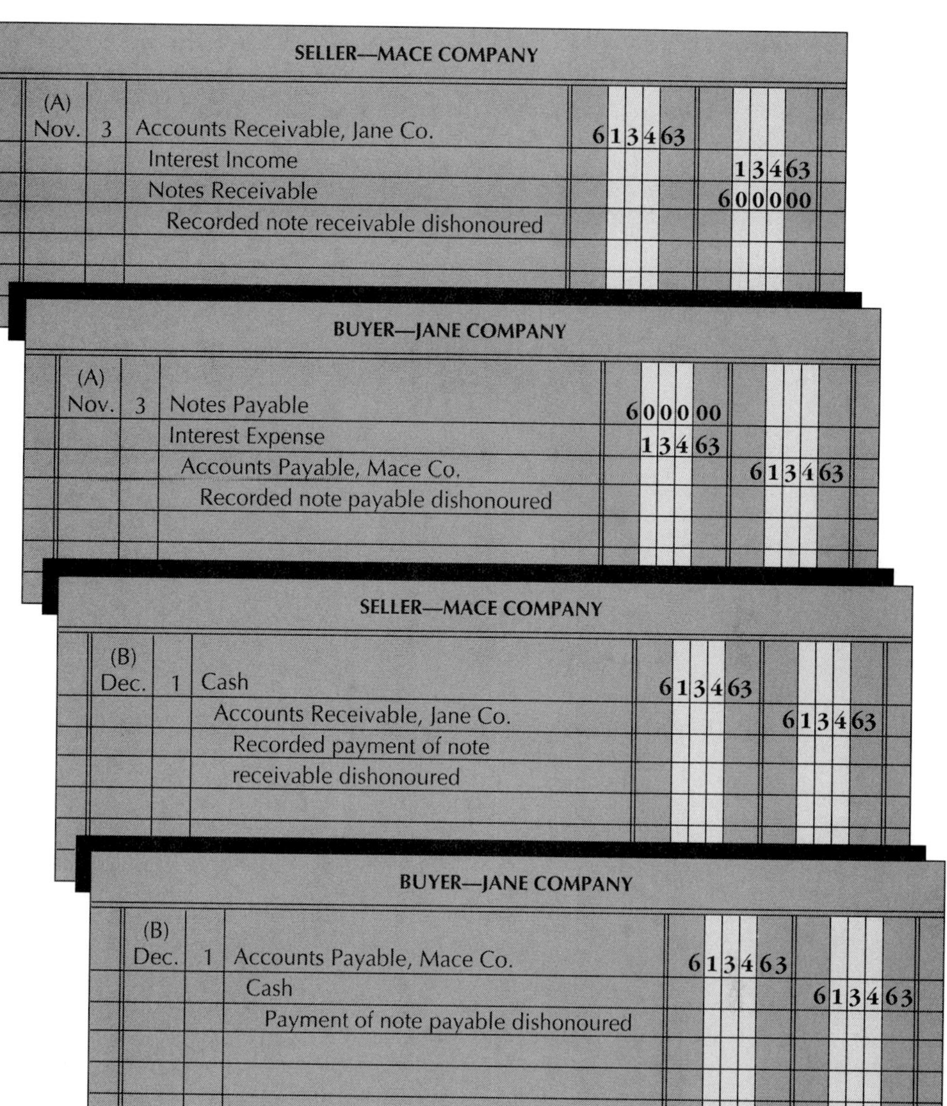

SELLER—MACE COMPANY

Date		Account	Debit	Credit
(A) Nov.	3	Accounts Receivable, Jane Co.	6134 63	
		Interest Income		134 63
		Notes Receivable		6000 00
		Recorded note receivable dishonoured		

BUYER—JANE COMPANY

Date		Account	Debit	Credit
(A) Nov.	3	Notes Payable	6000 00	
		Interest Expense	134 63	
		Accounts Payable, Mace Co.		6134 63
		Recorded note payable dishonoured		

SELLER—MACE COMPANY

Date		Account	Debit	Credit
(B) Dec.	1	Cash	6134 63	
		Accounts Receivable, Jane Co.		6134 63
		Recorded payment of note receivable dishonoured		

BUYER—JANE COMPANY

Date		Account	Debit	Credit
(B) Dec.	1	Accounts Payable, Mace Co.	6134 63	
		Cash		6134 63
		Payment of note payable dishonoured		

Before we conclude this Unit, let's discuss how a note may be given in exchange for an asset purchased.

NOTE GIVEN IN EXCHANGE FOR EQUIPMENT PURCHASED

Jane Company decided to buy from Ronald Company some display racks for $7,000. Because the price was high, Jane Company gave a note instead of buying the racks on account. The note issued by Jane Company was a 60-day, 9 percent interest-bearing note for $7,000. This transaction is recorded on the books of the buyer and seller as follows:

SELLER—RONALD COMPANY

May	9	Notes Receivable	7 0 0 0 00	
		Sales		7 0 0 0 00
		Sold display racks with a		
		60 day, 9% note		

BUYER—JANE COMPANY

May	9	Store Equipment	7 0 0 0 00	
		Notes Payable		7 0 0 0 00
		Purchased display racks with a		
		60 day, 9% note		

When the note is paid at maturity, the same transactions we previously discussed would result.

LEARNING UNIT 15-2 REVIEW

AT THIS POINT you should be able to

- Journalize entries for buyer and seller to record the extension of a past due account by issuing a note. (p. 578)
- Explain why a subsidiary ledger may not be needed with Notes Payable and Notes Receivable. (p. 579)
- Journalize entries for the buyer and seller to record renewal of a note, dishonouring of a note, eventual receipt of payment, and a note given in exchange for equipment purchased. (pp. 580–582)

SELF-REVIEW QUIZ 15-2

Journalize the following transactions for Action Company:

A. Action Company sold $8,000 of merchandise on account to Brian Company.

B. Action Company received a 60-day, $8,000, 12 percent note for a time extension of past due account of Brian Company.

C. Collected the Brian Company note on the maturity date.

D. Brian Company renewed the note for 90 days and paid interest on the old note. (Alternative to C.)

E. Assuming that Brian Company defaulted in C, record the note receivable dishonoured.

F. Brian Company paid note receivable dishonoured.

Solution to Self-Review Quiz 15-2

(A)		Accounts Receivable, Brian Co.	800000	
		Sales		800000
		Sold merchandise on account		
(B)		Notes Receivable	800000	
		Accounts Receivable, Brian Co.		800000
		Received 60 day note to extend payment		
(C)		Cash	816600	
		Interest Income		16600
		Notes Receivable		800000
		Received payment on note		
		[$8,000 × .012 × $\frac{63}{365}$ = $166]		
(D)		Cash	16600	
		Notes Receivable	800000	
		Notes Receivable		800000
		Interest Income		16600
		Received interest and renewed note		
		for 90 days		
(E)		Accounts Receivable, Brian Company	816600	
		Notes Receivable		800000
		Interest Income		16600
		Note dishonoured		
(F)		Cash	816600	
		Accounts Receivable, Brian Company		816600
		Payment of dishonoured note		

LEARNING UNIT 15-3

How to Discount Customers' Notes

Think of the bank discount as the cost of cashing in a note before maturity.

Many times a company that accepts notes from customers will not (or cannot) wait to receive its cash until the maturity date. Instead, it goes to a bank and exchanges the note for cash; this is called **discounting**. The company will endorse the note and receive the *maturity value* of the note (principal plus interest) less what the bank charges for holding the note from the date of discounting until the maturity date. The time period during which the bank holds the note (until maturity) is called the **discount period**.

What Marvin Company will receive from bank is called the proceeds.

The amount that the bank charges the company is called the **bank discount**. It is the difference between what the company receives from the bank and the maturity value of the note. The actual amount of money the company receives when a note is discounted is called the **proceeds** (maturity value less the bank discount).

Now let's take a look at Marvin Company and how it discounts an interest-bearing note receivable. The best way to understand the process is to take it step by step.

HOW TO DISCOUNT AN INTEREST-BEARING NOTE RECEIVABLE

Marvin Company received an $8,000, 90-day, 12 percent note from Jee Company dated October 1. On October 31 Marvin Company needed cash to finance its inventory, so it discounted the note to Royal Bank, which charges a bank discount rate of 14 percent. An overview of the process is shown in Figure 15-2.

FIGURE 15-2
Discounting an Interest-Bearing Note Receivable

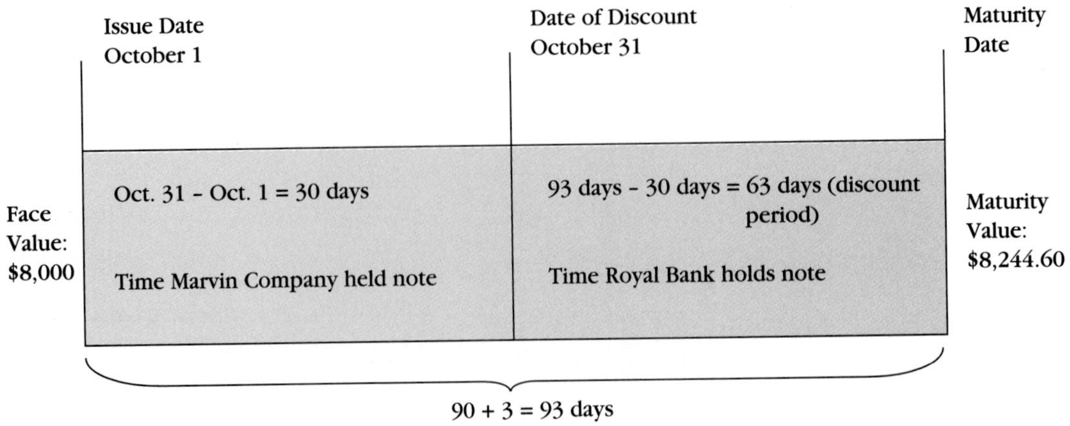

	Issue Date October 1	Date of Discount October 31	Maturity Date
Face Value: $8,000	Oct. 31 - Oct. 1 = 30 days Time Marvin Company held note	93 days - 30 days = 63 days (discount period) Time Royal Bank holds note	Maturity Value: $8,244.60

90 + 3 = 93 days

Find maturity value.

Step 1: Find the *maturity value* of the note:

a. $8,000 × 0.12 × 93/365 = $244.60 interest

b. Maturity value = Principal + Interest
= $8,000 + $244.60
= $8,244.60

Calculate discount period.

Step 2: Calculate the *discount period* (number of days from the date of discounting until the maturity date):

93 days note + grace period
− 30 days expired before discounting (Oct. 31 - Oct. 1)
= 63 days bank holds note until it comes due

Calculate bank discount.

Step 3: Calculate the *bank discount* (what the bank charges Marvin Company for holding the note until maturity):

Bank Discount = Maturity Value × Bank Discount Rate × No. of Days Bank Holds Note Until Maturity/365 days

= $8,244.60 × 0.14 × 63/365
= $199.23

Note that the bank discount is based on the maturity value, because we are borrowing the maturity value for the number of days in the discount period.

Calculate proceeds.

Step 4: Calculate the *proceeds* (what Marvin Company receives from the bank in the discounting process):

Proceeds = Maturity Value - Bank Discount
= $8,244.60 - $199.23
= $8,045.37

If Marvin Company could have waited until the maturity date, they would have received $8,244.60. By discounting the note the company lost interest of $199.23, or the cost charged by the bank to hold the note until maturity. Let's look at how Marvin Company would record this on its books (again for simplicity we use general journal entries rather than special journals).

Journalizing the discounted note receivable:

$ 8,045.37
− 8,000.00
$ 45.37
(Interest Income)

Oct.	31	Cash	8,045.37	
		Notes Receivable		8,000.00
		Interest Income		45.37
		Discounted Jee's Company		
		90-day, 12% note at 14%		

Now we use Interest Income, since the proceeds Marvin Company received were more than the face value of the note ($8,000). In actuality, if the proceeds had been *less* than the $8,000, Marvin Company would have incurred an interest expense. How could this happen? If Marvin Company held the note for only a short period of time and Royal Bank had a bank discount rate much higher than the original note, it is very possible that the proceeds to Marvin Company might have been less than the $8,000. For example, suppose this same note of Marvin Company was discounted after being held only two days, and the bank's discount rate was 18 percent. The bank discount, or amount the bank charges, would be calculated as follows:

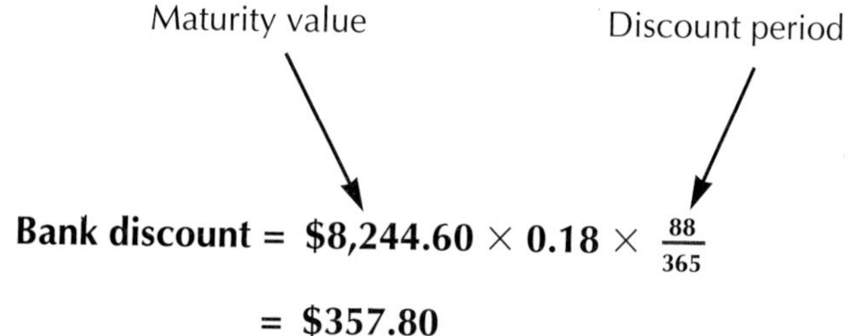

$$\textbf{Bank discount} = \$8{,}244.60 \times 0.18 \times \frac{88}{365}$$

$$= \$357.80$$

Thus the proceeds to Marvin Company would be:

$$\text{Proceeds} = \$8{,}244.60 - \$357.80$$
$$= \$7{,}886.80$$

Note that here Marvin Company is receiving *less* than the $8,000 face value of the note. The general journal entry of Marvin Company would thus look as follows:

Oct.	31	Cash	7,886.80	
		Interest Expense	113.20	
		Notes Receivable		8,000.00
		Discounted 12% note at 18%		

Now the question arises as to who is liable for the note if Jee Company fails to pay the note at maturity.

Procedure when a discounted note is dishonoured

When Marvin Company endorsed the note to Royal Bank, the company agreed to pay the note at maturity if Jee Company failed to pay. The potential liability that may result (or not) is called a **contingent liability**. Until the note is paid, Marvin Company will state this contingent liability as a footnote on its balance sheet. If the note had been endorsed *without recourse*, then Marvin Company would have no liability.

At some point before maturity, Jee Company is notified that Royal Bank is holding the note. Let's assume that the maturity date is reached and Jee Company defaults. Royal Bank notifies Marvin Company and charges Marvin Company the full amount of the note, including interest and a $5 protest fee, which is the charge made by Royal Bank for notifying Marvin Company that the note was presented to the maker for payment and was not received. Thus the bank charges Marvin Company (and Marvin will in turn charge Jee Company) the following:

Note	$8,000.00
Interest	244.60
Protest fee	5.00
	$8,249.60

The following entry is recorded on Marvin Company's books:

			Dr.	Cr.
Dec.	30	Accounts Receivable, Jee Co.	824960	
		Cash		824960
		To record default		

You can be sure that Marvin Company will try to collect this $8,249.60 from Jee Company. Marvin Company may charge additional interest for this delay in paying the $8,249.60. For simplicity we have left this step out. If the $8,249.60 becomes uncollectible, the account could be written off as a bad debt using the Allowance for Doubtful Accounts method discussed in Chapter 14.

Learning Unit 15-3 Review

AT THIS POINT you should be able to

- Define and explain discounting, maturity value, discount period, bank discount, proceeds. (p. 583)
- Explain the four steps required in discounting an interest-bearing note receivable. (p. 584)
- Prepare a journal entry to record the proceeds of a note. (p. 585)
- Define contingent liability and compare it with an endorsement without recourse. (p. 586)
- Journalize the entry to record a discounted note that has been dishonoured. (p. 586)

SELF-REVIEW QUIZ 15-3

Al Gene Company received a $10,000, 60-day, 12 percent note from Broom Company dated July 5. On August 3 Al Gene Company discounted the note to their Bank, which charged a bank discount rate of 15 percent.

a. Complete the four steps (p. 584) to discount the note.
b. Journalize the entry to record the proceeds.
c. Journalize the entry if a default occurs, assuming a $5 protest fee.

Solutions to Self-Review Quiz 15-3

a. Step 1: Maturity value (principal + interest):

$$I = \$10{,}000 \times 0.12 \times 63/365$$
$$= \$207.12$$
$$MV = \$10{,}000 + \$207.12$$
$$= \$10{,}207.12$$

Step 2: Discount period:

July 31
 -5
26 days Al Gene held note in July
 3 days Al Gene held note in August
29 days Al Gene held note

63 days
-29 days
34 days bank holds note

Step 3: Bank discount:

$$\text{Bank Discount} = \text{Maturity Value} \times \text{Bank Discount Rate} \times \frac{\text{No. of Days Bank Holds Note Until Maturity}}{365}$$

$$= \underset{\text{(Step 1)}}{\$10{,}207.12} \times \underset{\text{(Given in facts)}}{0.15} \times 34/365$$

$$= \$142.62$$

Step 4: Proceeds:

$$\text{Proceeds} = \text{Maturity Value} - \text{Bank Discount}$$
$$= \$10{,}207.12 - \$142.62$$
$$= \$10{,}064.50$$

				Debit	Credit
b.	Aug.	3	Cash	10 064 50	
			Notes Receivable		10 000 00
			Interest Income		64 50
			Discounted Broom Company		
			12% note at 15%.		
c.	Sept.	3	Accounts Receivable, Broom Company	10 212 12	
			Cash		10 212 12
			To record recourse on defaulted note.		

LEARNING UNIT 15-4

Discounting One's Own Note: Handling Adjustments for Interest Expense and Interest Income

DISCOUNTING ONE'S OWN NOTE

In the last Unit we looked at how a note of a customer was discounted. Now our attention shifts to Jones Company, which is borrowing $10,000 by giving Alberta Bank its own 12 percent, 60-day note on December 16, 19XX. In this case Alberta Bank deducts the interest *in advance*. The following is the formula to calculate the bank discount (cost of borrowing) and the proceeds (what Jones Company gets):

Note that maturity value here is the same as the original principal, since interest is deducted in advance.

Note also that when discounting one's own note, no days of grace are given.

$$\text{Bank Discount} = \left(\text{Maturity Value}\right) \times \left(\text{Interest Rate}\right) \times \left(\frac{\text{Discount Period}}{365}\right)$$

$$= \$10{,}000 \times 0.12 \times 60/365$$

$$= \$197.26$$

$$\text{Proceeds} = \text{Maturity Value} - \text{Discount}$$

$$= \$10{,}000 - \$197.26$$

$$= \$9{,}802.74$$

Discount on Notes Payable is a contra-liability.

Thus Jones Company receives $9,802.74 and at the time of maturity will pay back $10,000. The $197.26 of interest is recorded in a new account called **Discount on Notes Payable**. This is a contra-liability account that is subtracted from Notes Payable on the balance sheet, where it looks like this:

Current Liabilities:		
Notes Payable	$10,000.00	
Less: Discount on Notes Payable	197.26	
		$9,802.74

Later in this Unit, when we talk about adjustments, you will see that as the note matures, the discount will be reduced and then charged to Interest Expense. But for now let's record the journal entry for Jones Company as it discounts its own note with interest deducted in advance:

			Debit	Credit
Dec.	16	Cash	9 802 74	
		Discount on Notes Payable	197 46	
		Notes Payable		10 000 00
		Discounted own note at 12 percent		

Accounts Affected	Category	↑ ↓	Rules	
Cash	Asset	↑	Dr.	**$9,802.74**
Discount on Notes Payable	Liability (Contra)	↑	Dr.	**$197.46**
Notes Payable	Liability	↑	Cr.	**$10,000**

When the note is paid, the accountant will debit Notes Payable for $10,000 and credit Cash for $10,000.

Effective interest rate: the cost of borrowing the $10,000 is not 12 percent but really almost $12\frac{1}{4}$ percent.

Note: Although the bank interest rate is stated at 12 percent, the truth is that Jones Company really has the use of only $9,800. To calculate the true interest rate, which is called the effective interest rate, the following formula applies:

$$\text{Effective Interest Rate} = \frac{(\text{Maturity Value of Note}) \times (\text{Bank Interest Rate})}{\text{Amount of Cash Proceeds Received from Note}}$$

$$= \frac{\$10{,}000 \times 0.12}{\$9{,}802.74}$$

$$= 12.24\%$$

Now let's look at how adjustments will be handled for some of the transactions presented in this chapter.

INTEREST: THE NEED FOR ADJUSTMENTS

Because interest-bearing notes are often taken out and then paid off in different accounting periods, it is necessary to adjust or bring up to date Interest Income and Interest Expense. The following diagram shows why we need to adjust, as well as who does the adjusting:

ACCRUED INTEREST INCOME	ACCRUED INTEREST EXPENSE
Must adjust for income that has been earned during the period but has not been received or recorded because payment is not yet due.	Must adjust for interest that has been incurred during the period but has not been paid or recorded because payment is not yet due.
↓	↓
Note Receivable (*seller*)	(A) Note Payable (*buyer*) (B) Company's own discounted note

Let's look at how to record adjustments for Interest Income and Interest Expense from the following: Bog Company receives a $24,000, 60-day, 10 percent note on December 16 from Jan Company.

Step 1: Calculate interest on the note:

$$\text{Interest} = \$24{,}000 \times 0.10 \times 63/365$$
$$= \$414.25$$

Step 2: Calculate the number of days the note has already run before the end of the current period (see Figure 15-3):

Dec. 31 (end of period)
- Dec. 16 (starting date of note)
15 days

FIGURE 15-3 Adjusting for Interest Accrued

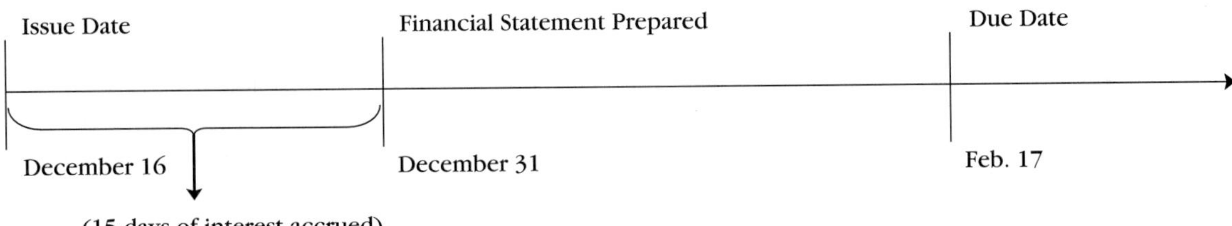

Step 3: Calculate interest incurred for this period:

$$\$24{,}000 \times 0.10 \times 15/365 = \$98.63$$

Step 4: Prepare the adjusting journal entries:

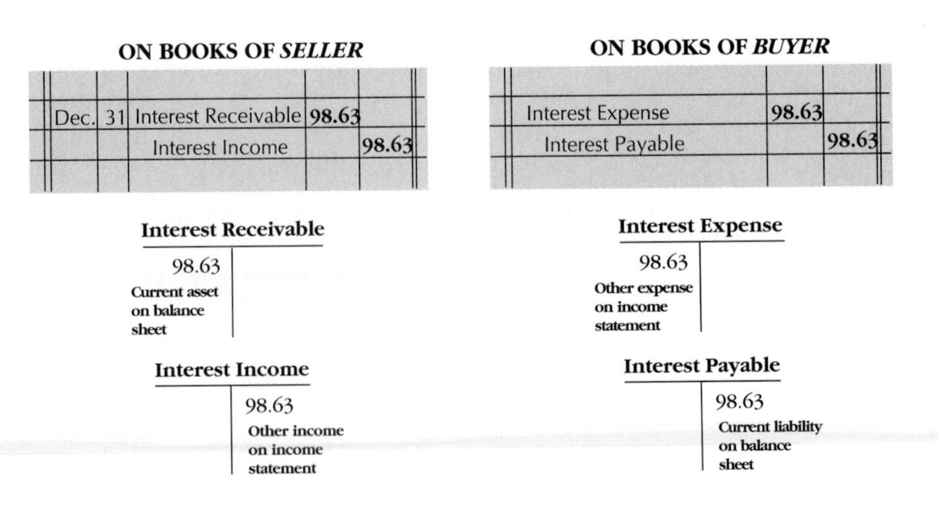

When the note is paid off on February 17, the following entries are made, assuming that no reversing entry is used.*

SELLER

Date		Account	Debit	Credit
Feb.	17	Cash	24414 25	
		Interest Receivable		98 63
		Notes Receivable		24000 00
		Interest Income		315 62
		Collection of note and interest to due date.		

BUYER

Date		Account	Debit	Credit
Feb.	17	Notes Payable	24000 00	
		Interest Expense	315 62	
		Interest Payable	98 63	
		Cash		24414 25
		Payment of note and interest to due date.		

Note that by *not* using reversing entries the bookkeeper of the buyer and seller had to recall the amount of accrued interest that was recorded in the *old* year so that this year's interest expense or income would not be overstated.

The last adjustment deals with a firm discounting its own note. At the beginning of this Unit, we saw Jones Company discounting its own note on December 16 for $10,000 for 60 days at 12 percent interest. Jones Company actually received $9,802.74 and recorded the $197.26 interest deducted in advance by the bank in a contra-liability account called Discount on Notes Payable.

Discount on Notes Payable

Dr.	Cr.
197.26	

Interest Expense

Dr.	Cr.

*If a reversing entry is used, the following entries are made:

SELLER

Date		Account	Debit	Credit
Feb.	17	Cash	24414 25	
		Notes Receivable		24000 00
		Interest Income		414 25
		Collection of note and interest to due date.		

BUYER

Date		Account	Debit	Credit
Feb.	17	Notes Payable	24000 00	
		Interest Expense	414 25	
		Cash		24414 25
		Payment of note and interest to due date.		

At the end of December, 15 days out of the 60 days have passed. Thus one-fourth of the interest on this note should be recorded in the old year. To record this interest we reduce the amount in the Discount on Notes Payable by \$49.32 (1/4 × \$197.26). The following journal entry is made:

			Dr.	Cr.
Dec.	31	Interest Expense	4932	
		Discount on Notes Payable		4932
		Recognition of expense incurred		

Accounts Affected	Category	↑ ↓	Rules	
Interest Expense	Expense	↑	Dr.	**\$49.32**
Discount on Notes Payable	Liability (Contra)	↓	Cr.	**\$49.32**

The current liability on the balance sheet will look as follows:

See p. 589 for comparison of this section before discount on note is reduced.

Current Liabilities

Notes Payable	\$10,000.00	
Less: Discount on Notes Payable	147.94	
		\$9,852.06

Alternate calculation:

$\frac{45 \text{ days}}{60 \text{ days}} \times \$197.26$

$= \$147.94$

When the note is paid the following journal entry will result:

			Dr.	Cr.
Feb.	14	Notes Payable	1000000	
		Interest Expense	14794	
		Discount on Notes Payable		14794
		Cash		1000000

LEARNING UNIT 15-4 REVIEW

AT THIS POINT you should be able to

- Explain the purpose of the Discount on Notes Payable account. (p. 588)
- Calculate the effective interest rate. (p. 589)
- Make adjustments for interest income and interest expense at end of period. (pp. 589–590)
- Adjust the Discount on Notes Payable account. (p. 592)

SELF-REVIEW QUIZ 15-4

Answer true or false to the following:

1. No bank deducts interest in advance.
2. Discount on Notes Payable is a contra-liability account.
3. When Discount on Notes Payable is reduced, Interest Expense results.
4. Effective rate of interest is lower than the stated rate.
5. Reversing entries are never used to adjust interest at the end of a period of time.

Solutions to Self-Review Quiz 15-4

1. False **2.** True **3.** True **4.** False **5.** False

Chapter Review

Learning Unit 15-1

1. A promissory note is a written promise by a borrower to pay a certain sum of money to a lender at a fixed future date. The note may be interest-bearing or non-interest-bearing.
2. The payee is the party to whom the note is payable.
3. The maker is the one who will pay the promissory note.
4. The maturity date is the time when note comes due.
5. $\text{Interest} = \text{Principal} \times \text{Rate} \times \dfrac{\text{Number of Days}}{365}$

Learning Unit 15-2

1. Notes Payable is a current liability on the balance sheet.
2. Notes do not need subsidiary ledgers.
3. Interest Income for the payee is Interest Expense for the maker.
4. A note that is not paid at maturity is said to be dishonoured.
5. Notes may be renewed as well as issued to buy assets.

Learning Unit 15-3

1. Maturity value = principal + interest.
2. Discount period = number of days from date of discounting until maturity date.
3. Bank discount = what the bank charges for holding a note until the maturity date, as shown in the formula:

$$\text{Bank Discount} = \text{Maturity Value} \times \text{Bank Discount Rate} \times \frac{\text{No. of Days Bank Holds Note (Until Maturity + 3 Days)}}{\text{365 Days}}$$

4. Proceeds = what one receives from bank in the discounting process (the maturity value minus the bank discount).
5. If a discounted note is dishonoured, the original holder of the note may be liable for payment unless the note was endorsed without recourse. This is called contingent liability.

Learning Unit 15-4

1. In discounting one's own note, the interest is usually deducted in advance.
2. The interest that is deducted in advance is recorded in a contra-liability account called Discount on Notes Payable.
3. The effective interest rate is higher than the stated rate.
4. At the end of the period, adjustments are made for Interest Income and Interest Expense that have accrued or built up. These entries can be reversed on the first day starting the next period to simplify recording when interest is paid or received in the new period.

5. The interest in the Discount on Notes Payable account is adjusted by reducing the Discount on Notes Payable and recording it as interest expense.

Key terms

Bank discount What the bank charges to hold a note until maturity (maturity value — proceeds).

Contingent liability Liability on the part of one who discounts a note to pay if the maker of the note defaults at maturity date.

Default Failure of maker to pay the maturity value of a note when due.

Discount on Notes Payable An account showing the amount of interest deducted in advance by the lender. This account reduces Notes Payable to actual cash value.

Discount period The amount of time the bank holds a note that was discounted until the maturity date.

Discounting a note The process or act of transferring the note to a bank before the maturity date.

Dishonoured note A note that was not paid at maturity by the maker.

Effective interest rate The true rate of simple interest.

Interest The cost of using money for a period of time.

Maker The one promising to pay a note.

Maturity date Due date of a promissory note.

Maturity value The value of the note that is due on the date of maturity (principal + interest).

Note payable A promissory note from the maker's point of view.

Note receivable A promissory note from the payee's point of view.

Payee The one to whom a note is payable.

Principal The face amount of a note.

Proceeds Maturity value less bank discount.

Promissory note or note A formal written promise by a borrower to pay a certain sum at a fixed future date.

Blueprint for Notes Payable and Notes Receivable

	SELLER	BUYER
Sales of merchandise on account	Accounts Receivable, XXX Sales	Purchases Accounts Payable, XXX
Time extension with a note	Notes Receivable Accounts Receivable, XXX	Accounts Payable, XXX Notes Payable
Note due and paid	Cash Interest Income Notes Receivable	Notes Payable Interest Expense Cash
Note renewed at maturity	Cash Notes Receivable (new) Notes Receivable (old) Interest Income	Notes Payable (old) Interest Expense Notes Payable (new) Cash
Note given in exchange for equipment purchased	Notes Receivable Sales	Store Equipment Notes Payable

(cont.)

BLUEPRINT (Cont.)

SITUATIONS AFFECTING SELLER ONLY

Discounting a note—receiving more than face value

Account	Debit	Credit
Cash		
Interest Income		
Notes Receivable		

Discounting a note—receiving less than face value

Account	Debit	Credit
Cash		
Interest Expense		
Notes Receivable		

Discounted note dishonoured

Account	Debit	Credit
Accounts Receivable, XXX		
Cash		

Discounting one's own note

Account	Debit	Credit
Cash		
Discount on Notes Payable		
Notes Payable		

(cont.)

BLUEPRINT (Cont.)

ADJUSTMENTS	SELLER			BUYER		
Adjust interest	19X1 Dec.	31	Interest Receivable	19X1 Dec.	31	Interest Expense
			Interest Income			Interest Payable
Note paid (no reversing entry was made)	19X2 Feb.	1	Cash	19X2 Feb.	1	Interest Expense
			Interest Receivable			Interest Payable
			Interest Income			Notes Payable
			Notes Receivable			Cash
Note paid (reversing entry was made)	Feb.	1	Cash	Feb.	1	Interest Expense
			Interest Income			Notes Payable
			Notes Receivable			Cash
Recognizing interest from discount on Notes Payable	Dec.	31	Interest Expense			
			Discount on Notes Payable			

Questions, Exercises, and Problems

Discussion Questions

1. List three reasons why a company may use Notes Payable instead of Accounts Payable.
2. Explain the parts of a promissory note.
3. What is the difference between finding a maturity date by (a) days or (b) months?
4. Notes Receivable is a current liability on the balance sheet. Accept or reject. Why?
5. Why is a subsidiary ledger not needed for notes?
6. Only matured notes are listed in the Notes Receivable account. Please discuss.
7. Explain what will happen if a maker defaults on a note. (Assume the note has not been discounted.)
8. List the four steps to arrive at proceeds in the process of discounting a note.
9. What is meant by contingent liability?
10. When could interest be deducted in advance by a lender?
11. What is the normal balance of the Discount on Notes Payable account?
12. How is the effective interest rate calculated?
13. How is Discount on Notes Payable usually adjusted?

Mini Exercises

(The forms you need are on pages 15-6 and 15-7 of the *Study Guide and Working Papers.*)

Determining Maturity Date

1. Find the maturity date of the following:
   - **a.** 120-day note dated July 8.
   - **b.** 90-day note dated October 8.

Calculate Maturity Value

2. Find the maturity value of the following:

a.	$6,000	6%	9 months
b.	$8,000	7%	70 days

Recording Notes for Buyer and Seller

3. For each of the following transactions for the Frank Co. (the seller), journalize what the entry would be for the buyer.

	Account	Debit	Credit
a.	Accounts Receivable, Bore Co.	700	
	Sales		700
b.	Notes Receivable	700	
	Accounts Receivable, Bore Co.		700
c.	Cash	7,140	
	Notes Receivable		7,000
	Interest Income		140

Discounting a Note

4. Pete Jones discounted a $9,000, 8 percent, 90-day note at the bank. He recorded the following entry:

Cash	9,100	
Notes Receivable		9,000
Interest Income		100

How much interest did Pete Jones lose by discounting the note?

Four Steps in the Discounting Process

5. Blue Co. received a $1,000, 6 percent, 60-day note from Aluin Co. dated August 10. On August 30 Blue discounted the note at their bank, which charged a discount rate of 8 percent. Calculate:

a. maturity value
b. discount period
c. bank discount
d. proceeds

Journal Entry for Discounting

6. Journalize the discounted note for Blue from Mini Exercise 5.

Defaulting

7. If Aluin defaults on the note, what would be the journal entry for Blue Co. assuming a $5 protest fee?

Discounting One's Own Note

8. Aster Co. discounts their own note at a bank. This $5,000 note results in the bank's deducting $300 interest in advance. Draw a transactional analysis box for this situation.

Adjusting the Discount

9. If in Mini Exercise 8 the discount needs to be adjusted at year-end, what would be the journalized adjusting entry? (Assume that the amount is $100.)

Exercises

Calculating interest.

15-1. Calculate the interest for the following:

a.	$14,000	8%	1 year
b.	$20,000	10%	7 months
c.	$ 9,000	12%	80 days

Determining maturity date without tables.

15-2. Determine the maturity date for each of the following without the use of tables:

Note Issued	*Length of Time*
a. January 17, 19X4	30 days
b. July 14, 19X4	90 days
c. May 31, 19X4	4 months
d. June 25, 19X4	75 days

Determining maturity date by table.

15-3. Using the Table 15-1 in Unit 15-1, prove your answers for Exercise 2.

Discounting a note and journalizing entry for proceeds.

15-4. On May 15, 19X4, Ralph Co. gave Blue Co. a 180-day, $9,000, 8 percent note. On July 21 Blue Co. discounted the note at 9 percent.

a. Journalize the entry for Blue to record the proceeds.

b. Record the entry for Blue if Ralph fails to pay at maturity. (Ignore dishonour fee.)

Discount on Notes Payable.

15-5. Howard Slater negotiated a bank loan for $30,000 for 120 days at a bank rate of 10 percent. Assuming the interest is deducted in advance, prepare the entry for Howard to record the bank loan.

Group A Problems

Journalizing notes receivable and notes payable along with note dishonoured.

15A-1. Journalize the following entries for (1) the buyer and (2) the seller. Record all entries for the buyer first.

19X9

June	11	Morgan Company sold $5,000 of merchandise on account to Connors Company (terms, net 30 days).
July	11	Morgan received a 90-day, $5,000, 8 percent note for a time extension of past due account of Connors Company.
Oct.	12	Collected the Connors Company note on the maturity date.
	12	Assuming Connors Company defaulted on its July 11 note, record the dishonoured note.
	18	Connors Company paid the note receivable that was dishonoured on October 12 (no additional interest is charged).

Identifying steps in discounting a note along with journal entry.

15A-2. On May 1, 19X4, Apples Company received a $30,000, 90-day, 9 percent note from Fletcher Company dated May 1. On June 20, 19X4, Apples discounted the note at their bank at a discount rate of 10 percent.

1. Calculate the following:

a. Maturity value of the note.

b. Number of days the bank will hold the note until maturity date.

c. Bank discount.

d. Proceeds.

2. Journalize the entry to record the proceeds.

Discounting of one's own note.

15A-3. Journalize the following transactions for Joye Company:

19X1

June	18	Joye discounted its own $40,000, 90-day note at Ontario Bank at 10 percent.
Sept.	16	Paid the amount due on the note of June 18. (Be sure to record interest expense from Discount on Notes Payable.)
Nov.	2	Joye discounted its own $20,000, 120-day note at Ontario Bank at 11 percent.
Dec.	31	Record the adjusting entry for interest expense.

Comprehensive problem: Integration of Notes Receivable and Notes Payable with Allowance for Doubtful Accounts and discounting.

15A-4. Journalize the following transactions for Rochester Company:

19XX

Apr.	18	Received $15,000, 80-day, 11 percent note from Mark Castle in payment of account past due.

May 9 Wrote off the Hal Balmer account as uncollectible for $600. (Rochester uses the Allowance method to record bad debts.)
July 10 Mark Castle paid Rochester the note in full.
Nov. 11 Gave Reech Company a $9,000, 30-day, 12 percent note as a time extension of account now past due.
15 Hal Balmer paid Rochester amount previously written off on May 9.
Dec. 3 Discounted its own $5,000, 90-day note at their bank at 10 percent.
5 Received a $10,000, 60-day, 12 percent note dated December 5 from Beverly Fields in payment of account past due.
14 Paid principal and interest due on note issued to Reech Company from November 11 note.
16 Received a $20,000, 60-day, 11 percent note from Larry Company in payment of account past due.
28 Discounted the Beverly Fields note to their bank at 13 percent.
31 Recorded adjusting entries as appropriate.

Group B Problems

Journalizing notes receivable and notes payable along with note dishonoured.

15B-1. Journalize the following entries for (1) the buyer and (2) the seller.

19X9

July 10 Morgan Company sold $8,000 of merchandise on account to Connors Company (terms, net 30 days).
Aug. 10 Morgan received a 90-day, $6,000, 9 percent note for a time extension of past due account of Connors Company.
Nov. 11 Collected the Connors Company note on the maturity date.
11 Assuming Connors Company defaulted on November 8, record the dishonoured note.
19 Connors Company paid the note receivable that was dishonoured on November 11 (no additional interest is charged).

Identifying steps in discounting a note along with journal entry.

15B-2. On June 2, 19X4, Apples Company received a $40,000, 90-day, 11 percent note from Fletcher Company dated June 2. On July 16, 19X4, Apples discounted the note at their bank at a discount rate of 12 percent.

1. Calculate the following:
a. Maturity value of the note.
b. Number of days the bank will hold the note until maturity date.
c. Bank discount.
d. Proceeds.

2. Journalize the entry to record the proceeds.

Discounting of one's own note.

15B-3. As the bookkeeper of Joye Company, record in the general journal the following transactions:

19X2

May 9 Joye discounted its own $25,000, 90-day note at Ontario Bank at 10 percent.
Aug. 7 Paid the amount due on the note of May 9. (Be sure to record interest expense from Discount on Note Payable.)
Oct. 7 Joye discounted its own $18,000, 120-day note at Ontario Bank at 11 percent.
Dec. 31 Record the adjusting entry for interest expense.

Comprehensive problem: Integration of Notes Receivable and Notes Payable with Allowance for Doubtful Accounts and discounting.

15B-4. Record the following entries into the general journal of Rochester Company:

19XX

May	12	Received $13,000, 90-day, 9 percent note from Mark Castle in payment of account past due.
June	15	Wrote off the Hal Balmer account as uncollectible for $900 using the Allowance method.
Aug.	13	Mark Castle paid Rochester the note in full.
Nov.	2	Gave Reech Company a $20,000, 30-day, 8 percent note as a time extension of account now past due.
	18	Hal Balmer paid Rochester amount previously written off on June 15.
Dec.	2	Discounted its own $10,000, 90-day note at their bank at 9 percent.
	2	Received a $6,000, 60-day, 11 percent note dated December 3 from Beverly Fields in payment of account past due.
	5	Paid principal and interest due on note issued to Reech Company from November 2 note.
	16	Received a $2,000, 60-day, 11 percent note from Larry Company in payment of account past due.
	28	Discounted the Beverly Fields note to their bank at 12 percent.
	31	Recorded adjusting entries as appropriate.

Group C Problems

Journalizing notes receivable and notes payable along with note dishonoured.

15C-1. Journalize the following entries for (1) the buyer and (2) the seller. Record all entries for the buyer first.

19X9

June	11	Campbell Company sold $8,000 of merchandise on account to Alexis Company (terms, net 30 days).
July	11	Campbell received a 90-day, $8,000, 9 percent note for a time extension of past due account of Alexis Company.
Oct.	12	Collected the Alexis Company note on the maturity date.
	12	Assuming Alexis Company defaulted on its July 11 note, record the dishonoured note.
	18	Alexis Company paid the note receivable that was dishonoured on October 12 (no additional interest is charged).

Identifying steps in discounting a note along with journal entry.

15C-2. On May 1, 19X4, Wynott Company received a $50,000, 120-day, 7 percent note from Flemming Company dated May 1. On June 20, 19X4, Wynott discounted the note at their bank at a discount rate of 9 percent.

1. Calculate the following:

- **a.** Maturity value of the note.
- **b.** Number of days the bank will hold the note until maturity date.
- **c.** Bank discount.
- **d.** Proceeds.

2. Journalize the entry to record the proceeds.

Discounting of one's own note.

15C-3. Journalize the following transactions for Ballis Company:

19X1

June	18	Ballis discounted its own $70,000, 60-day note at Ontario Bank at 12 percent.
Aug.	20	Paid the amount due on the note of June 18. (Be sure to record interest expense from Discount on Notes Payable.)

Nov. 2 Ballis discounted its own $40,000, 180-day note at Ontario Bank at 10 percent.

Dec. 31 Record the adjusting entry for interest expense.

Comprehensive problem: Integration of Notes Receivable and Notes Payable with Allowance for Doubtful Accounts and discounting.

15C-4. Journalize the following transactions for Dynamic Company:

19XX

Apr. 18 Received $25,000, 90-day, 10 percent note from Else Ellford in payment of account past due.

May 9 Wrote off the Vic Hallfor account as uncollectible for $800. (Dynamic uses the Allowance method to record bad debts.)

July 20 Else Ellford paid Dynamic the note in full.

Nov. 11 Gave Quincy Company a $12,000, 30-day, 11 percent note as a time extension of account now past due.

15 Vic Hall for paid Dynamic half of the amount previously written off on May 9.

Dec. 3 Discounted its own $15,000, 120-day note at their bank at 12 percent.

5 Received a $24,000, 90-day, 14 percent note dated December 5 from Angela Brown in payment of account past due.

14 Paid principal and interest due on note issued to Quincy Company from November 11 note.

16 Received a $27,500, 60-day, 12 percent note from Copper Company in payment of account past due.

28 Discounted the Angela Brown note to their bank at 15 percent.

31 Recorded adjusting entries as appropriate.

Real World Applications

15R-1.

Abby Scale, the bookkeeper of Roland Company, is having difficulty calculating the amount due Agent Company on March 19. Based on the following information, prepare a detailed calculation of the amount due Agent.

Roland issued Agent a $2,000, 60-day, 12 percent note dated December 19, 19X1. Roland was notified by Agent's bank that the note had been discounted by Agent and the note would be payable to them. On February 18 the bookkeeper of Roland became ill and the note wasn't paid. Agent's Bank notified Agent and charged them an additional $9 protest fee. On March 19 Abby decided to pay Agent the amount owed. Agent indicated they were charging the maturity value of the note, the protest fee, and interest on both for 30 days beyond maturity at 14 percent.

15R-2.

Moe Ring has left the following notes on your desk. As the new bookkeeper of Ryan Company you realize that no adjusting entries were made in 19X1.

Notes Receivable	
11/25/X1	$20,000
12%	150 days

Notes Payable	
12/16/X1	$33,600
15%	30 days

a. Prepare the appropriate adjusting entries.

b. Moe would like to know whether reversing entries are needed. Prepare a set of T accounts to show what would result on the books in the year 19X2 when the notes are paid (1) if there are no reversing entries and (2) if reversing entries are made.

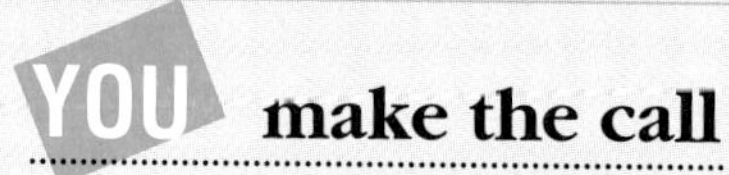

make the call

Critical Thinking/Ethical Case

15R-3.

Kevin Hoffaman works as a teller in a local bank. Yesterday he looked up confidential information concerning several friends. Kevin told his girlfriend all about the confidential information. Do you think Kevin acted appropriately? You make the call. Write down your recommendations to Kevin.

ACCOUNTING RECALL

A CUMULATIVE APPROACH

THIS EXAM REVIEWS CHAPTERS 1 THROUGH 15

Your *Study Guide and Working Papers* has forms to complete this exam, as well as worked-out solutions. The page references next to each question identify what page to turn back to if you answer the question incorrectly.

PART I Vocabulary Review

Match the terms to the appropriate definition or phrase.

Page Ref.

Page Ref.	Term		Definition
(583)	1. Proceeds	A.	Face amount of note
(548)	2. Allowance for doubtful accounts	B.	Principal and interest
(579)	3. Notes payable	C.	Cost of goods sold account
(584)	4. Maturity value	D.	Bank charge
(574)	5. Maker	E.	Contra-revenue account
(588)	6. Discount on notes payable	F.	A liability
(378)	7. Purchases	G.	Maturity value less bank discount
(584)	8. Bank discount	H.	Reduces notes payable to actual cash value
(328)	9. Sales returns and allowances	I.	Contra-asset
(573)	10. Principal	J.	One promising to pay a note

PART II True or False (Accounting Theory)

(588) 11. Discount on notes payable is a contra-asset account.

(584) 12. Maturity value less bank discount equals proceeds.

(585) 13. When a note is discounted and you receive more than face value it is interest expense.

(573) 14. The payee is the one who will pay the promissory note.

(257) 15. The three tax responsibilities of an employee include income tax, CPP, and UI.

PART III Applications Problem

From the following complete the four steps to discounting a note and provide the general journal entry.

On November 18, Broome Company discounted an $18,000, 12%, 120-day note dated September 8. Use ordinary interest in your calculation.

Accounting for Merchandise Inventory

16

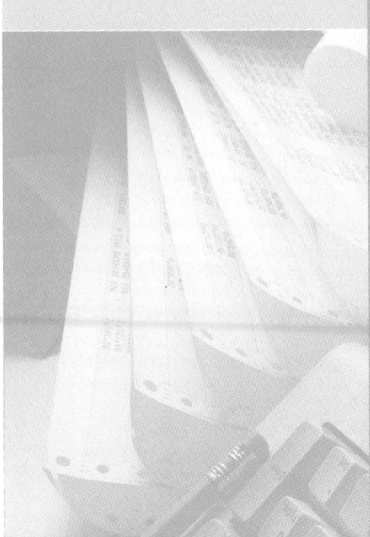

Chapter Objectives

- **Calculating the cost of ending inventory and cost of goods sold using four different methods: specific-invoice, weighted-average, first-in, first-out, and last-in, first-out. (p. 607)**
- **Calculating ending inventory by the retail method and the gross profit method. (p. 614)**
- **Journalizing transactions in a perpetual inventory system. (p. 618)**

Have you ever had the experience at Christmas time of thinking up the perfect present for someone, only to find that everyone else in the world had the same idea, and the stores were out of stock? In recent years we have seen this happen with home computers, video games, and so on. Having the right quantities of inventory is crucial to a retail business: it's bad to run out of stock and miss out on sales revenue, especially at Christmas, but it's also harmful to have too much of an item. A store must consider the cost of carrying inventory, and it must also worry about product obsolescence or the possibility of a fad's running out before all the products are sold.

In Chapter 12 we discussed the periodic inventory system, in which inventory is checked and counted only at the beginning and end of the accounting period. In this chapter we will look again at this inventory system, but we will look closer at how to assign a cost to ending inventory and the effect of this cost assignment on the financial reports.

In the last part of the chapter we will discuss how to assign costs to inventory using a *perpetual inventory system*—a system in which the inventory account is updated constantly by each sale or purchase of inventory made during the period.

LEARNING UNIT 16-1

How to Assign Costs to Ending Inventory Items

The method one uses to assign costs to ending inventory will have a direct effect on the company's cost of goods sold and profit. Look at the accompanying diagram and note that in each column ending inventory has a different value assigned to it. Note also how this affects gross profit in each of the four columns.

	A		B		C		D	
Net Sales		$50,000		$50,00		$50,000		$50,000
Beginning Inventory	$ 4,000		$ 4,000		$ 4,000		$ 4,000	
Net Purchases	20,000		20,000		20,000		20,000	
Cost of Goods Available for Sale	24,000		24,000		24,000		24,000	
Ending Inventory	5,000		6,000		7,000		8,000	
Cost of Goods Sold		19,000		18,000		17,000		16,000
Gross Profit		$31,000		$32,000		$33,000		$34,000

If all inventory brought into a store had the same cost, it would be simple to calculate ending inventory, and we would not have to have this chapter in the book. Unfortunately, things are not that easy; often the very same products are purchased and brought into the store at different costs during the same accounting period. Over the years there have been developed four generally accepted methods to assign a cost to ending inventory. They are: (1) specific-invoice, (2) weighted-average, (3) first-in, first-out, and (4) last-in, first-out. Each is based on the flow of costs, not the flow of goods (the actual physical movement of goods sold in a store).

SPECIFIC-INVOICE METHOD

Jones Hardware sells rakes. At the end of the period 12 rakes remain unsold. Notice in the accompanying diagram that on January 1, at the start of the accounting period, 10 rakes were on hand, but during the period additional purchases of rakes were made. The price given in the diagram is the purchase price paid by the store—it is not the same as the selling price, which is what the store charges its customers for the rakes. The selling price is not involved here. At the bottom of the diagram you can see that 44 rakes cost Jones Hardware $543.

	Goods Available for Sale			Calculating Cost of Ending Inventory		
	Units	**Cost**	**Total**	**Units**	**Cost**	**Total**
January 1 beg. inventory	10	@ $10 =	$100			
March 15 purchased	9	@ 12 =	108	6	@ $12	$72
August 18 purchased	20	@ 13 =	260	6	@ 13	78
November 15 purchased	5	@ 15 =	75			
	44		$543	12		$150

Cost of Goods Available for Sale	$543
Less: Cost of Ending Inventory	150
= Cost of Goods Sold	$393

In the **specific-invoice method**, one assigns the cost of ending inventory by identifying each item in that inventory by a specific purchase price and invoice number. Items can be identified by serial number, physical description, or location. Using this method, Jones Hardware knew that 6 of the rakes not sold were from the March 15 invoice and the other 6 were from the August 18 purchase. Thus $150 was assigned as the actual cost of ending inventory. If the total cost of goods available for sale is $543 and we subtract the actual cost of ending inventory ($150), this method provides a figure of $393 for cost of goods sold.

Let's look at pros and cons of this method:

Specific-Invoice Method

Pros

1. Simple to use if company has small amount of high-cost goods—for example, autos, jewels, boats, antiques, and so on.
2. Flow of goods and flow of cost are the same.
3. Costs are matched with the sales they helped to produce.

Cons

1. Difficult to use for goods with large unit volume and small unit prices—for example, nails at a hardware store, packages of toothpaste at a drug store.
2. Difficult to use for decision-making purposes—ordinarily an impractical approach.

WEIGHT-AVERAGE METHOD

The **weighted-average method** calculates an average unit cost by dividing the *total cost* of goods available for sale by the *total units* of goods available for sale. Since we don't know exactly *which* items are left in ending inventory, we will calculate the average of all the goods we have available in order to come up with a fair approximation of the cost of the ending inventory.

	Goods Available for Sale				
	Units		**Cost**		**Total**
January 1 beg. inventory	10	@	$10	=	$100
March 15 purchased	9	@	12	=	108
August 18 purchased	20	@	13	=	260
November 15 purchased	5	@	15	=	75
	44				$543

$\frac{\$543}{44}$ = $12.34 weighted-average cost per unit

12 rakes × $12.34 = $148.08

Cost of Goods Available for Sale	$543.00
Less: Cost of Ending Inventory	148.08
= Cost of Goods Sold	$394.92

Here are pros and cons of this method:

Weighted-Average Method

Pros

1. Takes into account the number of units purchased at each amount, not a simple average cost. Good for products sold in large volume, such as grains and fuels.
2. Accountant assigns an equal unit cost to each unit of inventory; thus, when the income statement is prepared, net income will not fluctuate as much as with other methods.

Cons

1. Current prices have no more significance than prices of goods bought months earlier.
2. Compared with other methods, the most recent costs are *not* matched with current sales.
3. Cost of ending inventory is not as up to date as it could be using another method.

FIRST-IN, FIRST-OUT METHOD (FIFO)

In the **FIFO method**, one assumes that the oldest goods (rakes, in this case) are sold first. In other words, the first merchandise brought into the store tends to be sold first. Indeed, it is often the sale of these items that prompts the store to buy more of them—as they start to run out, the store purchases more. When costs are assigned in the FIFO method, the cost of the last items brought into the store is assigned to ending inventory and the inventory sold is assigned to cost of goods sold. For example, using our Jones Hardware situation, the ending inventory of 12 rakes on hand is assigned a cost from the last two purchases of rakes (purchases made on November 15 and some purchases made on August 18), $166. Using the FIFO method, it is always assumed that it is the most recently purchased merchandise that has not been sold. Look at how this works out in the following diagram.

	Goods Available for Sale			Calculating Cost of Ending Inventory		
	Units	Cost	Total	Units	Cost	Total
January 1 beg. inventory	10	@ $10 =	$100			
March 15 purchased	9	@ 12 =	108			
August 18 purchased	20	@ 13 =	260	7	@ $13	$91
November 15 purchased	5	@ 15 =	75	5	@ 15	75
	44		$543	12		$166

Cost of Goods Available for Sale	$543
Less: Cost of Ending Inventory	166
= Cost of Goods Sold	$377

If you are having difficulty with this, think of the inventory as being taken from the bottom layer first, then the next one up, and the next one up, and so on.

The following are the pros and cons of this method:

FIFO Method

Pros

1. The cost flow tends to follow the physical flow (most businesses try to sell the old goods first—for example, perishables such as fruit or vegetables).
2. The figure for ending inventory is made up of current costs on the balance sheet (since inventory left over is assumed to be from goods last brought into the store).

Cons

1. During inflation this method will produce higher income on the income statement—thus more taxes to be paid. (We will discuss this later in the chapter.)
2. Recent costs are not matched with recent sales, since we assume *old* goods are sold first.

LAST-IN, FIRST-OUT METHOD (LIFO)

Cost of ending inventory is made up of the *old* inventory.

LIFO assumes *opposite* flow of FIFO.

Under the **LIFO method**, it is assumed that the rakes *most recently acquired* by Jones are sold first. In other words, the last merchandise brought into the store is the first to be sold. As an example of this method, think of a barrel of nails. It is the most recently purchased nails, which are at the top of the barrel, that are sold first—the nails at the bottom of the barrel are sold last. Note in the following table that the 12 rakes not sold were assigned costs on the basis of the old inventory of January and March that totalled $124, giving Jones a cost of goods sold of $419.

	Goods Available for Sale			Calculating Cost of Ending Inventory		
	Units	Cost	Total	Units	Cost	Total
January 1 beg. inventory	10	@ $10 =	$100	10	@ $10	$100
March 15 purchased	9	@ 12 =	108	2	@ 12	24
August 18 purchased	20	@ 13 =	260			
November 15 purchased	5	@ 15 =	75			
	44		$543	12		$124

Cost of Goods Available for Sale	$543
Less: Cost of Ending Inventory	124
= Cost of Goods Sold	$419

These are the pros and cons of this method:

LIFO Method

Pros

1. Cost of goods sold is stated at or near current costs, since costs of *latest* goods acquired are used.
2. Matches current costs with current selling prices.
3. During inflation this method produces the lowest net income, which is a tax advantage in countries which permit it (Canada does not). (The lower cost of ending inventory means a higher cost of goods sold; with a higher cost of goods sold, gross profit and ultimately net income are smaller, and thus taxes are lower.)

Cons

1. Ending inventory is valued at very old prices.
2. Doesn't match physical flow of goods (but can still be used to calculate flow of costs).

Now we will compare the methods that could be used by Jones Hardware to see the cost of ending inventory and the assigned cost of goods sold.

Comparison of Methods for Jones Hardware

Method	*Cost of Ending Inventory*	*Cost of Goods Sold*
Specific-invoice	$150.00	$393.00
Weighted-average	148.08	394.92
FIFO	166.00	377.00
LIFO	124.00	419.00

All four methods are acceptable accounting procedures,* and each has its own virtues:

1. This specific-invoice method matches exactly costs with revenue—as we have noted before, this is very important in the accrual basis of accounting.
2. The weighted-average method tends to smooth out the fluctuations between FIFO and LIFO.
3. FIFO provides an up-to-date picture of inventory on the balance sheet, since it uses the latest purchases to calculate ending inventory.
4. When prices are changing, LIFO shows the best match of cost of goods sold to net income.

In accounting there is a **principle of consistency**, which means that once a business selects a certain accounting method, it should follow it consistently from year to year without switching to another method. In the first part of this Unit we saw four methods of inventory valuations causing four different results for a business in terms of cost of goods sold and ultimately net income. Therefore, if a company kept switching from LIFO to FIFO each year, significant changes would result in the profit it reported. The financial reports would become undependable. Keeping to the same method lets readers of the financial reports make meaningful comparisons of cost of ending inventory, cost of goods sold, etc., from one year to the next.

The principle of consistency doesn't mean that a company can *never* change from one method of inventory valuation to another. If a change is decided upon, however, the company should fully disclose the change, the effects of the change on profit and inventory valuation, and the justification for change in a footnote on the financial report. This is called the **full disclosure principle** in accounting.

Let's look now at some situations in which a decision must be made about including certain items in the cost of inventory stated on the financial reports.

*but LIFO is not acceptable for income tax purposes in Canada,

Which items should be included in the cost of inventory

Situation 1: Goods in Transit

Goods in transit with terms F.O.B. shipping point are added to cost of inventory.

On the date that inventory is taken, goods in transit should be added to inventory if the firm has ownership of them. For example, goods that Alden Co. buys F.O.B. shipping point would be included in the firm's inventory, since title passes to Alden at shipping point, even though Alden has not yet received the goods.

Situation 2: Goods on Consignment

Goods should be added to the consignor's inventory and not the agent's.

Consignment means that a company (the **consignor**) is selling its goods through an agent (the **consignee**) who doesn't own the goods but has possession of them. Consigned goods belong to the consignor and thus will be added to the consignor's inventory and not to the consignee's.

Situation 3: Damaged or Obsolete Goods

Unsaleable goods are not added to the cost of inventory.

If the goods are not saleable, they should *not* be added to cost of inventory. For those goods that are saleable at a lower price, a conservative estimate should be made of their value and added to the cost of inventory.

LEARNING UNIT 16-1 REVIEW

AT THIS POINT you should be able to

- Calculate cost of ending inventory and cost of goods sold by the specific-invoice, weighted-average, first-in, first-out, and last-in, first-out methods. (pp. 607–610)
- Explain the pros and cons of each method used to calculate cost of ending inventory and cost of goods sold. (p. 611)
- Explain the principles of consistency and full disclosure. (p. 611)
- Explain how goods in transit, goods on consignment, and damaged or obsolete goods are counted in calculating inventory. (p. 612)

SELF-REVIEW QUIZ 16-1

1. From the information given below, calculate the cost of ending inventory as well as the cost of goods sold, using the (a) specific-invoice, (b) weighted-average, (c) first-in, first-out, and (d) last-in, first-out methods.

	Goods Available for Sale			Additional Fact:
	Units	Cost	Total	Inventory Not Sold
January 1 beg. inventory	40	@ $ 8 =	$320	
April 1 purchased	20	@ 9 =	180	40 from January 1
May 1 purchased	20	@ 10 =	200	4 from May 1
October 1 purchased	20	@ 12 =	240	4 from October 1
December 1 purchased	20	@ 13 =	260	
	120		$1,200	

2. Respond True or False to the following:
   a. It is possible for a company to change from LIFO to FIFO if it follows specific guidelines.
   b. Goods in transit (shipped F.O.B. shipping point) will not be included as part of the inventory for the purchaser.
   c. Damaged goods are always added to the cost of inventory.

Solutions to Self-Review Quiz 16-1

1. a.

Total cost of goods available for sale			$1,200
Less: Ending inventory based on specific invoices:			
40	units from January 1 purchased at $8	$320	
4	units from May 1 purchased at $10	40	
4	units from October 1 purchased at $12	48	
48	units in ending inventory		408
Cost of goods sold			$ 792

b.

$1,200 ÷ 120 units = $10 weighted-average cost per unit.

Total cost of goods available for sale	$1,200
Less: Ending inventory priced at weighted-average basis: 48 units at $10	480
Cost of goods sold	$ 720

c.

Total cost of goods available for sale			$1,200
Less: Ending inventory priced on FIFO:			
20	units from December 1 at $13	$260	
20	units from October 1 at $12	240	
8	units from May 1 at $10	80	
48	units in ending inventory		580
Cost of goods sold			$ 620

d.

Total cost of goods available for sale			$1,200
Less: Ending inventory priced on LIFO:			
40	units from Jan. 1 at $8	$320	
8	units from April 1 purchased at $9	72	
48	units in ending inventory		392
Cost of goods sold			$ 808

2. a. True **b.** False **c.** False

LEARNING UNIT 16-2

Lower-of-Cost-or-Market Principle; Retail Method; Gross Profit Method

Market doesn't mean what goods will sell for. It stands for *replacement cost.*

LOWER-OF-COST-OR-MARKET PRINCIPLE

So far we have estimated the value of ending inventory by looking at the cost that was paid to bring it into the store. Over the years a traditional conservative principle in accounting has been to price inventory at the **lower of cost or market.** The objective is to place all items on the balance sheet at a conservative figure. *Market* means what it *would have* cost to purchase or replace the goods on that inventory date. By choosing the lower of the two figures, we place a conservative figure for inventory on the balance sheet. In the USA, the procedure for determining the lower of cost and market can be quite complex. Here in Canada, the rule is actually fairly simple: use cost (LIFO, FIFO, or whatever) or market—whichever is the lower. Sometimes companies must make a decision as to whether to apply the rule to the whole of inventory, classes of inventory, or each item in inventory. As long as this decision is made carefully and the results applied in the same way from year to year, the financial results are not materially distorted.

Inventory is recorded below cost or replacement cost, since selling price less selling expense is less than current replacement cost.

If there were freight-in charges, they would be added to cost of net purchases.

RETAIL METHOD

Retail stores often will prepare interim financial reports (monthly or quarterly) to give managers a basis for decision making. Continually taking a physical inventory of their goods would be time-consuming and expensive. Thus many merchandising businesses estimate their inventory on hand by the **retail method,** a technique for estimating inventory for retail businesses. To use this method, a business must have the following information available:

1. Beginning inventory at cost and at retail (selling price).
2. Cost of net purchases at both cost and at retail.
3. The net sales at retail.

Let's look at the following diagram to see how French Company estimates ending inventory at cost by the retail method.

THE RETAIL INVENTORY METHOD

			Cost	Retail
	Goods available for sale:			
	Beginning inventory		$4,100	$6,900
	Net purchases		7,900	13,100
Step 1 ⟶	Cost of goods available for sale		$12,000	$20,000
Step 2 ⟶	Cost ratio (relationship between cost and retail)	$\frac{\$12,000}{\$20,000}$	= 60%	
Step 3 ⟶	Net sales at retail			14,000
⟶	Inventory at retail			$6,000
Step 4 ⟶	Ending inventory at cost, $6,000 × 0.6		$3,600	

French completed the following steps to arrive at the ending inventory cost of $3,600.

Step 1: Calculate cost of goods available for sale at cost and retail.

Step 2: Calculate the cost ratio (cost of goods available for sale at cost divided by cost of goods available for sale at retail). It cost French Company 60 cents for each $1 of sales for these goods.

Step 3: Deduct net sales from retail value of goods available for sale to arrive at an estimated ending inventory at retail.

Step 4: Multiply cost ratio (0.60) times ending inventory at retail to arrive at ending inventory at cost. In this case, since 60 cents for each $1 of retail represents cost and we have $6,000 at retail, the end result is $3,600 in cost.

Keep in mind that at year-end French will take a physical inventory.

GROSS PROFIT METHOD

Another method of estimating ending inventory without taking a physical count is the **gross profit method**. This method develops a relationship between sales, cost of goods sold, and gross profit in estimating the cost of ending inventory.

To use this method a company would have to keep track of the following:

Freight, if any, would be added to cost of net purchases.

1. Average gross profit rate.
2. Net sales, beginning inventory, net purchases.

The steps Moose Company takes to estimate its ending inventory are shown in the following diagram. We assume a normal gross profit rate of 30 percent of net sales. If 30 cents on a dollar is profit, 70 cents on a dollar is cost.

The Gross Profit Method

	Goods available for sale:		
	Inventory, January 1, 19XX		$10,000
	Net purchases		4,000
Step 1 →	Cost of goods available for sale		$14,000
	Less: Estimated cost of goods sold:		
	Net sales at retail	$6,000	
Step 2	Cost percentage (100% – 30%)	× 0.70	
	Estimated cost of goods sold		4,200
Step 3 →	Estimated inventory, January 31, 19XX		$9,800

Step 1: Moose determines cost of goods available for sale (beginning inventory plus net purchases).

Step 2: Moose estimates cost of goods sold by multiplying cost percentage (70 percent) times net sales.

Step 3: Moose subtracts cost of goods sold from cost of goods available for sale to arrive at an estimated inventory of $9,800.

This method, besides helping prepare financial reports, can help determine the amount of inventory on hand due to a fire or can verify at end of year the accuracy of the physical inventory.

Before concluding this Unit, let's look at how an error made in calculating ending inventory will affect financial reports.

HOW INCORRECT CALCULATION OF ENDING INVENTORY AFFECTS FINANCIAL REPORTS

As we have stated before, an incorrect figure in ending inventory can have an effect on cost of goods sold, gross profit, net income, and current assets as well as owner's capital. Let's look at the following diagram to see—if a mistake is in fact made—what items on the income statement will be affected and what the mistake's impact will be over time.

	Correct				Incorrect			
	19X1		19X2		19X1		19X2	
Sales		$200		$300		$200		$300
Cost of goods sold:								
Beginning inventory	$30		$70		$30		$60	
Purchases	95		85		95		85	
Goods available for sale	125		155		125		145	
Ending inventory	– 70	55	– 100	55	– 60	65	– 100	45
Gross profit		$145		$245		$135		$255

(Arrows: "Correct" from 19X1 ending inventory 70 to 19X2 beginning inventory $70; "Incorrect" from 19X1 ending inventory 60 to 19X2 beginning inventory $60.)

Summary

	Correct	Incorrect	Difference
Year X1, gross profit	$145	$135	–$10
Year X2, gross profit	245	255	+ 10
Total effect of mistake after 2 periods			0

Note in the diagram that when the *incorrect* figure of $60 is used for ending inventory in 19X1, it causes cost of goods sold to be $65 instead of $55 and profit to be $135 instead of $145. In other words, when ending inventory is understated ($60 instead of $70), cost of goods sold is overstated and profit is understated.

19X1

When ending inventory is understated	Cost of goods sold is overstated	Profit is understated
$60 instead of $70	$65 instead of $55	$135 instead of $145

As we look next at 19X2, we see that the ending incorrect inventory of 19X1 is carried as the beginning inventory of 19X2. Thus the understatement of beginning inventory in 19X2 of $60 (instead of $70) causes cost of goods sold to be understated and net income to be overstated.

19X2

When beginning inventory is understated	Cost of goods sold is understated	Profit is overstated
$60 instead of $70	$45 instead of $55	$255 instead of $245

Thus, at the end of 19X2, the error will be self-correcting.

To review, look at the table that follows and prove it to yourself by going back over the previous explanation.

Ending inventory works in same direction as profit. Beginning inventory is inversely related.

If This Item...	Is Overstated	Is Understated
Beginning inventory	Profit is understated.	Profit is overstated.
Ending inventory	Profit is overstated.	Profit is understated.

Keep in mind that since ending inventory is recorded as a current asset on the balance sheet, any mistake will cause the assets to be under- or overstated. The statement of owner's equity would also be affected, since we have seen that the net income will be over- or understated.

LEARNING UNIT 16-2 REVIEW

AT THIS POINT you should be able to

- Explain the lower-of-cost-or-market principle. (p. 614)
- Calculate ending inventory by the retail method. (p. 614)
- Calculate ending inventory by the gross profit method. (p. 615)
- Explain how understating or overstating ending inventory will affect financial reports. (pp. 615–616)

SELF-REVIEW QUIZ 16-2

1. Alon Company needs to estimate its month-end inventory. From the following, estimate the cost of ending inventory on September 30 by the retail method:

	Cost	*Retail*
Beginning inventory	$ 8,000	$10,000
Net purchases	40,000	60,000
Net sales		30,000

(Carry out the cost ratio to nearest hundredth percent.)

2. Respond True or False to the following:

a. Selling price does not necessarily follow cost decreases of goods.

b. The lower-of-cost-or-market is not modified to monitor the movement of the selling price.

c. Market cost means replacement cost, not selling price.

d. If ending inventory is overstated, net income will be overstated.

e. If beginning inventory is overstated, net income will be overstated.

Solutions to Self-Review Quiz 16-2

1.

	Cost	*Retail*
Beginning inventory	$ 8,000	$10,000
Net purchases	40,000	60,000
Cost of goods available for sale	$48,000	70,000
Cost ratio, $48,000/$70,000 = 68.57%		
Net sales at retail		30,000
Inventory at retail		$40,000
Ending inventory at cost, $40,000 × 0.6857	$27,428	

2. a. True **b.** False **c.** True **d.** True **e.** False

LEARNING UNIT 16-3

Perpetual Inventory System

Up to this point we have presented only periodic inventory systems. Many companies use instead a perpetual inventory system. A **perpetual inventory system** is an accounting system that keeps a continual running balance of the inventory account. Every time a company buys inventory, the Merchandise Inventory account is increased, and every time a company sells inventory, the Merchandise Inventory account is decreased, so that at any time the company will know how much inventory is on hand. Years ago this system was good only for companies that handled high-priced products in limited numbers. Companies with products such as autos, boats, heavy machinery, etc., would use a perpetual inventory system. However, with the use of the computer, many more businesses are able to continually monitor their inventory and thus provide better internal control.

To get a better idea of what makes up the perpetual system, let's look at the comparison chart below.

Cost of Goods Sold	
XXX Normal balance	

Will be closed at year's end.

This account records the cost of units sold.

Note in transaction A that in the periodic system the Merchandise Inventory account is not updated, while in the perpetual system the sale is recorded along with Merchandise Inventory reduced (sold), and Cost of Goods Sold is immediately recognized (when inventory is sold, the asset is reduced and shown as a cost). In transaction B, when more inventory is purchased, the perpetual system records additional purchases in the Inventory account, while in the periodic system there is a separate Purchases account. Note in transaction C that the freight in the perpetual system is added directly to Inventory. In transaction D, when goods are returned by the purchaser, the perpetual system reduces Inventory directly, while in the periodic system there is a separate account called Purchases Returns and Allowances. In other words, in a perpetual system, Purchases, Freight, and Purchases Returns and Allowances accounts *do not* exist; Inventory is updated immediately.

Transaction	Periodic System			Perpetual System		
(A) Sold merchandise on account for $20,000 that cost $8,000.	Accts. Rec.	2000000		Accts. Rec.	2000000	
	Sales		2000000	Sales		2000000
				Cost of Good Sold	800000	
				Merch. Inv.		800000
(B) Purchased $900 of merchandise on account.	Purchases	90000		Merch. Inv.	90000	
	Accts. Pay.		90000	Accts. Payable		90000
(C) Paid freight charge, $50.	Freight-in	5000		Merch. Inv.	5000	
	Cash		5000	Cash		5000
(D) Returned $400 of merchandise previously bought on account due to defects.	Accts. Pay.	40000		Accts. Payable	40000	
	Pur. Ret. and Allow.		40000	Merch. Inv.		40000

A perpetual system aids in preparing interim reports, because there is an up-to-date balance in Inventory and Cost of Goods Sold.

When a perpetual system is used, a detailed inventory record is kept manually or by computer. For some retail firms, the cash register is actually a point-of-sale computer, which records merchandise sold as well as updating the inventory records. Figure 16-1 shows an example of an inventory record.

Inventory Control

Item VX113 | Maximum 22
Description Digital Clock | Reorder Level 12
Location Storeroom 1 | Reorder Quantity 10

	Received			Sold			Balance		
Date	Units	Cost per Unit	Total	Units	Cost per Unit	Total	Units	Cost per Unit	Total
19XX Jan. 1	Balance		FWD				14	50	$ 700
12				2	50	100	12	50	600
19	10	60	600				{12	50	
							10	60	1,200
25				8	50	400	{4	50	
							10	60	800

FIGURE 16-1
An Inventory Record

Other companies could use LIFO, weighted-average, etc., in a perpetual system.

In this inventory control sheet the company is using the FIFO method to evaluate its inventory. Note on January 25, when 8 items were sold, they were assumed to be sold from the old inventory of 12 units, thus leaving a balance of 4 old units along with 10 of the new units. At end of year all the inventory cards' year-end balances are added, with the total equalling the Inventory account (the controlling account) in the general ledger. There may be need for adjustments due to theft, spoilage, and so on. Please remember that the perpetual inventory system does not eliminate the need for an annual physical count of inventory.

LEARNING UNIT 16-3 REVIEW

AT THIS POINT you should be able to

- Compare and contrast a perpetual inventory system to a periodic inventory system. (p. 618)
- Journalize entries for a perpetual inventory system. (pp. 618–619)
- Calculate cost of ending inventory using an inventory control sheet. (p. 619)

SELF-REVIEW QUIZ 16-3

Journalize the following transactions for a firm that uses a perpetual inventory system.

a. Sold $200 of merchandise on account that cost $50.
b. Purchased $250 of merchandise on account.
c. Paid freight of $30.
d. Returned $300 of merchandise previously bought on account.

Solutions to Self-Review Quiz 16-3

a. Accounts Receivable	200	
Sales		200
Cost of Goods Sold	50	
Merchandise Inventory		50
b. Merchandise Inventory	250	
Accounts Payable		250
c. Merchandise Inventory	30	
Cash		30
d. Accounts Payable	300	
Merchandise Inventory		300

Chapter Review

SUMMARY OF KEY POINTS

Learning Unit 16-1

1. In assigning a cost to ending inventory, the flow of goods may not follow the actual flow of costs.
2. The specific-invoice method identifies each item in inventory with a specific invoice in assigning a cost of ending inventory. It matches costs exactly with revenues.
3. The weighted-average method provides an average unit cost of all inventory. It is a compromise between LIFO and FIFO.
4. FIFO assumes the old goods are sold first. Since ending inventory is valued at most recent costs, FIFO provides the most realistic figure for ending merchandise inventory.
5. LIFO assumes the newest goods are sold first. It provides the most realistic figure for cost of goods sold.
6. During inflation LIFO offers the best tax break.

Learning Unit 16-2

1. In using the lower-of-cost-or-market principle, choose the lower of cost (FIFO, LIFO, or whatever) or replacement cost. While not as complex as the method used in the USA, it serves to place a conservative value on the asset—inventory.
2. The retail inventory method estimates inventory (rather than continually taking a physical count) by multiplying the cost ratio times ending inventory at retail.
3. The retail method can also reduce a physical inventory to cost.
4. The gross profit method is another way of estimating ending inventory without taking a physical count. This method requires calculating an estimated cost of goods sold, which is then subtracted from the cost of goods available for sale.
5. If ending inventory is overstated, net income will be overstated.
6. If beginning inventory is overstated, net income will be understated.
7. A mistake in calculating ending inventory will take two accounting periods to be self-correcting.

Learning Unit 16-3

1. In a perpetual inventory system the Inventory and Cost of Goods Sold accounts are continually updated.
2. Purchases, Purchases Discounts, Purchases Returns and Allowances, and Freight-In are not used in the perpetual inventory system.
3. The perpetual system has a subsidiary ledger of inventory control sheets to update each inventory item that is purchased or sold.

BLUEPRINT OF METHODS OF ESTIMATING ENDING INVENTORY

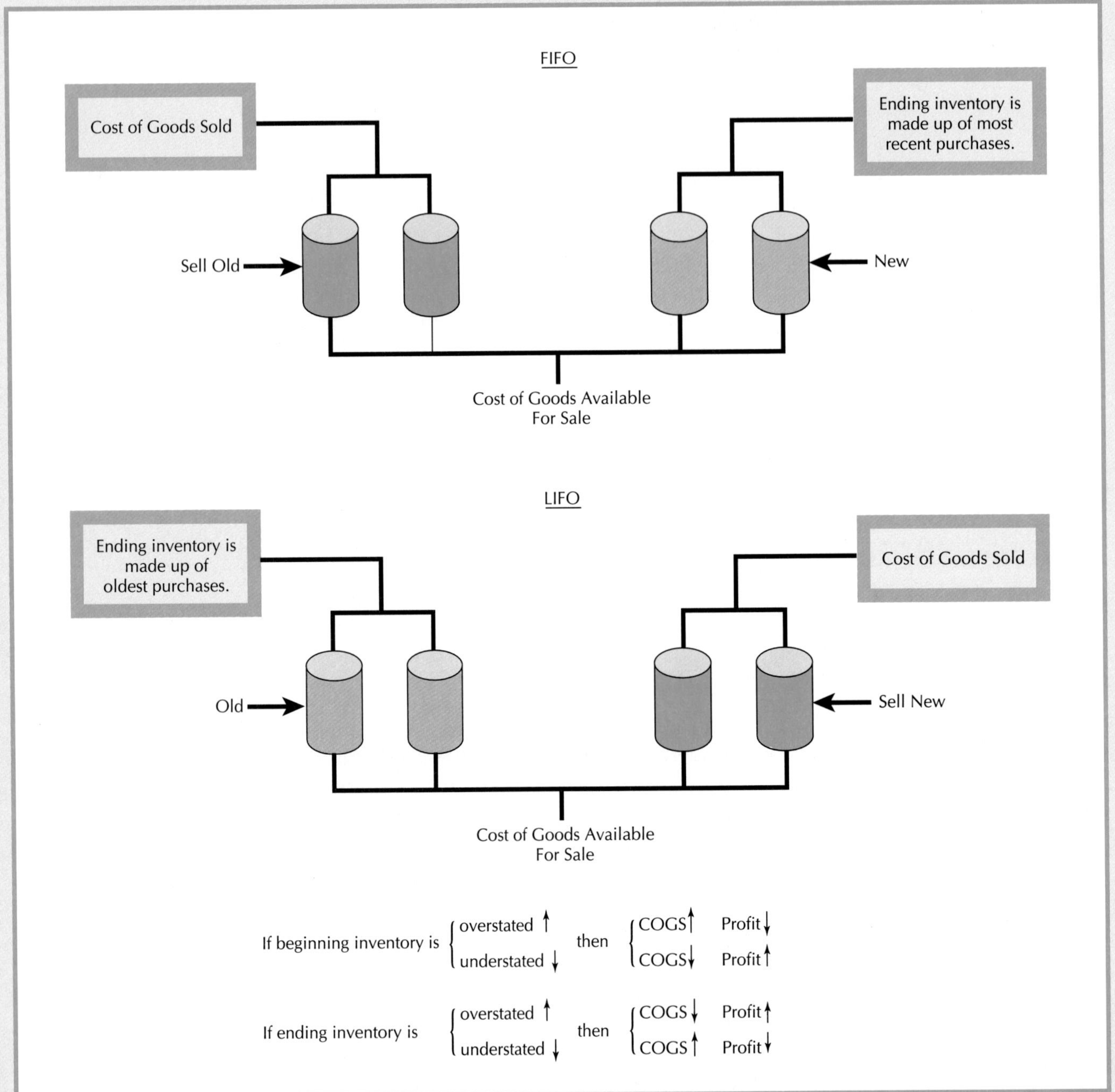

KEY TERMS

Consignee Company or person to whom goods are shipped but who doesn't have ownership.

Consignment Sales of goods through an agent who has possession but not ownership.

Consignor The one shipping goods to consignee.

Consistency The accounting principle that requires companies to follow the same accounting methods or procedures from period to period.

FIFO method Valuing of inventory assuming that the company sells the first goods received in the store.

Full disclosure principle The accounting principle that requires companies to fully disclose on their financial reports changes in accounting procedures and methods along with effects of the change, as well as justification for change.

Gross profit method A method for estimating the value of ending inventory. It is based on the assumption that the gross profit of a company remains approximately the same from period to period.

LIFO method Valuing of inventory with the assumption the last goods received in the store are the first to be sold.

Lower-of-cost-or-market Valuing of inventory at the lower of cost or replacement cost. This valuing depends on how selling price moves as well as on normal expected profit.

Perpetual inventory system The inventory system of a company that keeps a continuous inventory of merchandise on hand.

Retail method A method for estimating the value of ending inventory based on a cost ratio times the ending inventory at retail.

Specific invoice method Valuing of inventory where each item is identified with a specific invoice.

Weighted-average method Valuing of inventory where each item is assigned the same unit cost. This unit cost is found by dividing cost of goods available for sale by the total number of units for sale.

QUESTIONS, EXERCISES, AND PROBLEMS

Discussion Questions

1. How does flow of cost relate to the specific-invoice method?
2. What are the four methods of inventory valuation? Explain each.
3. During inflation, which inventory method will provide the lowest income on the income statement?
4. Which inventory method provides the most current valuation of inventory on the balance sheet? Explain.
5. Explain why goods in transit (F.O.B. shipping point) to buyer and goods issued on consignment are added to inventory valuations.
6. Explain why lower-of-cost-or-market valuation has been modified in recent years.
7. A mistake in ending inventory is self-correcting in the same period. Agree or disagree. Defend your position.
8. When ending inventory is understated, what effect will this have on cost of goods sold and net income?
9. What is the cost ratio in the retail inventory method?
10. Why must the average gross profit rate be used in the gross profit method?
11. What are the differences between the periodic and perpetual systems?

Mini Exercises

Calculate Cost of Goods Sold

1. From the following data calculate: (a) Cost of Goods Sold, (b) Gross Profit.

Net sales	100
Net purchases	10
Beginning inventory	40
Ending inventory	5

2. In Mini Exercise 1 what would be the figure for Cost of Goods Available for Sale?

3. Given the following, calculate the Cost of Goods Available for Sale. On December 31, 6 items were not sold.

		Units	*Cost*
January 1	Beginning Inventory	5	$1
March 6	Purchased	3	2
August 9	Purchased	2	3
December 10	Purchased	4	4

4. From Mini Exercise 3 calculate the Cost of Ending Inventory and Cost of Goods Sold using (a) the weighted-average method, (b) FIFO, (c) LIFO.

Retail Method

5. Complete the following using the retail method. (Round cost ratio to nearest whole percent.)

	Cost	*Retail*
Goods available for sale:		
Beg. inventory	$50	$100
Net purchases	70	90
Cost of goods available for sale	A	B
Cost ratio	C	
Net sales at retail		140
Inventory at retail		D
Ending inventory	E	

Gross Profit Method

6. Complete the following using the gross profit method. Assume a normal gross profit rate of 40 percent of net sales.

Goods available for sale:		
Inventory Jan. 1, 19XX		$50
Net purchases		10
Cost of goods available for sale		A
Less: Estimated cost of goods sold:		
Net sales at retail	$40	
Cost percentage	B	
Estimated cost of goods sold		C
Estimated inventory, Jan. 31, 19XX		D

Periodic vs. Perpetual

7. Journalize the transactions given below for
   a. A periodic system
   b. A perpetual system

19XX
Dec. 20 Sold merchandise on account for $100 that cost $30.
24 Purchases $20 of merchandise on account.
30 Paid freight charge, $4.

(The forms you need are on pages 16-4 and 16-16 of the *Study Guide and Working Papers*.)

Exercises

FIFO, LIFO, weighted average.

16-1. From the Loyola Company data given below, assuming a periodic inventory system, calculate the cost of ending inventory and cost of goods sold using the (a) first-in, first-out, (b) last-in, first-out, and (c) weighted-average methods. Loyola sells only one type of product.

		Units	*Cost per Unit*
Jan. 1	Beginning inventory	50	$ 9
Mar. 18	Purchased	12	10
Aug. 19	Purchased	40	12
Nov. 8	Purchased	48	13

Ending inventory is 52 units.

Consignment and freight in calculating cost of inventory.

16-2. From the following facts, calculate the correct cost of inventory for Ray Company.

- Cost of inventory on shelf, $4,000, which includes $300 of goods received on consignment.
- Goods in transit en route to Ray Company shipped F.O.B. shipping point, $22,000.
- Goods in transit en route to Ray shipped F.O.B. destination, $300. Ray has $600 worth of goods on consignment in Alice's Dress Shop.

Lower-of-cost-or-market.

16-3. Lyle Company uses the lower-of-cost-or-market principle in valuing inventory. From the following facts, record the cost of the inventory:

- Original selling price, $550.
- Cost, $400.
- Replacement cost has dropped to $300, but selling price remains at $550.

Retail inventory method.

16-4. Angel Company's May 1 inventory had a cost of $58,000 and a retail value of $72,000. During May, net purchases cost $255,000 with a retail value of $405,000. Net sales at retail for Angel for May were $225,000. Calculate the ending inventory at cost using the retail inventory method. (Round the cost ratio to the nearest hundredth percent.)

Gross profit method.

16-5. Amy Company on January 1 had inventory costing $30,000 and during January had net purchases of $67,000. Over recent years Amy's gross profit has averaged 40 percent on sales. Given that the company has net sales of $106,000, calculate an estimated cost of ending inventory using the gross profit method.

Group A Problems

FIFO, LIFO, weighted-average.

16A-1. Ashley Company began the year with 250 units of product B in inventory with a unit cost of $15. The following additional purchases of the product were made:

Apr. 1	300 units @	$18 each
Jul. 5	400 units @	20 each
Aug. 15	500 units @	22 each
Nov. 20	150 units @	24 each

At end of year Ashley Company had 525 units of its product unsold. Your task is to calculate cost of ending inventory as well as cost of goods sold by (a) FIFO, (b) LIFO, (c) weighted-average. (Round weighted-average to nearest cent.)

Retail inventory method.

16A-2. Marge Company uses the retail method to estimate cost of ending inventory for its monthly interim reports. From the following facts, estimate Marge's ending inventory at cost for the end of January. (Round the cost ratio to the nearest tenth percent.)

January 1 inventory at cost	$ 17,200
January 1 inventory at retail	33,000
Net purchases at cost	114,200
Net purchases at retail	197,000
Net sales at retail	193,600

Gross profit method.

16A-3. Over the past four years the gross profit rate for Hall Company was 30 percent. Last week a fire destroyed all of Hall's inventory. Luckily all the records for Hall were in a fireproof safe, and they indicated the following facts:

Inventory (January 1, 19XX)	$ 34,000
Sales	125,400
Sales Returns	1,940
Purchases	76,400
Purchases Returns and Allowances	1,280

Estimate the cost of inventory that was destroyed in the fire.

Perpetual inventory.

16A-4. Agree Company uses a perpetual inventory system on the FIFO basis. From the information given below, prepare an inventory control sheet. Assume on January 1, 19XX, a beginning inventory of 660 units at a cost of $7 each.

Received			*Sold*	
Date	*Quantity*	*Cost per Unit*	*Date*	*Quantity*
Apr. 15	280	$ 6	Mar. 8	620
Nov. 12	1,420	10	Oct. 5	240
Dec. 31	600	11	Nov. 30	300

Group B Problems

FIFO, LIFO, weighted-average.

16B-1. On January 1, 19XX, Ashley Company began with 200 units of product B in inventory with a unit cost of $24. The following additional purchases of the product were made:

Apr. 1	210 units @	$28 each
Jul. 5	500 units @	32 each
Aug. 15	450 units @	38 each
Nov. 20	200 units @	44 each

At end of year Ashley Company had 500 units of its product unsold. Your task is to calculate cost of ending inventory as well as cost of goods sold by (a) FIFO, (b) LIFO, (c) weighted-average. (Round weighted-average to nearest cent.)

Retail inventory method.

16B-2. Marge Company uses the retail method to estimate cost of ending inventory for its monthly interim reports. From the facts given below, estimate Marge's ending inventory at cost for end of January. (Round the cost ratio to the nearest hundredth percent.)

January 1 inventory at cost	$ 34,200
January 1 inventory at retail	69,800
Net purchases at cost	241,600
Net purchases at retail	407,000
Net sales at retail	396,000

Gross profit method.

16B-3. Over the past four years the gross profit rate for Hall Company was 32 percent. Last week a fire destroyed all of Hall's inventory. Luckily all the records for Hall were in a fireproof safe, and they indicated the following facts:

Inventory (January 1, 19XX)	$ 7,600
Sales	139,200
Sales Returns	2,450
Purchases	98,900
Purchases Returns and Allowances	1,810

Using the gross profit method, estimate the cost of inventory that was destroyed in the fire.

Perpetual inventory.

16B-4. Agree Company uses a perpetual inventory system on the FIFO basis. From the following information, prepare an inventory control sheet. Assume a beginning inventory of 600 units at a cost of $8 each.

Received			*Sold*	
Date	*Quantity*	*Cost per Unit*	*Date*	*Quantity*
Apr. 15	240	$ 7	Mar. 8	480
Nov. 12	1,420	11	Nov. 30	1,260
Dec. 31	500	12		

Group C Problems

FIFO, LIFO, weighted-average.

16C-1. Robbins Company began the year with 425 units of product B in inventory with a unit cost of $16.20. The following additional purchases of the product were made:

Apr. 15	340 units @	$18.46 each
Jul. 25	425 units @	21.12 each
Aug. 5	550 units @	24.86 each
Nov. 26	275 units @	27.10 each

At end of year Robbins Company had 520 units of its product unsold. Your task is to calculate cost of ending inventory as well as cost of goods sold by (a) FIFO, (b) LIFO, (c) weighted-average. (Round weighted-average to nearest cent.)

Retail inventory method.

16C-2. Pound Company uses the retail method to estimate cost of ending inventory for its monthly interim reports. From the following facts, estimate Pound's ending inventory at cost for the end of March. (Round the cost ratio to the nearest tenth percent.)

March 1 inventory at cost	$ 42,600
March 1 inventory at retail	78,200
Net purchases at cost	184,760
Net purchases at retail	337,400
Net sales at retail	356,200

Gross profit method.

16C-3. Over the past five years the gross profit rate for Genesis Company was 35 percent. Last week a fire destroyed all of their inventory. Luckily all the accounting records were in a fireproof safe and indicated the following facts:

Inventory (January 1, 19XX)	$ 47,000
Sales	141,200
Sales Returns	2,200
Purchases	79,600
Purchases Returns and Allowances	1,170

Estimate the cost of inventory that was destroyed in the fire.

Perpetual inventory.

16C-4. Sawyer Company uses a perpetual inventory system on the FIFO basis. From the information given below, prepare an inventory control sheet. Assume on January 1, 19XX, a beginning inventory of 600 units at a cost of $10 each.

Received			*Sold*	
Date	*Quantity*	*Cost per Unit*	*Date*	*Quantity*
Apr. 15	260	$ 9	Mar. 8	420
Nov. 12	1,400	13	Oct. 5	260
Dec. 31	600	15	Nov. 30	900

Real World Applications

16-R1.

To: Tom Hoover

From: Jennifer Ring

Re: Inventory Mistakes

The following mistakes have been found on our financial reports:

A. Beginning inventory was reported as $300 when it should have been $100.
B. The figure for ending inventory of $800 was understated by $200.
C. Purchases account of $18,000 was understated by $1,100.
D. Sales were overstated by $2,000.

Indicate what effect each of these mistakes will separately have on (1) cost of goods sold, (2) gross profit, and (3) owner's equity. Explain your answers.

Hints: Additional markups add to cost of goods available for sale at retail. Markdowns add to total sales.

16R-2.

Mike Sloy has completed his accounting course at Y College and was recently hired as the office manager of Reel Co. The firm estimates its inventory by the retail method. It has been brought to Mike's attention that Reel has additional markups as well as markdowns. In college Mike's instructor said, "In the retail method you don't have to worry about markups and markdowns—just get the concept." Now Mike is upset, since his job is to compute ending inventory at cost by the retail method that includes markups and markdowns. Could you take the following data and assist Mike? (Round the cost ratio to the nearest hundredth percent.)

Beginning inventory at cost (Jan. 1)	$20,000
Beginning inventory at retail (Jan. 1)	30,000
Additional markups	2,000
Net sales at retail	57,000
Net purchases at cost	36,000
Net purchases at retail	52,000
Markdowns	1,000

make the call

Critical Thinking/Ethical Case

16R-3.

Lyon Co. has used a perpetual inventory system for six months. The company president has issued a memo stating that the new computer system has failed to deliver acceptable standards in servicing his customers — too many goods out of stock. Fran, Lyon's accountant, blames the Computer Department and tells the president to fire the head of that department. The president wants to return immediately to a periodic inventory system. You make the call. Write down your recommendations to the president.

ACCOUNTING RECALL

A CUMULATIVE APPROACH

THIS EXAM REVIEWS CHAPTERS 1 THROUGH 16

Your *Study Guide and Working Papers* has forms to complete this exam, as well as worked-out solutions. The page references next to each question identify what page to turn back to if you answer the question incorrectly.

PART I Vocabulary Review

Match the terms to the appropriate definition or phrase.

Page Ref.		
(607)	1. Perpetual inventory system	A. Contra-cost-of-goods-sold
(588)	2. Discount on notes payable	B. Subtracted from cost of goods sold
(548)	3. Allow. for Doubtful Accts.	C. Uses a cost ratio
(610)	4. LIFO	D. Related to how selling price moves
(614)	5. Retail method	E. Last goods sold first
(614)	6. Lower of cost or market	F. Contra-asset
(379)	7. Purchases discount	G. Contra-liability
(383)	8. Controlling account	H. Accounts payable
(612)	9. Consignee	I. Continuous inventory of merchandise
(607)	10. Ending inventory	J. Doesn't have ownership

PART II True or False (Accounting Theory)

(616) 11. If ending inventory is overstated then cost of goods sold is overstated.

(609) 12. FIFO assumes the old goods are sold first.

(328) 13. Sales Returns and Allowances is a contra-cost-of-goods-sold account.

(607) 14. Net sales less cost of goods sold equals gross profit.

(618) 15. In the periodic system the Purchases account is not used.

PART III Applications Problem

From the following calculate the cost of ending inventory as well as cost of goods sold assuming the FIFO method. Assume an ending inventory of 75 units.

	Number Purchased	*Cost per Unit*	*Total*
January 1 inventory	40	$4	$160
April 1 inventory	60	7	420
July 1 inventory	50	8	400
December 1 inventory	55	9	495

HOW COMPANIES RECORD CREDIT CARD SALES IN THEIR SPECIAL JOURNALS

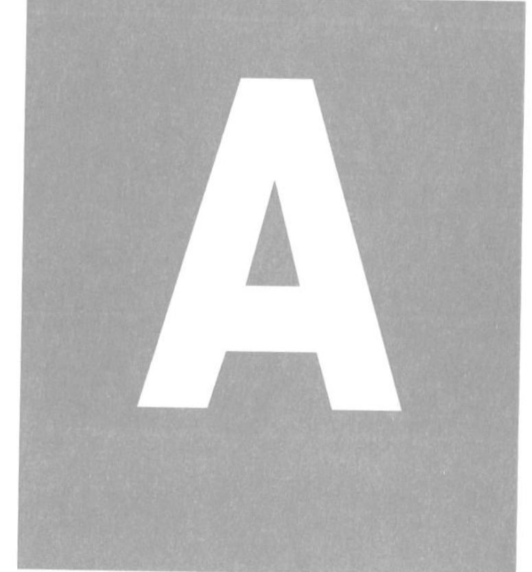

RECORDING BANK CREDIT CARDS

Example: Credit Card Sales of $100 MasterCard.

It is interesting to note that for bank credit cards (MasterCard, Visa) the sales are recorded in the seller's Cash Receipts Journal, since the slips are converted into cash immediately. Bank credit cards are not treated as accounts receivable. The fee the bank charges (about 2% to 5%) is deducted, and the bank credits the depositor's account immediately for the net. The end result for the seller is:

Accounts Affected	Category	↑ ↓	Rule
Cash	**Asset**	↑	**Dr. $97**
Credit Card Expense	**Expenses**	↑	**Dr. 3**
Sales	**Revenue**	↑	**Cr. 100**

CASH RECEIPTS JOURNAL

Date 19XX		Cash Dr.	Credit Card Expense Dr.	Accounts Receivable Cr.	Sales Credited	Sales Tax Payable Cr.	Sundry Account Name	Sundry Amount Cr.
		97 00	3 00		100 00			

It is the responsibility of the credit card company to sustain any losses (bad debts) from customers' nonpayment. If the bank waits to take the discount until the end of the month, the seller makes a nonpayment entry in the cash payment journal to record the credit card expense; the end result would be credit card expense up and cash balance down. Usually, the bank would send the charge on the monthly bank statement. *Remember: bank credit cards are not treated as accounts receivable.*

RECORDING PRIVATE COMPANY CREDIT CARDS

Private companies such as American Express and Diners Club are considered by most sellers as accounts receivable. The seller periodically summarizes the sales slips and submits them to the private credit card company for payment (these are usually paid within two weeks). Let's look at two situations to show how a company would handle its accounting procedures for these credit sales transactions.

Situation 1: On May 4, Morris Company sold merchandise on account $53.50 to Bill Blank. Bill used American Express. Assume Morris Company has low dollar volume and few transactions.

Note in Figure A-1 how the sale of $50 + GST is recorded in the sales journal. Keep in mind that Morris is treating American Express, not Bill Blank, as the accounts receivable. In Figure A-2 we see payment is received on June 8 from American Express and results in

1. Cash increasing by $50.82.
2. Credit card expense rising by $2.68.
3. Accounts receivable being reduced by the $53.50 originally owned by American Express.

SALES JOURNAL

Date 19XX		Invoice	Description of Accounts Receivable	PR	Accounts Receivable Dr.	GST Payable Cr.	Sales Cr.
May	4	692	American Express		5350	350	5000
			(Bill Blank)				

FIGURE A-1

CASH RECEIPTS JOURNAL

Date 19XX		Cash Dr.	Sales Discount Dr.	Credit Card Expense Dr.	Accounts Receivable Cr.	Sales Tax Payable Cr.	Sundry Account Name	Sundry PR	Sundry Amount Cr.
June	8	5082		268	5350		American Express		
							(Bill Blank)		

FIGURE A-2

Situation 2: On March 31, Blue Company summarized its credit card sales for American Express. Payment was received on April 13 from American Express. Assume Blue Company has high dollar volume and many transactions.

Note in Figure A-3 how each credit company has its own column set up. In the ledger there is an account set up for each as well; the posting to the ledger would be done at the end of the month. With high volume and the need to record many transactions, the use of these additional columns (versus Figure A-1) will result in increased efficiency. Figure A-4 shows the receipt of money from American Express less the credit card espense charge.

These new titles are found in the general ledger. Subsidiary ledgers are not needed, since a file is kept of all copies submitted for payment.

FIGURE A-3

BLUE COMPANY SALES JOURNAL

Date 19XX		Invoice	Description of Accounts Receivable	PR	Accounts Receivable Dr.	Credit Cards: American Express Dr.	Credit Cards: Diners Club Dr.	G.S.T. Payable Cr.	Credit Card Sales Cr.	Sales Cr.
Mar.	31		Summary of			121980 00		7980 00	114000 00	
			American Express							
						(112)	(113)		(401)	

Acc. Receivable American Express 112	
Total of column posted from sales journal at end of month	

Acc. Receivable Diners Club 113	
Total of column posted from sales journal at end of month	

Credit Card Sales 401	
	Total of column posted from sales journal at end of month

FIGURE A-4

BLUE COMPANY CASH RECEIPTS JOURNAL

Date 19XX		Cash Dr.	Sales Discount Dr.	Credit Card Expense Dr.	Credit Card Accounts Rec.: Accounts Receivable Cr.	Credit Card Accounts Rec.: American Express Cr.	Diners Club Cr.	Sales Cr.	G.S.T. Payable Cr.	Sundry: Account Name	Sundry: PR	Sundry: Amount Cr.
April	13	114661 20		7318 80		121980 00				Summary of		
										American		
										Express payments		
				(510)								

Credit Card Expense 510	
Total of columns posted from cash receipt journal at end of month	

COMPUTERIZED ACCOUNTING

PART A

An Introduction

Accounting procedures are essentially the same whether they are performed manually or on a computer. The following is a list of the accounting cycle steps in a manual accounting system as compared to the steps in a computerized accounting system.

STEPS OF THE ACCOUNTING CYCLE

Manual Accounting System	Computerized Accounting System
1. Business transactions occur and generate source documents.	1. Business transactions occur and generate source documents.
2. Analyse and record business transactions in a journal.	2. Analyse and record business transactions in a computerized journal.
3. Post or transfer information from journal to ledger.	3. Computer automatically posts information from journal to ledger.
4. Prepare a trial balance.	4. Trial balance is prepared automatically.
5. Prepare a worksheet.	5. No worksheet is necessary.
6. Prepare financial statements.	6. Financial statements are prepared automatically.
7. Journalize and post adjusting entries.	7. Record adjusting entries in a computerized journal; posting is automatic.
8. Journalize and post closing entries.	8. Closing procedures are completed automatically.
9. Prepare a post-closing trial balance.	9. Trial balance is prepared automatically.

The accounting cycle comparison shows that the accountant's task of initially analysing business transactions in terms of debits and credits (both routine business transactions and adjusting entries) is required in both manual and computerized accounting systems. However, in a computerized accounting system, the "drudge" work of posting transactions, creating and completing worksheets and financial statements, and performing the closing procedures is all handled automatically by the computerized accounting system.

In addition, computerized accounting systems can perform accounting procedures at greater speeds and with greater accuracy than can be achieved in a manual accounting system. It is important to recognize, however, that the computer is only a tool that can accept and process information supplied by the accountant. Each business transaction and adjusting entry must first be analysed and recorded in a computerized journal correctly; otherwise, the financial statements generated by the computerized accounting system will contain errors and will not be useful to the business.

Before a business can begin to use a computerized accounting system, and specifically the *CA-Simply Accounting for Windows* system, it must have the following items in place:

1. A computer system
2. Computer software
   a. Operating system software
   b. Applications software
      (1) Accounting applications software
      (2) *CA-Simply Accounting for Windows*

COMPUTER SYSTEM

A computer system is an electronic device that consists of several components that together have the ability to accept user-supplied data; input, store, and execute programmed instructions; and output results according to user specifications. The physical computer and its related devices are the hardware, while the stored program that supplies the instructions is called the software.

To understand how a computer system works, we must first look at a conceptual computer that demonstrates the major components and functions of a computer system. The conceptual computer shown in Figure B-1 has four major elements—input devices, processing/internal memory unit, secondary storage devices, and output devices. The illustration also shows the flow of data into the computer and of processed information out of the computer.

Input devices are used to feed data and instructions into the computer. Once the data and instructions are entered, the computer must be able to store them internally and then process the data based on the instructions. Storage and processing occur in the processing/internal memory unit.

There are two types of internal computer memory: random-access memory (RAM) and read-only memory (ROM). RAM is the largest portion of the memory but still has limited capacity; consequently, secondary storage devices are needed. In addition, RAM is temporary—anything stored in RAM is erased when power to the computer is interrupted. Therefore, data stored in RAM must be saved to a secondary storage medium through the use of a secondary storage device before the power is turned off. ROM is permanent memory and consists of those instruction sets necessary to start the computer and receive initial messages from input devices. ROM takes up only a small portion of the total internal memory capacity of a computer system.

FIGURE B-1
Conceptual Computer

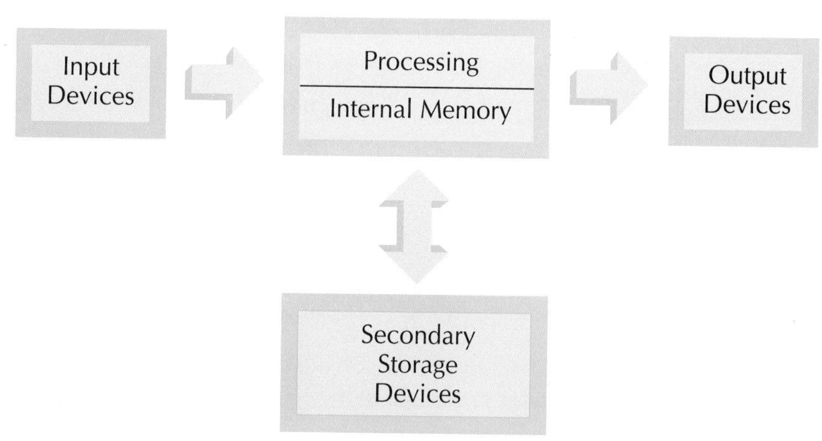

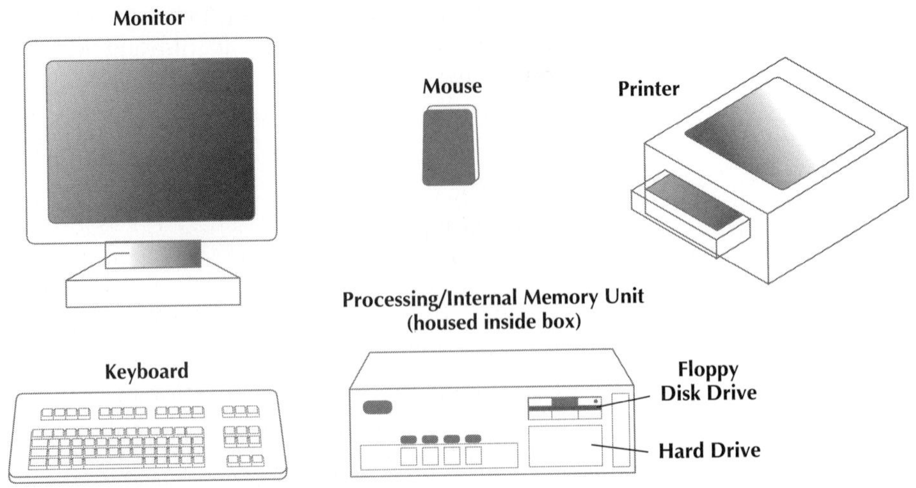

FIGURE B-2
Typical Configuration of a Microcomputer System

Finally, the results of processing must be made available to computer users through output devices. These components form a collection of devices referred to as computer hardware because they have physical substance.

In a typical microcomputer system (see Fig. B-2) a keyboard and mouse are used for input and a printer and monitor are used for output. The processing/internal memory unit is housed inside a box along with secondary storage devices consisting of a hard drive unit and one or more floppy disk drives.

Computer hardware can do nothing without a computer program. Computer programs are supplied on floppy disks, which are a secondary storage medium used in floppy disk drives. Figure B-3 shows two of the most common types of floppy disks. Handle these carefully! Do not bend them, fold them, or touch any of the exposed surfaces with your fingers!

To operate a particular computer program you must first load the program into the system's internal memory (RAM) either through the use of a floppy disk drive or by accessing the program that has been installed and stored on the system's hard drive. Once a program is accessed by RAM, the computer can execute the program instructions and process data as directed by the user through an input device. At the end of a processing session, the results may be viewed on the monitor, printed on the printer, and/or stored permanently on a secondary storage medium through the use of a secondary storage device.

COMPUTER SOFTWARE

The computer can do nothing without a computer program. Computer programs control the input, processing, storage, and output operations of a computer.

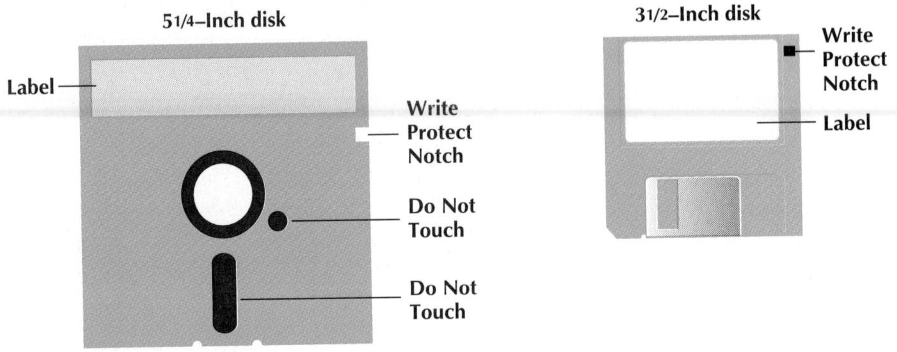

FIGURE B-3
Floppy Disks

Computer programmers write the instructions that tell the computer to execute certain procedures and process data. There are two broad categories of computer software: operating system software and applications software.

Operating System Software

Operating system software provides the link between the computer hardware, applications software, and the computer user. It consists of programs that start up the computer, retrieve applications programs, and allow the computer operator to store and retrieve data. Operating system software controls access to input and output devices and access to applications programs. There are several popular operating systems for microcomputers. They include DOS, DOS combined with Windows, OS/2, the Macintosh operating system (System 7), UNIX and, most recently, Windows 95 which is itself an operating system (it does not rely upon DOS as Windows 3.x did).

Applications Software

Applications software refers to programs designed for a specific use. The three most common types of business applications software are database management, spreadsheets, and word processing. Spreadsheet software allows the manipulation of data and has the ability to project answers to "what if" questions. For example, a spreadsheet program could project a company's profit next year if sales increased by 10 percent and expenses increased by 6 percent. Word processing software enables the user to write and print letters, memos, and other documents. Database management software stores, retrieves, sorts, and updates an organized body of information. Many computerized accounting systems are based upon database management software. Accounting information is data that must be organized and stored in a common base of data. This allows the entry of data and the retrieval of information in an organized and systematic way.

Applications software is frequently linked with a particular operating system. Database management, spreadsheet, word processing, accounting, and other software applications are available in versions that work with most of the popular operating systems. For example, if your computer system is using DOS you would purchase the DOS version of a word processing program. If you were using a Macintosh computer and operating system you would purchase the Macintosh version of a spreadsheet program. If you were using DOS in conjunction with Windows you would have the option of using either the DOS or Windows version of an applications program as Windows allows the use of non-Windows applications, although the additional functionality of Windows would be missing.

Accounting Applications Software Most computerized accounting software is organized into modules. Each module is designed to process a particular type of accounting data such as accounts receivable, accounts payable, or payroll. Each module is also designed to work in conjunction with the other modules. When modules are designed to work together in this manner, they are referred to as integrated software. In an integrated accounting system each module handles a different function but also communicates with the other modules. For example, to record a sale on account, you would make an entry into the accounts receivable module. The integration feature automatically records this entry in the sales journal, updates the customer's account in the accounts receivable subsidiary ledger, and posts all accounts affected in the general ledger. Thus in an integrated accounting system, transaction data are only entered once. All of the other accounting procedures required to bring the accounting records up-to-date are performed automatically through the integration function. Exceptions to this general rule include AccPac Plus, which does not integrate automatically, but is automated to some extent.

CA-Simply Accounting for Windows The version of *CA-Simply Accounting for Windows* chosen for use with this textbook has been selected to demonstrate and help you learn how to use a computerized accounting system. It is easy to use, fully integrated, and is also available in versions that work with the OS/2, Macintosh, and DOS operating systems. CA-Simply Accounting for Windows includes six modules: General Ledger, Receivables Ledger, Payables Ledger, Inventory Ledger, Payroll Ledger, and Project Ledger. Two modes of operation are available in CA-Simply Accounting for Windows: Ready and Not Ready. The Not Ready mode is used when you are converting a manual accounting system to a computerized accounting system. The Ready mode is used for regular accounting purposes. The payroll functions are based on the tax laws in effect as of January 1, 1996. If you are using a version later (or earlier) than this date, your payroll figures may differ slightly from those shown.

RELATIONSHIP OF THIS TEXTBOOK TO DATA SETS PROVIDED

In Canada, we are fortunate that most educational institutions have at least one of the two most popular accounting software packages available:

- CA-Simply Accounting for Windows Ver. 4.0
- CA ACCPAC Plus—Version 6.1

To allow students to learn computerized accounting as efficiently as possible, we have taken the position that it would not be very appropriate to duplicate software that is already owned by the majority of schools. Rather, we will concentrate on providing data sets, based on these two popular software products, which will permit students to master the essentials of computer accounting as quickly as possible.

This appendix, as well as the various computer exercises in the text, have been written to illustrate CA-Simply Accounting. If your school uses ACCPAC Plus, listen carefully to your instructor who will point out the steps necessary to complete the assignments using the software. There are many useful books available in bookstores to assist students who need more details. Most instructors will be happy to recommend a selection.

Remember that the supplied data disk has been compiled to assist you in learning the essentials of computer accounting. In preparing the disk, the authors' aim was to eliminate unnecessary data input and focus on only those tasks which seemed important to a student's education.

Another point worth making is that the field of business computing is dynamic. As these lines are being written, Windows 95 has been released but is not widely used yet. We decided to illustrate CA-Simply Accounting based upon Windows 3.x. Windows 95 might have been a better choice, but the decision was to stay with version 3.x for now. In any event, Windows 95 will itself be supplanted in due course and students are therefore advised to concentrate on the important principles, not on the various pretty screens which constitute the latest operating system. We are reasonably confident that the basics of CA-Simply Accounting will change only slightly over the next few years, so any investment by students learning this software will be worthwhile. In any event, the various screens within CA-Simply Accounting should not change much based on the operating system used.

Preparing to Work with CA-Simply Accounting for Windows

Before you begin to work with CA-Simply Accounting for Windows, you need to be familiar with your computer hardware and the DOS combined with Windows operating environment. When you are running Windows, your work takes place on the desktop. Think of this area as resembling the surface of a desk. There are physical objects on your real desk and there are windows and icons on the Windows desktop.

A mouse is an essential input device for all Windows applications. A mouse is a pointing device that assumes different shapes on your monitor as you move the mouse on your desk. According to the nature of the current action, the mouse pointer may appear as a small arrow head, an hourglass, or a hand. There are four basic mouse techniques:

- **Click** To quickly press and release the mouse button.
- **Double-click** To click the mouse button twice in rapid succession.
- **Drag** To hold down the mouse button while you move the mouse.
- **Point** To move the mouse until the mouse pointer on the screen rests on the item of choice.

The Windows Desktop

The following example contains a typical opening Windows screen. Your desktop may be different, just as your real desk is arranged differently from those of your colleagues. Regardless of the windows that are open on your desktop, most windows have certain elements in common. When you start Windows you can expect to see a window titled Program Manager. Program Manager is a special program crucial to the operation of Windows. It is the organizational tool that places applications in groups, then displays those groups as windows or icons. It starts automatically when Windows is loaded, and remains active throughout the current working session. Closing Program Manager closes Windows.

FIGURE B-4
A Typical Windows Desktop

A Windows 95 Desktop will appear much differently from the one shown for Windows 3.x.

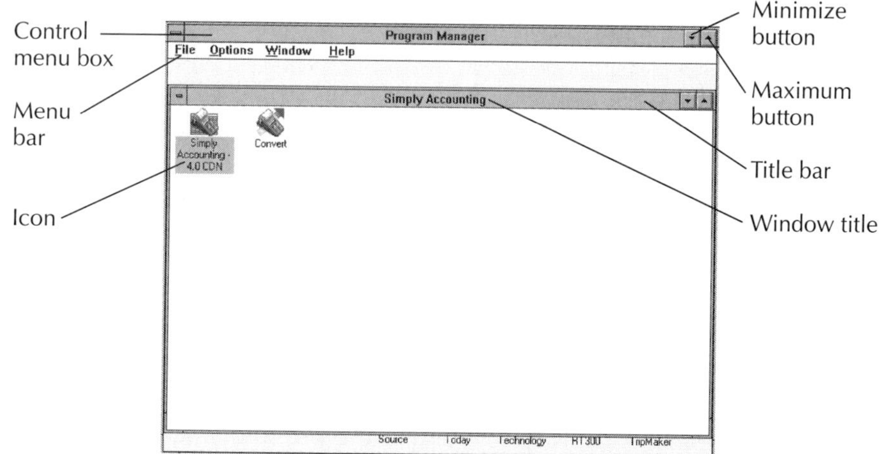

- **Minimize button:** Clicking on this button reduces a window to an icon.
- **Maximize button:** Clicking on this button enlarges the active window so that it fills the entire desktop. After you enlarge a window, the maximize button is replaced by a **Restore button** (a double arrow, not shown) that returns the window to the size it was before it was maximized.
- **Control menu box:** Double-clicking on this box will close the window. A single click will present a menu to resize, move, maximize, minimize, close, or switch to another window.

- **Menu bar:** This window element lists the available menus for the window.
- **Icon:** This is a small graphic symbol that represents various types of applications and files.
- **Title bar:** This window element displays the name of the window.
- **Window title:** This window element provides the name of the window. It appears in the title bar.

Application Window (the Company Window)

As you work with CA-Simply Accounting for Windows, two kinds of windows will appear on your desktop: the application window (called the Company Window), and windows contained within the Company Window (called dialog boxes). In Windows, an application window contains a running application. The name of the application and the application's menu bar will appear at the top of the application window.

FIGURE B-5
CA-Simply Accounting for Windows Application (Company) Window

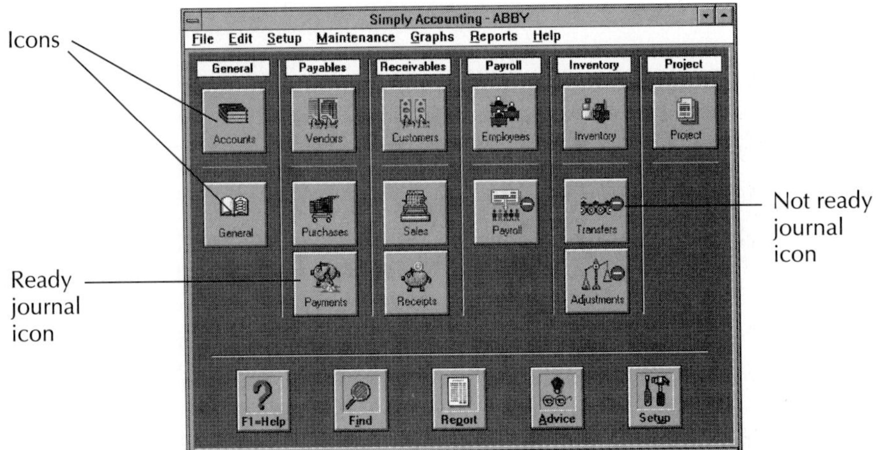

- **Icons:** The Company Window displays the icons that represent a company's accounting books — the full set of Ledgers and Journals that you use to record accounting transactions. The top row contains the Ledgers; the bottom two rows contain the Journals aligned vertically with their related Ledgers.
- **Highlighted (selected) icon:** The active icon in the Company Window.
- **Ready Journal icon:** A Journal icon is shown in the unlocked position if its status is Ready.
- **Not Ready Journal icon:** A Journal icon is shown with a lock if its status is Not Ready.

Dialog Boxes

A dialog box appears when additional information is needed to execute a command. There are different ways to supply that information; consequently, there are different types of dialog boxes. Most dialog boxes contain options you

Dialog Box 1

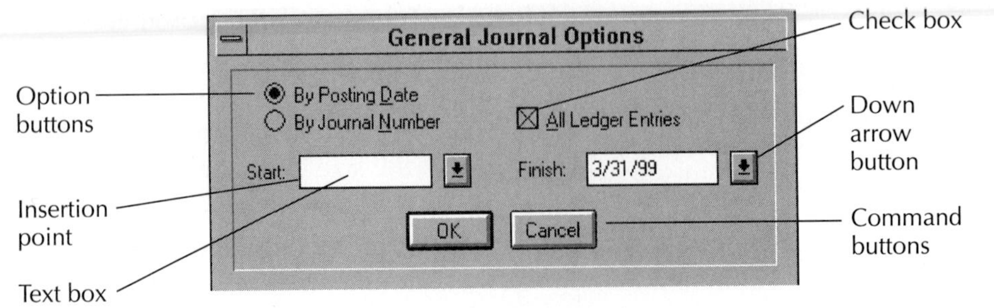

can select. After you specify options, you can choose a command button to carry out a command. Other dialog boxes may display additional information, warnings, or messages indicating why a requested task cannot be accomplished.

- **Insertion point:** This element shows where you are in the dialog box. It marks the place where text will appear when you begin typing.
- **Check box:** A small square that represents an option. When you select an option (click on the empty check box), the check box contains an X; when you turn off the option (click on the check box to remove the X), it is blank.
- **Option buttons:** A small circle that represents an option. When you select (click on the button) an option from a group, that button contains a large black dot; the remaining buttons in the group are blank. Option buttons represent mutually exclusive options. You can select only one option button at a time.
- **Text box:** When you move to an empty text box, an insertion point appears at the far left-hand side of the box. The text you type starts at the insertion point. If the box you move to already contains text, this text is selected (highlighted), and any text you type replaces it. You can also delete the selected text by pressing the DELETE or BACKSPACE key.
- **Command buttons:** Choose (click) on a command button to initiate an immediate action such as carrying out or canceling a command. The **OK, Cancel, Yes, No, Select,** and **Post** buttons are common command buttons.
- **Down arrow button:** Click on this button to display a list of choices.
- **Highlighted (selected) item:** To highlight or select an item in a displayed list, click on the item.
- **Scroll bar:** A bar that may appear at the bottom and/or right side of a window or dialog box if there is more text than can be displayed at one time within the window.
- **Scroll arrow:** A small arrow at the end of a scroll bar that you click on to move to the next item in the list. The top and left arrows scroll to the previous item; the bottom and right arrows scroll to the next item.
- **Scroll box:** A small box in a scroll bar. You can use the mouse to drag the scroll box left or right, or up or down. The scroll box indicates the relative position in the list.
- **Mouse pointer:** The mouse pointer is shown as a small arrow head in this example.

Dialog Box 2

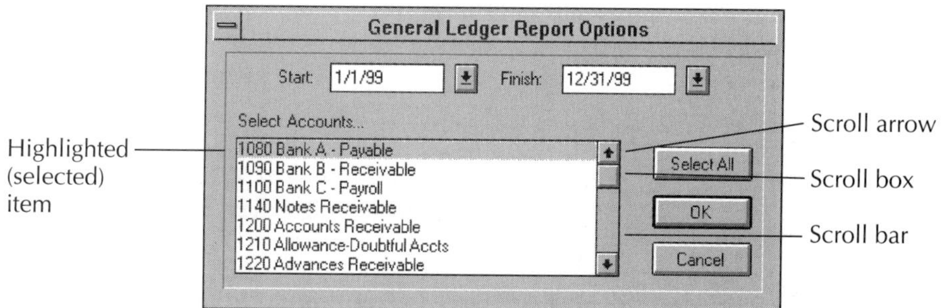

Using Menus

Windows commands are listed on menus. Each application has its own menus, which are listed on the **Application menu bar.** To display a complete menu, click on the **Menu title.** When a menu is displayed, choose a command by clicking on it or by typing the **Underlined letter** to execute the command. You can also bypass the menu entirely if you know the **Keystroke equivalent** shown to the right of the command when the menu is displayed.

A **Dimmed command** indicates that a command is not currently executable; some additional action has to be taken for the command to become available. Some commands are followed by an **Ellipsis** (. . .) to indicate that more information is required to execute the command. The additional information can be entered into a dialog box, which will appear immediately after the command has been selected.

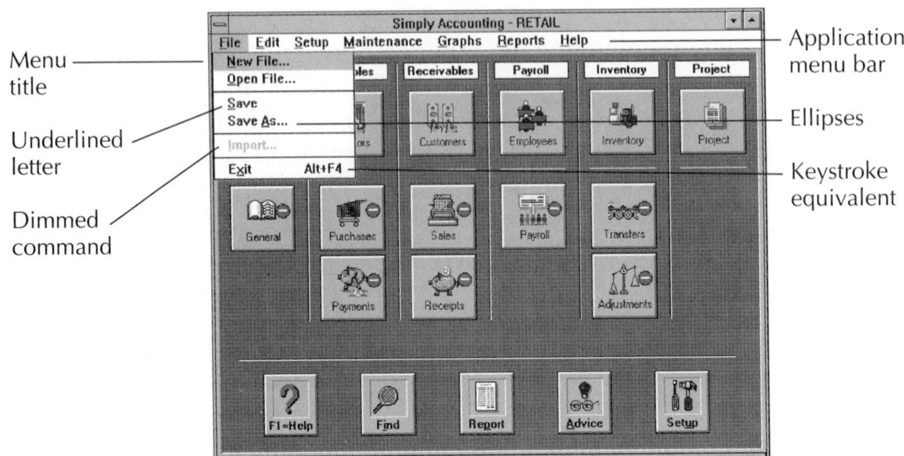

Working in the Windows Environment

You can use a combination of mouse and keyboard techniques to navigate within the Windows environment. For example, you can click on an item to select it, and then press the ENTER key to choose it, or you can just double-click on the item. CA-Simply Accounting for Windows is designed for a mouse, but it also provides keyboard equivalents for almost every command. It may seem confusing at first that there are several different ways to do the same thing. You will find this flexibility useful. For example, if your hands are already on the keyboard, it may be faster to use the keyboard equivalent of a mouse command. Alternatively, if your hand is already on the mouse, it may be faster to use a mouse technique to carry out a command. When a procedure in an assignment says to select or choose an item, generally use whichever method you prefer. Alternative procedures are often provided as well. It is not necessary to memorize any particular technique, just be flexible and willing to experiment. As you gain experience with the program, you will develop personal preferences, and the various techniques will become second nature.

Windows Tutorial

Windows includes a Windows Tutorial to acquaint new users with mouse techniques and the Windows operating environment. Use the following instructions to access the Windows Tutorial on your computer system.

1. Start Windows.
2. Click on the Help menu in the Program Manager window.
3. Click on the Windows Tutorial menu item; then follow the instructions on the screen.

PART B

Preparing to Use CA-Simply Accounting for Windows

This section of the appendix discusses several basic operations that you need to be familiar with to operate the CA-Simply Accounting for Windows program and complete the assignment material in this text. It is designed as a reference for such procedures as installing the CA-Simply Accounting program and making working copies of original disks. Each procedure is explained for a variety of common computer system configurations.

System requirements

The minimum software and hardware your computer system needs to run both Windows and CA-Simply Accounting for Windows are:

- MS-DOS or PC-DOS, version 3.1 or later.
- Windows, version 3.0 or later.
- A computer that can run Windows in standard or enhanced mode.
- 2 megabytes of RAM.
- A hard disk with 1.5 megabytes of free disk space.
- At least one 3.5 inch high density floppy disk drive.
- An EGA, VGA, or similar high-resolution monitor that is supported by Windows.
- A printer that is supported by Windows.
- A mouse that is supported by Windows.

Installation procedures are provided for several types of system configurations. Determine which instructions you should follow based on the following legend.

LEGEND

Computer Systems Configurations

- **System 1:** Your computer system has a hard drive and two floppy disk drives. Drive A is for high density 3.5 inch disks and drive B is for 5.25 inch disks.
- **System 2:** Your computer system has a hard drive with two floppy disk drives. Drive A is for 5.25 inch disks and drive B is for high density 3.5 inch disks.
- **System 3:** Your computer system has a hard drive and a single high density 3.5 inch disk drive (drive A).

Disk contents

One high density 3.5 inch floppy disk packaged with this text contains the company files for use in completing each assignment in both CA-Simply Accounting and AccPac Plus format. All files are in one of two sub-directories labeled "Simply" and "AccPac".

Making working copies of original disks

Making a working copy of an original disk is always a good practice. Should anything happen to your working copy while installing a program, running a program, or accessing data files, you will always have another copy of the disk to use. Should this occur, always make a new working copy of your original disk

Warning! Always use caution when using the Copy Disk command; if you accidentally reverse the two disks, you will erase the data on your original disk.

Definitions: The "source disk" is your original disk. The "destination disk" is your working copy.

before attempting to repeat the action that caused your first working copy to fail. After making a working copy of an original disk, store your original disk in a safe place.

To make working copies of your Student Data Files disk, use the following instructions:

1. Start Windows.
2. From Program Manager on your Windows desktop, double-click on the File Manager icon (Note: You may need to double-click on the Main icon to display the File Manager icon.).
3. Insert the source disk in the drive from which you wish to copy.
   - **System 1:** A
   - **System 2:** B
   - **System 3:** A
4. Click on the File Manager Disk menu; then click on Copy Disk.
5. If your computer has two floppy disk drives, the Copy Disk dialog box will appear. Select the letter of the source drive and the destination drive.
   - **System 1: Source In:** A **Destination In:** A
   - **System 2: Source In:** B **Destination In:** B
   - **System 3:** No dialog box will appear.
6. Click on the **OK** button.
7. A confirmation dialog box will appear asking you to verify that you want to copy the disk. Click on the **Yes** button. A message will appear informing you of the percentage of your disk that has been copied. Follow the instructions on the screen to switch source and destination disks as needed.
8. Click on the File Manager File menu; then click on Exit to close File Manager and return to your Windows desktop.

INSTALLING THE CA-SIMPLY ACCOUNTING FOR WINDOWS PROGRAM

If you need to install the CA-Simply Accounting for Windows program on your hard disk, follow these instructions:

1. Start Windows.
2. Insert disk one of the CA-Simply Accounting for Windows Program in drive A (**System 1** and **System 3**) or in drive B **(System 2).**
3. Click on the Program Manager File menu; then click on Run. The Run dialog box will appear.
4. Type A:\install (**System 1** and **System 3**) or B:\install **(System 2)** in the **Command Line** text box; then click on the **OK** button.
5. Follow the step-by-step instructions as they appear on the screen.
   - You can install one or more of the following in the C:\Winsim subdirectory:
   - *Program Files:* To install the CA-Simply Accounting for Windows program, select Program Files.
   - *Conversion:* If you want to convert company data files created using CA-Simply Accounting for DOS (formerly called ACCPAC Bedford Integrated Accounting), select Conversion.
   - The program components you select will be copied to your hard disk.
6. Click on the **OK** button when the Installation Complete! message appears.

7. When the Notepad-README.TXT window appears you can read the information by advancing the text using the scroll bar to the right of the window; then close the Notepad-README.TXT window by double-clicking on the control menu box.
8. The CA-Simply Accounting icon will appear in the CA-Simply Accounting program group on your Windows desktop. If you selected conversion, the Convert icon will also appear.
9. Put your copy of the CA-Simply Accounting for Windows Program disk away for safekeeping.
10. You must test your print and display settings in the CA-Simply Accounting for Windows Program prior to starting on any of the assignments in the text. Refer to Part F-Print and Display Settings in CA-Simply Accounting for Windows in this appendix for information on how to test and adjust your print and display settings.

INSTALLING CA-SIMPLY ACCOUNTING FOR WINDOWS ON A NETWORK

CA-Simply Accounting for Windows can be used in a network environment as long as each student uses a separate Student Data Files disk to store their data files. It is assumed that any network versions of this software will already be installed.

Students should consult with their instructor and/or network administrator for specific procedures regarding program installation and any special printing procedures required for proper network operation.

PART C Correcting a Posted Transaction

Important Note: *All students should be aware of one of the major differences between CA-Simply Accounting and AccPac Plus. AccPac Plus is a batch system (transactions are saved in "batches" and posted as a group) whereas CA-Simply Accounting posts each entry just after it is made. If you are using AccPac Plus, be aware that the procedures for correcting entries is much different than with CA-Simply Accounting as described below.*

Once a transaction is posted in the CA-Simply Accounting for Windows program, the journal entry will be permanently reflected in the accounting records. This feature of CA-Simply Accounting for Windows is designed to ensure that a good audit trail of all transactions is constantly maintained within the program. Consequently, the only way to correct a posted transaction is to reverse the original entry. After this is accomplished, the accounting records will be in the same position as if the transaction had not been posted in the first place, but a complete record of the original entry and the reversing entry will be maintained by the CA-Simply Accounting for Windows program. After the reversing entry is posted, enter the correct journal entry.

The term reversing entry as it is used here should not be confused with the optional way of handling certain adjusting entries. The optional reversing entry procedure for adjusting entries is designed to help prevent errors. Reversing an incorrect entry in a computerized accounting system is a required procedure designed to correct an error that has already occurred.

The following procedures for reversing an incorrect journal entry and re-entering the correct journal entry are not intended to be exhaustive, but to give you the general idea of how to correct transactions posted in error. It is impossible to predict the particular error or combination of errors you might make in an assignment.

REVERSING AN ENTRY MADE IN THE GENERAL JOURNAL DIALOG BOX: USE THE GENERAL JOURNAL

You will need to have a printed copy of a General Journal report listing the entry you intend to reverse on hand as you work through the following reversing and correcting procedures.

1. Open the General Journal; enter the word "Reverse" into the **Source** text box; press the TAB key; enter the **Using** date into the **Date** text box; press the TAB key; enter an explanation for the transaction into the **Comment** text box; then press the TAB key.
2. Refer to your printed copy of the General Journal report. With the flashing insertion point positioned in the **Account** text box press the ENTER key to bring up the Select Account dialog box. Double-click on the account that you credited in the incorrect journal entry; enter the amount used in the credit portion of the incorrect journal entry into the **Debits** text box; then press the TAB key.
3. If you are reversing a compound journal entry, skip this step and go to the next step. With the flashing insertion point positioned in the **Account** text box, press the ENTER key to bring up the Select Account dialog box. Double-click on the account that you debited in the incorrect journal entry; then press the TAB key to accept the default **Credits** amount.
4. If you are reversing a compound journal entry, press the ENTER key with the flashing insertion point positioned in the **Account** text box to bring up the Select Account dialog box. Double-click on the first account that you debited in the incorrect compound journal entry. The program will offer a default **Credits** amount and the **Credits** amount will remain highlighted. Override the default **Credits** amount by entering the amount used in the debit portion of the incorrect compound journal entry. Press the TAB key; then press the ENTER key to bring up the Select Account dialog box. Double-click on the second account that you debited in the incorrect compound journal entry. The program will offer a default **Credits** amount; press the TAB key to accept the default **Credits** amount.
5. Click on the General Journal Report menu; then click on Display General Journal Entry. Verify that the reversing entry is correct. The reversing entry should be the exact opposite of your incorrect journal entry. Accounts and amounts originally debited should be credited, and accounts and amounts originally credited should be debited.
6. Close the General Journal Entry Display window. Make editing corrections if necessary.
7. Click on the **Post** button to post the entry.
8. Re-enter the journal entry correctly. Enter the word "Correct" in the **Source** text box to indicate that it is a correcting entry; enter the **Using** date into the **Date** text box.

NOTE: The CA-Simply Accounting for Windows program will not accept duplicate invoice or cheque numbers in the Sales, Receipts, Purchases, Payments, or Payroll Journals. This feature of the program is designed to prevent the error of entering invoices and cheques twice. Consequently, invoice and check numbers must be modified when reversing and correcting entries are entered. Insert the letter R after the invoice or cheque number to indicate a reversing entry. Insert the letter C after the invoice or cheque number to indicate a correcting entry.

Reversing an Entry Made in the Payroll Journal Dialog Box: Use the Payroll Journal

1. Click on the Company Window Setup Menu; then click on Settings. The Settings dialog box will appear. Click on the **Payroll** option button; click on the **Automatic Payroll Deductions** check box to de-select this option (the X will disappear from the check box); then click on the **OK** button.
2. Open the Payroll Journal; click on the arrow key to the right of the **To the order of** text box; select the employee from the list displayed; then press the TAB key.
3. Enter the cheque number into the **No.** text box inserting the letter R after the cheque number to indicate that this is a reversing entry; then press the TAB key.
4. Enter the Using date into the **Date** text box; then press the TAB key.
5. Accept the **Period Start** and **Period End** dates offered by pressing the TAB key.
6. Refer to your General Journal report listing the incorrect payroll journal entry. Enter amounts into the following text boxes overriding any default amounts offered:

   Wages Enter the amount debited to the Wages account as a negative number.

   FIT Enter the amount credited to the FIT Payable account as a negative number.

   CPP Enter the amount credited to the CPP Payable account as a negative number.

   UI Enter the amount debited to the Medicare Tax Expense account as a negative number.
7. Press the TAB key; click on the Payroll Journal Report menu; then click on Display Payroll Journal Entry. Verify that the entry is correct. It should be the exact opposite of your incorrect payroll entry. Accounts and amounts originally debited should be credited, and accounts and amounts originally credited should be debited.
8. Close the Payroll Journal Entry window. Make editing corrections if necessary.
9. Click on the **Post** button to post the entry.
10. Click on the Company Window Setup menu; then click on Settings. The Settings dialog box will appear. Click on the **Payroll** option button; click on the **Automatic Payroll Deductions** check box to re-select this option (the X will re-appear in the check box); then click on the **OK** button.
11. Re-enter the payroll journal entry correctly. Insert the letter C after the cheque number in the **No.** text box to indicate that this is a correcting entry; enter the **Using** date into the **Date** text box.

Reversing and Correcting Entries Made in Special Journals

You must know for certain which dialog box you originally used (Sales Journal, Receipts Journal, Purchases Journal, or Payments Journal) to record a transaction prior to attempting to use the reversing procedures described in the following sections for special journals. If you are uncertain about which dialog box you used to record the journal entry you wish to reverse and correct, print a Sales Journal, Receipts Journal, Purchases Journal, and Payments Journal report.

1. **To print a Sales Journal,** click on the Sales Journal icon to highlight the icon;

click on the Company Window Report menu; then click on Display Sales Journal. Enter 3/1/99 into the **Start** date text box; leave the **Finish** date text box set at 3/31/99; then click on the **OK** button. The Sales Journal Display window will appear. Click on the Sales Journal Display File menu; then click on Print to print the report. After you have printed the report, click on the control menu box to close the Sales Journal Display window and return to the Company Window.

2. **To print a Receipts Journal,** click on the Receipts Journal icon to highlight the icon; click on the Company Window Report menu; then click on Display Receipts Journal. Enter 3/1/99 into the **Start** date text box; leave the **Finish** date text box set at 3/31/99; then click on the **OK** button. The Receipts Journal Display window will appear. Click on the Receipts Journal Display File menu; then click on Print to print the report. After you have printed the report, click on the control menu box to close the Receipts Journal Display window and return to the Company Window.
3. **To print a Purchases Journal,** click on the Purchases Journal icon to highlight the icon; click on the Company Window Report menu; then click on Display Purchases Journal. Enter 3/1/99 into the **Start** date text box; leave the **Finish** date text box set at 3/31/99; then click on the **OK** button. The Purchases Journal Display window will appear. Click on the Purchases Journal Display File menu; then click on Print to print the report. After you have printed the report, click on the control menu box to close the Purchases Journal Display window and return to the Company Window.
4. **To print a Payments Journal,** click on the Payments Journal icon to highlight the icon; click on the Company Window Report menu; then click on Display Payments Journal. Enter 3/1/99 into the **Start** date text box; leave the **Finish** date text box set at 3/31/99; then click on the **OK** button. The Payments Journal Display window will appear. Click on the Payments Journal Display File menu; then click on Print to print the report. After you have printed the report, click on the control menu box to close the Payments Journal Display window and return to the Company Window.

Review each report to determine which contains the journal entry you wish to reverse; then use the following chart to determine which set of instructions to use for reversing the journal entry and entering the correct entry.

If the journal entry you wish to reverse appears on the:	Use these instructions to reverse the entry and enter the correct entry:
Sales Journal	Reversing an Entry Made in the Sales Journal Dialog Box: Use the Sales Journal
Receipts Journal	Reversing an Entry Made in the Receipts Journal: Use the Sales Journal
Purchases Journal	Reversing an Entry Made in the Purchases Journal: Use the Purchases Journal
Payments Journal	Reversing an Entry Made in the Payments Journal: Use the Purchases Journal

Reversing an Entry Made in the Sales Journal Dialog Box: Use the Sales Journal

1. Open the Sales Journal; click on the arrow button to the right of the **Sold to** text box; select the customer from the list displayed; then press the TAB key until the **Invoice** text box is highlighted.
2. Enter the invoice number used in the incorrect entry into the **Invoice** text box followed by the letter R to show that you are reversing this entry; then press the TAB key.
3. Enter the Using date into the **Date** text box; then press the TAB key until the insertion point is positioned in the **Amount** text box.
4. Enter the same **Amount** as used in the incorrect entry, preceded by a minus sign if the incorrect amount was originally entered as a positive amount. Enter the amount as a positive amount if the original amount entered was negative. Press the TAB key.
5. Enter the same **Acct** number as used in the incorrect entry (do not use the Accounts Receivable account number); then press the TAB key.
6. Click on the Sales Journal Report menu; then click on Display Sales Journal Entry. Verify that the entry is correct. The entry should be the exact opposite of your incorrect entry. Accounts and amounts originally debited should be credited, and accounts and amounts originally credited should be debited.
7. Close the Sales Journal Entry window. Make editing corrections if necessary.
8. Click on the **Post** button to post the entry.
9. Re-enter the journal entry correctly. Insert the letter C after the invoice number to show that this is a correcting entry; enter the **Using** date into the **Date** text box.

Reversing an Entry Made in the Receipts Journal Dialog Box: Use the Sales Journal

1. Open the Sales Journal; click on the arrow button to the right of the **Sold to** text box; select the customer from the list displayed; then press the TAB key until the **Invoice** text box is highlighted.
2. Enter the customer's cheque number used in the incorrect entry into the **Invoice** text box followed by the letter R to show that you are reversing this entry; then press the TAB key.
3. Enter the Using date into the **Date** text box; then press the TAB key until the flashing insertion point is positioned in the **Amount** text box.
4. Enter the amount debited to the Cash account in the incorrect journal entry into the **Amount** text box; then press the TAB key.
5. Enter the Cash account number into the **Acct** text box; then press the TAB key.
6. Click on the Sales Journal Report menu; then click on Display Sales Journal Entry. The entry should debit the Accounts Receivable account and credit the Cash account for the amount of the entry you are reversing. Verify that the entry is correct.
7. Close the Sales Journal Entry window. Make editing corrections if necessary.
8. Click on the **Post** button to post the entry.
9. Re-enter the customer's payment correctly using the Receipts Journal dialog box. Insert the letter C after the customer's cheque number to show that this is a correcting entry; enter the **Using** date into the **Date** text box. Accept the default amounts offered in the **Payment Amt.** text box as necessary to record the correct amount received from the customer.

Reversing an Entry Made in the Purchases Journal Dialog Box: Use the Purchases Journal

1. Open the Purchases Journal; click on the arrow button to the right of the **Purchased from** text box; select the vendor from the list displayed; then press the TAB key until the flashing insertion point is positioned in the **Invoice** text box.
2. Enter the invoice number used in the incorrect entry into the **Invoice** text box followed by the letter R to show that you are reversing this entry; then press the TAB key.
3. Enter the Using date into the **Date** text box; then press the TAB key until the insertion point is positioned in the **Amount** text box.
4. Enter the same **Amount** as used in the incorrect entry, preceded by a minus sign if the incorrect amount was originally entered as a positive amount. Enter the amount as a positive amount if the original amount entered was negative. Press the TAB key.
5. Enter the same **Acct** number as used in the incorrect entry (do not use the Accounts Payable account number); then press the TAB key.
6. Click on the Purchases Journal Report menu; then click on Display Purchases Journal Entry. Verify that the entry is correct. The entry should be the exact opposite of your incorrect entry. Accounts and amounts originally debited should be credited, and accounts and amounts originally credited should be debited.
7. Close the Purchases Journal Entry window. Make editing corrections if necessary.
8. Click on the **Post** button to post the entry.
9. Re-enter the journal entry correctly. Insert the letter C after the invoice number to show that this is a correcting entry; enter the **Using** date into the **Date** text box.

Reversing an Entry Made in the Payments Journal Dialog Box: Use the Purchases Journal

1. Open the Purchases Journal; click on the arrow button to the right of the **Purchased from** text box; select the vendor from the list displayed; then press the TAB key until the flashing insertion point is positioned in the **Invoice** text box.
2. Enter the cheque number used in the incorrect entry into the **Invoice** text box followed by the letter R to show that you are reversing this entry; then press the TAB key.
3. Enter the Using date into the **Date** text box; then press the TAB key until the insertion point is positioned in the **Amount** text box.
4. Enter the amount credited to the Cash account in the incorrect journal entry into the **Amount** text box; then press the TAB key.
5. Enter the Cash account number into the **Acct** text box; then press the TAB key.
6. Click on the Purchases Journal Report menu; then click on Display Purchases Journal Entry. The entry should debit the Cash account and credit the Accounts Payable account for the amount of the entry you are reversing. Verify that the entry is correct.
7. Close the Purchases Journal Entry window. Make editing corrections if necessary.
8. Click on the **Post** button to post the entry.

9. Re-enter the payment issued to the vendor correctly using the Payments Journal dialog box. Insert the letter C after the cheque number to show that this is a correcting entry; enter the **Using** date into the **Date** text box. Accept the default amounts offered in the **Payment Amt.** text box as necessary to record the correct amount of the payment issued to the vendor.

PART *D*

How to Repeat or Start Over on an Assignment

You always have the option to repeat an assignment for additional practice or to start over on an assignment. To repeat or start over on an assignment, make a new working copy of your original Student Data Files disk using the procedures listed in the Making Working Copies of Original Disks section of this appendix. Relabel your first working copy of the Student Data Files disk "Working copy of Student Data Files #1" and label your new working copy "Working copy of Student Data Files #2." Store your disk labeled "Working copy of Student Data Files #1" in a safe place; then use the disk labeled "Working copy of Student Data Files #2" to repeat the assignment or start over on the assignment.

After you have repeated or started over on an assignment, you can continue to use the disk labeled "Working copy of Student Data Files #2" to complete the remaining assignments in this text.

Sometimes students find it is easier to begin a given assignment again rather than struggle with the somewhat tedious process of correcting an error in CA-Simply Accounting. Remember that in the business world it is not always possible to begin again because the volume of transactions is often too large. See also the next session.

PART *E*

How and When to Use the Backup Copy of a Company's Data Files

At certain times in the assignments you are asked to make a backup copy of a company's data files. There are several reasons why you might wish to access the backup copy of a company's data files. For example, you may not have printed a required report in an assignment before advancing the **Using** date to a new month, or you may want to start an assignment over at the point where the backup copy was made rather than at the beginning of an assignment.

To use the backup copy of a company's data files complete the following procedures. The backup data files for Valdez Realty for June are used to explain the process in the following procedures.

1. Start Windows; insert your Student Data Files disk into disk drive A or B; then double-click on the CA-Simply Accounting icon. The CA-Simply Accounting–Open File dialog box will appear.
2. Enter one of the following paths into the **Open file name** text box:

   A:\Valdjune.asc (if you are storing your student data files on the disk in drive A)

   B:\Valdjune.asc (if you are storing your student data files on the disk in drive B)

3. Click on the **Open** button; leave the **Using date for this session** set at 6/30/99; then click on the **OK** button. The Company Window for Valdjune will appear on your screen. If you only need to print reports for Valdez Realty for June, print those reports now; click on the Company Window File menu; then click on Exit to end the current work session and return to your Windows desktop. If you want to start the Valdez Realty assignment over at the point where you made the June backup copy (i.e., you completed the June transactions and adjusting entries correctly, but made an error in the June closing process and/or made errors in the July transactions) continue with the following instructions.
4. Click on the Company Window File menu; click on Save As; then enter one of the following new file names into the **Save file as** text box:

   A:\valdez.asc (if you are storing your student data files on the disk in drive A)

   B:\valdez.asc (if you are storing your student data files on the disk in drive B)
5. Click on the **Save** button. Click on the **OK** button in response to the question "Replace existing data files with the same name?" Note that the company name in the Company Window has changed from Valdjune to Valdez.
6. Continue with the Valdez Realty Mini Practice Set starting with instruction #17 under Part A: The June Accounting Cycle.

If you want to use the backup copy of a company's data files in a situation other than that described in the preceding section, substitute the desired backup file name for valdjune. asc and the desired current data file name for valdez. asc into the procedures described in the preceding section. A summary of the substitutions appears below:

Backup You Want to Use	Substitute in Prior Procedures	Using Date	Continue Assignment Starting With
1. valdjuly.asc	valdjuly.asc for valdjune.asc	7/31/99	Valdez Realty Mini Practice Set Part B, instruction #15
2. petejan.asc	petejan.asc for valdjune.asc pete.asc for valdez.asc	1/31/99	Pete's Market Mini Practice Set, instruction #20
3. petefeb.asc	petefeb.asc for valdjune.asc pete.asc for valdez.asc	2/29/99	Pete's Market Mini Practice Set, instruction #30
4. petemar.asc	petemar.asc for valdjune.asc pete.asc for valdez.asc	3/31/99	Pete's Market Mini Practice Set instruction #42
5. dressmar.asc	dressmar.asc for valdjune.asc dress.asc for valdez.asc	3/31/99	The Corner Dress Shop Mini Practice Set instruction #15

Print and Display Settings in CA-Simply Accounting for Windows

When you install CA-Simply Accounting for Windows, the program automatically installs the default printer established in Windows as the default printer for CA-Simply Accounting for Windows. If you have not yet installed a default printer in

Windows, you will need to do so prior to attempting to print any reports from the CA-Simply Accounting for Windows program. Refer to your Windows manual for information on installing a printer. You do not need to re-install CA-Simply Accounting for Windows. The next time you access the CA-Simply Accounting for Windows program, the Windows default printer will automatically be established as the default printer for CA-Simply Accounting for Windows.

The installation process for the Windows default printer does not ensure that the default printer and display settings within the CA-Simply Accounting for Windows program will work to your satisfaction; consequently, you must test and, if necessary, adjust your printer and display settings before you complete any of the assignments in the text. Once the print and display settings are adjusted, they will become the default printer and display settings for each set of company data files. You need only make these adjustments once.

How to Test and Adjust the Default Printer and Display Settings for CA-Simply Accounting for Windows

1. Start Windows; insert your Student Data Files disk into disk drive A or B; then double-click on the CA-Simply Accounting icon.
2. The CA-Simply Accounting copyright screen will appear briefly; then the CA-Simply Accounting–Open File dialog box will appear. Enter one of the following paths into the **Open file name** text box:

   A:\printest.asc (if you are storing your student data files on the disk in drive A)

   B:\printest.asc (if you are storing your student data files on the disk in drive B)
3. Click on the **Open** button. The program will respond with a request for the **Using date for this session.** Leave the **Using date for this session** text box set at 12/1/99; then click on the **OK** button. The Company Window for Printest will appear.
4. Click on the Company Window Setup menu; then click on Settings. The Settings dialog box will appear.
5. Click on the **Other** option button; then adjust the display features based on the folowing definitions and suggestions:
   - **Display Font:** Click on the arrow button to the right of the **Display Font** text box to display a list of available fonts. Select the font you want to see on the screen when you display reports.
   - **Size:** Click on the arrow button to the right of the **Size** text box to display a list of available type sizes. Select the type size you want to see on the screen when you display reports.

   NOTE: It is suggested that you adjust the display settings to agree with **Display Font** and **Size** used for the screen illustrations in the text. These settings are:

   - **Display Font:** MS Sans Serif
   - **Size:** 8
6. Click on the **OK** button to return to the Company Window. These display settings will become the new display settings for all sets of company data files.
7. Click on the Company Window Report menu; then click on Trial Balance. The Trial Balance Options dialog box will appear. Leave the **As at** date set at 12/1/99; then click on the **OK** button.

8. The scroll bar can be used to advance the display to view other portions of the report.
9. Click on the Trial Balance File menu; then click on Print to print the Trial Balance.
10. Double-click on the control menu box to close the Trial Balance window and return to the Company Window.
11. Review your printed Trial Balance report. If the font, type size, and/or margins are not satisfactory continue with the following instructions. If the font, type size, and margins are satisfactory, click on the Company Window File menu; then click on Exit to end your current work session and return to your Windows desktop.
12. To adjust the printer settings, click on the Company Window Setup menu; then click on Printers. The Printers dialog box will appear.
13. Adjust the printer settings as necessary based on the following definitions:
    - **Set Printer For:** Click on the **Reports** option button to establish the printer for standard reports and lists, such as a balance sheet or trial balance. Note: The **Checks, Invoices, Labels, Statements,** and **T-4s** printing options are not used in the assignments in this text; consequently you do not need to adjust the printer settings for these options.
    - **Margins:** Enter the top and left margins for the printout:
        - **Top:** Enter the amount you want the top margin of the text to be lowered or raised if your reports are being printed too high or too low on the page. The amount should be expressed in inches and decimal fractions of an inch (up to two decimal places). Positive amounts lower the top margin; negative amounts raise it.
        - **Left:** Enter the amount you want the left margin of the text to be moved to the right or left if your reports are being printed too far to the left or right. The amount should be expressed in inches and decimal fractions of an inch (up to two decimal places). Positive amounts move the left margin to the right, negative amounts move it to the left.
    - **Printer:** Click on the arrow button to the right of the **Printer** text box to display a list of available printers. These are the printers you set up in Windows. If you want to use a printer that is not on the list, you must install the new printer in Windows. Select the printer you want to use.
    - **Font:** Click on the arrow button to the right of the **Font** text box to display a list of available fonts. Select the font you want to use.
    - **Size:** Click on the arrow button to the right of the **Size** text box to display a list of available type sizes. Select the type size you want to use. The larger the type size selected, the larger the type will appear on your printed reports. If no type size options appear, make sure that you have selected a font in the **Font** text box; then select the type size for the **Font** you have selected.
14. After you have established the desired printer settings, click on the **OK** button to return to the Company Window. These printer settings will become the new printer settings for all sets of company data files.
15. To test your adjusted printer settings, click on the Company Window Report menu; then click on Trial Balance. The Trial Balance Options dialog box will appear. Leave the **As at** date set at 12/1/99; then click on the **OK** button.
16. Click on the Trial Balance File menu; then click on Print to print the Trial Balance.

17. Double-click on the control menu box to close the Trial Balance window and return to the Company Window.
18. Review your printed Trial Balance report. If the font, type size, and/or margins are still not satisfactory go back to instruction #12 and make new adjustments. If the font, type size, and margins are satisfactory, click on the Company Window File menu; then click on Exit to end your current work session and return to your Windows desktop.

INDEX

D

E

F

G

H

N

O

P

Q

R

S

T

U

W